Essentials of Marketing Research

A Hands-On Orientation

Global Edition

Naresh K. Malhotra
Georgia Institute of Technology

PEARSON

Boston   Columbus   Indianapolis   New York   San Francisco
Upper Saddle River   Amsterdam   Cape Town   Dubai   London
Madrid   Milan   Munich   Paris   Montreal   Toronto   Delhi   Mexico City
Sao Paulo   Sydney   Hong Kong   Seoul   Singapore   Taipei   Tokyo

Editor in Chief: Stephanie Wall
Head of Learning Asset Acquisition: Laura Dent
Acquisitions Editor: Mark Gaffney
Senior Acquisitions Editor, Global Editions: Steven Jackson
Program Manager Team Lead: Ashley Santora
Program Manager: Jennifer M. Collins
Editorial Assistant: Daniel Petrino
Director of Marketing: Maggie Moylan
Executive Marketing Manager: Anne Fahlgren
Project Manager Team Lead: Judy Leale
Project Manager: Becca Groves

Media Producer, Global Editions: M Vikram Kumar
Project Editor, Global Editions: K.K. Neelakantan
Senior Production Manufacturing Controller, Global Editions: Trudy Kimber
Procurement Specialist: Nancy Maneri
Creative Director: Blair Brown
Sr. Art Director: Janet Slowik
Interior and Cover Designer: Karen Quigley
Cover Art: © carlos castilla/shutterstock
Digital Production Project Manager: Lisa Rinaldi

Credits and acknowledgments borrowed from other sources and reproduced, with permission, in this textbook appear on the appropriate page within text.

Pearson Education Limited
Edinburgh Gate
Harlow
Essex CM20 2JE
England

and Associated Companies throughout the world

Visit us on the World Wide Web at: www.pearsonglobaleditions.com

© Pearson Education Limited 2015

British Library Cataloguing-in-Publication Data

A catalogue record for this book is available from the British Library

10 9 8 7 6 5 4 3 2 1
15 14

ISBN 10: 1-292-06016-6
ISBN 13: 978-1-292-06016-3

Typeset in Utopia, 9.5/13 by Integra.
Printed by CPI UK

To my precious and beloved children, Ruth and Paul, with love.

"And all thy children shall be taught of the LORD;
and great shall be the peace of thy children."

ISAIAH 54:13

"For ye are all the children of God by faith in Christ Jesus."

GALATIANS 3:26

The Holy Bible

Brief Contents

Contents

Foreword

I am very pleased to write this foreword. Dr. Naresh K. Malhotra is an extremely well-known and highly regarded author, researcher, and teacher whom I have known for over 33 years. This first edition of *Essentials of Marketing Research: A Hands-On Orientation* is yet another outstanding textbook written by him. His other two marketing research books, *Basic Marketing Research: Integration of Social Media*, fourth edition and *Marketing Research: An Applied Orientation*, now in its sixth edition, have been very successful and have been translated into several languages and have been published in several English editions. Both those books are global leaders and I am confident that his new book, *Essentials of Marketing Research*, will also join their rank.

Essentials of Marketing Research: A Hands-On Orientation presents the essential marketing research concepts in a clear, concise, and elementary way without getting bogged down with technical details, statistics, and formulas. It carries Dr. Malhotra's expertise in marketing research and pedagogical skills even further with a simple yet forceful presentation. With its focus on contemporary issues like international marketing research, social media and new technologies, and ethics, the book is very relevant to the current environment. The application of Internet-based marketing research is integrated in a pervasive way throughout the book with ample opportunities for students to experience these concepts. Just one of the ways in which this book is leading the field of marketing research is the innovative emphasis on social media, both as a domain in which to conduct marketing research and as an application of marketing research.

This book is rich in meaningful and illustrative examples that show how researchers are capturing the realities of the marketplace and how managers are making decisions based on them. The iResearch, Applied Problems, and Internet Exercises provide rich hands-on experience. The Research in Practice examples, cases, and Online Video Cases are great learning tools that further reinforce the highly-applied and managerial orientation of the text. Particularly noteworthy are the Running Case, Comprehensive Critical Thinking Case, and other cases that include questionnaires and real-life data. The book has an abundance of diagrams, figures, and tables that truly enhance learning. Dr. Malhotra has succeeded in presenting the elementary research concepts with simplicity and clarity while yet upholding the technical accuracy for which he is most famous. The book is strong in qualitative concepts and imparts the necessary quantitative knowledge and skills with the use of SPSS and Excel. The SPSS and Excel demonstration movies, screen captures, step-by-step instructions, and online Student Resource Manual provide the greatest resources available anywhere for students to learn these programs.

Essentials of Marketing Research: A Hands-On Orientation provides an exceptionally solid foundation that students and practitioners need in order to understand and manage the marketing research function.

William D. Neal
Senior Partner
SDR Consulting
Former Chairman of the Board,
American Marketing Association
Recipient of the Charles Coolidge Parlin
Marketing Research Award (2001)

Preface

Enabling the Learning of Marketing Research

Teaching marketing research can be a challenging task for instructors and learning the subject can be equally daunting for the students, especially for those taking an introductory course in marketing research. We enable learning by giving a simple, easy to understand exposition of the basic concepts and by adopting a hands-on, do-it-yourself orientation. This first edition is current, contemporary, illustrative, and sensitive to the needs of undergraduate students, integrating the Internet, social media and new technologies, international marketing research, and ethics in a pervasive way.

Thanks to your feedback and encouragement, *Essentials of Marketing Research: A Hands-On Orientation,* first edition, builds on the success of my first four editions of *Basic Marketing Research: Integration of Social Media* and on the success of the six editions of my book *Marketing Research: An Applied Orientation.* The latter is the most widely used graduate marketing research title, with more than 150 universities adopting the book in the United States. It has been translated into Chinese, Spanish, Portuguese, Russian, French, Hungarian, Indonesian, and Japanese. In addition to these eight translations, there are several English-language editions, including North American, International, European, Indian, Arabian, and Australian editions. The book is being used in more than 100 countries. Please accept my personal gratitude and thanks for your support of my marketing research books. Truly, I owe you a lot!

Audience

Essentials of Marketing Research: A Hands-On Orientation is suitable for use in the introductory marketing research course at the undergraduate level in two- or four-year colleges and in schools that do not want to emphasize the technical and statistical methodology, but teach marketing research with a managerial orientation. With plenty of self-help for students, it not only facilitates classroom learning, but is also very suitable for online marketing research courses. I have presented the marketing research concepts and principles at an elementary level, in a manner that is easy to read and understand. There is an abundance of diagrams, pictures, illustrations, and examples that help to explain the elementary concepts. The relative positioning of my three books is as follows.

Textbook	Number of Chapters	Depth of Coverage. Statistics and Formulas.	Positioning
Essentials of Marketing Research, First Edition	13	Covers concepts at an elementary level. Deemphasizes statistics and formulas.	Two-year, four-year, and schools emphasizing a nontechnical and nonstatistical orientation to marketing research. Online marketing research courses.
Basic Marketing Research, Fourth Edition	19	Covers concepts at a medium level. Moderate emphasis on statistics and formulas; only basic statistical techniques are covered.	Upper level undergraduate textbook.
Marketing Research, Sixth Edition	24	Covers concepts at a deep level. Heavy emphasis on statistics and formulas; all the advanced statistical techniques are covered including SEM.	Mainstream MBA level textbook.

Organization

I have organized this book into three main parts, based on a six-step framework for conducting marketing research. Part 1 provides an introduction to marketing research (Chapter 1). It also discusses problem definition—the first and the most important step—and developing an approach to the problem—the second step in the marketing research process (Chapter 2).

Part 2 covers research design—the third step—describing the following research designs in detail: exploratory (secondary and syndicated data, qualitative research, Chapters 3 and 4); descriptive (survey and observation, Chapter 5); and causal (experiment, Chapter 6). The types of information commonly obtained in marketing research, as well as the appropriate scales for obtaining such information, are described (Chapter 7). Guidelines for designing questionnaires are given (Chapter 8) and sampling design and procedures are explained (Chapter 9).

Part 3 presents a practical and managerially oriented discussion of field work—the fourth step in the marketing research process. It also covers data preparation and analysis—the fifth step (Chapter 10). Basic statistical techniques are discussed in detail, with emphasis on explaining the procedures, interpreting the results, and understanding managerial implications (Chapters 11 and 12). Two statistical packages, SPSS and Excel, are featured. Here, I provide detailed, step-by-step instructions for running SPSS, including illustrations, demonstration movies, and screen captures. Detailed instructions, data files, demonstration movies, and screen captures are also provided for Excel. Communicating the research by preparing and presenting a formal report constitutes the sixth step in the marketing research process, which I also discuss in Part 3 (Chapter 13).

Distinctive Features of the Text

This book has several salient or distinctive features that set it apart from competing books.

1. *A Hands-On Orientation.* It emphasizes a hands-on, do-it-yourself approach, affording students several opportunities to experience marketing research. iResearch scenarios require students to actually do research and make marketing research and marketing management decisions through a hands-on orientation. This hands-on orientation is further reinforced by cases, Online Video Cases, Review Questions, Applied Problems, and Internet Exercises.
2. *Extensive Self-Help for Students.* As compared to competing texts, this book provides extensive self-help for students that is posted on the open access (no password required) Companion website. This includes a comprehensive Student Resource Manual, SPSS and Excel Demonstration Movies, SPSS and Excel Screen Captures with Notes, and other resources mentioned later. This makes the book very suitable for use in the classroom and for use in online marketing research courses.
3. *Interaction between Marketing Research Decisions and Marketing Management Decisions.* This book is unique in the way it illustrates the interaction between marketing research decisions and marketing management decisions. Each chapter shows how marketing research decisions influence marketing management decisions and vice versa. This interaction is illustrated through several pedagogical tools mentioned earlier. Thus, the book has a highly applied and managerial orientation. In it, I illustrate how marketing researchers apply the various marketing concepts and techniques, and how managers implement the marketing research findings in order to improve marketing practice.

4. *Extensive and Pervasive Social Media Coverage.* There is an innovative and extensive integration of social media and new technologies. Here I focus on social media as an application of marketing research and as a domain through which to conduct marketing research. Each and every chapter, excluding the data analysis in Chapters 11 and 12, has a separate section entitled "Marketing Research and Social Media." However, the use of social media is not limited to this section but is discussed in several other sections of the chapter, including end of chapter questions, Dell Running Case, and all the cases and video cases. The major occurrences of social media are highlighted with an icon in the margin.

5. *International Focus.* Apart from the data analysis in Chapters 11 and 12, every chapter has a section titled International Marketing Research and an example illustrating the concepts in an international setting.

6. *Ethics Focus.* Ethical issues are prevalent in marketing research. Every chapter has a section titled Ethics in Marketing Research and an example that illustrates marketing research ethical issues. I'll talk about ethics from the perspectives of the four stakeholders: the client, the marketing research firm, the respondents, and the general public.

7. *Contemporary Focus.* A contemporary focus has been achieved by applying marketing research to current topics such as customer value, satisfaction, loyalty, customer equity, brand equity and management, innovation, entrepreneurship, return on marketing, relationship marketing, sustainability, and socially responsible marketing throughout the text.

8. *Six-Step Marketing Research Process.* This book is organized around the well-accepted six-step framework for conducting marketing research. A six-step process diagram appears in each chapter, showing how the chapter content relates to this framework. Thus, the six-step marketing research process serves as a unifying framework that imparts structure. There is ample evidence suggesting undergraduate students learn structured material more easily.

9. *Extensive and Pervasive Internet Coverage.* The text discusses how the Internet can be integrated in each step of the marketing research process and how it can be used to implement the concepts discussed in each chapter. The coverage of the Internet is so extensive that it has not been singled out. Internet applications are ubiquitous. For example, all the iResearch exercises require the students to do Internet research including social media. In addition, a section entitled Internet Exercises is featured in each chapter.

10. *Stimulating Critical Thinking.* The principles for critical thinking (including Socratic questioning, critical reading and writing, higher order thinking, and assessment) have been embodied in a Comprehensive Critical Thinking Case (Case 2.1 American Idol), end of chapter Review Questions, Applied Problems, and Internet Exercises. These materials have been designed based on the guidelines provided by the Foundation for Critical Thinking.

11. *Real-life Examples and Illustrations.* Several real-life examples are presented in each chapter, entitled Research in Practice. These examples describe in detail the kind of marketing research conducted to address specific managerial problems and the decisions that were based on the findings. Where appropriate, the sources cited have been supplemented by additional marketing research information to enhance the usefulness of these examples. In addition, there are several other examples and illustrations that are blended in the text.

12. *Research Recipe.* Every major section in each chapter ends with an active summary entitled Research Recipe. This feature not only summarizes the main concepts in that section but also provides guidelines on how those concepts should be implemented in actual practice.

13. *Comprehensive Cases with Actual Questionnaires and Real Data.* Each chapter contains the Dell Running Case (Case 1.1) featuring an actual questionnaire and real-life data. While the questions for Dell appear in each chapter, the case itself appears toward the end of the book. There I have included additional comprehensive cases with actual questionnaires and real-life data (Case 3.1 JP Morgan Chase, Case 3.2 Wendy's).

14. *Online Video Cases.* Each chapter of this book contains an Online Video Case. The video cases have been drawn from the Pearson video library, and have been written from a marketing research perspective. The questions at the end of each video case are all marketing research questions. The questions are cumulative and cover the contents of that chapter as well as the previous chapters. The cases and videos are available online to instructors and students.

15. *Learning Objectives and Opening Research in Practice Examples.* Each chapter opens with a set of objectives to arouse curiosity and to impart structure. Each chapter also contains an Opening Research in Practice feature that I use as a running example throughout the chapter.

16. *SPSS and Excel.* Data analysis procedures are illustrated with respect to SPSS and Excel. SPSS and Excel files are provided for all datasets.

17. ***SPSS and Excel Computerized Demonstration Movies.*** I have created computerized demonstration movies illustrating step-by-step instructions for each data analysis procedure using SPSS and Excel that can be downloaded or viewed on the website for this book (see Exhibit 10.1). Students can watch these movies on their own to promote self-learning and/or they can be shown in class.

18. ***SPSS and Excel Screen Captures with Notes.*** In addition to the demonstration movies, I have also provided screen captures with notes illustrating step-by-step instructions for running each data analysis procedure presented in the book using SPSS as well as Excel. These are available on the text website for downloading.

19. ***SPSS and Excel Step-by-Step Instructions.*** Each chapter contains separate step-by-step instructions for SPSS and Excel for conducting the data analysis presented in that chapter.

20. ***Conducting a Live Marketing Research Project.*** Toward the end of each chapter there is a section entitled, "Live Research: Conducting a Marketing Research Project." These sections show how to implement one or more live marketing research projects in the course. The approach is flexible and can handle a variety of organizations and formats. The entire class could be working on the same project with each team working on all aspects of the project, or each team could be assigned a specific responsibility (e.g., a specific component of the problem or a specific aspect of the project like collection and analysis of secondary data). Alternatively, the class could be working on multiple projects with specific teams assigned to a specific project.

21. ***Acronyms.*** Each chapter contains one or more helpful acronyms that summarize the salient concepts. Acronyms are the most popular mnemonic technique college students use. Theoretical and empirical evidence supporting the effectiveness of mnemonic techniques and their usefulness as a pedagogical tool has been discussed in a paper I published in the *Journal of the Academy of Marketing Science,* (spring 1991): 141–150.

22. ***AACSB Learning Standards.*** All the pedagogical tools, end of chapter exercises, and the test item file have been designed to incorporate the AACSB learning standards with respect to: Written and oral communication, ethical understanding and reasoning, information technology, analytical thinking, diverse and multicultural work environments, reflective thinking, application of knowledge, and interpersonal relations and teamwork.

Students Can Learn SPSS® and Excel on Their Own!

SPSS and Excel files are provided for all chapter datasets; outputs and screen captures are posted on the Companion website (www.pearsonglobaleditions.com/malhotra). Help for running the SPSS and Excel programs used in each data analysis chapter is provided in four ways:

1. Detailed step-by-step instructions are given in the chapter.
2. Download or view online computerized demonstration movies illustrating these step-by-step instructions from www.pearsonglobaleditions.com/malhotra. For each data analysis procedure I have provided a movie illustrating SPSS and another illustrating Excel.
3. Download screen captures with notes illustrating these step-by-step instructions.
4. Extensive instructions for SPSS and Excel are given in the Student Resource Manual that is also posted on the Companion website and can be accessed without a password.

Thus, we provide **the most extensive help** available anywhere to learn SPSS and Excel!

Teaching Aids for Instructors

The password-protected Instructor Resource Center offers several teaching aids that can be accessed only by instructors. These include:

PowerPoint Presentations

A comprehensive set of PowerPoint slides can be used by instructors for class presentations or by students for lecture preview or review. These slides contain extensive materials including the major concepts, all the figures, and all the tables for each chapter of the book. The instructor slides are distinct in that: (1) some slides contain notes that are identified with a scarlet border, (2) some slides contain images, and (3) there are additional slides containing material not covered in the book. These extra slides have been identified with "Review Comments," a feature of PowerPoint.

Instructor's Manual

A complete instructor's manual (IM), prepared by me, can be used to prepare lectures or class presentations, find answers, and even to design the course syllabus. I personally wrote the entire instructor's manual so that it is very closely tied to the text. Each chapter contains Learning Objectives; Author's Notes; Chapter Outline; Teaching Suggestions organized by Leraning Objectives; and answers to all end-of-chapter Review Questions, Applied Problems, and Internet Exercises. Answers are also provided to the iResearch scenarios. In addition, solutions are provided for all the cases, including those that involve data analysis. Solutions are also provided for all the Online Video Cases. Each chapter in the IM contains an additional feature (not contained in the book) entitled Decision Research that describes a real-life scenario with specific questions that require students to make marketing research and marketing management decisions and the answers are given. Additional exercises and answers entitled Role Playing, Field Work, and Group Discussions are also provided.

Test Item File

The test bank contains multiple-choice, true/false, and essay questions for every chapter. I personally wrote the test item file. This valuable resource contains a wide variety of questions for each chapter that allows you to create your own exams.

This Test Item File supports Association to Advance Collegiate Schools of Business (AACSB) International Accreditation. Each chapter of the Test Item File was prepared with the AACSB learning standards in mind. Where appropriate, the answer line of each question indicates a category within which the question falls. This AACSB reference helps instructors identify those test questions that support that organization's learning goals.

The eight categories of AACSB Learning Standards were identified earlier. Questions that test skills relevant to these standards are tagged with the appropriate standard. For example, a question testing the moral issues associated with externalities would receive the ethical understanding and reasoning abilities tag.

How can I use these tags? Tagged questions help you measure whether students are grasping the course content that aligns with AACSB guidelines. In addition, the tagged questions may help to identify potential applications of these skills. This, in turn, may suggest enrichment activities or other educational experiences to help students achieve these goals.

Online Video Cases

A set of cases and videos accompanying these cases is available online. The viewing time for many of these videos is less than 10 minutes so that they can be conveniently shown in class. These video cases are posted online and the solutions to these cases are provided in the instructor's manual.

Other Teaching Aids

The password-protected Instructor Resource Center also contains the following:

- Data files for Cases 1.1 Dell, 3.1 JP Morgan Chase, and 3.2 Wendy's, given in the book (SPSS and Excel)
- Data files for all the Applied Problems (SPSS and Excel)
- Data file for the data set(s) used in each data analysis chapter (SPSS and Excel)
- SPSS and Excel Computerized Demonstration Movies
- SPSS and Excel Screen Captures with Notes
- SPSS and Excel output files for data analyses presented in Chapters 10 to 12, and for solutions to all Applied Problems and Cases (1.1 Dell, 3.1 JPMorgan Chase, and 3.2 Wendy's)
- Additional materials that supplement the topics discussed in the book.

Student Resource Manual

It enables students to study more effectively. This online resource manual contains chapter outlines, learning tips organized by objectives, practice true and false and multiple choice questions, additional figures and tables, and hints for selected Applied Problems. It also gives detailed instructions for running the data analysis procedures using SPSS and Excel along with an additional practice dataset.

CourseSmart eTextbooks*

Developed for students looking to save on required or recommended textbooks, CourseSmart eTextbooks Online shaves money off the suggested list prices of the print text. Students simply select their eText by title or author and purchase immediate access to the content for the duration of the course using any major credit card. With a CourseSmart eText, students can search for specific keywords or page numbers, make notes online, print out reading assignments that incorporate lecture notes, and bookmark important passages for later review.

Learning Aids for Students

Companion Website

Housed at www.pearsonglobaleditions.com/malhotra, the Companion website offers valuable additional resources for *Essentials of Marketing Research*, First Edition, for instructors as well as students. This site is not password protected so that these materials can be accessed freely. Video cases are located on this companion website and include the accompanying streaming video. This site also offers downloads of data files and additional material for use in conjunction with the textbook. Specifically, the Companion website contains the following materials:

- Student Resource Manual
- Data files for Cases 1.1 Dell, 3.1 JP Morgan Chase, and 3.2 Wendy's, given in the book (SPSS and Excel)
- Online Video Cases, including streaming video
- Data files for all the Applied Problems (SPSS and Excel)
- Data files for the data set(s) used in each data analysis chapter (SPSS and Excel)
- Output files for the analysis in each data analysis chapter (SPSS and Excel)
- SPSS and Excel Computerized Demonstration Movies
- SPSS and Excel Screen Captures with Notes
- Additional materials that supplement the topic discussed in the book

Tips to Students on How to Use This Textbook

I want to offer you a few tips on how to use this book and suggestions on how to master the material presented.

- Read the Chapter. Start by reading the chapter. Be sure to look at the Overview, Learning Objectives and opening Research in Practice examples, and reread the Overview so you will know what is in the chapter. Often this is skipped because students don't believe it is important. Read the Research Recipe feature twice. Each recipe is very short but effectively summarizes that section and provides guidelines on how to implement the concepts in practice.
- Review the Key Terms. It is important to read through these new terms to be sure you understand each one. Key Terms are often targets of quiz and exam questions.
- Answer the Review Questions. Go through the Review Questions and see if you can answer them without looking in the chapter. When you are finished, go back and check to see if you got each one correct. For the ones you couldn't answer, go back and locate the correct information in the chapter.
- Do the Applied Problems. Pick several problems you believe would be interesting. Spend some time thinking about the question and the concepts being explored. You can make these problems fun to do as you analyze the concepts at a deeper level.

*This product may not be available in all markets. For more details, please visit www.coursesmart.co.uk or contact your local Pearson representative.

- Have Some Fun with Critical Thinking. Go to the Critical Thinking Case (2.1 American Idol). This case is comprehensive and contains questions on all the chapters except the data analysis chapters. Based on the knowledge you have learned in the chapter and the case information, answer the critical thinking questions as well as the technical questions. Doing this case will help you understand and apply the concepts in real-life situations from a critical thinking perspective.
- Hone your Internet skills. Select a few iResearch and Internet Exercises that you find interesting and complete them. This will sharpen your Internet marketing research skills.
- Experience case analysis and problem solving. Pick one of the Comprehensive Cases with Real Data and Questionnaires that interests you the most. Answer the marketing research questions that have been posed for each chapter, including the data analysis chapters. These will help you apply the marketing research concepts to real-life situations and also give you a taste of case analysis and problem solving.

Suggestions to Students for Preparing for Exams

If you have followed the tips provided in the previous section, you will almost be ready for the exam. A brief review of the Key Terms, Research Recipes, and a scan of the chapter will be all that you need. But, if you have not followed all of the tips, here is a sequence of activities you can follow that will aid in learning the material.

- Read the chapter.
- Review the Research Recipes.
- Review the Key Terms.
- Read the chapter Overview.
- Read the chapter Summary.
- Answer the Review Questions.
- Go through the chapter and locate all of the bold and italic words. Read the context of each term to make sure you understand that term.
- Start at the beginning of the chapter and read the topic sentence of each paragraph. These sentences should provide a good summary of that paragraph. Reread the Research Recipes.
- Reread the chapter Summary.

Congratulations! You are now ready for the exam. Relax—you will do well.

Reviewers for the First Edition

The reviewers have provided many constructive and valuable suggestions. Among others, the help of the following reviewers is gratefully acknowledged.

Erika Matulich
University of Tampa

Anthony Di Benedetto
Temple University

Wolfgang Grassl
St. Norbert College

Doreen Sams
Georgia College & State University

Jennifer Barr
Stockton College

Audhesh Paswan
University of North Texas

Jared Hansen
University of North Carolina at Charlotte

Aliosha Alexandrov
University of Wisconsin at Oshkosh

Connie Bateman
University of North Dakota

Amit Ghosh
Cleveland State University

James Gould
Pace University

Norman McElvany
Johnson State College

Sangkil Moon
North Carolina State University

Acknowledgments

Several people have been extremely helpful in writing this textbook. I would like to acknowledge Professor Arun K. Jain (State University of New York at Buffalo) who taught me marketing research in a way I will never forget. My son Paul Malhotra provided valuable research assistance and proofread the manuscript. The students in my marketing research courses have provided useful feedback, as the material was class-tested for several years. Jeff Miller, President and CEO, Burke Inc., William D. Neal, Founder and Senior Executive Officer of SDR Consulting, Terry Grapentine, Principal at Grapentine Company LLC, and Ken Athaide, Senior Vice President, Market Strategies International, have been very helpful and supportive over the years.

The team at Pearson provided outstanding support. Special thanks are due to Stephanie Wall, editor in chief; Mark Gaffney, acquisitions editor, Jennifer M. Collins, program manager, Ashley Santora, program manager team lead; Anne Fahlgren, executive marketing manager; Becca Groves, project manager; and Erica Gordon, photo researcher. Special recognition is due to the several field representatives and sales people who have done an outstanding job.

I want to acknowledge, with great respect, my parents, the late Mr. H. N. Malhotra, and Mrs. S. Malhotra. Their love, encouragement, support, and the sacrificial giving of themselves have been exemplary. My heartfelt love and gratitude go to my wife Veena, and my children Ruth and Paul, for their faith, hope, and love.

Most of all, I want to acknowledge and thank my Savior and Lord, Jesus Christ, for the abundant grace and favor He has bestowed upon me. This book is, truly, the result of His grace and mercy—"Grace, mercy, and peace, from God our Father and Jesus Christ our Lord" (I Timothy 1:2). I praise God and give Him all the glory. Undoubtedly, the most significant event in my life was when I accepted the Lord Jesus Christ as my personal Savior and Lord. "For whosoever shall call upon the name of the Lord shall be saved" (Romans 10:13).

Naresh K. Malhotra

Pearson would like to thank and acknowledge the following people for their work on the Global Edition:

Contributor

Hammed Shamma, *The American University in Cairo*

Reviewers

Dalia Farrag, *Qatar University*

Daryanto Ahmad, *Lancaster University Management School*

Nor Azila Mohd. Noor, *Othman Yeop Abdullah Graduate School of Business*

Christof Backhaus, *Newcastle University Business School*

Yoosuf A. Cader, *Zayed University*

About the Author

Dr. Naresh K. Malhotra is Senior Fellow, Georgia Tech CIBER and Regents' Professor Emeritus, Scheller College of Business, Georgia Institute of Technology, USA. He has been listed in Marquis *Who's Who in America* continuously since the 51st Edition in 1997 and in *Who's Who in the World* since 2000. He received the prestigious Academy of Marketing Science CUTCO/Vector Distinguished Marketing Educator Award in 2005. In 2010, he was selected as a Marketing Legend, and his refereed journal articles were published in nine volumes by Sage with tributes by other leading scholars in the field. In 2011, he received the Best Professor in Marketing Management, Asia Best B-School Award.

In an article by Wheatley and Wilson (1987 AMA Educators' Proceedings), Professor Malhotra was ranked number one in the country based on articles published in the *Journal of*

Marketing Research (JMR) during 1980–1985. He also holds the all-time record for the maximum number of publications in the *Journal of Health Care Marketing*. He is ranked number one based on publications in the *Journal of the Academy of Marketing Science* (JAMS) since its inception through Volume 23, 1995. He is also number one based on publications in JAMS during the 10-year period 1986–1995. (See Tables 6 and 7 of JAMS, Vol. 24, No. 4, Fall 1996, p. 297). In an editorial by Schlegelmilch (JIM, 11(1), 2003), Malhotra was ranked number one based on publications in the *International Marketing Review* (IMR) from 1992–2002. He is also ranked number one based on publications in the *International Marketing Review* since its inception (1983) to 2003 (Table V, IMR, 22(4) (2005), p. 396), and from 1983 to 2011 (Table VI, IMR, 30(1) (2013), p. 14.) He is also ranked number one based on publications in the *International Marketing Review* from 1996–2006 based on a study by Xu et al., published in the *Asia Pacific Journal of Management* (2008) 25: 189–207. In a landmark study by Ford et al. (2010) examining publications in the top four marketing journals (JMR, JM, JAMS, and JCR) over a 25-year period from 1977–2002, Professor Malhotra has three top-three rankings: ranked number three based on publications in all the four journals combined, ranked number three based on publications in JMR, and ranked number one based on publications in JAMS. He has published 10 papers in JMR.

He has published more than 130 papers in major refereed journals, including the *Journal of Marketing Research, Journal of Consumer Research, Marketing Science, Management Science, Journal of Marketing, Journal of Academy of Marketing Science, Journal of Retailing, Journal of Health Care Marketing*, and leading journals in statistics, management science, information systems, and psychology. In addition, he has also published numerous refereed articles in the proceedings of major national and international conferences. Several articles have received best paper research awards.

He was Chairman, Academy of Marketing Science Foundation, 1996–1998; President, Academy of Marketing Science, 1994–1996; and Chairman, Board of Governors, 1990–1992. He is a Distinguished Fellow of the Academy and Fellow, Decision Sciences Institute. He is the founding editor of *Review of Marketing Research* (published by the Emerald Group); served as an associate editor of *Decision Sciences* for 18 years; and has served as section editor, Health Care Marketing Abstracts, *Journal of Health Care Marketing*. Also, he serves on the editorial board of eight journals.

He has traveled and taught in 33 countries. His book titled *Marketing Research: An Applied Orientation*, Sixth Edition, was published by Prentice Hall, Inc., in 2010. This book has been translated into Chinese, Spanish, Russian, Portuguese, Hungarian, French, Bahasa Indonesia, and Japanese. In addition to the eight translations, this book also has several English editions, including North America, International, Europe, India, Arab, and Australia and New Zealand. The book has received widespread adoption at both the graduate and undergraduate levels with more than 150 schools using it in the United States and is being studied in over 100 countries. His book, *Basic Marketing Research: Integration of Social Media,* Fourth Edition, was published by Prentice Hall in 2011 and is likewise a global leader in the field.

Dr. Malhotra has consulted for business, nonprofit, and government organizations in the United States and abroad and has served as an expert witness in legal and regulatory proceedings. He has special expertise in data analysis and statistical methods. He is the winner of numerous awards and honors for research, teaching, and service to the profession, including the Academy of Marketing Science, Outstanding Marketing Teaching Excellence Award, 2003.

Dr. Malhotra is an ordained minister of the Gospel, a member and Deacon of the First Baptist Church, Atlanta, and President of Global Evangelistic Ministries, Inc. He has been married to Veena for more than 33 years, and they have two children, Ruth and Paul.

Introduction to Marketing Research

∨ Overview

Marketing research is one of the most important and fascinating aspects of marketing. In this chapter, we give a formal definition of marketing research and classify marketing research into two areas: problem-identification and problem-solving research. We describe the marketing research process and the six steps that are involved in conducting research, and discuss the nature of marketing research, emphasizing its role of providing information for marketing decision making. Next we provide an overview of marketing research suppliers who collectively make up the marketing research industry, along with guidelines for selecting a supplier. The demand for well-executed marketing research leads to many exciting career opportunities that are described. We show the relationship of marketing research to marketing information systems and decision support systems.

Information on the use of the Internet in marketing research is interwoven into each chapter. The topic of international marketing research is introduced and discussed systematically in the subsequent chapters, as is the subject of marketing research and social media. The major occurrences of social media research are highlighted throughout the book with the use of an icon in the margin. This book is on the leading edge in terms of integrating social media as an additional domain to conduct marketing research. The ethical aspects of marketing research and the responsibilities each of the marketing research stakeholders have to themselves, one another, and the research process are presented and developed in more detail throughout the text. The major takeaways from key sections are summarized by way of "Research Recipe" boxes. This and all subsequent chapters include several Internet and hands-on applications of marketing research in the form of "Research in Practice," "iResearch," cases, online video cases, review questions, applied problems and Internet exercises. To further reinforce student learning, we present a running case on Dell toward the end of each chapter. For instructors wishing to implement a real-life marketing research project, we include a section entitled "Live Research: Conducting a Marketing Research Project." Perhaps there is no better way to present an overview than to give an example that provides a flavor of the nature of marketing research.

The role of a marketing researcher must include consulting skills, technical proficiency and sound management. The focus of the role is to provide information to identify marketing problems and solutions in such a way that action can be taken."

> **Jeff Miller, President and CEO, Burke, Inc., Cincinnati, Ohio**

⌄ Learning Objectives

After reading this chapter, the student should be able to:

1. Define marketing research and distinguish between problem-identification and problem-solving research.

2. Describe a framework for conducting marketing research as well as the six steps of the marketing research process.

3. Understand the nature and scope of marketing research and its role in designing and implementing successful marketing programs.

4. Explain how the decision to conduct marketing research is made.

5. Discuss the marketing research industry and the types of research suppliers, including internal, external, full-service, and limited-service suppliers.

6. Describe careers available in marketing research and the background and skills needed to succeed in them.

7. Explain the role of marketing research in decision support systems.

8. Acquire an appreciation of the international dimension and the complexity involved in international marketing research.

9. Describe the use of social media as a domain to conduct marketing research.

10. Gain an understanding of the ethical aspects of marketing research and the responsibilities each of the marketing research stakeholders have to themselves, one another, and the research project.

Research in Practice
Apple: Combining Marketing Research and Technological Innovation

Apple launched the iPad in 2010 and sold 300,000 of the tablets on the first day, 1 million iPads in twenty-eight days—less than half of the seventy-four days it took to sell 1 million iPhones. Consumers watched more than 30 billion videos online in one month. As in the case of other innovative products it had introduced in the past (iPod, iTunes Music Store, iPhone), marketing research played a significant role in the design and successful introduction of the iPad. Marketing research in the form of focus groups (interviews with a small group of consumers), analysis of social media, and surveys indicated that in this electronic age of multitasking, consumers were looking for electronic devices that integrate numerous functions on one platform. Consumers were also looking for a device that filled the gap between smartphones and laptops. The iPad was designed to meet this need and succeeded in creating a new mobile device category on its own. With over 15 million iPads sold in its first nine months of availability, the late Apple CEO Steve Jobs said 2010 was "The Year of the iPad." Capitalizing on this great success, Apple launched the iPad2 in March 2011. The company launched a new version of the iPad on March 16, 2012, and sold more than 3 million units in four days, making this the most successful launch yet for Apple's tablet. On September 12, 2012, Apple unveiled a new thinner iPhone 5 and pre-orders sold out in less than an hour. The iPhone 5 set a new sales record as customers placed more than 2 million pre-orders for the iPhone 5 on the first day it was available, doubling previous results and exceeding initial supply of the smartphone.

Apple undertakes extensive research to identify marketing opportunities and also to develop products and marketing programs to exploit those opportunities. While, it maintains an in-house staff of

Source: Jeff Miller, President and CEO, Burke, Inc.

marketing researchers, the company relies heavily on external marketing research suppliers. All the information generated by marketing research becomes a part of Apple's decision support system.

Despite the passing away of Steve Jobs on October 5, 2011, consumers can expect the stream of innovative new products from Apple to continue given the company's continued reliance on marketing research and technological innovation. In fact, during 2013 and 2014, Apple was expected to launch many new innovative products including the highly anticipated Apple television that has been developed based on extensive marketing research.[1] **<**

This example illustrates the crucial role played by marketing research in designing and implementing successful marketing programs. It illustrates only a few of the methods used to conduct marketing research: focus groups, analysis of social media, and surveys. This book will introduce you to all types of marketing research techniques and illustrate their applications in designing effective marketing strategies. The role of marketing research can be better understood through its definition.

DEFINITION OF MARKETING RESEARCH

In this book, we emphasize the need for information for decision making and therefore define marketing research as follows:

marketing research

The systematic and objective identification, collection, analysis, dissemination, and use of information for the purpose of assisting management in decision making related to the identification and solution of problems and opportunities in marketing.

Marketing research is the systematic and objective identification, collection, analysis, dissemination, and use of information for the purpose of improving decision making related to the identification and solution of problems and opportunities in marketing.

Several aspects of this definition are noteworthy. First, marketing research is systematic. Thus, systematic planning is required at all stages of the marketing research process. The procedures followed at each stage are methodologically sound; well documented; and, as much as possible, planned in advance. Marketing research uses the scientific method in that data are collected and analyzed to test prior thinking that may be formulated into specific hypotheses.

Marketing research attempts to provide accurate information that reflects a true state of affairs. It is objective and should be conducted impartially. Although research is always influenced by the researcher's philosophy, it should be free from the personal or political biases of the researcher or management. The motto of every researcher should be, "Find it and tell it like it is."

Marketing research involves the identification, collection, analysis, dissemination, and use of information, as described in Figure 1.1.

Each phase of this process is important. We identify or define the marketing research problem or opportunity and then determine what information is needed to investigate it. Because every marketing opportunity translates into a research problem to be investigated, we use the terms *problem* and *opportunity* interchangeably. Next, the relevant information sources are identified and a range of data collection methods varying in sophistication and complexity are evaluated for their usefulness. The data are collected using the most appropriate method; they are analyzed and interpreted, and inferences are drawn. Finally, the findings, implications, and recommendations are provided in a format that enables the managers to use the information for marketing decision making and to take appropriate actions.

> ## Research Recipe
>
> Conduct marketing research in an objective and systematic way. It should be free from the personal and political biases of the researcher and management. The procedures used should be methodologically sound; well documented; and, as much as possible, planned in advance.

The Internet is quickly becoming a useful tool in the identification, collection, analysis, and dissemination of information related to marketing research. The Marketing Research Association (**www.marketingresearch.org**) is a worldwide association of researchers dedicated to providing

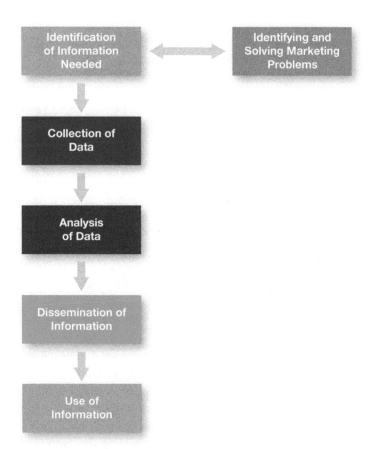

FIGURE 1.1

DEFINING MARKETING
RESEARCH

an open forum for the discussion of best practices and ethical approaches to research being conducted via the Internet, social media, and traditional methodologies. The next section further clarifies this definition by classifying different types of marketing research.

iResearch
Coca-Cola on the Web

Visit Coca-Cola's website at **www.coca-cola.com**. How does this site collect marketing research information? How would you improve the website in order to collect more or better marketing research information?

As the brand manager for Coca-Cola, how would you use information collected on the website to market your brand more effectively? **‹**

A CLASSIFICATION OF MARKETING RESEARCH

Our definition states that organizations engage in marketing research for two reasons: (1) to identify and (2) to solve marketing problems. This distinction serves as a basis for classifying marketing research into problem-identification research and problem-solving research, as shown in Figure 1.2.

Problem-identification research is undertaken to help identify problems that are, perhaps, not apparent on the surface and yet exist or are likely to arise in the future. Examples of problem-identification research include market potential, market share, brand or company image, market characteristics, sales analysis, short-range forecasting, long-range forecasting, and business trends research. A survey of companies conducting marketing research indicated that 97 percent of those who responded were conducting market potential, market share, and market characteristics research. About 90 percent also reported that they were using other types of problem-identification research. Research of this type provides information about the marketing environment and helps

**problem-identification
research**
*Research undertaken to help
identify problems that are not
necessarily apparent on the
surface and yet exist or are likely
to arise in the future.*

FIGURE 1.2

A CLASSIFICATION OF
MARKETING RESEARCH

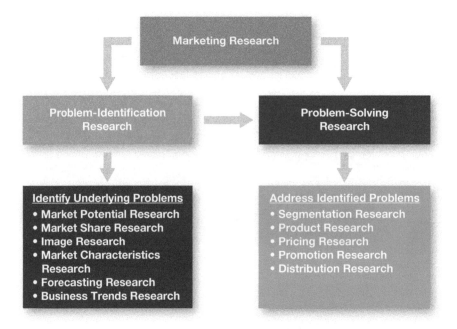

diagnose a problem. For example, a declining market potential indicates that the firm is likely to have a problem achieving its growth targets. It is very difficult to grow in a declining market. Similarly, a problem exists if the market potential is increasing but the firm is losing market share. That was indeed the situation confronting Scott Products, a brand of the Kimberly-Clark Corporation (**www.kimberly-clark.com**). Sales of Scott products were increasing but the brand was losing market share. While the brand's sales were increasing, they were not increasing as fast as its competitors. Upon further analysis, the problem was identified as price competition from lower-priced regional brands. Similarly, the recognition of economic, social, or cultural trends, such as changes in consumer behavior, may also point to underlying problems or opportunities.

problem-solving research
Research undertaken to help solve specific marketing problems.

Once a problem or opportunity has been identified, **problem-solving research** is undertaken to arrive at a solution. Thus, problem-identification research is generally followed by problem-solving research. The findings of problem-solving research are used in making decisions that will solve specific marketing problems. Most companies conduct problem-solving research. The different types of issues that are addressed by problem-solving research include segmentation, product, pricing, promotion, and distribution research.

Classifying marketing research into two main types is useful from a conceptual as well as a practical viewpoint. However, problem-identification research and problem-solving research go hand in hand, and a given marketing research project may combine both types of research. Once it identified the problem as priced competition from regional brands, Kimberly-Clark undertook problem-solving research, specifically product research. Based on the findings of product research, the company introduced a lower-priced line of paper products, under a new brand name, in markets where it was facing stiff competition from regional brands. As mentioned in the first Research in Practice feature, Apple undertakes both problem-identification and problem-solving research. Another illustration is provided by Kellogg's.

Research in Practice
Nutri-Grain Cereal Bars Add Nutrition to Kellogg's Sales

Kellogg's (**www.kelloggs.com**) marketed its products in more than 180 countries as of 2014. During the economic slowdown of 2009-2012, it had experienced a slump in the market and faced the challenge of reviving low cereal sales. Through problem-identification research, Kellogg's was able to identify the problem and, through problem-solving research, develop several solutions to increase cereal sales.

Kellogg's performed several tasks to identify the problem. The researchers spoke to decision makers within the company, interviewed industry experts, conducted analysis of available secondary data including social media, performed focus groups and surveyed consumers about their perceptions and preferences for cereals. Several important issues or problems were identified by this research. Current products were being targeted to children, bagels and muffins were winning for favored breakfast foods, and high prices were turning consumers to generic brands. Some other information also came to light during the research. Adults wanted quick foods that required very little or no preparation. These issues helped Kellogg's identify the problem. It was not being creative in introducing new products to meet the needs of the adult market.

After defining the problem, Kellogg's conducted problem-solving research and went to work on solutions. Specifically, product research was conducted by developing and testing several new flavors of cereals using mall intercept interviews with adult consumers. Based on the results, Kellogg's introduced new flavors that were more suited to the adult palate but were not the tasteless varieties of the past. For example, it introduced Kellogg's Nutri-Grain Cereal Bar Blackberry, a new cereal bar filled with blackberries. This new cereal bar was supported by an ad campaign and major in-store promotions. Kellogg's kept expanding this line successfully and, as of 2014, Nutri-Grain Cereal Bars were available in seven different varieties.

Through creative problem-identification research followed by problem-solving research, Kellogg's has not only seen an increase in sales, but also increased consumption of cereal at times other than breakfast.[2] <

R e s e a r c h   R e c i p e

Conduct problem-identification research on an ongoing basis. In general, problem-identification research should be followed by problem-solving research.

iResearch
NFL is Tickled Pink

Visit **www.nfl.com** and search the Internet, including social media and your library's online databases, to obtain information on women's attitudes toward the National Football League (NFL).

As the marketing director of the NFL, what marketing strategies would you formulate to target female fans?

The NFL would like to appeal to more female fans. What kind of marketing research would you recommend? <

Problem-identification and problem-solving research not only go hand in hand, as shown by the Kellogg's example, but they also follow a common marketing research process.

THE MARKETING RESEARCH PROCESS

We conceptualize the **marketing research process** as consisting of six steps (Figure 1.3): defining the problem, developing an approach to the problem, formulating a research design, doing field work or collecting data, preparing and analyzing data, and preparing and presenting the report. Each of these steps is discussed in great detail in the subsequent chapters; thus, the discussion here is brief.

marketing research process
A set of six steps that define the tasks to be accomplished in conducting a marketing research study. These steps consist of defining the problem, developing an approach to the problem, formulating a research design, doing field work or collecting data, preparing and analyzing data, and preparing and presenting the report.

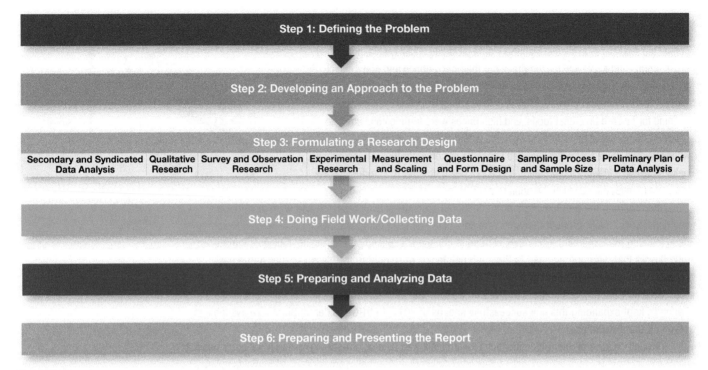

FIGURE 1.3 | THE MARKETING RESEARCH PROCESS

Step 1: Defining the Problem

The first step in any marketing research project is to define the problem. In defining the problem, the researcher should take into account the purpose of the study, the relevant background information, the information needed, and how it will be used by managers in making decisions. Once the problem has been defined precisely, the research can be designed and conducted properly. (See Chapter 2.)

Step 2: Developing an Approach to the Problem

Development of an approach to the problem involves a broad determination of how the problem will be addressed without going into the details. It consists of formulating an analytical framework and models, and research questions and hypotheses, and identifying the information needed. (See Chapter 2.)

Step 3: Formulating a Research Design

A research design gives details of the procedures that must be implemented for obtaining the required information. Its purpose is to design a study that will test the hypotheses of interest, determine possible answers to the research questions, and provide the information needed by managers for making decisions. Determining the type of research to be conducted, defining the variables precisely, and designing appropriate scales to measure them are also part of the research design. The issue of how the data should be obtained from the respondents (for example, by conducting a survey or an experiment) must be addressed. It is also necessary to design a questionnaire. The researcher has to develop a sampling plan that specifies how to select respondents for the study and must prepare a preliminary plan of data analysis. (See Chapters 3 through 10.)

Step 4: Doing Field Work or Collecting Data

Field work, or data collection, involves a field force or staff that operates either in the field, as in the case of personal interviewing, or from an office by telephone, through mail, or electronically as in the case of e-mail and Internet surveys. Proper selection, training, supervision, and evaluation of the field force help minimize data collection errors. (See Chapter 10.)

Step 5: Preparing and Analyzing Data

Data preparation involves adequately preparing the data for analysis. Each questionnaire or observation form is inspected or edited and, if necessary, corrected for any errors. Number or letter codes are assigned to represent each response to each question in the questionnaire; this procedure is called coding. The data from the questionnaires are transcribed or keyed onto disks or storage devices, or input directly into the computer. The data are then analyzed to derive information related to the components of the marketing research problem and thus to provide input into management decision making. (See Chapters 10 through 12.)

Step 6: Preparing and Presenting the Report

The entire project should be documented in a written report that addresses the research questions; describes the approach, the research design, data collection, and data analysis procedures; and presents the results and the major findings. The findings should be presented in a comprehensible format so that management can readily use them in the decision-making process. In addition, an oral presentation should be made to management using tables, figures, and graphs to enhance clarity and impact. (See Chapter 13.)

Although we have described the research process as a sequence of steps, it should be noted that these steps are interdependent and iterative (Figure 1.3). Thus, at each step, the researcher should not only look back at the previous steps but also look ahead to the following steps. Our description of the marketing research process is fairly typical of the research being done by major corporations such as Apple, in the introductory Research in Practice example.

R e s e a r c h   R e c i p e

Follow the marketing research process systematically. All the six steps are important and should be diligently conducted to obtain high-quality findings that add value to the client. While there is a logical sequence, these steps are also interdependent and should be performed iteratively.

THE ROLE OF MARKETING RESEARCH IN MARKETING DECISION MAKING

The nature and role of marketing research can be better understood in light of the basic marketing paradigm depicted in Figure 1.4.

The emphasis in marketing is on the identification and satisfaction of customer needs. To determine customer needs and to implement marketing strategies and programs aimed at satisfying those needs, marketing managers need information. They need information about customers, competitors, and other forces in the marketplace. In recent years, many factors have increased the need for more and better information. As consumers have become more affluent and sophisticated, marketing managers need better information on how they will respond to products and other marketing offerings. As competition has become more intense, managers need information on the effectiveness of their marketing tools relative to competitors. The environment changes more rapidly, and marketing managers need current information.

The task of marketing research is to assess the information needs and provide management with relevant, accurate, reliable, valid, current, and actionable information. Today's competitive marketing environment and the ever-increasing costs attributed to poor decision making require marketing research to provide sound information. Sound decisions are not based on gut feeling, intuition, or even pure judgment. In the absence of sound information, an incorrect management decision may be made.

FIGURE 1.4 |

THE ROLE OF MARKETING
RESEARCH IN MARKETING
DECISION MAKING |

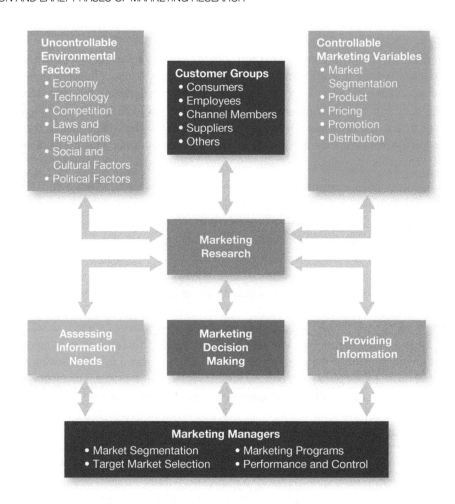

Marketing managers make numerous strategic and tactical decisions in the process of identifying and satisfying customer needs. As shown in Figure 1.4, they make decisions about potential opportunities, target market selection, market segmentation, planning and implementing marketing programs, marketing performance, and control. These decisions are complicated by interactions among the controllable marketing variables of product, pricing, promotion, and distribution, variables that are under the control of the marketing manager. Additional complications come from uncontrollable environmental factors such as general economic conditions, technology, public policies and laws, the political environment, competition, and social and cultural changes. These factors are not under the control of managers. Another factor in this mix is the complexity of the various customer groups: consumers, employees, channel members, shareholders, and suppliers. Marketing research helps the marketing manager link the marketing variables with the environment and the customer groups. It helps remove some of the uncertainty by providing relevant information about the marketing variables, environment, and customer groups. In the absence of relevant information, consumers' response to marketing programs cannot be predicted reliably or accurately. Ongoing marketing research programs provide information on controllable and noncontrollable factors and consumers; this information enhances the effectiveness of decisions made by marketing managers. Marketing researchers also participate in decision making.

In essence, marketing research must add value to marketing decision making, indeed to the entire organization. It should be emphasized that marketing managers do not work in isolation from other functions in the organization. Rather, the marketing orientation embodies a cross-functional perspective to meet consumer needs and attain long-term profitability. Therefore, marketing research should interface with the other functions in the organization such as manufacturing, research and development, finance, accounting, and other areas as may be relevant in a given project.

Research Recipe

Marketing researchers should assess the information needs of the organization, and they should provide management with relevant, accurate, reliable, valid, current, and actionable information. They should actively participate in marketing decision making and also interface with other functional areas in the organization.

As illustrated by the preceding Research in Practice examples, marketing and marketing research are becoming more and more integrated. However, the decision to conduct research has to be made carefully.

THE DECISION TO CONDUCT MARKETING RESEARCH

Marketing research can be beneficial in a variety of situations, but the decision to conduct research is not automatic. Rather, this decision should be guided by a number of considerations, including the costs versus the benefits, the resources available to conduct the research, the resources available to implement the research findings, and management's attitude toward research. Marketing research should be undertaken when the expected value of information it generates exceeds the costs of conducting the marketing research project. In general, the more important the decision confronting management and the greater the uncertainty or risk, the greater the value of information obtained. Formal procedures are available for quantifying the expected value as well as the costs of a marketing research project. Although in most instances the value of information exceeds the costs, the reverse may sometimes be true. A pie manufacturer, for example, wanted to understand consumers' purchase of pies in convenience stores. I advised against a major marketing research project when I discovered that less than 1 percent of the sales were coming from convenience stores and that this situation was unlikely to change in the next five years.

Resources, especially time and money, are always limited. However, if either time or money is not available in adequate amounts to conduct a quality project, that project probably should not be undertaken. It is better not to do a formal project than to undertake one in which the integrity of the research is compromised because of lack of resources. Other instances may constitute arguments against conducting a marketing research project. If the required information is already available within the organization, the decision for which the research is to be conducted has already been made, management does not have a positive attitude toward research, or the research is going to be used for gaining political ends, then the value of information generated is greatly reduced and the project is generally not warranted. However, if the decision is made to conduct marketing research, then management may also rely on marketing research industry suppliers and services to obtain the specific information needed.

Research Recipe

The decision to conduct marketing research is not automatic and should be made carefully. In general, conduct marketing research when the value of information it generates will exceed the cost of doing research and there are no seriously inhibiting constraints.

THE MARKETING RESEARCH INDUSTRY

marketing research industry
The marketing research industry consists of all internal and external suppliers who provide marketing research services.

internal suppliers
Marketing research departments located within firms.

external suppliers
Outside marketing research companies hired to supply marketing research services.

full-service suppliers
Companies that offer the full range of marketing research activities and perform all the six steps of the marketing research process.

customized services
Companies that tailor the research procedures to best meet the needs of each client.

The **marketing research industry** consists of all internal and external suppliers who provide marketing research services. Marketing research suppliers and services provide most of the information needed for making marketing decisions and it is useful to classify them. Broadly, research suppliers can be classified as internal or external (see Figure 1.5). An **internal supplier** is a marketing research department within the firm. Many firms, particularly the big ones, ranging from automobile companies (GM, Ford) to consumer products firms (Procter & Gamble, Colgate Palmolive, Coca-Cola), to banks (JPMorgan Chase, Bank of America), maintain in-house marketing research departments. The marketing research department's place in the organizational structure may vary considerably. At one extreme, the research function may be centralized and located at the corporate headquarters. At the other extreme is a decentralized structure in which the marketing research function is organized along divisional lines. The best organization for a firm depends on its marketing research needs and the structure of marketing and other functions, although in recent years there has been a trend toward centralization and a trimming of the marketing research staff. The involvement of internal client personnel is critical to the success of a marketing research project. Internal suppliers often rely on external suppliers to perform specific marketing research tasks.

External suppliers are outside firms hired to supply marketing research services. These external suppliers range from small (one or a few persons) operations to very large global corporations. Table 1.1 lists the top ten global marketing research suppliers. External suppliers can be classified as full-service or limited-service suppliers. **Full-service suppliers** offer the entire range of marketing research services: problem definition, approach development, questionnaire design, sampling, data collection, data analysis, interpretation, and report preparation and presentation. Thus, these suppliers have the capability to perform all six steps of the marketing research process. The services provided by these suppliers can be further broken down into customized services, syndicated services, and Internet/social media services (Figure 1.5).

Customized services offer a wide variety of marketing research services customized to suit a client's specific needs. Each marketing research project is designed to meet the client's unique

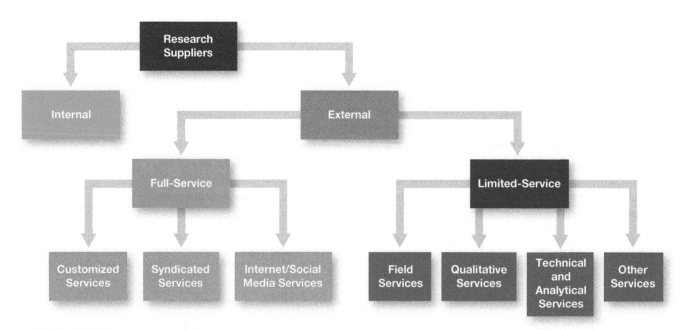

FIGURE 1.5 | MARKETING RESEARCH INDUSTRY: SUPPLIERS AND SERVICES

Table 1.1 > Top Ten Global Research Suppliers

Rank 2012	Rank 2011	Organization	Headquarters	Parent country	Website	Number of Countries with Subsidiaries/ Branch Offices	Global Revenue (US$ millions)	Percent of Global Revenue from Outside Home Country (%)
1	1	Nielsen Holdings N.V.	New York	U.S.	Nielsen.com	100	$5,429.0	51.2%
2	2	Kantar	London & Fairfield, Conn.	U.K.	Kantar.com	80	3,338.6	72.2
3	3	Ipsos SA	Paris	France	Ipsos.com	85	2,301.1	93.2
4	4	GfK SE	Nuremberg	Germany	Gfk.com	68	1,947.8	70.0
5	6	IMS Health Inc.	Parsippany, N.J.	U.S.	IMSHealth.com	74	775.0	65.0
6	5	Information Resources Inc.	Chicago	U.S.	IRIworldwide.com	8	763.8	37.3
7	8	INTAGE Inc.	Tokyo	Japan	Intage.co.jp	7	500.3	2.6
8	7	Westat Inc.	Rockville, Md.	U.S.	Westat.com	8	495.9	1.0
9	9	Arbitron Inc.	Columbia, VA	U.S.	Arbitron.com	3	449.9	1.3
10	10	The NPD Group Inc.	Port Washington, N.Y.	U.S.	NPD.com	13	272.0	29.5

Source: Marketing News (August 2013):24, American Marketing Association.

needs. All the costs are paid by the client and the information generated becomes the intellectual property of that client. Some of the marketing research firms that offer these services are Kantar, Westat, and Burke, Inc.

Syndicated services are companies that collect and sell common pools of data designed to serve information needs that are shared by a number of clients. These data are collected primarily through surveys, purchase and media panels, scanners, and audits. For example, Nielsen provides information on audience size and demographic characteristics of households watching specific television programs (**www.nielsen.com**). The Nielsen Company also provides scanner tracking data, such as that generated by electronic scanners at checkout counters in supermarkets. The NPD Group (**www.npd.com**), another example of a syndicated service, maintains one of the largest consumer panels in the United States. Syndicated services are discussed in more detail in Chapter 3.

Several marketing research firms, including some that have specialized in conducting marketing research on the Internet, offer **Internet services** including social media research. For example, the Toluna Group (**www.toluna-group.com**), which acquired Greenfield Online and Ciao Surveys in 2009, offers a broad range of customized qualitative and quantitative online marketing research for consumer, business-to-business, and professional markets. Using large, proprietary databases, studies are conducted within the company's secure website. Forrester Research (**www.forrester.com**), which acquired Jupiter Research in 2008, offers research and consulting services that focus on consumer online behavior and interactive technologies. A special class of Internet services focuses on social media research, and these companies are discussed later in the chapter.

Limited-service suppliers specialize in one or a few steps of the marketing research process. Limited-service suppliers specialize in field services, qualitative services, technical and analytical services, and other services. **Field services** collect data. They might use the full range of data collection methods (i.e., mail, personal, telephone, and electronic interviewing), or they might specialize in only one method. Some field service organizations maintain extensive interviewing facilities across the country for interviewing shoppers in malls. Firms that offer field services include Field Work, Inc., (**www.fieldwork.com**), Booth Research Services (**www.boothresearch.com**), and WorldOne (**www.worldone.com**).

syndicated services
Companies that collect and sell common pools of data designed to serve information needs shared by a number of clients.

Internet services
Companies that specialize in conducting marketing research on the Internet, including social media.

limited-service suppliers
Companies that specialize in one or a few steps of the marketing research process.

field services
Companies whose primary service offering is their expertise in collecting data for research projects.

qualitative services
Services related to facilities, recruitment, and other services for focus groups and other forms of qualitative research such as one-on-one depth interviews.

technical and analytical services
Companies that provide guidance in the development of the research design and computer analysis of qualitative and quantitative data.

data analysis services
Firms whose primary service is to conduct statistical analysis of data.

branded marketing research products
Specialized data collection and analysis procedures developed to address specific types of marketing research problems.

Qualitative services provide facilities and recruit respondents for focus groups and other forms of qualitative research, such as one-on-one depth interviews (discussed in Chapter 4). Some firms might provide additional services, such as moderators, and prepare focus group reports. Examples of such firms include Jackson Associates (**www.jacksonassociates.com**) and 20|20 Research, Inc. (**www.2020research.com**).

Technical and analytical services are offered by firms that specialize in design issues and computer analysis of qualitative and quantitative data, such as those obtained in large surveys. Firms such as SDR of Atlanta (**www.sdr-consulting.com**) offer sophisticated data analysis using advanced statistical techniques. Sawtooth Technologies (**www.sawtooth.com**) provides software for research data collection and analysis. Statistical software packages enable firms to perform data analysis in-house. However, **data analysis services** of outside suppliers that provide specialized data-analysis expertise are still in demand. Other services include **branded marketing research products** that are specialized data collection and analysis procedures developed to address specific types of marketing research problems. For example, Survey Sampling International (**www.surveysampling.com**) specializes in sampling design and distribution. Some firms focus on specialized services, such as research in ethnic markets (i.e., Hispanic, African, multicultural). Two firms that focus on research in ethnic markets are Latin Facts Research, a subsidiary of Facts 'n' Figures, Inc. (**www.factsnfiguresinc.com**) and Multicultural Insights (**www.multicultural-insights.com**).

A firm without an internal marketing research department or specialists is forced to rely on external, full-service suppliers. A firm with an internal marketing research staff can use both full- and limited-service suppliers. While Apple employs its own marketing researchers, it also relies heavily on both full- and limited-service suppliers. Certain guidelines should be followed when selecting a research supplier, whether it is a full-service or a limited-service supplier.

Research Recipe

The involvement of internal client personnel is critical to the success of a marketing research project. It is often desirable to have external suppliers conduct one or more steps of the marketing research process. Consider the services of both full-service and limited-service suppliers to best meet the needs of a marketing research project.

SELECTING A RESEARCH SUPPLIER

A firm that cannot conduct an entire marketing research project in-house must select an external supplier for one or more phases of the project. The firm should compile a list of prospective suppliers from sources such as trade publications, professional directories, and word of mouth. When deciding on criteria for selecting an outside supplier, a firm should ask itself why it is seeking outside marketing research support. For example, a small firm that needs one project investigated may find it economically efficient to employ an outside source. A firm may not have the resources or the technical expertise to undertake certain phases of a project, or political conflict-of-interest issues may determine that a project be conducted by an outside supplier.

When developing criteria for selecting an outside supplier, a firm should keep some basics in mind. What is the reputation of the supplier? Does it complete projects on schedule? Is it known for maintaining ethical standards? Is it flexible? Are its research projects of high quality? What kind and how much experience does the supplier have? Has the firm had experience with projects similar to this one? Do the supplier's personnel have both technical and nontechnical expertise? In other words, in addition to technical skills, are the personnel assigned to the task sensitive to the client's needs, and do they share the client's research ideology? Do they have Professional Researcher Certification offered by the Marketing Research Association (**www.marketingresearch.org**)? Can they communicate well with the client? You can also find checklists for qualifying marketing research suppliers at the websites of prominent marketing research associations (e.g., **www.esomar.org**).

A competitive bidding process is often used in selecting external suppliers, particularly for large jobs. Often an organization commissioning research to external suppliers issues a request for proposal (RFP), or a similar call, inviting suppliers to submit bids. You can locate actual RFPs on the Internet by doing a Google advanced search using "RFP" and "marketing research." Some marketing research firms, such as Marketing Research Services, Inc. (**www.mrsi.com**), post a RFP format on their websites that prospective clients can use to issue RFPs. Awarding projects based on lowest price is not a good rule of thumb. The completeness of the research proposal and the criteria discussed above must all be factored into the hiring decision. Long-term contracts with research suppliers are preferable to selection on a project-by-project basis.

Research Recipe

Awarding marketing research projects based on the lowest bid is not a good rule of thumb. Rather, consider several factors in selecting a supplier. In general, long-term contracts with research suppliers are preferable to selection on a project-by-project basis.

The Internet is very efficient for identifying marketing research firms that supply specific services. Using a search engine, such as Yahoo!, several research firms can be identified, and it is easy to find information on the suppliers at their websites. Many sites include information on company history, products, clients, and employees. For example, **www.greenbook.org** lists thousands of market research companies, and specific firms can be conveniently located using their search procedures.

Career opportunities are available with marketing research suppliers, as well as with marketing and advertising firms.

iResearch
Google: Shopping for Shoppers

Visit **www.greenbook.org** and identify all the marketing research firms in your state that conduct Internet-based surveys.

As the research director for Google, you need to select a marketing research firm that specializes in researching consumer shopping on the Internet. Make a list of five such firms. Which one will you select and why?

As the director of marketing, how would you use information on consumer shopping on the Internet to increase Google's penetration of this segment? ‹

CAREERS IN MARKETING RESEARCH

Promising career opportunities are available with marketing research firms (e.g., the Nielsen Co., Burke, Inc., and The Kantar Group). Equally appealing are careers in business and nonbusiness firms and agencies with in-house marketing research departments (e.g., Procter & Gamble, Coca-Cola, GM, the Federal Trade Commission, and United States Census Bureau). Advertising agencies (e.g., BBDO International, J. Walter Thompson, and Young & Rubicam) also conduct substantial marketing research and employ professionals in this field. Some of the positions available in marketing research include vice president of marketing research, research director, assistant director of research, project manager, statistician/data processing specialist, senior analyst, analyst, junior analyst, field work director, and operational supervisor.

The most common entry-level position in marketing research for people with bachelor's degrees (e.g., bachelor of business administration [BBA]) is an operational supervisor. These people are responsible for supervising a well-defined set of operations, including field work, data editing, and coding, and may be involved in programming and data analysis. In the marketing research industry, however, there is a growing preference for people with master's degrees. Those with MBA or equivalent degrees are likely to be employed as project managers. The typical entry-level position in a business firm would be junior research analyst (for BBAs) or research analyst (for MBAs). The junior analyst and the research analyst learn about the particular industry and receive training from a senior staff member, usually the marketing research manager. The junior analyst position includes a training program to prepare individuals for the responsibilities of a research analyst, including coordinating with the marketing department and sales force to develop goals for product exposure. The research analyst responsibilities include checking all data for accuracy, comparing and contrasting new research findings with established norms, and analyzing primary and secondary data for the purpose of market forecasting.

As these job titles indicate, people with a variety of backgrounds and skills are needed in marketing research. For descriptions of other marketing research positions and current salaries, visit **www.marketresearchcareers.com**. To prepare for a career in marketing research, you should:

- Take all the marketing courses you can.
- Take courses in statistics and quantitative methods.
- Acquire Internet, social media, and computer skills. Knowledge of programming languages is an added asset.
- Take courses in psychology, sociology, and consumer behavior.
- Acquire effective written and verbal communication skills.
- Think creatively. Creativity and common sense command a premium in marketing research.

Marketing researchers should be liberally educated so that they can understand the problems confronting managers and address them from a broad perspective. The following Research in Practice feature shows what makes a successful marketing researcher and marketing manager.

Research in Practice
Eric Kim: A Career in Marketing and Marketing Research Can Take You to the Top

Eric B. Kim earned an undergraduate degree in physics at Harvey Mudd College in Claremont, California; a master's degree in engineering at UCLA; and an MBA at Harvard. He learned his current craft at places such as Lotus Development Corp.; D&B; and Spencer Trask Software Group, a technology-focused venture capital firm in New York City. Spencer Trask CEO Kevin Kimberlin remembers Kim as the rare executive who knows software and electronics and is also skilled in marketing and marketing research.

When Kim arrived at Samsung in 1999, he realized that the basic problem lay in the brand image and that the Samsung brand was perceived to be inferior to other brands with comparable products. To confirm his intuition and dig out specific, actionable issues, he conducted marketing research involving focus groups, in-depth interviews, and surveys of channel partners and customers. The research revealed that brand image was fuzzy and inconsistent from market to market. One reason was that Samsung employed a gaggle of fifty-five ad agencies. Kim consolidated advertising, assigning Madison Avenue's Foote, Cone & Belding Worldwide to coordinate Samsung's global marketing. Kim made another smart move by sponsoring big-ticket events like the Salt Lake City Olympics in 2002, gaining quick, cost-effective global exposure. When Kim left Samsung in 2004, the company earned $12.04 billion in net profits that year (while many retail-tech stars fizzled), and business in the United States had more than tripled since 1999.

On November 4, 2004, Intel poached Samsung executive Eric Kim and used him to invigorate its advertising and inject more consumer values into the chip giant's brand. Kim's secret lies in his broad-based education and very good knowledge of marketing and marketing research. In June 2010, Kim became the CEO and president of Soraa, a clean-tech semiconductor company. Yes, a career in marketing and marketing research can take you to the top![3] <

Research Recipe

To prepare for a career in marketing research, you should take courses in marketing, psychology, and quantitative methods, and acquire verbal and written communication and Internet skills. A liberal, broad-based education will serve you well.

THE ROLE OF MARKETING RESEARCH IN MIS AND DSS

Earlier, we defined *marketing research* as the systematic and objective identification, collection, analysis, dissemination, and use of information for making marketing decisions. Combining external marketing information with internal billing, production, and other records results in a powerful marketing information system (MIS) (Figure 1.6).

A **marketing information system (MIS)** is a formalized set of procedures for generating, analyzing, storing, and distributing information to marketing decision makers on an ongoing basis. Such systems are differentiated from marketing research in that they are continuously available. Marketing information systems are designed to complement the decision maker's responsibilities, style, and information needs. The power of an MIS is in the access it gives managers to vast amounts of information by combining production, invoice, and billing information with marketing intelligence, including marketing research, into a centralized data warehouse. An MIS offers the potential of much more information than can be obtained from ad hoc marketing research projects. However, that potential often is not achieved when the information is structured so rigidly that it cannot be easily manipulated. Developed to overcome the limitations of MIS, **decision support systems (DSS)** have built-in flexibility that allows decision makers to interact directly with databases and analysis models. Information generated by marketing research should become a part of a MIS and a DSS, as illustrated by Apple in the first Research in Practice. All these systems can greatly enhance the effectiveness of marketing decision making.

marketing information system (MIS)
A formalized set of procedures for generating, analyzing, storing, and distributing pertinent information to marketing decision makers on an ongoing basis.

decision support system (DSS)
An information system that enables decision makers to interact directly with both databases and analysis models.

FIGURE 1.6
THE DEVELOPMENT OF MIS AND DSS

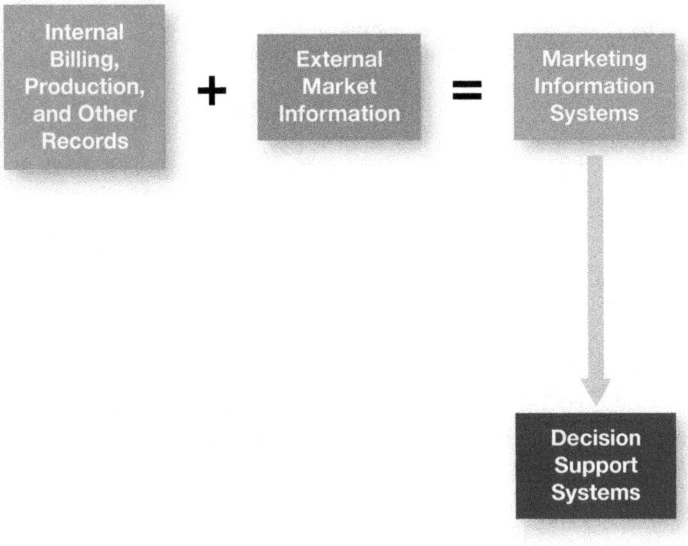

> **Research Recipe**
>
> Information generated by marketing research should be made a part of a MIS and a DSS. The integration with these systems can greatly enhance the value of marketing research and improve decision making.

INTERNATIONAL MARKETING RESEARCH

We use the term *international marketing research* broadly to denote all research conducted in markets other than the domestic market of the research commissioning organization. The United States accounts for 40 percent of the marketing research expenditures worldwide. About 40 percent of all marketing research is conducted in western Europe, 10 percent in Japan, and 10 percent in other parts of the world. Most of the research in Europe is done in Germany, the United Kingdom, France, Italy, and Spain. With the globalization of markets, marketing research has assumed a truly international character, and this trend is likely to continue. Several U.S. firms conduct international marketing research, including Nielsen, IMS Health, and SymphonyIRI (see Table 1.1). Foreign-based firms include Kantar (United Kingdom), GfK (Germany), and INTAGE (Japan).

Conducting international marketing research is much more complex than domestic marketing research. The environment prevailing in the countries or international markets that are being researched influences the way the six steps of the marketing research process should be performed. These environmental factors consist of the marketing, government, legal, economic, structural, informational and technological, and the sociocultural environments (see Figure 1.7). The impact of these factors on the marketing research process is discussed in detail in subsequent chapters.

Despite the complexity involved, international marketing research is expected to grow at a faster rate than domestic research. A major contributing factor is that markets for many products in the

FIGURE 1.7 |
FRAMEWORK FOR
INTERNATIONAL
MARKETING RESEARCH

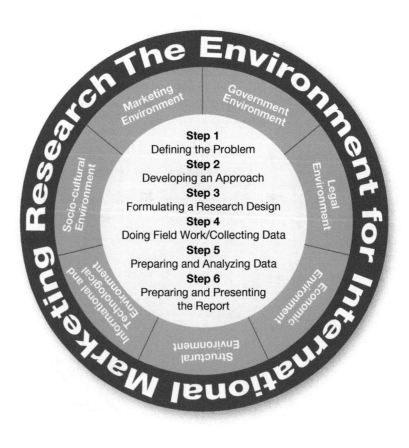

United States are approaching saturation. In contrast, the markets for these products in other countries are in the early stages of development, as illustrated by the following Research in Practice feature.

Research in Practice
McDonald's: Adapting to Local Culture with Its Global Image

In markets across the globe, McDonald's respects local cultures and has adopted its menu and dining experience to local preferences. Marketing research showed that, in India, food consumption was influenced by people's religious beliefs. Accordingly, McDonald's dropped beef and pork from its menus, conforming to the religious beliefs of Hindus and Muslims, who make up most of India's population. Instead, it has numerous vegetarian versions of some of its American classics, like the McVeggie burger and McSpicy Paneer, as well as chicken offerings. On the value menu, the McAloo Tikki burger, made from a potato-based patty, is a top seller, accounting for as much as 25 percent of the restaurants' total sales in India.

Source: david pearson / Alamy.

Marketing research also revealed that vegetarians in India are strict in observing food habits and practices. Therefore, McDonald's kitchens in this country are divided into separate sections for cooking vegetarian and nonvegetarian food. In September 2012, the fast-food giant announced that the new restaurants in some pilgrimage areas in India will be vegetarian-only to cater to the preferences of the local customer base.

In part, McDonald's success globally has been attributed to its ability to adapt to local culture and preferences while retaining its global brand image, which is made possible by its reliance on marketing research.[4] <

Research Recipe

In international marketing research, take into account the environmental factors in the countries where research is being conducted. The same six steps of the marketing research process have to be performed but within the context of the environment of international markets or countries.

iResearch
Levi's: Increasing Global Market Share

Visit **www.levis.com** and search the Internet, including social media, and your library's online databases to find information on consumer preferences for jeans. Levi's would like to conduct marketing research to increase its share of the jeans market in the United States and India. How would you conduct marketing research in the two countries?

As Levi's marketing chief, what information would you need to formulate strategies aimed at increasing global market share? <

MARKETING RESEARCH AND SOCIAL MEDIA

Social media embody social computing tools commonly referred to as Web 2.0. These are Web applications that facilitate interactive information sharing, user-centered design, and collaboration on the World Wide Web. Examples of social media include social-networking sites (e.g., Facebook), video sharing (e.g., YouTube), photo sharing (e.g., Flickr, Instagram), music sharing (e.g., Last FM), bookmarking (e.g., Delicious), voice networking (e.g., Skype), wikis (e.g., Wikipedia), product and service reviews (e.g., TripAdvisor), virtual worlds (e.g., Second Life), multiplayer games (e.g., Farmville), Web-based communities (e.g., ivillage), blogs (e.g., Direct2Dell), and microblogs (e.g., Twitter).

Marketing researchers can make use of these new social networks to conduct marketing research in a way that complements the use of the traditional methods. These social communities open new avenues for understanding, explaining, influencing, and predicting the behaviors of consumers in the marketplace. Thus, they can be used in a variety of marketing research applications, including segmentation, idea generation, product development and testing, brand launches, pricing, and integrated marketing communications.

Social media are not without limitations. Although the standard for objectivity is high for journalists, expectations about objectivity among bloggers and other social media users are lower. Social media users may not be representative of the target population in many marketing research applications. Social media as a source of samples suffers from at least two biases: from self-selection (the respondents can self-select themselves into the sample) and from advocacy. As long as these limitations are understood, however, insights from social media analysis can uncover useful information that can inform marketing decisions. In this book, we advocate the use of social media as an additional domain in which to conduct marketing research to supplement and complement, but not to replace, the traditional ways in which research is conducted. We illustrate how one firm, namely, Starbucks, is using social media to obtain information and connect with consumers in the target market.

Research in Practice
Starbucks: The Star of Social Media

Starbucks has a blog, My Starbucks Idea (MSI) (**mystarbucksidea.force.com**), where it not only connects with customers but also co-creates the company's future with them. Customers can share ideas, vote on ideas others have suggested, discuss ideas with other customers, and view the ideas Starbucks has announced. Starbucks's Idea Partners from different departments within the company take part in answering queries and providing insights to discussions. Starbucks can then get ideas and feedback on how to improve its products to satisfy the needs of customers. The brand takes suggestions posted on the site seriously and publishes implemented suggestions for all to see. It encourages feedback from customers by providing online incentives in the form of virtual vouchers or purchase points. This enables the brand to interact with its loyal customers. Starbucks also includes qualitative and quantitative types of survey questions in the form of polls along the sidelines of the blog to solicit marketing research data. My Starbucks Idea has a significant impact: On average, one in three suggestions is implemented. All suggestions are acknowledged and commented on within an hour of uploading; an average of four suggestions are made every hour.

Starbucks's Facebook page (**www.facebook.com/starbucks**) has more than 34 million fans, and the number is still growing. It uses this site to promote new products and gain the feedback of customers. It also organizes events and uses Facebook's technology to invite customers to attend its events. It has a collection of photos from its products and events, among many others uploaded by fans. Starbucks updates its Facebook page approximately once every two days, and every update sees thousands of users responding to it. The company actively comments on or replies to its followers' posts or photo tags of them, increasing its presence on social media. Starbucks also uses its Facebook page to develop a target market's profile.

Starbucks also uses Twitter (**www.twitter.com/starbucks**) to promote products and connect with customers. The firm uses Twitter to update customers about new products and services with short messages. Tools like retweets allow users to spread messages originally Tweeted by Starbucks to others. Starbucks's Twitter account often directs followers to MSI for polls, surveys, or opinions-casting.

Starbucks also uses many other forms of social media. An example of how social media have helped Starbucks improve its service is the recurring requests for free wireless and the final move made by Starbucks to offer free unlimited wireless to all its customers. Likewise, several members of the MSI community posted ideas requesting that fresh fruit be served at Starbucks. In response, Starbucks began producing a new drink with a fruity touch, alongside its new iced coffee beverage, to help beat the summer heat. From the tropics of the Bahamas to the Forbidden City in Beijing, social media have helped Starbucks serve its corporate logo alongside freshly brewed coffees in meeting the needs of customers. As of 2014, the brand is represented in more than sixty countries and continues to grow.[5] <

Source: David Adamson/Alamy.

Research Recipe

As long as you understand the limitations of social media, they can be valuable as an additional domain in which to conduct marketing research. Analysis of social media can complement the traditional methods of doing research and add value to the marketing research project.

ETHICS IN MARKETING RESEARCH

Marketing research has often been described as having four stakeholders: (1) the marketing researcher, (2) the client, (3) the respondent, and (4) the public (Figure 1.8). These stakeholders have certain responsibilities to each other and to the research project. Ethical issues arise when the interests of these stakeholders are in conflict and when one or more of the stakeholders is lacking in its responsibilities. For example, if the researcher does not follow appropriate marketing research procedures, or if the client misrepresents the findings in the company's advertising, ethical norms are violated. Ethical issues are best resolved by the stakeholders behaving honorably. Codes of conduct, by professional associations such as the American Marketing Association code of ethics, are available to guide behavior and help resolve ethical dilemmas. Ethical issues are discussed in more detail in the subsequent chapters. We give the URLs of important marketing research associations that provide ethical codes in the following Research in Practice feature.

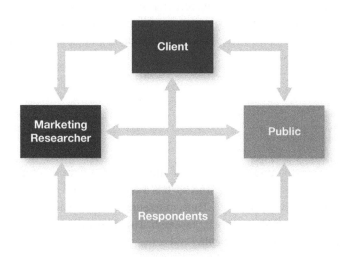

FIGURE 1.8

STAKEHOLDERS IN MARKETING RESEARCH: AN ETHICAL PERSPECTIVE

Research in Practice
Marketing Research Associations Online

Domestic

AAPOR: American Association for Public Opinion Research (**www.aapor.org**)

AMA: American Marketing Association (**www.marketingpower.com**)

ARF: The Advertising Research Foundation (**www.thearf.org**)

CASRO: The Council of American Survey Research Organizations (**www.casro.org**)

MRA: Marketing Research Association (**www.marketingresearch.org**)

QRCA: Qualitative Research Consultants Association (**www.qrca.org**)

International

ESOMAR: European Society for Opinion and Marketing Research (**www.esomar.org**)

MRS: The Market Research Society (UK) (**www.mrs.org.uk**)

AMSRS: The Australian Market & Social Research Society (**www.amsrs.com.au**)

CMA: The Canadian Marketing Association (**www.the-cma.org**) <

Research Recipe

It is imperative that the marketing researcher behaves ethically with respect to the other stakeholders: the client, the respondents, and the general public. The marketing research firm should follow the codes of conduct from the various professional associations. The other stakeholders also have a responsibility to behave ethically.

Dell Running Case

Review the Dell Direct case, Case 1.1, and questionnaire given toward the end of the book. Answer the following questions.

1. Discuss the role that marketing research can play in helping Dell maintain and build on its leadership position in the personal computers market.
2. What problem-identification research should Dell undertake?
3. What problem-solving research should Dell undertake?
4. Would you like to pursue a marketing research career with Dell? Explain.
5. How can Dell use social media to obtain marketing research information?

Summary

Marketing research assesses information needs and provides relevant information in order to improve the marketing decision-making process. It is a systematic and objective process designed to identify and solve marketing problems. Thus, marketing research can be classified as problem-identification research and problem-solving research. The marketing research process consists of six steps that must be followed systematically.

Marketing research provides information about consumers, channel members, competitors, changes and trends in the marketplace, and other aspects of the firm's environment. The decision to conduct marketing research should be guided by a number of considerations, including costs versus benefits, the resources available to conduct the research, the resources available to implement the research findings, and management's attitude toward research.

A firm can conduct its own marketing research or purchase it from external suppliers. External suppliers might provide full-service or specialize in one or more aspects of the process. Full-service suppliers provide the entire range of marketing research services, from problem definition to report preparation and presentation. The services provided by these suppliers can be classified as customized services, syndicated services, or Internet services. Limited-service suppliers specialize in one or a few phases of the marketing research project. These suppliers might offer field services; qualitative services; technical and analytical services; and other specialized services, such as sampling.

The marketing research industry offers a wide range of careers in both corporate and independent research organizations. Marketing research firms, business and nonbusiness firms, and advertising agencies all employ research professionals. Information obtained using marketing research should be made part of MIS and DSS.

International marketing research is much more complex than domestic research because researchers must consider the environment in the international markets they are researching. Social media are emerging as an important domain in which to conduct marketing research. The ethical issues in marketing research involve four stakeholders: (1) the marketing researcher, (2) the client, (3) the respondent, and (4) the public.

∨ Companion Website

This textbook includes numerous student resources that can be found at **www.pearsonglobaleditions.com/malhotra**. At this Companion website, you'll find:

- Student Resource Manual
- Demo movies of statistical procedures using SPSS and Microsoft Excel
- Screen captures of statistical procedures using SPSS and Microsoft Excel
- Data files for all datasets in SPSS and Microsoft Excel
- Additional figures and tables
- Videos and write-ups for all video cases
- Other valuable resources

∨ Key Terms and Concepts

Marketing research	External suppliers	Qualitative services
Problem-identification research	Full-service suppliers	Technical and analytical services
Problem-solving research	Syndicated services	Data analysis services
Marketing information system	Customized services	Branded marketing research products
Decision support system	Limited-service suppliers	Marketing research process
Internal suppliers	Internet services	
	Field services	

⌄ Suggested Cases and Video Cases

Running Case with Real Data and Questionnaire
    1.1 Dell

Comprehensive Critical Thinking Cases
    2.1 American Idol

Comprehensive Cases with Real Data and Questionnaires
    3.1 JPMorgan Chase   3.2 Wendy's

Online Video Cases
    1.1 Burke   2.1 Accenture   3.1 NFL   7.1 P&G   8.1 Dunkin' Donuts
    9.1 Subaru   10.1 Intel   13.1 Marriott

⌄ Live Research: Conducting a Marketing Research Project

1. Give the background of the client organization.
2. Discuss the client's marketing organization and operations.
3. Explain how the project's result will help the client make specific marketing decisions.
4. Organize the class. This might require the formation of project teams. The entire class could be working on the same project, with each team working on all aspects of the project, or each team could be assigned a specific responsibility (e.g., a specific component of the problem or a specific aspect of the project, such as collection and analysis of secondary data). Each student should participate in primary data collection. Alternatively, the class could be working on multiple projects with specific teams assigned to a specific project. The approach is flexible and can handle a variety of organizations and formats.
5. Develop a project schedule that clearly specifies the deadlines for the different steps.
6. Explain how the teams will be evaluated.
7. One or a few students should be selected as project coordinators.

⌄ Acronyms

The role and salient characteristics of marketing research may be described by the acronym RESEARCH:

R ecognition of information needs

E ffective decision making

S ystematic and objective

E xude/disseminate information

A nalysis of information

R ecommendations for action

C ollection of information

H elpful to managers

⌄ Review Questions

1-1. Describe the task of marketing research.

1-2. What decisions are made by marketing managers? How does marketing research help in making these decisions?

1-3. Define marketing research.

1-4. What are the different methods of conducting marketing research?

1-5. What are some of the issues that should be considered when conducting marketing research?

1-6. Why do organizations conduct marketing research?

1-7. What are syndicated services?

1-8. What is the main difference between a full-service and a limited-service supplier?

1-9. What are some of the reasons for the increased need for marketing research?

1-10. List five guidelines for selecting an external marketing research supplier.

1-11. What career opportunities are available in marketing research?

1-12. What is a marketing information system?

1-13. How is a DSS different from an MIS?

1-14. List two possible limitations when using social media for marketing research.

1-15. Discuss an ethical issue in marketing research that relates to each of the following stakeholders: (1) client, (2) the supplier, and (3) the respondent.

⌄ Applied Problems

1-16. Search the Internet, including social media, to identify five examples of problem-identification research and five examples of problem-solving research.

1-17. List one kind of marketing research that would be useful to each of the following organizations:

    a. Your campus bookstore

    b. The public transportation authority in your city

    c. A major department store in your area

    d. A restaurant located near your campus

    e. A zoo in a major city

⌄ Internet Exercises

1-18. Visit the websites of the top three marketing research firms in Table 1.1. Write a report on the services offered by these firms. Use the framework of Figure 1.5. What statements can you make about the structure of the marketing research industry?

1-19. Visit the Vodafone website for your region. Write a report on the marketing and promotional activities done by the company.

1-20. Check the websites of the American Marketing Association, the Interactive Market Research Association and the Advertising Research Association. From these websites, can you determine the main trends occurring in marketing research?

1-21. Visit **www.marketresearchcareers.com**. What are some of the common career paths in marketing research?

1-22. Examine recent issues of magazines such as *Marketing News, Advertising Age, Quirk's Marketing Research Review*, and *Marketing Research: A Magazine of Management and Applications* to identify an Internet application in each of the following areas:

    a. Identification of information needs

    b. Collection of information

    c. Analysis of information

    d. Provision of information (report preparation)

NOTES

1. Mark Prigg, "Apple will launch FIVE new products in 2013 (including their first TV), analysts claim," online at **www.dailymail.co.uk/sciencetech/article-2260097/5-new-Apple-products-coming-2013-including-TV--analysts-claim.html**, accessed May 5, 2013; Philip Elmer-DeWitt, (September 14, 2012), "Pre-orders for Apple's iPhone 5 Sell Out in Less Than an Hour," online at **http://tech.fortune.cnn.com/2012/09/14/pre-orders-for-apples-iphone-5-sell-out-in-less-than-an-hour/?iid=HP_LN**, accessed May 6, 2013; David Goldman, "Apple sells 3 million new iPads in 4 days," online at **http://money.cnn.com/2012/03/19/technology/apple-ipad-sales/index.htm?iid=Lead**, accessed March 20, 2013; and Yukari I. Kane and Geoffrey A. Fowler, "Steven Paul Jobs, 1955–2011," *Wall Street Journal* (October 6, 2011): A1, A7.
2. www.kelloggs.com, accessed May 5, 2013; and Catherine Boal, "Kellogg Rolls Out New Cereal and Snacking Options," *Bakery & Snacks*, online at **www.bakeryandsnacks.com/news/ng.asp?id=74110-kellogg-leatherhead-breakfast-snacks,** accessed May 5, 2013.
3. "Soraa Hires Eric Kim As New President, CEO," online at **www.freshnews.com/news/340726/soraa-hires-eric-kim-new-president-ceo**, accessed January 10, 2013; and "CEO Interview: Eric Kim of Twylah," online at **www.rickliebling.com/2011/09/05/ceo-interview-eric-kim-of-twylah/**, accessed January 10, 2013.
4. Annie Gasparro and Julie Jargon, "McDonald's to Go Vegetarian in India," *Wall Street Journal* (Wednesday, September 5, 2012): B7.
5. Starbucks Facebook page, online at **www.facebook.com/Starbucks**, accessed May 5, 2013; My Starbucks Idea, online at **http://mystarbucksidea.force.com/**, accessed April 8, 2013; and Seattle's Best Coffee Introduces New Specialty Iced Drinks to Help Beat the Summer Heat, online at **http://news.starbucks.com/article_display.cfm?article_id=394,** accessed October 8, 2012.

Online Video Case 1.1

BURKE: Learning and Growing Through Marketing Research

Visit **www.pearsonglobaleditions.com/malhotra** to read the video case and view the accompanying video. Burke: Learning and Growing Through Marketing Research traces the evolution of marketing research and how Burke implements the various steps of the marketing research process. Burke's approach to all the six steps of the marketing research process is highlighted: defining the marketing research problem, developing an approach to the problem, formulating a research design, collecting data, analyzing the data, and preparing and presenting the report. This case can be used to discuss the role of marketing research in marketing decision making and the steps of the marketing research process. Specific marketing research questions are posed in the video case.

Defining the Marketing Research Problem and Developing an Approach

∨ Overview

This chapter covers the first two of the six steps of the marketing research process described in Chapter 1: defining the marketing research problem and developing an approach to the problem. Defining the problem is the first and most important step because only when a problem has been clearly and accurately identified can a research project be conducted properly. Defining the marketing research problem sets the course of the entire project. In this chapter, we want you to appreciate the complexities involved in defining a problem by identifying the tasks involved and the factors to be considered. We also provide guidelines for appropriately defining the marketing research problem and avoiding common types of errors. We discuss in detail the components of an approach to the problem: analytical framework and models, research questions and hypotheses, and specification of the information needed. The special considerations involved in defining the problem and developing an approach in international marketing research are presented. Finally, we discuss the impact of social media and the ethical issues that arise at this stage of the marketing research process.

Figure 2.1 gives the relationship of this chapter to the marketing research process discussed in Chapter 1. We introduce our discussion with an example from Harley-Davidson, which needed specific information about its customers.

The most challenging part of any research project is defining the problem in the terms management understands and in a way that ensures the desired information is obtained."

> **Chet Zalesky, President, CMI, Atlanta, Georgia**

∨ Learning Objectives

After reading this chapter, the student should be able to:

1. Understand the importance of and process used for defining the marketing research problem.

2. Describe the tasks involved in problem definition, including discussion with decision maker(s), interview with industry experts, secondary data analysis, and qualitative research.

3. Discuss the environmental factors affecting the definition of the research problem: past information and forecasts, resources and constraints, objectives of the decision maker, buyer behavior, legal environment, economic environment, and marketing and technological skills of the firm.

4. Clarify the distinction between the management decision problem and the marketing research problem.

5. Explain the structure of a well-defined marketing research problem, including the broad statement and the specific components.

6. Discuss in detail the various components of the approach: analytical framework and models, research questions and hypotheses, and identification of the information needed.

7. Acquire an appreciation of the complexity involved in defining the problem and developing an approach in international marketing research.

8. Describe how social media can be used to identify and define the marketing research problem and aid in developing an approach.

9. Understand the ethical issues and conflicts that arise in defining the problem and developing the approach.

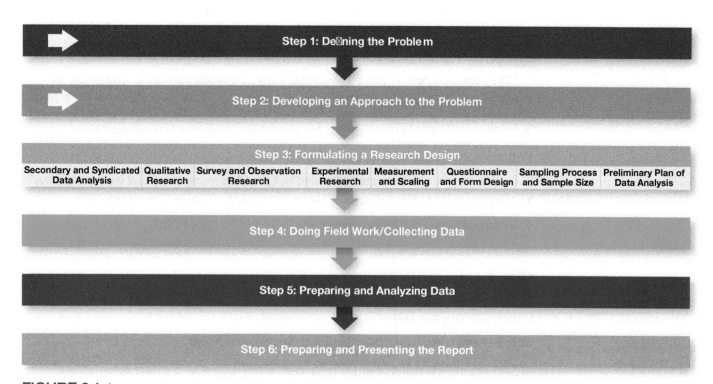

FIGURE 2.1 | RELATIONSHIP OF THIS CHAPTER TO THE MARKETING RESEARCH PROCESS

Research in Practice
Harley Goes Whole Hog

The motorcycle manufacturer Harley-Davidson (**www.harleydavidson.com**) made such an important comeback in the early 2000s that there was a long waiting list to get a bike. Harley-Davidson's revenues were $5.58 billion in 2012, and it was the U.S. market leader in the heavyweight category in 2013. Although distributors urged Harley-Davidson to build more motorcycles, the company was skeptical about investing in new production facilities.

Past years of declining sales had taught top management to be more risk-averse than risk-prone. Harley-Davidson was now performing well again, and investing in new facilities meant taking risks. Would the demand follow in the long run or would customers stop wanting Harleys when the next fad came along? The decrease in motorcycles' quality linked to Harley's fast growth had cost the company all its bad years. Top management was afraid that the decision to invest was too early. On the other hand, investing would help Harley-Davidson expand and possibly become the dominant market leader in the heavyweight segment. Discussions with industry experts indicated that brand loyalty was a major factor influencing the sales and repeat sales of motorcycles. Secondary data revealed that the vast majority of motorcycle owners also owned automobiles such as cars, SUVs, and trucks. Focus groups with motorcycle owners further indicated that in the United States, motorcycles were not used primarily as a means of basic transportation but as a means of recreation. The focus groups and social media also highlighted the role of brand loyalty in motorcycle purchase.

Source: Helen Sessions / Alamy

Forecasts called for an increase in consumer spending on recreation and entertainment well into the year 2020. Empowered by the Internet and social media, consumers in the twenty-first century had become increasingly sophisticated and value-conscious. Yet brand image and brand loyalty played a significant role in buyer behavior, with well-known brands continuing to command a premium. Clearly, Harley-Davidson had the necessary resources and marketing and technological skills to achieve its objective of being the dominant motorcycle brand on a global basis.

This process and the findings that emerged helped define the management decision problem and the marketing research problem. The management decision problem was: Should Harley-Davidson invest to produce more motorcycles? The marketing research problem was to determine if customers would be loyal buyers of Harley-Davidson in the long term. Specifically, the research had to address the following questions:

1. Who are the customers? What are their demographic and psychographic (lifestyle) characteristics?
2. Can different types of customers be distinguished? Is it possible to segment the market in a meaningful way?
3. How do customers feel regarding their Harleys? Are all customers motivated by the same appeal?
4. Are the customers loyal to Harley-Davidson? What is the extent of brand loyalty?

One of the research questions (RQs) examined and its associated hypotheses (Hs) were:

RQ: Can the motorcycle buyers be segmented based on psychographic characteristics?

H1: There are distinct segments of motorcycle buyers.

H2: Each segment is motivated to own a Harley for a different reason.

H3: Brand loyalty is high among Harley-Davidson customers in all segments.

This research was guided by the theory that brand loyalty is the result of positive beliefs, attitude, emotions, and experience with the brand. Both qualitative research and quantitative research were conducted. First, focus groups of current owners, would-be owners, and owners of other brands were conducted to understand their feelings about Harley-Davidson. Then a survey was conducted to get the demographic and psychographic profiles of customers and also their subjective appraisal of Harley.

Some of the major findings follow:

- Seven categories of customers could be distinguished: (1) the adventure-loving traditionalist, (2) the sensitive pragmatist, (3) the stylish status seeker, (4) the laid-back camper, (5) the classy capitalist, (6) the cool-headed loner, and (7) the cocky misfit. Thus, H1 was supported.
- All customers, however, had the same desire to own a Harley: It was a symbol of independence, freedom, and power. (This uniformity across segments was surprising, contradicting H2.)
- All customers were long-term loyal customers of Harley-Davidson, supporting H3.

Based on these findings, the decision was taken to invest and thus increase the number as well as the quality of Harleys built.[1] <

This example shows the importance of correctly defining the marketing research problem and developing an appropriate approach.

THE IMPORTANCE OF DEFINING THE PROBLEM

Although every step in a marketing research project is important, problem definition is the most important step. As mentioned in Chapter 1, marketing researchers consider problems and opportunities confronting management to be interchangeable because the investigation of each follows the same research process. **Problem definition** involves stating the problem confronting the managers (the management decision problem) and the marketing research problem that the researcher will address. The latter should be broken down into a broad statement and the specific components of the marketing research problem, as illustrated by the opening feature about Harley-Davidson. This example provided the problem confronting Harley-Davidson management and a broad statement of the marketing research problem, and identified its four specific components. The researcher and the key decision makers on the client side should agree on the definition of the problem. The *client* is the individual or organization commissioning the research. The client might be an internal person, as in the case of a research director dealing with a decision maker in her or his own organization. Alternatively, the client might be an external entity if the research is being conducted by a marketing research firm. (See Chapter 1.) Only when both parties have clearly defined and agreed on the marketing research problem can research be designed and conducted properly. The basic message here is that it is critical to clearly identify and define the marketing research problem. The problem-definition process provides guidelines on how to define the marketing research problem correctly.

problem definition
A statement of the management decision problem and the marketing research problem. The marketing research problem is broken down into a broad statement and specific components.

Research Recipe

You should not proceed beyond the initial stages of the project unless there is a written statement of the management decision problem and the corresponding marketing research problem that is agreed upon by the client and the research organization.

THE PROCESS OF DEFINING THE PROBLEM AND DEVELOPING AN APPROACH

The problem definition and approach development process is illustrated in Figure 2.2. To define a research problem correctly, the researcher must perform a number of tasks. The researcher must discuss the problem with the decision makers in the client organization, interview

FIGURE 2.2

THE PROBLEM DEFINITION &
APPROACH DEVELOPMENT
PROCESS

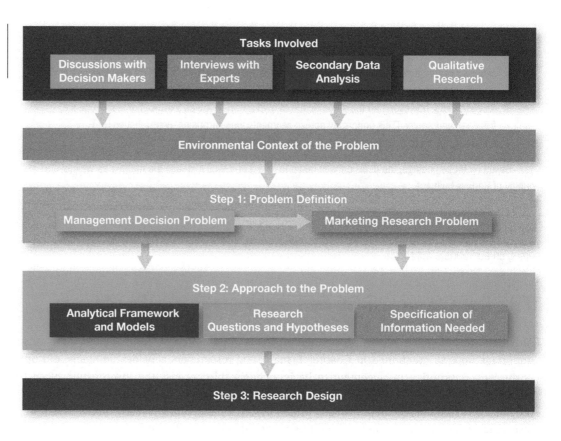

**problem-definition
process**
*The process of defining the
management decision problem
and the marketing research
problem.*

industry experts and other knowledgeable individuals, analyze secondary data, and sometimes conduct qualitative research. This informal data collection helps the researcher understand the context or environment within which the problem has arisen. A clear understanding of the marketing environment also provides a framework for identifying the management decision problem: What should management do? The management decision problem is then translated into a marketing research problem, the problem that the researcher must investigate. Based on the definition of the marketing research problem, the researcher develops an appropriate approach. Further explanation of the **problem-definition process** follows, with a discussion of the tasks involved.

TASKS INVOLVED IN PROBLEM DEFINITION

As mentioned earlier, the tasks involved in problem definition include discussions with the decision makers, interviews with industry experts, analysis of secondary data, and qualitative research. The purpose of performing these tasks is to obtain information on the environmental factors that are relevant to the problem and to help define the management decision problem and the corresponding marketing research problem, as well as to develop an approach. We will discuss and illustrate each of these tasks.

Discussions with Decision Makers

It is essential that the researcher understand the nature of the decision faced by the firm's managers—the management decision problem—as well as management's expectations of the research. This discussion gives the researcher an opportunity to establish achievable expectations. The decision maker (DM) needs to understand the capabilities, as well as the limitations, of the research. Research does not provide automatic solutions to problems; rather, it serves as an additional source of information that the manager should consider in making decisions.

To identify the management decision problem, the researcher must possess considerable skill in interacting with the decision maker and maneuvering through the organization. When the ultimate decision maker is a senior executive, the researcher might have difficulty gaining access to that individual. To complicate the situation even further, several individuals might be involved in the final decision. All individuals responsible for resolving the marketing problem should be consulted in this early phase of the project. Key insights will be discovered and the quality of the project will be dramatically improved when the researcher is given the opportunity to interact directly with the key decision makers. In the Harley-Davidson Research in Practice given in the Overview, discussions revealed that top management had become more risk-averse than risk-prone and was concerned that the decision to invest was too early.

Discussions with the decision maker can be structured around the **problem audit**, which helps to identify the underlying causes of the problem. The problem audit, like any other type of audit, is a comprehensive examination of a marketing problem with the purpose of understanding its origin and nature.

The problem audit involves discussions with the DM on the history of the problem, the alternative courses of action available to the DM, and the information that is needed to answer the DM's questions.

Conducting a problem audit is essential in order to clarify the problem for the researcher. Not surprisingly, it may serve the same function for the decision maker. Often, the decision maker has only a vague idea of the real problem. For example, the decision maker might know that the firm is losing market share but might not know why. This is because most decision makers focus on the symptoms of a problem rather than its causes. An inability to meet sales forecasts, loss of market share, and a decline in profits are all symptoms. The reason the DMs focus on the symptoms (sales, market share, profits, etc.) is because their performance is judged in these terms. Research that adds value goes beyond the symptoms to address the underlying causes. For example, loss of market share might be caused by superior promotion on the part of the competition, inadequate distribution of the company's products, lower product quality, price undercutting by a major competitor, or any number of factors (see Figure 2.3). A problem audit can help identify the underlying causes. As shown in Table 2.1, a definition of the problem based on symptoms can be misleading. Only when the underlying causes are identified can the problem be addressed successfully, as exemplified by the effort of store-brand jeans.

problem audit
A comprehensive examination of a marketing problem to understand its origin and nature.

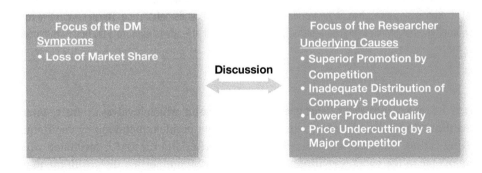

Focus of the DM
Symptoms
• Loss of Market Share

Discussion

Focus of the Researcher
Underlying Causes
• Superior Promotion by Competition
• Inadequate Distribution of Company's Products
• Lower Product Quality
• Price Undercutting by a Major Competitor

FIGURE 2.3
DISCUSSION BETWEEN THE RESEARCHER AND THE DECISION MAKER

Table 2.1 > Problem Definition Based on Symptoms Can be Misleading

Firm	Symptoms	Problem Definition	
		Based on Symptoms	Based on Underlying Causes
Manufacturer of orange soft drinks	Consumers say the sugar content is too high	Determine consumer preferences for alternative levels of sugar content.	Color. The color of the drink is a dark shade of orange, giving the perception that the product is too "sugary."
Manufacturer of machine tools	Customers complain prices are too high	Determine the price elasticity of demand.	Channel management. Distributors do not have adequate product knowledge to communicate product benefits to customers.

Research in Practice
Turning "Uncool" to "Cool": It's a Matter of Image

For years, teenagers have considered store-label jeans "uncool." While the lower price tag of store-brand jeans, such as JCPenney Arizona brand jeans or the Gap's in-house brand, has long appealed to value-conscious parents, teenagers have preferred big-name brands such as Levi's, Lee, and Wrangler. The big-name brands have historically dominated the $11 billion industry as a result. Through marketing research problem audits, the private labels determined that the real cause for their low market share was lack of image. Therefore, the marketing research problem was defined as enhancing their image in the eyes of the target market—the lucrative teenage segment.

Arizona jeans and Gap's in-house brands have led the charge among the generics in changing their image. These store-brand jeans, along with other store-label jeans, now target the teenage market with cutting-edge advertising. Their advertisements feature rock bands such as Aerosmith along with high-tech imagery to attract teenagers. The brands also promote their trendy websites—where their target market should go and visit to be "cool."

Gap jeans have also scored big. The chain's strategy has been to distance their store-brand jeans from the store itself. Teenagers think of the Gap as a place where older people or their parents shop, thus making it "uncool." Gap's marketing campaign now aims to separate their store name and image from their jeans that are aimed at teens. This is the opposite of a more typical or traditional brand-name leveraging strategy. The results, according to a global leader in youth research TRU (**www.tru-insight.com**), are that teens are not putting it together that this is the house brand.

The results for the store-brand jeans have been quite successful. According to the marketing research firm NPD Group, private label jeans' market share has risen. Levi's, the market leader, has seen their market share drop. Levi's drop is also indicative of the trends for the big-name brands nationwide. These impressive results are encouraging other stores to consider introducing their own label jeans to capture a portion of the teenage market.[2] <

As in the case of the private-label jeans, a problem audit, which involves extensive interaction between the DM and the researcher, can greatly facilitate problem definition by determining the underlying causes. The interaction between the researcher and the DM is facilitated when one or more people in the client organization serve as a liaison and form a team with the marketing researcher.

The Internet provides several mechanisms that can help the researcher communicate with decision makers. The first and most obvious is e-mail. Researchers can use e-mail to reach decision makers at any place or time. Chat rooms also are good forums for discussion with decision makers. For instance, a chat room discussion with multiple decision makers could be developed around a problem audit. The researcher could introduce the audit issues in the chat, and then the decision makers could respond to the issues and to each other's ideas. Chat rooms can be secured with a password if there is a need to protect the contents of the discussion.

Research Recipe

The decision makers tend to focus on the symptoms. However, it is critical that you define the marketing research problem in terms of the underlying causes and not in terms of the symptoms. A problem audit can help identify the underlying causes.

Interviews with Industry Experts

In addition to discussions with the DM, interviews with industry experts and individuals knowledgeable about the firm and the industry may help formulate the marketing research problem. These experts may be found both inside and outside the firm. Typically, expert information is obtained by unstructured personal interviews, without administering a formal questionnaire. It is helpful, however, to prepare a list of topics to be covered during the interview. The order in which these topics are covered and the questions to ask should not be predetermined but decided as the interview progresses. This allows greater flexibility in capturing the insights of the experts. The purpose of interviewing experts is to help define the marketing research problem rather than to develop a conclusive solution. In the Harley-Davidson Research in Practice, discussions with industry experts indicated that brand loyalty was a major factor in the purchase of motorcycles. Thus, the investigation of brand loyalty became a major component of the problem definition.

Interviews with experts are more useful in conducting marketing research for industrial firms and for products of a technical nature, where it is relatively easy to identify and approach the experts. This method is also helpful in situations where little information is available from other sources, as in the case of radically new products.

Researchers can also use the Internet to enhance their ability to obtain information from experts in a specific industry. One approach to finding experts is to use newsgroups. Due to the large amount of information available, searching through the newsgroups for specific information can be an arduous task. A good place to start is Google Groups (**groups.google.com**), which provides categorized lists of newsgroups. After finding a relevant newsgroup, access the newsgroup and search for postings about the topics in which you are interested. Surveying the postings in a newsgroup would provide a good starting point for making contacts with the experts in that industry.

Research Recipe

Conduct interviews with experts particularly in marketing research for industrial firms, for products of a technical nature, and where little information is available from other sources, as in the case of radically new products.

iResearch
Wal-Mart: The Largest Retailer in the World

Visit **www.walmart.com** and search the Internet, including social media, as well as your library's online databases to identify the challenges and opportunities facing Wal-Mart, the largest retailer in the United States and the world.

Visit **groups.google.com** and browse retailing newsgroups to identify an expert in online retailing. Interview this expert (via telephone or online) to identify the challenges and opportunities facing Wal-Mart. Alternatively, you can search for and analyze this expert's comments by searching the Internet and social media.

As the CEO of Wal-Mart, what marketing strategies would you formulate to overcome the challenges and capitalize on the opportunities identified by the marketing researcher? **❮**

Secondary Data Analysis

secondary data
Data collected for some purpose other than the problem at hand.

primary data
Data originated by the researcher specifically to address the research problem.

The information that researchers obtain from decision makers and industry experts should be supplemented with available secondary data. **Secondary data** are data collected for some purpose other than the problem at hand, such as data available from trade organizations, the U.S. Census Bureau (**www.census.gov**), and the Internet. In contrast, **primary data** are originated by the researcher for the specific problem under study, such as survey data. Secondary data include information made available by business and government sources, social media and computerized databases. Secondary data are an economical and quick source of background information.

Analyzing available secondary data is an essential step in the problem-definition process and should always precede primary data collection. Secondary data can provide valuable insights into the problem situation and lead to the identification of innovative courses of action. In the case of Harley-Davidson, secondary data revealed that the vast majority of motorcycle owners also owned automobiles such as cars, SUVs, and trucks. As another example, the U.S. Department of Labor says that the median age of the U.S. labor force is increasing. This is, in part, the result of the maturation of the "baby bust" generation (those born between 1965 and 1976), which will cause a decline in the number of young (age 16 to 24) workers available to fill entry-level positions. This potential shortage of young workers has caused many marketers, particularly those in the service industries, to investigate the problem of consumer response to self-service. Some companies, such as fast-food restaurants, have switched from a high-touch to a high-tech service orientation. By using high-tech equipment, consumers now perform many of the services formerly done by workers, such as placing their own orders by entering them directly into the electronic terminal. Given the tremendous importance of secondary data, this topic will be discussed in detail in Chapter 3.

Always analyze available secondary data. The cost and the effort required are marginal but the insights gained can be invaluable in defining the problem.

iResearch
Wendy's Battle for Market Share

As the marketing director for Wendy's, what significance do you attach to secondary data showing the aging of the U.S. population? What are the implications of these data for increasing Wendy's market share?

Identify the sources of secondary data that would be helpful in defining the problem of Wendy's increasing its share of the fast-food market. Visit **www.wendys.com** and search the Internet, including social media, as well as your library's online databases to determine Wendy's market share for the past three years. **❮**

Qualitative Research

Information obtained from the DM, industry experts, and secondary data may not be sufficient to define the research problem. Sometimes qualitative research must be undertaken to gain an understanding of the problem and its underlying factors. **Qualitative research** is exploratory in nature; is based on small samples; and may utilize popular qualitative techniques such as focus groups (group interviews), word association (asking respondents to indicate their first responses to stimulus words), and depth interviews (one-on-one interviews that probe the respondents' thoughts in detail). Other exploratory research techniques, such as pilot surveys with small samples of respondents, may also be undertaken. Exploratory research is discussed in more detail in Chapter 3, and qualitative research techniques are discussed in detail in Chapter 4. While research undertaken at this stage may not be conducted in a formal way, it can provide valuable insights. Qualitative research played an important part in in the Harley-Davidson Research in Practice. Focus groups with motorcycle owners indicated that in the United States, motorcycles were not used primarily as a means of basic transportation but as a means of recreation. Qualitative research also reaffirmed the role of brand loyalty in motorcycle purchase and ownership.

The importance of performing these tasks to identify the problem correctly is further illustrated by Amtrak.

qualitative research
An unstructured, exploratory research methodology based on small samples intended to provide insight and understanding of the problem setting.

Research in Practice
Qualitative Research Helps Amtrak Stay on Track

Amtrak created a high-speed, premium railroad service for its Boston-New York-Washington route. In designing this service, the researchers consulted with decision makers (DMs) within the firm as well as industry experts. The industry experts pointed out that, in order to be successful on this route, Amtrak will have to compete with the airlines and this became an important component of the problem. Analysis of internal and external secondary data indicated good potential for Amtrak on the Boston-New York-Washington route. Qualitative research in the form of focus groups helped to identify the important aspects of the problem. Initial focus groups revealed that travel time, seating, lighting, color schemes, and food beverage services would be important to customers who were looking for a comfortable and enjoyable ride. Determining the importance consumers attached to these factors in selecting a mode of transportation became another important component of the problem. Additional focus groups were held to further explore these factors, followed by several large sample surveys. In total, Amtrak utilized the opinions of more than 20,000 customers in the design of their new train service.

This research indicated that a travel time of less than three hours would be required to compete with the airlines. Seat characteristics valued by the participants included back support, conformation to the body, provision of personal space, and comfort. The results of this research led Amtrak to consider designing comfortable and spacious seating. Results also showed that participants preferred lighting that was adequate for reading and conducting work, but not too bright. They preferred classic color schemes. Specifically, the majority preferred white or off-white walls, and green, maroon, and blue upholstery. Questions regarding food and beverage service lead Amtrak to include a bistro-style train car as well as "service at your seat" such as that provided by airlines.

Amtrak has continued conducting research, including analysis of social media, thus allowing it to stay in touch with customers' preferences and opinions regarding this service and to make adjustments as necessary. On September 28, 2010, the company presented an initial look at how next-generation (next-gen) high-speed rail service could be successfully developed in the Northeast with sustained maximum speeds of 220 mph (354 kph) and three-hour trip times between Washington and Boston to get passengers where they need to be—when they need to be there—fast, safely, and efficiently. The first of Amtrak's new 70 high-tech trains, built

Source: Neil Setchfield / Alamy

by Siemens, rolled off the assembly line in 2013. As of 2013, Amtrak had set ridership records nine out of the last ten years. Amtrak continued to benefit from heavy passenger traffic in 2014. Continued reliance on marketing research will serve Amtrak well into the future.[3] ‹

Research Recipe

Some form of qualitative research is warranted in most marketing research projects. It gives you a much better understanding about the underlying issues, issues that may not be apparent otherwise.

The insights gained from qualitative research, along with discussion with decision maker(s), interviews with industry experts, and secondary data analysis, help the researcher to understand the environmental context of the problem.

environmental context of the problem

Consists of the factors that have an impact on the definition of the marketing research problem, including past information and forecasts, resources and constraints of the firm, objectives of the decision maker, buyer behavior, legal environment, economic environment, and marketing and technological skills of the firm.

ENVIRONMENTAL CONTEXT OF THE PROBLEM

To understand the background to a marketing research problem, the researcher must understand the client's firm and industry. In particular, the researcher should analyze the factors that have an impact on the definition of the marketing research problem. These factors, encompassing the **environmental context of the problem**, include past information and forecasts pertaining to the industry and the firm, resources and constraints of the firm, objectives of the decision maker, buyer behavior, legal environment, economic environment, and marketing and technological skills of the firm, as shown in Figure 2.4. Each of these factors is discussed briefly.

FIGURE 2.4

FACTORS TO BE CONSIDERED IN THE ENVIRONMENTAL CONTEXT OF THE PROBLEM

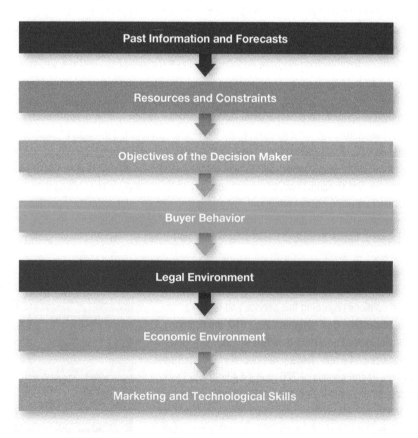

Past Information and Forecasts

Resources and Constraints

Objectives of the Decision Maker

Buyer Behavior

Legal Environment

Economic Environment

Marketing and Technological Skills

Past Information and Forecasts

Past information and forecasts of trends with respect to sales, market share, profitability, technology, population, demographics, and lifestyle can help the researcher understand the underlying marketing research problem. Where appropriate, this kind of analysis should be carried out at the industry and firm levels. For example, if a firm's sales have decreased but industry sales have increased, the problems will be very different than if the industry sales have also decreased. In the former case, the problems are likely to be specific to the firm. In the latter case, the problems affect not only the firm but also its competitors, that is, the whole industry.

Past information and forecasts can be valuable in uncovering potential opportunities and problems, as the fast-food industry has discovered. Fast-food chains, pizza restaurants, and other outlets for takeout food have sought to exploit potential opportunities in the recent trend toward takeout food and home delivery. For example, Pizza Hut opened several takeout only (with no dine-in service) outlets to better serve this market. In the Harley-Davidson Research in Practice, forecasts called for an increase in consumer spending on recreation and entertainment well into the year 2020.

Past information and forecasts can be especially valuable if resources are limited and there are other constraints on the organization.

Resources and Constraints

To formulate a marketing research problem of appropriate scope, it is necessary to take into account both the resources available, such as money and research skills, and the constraints on the organization, such as cost and time. Proposing a large-scale project that would cost $100,000 when only $40,000 has been budgeted obviously will not meet management approval. In many instances, the scope of the marketing research problem may have to be reduced to accommodate budget constraints. This might be done, for example, by confining the investigation to major geographical markets rather than conducting the project on a national basis or by having a more focused problem definition.

Conversely, it might be possible to extend the scope of a project appreciably with only a marginal increase in costs. This can considerably enhance the usefulness of the project, thereby increasing the probability that management will approve it. Time constraints can be important when decisions must be made quickly. I conducted a project for Fisher-Price, a major toy manufacturer, involving mall-intercept interviews in six major cities (Chicago, Fresno, Kansas City, New York, Philadelphia, and San Diego) that had to be completed in six weeks. Why this rush? The results had to be presented at an upcoming board meeting where a major (go or no go) decision was to be made about a new product introduction. The resources and constraints can be better understood when examined in light of the objectives of the organization and the decision maker.

Objectives

Decisions are made to accomplish **objectives**. The formulation of the management decision problem must be based on a clear understanding of two types of objectives: (1) the organizational objectives (the goals of the organization), and (2) the personal objectives of the decision maker (DM). For the project to be successful, it must serve the objectives of the organization and of the DM. In the first Research in Practice feature, the objective of Harley-Davidson was to become the dominant motorcycle brand on a global basis.

objectives
The goals of the organization and of the decision maker that must be considered in order to conduct successful marketing research.

Buyer Behavior

Buyer behavior is a central component of the environmental context. In most marketing decisions, the problem can ultimately be traced to predicting the response of buyers to specific actions

buyer behavior
A body of knowledge that tries to understand and predict consumers' reactions based on specific characteristics of individuals.

by the marketer. An understanding of the underlying buyer behavior can provide valuable insights into the problem. The buyer behavior factors that should be considered include:

1. The number and geographical location of the buyers and nonbuyers.
2. Demographic and psychographic (lifestyle) characteristics.
3. Product consumption habits and the consumption of related product categories.
4. Media consumption behavior and response to promotions.
5. Price sensitivity.
6. Retail outlets patronized.
7. Buyer preferences.

The Harley-Davidson example showed that taking buyer behavior into account while defining the problem can be very rewarding. Empowered by the Internet, consumers in the twenty-first century had become increasingly sophisticated and value-conscious. Yet brand image and brand loyalty played a significant role in buyer behavior, with well-known brands continuing to command a premium, a factor that was very important to the motorcycle manufacturer. The Puma Research in Practice provides another illustration.

Research in Practice
PUMA: Start in Sport and End in Fashion

PUMA (**www.puma.com**) is one of the world's leading sport lifestyle companies that designs and develops footwear, apparel, and accessories. The company has achieved this position by relying on marketing research to understand the behavior of its target consumers and formulating its marketing strategies accordingly. Secondary data revealed that only 20 percent of customers wear the shoes for the main purpose of the shoe, for example, tennis, running, and so on. Qualitative research revealed that most people used athletic shoes for street wear. Furthermore, many of these users wanted to make a fashion statement with their shoes. Accordingly, PUMA investigated the marketing research problem of determining the demand potential for fashionable athletic shoes. The findings of this research were encouraging. Therefore, instead of competing directly with bigger brands like Nike and Adidas in areas of performance-enhancing equipment, PUMA decided that it would focus on designing and producing what consumers wanted, thus embracing fashion and producing fashionable footwear for their customers. This strategy has been successful for the company. PUMA is constantly conducting marketing research to monitor the changing tastes and preferences of consumers. In 2012, the company introduced The Blaze of Glory LWT that features natural cushioning, soft materials, and pop color aplenty—more or less everything needed to make a few solid, snappy fashion statements. The shoe has been a major hit with both fashionistas and weekend warriors. Continuing this strategy, in 2013 the Puma Social line was being marketed as meant "for surfing the crowd." As of 2014, PUMA's products were being marketed in more than 120 countries.[4] **<**

In addition to buyer behavior, the legal environment and the economic environment can have an impact on the behavior of the consumers and the definition of the marketing research problem.

Legal Environment

legal environment
Regulatory policies and norms within which organizations must operate.

The **legal environment** includes public policies, laws, government agencies, and pressure groups that influence and regulate various organizations and individuals in society. Important areas of law include patents, trademarks, royalties, trade agreements, taxes, and tariffs. Federal laws have an impact on each element of the marketing mix. In addition, laws have been passed to regulate specific industries. The legal environment can have an important bearing on the definition of the marketing research problem.

Economic Environment

Along with the legal environment, another important component of the environmental context is the **economic environment**, which is comprised of purchasing power, gross income, disposable income, discretionary income, prices, savings, credit availability, and general economic conditions. The general state of the economy (rapid growth, slow growth, or recession) influences the willingness of consumers and businesses to take on credit and spend on big-ticket items, as was seen in the global recession of 2008 to 2010. To induce reluctant consumers to purchase automobiles, the U.S. government came up with Cash for Clunkers program in 2009. The Cash for Clunkers program gave car buyers rebates of up to $4,500 if they traded in less fuel-efficient vehicles for new vehicles that met certain fuel economy requirements. A total of $3 billion was allotted for those rebates. Thus, the economic environment can have important implications for marketing research problems.

economic environment
The economic environment is composed of purchasing power, income, prices, savings, credit availability, and general economic conditions.

Marketing and Technological Skills

A company's expertise with each element of the marketing mix and its general level of marketing and technological skills affect the nature and scope of the marketing research project. For example, the introduction of a new product that requires sophisticated technology may not be a viable course if the firm lacks the skills to manufacture or market it. In the first Research in Practice feature, Harley-Davidson had the necessary resources and marketing and technological skills to achieve its objective of being the dominant motorcycle brand on a global basis.

Many of the factors to be considered in determining the environmental context of the problem can be researched via the Internet. Past information and trend forecasts can be found by searching for the appropriate information via search engines. For company-specific information pertaining to the client or a competitor, the researcher can go to the company's homepage.

> ## Research Recipe
>
> It is essential to gain a thorough understanding of the environmental context if the problem is to be defined correctly. All the factors of the environmental context are important and you should thoroughly research and understand them.

After gaining an adequate understanding of the environmental context of the problem, the researcher can define the management decision problem and the marketing research problem.

MANAGEMENT DECISION PROBLEM AND MARKETING RESEARCH PROBLEM

The **management decision problem** asks what the decision maker needs to do, whereas the **marketing research problem** asks what information is needed and how it can best be obtained (see Table 2.2). Research is directed at providing the information necessary to make a sound decision. The management decision problem is action-oriented, framed from the perspective of what should be done. How should the loss of market share be arrested? Should the market be segmented differently? Should a new product be introduced? Should the promotional budget be increased?

In contrast, the marketing research problem is information-oriented. Research is directed at providing the information necessary to make a sound decision. The management decision problem focuses on the symptoms, whereas the marketing research problem is concerned with the underlying causes (see Table 2.2). Of course, the marketing research problem should be closely linked to the management decision problem. If the researcher addresses the marketing research problem,

management decision problem
The problem confronting the decision maker. It asks what the decision maker needs to do.

marketing research problem
A problem that entails determining what information is needed and how it can be obtained in the most feasible way.

Table 2.2 > Management Decision Problem Versus Marketing Research Problem

Management Decision Problem	Marketing Research Problem
• Asks what the decision maker needs to do	• Asks what information is needed and how it should be obtained
• Action-oriented	• Information-oriented
• Focuses on symptoms	• Focuses on the underlying causes

then the findings should help the decision maker(s) address the management decision problem; that is, effectively make the decision confronting management.

To further illustrate the distinction between the two orientations, consider an illustrative problem: the loss of market share for the Old Spice product line (aftershave, cologne, deodorant). The decision maker is faced with the problem of how to recover this loss (the management decision problem). Possible responses include modifying existing products, introducing new products, reducing prices, changing other elements in the marketing mix, and segmenting the market. Suppose the decision maker and the researcher believe that the problem can be traced to market segmentation; that is, Old Spice should be targeted at a specific segment. They decide to conduct research to explore that issue. The marketing research problem would then become the identification and evaluation of different ways to segment or group the market. As the research process progresses, problem definition can be modified to reflect emerging information. Table 2.3 provides additional examples, including that of Harley-Davidson from the first Research in Practice feature in this chapter, that further clarify the distinction between the management decision problem and the marketing research problem.

Research Recipe

You should define the marketing research problem so that its solution will directly help the decision maker to address the management decision problem. The marketing research problem, while focusing on the underlying causes, should be closely interlinked with the symptoms that characterize the management decision problem.

Table 2.3 > Management Decision Problem and the Corresponding Marketing Research Problem

Management Decision Problem	Marketing Research Problem
• Should a new product be introduced?	• To determine consumer preferences and purchase intentions for the proposed new product.
• Should the advertising campaign be changed?	• To determine the effectiveness of the current advertising campaign.
• Should the price of the brand be increased?	• To determine the price elasticity of demand and the impact on sales and profits of various levels of price changes.
• Should Harley-Davidson invest to produce more motor cycles?	• To determine if customers would be loyal buyers of Harley-Davidson in the long term.

DEFINING THE MARKETING RESEARCH PROBLEM

The general rule to be followed in defining the research problem is that the definition should (1) allow the researcher to obtain all the information needed to address the management decision problem, and (2) guide the researcher in proceeding with the project. Researchers make two common errors in problem definition (Figure 2.5). The first arises when the research problem is defined too broadly. A broad definition does not provide clear guidelines for the subsequent steps involved in the project. Some examples of overly broad marketing research problem definitions are (1) developing a marketing strategy for the brand, (2) improving the competitive position of the firm, or (3) improving the company's image. These are not specific enough to suggest an approach to the problem or a research design.

The second type of error is just the opposite: The marketing research problem is defined too narrowly. A narrow focus may preclude consideration of some courses of action, particularly those that are innovative and not obvious. It may also prevent the researcher from addressing important components of the management decision problem. For example, in a project conducted for a major consumer products firm, the management problem was how to respond to a price cut initiated by a competitor. The alternative courses of action initially identified by the firm's research staff were (1) decrease the price of the firm's brand to match the competitor's price cut; (2) maintain price but increase advertising heavily; and (3) decrease the price somewhat, without matching the competitor's price, and moderately increase advertising. None of these alternatives seemed promising. When outside marketing research experts were brought in, the problem was redefined as improving the market share and profitability of the product line. Qualitative research indicated that, in blind tests, consumers could not differentiate products offered under different brand names. Consumers also relied on price as an indicator of product quality reasoning that if costs more it must be of a higher quality. These findings led to a creative alternative: Increase the price of the existing brand and introduce two new brands—one priced to match the competitor and the other priced to undercut it. This strategy was implemented, leading to an increase in market share and profitability.

The likelihood of committing either error of problem definition can be reduced by stating the marketing research problem in broad, general terms and identifying its specific components (see Figure 2.6). The **broad statement** provides perspective on the problem and acts as a safeguard against committing the second type of error. The **specific components** focus on the key aspects of the problem and provide clear guidelines on how to proceed. They act as a safeguard against committing the first type of error.

The relationship between the marketing research problem and the management decision problem is further illustrated by Figure 2.7. Examples of appropriate marketing research problem definitions are provided by Harley-Davidson and the *Tennis* magazine Research in Practice features.

broad statement of the problem
The initial statement of the marketing research problem that provides an appropriate perspective on the problem.

specific components of the problem
The second part of the marketing research problem definition. The specific components focus on the key aspects of the problem and provide clear guidelines on how to proceed.

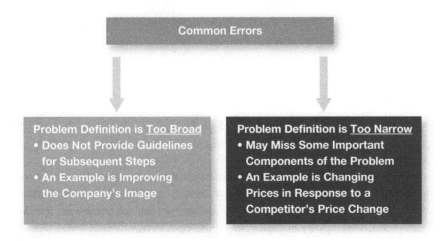

FIGURE 2.5
ERROS IN DEFINING THE MARKET RESEARCH PROBLEM

FIGURE 2.6
PROPER DEFINITION OF THE
MARKETING RESEARCH
PROBLEM

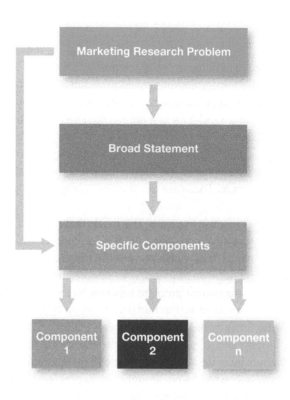

FIGURE 2.7
MANAGEMENT DECISION
PROBLEM AND MARKETING
RESEARCH PROBLEM

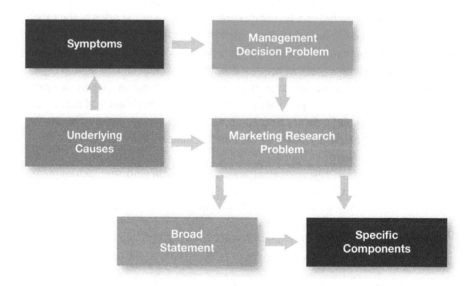

Research in Practice
Research Serves *Tennis* Magazine

Tennis magazine (**www.tennis.com**), a Miller Sports Group publication, wanted to obtain information about its readers. They hired Signet Research, Inc. (**www.signetresearch.com**), an independent research company in Cliffside Park, New Jersey, to conduct marketing research. The management decision problem was this: What changes should be made in *Tennis* magazine to make it more appealing to its readers?

The broad marketing research problem was defined as gathering information about the subscribers of *Tennis* magazine. Specific components of the problem included the following:

1. Demographics. Who are the men and women who subscribe to the magazine?

2. Psychological characteristics and lifestyles. How do subscribers spend their money and their free time? Lifestyle indicators to be examined were fitness, travel, car rental, apparel, consumer electronics, credit cards, and financial investments.

3. Tennis activity. Where and how often do subscribers play tennis? What are their skill levels?

4. Relationship to *Tennis* magazine. How much time do subscribers spend with the issues? How long do they keep them? Do they share the magazine with other tennis players?

Because the questions were so clearly defined, the information provided by this research helped management design specific features on tennis instruction, equipment, famous tennis players, and locations to play tennis to meet readers' specific needs. These changes made *Tennis* magazine more appealing to its readers.[5] <

In the *Tennis* magazine example, the broad statement of the problem focused on gathering information about the subscribers, and the specific components identified the specific items of information that should be obtained. An appropriate definition of the problem helped *Tennis* magazine to make changes that met specific needs in the marketplace.

Research Recipe

Define the marketing research problem in broad, general terms and identify its specific components. The broad statement provides a perspective on the problem and acts as a safeguard against defining the problem too narrowly. The specific components focus on the key aspects of the problem and provide clear guidelines on how to proceed further.

iResearch
TiVo: The World's First Smart DVR

A TiVo digital video recorder (DVR) is like a video cassette recorder (VCR), but without the hassles of videotapes or timers. Browse the TiVo website (**www.tivo.com**) to get a better idea of this innovative product/service.

As the marketing manager, you want to increase TiVo's market share. What information do you need in accomplishing this goal? Broadly define and identify the specific components of the marketing research problem facing TiVo. <

Once the marketing research problem has been broadly stated and its specific components identified, the researcher is in a position to develop a suitable approach.

COMPONENTS OF THE APPROACH

The tasks performed earlier also help in developing an approach. An approach to a marketing research problem should include the following components: analytical framework and models, research questions and hypotheses, and a specification of the information needed (see Figure 2.2). Each of these components is discussed in the following sections.

Analytical Framework and Models

In general, marketing research should be based on objective evidence and supported by theory. **Objective evidence** (evidence that is unbiased and supported by empirical findings) is gathered

objective evidence
Unbiased evidence that is supported by empirical findings.

theory
A conceptual scheme based on foundational statements, or axioms, that are assumed to be true.

analytical framework
An analytical framework is a statement of the theory as applied to the marketing research problem.

analytical model
An explicit specification of a set of variables and their interrelationships designed to represent some real system or process in whole or in part.

graphical model
An analytical model that provide a visual picture of the relationships between variables.

by compiling relevant findings from secondary sources. A **theory** is a conceptual framework based on foundational statements that are assumed to be true and that guide the collection of this data. Theory may come from academic literature contained in books, journals, and monographs. For example, according to attitude theory, attitude toward a brand, such as Nike sneakers, is determined by an evaluation of the brand on salient attributes (e.g., price, performance, durability, and style). Relevant theory provides insight regarding which variables should be investigated and which should be treated as dependent variables (those whose values depend on the values of other variables) and which should be treated as independent variables (those whose values affect the values of other variables). Thus, attitude toward Nike will be the dependent variable; price, performance, durability, and style will be independent variables. The Harley-Davidson research was guided by the theory that brand loyalty is the result of positive beliefs, attitude, emotions, and experience with the brand. The approach should be based on some kind of working theory or **analytical framework**. An analytical framework is a statement of the theory as applied to the marketing research problem. This is also helpful in developing an appropriate model.

An **analytical model** consists of a set of variables related in a specified manner to represent all or a part of some real system or process. Models can take many forms, but here we will focus on graphical models. **Graphical models** are visual and pictorially represent the theory. They are used to isolate variables and to suggest directions of relationships; however, they are not designed to provide numerical results. Graphical models are particularly helpful in conceptualizing an approach to the problem, as the following new car purchase model illustrates.

Research in Practice
The True Definition of Luxury. Yours.

The following graphical model illustrates the new car purchase decision process. A person starts as a passive consumer ("I am not now interested in considering the purchase of a new vehicle"). When the consumer is actively interested in purchasing a new car, the consumer creates a consideration set (limits the brands to be considered). This is followed by shopping, buying (sale), and assessing the value of products and services. Automobile firms such as BMW have used the new car purchase model to formulate marketing strategies that are consonant with consumers' underlying decision-making process. In this model, BMW is part of the consideration set for a certain group of consumers who are interested in luxury and innovation. The 2013 marketing theme of BMW, "BMW Efficient Dynamics. Less emissions. More Driving Pleasure," was based on this model (**www.bmwusa.com**).[6] <

New Car Purchase Model

Passive Population

↓

Active Consumers

↓

Consideration Set

↓

Shopping

↓

Sale

↓

Assessment of Product/Services

iResearch!
GM: Targeting Car Buyers

Visit **www.gm.com** and write a report about GM's automobile brands. Develop a graphical model explaining consumers' selection of an automobile brand.

As the marketing chief of GM, how can you develop a graphical model explaining consumers' selection of an automobile brand to help you to position GM's various brands? **<**

Research Questions and Hypotheses

Research questions (RQs) are refined statements of the specific components of the problem. A problem component might break into several research questions. Research questions are designed to ask the specific information required to address each problem component. Research questions that address the problem components successfully provide valuable information for the decision maker.

The formulation of the research questions should be guided, not only by the problem definition, but also by the analytical framework and the model adopted. In the new car purchase model, the factors that influenced consumers' selection of an automobile brand may be postulated based on theoretical framework as brand name, price, performance, styling, options (features), and quality. Several research questions can be posed related to these factors: What is the relative importance of these factors in influencing consumers' selection of automobiles? Which factor is the most important? Which factor is the least important? Does the relative importance of these factors vary across consumers?

A **hypothesis (H)** is an unproven statement or proposition about a factor or phenomenon that is of interest to the researcher. It may be a tentative statement about the relationships discussed in the theory or analytical framework or represented in the analytic model. The hypothesis can also be stated as a possible answer to the research question. Hypotheses are statements about proposed relationships rather than merely questions to be answered. They reflect the researchers' expectation and can be tested empirically. (See Chapters 11 to 13.) Hypotheses also play the important role of suggesting variables to be included in the research design. In commercial marketing research, the hypotheses are not formulated as rigorously as they are in academic research. The relationships among the marketing research problem, research questions, and hypotheses, along with the influence of the framework and models, is described in Figure 2.8. The

research questions (RQs)
Research questions are refined statements of the specific components of the problem.

hypothesis (H)
An unproven statement or proposition about a factor or phenomenon that is of interest to the researcher.

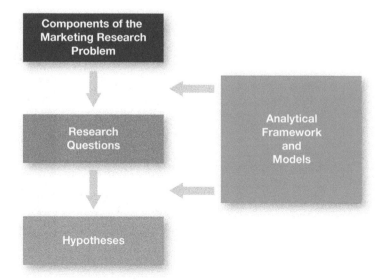

FIGURE 2.8
DEVELOPMENT OF
RESEARCH QUESTIONS &
HYPOTHESIS

first Research in Practice feature in this chapter about Harley-Davidson illustrated the role of research questions and hypotheses. One research question and three associated hypotheses were formulated for motorcycle buyers.

Specification of Information Needed

By focusing on each component of the problem, the research questions and hypotheses, the researcher can determine what information should be obtained (see Figure 2.9). It is helpful to carry out this exercise for each component of the problem and to make a list specifying all the information that should be collected. We illustrate this process with respect to the Harley-Davidson example.

Information Needed for Component 1

- Ownership of motorcycles (Harley-Davidson and its competitors). Interest in potentially owning a motorcycle if they do not currently have one.
- Standard demographic characteristics (e.g., gender, marital status, household size, age, education, occupation, income, and type and number of automobiles owned) and psychographic characteristics. Psychographic characteristics include outdoor and recreational activities, family orientation, and attitude toward adventure.

Information Needed for Component 2

- No new information to be collected. The segments can be identified based on information obtained for the first component.

Information Needed for Component 3

- Ratings of Harley-Davidson motorcycles on image, features, brand name, and subjective perceptions.

Information Needed for Component 4

- Attitudes toward, preferences for, and repurchase of Harley-Davidson motorcycles.

This process is further illustrated by the United Airlines Research in Practice.

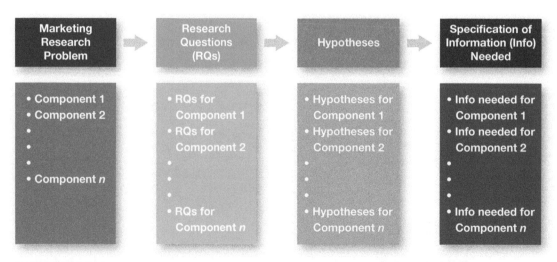

FIGURE 2.9 | SPECIFICATION OF INFORMATION NEEDED

Research in Practice
At United, Food Is Uniting the Airline with Travelers

United Airlines, the world's leading airline as of 2014, had to deal with passenger loyalty, as did other major airlines. Its management decision problem: how to attract more and more loyal passengers? The broad marketing research problem was to identify the factors that influence the loyalty of airline travelers. The basic answer is to improve service. Exploratory research, theoretical framework, and empirical evidence reveal that the consumers' choice of an airline is influenced by safety, the price of the ticket, the frequent-flyer program, convenience of scheduling, and brand name.

A graphical model stipulated that consumers evaluate competing airlines based on factors of the choice criteria for selecting a preferred airline. The problem was that major airlines were quite similar on these factors. Indeed, "airlines offer the same schedules, the same service, and the same fares." Consequently, United Airlines had to find a way to differentiate itself. Food turned out to be the solution.

Secondary data, like the J. D. Power & Associates survey on "current and future trends in the airline food industry," and analysis of social media indicated that "food service is a major contributor to customer loyalty." This survey also emphasized the importance of food brands. The airline's Marketrak survey told United Airlines that "customers wanted more varied and up-to-date food."

The following research questions and hypotheses may be posed.

RQ1 How important is food for airline customers?

H1: Food is an important factor for airline travelers.

H2: Travelers value branded food.

H3: Travelers prefer larger food portions but with consistent quality.

H4: Travelers prefer exotic food.

Specification of information needed included the identification of competing airlines (Delta, American, etc.), factors of the choice criteria (already identified), measurement of airline travel, and loyalty.

This kind of research helped United Airlines to define their marketing research problem and develop the approach. Focus groups and surveys were conducted to check customers' perceptions of food in United Airlines' aircraft. The results provided support for all the hypotheses (H1 to H4). United Airlines then made a few changes: new "culinary menus," larger portions of food, new coffee, and branded products (e.g., Godiva chocolates). As of 2014, snack offerings were available for purchase on most flights longer than two hours. This resulted in better service, increasing customer satisfaction and fostering loyalty.[7] <

Source: David Lyons / Alamy

R e s e a r c h   R e c i p e

Develop a broad approach to the problem consisting of three components.

1. Develop a graphical model that visually portrays an underlying process or phenomenon that is of central interest in the research.

2. Further refine each specific component of the marketing research problem by developing one or more research questions and associated hypotheses.

3. Determine all the information needed to address the marketing research problem. This can best be done on a component by component basis.

INTERNATIONAL MARKETING RESEARCH

Conducting research in international markets often means working within unfamiliar environments. This lack of familiarity with the environmental factors of the country in which the research is being conducted can greatly increase the difficulty of appropriately defining the problem. Many international marketing efforts fail because a problem audit is not conducted prior to entering the foreign market, and the relevant environmental factors are not taken into account. This leads to an incorrect definition of the marketing research problem and an inappropriate approach. While developing models, research questions, and hypotheses, remember that differences in the environmental factors, especially the sociocultural environment, can lead to differences in the formation of perceptions, attitudes, preferences, and choice behavior.

For example, orientation toward time varies considerably across cultures. In Asia, Latin America, and the Middle East, people are not as time conscious as westerners, which can influence perceptions and preferences for convenience foods, such as frozen foods and prepared dinners. In defining the problem and developing an approach, the researcher must be sensitive to the underlying factors that influence consumption and purchase behavior, as illustrated by Apple's iPhone in India. <

Research in Practice
Apple iPhone: A Different Story in India

Apple's iPhone has been astoundingly successful in many parts of the globe. Unfortunately, this is not the case in India. The iPhone has been anything but a success because Apple failed to properly assess the environmental context of the problem when considering the launch in India.

Apple assumed that the Indian mobile phone market works similar to the U.S. market. However, the market in India is very different from that in the United States. India is largely a prepaid market, and consumers buy handsets without any contracts or plans. This difference resulted in the high price of the iPhone in India of about US$700. On the other hand, the United States is a postpaid market, allowing service providers to bundle the iPhone at US$199 with their service plans. In addition, it was announced that the iPhone would be priced at US$199 globally, and the failure to offer this same price in India led to consumers thinking they were shortchanged.

Another mistake was Apple's failure to conduct advertising and marketing campaigns. Compared to its month-long marketing campaign in the United States, Apple did not run any marketing campaign in India, choosing to leave it to the licensed holders, Vodafone and Airtel. Both these licensees did not adequately promote the iPhone, leaving the Indian population unenthusiastic and apathetic.

Source: Bloomberg / Getty Images

This problem has continued to persist in India. The iPhone 4S was launched in India on November 26, 2011, and met with a tepid response. Again, price was a major factor. The iPhone 4S, with storage space of 16 gigabytes, cost 44,500 rupees (Rs) (about US$900) apiece, while the 32-gigabyte model was priced at Rs50,900 and the 64-gigabyte version at Rs57,500.

Secondary data show that the Indian market for mobile phones priced at more than US$300 constitutes just 2 percent of the total sale of mobile handsets, but it is expected to grow at nearly 20 percent a year for the next five years. Apple should conduct ongoing marketing research in India if it wants to succeed.[8] <

┌─────────────────────────┐
│ R e s e a r c h   R e c i p e │
└─────────────────────────┘

While defining the problem and developing an approach in an international context, account for the differences in the environmental factors, especially the sociocultural environment.

MARKETING RESEARCH AND SOCIAL MEDIA

Social media can be used to aid in all the tasks that need to be performed in order to define the problem. If the decision maker maintains a blog or has a Facebook page, these sources provide additional information in understanding the DM and her or his objectives. It is also possible to identify industry experts, and an analysis of their social media sites can provide insights into their thinking as it relates to the problem. Social media are a natural source of qualitative secondary data and qualitative research, as discussed further in Chapters 3 and 4.

Social media can also help in gaining an understanding of the environmental context of the problem, especially consumer behavior. We can look at the way consumers interact with each other, over time. We can also study the environmental context within which they interact, and how environmental changes cause their behavior to change.

In defining the marketing research problem, analysis of social media content can provide a good idea of the broad scope of the problem and aid in identifying the specific components. For example, analysis of blogs and Facebook postings revealed to Hewlett-Packard (HP) that many customers who purchased its computers were having issues with service support. Hence, evaluation of HP and competitors on service support was identified as an important component of the problem. Subsequent research, indeed, confirmed this initial discovery, leading HP to revamp its service function.

Approach to the Problem

An analysis of social media data can also be useful in developing an approach to the problem. With the use of relevant media such as blogs, Facebook, or Twitter, researchers can update consumers on the research that has been ongoing and the actions that have been taken. As such, the use of these media can then be extended to incorporate feedback from consumers about whether the researchers are on the right track: whether the analytical models developed and the research questions posed by the firm were consistent with and based on consumer thinking and insights. Researchers can then assess the appropriateness of their models or whether they are asking the right research questions. Marketing researchers can also choose to openly discuss their derived hypothesis for feedback among closed social media consumer panels. Thus, the use of social media facilitates problem definition and the development of an approach, as illustrated by the case of Dell.

Research in Practice
From Dell Hell to Tell Dell Through Social Media

In June 2005, Dell saw erosion in their profits and a drop in share prices because of public outrage over their products' poor functionality and safety features, from faulty network cards to battery explosions. Popular blogger Jeff Jarvis coined the term *Dell Hell* to describe consumers' experiences of Dell products. However, these were but the tip of the iceberg—the symptoms of the underlying problems faced by Dell. Therefore, it was crucial for Dell to identify the problem and develop a research approach.

As negative comments and online posts proliferated, Dell analyzed the secondary data available on social media sites. The analysis of social media data indicated that the underlying problems were (1) the poor components of Dell laptops (product fault) and (2) Dell's poor support and response to consumer complaints. As product fault was more of a technical problem, marketing researchers decided to focus on Dell's other problem. The management decision problem was this: What should Dell do to address consumer complaints? The broad marketing research problem was to determine the effectiveness of traditional media and social media as platforms for supporting and responding to consumer complaints. The specific components of the problem were to determine the following:

1. The effectiveness of the current system in addressing consumer complaints
2. Whether social media would be an effective support system for addressing consumer complaints
3. Whether social media could meet any other consumer needs

Analysis of social media, along with secondary data from traditional sources, helped Dell to formulate the enclosed graphical model to explain consumers' choice of a preferred medium to address their complaints.

Based on the graphical model, specific research questions and hypotheses were formulated. When the results of this research favored the use of social media, Dell set up the Online Tech support team to offer assistance to Dell consumers through social media. In July 2006, the Direct2Dell blog was set up to listen to and connect with Dell consumers. Direct2Dell became a moderated medium for Dell to be connected directly to consumers, to hear their complaints, and to provide feedback and support to consumers in the fastest, quickest way.

With the success of Direct2Dell in gathering feedback and control of negative comments, IdeaStorm (**www.ideastorm.com**) was created in February 2007 as a social media platform that involves the consumers in generating ideas and suggestions. By 2008, Dell had emerged from the public outrage of 2005 through the use of social media tools as marketing research tools, successfully controlling and reducing unfavorable comments online from 49 percent to 20 percent. In early 2008, Dell stated that as many as twenty-seven product and process innovations had been developed as a direct result of ideas submitted on IdeaStorm by consumers. For example, Dell's offering of the Linux operating system on its desktop computers was motivated by several suggestions posted on IdeaStorm. As of May 31, 2013, the Dell community had contributed more than 18,886 ideas through IdeaStorm, and more than 531 ideas had been implemented by Dell.[9] **<**

Consumer Encounters a Problem with Dell

↓

Awareness of Different Feedback Media

↓

Convenience of Expression

↓

Preference for a Medium

↓

Choice of a Medium

Research Recipe

Analyze the relevant social media content to obtain additional insights that can be helpful in defining the problem and developing an approach.

ETHICS IN MARKETING RESEARCH

Ethical issues arise if the process of defining the problem and developing an approach is compromised by the personal agendas of the client (DM) or the researcher. This process is adversely affected when the DM has hidden objectives, such as gaining a promotion or justifying a decision that has been already made. The DM has an obligation to be candid and disclose to the researcher all the relevant information that will enable a proper definition of the marketing research problem.

Likewise the researcher is ethically bound to define the problem to further the best interest of the client rather than the interest of the research firm. At times this may involve making the interest of the research firm subservient to the client, leading to an ethical dilemma.

Research in Practice
Ethical or More Profitable?

A marketing research firm is hired by a major consumer electronics company (e.g., Philips) to conduct a large-scale segmentation study with the objective of improving market share. The researcher, after following the process outlined in this chapter, determines that the problem is not market segmentation but distribution. The company appears to be lacking an effective distribution system, which is limiting market share. However, the distribution problem requires a much simpler approach that will greatly reduce the cost of the project and the research firm's profits. What should the researcher do? Should the research firm conduct the research the client wants rather than the research the client needs? Ethical guidelines indicate that the research firm has an obligation to disclose the actual problem to the client. If, after the distribution problem has been discussed, the client still desires the segmentation research, the research firm should feel free to conduct the study because the researcher cannot know for certain the motivations underlying the client's behavior.[10] ◄

Several ethical issues are also pertinent in developing an approach. When a client solicits proposals, not with the intent of contracting the research but with the intent of gaining the expertise of research firms without pay, an ethical breach has occurred. If the client rejects the proposal of a research firm, then the approach specified in that proposal should not be implemented by the client, unless the client has paid for the development of the proposal. Likewise, the research firm has the ethical obligation to develop an appropriate approach. If the approach will use models developed in another context, then this should be disclosed to the client. For example, if the researcher will use a customer satisfaction model that was previously developed for an insurance company in a customer satisfaction study for a bank, then this information should be made known. Proprietary models and approaches developed by a research firm are the property of that firm and should not be reused by the client in subsequent studies without the permission of the research firm.

Research Recipe

Take into account the rights and responsibilities of the client and the research firm when dealing with the ethical issues that arise while defining the problem and developing an approach.

Dell Running Case

Review the Dell case, Case 1.1, and the questionnaire provided toward the end of the book.

1. Search the Internet, including social media, on Dell and briefly describe the environmental context of the problem surrounding the company.
2. Define the management decision problem facing Dell as it seeks to maintain and build on its leadership position in the personal computer market.
3. Define an appropriate marketing research problem that corresponds to your definition of the management decision problem.
4. Present a graphical model describing consumers' selection of a personal computer brand.
5. Describe three research questions, with one or more hypotheses associated with each.

Summary

Defining the marketing research problem is the most important step in a research project. It is a difficult step because management frequently has not determined the actual problem or has only a vague notion about it. The researcher's role is to help management identify and isolate the problem.

The tasks involved in formulating the marketing research problem include discussions with management, including the key decision makers, interviews with industry experts, analysis of secondary data, and qualitative research. These tasks should lead to an understanding of the environmental context of the problem. The environmental context of the problem should be analyzed and certain essential factors evaluated. These factors include past information and forecasts about the industry and the firm, objectives of the DM, buyer behavior, resources and constraints of the firm, the legal and economic environment, and marketing and technological skills of the firm.

Analysis of the environmental context should assist in the identification of the management decision problem, which should then be translated into a marketing research problem. The management decision problem asks what the DM needs to do, whereas the marketing research problem asks what information is needed and how it can be obtained effectively and efficiently. The researcher should avoid defining the marketing research problem either too broadly or too narrowly. An appropriate way of defining the marketing research problem is to make a broad statement of the problem and then identify its specific components.

Developing an approach to the problem is the second step in the marketing research process. The components of an approach consist of an analytical framework and models, research questions and hypotheses, and specification of the information needed. It is necessary that the approach developed be based on theory or an analytical framework. The relevant variables and their interrelationships may be neatly summarized by a graphical model. The research questions are refined statements of the specific components of the problem that ask what specific information is required with respect to the problem components. Research questions may lead to specific hypotheses. Finally, given the problem definition, research questions, and hypotheses, the information needed can be specified.

When defining the problem or developing an approach in international marketing research, the researcher must consider the differences in the environment prevailing in the domestic market and the foreign markets. Analysis of social media content can facilitate problem definition and the development of an approach. Several ethical issues that have an impact on the client and the researcher can arise at this stage, but they can be resolved by adhering to the codes of ethics of marketing research associations.

⌄ Companion Website

This textbook includes numerous student resources that can be found at **www.pearsonglobaleditions.com/malhotra**. At this Companion website, you'll find:

- Student Resource Manual
- Demo movies of statistical procedures using SPSS and Microsoft Excel
- Screen captures of statistical procedures using SPSS and Microsoft Excel
- Data files for all datasets in SPSS and Microsoft Excel
- Additional figures and tables
- Videos and write-ups for all video cases
- Other valuable resources

⌄ Key Terms and Concepts

Problem definition	Buyer behavior	Theory
Problem-definition process	Legal environment	Objective evidence
Problem audit	Management decision	Analytical model
Secondary data	problem	Analytical
Primary data	Marketing research problem	framework
Qualitative research	Broad statement of the	Graphical model
Environmental context of the	problem	Research
problem	Specific components of the	questions (RQs)
Objectives	problem	Hypothesis (H)

⌄ Suggested Cases and Video Cases

Running Case with Real Data and Questionnaire
   1.1 Dell

Comprehensive Critical Thinking Cases
   2.1 American Idol

Comprehensive Cases with Real Data and Questionnaires
   3.1 JPMorgan Chase   3.2 Wendy's

Online Video Cases
   2.1 Accenture   3.1 NFL   4.1 Nike   7.1 P&G   8.1 Dunkin' Donuts
   9.1 Subaru   10.1 Intel   13.1 Marriott

⌄ Live Research: Conducting a Marketing Research Project

1. Invite the client to discuss the project with the class.
2. Have the class (or different teams) analyze the environmental context of the problem: past information and forecasts, resources and constraints, objectives, buyer behavior, legal environment, economic environment, and marketing and technological skills.
3. The instructor should make a joint presentation—with the client—to the class discussing the management decision problem and the marketing research problem. The students should think of formal definitions of the management decision problem and the marketing research problem. In conjunction with the client, arrive at consensual definitions.
4. Ask the class or specific teams to develop an approach (analytical framework and models, research questions and hypotheses, and identification of the information needed). Through class discussion, arrive at a consensus.

⌄ Acronyms

The factors to be considered while analyzing the environmental context of the problem may be summed up by the acronym PROBLEM:

P ast information and forecasts

R esources and constraints

O bjectives of the decision maker

B uyer behavior

L egal environment

E conomic environment

M arketing and technological skills

∨ Review Questions

2-1. What is the first step in conducting a marketing research project?

2-2. Why is it important to define the marketing research problem appropriately?

2-3. What are some reasons why management is often not clear about the real problem?

2-4. What is the role of the researcher in the problem-definition process?

2-5. What is the difference between primary data and secondary data?

2-6. What is the environmental context of a marketing research problem?

2-7. What are some differences between a management decision problem and a marketing research problem?

2-8. What are the common types of errors encountered in defining a marketing research problem? What can be done to reduce the incidence of such errors?

2-9. What guides the formulation of a research question?

2-10. What is the importance of secondary data analysis?

2-11. Is it necessary for every research project to have a set of hypotheses? Why or why not?

2-12. What is the most common form of analytical models?

2-13. Discuss the role of social media in enabling the researcher to define the marketing research problem and in developing an approach.

∨ Applied Problems

2-14. State the research problems for each of the following management decision problems.
  a. Should a new product be introduced?
  b. Should a three-year-old advertising campaign be changed?
  c. Should the in-store promotion for an existing product line be increased?
  d. What pricing strategy should be adopted for a new product?
  e. Should the compensation package be changed to motivate the sales force better?

2-15. State management decision problems for which the following research problems might provide useful information.
  a. Estimate the sales and market share of department stores in a certain metropolitan area.
  b. Determine the design features for a new product that would result in maximum market share.
  c. Evaluate the effectiveness of alternative television commercials.
  d. Assess current and proposed sales territories with respect to their sales potential and workload.
  e. Determine the prices for each item in a product line to maximize total sales for the product line.

2-16. Identify five symptoms, each pertaining to a management decision problem, and a plausible cause for each one.

2-17. For the second component of the marketing research problem given in the *Tennis* magazine Research in Practice, identify two relevant research questions and develop suitable hypotheses.

2-18. Suppose you are doing a project for Delta Airlines. From secondary sources and an analysis of social media, identify the attributes or factors passengers consider when selecting an airline.

∨ Internet Exercises

2-19. You are a consultant to Coca-Cola USA working on a marketing research project for Diet Coke.

    a. Use the online databases in your library and conduct an analysis of social media to compile a list of articles related to the Coca-Cola Company, Diet Coke, and the soft drink industry published during the past year.

    b. Visit the Coca-Cola and PepsiCo websites and compare the information available at each.

    c. Based on the information you collect from the Internet, write a report on the environmental context surrounding Diet Coke.

2-20. Visit the BMW group's website. What information could you obtain about their sales for the year 2012? How do they compare to their main competitors, Audi and Mercedes, for the same year?

2-21. You are conducting a marketing research project for Starbucks Coffee. Research online to determine the main factors affecting consumer preference for certain coffee brands. Also, determine the current performance of Starbucks coffee with respect to the whole industry.

2-22. adidas, ranked after Nike in the global market for athletic footwear, wants to conduct marketing research to find out how to increase its market share. Conduct research online to identify the environmental factors that would affect achieving such a goal for adidas.

NOTES

1. **www.harley-davidson.com**, accessed February 4, 2013; Henny Ray Abrams, "Harley-Davidson Increases U.S. Market Share," *Cycle News*, January 25, 2011, online at **www.cyclenews.com/articles/industry-news/2011/01/25/harley-davidson-increases-u-s-market-share**, accessed February 11, 2012; and Ian Murphy, "Aided by Research, Harley Goes Whole Hog," *Marketing News* (December 2, 1996): 16–17.

2. "Upscale Jeans Focused on Market Share Gains," online at **www.retailwire.com/Discussions/sngl_discussion.cfm/13079**, accessed May 16, 2013; Ellen Neuborne and Stephanie Anderson Forest, "Look Who's Picking Levi's Pocket," *Business Week* (September 8, 1997): 68, 72.

3. **www.amtrak.com**, accessed February 3, 2013; Associated Press, "Amtrak Says Ridership Reaches a New Record," *Wall Street Journal*, (October 14, 2011): A6; and "Obama talks up high speed rail, Amtrak," online at **http://trains4america.wordpress.com/2008/05/03/obama-talks-up-high-speed-rail-amtrak/**, accessed 2009May 16, 2013.

4. **www.puma.com**, accessed March 23, 2013.

5. **www.tennis.com**, accessed January 2, 2013.

6. **www.bmwusa.com**, accessed May 12, 2013.

7. "Choice Menu—onboard meals," online at **https://store.united.com/traveloptions/control/category?category_id=UM_CHOICEMEU,** accessed January 2, 2012.

8. "Pricey iPhone 4S Gets Tepid Response on First Day of Launch," online at **www.indianexpress.com/news/pricey-iphone-4s-gets-tepid-response-on-first-day-of-launch/880669**, accessed May 16, 2013.

9. **www.dell.com**, accessed May 9, 2013.

10. Anonymous, "Closing the Gap Between the Ethical and Profitable," *Marketing Week* (October 16, 2003): P32.

Online Video Case 2.1

ACCENTURE: The Accent Is in the Name

Visit **www.pearsonglobaleditions.com/malhotra** to read the video case and view the accompanying video. Accenture: The Accent Is in the Name describes the marketing research conducted by Andersen Consulting to change its name, while at the same time maintain the brand equity and the goodwill of its previous name. The case can be used to prompt discussion on the various environmental factors affecting the formulation of a well-defined research problem, as well as discussion on clarifying the distinction between the management decision problem and the marketing research problem. Specific marketing research questions on this and the previous chapter are posed in the video case.

3 Research Design, Secondary and Syndicated Data

∨ Overview

Chapter 2 discussed how to define a marketing research problem and develop a suitable approach that are, respectively, the first and the second step of the marketing research process. These first two steps are critical to the success of the entire marketing research project. Once they have been completed, attention should be devoted to designing the formal research project by formulating a detailed research design (see Figure 2.2 in Chapter 2). This chapter defines and classifies research designs. We describe the two major types of research designs: exploratory and conclusive. We further classify conclusive research designs as descriptive or causal and discuss both types. Then we present a detailed discussion of secondary data, including syndicated sources.

We discuss the distinction between primary and secondary data (see Chapter 2). The advantages and disadvantages of secondary data are considered and criteria for evaluating secondary data are presented, along with a classification of secondary data. Internal secondary data are described and major sources of external secondary data, including syndicated services, are also discussed. We give a practical procedure for conducting an online search for external secondary data. The sources of secondary data useful in international marketing research are covered. We explain how an analysis of social media can be helpful in formulating a research design and in collecting secondary data. Several ethical issues that arise in the use of secondary data are identified.

Figure 3.1 shows how this chapter relates to the marketing research process described in Chapter 1. We begin by citing an example to give you a flavor of secondary data.

∨ Learning Objectives

After reading this chapter, the student should be able to:

1. Define and classify various research designs, and explain the differences between exploratory and conclusive research.

2. Define the nature and scope of secondary data and distinguish secondary data from primary data.

3. Analyze the advantages and disadvantages of secondary data and their uses in the various steps of the marketing research process.

4. Evaluate secondary data using the criteria of specifications, error, currency, objectives, nature, and dependability.

5. Describe in detail the different sources of secondary data, including internal sources and external sources.

6. Discuss in detail the syndicated sources of secondary data, including household/consumer data obtained via surveys, mail panels, and electronic scanner services, as well as institutional data related to retailers, wholesalers, and industrial/service firms.

7. Explain the need to use multiple sources of secondary data and describe single-source data.

8. Discuss research design formulation, and identify and evaluate the sources of secondary and syndicated data useful in international marketing research.

9. Discuss how the analysis of social media content can facilitate the research design process and the collection of secondary and syndicated data.

10. Understand the ethical issues involved in the formulation of research design and the use of secondary and syndicated data.

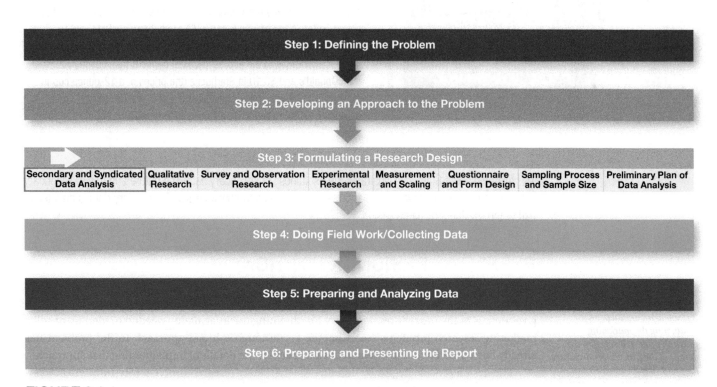

FIGURE 3.1 | RELATIONSHIP OF THIS CHAPTER TO THE MARKETING RESEARCH PROCESS

Research in Practice
Starbucks: Instant Success for VIA Instant Coffee

In 2009, Starbucks introduced a new product: Starbucks VIA ready brew. The decision of Starbucks to venture into the instant coffee market was made based on intensive market research that included secondary data analysis. However, before using secondary data, they were carefully evaluated to determine their relevance, currency, accuracy, and dependability. Analysis of internal and external secondary data, social media, and syndicated data revealed the following:

Source: studiomode / Alamy

- In many markets, Starbuck was losing market share to McDonald's, Panera Bread Co., and Dunkin' Donuts. McDonald's was rolling out its McCafe espresso drinks, and Panera Bread Co. offered new coffee and breakfast items.
- The global instant coffee market was worth US$17 billion. This market was primarily dominated by established brands such Nestle SA's Nescafe and Kraft Foods Inc.'s Sanka. There was room for another major player to enter this market.
- Instant coffee, while not exceptionally popular in the United States, accounted for about 40 percent of coffee sales outside the United States. This percentage was as high as 81 percent of coffee sold in the United Kingdom and 63 percent of coffee sales in Japan.
- Customers want high-quality coffee that was more affordable.

Instead of slashing prices of their Starbucks coffee to compete directly with McDonald's and Dunkin' Donuts, Starbucks created a new product in 2009. Their VIA ready brew was set to compete in a whole new market—instant coffee. A trio of single-serve VIA ready brew packets sold for $2.95, and twelve packets were priced at $9.95. VIA ready brew is a much cheaper alternative to the espresso-based coffee drinks costing $2.29 at McDonald's and $3.10 in Starbucks (the prices of a 12-ounce cup in Chicago). The launch was a big success, and Starbucks racked up an impressive $100 million in global sales in ten months.[1] ◄

This example about Starbucks illustrates the usefulness of secondary data. The nature and role of secondary data become clear when we understand research design and how analysis of secondary data is an integral part of formulating a research design.

RESEARCH DESIGN DEFINITION

research design
A framework or blueprint for conducting the marketing research project. It specifies the details of the procedures necessary for obtaining the information needed to structure and/or solve marketing research problems.

A **research design** is a framework or blueprint for conducting the marketing research project. It gives details of the procedures necessary for obtaining the information needed to identify or solve marketing research problems (see Chapter 1). Although a broad approach to the problem has already been developed, the research design specifies the details of implementing that approach.

The design process begins by defining the marketing research problem (Step 1 of the marketing research process). Next comes the approach to the problem consisting of a framework and models, research questions and hypotheses, and the information needed (Step 2 of the marketing research process) (see Chapter 2). The research design is based on the results of these first two steps and is the third step of the marketing research process. Yet the process is iterative, with feedback from research design to the earlier steps (Figure 3.2). A research design lays the foundation

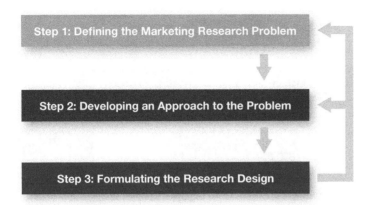

FIGURE 3.2
STEPS LEADING TO
THE FORMULATION OF
A RESEARCH DESIGN

for conducting the project. Many different designs might be appropriate for a given marketing research problem. A good research design ensures that the information collected will be relevant and useful to management and that all of the necessary information will be obtained.

Typically, a research design involves all or most of the following components, or tasks:

1. Analysis of secondary and syndicated data (Chapter 3)
2. Qualitative research (Chapter 4)
3. Survey and observation research (Chapter 5)
4. Experimental research (Chapter 6)
5. Measurement and scaling procedures (Chapter 7)
6. Design and pretest of a questionnaire (interviewing form) or an observation form for data collection (Chapter 8)
7. Sampling process and sample size determination (Chapter 9)
8. Development of a preliminary plan of data analysis (Chapter 10)

Depending on the nature of the research project, not all of the eight tasks may be involved, and the order or the sequence in which these tasks are performed could also vary. Each of these components will be discussed in great detail in the subsequent chapters. First, we must further our understanding of research design with a classification of the basic types.

Research Recipe

Formulate the research design only after defining the problem and developing an approach. However, this process is iterative, with feedback from research design to the earlier steps.

BASIC RESEARCH DESIGNS

Research designs are of two broad types: exploratory and conclusive. Conclusive designs are either descriptive or causal. Exploratory, descriptive, and causal are the basic research designs we examine in this chapter (see Figure 3.3). Descriptive designs can be further categorized as either cross-sectional or longitudinal.

Exploratory Research

The differences between exploratory and conclusive research are summarized in Table 3.1. The primary objective of **exploratory research** is to provide insights into, and an understanding of, the problem confronting the researcher. Exploratory research is used in cases when you must define

exploratory research
One type of research design that has as its primary objective the provision of insights into and comprehension of the problem situation confronting the researcher.

FIGURE 3.3
A CLASSIFICATION OF
MARKETING RESEARCH
DESIGNS

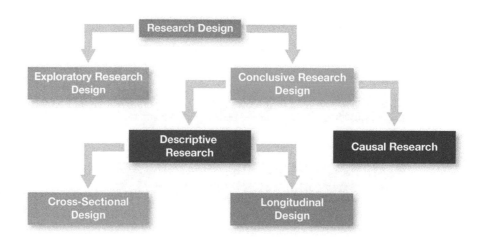

the problem more precisely, identify relevant courses of action, or gain additional insights before an approach can be developed. The information needed is only loosely defined at this stage, and the research process that is adopted is flexible and unstructured. For example, it may consist of personal interviews with a few industry experts (see Chapter 2). The sample, selected to generate maximum insights, is small and nonrepresentative. The primary data are qualitative in nature and are analyzed accordingly. Given these characteristics of the research process, the findings of exploratory research should be regarded as tentative. Typically, such research is followed by further exploratory or conclusive research. Thus, it is a good idea to begin a marketing research project by first conducting exploratory research and then some form of conclusive research. Sometimes, exploratory research is all the research that is conducted. In these cases, caution should be exercised in utilizing the findings. Secondary data including social media (discussed later in this chapter) and qualitative research (Chapter 4) are the main methods of exploratory research. The research conducted by Starbucks to introduce VIA in the first Research in Practice included an analysis of secondary data.

The insights gained from exploratory research might be verified by conclusive research because the objective of conclusive research is to test specific hypotheses and examine specific relationships. This requires that the information needed is clearly specified. **Conclusive research** is typically more formal and structured than exploratory research. It is based on large, representative samples, and the data obtained are subjected to quantitative analysis. The findings from this research are considered to be conclusive in nature in that they are used as input into managerial decision making. As shown in Figure 3.3, conclusive research designs may be either descriptive or causal.

conclusive research
Research designed to assist the decision maker in determining, evaluating, and selecting the best course of action to take in a given situation.

Table 3.1 > Differences Between Exploratory and Conclusive Research

	Exploratory	Conclusive
Objective:	To provide insights and understanding.	To test specific hypotheses and examine relationships.
Characteristics:	Information needed is defined only loosely.	Information needed is clearly defined.
	Research process is flexible and unstructured.	Research process is formal and structured.
	Sample is small and nonrepresentative.	Sample is large and representative.
	Data analysis is qualitative.	Data analysis is quantitative.
Findings:	Tentative.	Conclusive.
Outcome:	Generally followed by further exploratory or conclusive research.	Findings used as input into decision making.

Research Recipe

Begin most marketing research projects by first conducting exploratory research and then some form of conclusive research. Exploratory research is often necessary to gain an adequate understanding of the problem context so that meaningful conclusive research can be conducted.

Descriptive Research

As the name implies, the major objective of **descriptive research** is to describe something—usually the characteristics of relevant groups, such as consumers, salespeople, organizations, or market areas. For example, we could develop a profile of the "heavy users" (frequent shoppers) of prestigious department stores like Saks Fifth Avenue and Neiman Marcus. A vast majority of marketing research studies involve descriptive research, which makes use of surveys and observations as major methods. **Surveys** involve questioning of respondents by administering a questionnaire. **Observations** involve recording people's behavior without asking them questions. (These methods are discussed further in Chapter 5.) Descriptive research can be further classified into cross-sectional and longitudinal research (Figure 3.3).

Cross-sectional designs involve the collection of information from any given sample of population elements only once. For example, a survey may be conducted at a given point in time, the data are analyzed, and a report is prepared. The cross-sectional study is the most frequently used descriptive design in marketing research. In **longitudinal designs**, a fixed sample of population elements is measured repeatedly (two or more times) on the same variables. A longitudinal design differs from a cross-sectional design in that the sample remains the same over time. In other words, the same people are studied over time and the same variables are measured (see Figure 3.4). In contrast to the typical cross-sectional design, which gives a snapshot of the variables of interest at a single point in time, a longitudinal study provides a series of pictures that give the changes that take place over time. Thus, a longitudinal design enables us to examine changes over time. For example, the question, "How did the American people rate the U.S. economy at the beginning of 2014?" would be addressed using a cross-sectional design. A survey of a representative sample of the U.S. population will have to be conducted only at the beginning of 2014. However, a longitudinal design would be used to address the question, "How did the American people change their view of the U.S. economy during 2014?" A survey of a representative sample of the U.S. population will have to be conducted at the beginning of 2014, and the same survey will have to be repeated on the same sample at the end of 2014. Longitudinal designs can be implemented using panels. Sometimes, the term *panel* is used interchangeably with the term longitudinal design. A **panel** consists of a sample of respondents, generally households that have agreed to provide information at specified intervals over an extended period. Panels are maintained by marketing research firms, and panel

descriptive research
A type of conclusive research that has as its major objective the description of something—usually market characteristics or functions.

surveys
Interviews with a large number of respondents using a predesigned questionnaire.

observations
The recording of people's behavior to obtain information about the phenomenon of interest.

cross-sectional design
A type of research design involving the collection of information from any given sample of population elements only once.

longitudinal design
A type of research design, involving a fixed sample of population elements, that is measured repeatedly. The sample remains the same over time. Thus it provides a series of pictures that, when viewed together, portray a vivid illustration of the situation and the changes taking place over time.

panel
A sample of respondents who have agreed to provide information at specified intervals over an extended period.

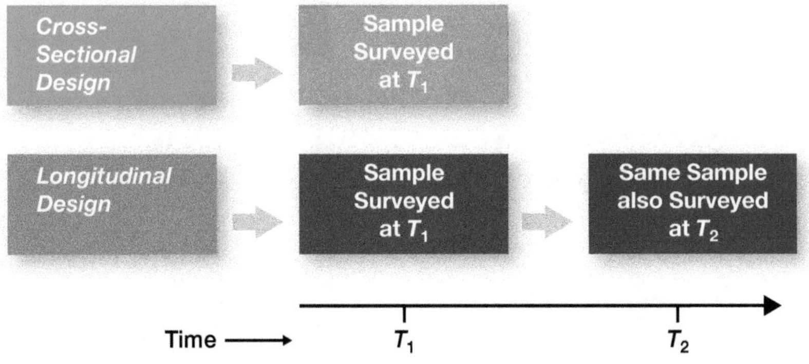

FIGURE 3.4
CROSS-SECTIONAL VERSUS LONGITUDINAL DESIGNS

members are compensated for their participation with gifts, coupons, information, or cash. Panels are discussed further later in this chapter.

Research Recipe

When conducting descriptive research, a cross-sectional design is all you need unless you want to examine changes over time. In the latter case, use a longitudinal design.

Causal Research

causal research
A type of conclusive research where the major objective is to obtain evidence regarding cause-and-effect (causal) relationships.

Causal research is used to obtain evidence of cause-and-effect (causal) relationships. Marketing managers continually make decisions based on assumed causal relationships. These assumptions may not be justifiable, and the validity of the causal relationships should be examined via formal research. For example, the common assumption that a decrease in price will lead to increased sales and market share does not hold in certain competitive environments.

Like descriptive research, causal research requires a planned and structured design. While descriptive research can determine the degree of association or correlation between variables (i.e., the two variables vary together or are related), it is not appropriate for examining causal relationships (i.e., one variable is a cause of the other variable). Such an examination requires a causal design (Figure 3.5). The main method of causal research is experimentation, which is discussed further in Chapter 6.

Research Recipe

If cause-and-effect relationships have to be examined, use a causal design rather than a descriptive design. You can implement a causal design by conducting an experiment.

Exploratory and descriptive research is being used by companies such as Procter & Gamble (P&G) to gain a better understanding of consumers and to formulate targeted marketing strategies, as illustrated in the following Research in Practice feature.

FIGURE 3.5 |
DESCRIPTIVE VERSUS
CAUSAL RESEARCH

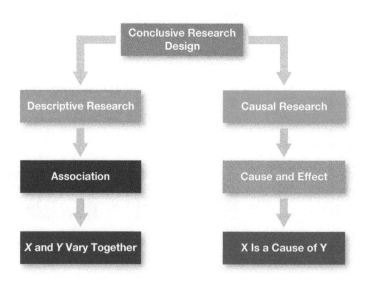

Research in Practice
Hola: P&G Woos Latino Shoppers

Procter & Gamble Co. (**www.pg.com**), looking for ways to boost its sluggish U.S. business, is targeting Hispanic shoppers. This strategy was guided by extensive marketing research that involved both exploratory and descriptive phases.

Exploratory research involved the analysis of secondary and syndicated data as well as focus groups. According to secondary (publicly available) data from the U.S. Census Bureau (**www.census.gov**), Hispanics accounted for more than half of the gains in the U.S. population from 2000 to 2010. Furthermore, secondary data showed that Hispanics spent about $1 trillion in 2010, accounting for some 9 percent of total consumer buying power in the United States, and are expected to shell out $1.5 billion by 2015, outpacing growth in spending by non-Hispanic consumers. Syndicated research (made available for purchase on a subscription basis) from Packaged Facts (**www.packagedfacts.com**) revealed that, from 2000 to 2010, the spending on laundry, household cleaning supplies, and personal-care products by Hispanic households grew nearly three times faster than non-Hispanic outlays. P&G also conducted its own research using qualitative method such as focus groups and depth interviews.

Descriptive research included computer analysis of Hispanic social media, as well as a variety of survey methods (telephone, mall intercept, and Internet interviews). P&G found that, while they are generally frugal spenders, Hispanics are willing to splurge on the types of premium household goods that P&G makes, subscribing to the phrase *lo barato sale caro*, meaning "cheap things may ultimately prove costly."

Source: Spencer Grant / PhotoEdit

Based on these findings, P&G is tweaking products, retargeting its marketing, changing its mix of celebrity spokeswomen, and making greater use of Spanish on its products. For example, P&G's Pantene shampoo and Gillette Venus razors now include actress Eva Mendes as well as singer and actress Jennifer Lopez, respectively, as spokeswomen. This effort is paying off, leading to a revival of sales in the United States.[2] ◄

As discussed in Chapter 2, the Internet offers many resources for marketing research. Newsgroups, listservs, and other bulletin-board-type services can be very useful in the exploratory phase of research. Messages posted to newsgroups can often direct the researcher to other valid sources of information. Newsgroups can be used to set up more formal focus groups with experts or individuals representing the target audience in order to obtain initial information on a subject. In Chapter 4, we discuss in more detail the use of the Internet for conducting focus groups.

We next focus our attention on secondary data, the first major component of a research design.

PRIMARY VERSUS SECONDARY DATA

An early outcome of the research process is to define the marketing research problem and to identify specific research questions and hypotheses (see Chapter 2). When data are collected to address a specific marketing research problem, they are referred to as **primary data**. Obtaining primary data can be expensive and time-consuming because it involves all six steps of the marketing research process (Figure 3.1).

Before initiating primary data collection, a researcher should remember that the problem under study might not be unique. It is possible that someone else has investigated the same or a similar marketing research problem. A search through existing data might lead to relevant information. **Secondary data** represent any data that have already been collected for purposes other than the problem at hand. Relative to primary data collection, these data can be located quickly

primary data
Data originated by the researcher for the specific purpose of addressing the marketing research problem.

secondary data
Data collected for some purpose other than the problem at hand.

Table 3.2 > A Comparison of Primary and Secondary Data

	Primary Data	Secondary Data
Collection purpose	For the problem at hand	For other problems
Collection process	Very involved	Rapid and easy
Collection cost	High	Relatively low
Collection time	Long	Short

and inexpensively, as in the opening Research in Practice featuring Starbucks. The differences between primary and secondary data are summarized in Table 3.2.

ADVANTAGES AND DISADVANTAGES OF SECONDARY DATA

The main advantages of secondary data are the time and money they can save because the researcher does not have to go through the six steps of the marketing research process; someone else has already done that. The collection of some secondary data, such as those provided by the U.S. Department of Labor or the Census Bureau, would not be feasible for individual firms such as GM or Ford. In some projects, particularly those with limited budgets, research may be largely confined to the analysis of secondary data because some routine problems may be addressed based only on secondary data. Although it is rare for secondary data to provide all the answers to a nonroutine research problem, analysis of secondary data should always be the first step taken toward solving any research problem. Given these advantages and uses of secondary data, we state a basic rule of research:

> Examine available secondary data first. The research project should proceed to primary data collection only when the secondary data sources have been reasonably exhausted or yield marginal returns.

An example of the use of secondary data was given at the beginning of this chapter where Starbucks made extensive use of secondary and syndicated data to introduce VIA ready brew successfully. Analysis of secondary data can provide valuable insights and lay the foundation for conducting more formal research, such as focus groups and surveys. However, the researcher should be cautious when using secondary data because they have some disadvantages as well.

The value of secondary data is typically limited by their degree of fit with the current research problem. Because secondary data have been collected by someone else for purposes other than the problem at hand, they may have only limited applicability to the current problem. The objectives, nature, and methods used to collect secondary data might not be compatible with the present situation. Also, secondary data might be lacking in terms of accuracy, compatibility of units of measurement, or timeframe. Before using secondary data, it is important to evaluate their usefulness and fit.

R e s e a r c h   R e c i p e

Analyze available secondary data before collecting primary data. Secondary data are abundantly available and can be obtained quickly and at a relatively low cost.

CRITERIA FOR EVALUATING SECONDARY DATA

The criteria used for evaluating secondary data consist of specifications, error, currency, objective, nature and dependability. Starbucks used similar criteria for evaluating secondary data in the research conducted to introduce VIA.

Specifications: Methodology Used to Collect the Data

The research design specifications—that is, the methodology used to collect the data—should be examined to identify possible sources of bias. Factors that are important in identifying potential error, as well as relevance of the data, include the size and nature of the sample, response rate and quality, questionnaire design and administration, procedures used for field work, and data analysis and reporting procedures. These issues are discussed in detail in the subsequent chapters. One reason it is advantageous to use data from the originating source is that a description of the research design is typically provided as part of the original published study.

Error: Accuracy of the Data

Both secondary and primary data can have errors, but it is more difficult to evaluate the accuracy of secondary data because the researcher has not directly participated in the research. One approach to ascertaining the accuracy is to find data from multiple sources and compare them. The data are accurate to the extent that the different sources agree. Data obtained from different sources might not agree, however. In these cases, the researcher should verify the accuracy of secondary data by conducting pilot studies or by other appropriate methods. With a little creativity, verification can often be accomplished with little expense and effort.

Currency: When the Data Were Collected

Secondary data might not be current. A time lag might exist between data collection and publication, as with census data. The data might not be updated frequently enough to answer questions related to the problem at hand. For instance, data from the 2010 census might not be current enough for use by Home Depot in predicting potential demand for the year 2015. Fortunately, several marketing research firms update census data periodically and make the current information available for a fee.

Objective: The Purpose for the Study

Understanding why secondary data were originally collected can help the researcher understand the limitations of using them for the current marketing problem. *Time* magazine surveyed its renewing subscriber base regarding reading of its articles and recall of its advertising. One objective of this study was to use the information to sell advertising space. With that in mind, the results of the study were made available to advertising managers, who would likely make decisions regarding advertising placement. This type of secondary information might be relevant to the question of where to place future advertising. The results of this survey from *Time* would be biased, however, because they would reflect the behavior of its renewing subscribers, a group that might be more involved with the magazine than the general subscribers. To interpret this secondary data accurately, the advertising manager would have to understand how closely the *Time* magazine renewing segment represents its total subscribing population.

Nature: The Content of the Data

The *nature*, or *content*, of the data should be examined, with special attention to the definition of key variables, the units of measurement, the categories used, and the relationships examined. One of the most frustrating limitations of secondary data comes from differences in definition, units of measurement, or the timeframe examined. If the key variables have not been defined or are defined in a manner inconsistent with the researcher's definition, then the usefulness of the data is limited. If Mercedes is interested in high-income consumers with gross annual household incomes of more than $100,000, then secondary data with income categories of less than $15,000, $15,001 to $35,000, $35,001 to $50,000, and more than $50,000 will not be of much use.

Dependability: How Dependable Are the Data?

An overall indication of the dependability of the data can be obtained by examining the expertise, credibility, reputation, and trustworthiness of the source. This information can be obtained by checking with others who have used information from this source. Data published to promote sales, advance specific interests, or carry on propaganda should be viewed with suspicion. In contrast, secondary data published by reputable organizations, such as the U.S. Census Bureau, are very dependable and of high quality.

R e s e a r c h   R e c i p e

Always evaluate secondary data to determine their applicability to the problem at hand before using them. This is essential because secondary data were collected for some purpose other than the problem at hand. Thus, their relevance and applicability for your particular purposes may be limited and you should ascertain this information in advance.

iResearch
At Home in Home Depot

As the CEO of Home Depot, you come across a Gallup poll reporting that an increasing number of women are shopping for home improvement products and services. How will you use this information to improve the competitiveness of Home Depot?

Visit **www.gallup.com**. Examine the information on how Gallup conducts its polls. By applying the criteria we have considered, evaluate the quality of Gallup polls. Would you use Gallup data to make marketing decisions pertaining to Home Depot? How would you apply these criteria to evaluate the quality of secondary data available in social media? **<**

It is easy to overlook the many sources of secondary data when developing a formal research design. Once a secondary data search is initiated, however, the volume of existing information can be overwhelming. To browse efficiently through this mountain of information, it is important that the researcher be familiar with various sources of secondary data. It would be very useful to classify them.

CLASSIFICATION OF SECONDARY DATA

internal data
Data available within the organization for which the research is being conducted.

external data
Data that originate external to the organization for which the research is being conducted.

As represented in Figure 3.6, the two primary sources of secondary data are internal and external data. **Internal data** are data generated within the organization for which the research is being conducted. Many organizations are engaged in building large customer databases, data warehousing and data mining, and customer relationship management (CRM) and database marketing. They are also using social media to generate internal secondary data. **External data** are data generated by sources outside the organization. These data are available in the form of business/nongovernment

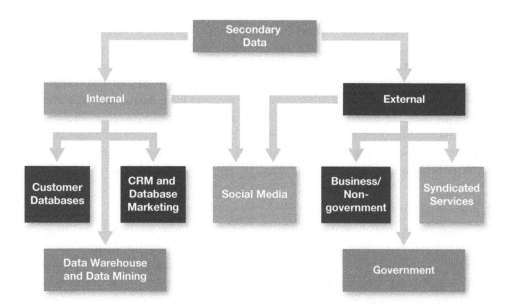

FIGURE 3.6
A CLASSIFICATION OF
SECONDARY DATA

sources, government sources, syndicated services, and social media. Thus, social media are sources of both internal and external secondary data and are discussed later in this chapter. We next focus on the sources of internal secondary data.

INTERNAL SECONDARY DATA

Before collecting external secondary data, it is always useful to analyze internal secondary data. Internal data are typically generated as part of the ongoing process of doing business. These data can come from accounting records, sales reports, production or operation reports, or internal experts. Although it is possible that internal secondary data might be available in usable form, it is more typical that considerable processing effort will be required before such data can be used. For example, cash register receipts of a department store might contain a wealth of information, such as sales by product line, sales by specific store, sales by geographical region, sales by cash versus credit purchases, sales in specific time periods, sales by size of purchase, and so on. To derive this information, however, data must be transcribed from the paper-based sales receipts to a computer database and analyzed extensively. Many organizations are building sophisticated customer databases as platforms for their marketing efforts.

Customer Databases

For many companies, the first step in creating a customer database is to transfer raw sales information, such as that found on sales call reports or invoices, to a personal computer. Customer information is also obtained from other sources, such as warranty cards and loyalty programs (e.g., frequent flier programs of airlines). This is augmented with demographic and psychographic information about the customers obtained from external secondary sources. **Psychographics** refers to quantified psychological profiles of individuals. Several companies in this business, such as Experian (**www.experian.com**), have compiled household lists that include names, addresses, and a great deal of individual-specific data. The size of these customer databases can be staggering. Sears, for example, has more than 75 percent of U.S. households in its customer database. In the first Research in Practice example in this chapter, Starbucks analyzed its own customer databases to determine that consumers wanted high quality coffee that was more affordable. These customer databases reside in a data warehouse.

psychographics
Quantified psychological profiles of individuals.

Data Warehouse and Data Mining

data warehouse
A centralized database that consolidates company-wide data from a variety of operational systems.

data mining
Technique involving the use of powerful computers and advanced statistical and other software to analyze large databases in order to discover hidden patterns in the data.

customer relationship management (CRM) system
A decision support system that is used for managing the interactions between an organization and its customers.

database marketing
The use of CRM databases to develop relationships and highly targeted marketing efforts with individuals and customer groups.

A **data warehouse** is a centralized database that consolidates companywide data from a variety of operational systems. The analysis of such large databases requires special skills and resources and has been termed *data mining*. **Data mining** involves the use of powerful computers with advanced statistical packages and other software to analyze large databases to discover hidden patterns in the data. The patterns discovered can be very useful for targeting marketing effort. For example, data mining revealed that husbands tend to buy additional life insurance immediately after the birth of their first child. Therefore, Allstate's (**www.allstate.com**) slogan, "You're in good hands," is particularly appropriate for targeting first-time fathers with life insurance products.

CRM and Database Marketing

Customer databases and data mining are the building blocks for **customer relationship management (CRM) systems**. A CRM is a decision support system (see Chapter 1) that is used for managing the interactions between an organization and its customers. **Database marketing** is the practice of using CRM databases to develop relationships and highly targeted marketing efforts with individuals and customer groups. For example, recently Whirlpool used its massive database to identify families of four or more who had bought Whirlpool washers and/or dryers five years ago and offered them special discounts to replace their machines with newer models. This effort was successful as the targeted household realized that their machines had lived the average life span and needed to be replaced.

Research Recipe

Analyze internal secondary data before collecting external secondary data. Organizations should process internal secondary data that are generated routinely. Efforts to build large customer databases will yield high dividends.

EXTERNAL SECONDARY DATA

As mentioned earlier, external secondary data may be classified as business/nongovernment, government, and syndicated services (Figure 3.6). External secondary data, particularly those available from business/nongovernment sources, have grown dramatically over the past twenty years. This growth has been stimulated, in part, by the Internet and personal computers in the workplace, which gives employees easy access to commercial databases. The following section provides an overview of some of the business/nongovernment sources of external secondary data.

Business/Nongovernment Data

Business/nongovernment sources are used as a broad category and encompass nonprofit organizations (e.g., chambers of commerce), trade and professional organizations, commercial publishers, investment brokerage firms, and for-profit firms. Most of these data can be accessed conveniently over the Internet. Businesses publish a great deal of information in the form of books, periodicals, journals, newspapers, magazines, reports, and trade literature. Moody's (**www.moodys.com**) and Standard & Poor's (**www.standardandpoors.com**) provide information on U.S. and foreign companies. Another useful source for industrial brand and trade information is ThomasNet (**www.thomasnet.com**). Valuable marketing and marketing research information can be obtained from **SecondaryData.com** (**www.secondarydata.com**).

A variety of business-related sites can provide sales leads, mailing lists, business profiles, and credit ratings for U.S. businesses. Many sites supply information on businesses within a specific industry. For example, all of the American Marketing Association's publications can be searched by keywords at **www.marketingpower.com**. Encyclopedia Britannica provides free online access to its entire thirty-two-volume set (**www.britannica.com**). Data on U.S. manufacturers and key decision makers can be obtained from Hoovers (**www.hoovers.com**), a D&B company. Another good source is Infogroup (**www.infogroup.com**).

Business/nongovernment data can be found conveniently by using bibliographies and indexes. Bibliographies, which are organized alphabetically by topic, are a good place to start the search. Current or historic discussion of a particular topic of interest will be indexed in these references, leading you to a number of authors. Several indexes are available for referencing both academic and business topics. *Business Periodicals Index* (**www.ebscohost.com**) is a bibliographic database that cites articles of at least one column in length from English-language periodicals published in the United States and elsewhere. *Social Sciences Citation Index*® (**www.thomsonreuters.com**), provides you with quick, powerful access to the bibliographic and citation information you need to find research data, analyze trends, and locate journals and researchers. Several newspapers, for example the *Wall Street Journal* (**www.wsj.com**), have an index to conduct a guided search. *CI Resource Index* (**www.bidigital.com/ci**) features sites for competitive intelligence information.

The website "ipl2: information you can trust" (**www.ipl.org**) was launched in January 2010, merging the collections of resources from the Internet Public Library (IPL) and the Librarians' Internet Index (LII) websites. This new ipl2 website is a public service organization; it features an "Ask an ipl2 Librarian" service and is a useful source for indexes and bibliographies.

Firmographics are the business equivalent of demographics. They include variables such as market share, corporate location, industry classification, and employment size. D&B (**www.dnb.com**) provides this type of data. YP launched in May 2012 (**www.yellowpages.com**) has a large database of U.S. companies.

Research in Practice
Market Research Library

Customers can purchase report information online from the LexisNexis Market Research Library (**www.lexisnexis.com**) by subsection, eliminating the cost of buying an entire report. Users can browse the entire table of contents and study the methodology of most reports as well as view actual tables, minus the data, before purchasing the information. The subsections of the marketing research reports on the LexisNexis Market Research Product have been formatted by the marketing research providers as complete, stand-alone units of information. The product offers research data from sources such as The Nielsen Company, Datamonitor, Euromonitor, and Packaged Facts. Visit the company's website for more information.[3] **‹**

Government Sources

The U.S. government is the largest source of secondary data in this country and in the world. The data the government collects could not feasibly be collected by private industry. Its value ranges from use in developing sales forecasts and market potential estimates to simply locating specific retailers, wholesalers, or manufacturers. The breadth and accuracy of government sources make it a rich source of secondary data. Government sources can be divided into census data and other types.

CENSUS DATA   Census data are useful in a variety of marketing research projects. The demographic data collected by the U.S. Census Bureau include information about household types, sex, age, marital status, and race. Consumption detail related to automobile ownership, housing characteristics, work status, and practices as well as occupations are just a few of the categories of information available. What makes this demographic information particularly valuable to marketers is that it can be categorized geographically at various levels of detail. These data can be summarized at various levels, such as city block, block group, census tract, metropolitan statistical area (MSA), consolidated metropolitan statistical area (CMSA), and region (Northeast, Midwest, South, and West), or they can be aggregated for the nation as a whole.

In general, the quality of census data is high, and the data are often extremely detailed. Important census data include Census of Housing, Census of Manufacturers, Census of Population, Census of Retail Trade, Census of Service Industries, and Census of Wholesale Trade. Nielsen (**www.nielsen.com**) has created a number of research tools using census and other lifestyle data. Integrating enhanced census data with internal company databases is a useful application of multiple secondary sources. This integration of secondary data is discussed later in the chapter.

U.S. Census Bureau

The 2010 census of the United States provides insight into the demographic profile of not only the United States in full, but also smaller U.S. regions, such as states and MSAs. Go to the home page for the U.S. Census Bureau (**www.census.gov**) and find out the following:

1. What is the current population estimate for the United States? For the world?

2. Compare your home state's "population percentage change from 2000 to 2010" with that of the United States as a whole. Which grew faster?

3. Find out how many "singles without children living at home" were counted in your zip code in the 2010 census. ❮

OTHER GOVERNMENT SOURCES   In addition to the census, the federal government collects and publishes a great deal of statistical data, much of it relevant to business. The United States, Mexico, and Canada have created a new common classification system to replace the previous classification of each country. The four-digit Standard Industrial Classification (SIC) code of the United States has been replaced by a six-digit North American Industry Classification System (NAICS). The two extra digits in the NAICS accommodate a larger number of sectors, making the classification system more flexible in designating subsections. NAICS is organized in a hierarchical structure, much like the SIC. The new codes will be reviewed every five years.

Other useful government publications include *County and City Data Book, Statistical Abstract of the United States, State and Metropolitan Area Data Book*, and *World Factbook*. Several U.S. government sources can be accessed at FedWorld (**www.fedworld.gov**). Extensive business statistics can be obtained from FedStats (**www.fedstats.gov**). FedStats compiles statistical information from more than 100 agencies. The U.S. Department of Commerce can be reached at **www.doc.gov**. The Bureau of Labor Statistics (**www.bls.gov**) provides useful information, especially consumer expenditure surveys. A wide range of economic statistics can be obtained from the Bureau of Economic Analysis (**www.bea.gov**). Information about public companies can be obtained from the EDGAR Database of Corporate Information, which contains Securities and Exchange Commission (SEC) filings (**www.sec.gov/edgar.shtml**). Information about small businesses can be obtained at **www.sbaonline.sba.gov**.

Research Recipe

External secondary data may be classified as business/nongovernment, government, and syndicated services. Data available from business/nongovernment sources have grown tremendously. The U.S. government is the largest source of secondary data in the world and the quality of these data is high.

THE NATURE OF SYNDICATED DATA

In addition to data available from business and government, syndicated sources constitute the other major source of external secondary data. **Syndicated sources**, also referred to as *syndicated services*, are companies that collect and sell common pools of data of known commercial value and designed to serve information needs shared by a number of clients, including competing firms in the same industry. These data differ from customized research in that the objective guiding the research is common to several client firms (see Chapter 1). Syndicated firms make their money by collecting data and designing research products that fit the information needs of more than one organization. Any client, even two competitors in the same industry (e.g., Coca-Cola Company and PepsiCo) can purchase the same syndicated data, typically through a subscription process. In the first Research in Practice, the syndicated data purchased by Starbucks were also available to its competitors, namely, Nestle and Kraft Foods. The data and reports that syndicated services supply to client companies can be personalized to fit their specific needs. For example, reports could be organized on the basis of the client's sales territories or product lines. The cost of syndicated data is marginal compared to the cost of collecting primary data. Hence, it is useful to examine applicable syndicated data before collecting primary data.

syndicated sources
Companies that collect and sell common pools of data designed to serve information needs shared by a number of clients, including competing firms in the same industry.

Research Recipe

Syndicated data are a special form of secondary data that are meant for use by multiple clients and you can purchase them on a subscription basis. Hence, the cost of syndicated data is low compared to the cost of collecting primary data. Analyze applicable syndicated data before collecting primary data.

A CLASSIFICATION OF SYNDICATED SERVICES

Figure 3.7 presents a classification of syndicated sources based on either a household/consumer or institutional unit of measurement. Household/consumer data can be collected through a survey process, recorded by panel respondents in diaries (paper or electronic), or captured electronically via scanners. Consumer surveys are used to obtain information on beliefs, values, attitudes, preferences, and intentions. Panels used in consumer research emphasize information on purchases or media consumption. Electronic scanner services track purchases at the point of sale or in the home through handheld scanners. These data collection techniques can also be integrated, linking electronic scanner data with panels, survey data, or targeted television advertising through cable.

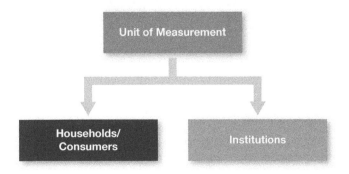

FIGURE 3.7
A CLASSIFICATION OF SYNDICATED SERVICES

When syndicated services obtain data from institutions rather than households, the primary subjects they track are product movement through the distribution channel (retailers and wholesalers) or corporate statistics. These sources will be discussed in the following sections, beginning with syndicated services for consumer data.

SYNDICATED SERVICES FOR CONSUMER DATA

Syndicated consumer data are collected primarily through surveys, purchase and media panels, and electronic scanner services (Figure 3.8).

Surveys

At a general level, surveys are of two types: periodic and panel.

periodic surveys

Surveys that collect data on the same set of variables at regular intervals, each time sampling from a new group of respondents.

PERIODIC SURVEYS   **Periodic surveys** collect data on the same set of variables at regular intervals, each time sampling a new group of respondents from the target population. Like longitudinal research, periodic surveys track change over time. However, the change due to variation in the respondent pool is not controlled in the way it is for true longitudinal studies. A new sample of respondents is chosen with each survey. Once analyzed, the data are made available to subscribers.

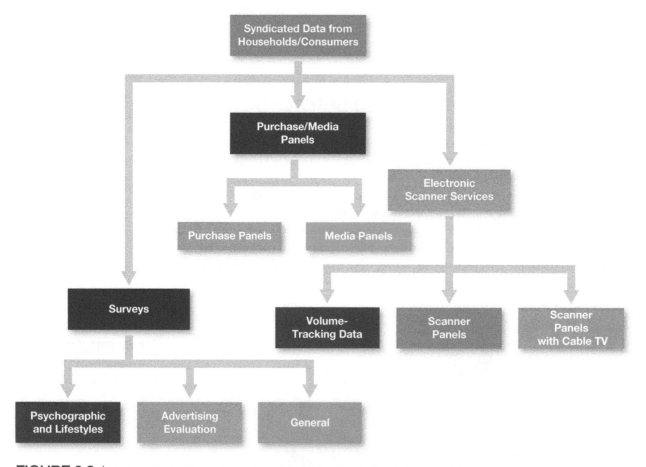

FIGURE 3.8 | A CLASSIFICATION OF SYNDICATE SERVICES: HOUSEHOLDS/CONSUMERS

PANEL SURVEYS   Syndicated **panel surveys** measure the same group of respondents over time, but not necessarily on the same variables. A large pool of respondents is recruited to participate on the panel. From this pool, different subsamples of respondents might be drawn for different surveys. Any survey technique can be used, including telephone, personal, mail, or electronic interviewing. The content and topics of the surveys vary and cover a wide range. Also known as *omnibus panels*, these panels are used to implement different cross-sectional designs at different points in time, generally for different surveys. Omnibus panels are different from panels that use longitudinal designs, which were discussed earlier in this chapter. Recall that in a longitudinal design, repeated measurements on the same variables are made on the same sample. Such panels are sometimes referred to as *true panels* to distinguish them from omnibus panels.

Surveys, whether they are periodic or panel, can be broadly classified on the basis of their content as psychographics and lifestyles, advertising evaluation, or general surveys (see Figure 3.8).

PSYCHOGRAPHICS AND LIFESTYLES SURVEYS   As stated earlier, the term psychographics refers to psychological profiles of individuals and to psychologically based measures of lifestyle, such as brand loyalty and risk taking. The term *lifestyle* refers to the distinctive modes of living within a society or some of its segments, such as the double income no kids (DINKs) lifestyle characterized as being money rich and time poor. Together, these measures are generally referred to as *activities, interests,* and *opinions,* or simply as AIOs. As an example, Strategic Business Insights (**www.strategicbusinessinsights.com**) conducts an annual survey of consumers that is used to classify persons into values and lifestyles (VALs) types for segmentation purposes. Information on specific aspects of consumers' lifestyles is also available. GfK (**www.gfk.com**) conducts an annual survey of 5,000 consumers who participate in leisure sports and recreational activities. Several firms conduct surveys to compile demographic and psychographic information at the household, sub–Zip code (e.g., 30308-1149), and Zip code level, which is then made available on a subscription basis. Such information is particularly valuable for client firms seeking to enhance internally generated customer data for database marketing. Starbuck's decision to introduce VIA was partly influences by syndicated lifestyle surveys that indicated consumers in many parts of the world wanted high quality coffee that was more affordable. Also, many consumers outside of the United States consumed instant coffee because it is easy to prepare.

ADVERTISING EVALUATION SURVEYS   The purpose of these surveys is to measure the size and profile of the advertising audience and to assess the effectiveness of advertising using print and broadcast media. A well-known survey is the Gallup and Robinson Magazine Impact Research Service (MIRS), which measures the effectiveness of magazine ads (**www.gallup-robinson.com**).

Gallup & Robinson also offers testing of television commercials and of advertising in other media, such as radio, newspapers, and direct mail. Experian Simmons (**www.experian.com**) conducts four different surveys with a large sample of respondents to monitor magazine, TV, newspaper, and radio media. GfK MRI (**www.gfkmri.com**) is another firm that makes available information on the consumption of media, products, and services by households.

GENERAL SURVEYS   Surveys are also conducted for a variety of other purposes, including examination of purchase and consumption behavior. Gallup (**www.gallup.com**) surveys a random sample of 1,000 households by telephone about a variety of topics. The weekly Harris Poll by Harris Interactive (**www.harrisinteractive.com**) is also based on a nationally representative telephone survey of 1,000 adults age 18 years or over. Again, a wide range of topics is considered. Ipsos (**www.ipsos.com**) also conducts general surveys on a variety of topics using its omnibus panels, as shown in the following Research in Practice feature.

panel surveys
Surveys that measure the same group of respondents over time, but not necessarily on the same variables.

Research in Practice
The Cure for the Flu

About 200,000 people are hospitalized every year with influenza (flu) complications. About 36,000 die as a result of these complications of the flu. The majority of the deaths and hospitalizations are among the elderly and chronically ill. Nationally, up to 20 percent of people can be affected by influenza.

A survey was conducted by Ipsos Healthcare (a global health-care market research firm) via its Omnibus service with a nationally representative sample of 879 heads of household age 18 years and over. The objective was to determine where and how often people go to get their flu vaccine.

Among respondents with at least one dependent in their household, less than half (42 percent) report that their dependent(s) received the flu vaccine in the past six months, according to the findings. Of those who had obtained the flu vaccine in the past six months, the majority report having received the vaccine either from their doctor's office (43 percent) or from their employer (23 percent). Pharmacies and retail clinics in large stores were less popular venues, especially among those age 18 to 44, suggesting either low patient awareness or low acceptance of such venues for health-care access. Given that less than half the people get flu shots, the government should launch an educational campaign citing the flu statistics and promoting the flu shot. Pharmacies and retail clinics in large stores should launch marketing campaigns aimed at boosting patient awareness and acceptance of such venues for taking flu shots.[4] ◄

USES, ADVANTAGES, AND DISADVANTAGES OF SURVEYS   Surveys are the primary means of obtaining information about consumers' motives, attitudes, and preferences. Surveys that are designed to collect psychographic and lifestyle data can be used for market segmentation, developing consumer profiles, or determining consumer preferences. A major advantage is that surveys are flexible: A variety of questions can be asked and visual aids, packages, products, or other props can be used during the interviews. The sampling process also allows targeting of respondents with very specific characteristics.

Because survey researchers rely primarily on what the respondents say (self-reports), data gathered in this way can have serious limitations. What people say is not always what they actually do. Errors might occur because respondents remember incorrectly or feel pressured to give the "right" answer. Furthermore, samples might be biased, the questions poorly phrased, interviewers not properly instructed or supervised, and results misinterpreted.

Although surveys remain popular for both primary and secondary research, purchase and media panels do a much better job of tracking consumer behavior.

Research Recipe

When looking for data pertaining to activities, interests, opinions, beliefs, attitudes, motivations and preferences, surveys are your best bet. Surveys remain popular for primary, secondary, and syndicated data collection. Surveys can be conducted on samples that are representative of the general population or specified target populations.

iResearch
J.D. Power Powers Ford

As the CEO of Ford Motor Company, what marketing strategies would you adopt to increase the dependability and image of Ford vehicles?

Visit the J.D. Power website at **www.jdpower.com** and write a brief report about its latest vehicle-dependability study findings and methodology. How can you make use of the J.D. Power vehicle-dependability study and other secondary and syndicated data to help Ford improve the image of its vehicles? How will you use social media to recommend marketing strategies to Ford? **<**

Purchase and Media Panels

Purchase and media panels are composed of a group of individuals, households, or organizations that record their purchases and behavior in a diary or on the Internet over time. Although panels are also maintained for conducting surveys, the distinguishing feature of purchase and media panels is that the respondents or electronic devices record specific behaviors (e.g., product purchases or media consumption) as they occur. This makes the information more accurate. Previously, behavior was recorded in a diary, and the diary was returned to the research organization every one to four weeks. Paper diaries have been gradually replaced by electronic diaries. Now, most of the panels are online, and the behavior is recorded electronically, either entered online by the respondents or recorded automatically by electronic devices. Based on the type of information recorded, these panels can be classified as either purchase panels or media panels. Media panels are further characterized by the type of media consumption recorded as television, radio, Internet, mobile, or social media.

It should be mentioned that survey, purchase, and media panels are not mutually exclusive categories. Some panels may well combine two or even all three types. For example, TNS Global (**www.tnsglobal.com**) (a member of Kantar Group) uses a digital panel that combines survey information with click-stream data that passively measures actual behavior to obtain a more accurate and complete picture of what consumers are doing and why.

PURCHASE PANELS   Survey data can often be complemented with data obtained from **purchase panels**, in which respondents record their purchases in a diary or on the Internet. The NPD Group (**www.npd.com**) is a leading provider of market information collected and delivered online for a wide range of industries and markets. The NPD Group combines information obtained via surveys with that recorded by respondents about their behaviors to generate reports on consumption behaviors, industry sales, market share, and key demographic trends. Consumer information is collected from its online panel of about 2 million registered adults and teens on a wide range of product categories, including fashion, food, fun, house and home, technology, and automobile. Respondents provide detailed information regarding the brand and amount purchased, the price paid, whether any special deals were involved, the point of purchase, and the product's intended use. The composition of the panel is representative of the U.S. population as a whole. Information provided by the panel is used by consumer product firms, such as Colgate Palmolive, to determine brand loyalty and brand switching and to profile heavy users of various brands.

purchase panels
A data-gathering technique in which respondents record their purchases in a diary or on the Internet.

MEDIA PANELS   In **media panels**, electronic devices automatically record the media consumption behavior of members, supplementing a diary. We classify media panels as measuring television, radio, Internet, mobile, and social media consumption. Again, these classifications are not mutually exclusive, and a panel may well be set up to monitor consumption of multiple media so that client companies can determine the optimal media mix. This is becoming all the more relevant as some forms of entertainment are consumed over multiple media. For example, television programming can be viewed over a TV set, mobile handset, or the Internet using a computer. Perhaps the most familiar television panel is by the Nielsen company (**www.nielsen.com**). Nielsen tracks a program's minute-to-minute and second-by-second audiences, measuring how long consumers spend with a program and how often they return. This type of information enables television stations to cultivate relationships, maximize programming effectiveness, and establish advertising rates. Nielsen TV Audience Measurement data provide a richer view of TV audiences because of the breadth of their panel as well as the methodologies they employ.

media panels
A data-gathering technique that involves samples of respondents whose television viewing behavior is automatically recorded by electronic devices, supplementing the purchase information recorded in a diary.

Nielsen, through its Nielsen Online service, tracks and collects Internet usage in real time from home and work users. It reports site and e-commerce activity, including the number of visits to properties, domains, and unique sites; rankings by site and by category; time and frequency statistics; traffic patterns; and e-commerce transactions. On September 27, 2010, Nielsen announced the development of Nielsen Online Campaign Ratings, which for the first time provided audience data comparable to Nielsen's television ratings. Nielsen Mobile, the mobile arm of The Nielsen Company, measures billing activity through an opt-in panel of more than 50,000 mobile subscribers. From the billing data, Nielsen reports on many things, from how many text messages mobile users send to what ring tones and games they download.

USES, ADVANTAGES, AND DISADVANTAGES OF PURCHASE AND MEDIA PANELS   Purchase panels provide information that is useful for forecasting sales, estimating market shares, assessing brand-loyalty and brand-switching behavior, establishing profiles of specific user groups, measuring promotional effectiveness, and conducting controlled store tests. In the first Starbucks Research in Practice, purchase panel data revealed that Instant coffee accounted for about 40 percent of coffee sales outside the United States. Media panels yield information helpful for establishing advertising rates by radio and TV networks, selecting appropriate programming, and profiling viewer or listener subgroups. Advertisers, media planners, and buyers find panel information to be particularly useful.

The advantages of panel data over survey data relate to data accuracy and the generation of longitudinal data. Purchase panels that record information at the time of purchase also eliminate recall errors. Information recorded by electronic devices is even more accurate because the devices eliminate human error.

The disadvantages of panel data can be traced to the fact that panel members might not be representative of the larger population and to increased response errors uniquely associated with the process of maintaining a panel. Recruiters for purchase and media panels attempt to mirror the population in the panel makeup. However, certain groups tend to be underrepresented, such as minorities and those with low education levels. Response biases can occur because simply being on the panel might alter a panel member's behavior.

Research Recipe

You can best obtain information on certain purchases and media consumption habits from panels. Panels can yield longitudinal data that allow the examination of changes, such as brand loyalty and brand switching, over time.

iResearch
Nielsen Online

Nielsen Online reports on more than 90 percent of global Internet activity and provides insights about the online universe, including audiences, advertising, video, e-commerce, and consumer behavior.

Go to the Nielsen homepage **www.nielsen.com**. On the top menu bar, select "Measurement" and then select "Online." (If this has changed, search the Nielsen site for "online measurement.") Answer the following questions:

1. Describe Nielsen's online measurement methodology.

2. How does Nielsen recruit online panel members?

3. Under "Featured News & Insights" given at the bottom of the page, identify and discuss a recent application of Nielsen's online measurement. ‹

Electronic Scanner Services

We now describe various forms of scanner data and discuss their uses, advantages, and disadvantages. **Scanner data** are obtained by using electronic scanners at the cash register that read the Universal Product Code (UPC) from consumer purchases. Among the largest syndicated firms specializing in this type of data collection are Nielsen (**www.nielsen.com**) and Information Resources (**www.iriworldwide.com**). These companies compile and sell data, which tell subscribers how well their products are selling relative to the competition. This analysis can be conducted for each item with a unique UPC. The type of information that can be collected includes, for example, brand, flavor, and package size. Three types of scanner data are available: volume-tracking data, scanner panels, and scanner panels with cable TV (see Figure 3.8).

scanner data
Data obtained by passing merchandise over a laser scanner that reads the UPC code from the packages.

VOLUME-TRACKING DATA **Volume-tracking data** are routinely collected by supermarkets and other outlets with electronic checkout counters. When the consumer's purchases are scanned, the data are automatically entered into a computer. These data provide information on purchases by brand, size, price, and flavor or formulation based on sales data collected from the checkout scanner tapes. However, this information cannot be linked to consumers' background characteristics because their identities are not recorded when their purchases are scanned. This information is collected nationally from a sample of supermarkets with electronic scanners. Scanner services providing volume-tracking data include SCANTRACK (Nielsen) and InfoScan (Information Resources). The SCANTRACK service gathers data weekly from a sample of more than 4,800 stores representing more than 800 retailers in fifty-two major markets. The InfoScan Syndicated Store Tracking service monitors more than 34,000 supermarket, drugstore, and mass-merchandise outlets.

volume-tracking data
Scanner data that provide information on purchases by brand, size, price, and flavor or formulation.

SCANNER PANEL DATA With **scanner panels**, each household member is given an ID card that can be read by the electronic scanner at a cash register. Scanner panel members simply present the ID card at the checkout counter each time they shop. In this way, the consumer's identity is linked to product purchases as well as the time and day of the shopping trip. This enables the firm to build a shopping record for that individual resulting in longitudinal data. Alternatively, some firms provide handheld scanners to panel members. These members scan their purchases once they are home, as in Nielsen's Homescan global consumer panel that records the purchases of more than 250,000 households across twenty-seven countries.

scanner panels
Scanner data collected from panel members who are issued an ID card that enables their purchases to be linked to their identities.

SCANNER PANELS WITH CABLE TV An even more advanced use of scanning technology, **scanner panels with cable TV**, combines scanner panels with new technologies that have grown out of the cable TV industry. Households on these panels subscribe to one of the cable TV systems in their market. By means of a cable TV "split," the researcher targets various commercials into panel members' homes. For example, half the households might see test commercial A during the 6 P.M. newscast, while the other half views test commercial B. The purchases of both groups are tracked via scanner data and compared to determine which test commercial was more effective. This enables marketing researchers to conduct fairly controlled experiments in a relatively natural environment. The technology also offers a way to target marketing effort. For example, it is possible to transmit a Pepsi commercial only to Coke consumers to determine whether they can be induced to switch brands. Information Resources's BehaviorScan system contains such a panel. Systems have been developed to allow transmission of advertising into participating households without the use of a cable TV system. Because these panels can be selected from all available TV households, not just those with cable TV, the bias of cable-only testing is eliminated.

scanner panels with cable TV
The combination of a scanner panel with manipulation of the advertising that is being broadcast by cable television companies.

USES, ADVANTAGES, AND DISADVANTAGES OF SCANNER DATA Scanner data are useful for a variety of purposes. National volume-tracking data can be used for tracking sales, prices, and distribution and for modeling and analyzing early warning signals. Scanner panels with cable TV can be used for testing new products, repositioning products, analyzing promotional mix, and making advertising and pricing decisions. The prompt feedback about point-of-sale product activity enables managers to evaluate existing marketing programs and to formulate new ones.

Scanner data are not only available more quickly, they are also typically more accurate than data collected through either surveys or purchase panels. The response bias that plagues manual data collection is lessened because the respondents are much less conscious of their role as members of a scanner panel. Errors due to failures in recall are also eliminated with electronic data collection. Scanners offer the ability to study very short time periods of sales activity.

Another advantage of scanners is that in-store variables, such as pricing, promotions, and displays, are also recorded. Finally, a scanner panel with cable TV provides a highly controlled environment for testing alternate promotional messages.

A major weakness of scanner data is its lack of representativeness. Only retailers equipped with scanners are included in the research. Entire retail categories, such as food warehouses and mass merchandisers, might be excluded. Likewise, the availability of scanners might be lacking in certain geographical areas. Although scanner data provide behavioral and sales information, they do not provide information on underlying attitudes, preferences, and reasons for specific choices.

Research Recipe

Scanner services are fast and accurate sources of information on purchases of consumer packaged goods. Scanner panels collect longitudinal data that you can analyze at a great level of detail because purchases are linked to consumer characteristics.

iResearch
Scanning Potato Chips

As the marketing manager for Lay's potato chips, how would you determine the right price?

Visit the Nielsen Company at **www.nielsen.com** and write a brief report about its SCANTRACK service. How can you use SCANTRACK to determine the optimal price for Lay's potato chips? Will the analysis of social media be useful in this respect? Why or why not? ‹

SYNDICATED SERVICES FOR INSTITUTIONAL DATA

We have already discussed syndicated data collected from consumers and households. Parallel electronic and manual systems are also used to collect institutional and industrial data. As Figure 3.9 shows, syndicated data are collected by performing audits of retailers and wholesalers. Data are also collected by industry services on industrial firms and organizations.

Retailer and Wholesaler Audits

audit
A data-collection process derived from physical records or inventory analysis. Data are collected personally by the researcher or by representatives of the researcher, and the data are based on counts, usually of physical objects.

Collecting product movement data for wholesalers and retailers is referred to as an **audit**. These periodic audits can be a physical count of the inventory or managed through a link to the scanning process. These audits track inventory flow, current inventory levels, and the impact of both promotional and pricing programs on inventory levels.

A physical audit is a formal examination and verification of product movement carried out by examining physical records or analyzing inventory. An example of the traditional audit is the

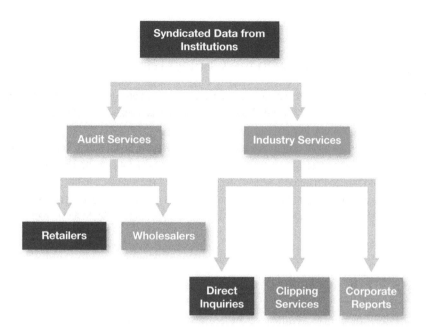

FIGURE 3.9
A CLASSIFICATION OF
SYNDICATE SERVICES:
INSTITUTIONS

Nielsen Convenience Track, which is a retail audit of convenience stores in thirty local markets. Retail audits are also provided by GfK (**www.gfk.com**) that provide updated measurements of product distribution in all types of retail and service outlets. Their audits covers point-of-sale (POS) audits, POS displays, brand audits, price checking, promotional compliance, product audits, and stock availability audits. For high speed and accuracy, the in-store audits use handheld computers to capture UPC information electronically. Retail audit data can be useful to consumer product firms. For example, say that Procter & Gamble is contemplating introducing a new toothpaste brand. A retail audit can help determine the size of the total market and distribution of sales by type of outlet and by different regions.

Wholesale audit services, the counterpart of retail audits, monitor warehouse withdrawals. Participating operators, which include supermarket chains, wholesalers, and frozen-food warehouses, typically account for more than 80 percent of the volume in this area. Audits are now being increasingly conducted via scanner data and electronic records rather than by physical examination and verification.

USES, ADVANTAGES, AND DISADVANTAGES OF AUDIT DATA   Audit information can be used to (1) determine market size and share for both categories and brands by type of outlet, region, or city; (2) assess competitive activity; (3) identify distribution problems, including shelf-space allocation and inventory issues; (4) develop sales potentials and forecasts; and (5) develop and monitor promotional allocations based on sales volume. Audits provide relatively accurate information on the movement of many products at the wholesale and retail levels. This information can be broken down by several important variables, such as brand, type of outlet, and size of market. In the Starbucks Research in Practice, the size of the global instant coffee market amounting to US$17 billion was determined by retail audits.

A major disadvantage of physical audits, however, is the limited retail coverage and delay associated with compiling and reporting inventory data. Typically, a two-month gap exists between the completion of the audit cycle and the publication of reports. Another disadvantage of physical audits is that, unlike scanner data, audit data cannot be linked to consumer characteristics. In fact, it can be difficult to relate audit data to advertising expenditures and other marketing efforts.

Research in Practice
Staying in Contact with the Contact Lens Market

Global demand for contact lens remains strong with a consistent upward growth in market value in the US, Europe and Asia. A recent GfK contact lens retail audit for these regions revealed sustained expansion across the board in the 12 month period from July 2011 to June 2012.

According to findings, the Asian countries tracked—China, Malaysia, South Korea, Taiwan, Hong Kong and Singapore, achieved the highest value growth among the three regions at 7.4 percent. The US and Europe trailed at a lower value growth rate of 4.8 and 3.2 percent, respectively, but still managed to turn in slightly better results by around one percentage point from a year ago. Such findings are valuable to contact lens companies such as Bausch + Lomb (**www.bausch.com**) that are seeking to penetrate the South Asian market.[5] **<**

Research Recipe

Use audit services to obtain syndicated information on retailers and wholesalers. Audit information is helpful in determining market potential, size, and share, and for assessing competitive activity.

Industry Services

industry services
Secondary data derived from industrial firms and organizational sources and intended for industrial or institutional use.

Industry services provide syndicated data about industrial firms, businesses, and other institutions, including nonprofit organizations. Financial, operating, and employment data are also collected by these syndicated research services for almost every North American Industry Classification System (NAICS) category. These data are collected by making direct inquiries, from clipping services that monitor newspapers, the trade press, or broadcasts, and from corporate reports. The range and sources of syndicated data available for institutional firms are more limited than those available to consumer goods firms. D&B can provide reports of businesses located in the United States and abroad.

The D&B (**www.dnb.com**) global commercial database provides one-click access to more than 225 million public and private companies located around the world. After locating a business, you can get key business data, including full address information; NAICS line-of-business details; business size (sales, net worth, and employees); names of key principals; and identification of this location's headquarters, domestic parent company, and/or global parent company.

These data are very useful in developing business-to-business sales plans and direct-marketing lists, estimating market potential and share within industries, and devising overall marketing strategies. Business statistics related to annual sales, geographic coverage, supplier relationships, and distribution channels are just a few of the categories of information available to business-to-business market planners.

USES, ADVANTAGES, AND DISADVANTAGES OF INDUSTRY SERVICES   Information provided by industry services is useful for sales management decisions, including identifying prospects, defining territories, setting quotas, and measuring market potential by geographic areas. It can also aid in advertising decisions, such as targeting prospects, allocating advertising budgets, selecting media, and measuring advertising effectiveness. This kind of information is also useful for segmenting the market and designing custom products and services for segments in the target markets.

Information provided by industrial services is useful for formulating the research design in business-to-business marketing. Moreover, the data are accurate. The information is typically limited to publicly traded firms, however, and dissemination of that data is typically controlled by the reporting firm itself. A researcher has to be wary of the completeness of reported data as well as the bias introduced by this form of respondent self-report. These data are limited in the nature, content, quantity, and quality of information.

Research Recipe

Use industry services to obtain information on industrial firms and institutions. This type of information is helpful in conducting research in business-to-business markets.

COMBINING INFORMATION FROM A VARIETY OF SOURCES: SINGLE-SOURCE DATA

Combining data from different sources can enhance the value of secondary data. This practice in syndicated services is referred to as *single-source research*. Single-source research tracks the full marketing process from initial advertising communication through product purchase. The process links a person's demographic and psychographic information with television, reading, and shopping habits. A combination of surveys, purchase and media panels, and electronic scanners is used to integrate such information. Manufacturer pricing and promotional activities are overlaid on this consumer data as well. Thus, **single-source data** provide integrated information on household variables, such as media consumption and purchases, and on marketing variables, such as product sales, price, advertising, promotion, and in-store marketing effort.

single-source data
An effort to combine data from different sources by gathering integrated information on household and marketing variables applicable to the same set of respondents.

Information Resources collects consumer purchase information from a nationally representative household panel of approximately 70,000 recruited households with coverage at the regional, national, and individual market level. It is designed to supply strategic direction to marketers by focusing on the consumer dynamics that drive brand and category performance. Complete multi-outlet purchase information on these households is tracked electronically. Panel households use a simple in-home scanning device, called a ScanKey, to record their purchases from all outlets. Panelists are not required to record any causal information except for manufacturer coupons. Price reductions are recorded by scanner, and features and displays are captured by Information Resources's in-store personnel, ensuring an accurate and unbiased record of sales. Other examples of single-source data include I Consumer Insights by GfK MRI (**www.gfkmri.com**) and Nielsen Segmentation Solutions (**www.nielsen.com**). Nielsen combines census data, consumer surveys about shopping and lifestyles, and purchase data to identify segments. Starbucks made use of single-source data while deciding on the introduction of VIA.

Research Recipe

When using syndicated services, consider single-source data for obtaining integrated information on households. Single-source data add value by providing a more complete picture of the consumers at marginal additional cost. Marketing management variables, such as price and promotion, are often part of single-source data, which further enhances the usefulness of such data.

HOW TO CONDUCT AN ONLINE SEARCH FOR EXTERNAL SECONDARY DATA

The following is a general search procedure for conducting an online search for relevant, external secondary data, including social media:

1. Search the online database(s) of your library using keywords. Your library provides access to a rich set of databases, and this should be the starting point for your search.

2. Run the search in Google (**www.google.com**), Yahoo! (**www.yahoo.com**), **Ask.com**, Bing (**www.bing.com**), and possibly other search engines. Use the advanced search option to conduct a more specific search and to narrow the list.

3. For industry and company financial information, search financial websites such as Google Finance (**www.google.com/finance**), CNNMoney (**money.cnn.com**), Yahoo! Finance (**finance.yahoo.com**), Bloomberg (**www.bloomberg.com**), Wikinvest (**www.wikinvest.com**), or similar sites. For information on a specific company, it is helpful to use the trading symbol to get a quote on the stock price. The stock price information contains links to other financial data. Each of the financial websites listed here has a provision for obtaining the trading symbol for a specific company.

4. Vertical search engines are available for searching specific industries. For example, **ChemIndustry.com** searches articles about the chemical industry, Ebuild (**www.ebuild.com**) contains information about the construction industry, ThomasNet (**www.thomasnet.net**) searches industrial parts, and **Lawyers.com** and **Findlaw.com** mine legal information.

5. Conduct a search of the social media, if appropriate.
   a. Blogs can be searched by using blog search engines: Technorati (**www.technorati.com**), IceRocket (**www.icerocket.com**), Bloglines (**www.bloglines.com**), or Google Blog Search (**www.google.com/blogsearch**). Blogpulse (**blog.pulse.me**) is powered by Nielsen Online and tracks well over 100 million blogs.
   b. Search Facebook and MySpace. Facebook is focusing on the development of analytical tools for page owners, advertisers, and platform developers. IceRocket has dedicated searches for **MySpace.com** (Classic Myspace or New Myspace).
   c. Conduct a Twitter search. A prominent set of social media trends is Twitter's Trending Topics (**www.twitter.com**). These are the words most used in Tweets.
   d. Search YouTube (**www.youtube.com**) for videos and Flickr (**www.flickr.com**) to locate relevant photos. If photos are of particular interest, search other photo-sharing sites such as Snapfish (**www.snapfish.com**), Shutterfly (**www.shutterfly.com**), Photobucket (**www.photobucket.com**).
   e. If podcasts are of interest, search Apple's iTunes (**www.apple.com/itunes**), the who's who of podcasting. Podnova (**www.podnova.com**) and Podcast Alley (**www.podcastalley.com**) should also be searched.
   f. Search social-bookmarking sites like Delicious (**www.delicious.com**), Digg (**www.digg.com**), Mixx (**www.mixx.com**), Chipmark (**www.chipmark.com**), Linkroll (**www.linkroll.com**), and StumbleUpon (**www.stumbleupon.com**).
   g. Web-based news aggregators (such as Bloglines) make it easy to collect and read information published using really simple syndication (RSS). Use them to aggregate and simplify your search.

6. Marketing research reports may be obtained from Mintel (**www.mintel.com**) and **MarketResearch.com**. Other companies provide more specialized reports. For example, Packaged Facts (**www.packagedfacts.com**) compiles marketing research related to the food, beverage, consumer packaged goods, and demographic sectors. General news

sites such as Dow Jones Factiva (**www.dowjones.com/factiva**) also contain useful information.

7. Reports and information are also available for purchase from syndicated firms as described in this chapter.

Research Recipe

When searching online for external secondary data, begin with your library's databases and then use the popular search engines. Search financial websites and use vertical search engines for searching specific industries. Conduct a search of social media, if appropriate. Search for marketing research reports and search syndicated sources.

INTERNATIONAL MARKETING RESEARCH

The various methods associated with implementing each step of the research design discussed in this chapter must be reassessed within the context of cultural differences before they can be used internationally. Given environmental and cultural differences, a research design appropriate for one country might not be suitable for another. Consider the problem of determining household attitudes toward major appliances in the United States and Saudi Arabia. When conducting exploratory research in the United States, it is appropriate to conduct focus groups jointly with male and female heads of households. It would not be appropriate to conduct such focus groups in Saudi Arabia. As a result of their traditional culture, wives are unlikely to participate freely in the presence of their husbands. It would be more useful to conduct one-on-one, in-depth interviews with both male and female heads of households included in the sample. A wide variety of secondary data are available for international marketing research. As in the case of domestic research, the problem is not one of lack of data but of the plethora of information available, and it is useful to classify the various sources. Secondary international data are available from both domestic government and nongovernment sources. The most important government sources are the Department of Commerce (**www.commerce.gov**), the Agency for International Development (**www.usaid.gov**), the Small Business Administration (**www.sba.gov**), the Export-Import Bank of the United States (**www.exim.gov**), the Department of Agriculture (**www.usda.gov**), the Department of State (**www.state.gov**), the Department of Labor (**www.dol.gov**), and the Port Authority of New York and New Jersey (**www.panynj.gov**). The Department of Commerce offers not only a number of publications but also a variety of other services, such as the foreign buyer program, matchmaker events, trade missions, export contact list service, the foreign commercial service, and custom statistical service for exporters. Another very useful source is the CIA World Factbook (**https://www.cia.gov**).

Nongovernment organizations, including international organizations located in the United States, can also provide information about international markets. These data sources include the United Nations (**www.un.org**), the Organization for Economic Cooperation and Development (**www.oecd.org**), the International Monetary Fund (**www.imf.org**), the World Bank (**www.worldbank.org**), the International Chambers of Commerce (**www.iccwbo.org**), the Commission of the European Union to the United States (**www.eurunion.org**), and the Japanese External Trade Organization (**www.jetro.org**). Finally, locally sourced secondary data are available from foreign governments, international organizations located abroad, trade associations, and private services such as syndicated firms.

Evaluation of secondary data is even more critical for international than for domestic projects, yet it may also be more difficult because the relevant details on the methodology may not be available. Fortunately, several syndicated firms are developing huge sources of international secondary data, and obtaining information from a reputable firm may be more desirable than collecting the information yourself.

Research in Practice
Dunkin' Donuts Eyes Asian Expansion

Before launching in South Korea, Dunkin' Donuts undertook exploratory research followed by descriptive research to understand the psychographic and lifestyle trends of South Koreans. Exploratory research consisted of an analysis of secondary and syndicated data followed by focus groups. The descriptive research consisted of personal interviews administered at important shopping and street locations. This research yielded some important findings:

- Breakfast is traditionally eaten at home.
- Young men and women and teenagers visit the stores in the afternoon or evening.
- Koreans like savoring their meals and beverages.
- Young Koreans are technology savvy, heavy users of social media, and Internet penetration is high.
- Koreans age 18 to 29 are more open to trying new products. The reason for this is that they "[want] to be different than their parents." They are also brand conscious.
- Koreans aren't typically as large consumers of coffee as Americans are and often prefer tea.

Armed with these insights, the company initially targeted 18- to 29-year-olds. As a result, Dunkin' Donuts stores were furnished with plush chairs, Wi-Fi access, and plasma-screen televisions. Among

Source: John Van Hasselt / Sygma / Corbis

other efforts to promote coffee, the company hired celebrities to endorse the brand. In keeping with the importance of image and appearance, Dunkin' Donuts used its "Natural and Organic ingredients" to appeal to health-conscious consumers. Local flavors such as green tea lattes and sweet soybean doughnuts were also on the menu.

As of 2014, Dunkin' Donuts had over 3,100 stores in thirty countries outside the United States. South Korea was one of its success stories thanks to the company's use of exploratory and descriptive research.[6] ◄

Research Recipe

When collecting international secondary data, try syndicated firms and other domestic and foreign sources. It is critical to evaluate international secondary data for their relevance and applicability using the same criteria as that used for evaluating domestic secondary data.

MARKETING RESEARCH AND SOCIAL MEDIA

Social media can be appropriate for conducting exploratory, descriptive, and causal research. One reason why social networks can be suitable for conducting marketing research is that they eliminate the onerous cost of building and maintaining traditional panels. For example, there are more than 100,000 members of various Starbucks communities on Facebook, and none of them are sponsored by the coffee retailer. Such panels based on brand communities may not be suitable for all kinds of marketing research. Nevertheless, such panels could be useful for investigating a host of marketing research issues, such as developing new products targeted at core users of the brand. The key is to analyze the characteristics of each social network and choose the network that most closely matches your research objectives. For instance, MySpace is heavily slanted toward an audience under age 20. In contrast, 40 percent of Facebook members are over 35 years old, and the Facebook community tends to be more affluent and better educated than MySpace users. These network communities can be used to recruit marketing research panels, as illustrated by Disney.

Research in Practice
Disney Moms

Disney set up the Walt Disney Moms Panel, featuring moms who answer questions about the company's theme parks and vacation resorts from prospective visitors. In 2008, Disney launched the Mickey Moms Club, an online community capped at 10,000 members. This community has become one of the most frequently visited of all Disney sites. Visitors spend an average of eight to ten minutes per visit, which is more than they spend on any other Disney site. Site visitors also spend more on their Disney vacations than nonmembers. Disney uses the information collected at this site to monitor longitudinally visitors' reactions and feedback about its theme parks and vacation resorts.[7] **<**

As you saw in Figure 3.6, social media can be a rich source of both internal as well as external secondary data. A company's blog, Facebook page, or Twitter account can generate rich internal secondary data. External social media tools and sites provide a valuable database that researchers can sift through in a bid to analyze relevant consumer information. The archival information and posts from social media such as blogs or Facebook fan pages give an informative account of consumer perception and preference with regard to the problem at hand. Although it is important for researchers to analyze secondary data from typical and traditional sources such as journals, periodicals, and the Internet, it is essential that social media not be ignored in light of their significance in representing the voice of the consumer. Insights from various discussion threads within social media provide credible information that marketing researchers should consider when analyzing secondary data.

The emergence of social media has greatly increased syndicated firms' ability to reach out to the once-unreachable and hear conversations that used to be restricted among neighborhoods and personal physical social networks. Rapid advances in technology have created a new source of information and communication for firms like the Nielsen Company. Social media are rich in qualitative and quantitative data that traditional data collection methods may not be able to collect, and gathering this type of data could be a more time-consuming and costly process for traditional data collection methods. Information gathered from social media is used by syndicated firms to understand the market, answer clients' concerns, connect to consumers and potential participants, conduct online research, and publicize reports and company information.

Research Recipe

You can implement all types of research designs—exploratory, descriptive, and causal—in social media. Social media are sources of both internal and external secondary data. Social media have created a new source of information and communication for syndicated firms.

ETHICS IN MARKETING RESEARCH

Researchers must ensure that the research design provides the information needed to address the marketing research problem. The client should have the integrity not to misrepresent the project, should describe the constraints under which the researcher must operate, and should not make unreasonable demands. If customer contact has to be restricted or if time is an issue, the client should make these constraints known at the start of the project. It would be unethical for a client to extract details from a proposal submitted by one research firm and pass them to another firm that would actually conduct the project for the client. A proposal is the property of the research firm that prepared it, unless the client has paid for it. The client should not take advantage of the research firm by making false promises of future research contracts in order to solicit concessions for the current project.

The researcher is ethically obligated to ensure the relevance and usefulness of secondary data for the problem at hand. The secondary data should be evaluated by the criteria discussed earlier in this chapter. Only data judged to be appropriate should be used. It is also important that the data are collected using procedures that are morally appropriate. Data can be judged unethical if they were gathered in a way that harms the respondents or invades their privacy. Ethical issues also arise if the users of secondary data are unduly critical of the data that do not support their interests and viewpoints.

Research in Practice
The Ethical Pill Can Be Bitter to Swallow

ABC, NBC, and CBS (the Big Three); some advertising agencies; and major advertisers are at odds with Nielsen's (**www.nielsen.com**) television ratings. They criticize Nielsen's sampling scheme and intrusive data recording methodologies. A central issue in the criticisms of Nielsen is that the Big Three have received declining viewership ratings. As of 2013, prime-time viewership for the broadcast networks has declined. For example, according to Nielsen, the badly slumping NBC had its lowest prime-time viewership average ever, for the week of March 4–10, 2013.

Rather than accept the idea that the broadcast network audience is shrinking, the networks would prefer a more flattering assessment of their audiences. Ratings translate directly into advertising revenues. The more viewers a television show draws, the higher fees a network can charge for airing advertising at that spot. Advertising charges can differ dramatically between time slots, so accurate (or aggressive) viewer ratings are desirable from the network's perspective.

Monopolies like the networks tend to resist innovation and lack incentive to improve processes. Complacency rules, as long as the money keeps coming. As a professional marketing research supplier, however, Nielsen is ethically bound to provide accurate and representative data—to the best of its ability. Users also have the ethical responsibility of not criticizing secondary data simply because the data do not support their own viewpoints. Eventually network executives will have to swallow the bitter pill of reality: cable TV, direct-broadcast satellite TV, and the Internet are all gaining ground over broadcast television viewership.[8] ◄

Given the limitations of secondary data, it is often necessary to collect primary data to obtain the information needed to address the management decision problem. The use of secondary data alone when the research problem requires primary data collection could raise ethical concerns. Such concerns are heightened when the client is being billed a fixed fee for the project, and the proposal submitted to get the project did not adequately specify the data collection methodology. On the other hand, in some cases it may be possible to obtain the information needed from secondary sources alone, making it unnecessary to collect primary data. The unnecessary collection of expensive primary data, when the research problem can be addressed based on secondary data alone, may be unethical. These ethical issues become more salient if the research firm's billings increase, but at the expense of the client.

R e s e a r c h   R e c i p e

The researcher is ethically obligated to formulate a research design that will obtain all the information that is needed in an effective and efficient manner. You should also evaluate the relevance of secondary data and ensure that the data were collected using ethical and moral procedures. The collection of secondary, syndicated, and primary data should be done with the interest of the client at the forefront. The users of secondary data are also obligated to use them in an ethical manner.

Dell Running Case

Review the Dell case, Case 1.1, and questionnaire given toward the end of the book. Answer the following questions.

1. How can Dell use exploratory research to understand how household consumers buy personal computers and related equipment?
2. Describe one way in which Dell can use descriptive research.
3. Describe one way in which Dell can use causal research.
4. Search the Internet to find information on the latest U.S. market share of Dell and other PC marketers.
5. Visit the U.S. Census Bureau at **www.census.gov**. As Dell seeks to increase its penetration of U.S. households, what information available from the U.S. Census Bureau would be helpful?
6. What information available from social media would be useful to Dell as it seeks to increase its penetration of U.S. households?
7. What information is available on consumer technology usage from syndicated firms? How can Dell use this information? (*Hint:* Visit **www.npd.com**; under "Industries," select "Technology.")
8. What information available from Nielsen at **www.nielsen.com** can help Dell evaluate the effectiveness of its website?

 # Summary

A research design is a framework or blueprint for conducting the marketing research project. It specifies the details of how the project should be conducted. Research designs may be broadly classified as exploratory or conclusive. The primary purpose of exploratory research is to provide insights into the problem. Conclusive research is conducted to test specific hypotheses and examine specific relationships. The findings from conclusive research are used as input into managerial decision making. Conclusive research may be either descriptive or causal.

The major objective of descriptive research is to describe market characteristics or functions. Descriptive research can be further classified into cross-sectional and longitudinal research. Cross-sectional designs involve the collection of information from a sample of population elements at a single point in time. In longitudinal designs, repeated measurements are taken on a fixed sample. Causal research is designed for the primary purpose of obtaining evidence about cause-and-effect (causal) relationships.

In contrast to primary data, which originate with the researcher for the specific purpose of the problem at hand, secondary data are originally collected for other purposes. Secondary data can be obtained quickly and are relatively inexpensive. However, they have limitations and should be evaluated carefully to determine their appropriateness for the problem at hand. The evaluation criteria consist of specifications, error, currency, objectivity, nature, and dependability.

A wealth of information exists in the organization for which the research is being conducted. This information constitutes internal secondary data. External data are generated by sources outside the organization. These data may be classified as business/nongovernment, government, and syndicated services. Government sources may be broadly categorized as census data and other data.

Syndicated sources are companies that collect and sell common pools of data designed to serve a number of clients. Syndicated sources can be classified based on the unit of measurement (households/consumers or institutions). Household/consumer data may be obtained via surveys, purchase and media panels, or electronic scanner services. When institutions are the unit of measurement, the data may be obtained from retailers, wholesalers, or industrial firms and organizations. It is desirable to combine information obtained from different secondary sources.

The various methods associated with implementing each step of the research design discussed in this chapter must be reassessed within the context of cultural differences before they can be used internationally. Several specialized sources of secondary data are useful for conducting international marketing research. However, the evaluation of secondary data becomes even more critical because the usefulness and accuracy of these data can vary widely. Social media can be appropriate for conducting exploratory, descriptive, and causal research. Social media are sources of both internal and external secondary data and can also be used to collect primary data. The researcher has the ethical responsibility to ensure that the research design will provide the information needed to address the marketing research problem. Ethical dilemmas that can arise include the unnecessary collection of primary data, the use of only secondary data when primary data are needed, the use of secondary data that are not applicable, and the use of secondary data that have been gathered through morally questionable means.

⌄ Companion Website

This textbook includes numerous student resources that can be found at **www.pearsonglobaleditions.com/malhotra**. At this Companion website, you'll find:

- Student Resource Manual
- Demo movies of statistical procedures using SPSS and Microsoft Excel
- Screen captures of statistical procedures using SPSS and Microsoft Excel
- Data files for all datasets in SPSS and Microsoft Excel
- Additional figures and tables
- Videos and write-ups for all video cases
- Other valuable resources

⌄ Key Terms and Concepts

Research design	Secondary data	Media panels
Exploratory research	Internal data	Scanner data
Conclusive research	External data	Volume-tracking data
Descriptive research	Database marketing	Scanner panels
Cross-sectional design	Syndicated sources	Scanner panels with
Longitudinal design	Surveys	cable TV
Panel	Observations	Audit
Causal research	Psychographics	Industry services
Primary data	Purchase panels	Single-source data

⌄ Suggested Cases and Video Cases

Running Case with Real Data and Questionnaire
    1.1 Dell

Comprehensive Critical Thinking Cases
    2.1 American Idol

Comprehensive Cases with Real Data and Questionnaires
    3.1 JPMorgan Chase   3.2 Wendy's

Online Video Cases

3.1 NFL   6.1 AFLAC   7.1 P&G   8.1 Dunkin' Donuts
9.1 Subaru   13.1 Marriott

∨ Live Research: Conducting a Marketing Research Project

1. Teams should present to the class the type of research design they think is appropriate. Normally, the teams will end up with similar research designs unless they are working on different projects.
2. As a class, discuss and select the research design for this project. It is helpful to invite the client to this session.
3. Assign one, some, or all teams the responsibility of collecting and analyzing secondary data.
4. If this work is divided, one or some teams could search the library's electronic database, others could search government sources, and other teams could visit the library and work with a reference librarian to identify relevant sources.
5. Encourage the students to visit relevant websites of the client and its competitors as well to conduct a thorough online search using search engines.
6. Visit the websites of syndicated firms to identify the relevant information, some of which can be obtained without cost.
7. If the project is supported by a budget, then relevant information can be purchased from syndicated sources.

∨ Acronyms

The components of research designs may be summarized by the acronym R DESIGNS:

R evisable plan of data analysis

D ata from secondary and syndicate sources

E xperimentation: causal research design

S caling and measurement

I nterviewing forms: questionnaire design

G roups (focus): qualitative research

N Sample size and plan

S urvey and observation

The criteria used for evaluating secondary data may be described by the acronym SECOND:

S pecifications: methodology used to collect the data

E rror: accuracy of the data

C urrency: when the data were collected

O bjective: purpose for which the data were collected

N ature: content of the data

D ependability: overall, how dependable are the data

The salient characteristics of syndicated data may be described by the acronym SYNDICATED:

S urveys

Y ields data of known commercial value

N umber of clients use the data

D iary, online and media panels

I nstitutional services

C ost is low

A udits

T imely and current

E lectronic scanner services

D ata combined from different sources: single-source data

⌄ Review Questions

3-1. Define "research design" in your own words.

3-2. How does formulating a research design differ from developing an approach to a problem?

3-3. List the major components of a research design.

3-4. Differentiate between exploratory and conclusive research.

3-5. Compare and contrast cross-sectional and longitudinal designs.

3-6. Why should secondary data always be assessed before primary data?

3-7. What are the differences between primary and secondary data?

3-8. What is the difference between a data warehouse and data mining?

3-9. Differentiate between internal and external secondary data.

3-10. List and describe the various syndicated sources of secondary data.

3-11. What is the nature of information collected by surveys?

3-12. Explain what a panel is. What is the difference between purchase panels and media panels?

3-13. Why would a researcher decide to resort to panel data over survey data?

3-14. What is one way to increase the value of syndicated data?

3-15. What is an audit? Discuss the advantages and disadvantages of audits.

3-16. Describe the information provided by industry services.

3-17. Why is it desirable to use multiple sources of secondary data?

3-18. How can exploratory and descriptive research be implemented in social media?

3-19. Discuss the use of social media as a source of secondary data.

⌄ Applied Problems

3-20. Sweet Cookies is planning to launch a new line of cookies and wants to assess the market size. The cookies have a mixed chocolate-pineapple flavor and will be targeted at the premium end of the market. Analyze social media to determine consumer preferences for cookies. Discuss the research design that should be adopted.

3-21. Obtain automobile industry sales and sales of major automobile manufacturers for the last five years from secondary sources.

3-22. Select an industry of your choice. Using secondary sources, obtain industry sales and the sales of the major firms in that industry for the past year. Estimate the market shares of each major firm. From another source, obtain information on the market shares of these same firms. Do the two estimates agree?

⌄ Internet Exercises

3-23. Visit Anderson Analytics's website (**http://www.andersonanalytics.com/**).

  a. What are the services provided by Anderson Analytics?

  b. What edge do their services provide when it comes to social media data analysis?

3-24. Visit the webpage of three of the marketing research firms listed in Table 1.1 in Chapter 1. What types of research designs have been implemented recently by these firms?

3-25. You are conducting an image study for Carnival Cruise Lines. As part of exploratory research, analyze general social media and the messages posted to a relevant newsgroup to determine the factors that consumers use in evaluating cruise companies. You can locate a newsgroup by performing a search for forums/cruises.

3-26. Visit the website of a company of your choice. Suppose the management decision problem facing this company was to expand its share of the market. Obtain as much secondary data from the website of this company and other sources on the Internet including social media as are relevant to this problem.

3-27. Visit the website of the U.S. Census Bureau (**www.census.gov**). Write a report about the secondary data available from the bureau that would be useful to a fast-food firm such as McDonald's for the purpose of formulating domestic marketing strategy.

3-28. Visit **www.npd.com** and write a description of the panels maintained by NPD.

3-29. Visit **www.standardandpoors.com**. What kind of information does it provide about organizations?

NOTES

1. **www.reuters.com/article/rbssRestaurants/idUSN1733179320090217**, accessed May 22, 2013; and **http://foodbeverage.about.com/od/Food_Entreprenur_Spotlight/a/Most-Memorable-New-Product-Launches-Part-2_3.htm**, accessed March 22, 2012.
2. Ellen Byron, "Hola: P&G Seeks Latino Shoppers," *Wall Street Journal* (September 15, 2011): B1–B2.
3. **www.lexisnexis.com**, accessed May 4, 2013.
4. **www.ipsos.com**, accessed May 20, 2013; Synovate, "New Survey: Flu Shot Still Not Catching on, Especially at Retail Clinics," **www.synovate.com/news/article/2009/02/new-survey-flu-shot-still-not-catching-on-especially-at-retail-clinics.html**, accessed January 4, 2012.
5. **www.gfk.com**, accessed May 20, 2013.
6. **www.dunkindonuts.com**, accessed March 23, 2013; and Julie Jargon and Sungha Park, "Dunkin' Brands Eyes Asian Expansion," online at **http://online.wsj.com/article/SB124405624845382149.html**, accessed March 23, 2012.
7. **http://disneyworld.disney.go.com/wdw/mmc/index?id=MMCLoginPage&bhcp=1**, accessed January 4, 2013; and Paul Gillin, *Secrets of Social Media Marketing* (Fresno, CA: Quill Driver Books, 2009).
8. David Bauder, "NBC Ratings Sink Even Lower: Peacock Network Posts Its Lowest Prime-Time Viewership Average Ever," online at **www.huffingtonpost.com/2013/03/12/nbc-ratings-lowest-ever_n_2862714.html**, accessed May 20, 2013; Sam Schechner and Lauren A. E. Schuker, "NBC Unable to Shake Slide in Ratings," *Wall Street Journal* (October 24, 2011): B1, B11; Katy Bachman, "Arbitron, Nielsen Face Off in Out-of-Home TV Ratings," *MediaWeek*, 17(29) (August 6, 2007): 6; Anonymous, "Ratings Broken? Demand Better," *Advertising Age*, 74(49) (December 8, 2003): 22; Donna Petrozzello, "Arbitron Moves to Offer Audio Measuring," *Broadcasting & Cable*, 126(36) (August 26, 1996): 38; Steve McClellan, "New Nielsen System Is Turning Heads," *Broadcasting* (May 18, 1992): 8.

Online Video Case 3.1

NATIONAL FOOTBALL LEAGUE: The King of Professional Sports

Visit **www.pearsonglobaleditions.com/malhotra** to read the video case and view the accompanying video. National Football League: The King of Professional Sports highlights the NFL's use of marketing research to foster immense goodwill and influence to make a difference to the community. The description of focus groups and consumer perception and attitudinal surveys in the video can stimulate discussion of the three basic research designs (exploratory, descriptive, and causal) and their role in helping the NFL's various social initiatives and programs. Specific marketing research questions on this and the previous chapters are posed in the video case.

4 Qualitative Research

∨ Overview

qualitative research

An unstructured, exploratory research methodology based on small samples that provides insights and understanding of the problem setting.

As discussed in Chapter 2, **qualitative research** is an unstructured, exploratory research methodology based on small samples that provides insights and understanding of the problem setting. Like secondary data analysis (see Chapter 3), qualitative research is a major methodology used in exploratory research. Researchers undertake qualitative research to define the problem or develop an approach (Chapter 2). In developing an approach, qualitative research is often used for generating hypotheses and identifying variables that should be included in the research. In cases where conclusive or quantitative research is not done, qualitative research and secondary data comprise the major part of the research project. In this chapter, we discuss the differences between qualitative and quantitative research and the role of each in the marketing research project. We present a classification of qualitative research and cover the major techniques, focus groups and depth interviews, in detail. We also consider the indirect procedures called projective techniques. The considerations involved in conducting qualitative research when researching international markets, as well as in social media, are discussed. Several ethical issues that arise in qualitative research are identified. Figure 4.1 gives the relationship of this chapter to the marketing research process. The following examples give a flavor of qualitative research and its applications in marketing research.

⌄ Learning Objectives

After reading this chapter, the student should be able to:

1. Explain the difference between qualitative and quantitative research in terms of the objectives, sampling, data collection and analysis, and outcomes.

2. Understand the various forms of qualitative research, including direct procedures such as focus groups and depth interviews, and indirect methods such as projective techniques.

3. Describe focus groups in detail, with emphasis on planning and conducting focus groups, and their advantages, disadvantages, and applications.

4. Describe depth interview techniques in detail, citing their advantages, disadvantages, and applications.

5. Explain projective techniques in detail and discuss their advantages, disadvantages and applications.

6. Discuss the considerations involved in conducting qualitative research in an international setting.

7. Discuss the use of social media in obtaining and analyzing qualitative data.

8. Understand the ethical issues involved in conducting qualitative research.

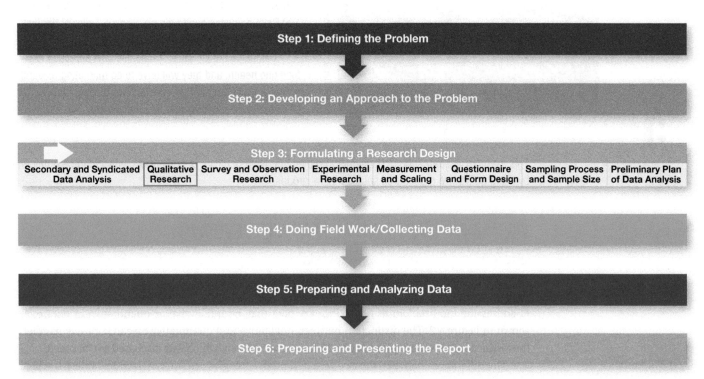

FIGURE 4.1 | RELATIONSHIP OF THIS CHAPTER TO THE MARKETING RESEARCH PROCESS

Research in Practice
The 100-Calorie Snack Attack

Analysis of current U.S. food consumption indicates that Americans are becoming more concerned about their health. The shrinking waistlines also mean a shrinking bottom line for junk-food companies such as Mondelēz International (**www.mondelezinternational.com**) that markets brands such as Nabisco. This in turn sparked a need to conduct marketing research in order to turn around the problem.

First, qualitative research was conducted with the objective of understanding the motivations and snack purchase behavior of mothers. Nabisco conducted focus groups to uncover how mothers felt about lunches and snacking for their children. The screening criteria for selecting focus group respondents consisted of mothers with young children at home who served snacks at least twice a week. A detailed moderator's outline was prepared to understand the motivations and concerns of mothers while serving snacks to their children. Nabisco conducted focus groups with the size of each group varying between 8 to 12 respondents. The findings indicated that families, especially mothers, were trying to portion out snack foods to their children to cut down on caloric intake. Mothers especially were found to appreciate snacks in small portions with fewer calories. Also, convenience was very important. Portioning out snacks into individual bags makes for a quick snack on the go.

When these findings were verified by survey research, Nabisco introduced their 100 Calorie Snack Pack. The packs consist of waferlike, low-calorie versions of Nabisco's famous Oreos, Chips Ahoy, Ritz crackers,

Source: Tim Roske / AP Images

and several other snack foods. These snacks proved to be successful: They brought in over $100 million in revenue for Nabisco after one year since their launch, a feat that less than 1 percent of snack companies have been able to achieve. As of 2014, Nabisco marketed an extended line of 100 Calorie Snacks due to the immense success of the first launch.

Companies today must realize this new approach to food and health, and they will have to do marketing research of their own to discover new ways of positioning their products in order to stay afloat in the market.[1] ◄

This example illustrates the rich insights into the underlying behavior of consumers, which can be obtained by using qualitative procedures such as focus groups.

PRIMARY DATA: QUALITATIVE VERSUS QUANTITATIVE RESEARCH

As was explained in Chapter 3, primary data are originated by the researcher for the specific purpose of addressing the problem at hand. Primary data may be qualitative or quantitative in nature, as shown in Figure 4.2. The distinction between qualitative and quantitative research closely parallels the distinction between exploratory and conclusive research, which was discussed in Chapter 3.

The differences between the two research methodologies are summarized in Table 4.1, which parallels Table 3.1. Qualitative research provides insights and understanding of the problem setting, while **quantitative research** seeks to quantify the data and typically applies some form of statistical analysis. Whenever a new marketing research problem is addressed, quantitative research must be preceded by appropriate qualitative research. Qualitative research provides a greater understanding of the environmental context of the problem (see Chapter 2) and the underlying issues and lays the foundation for quantitative research. In most new or nonroutine marketing research projects, qualitative research is conducted first followed by quantitative research.

quantitative research
A research methodology that seeks to quantify the data and typically applies some form of statistical analysis.

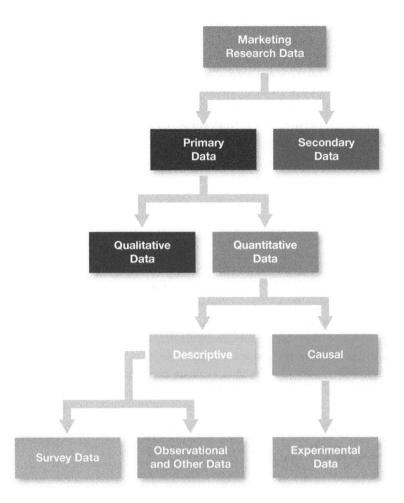

FIGURE 4.2
A CLASSIFICATION
OF MARKETING
RESEARCH DATA

This was illustrated in the first Research in Practice feature in this chapter. Nabisco first conducted qualitative research in the form of focus groups. This was followed by quantitative research in the form of a survey.

It may not be necessary to conduct qualitative research if a marketing research project is being repeated. An example would be a routine monthly customer satisfaction survey and there are no changes in the environmental context since the last survey. However, the findings of qualitative research are misused when they are regarded as conclusive and are used to make quantitative estimates and generalizations to the population of interest. It is a sound principle of marketing research to view qualitative and quantitative research as complementary rather than in competition with each other.

Table 4.1 ❯ Qualitative Versus Quantitative Research

	Qualitative Research	Quantitative Research
Objective	To gain a qualitative understanding of the underlying reasons and motivations	To quantify the data and generalize the results from the sample to the population of interest
Sample	Small number of non-representative cases	Large number of representative cases
Data Collection	Unstructured	Structured
Data Analysis	Nonstatistical	Statistical
Outcome	Develop an initial understanding	Recommend a final course of action

Research Recipe

When conducting a new marketing research project, you should conduct appropriate qualitative research before undertaking quantitative research. Qualitative research provides a deeper understanding of the environmental context of the problem and the underlying issues, and lays the foundation for quantitative research. However, qualitative research may not be necessary if a marketing research project is being repeated.

A CLASSIFICATION OF QUALITATIVE RESEARCH PROCEDURES

direct approach
One type of qualitative research in which the purposes of the project are disclosed to the respondent or are obvious given the nature of the interview.

indirect approach
A type of qualitative research in which the purposes of the project are disguised from the respondents.

A classification of qualitative research procedures is presented in Figure 4.3. These procedures are classified as either direct or indirect based on whether the true purpose of the project is known to the respondents. A **direct approach** is not disguised. The purpose of the project is disclosed to the respondents or is otherwise obvious to them from the questions asked. Focus groups and depth interviews are the major direct techniques. In contrast, research that takes an **indirect approach** disguises the true purpose of the project. For example, in a study evaluating Pepsi (test) commercials, the respondents are also asked to evaluate commercials of other food products (filler commercials). This is done to disguise the true purpose of the study, which is to evaluate Pepsi commercials. Projective techniques are the common indirect procedures. Each of these techniques is discussed in detail, beginning with focus groups.

FOCUS GROUP INTERVIEWS

focus group
An interview conducted by a trained moderator among a small group of respondents in an unstructured and natural manner.

A **focus group** is an interview conducted by a trained moderator in an unstructured and natural manner with a small group of respondents. The moderator leads the discussion. The main purpose of focus groups is to gain insights by listening to a group of people from the appropriate target market talk about issues of interest to the researcher. The value of the technique lies in the unexpected findings often obtained from a free-flowing group discussion.

Focus groups are the most important qualitative research procedure. They are so popular that many marketing research practitioners consider this technique synonymous with

FIGURE 4.3
A CLASSIFICATION OF
QUALITATIVE RESEARCH
PROCEDURES

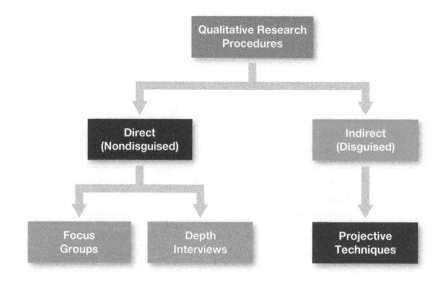

qualitative research. An application of focus groups was illustrated in the first Research in Practice where Nabisco developed their 100 Calorie Snack Pack. Several hundred facilities around the country now conduct focus groups several times a week. The typical focus group costs range between $6,000 to $8,000. Given their importance and popularity, we describe the salient characteristics of focus groups in detail.

Characteristics

The major characteristics of a focus group are summarized in Table 4.2. A focus group generally includes eight to twelve members. Groups of fewer than eight are unlikely to generate the momentum and group dynamics necessary for a successful session. Likewise, groups of more than twelve may be too crowded and may not be conducive to a cohesive and natural discussion. The focus groups conducted by Nabisco conformed to this guideline.

Viewing room looking into the focus group room through the one-way mirror.
Source: Marmaduke St. John / Alamy

Table 4.2 > Characteristics of Focus Groups

Group size	8–12
Group composition	Homogeneous; respondents prescreened
Physical setting	Relaxed, informal atmosphere
Time duration	1–3 hours
Recording	Use of audio and video recording
Moderator	Observational, interpersonal, and communication skills of the moderator

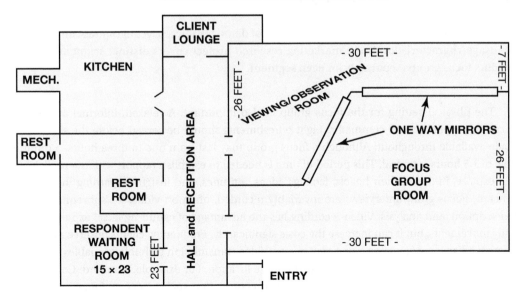

BALTIMORE RESEARCH SUITE #140

Layout of a focus group facility. Baltimore Research: facility overview.
Source: http://www.baltimoreresearch.com/marketing_research_facility.php?sPage=Facility

Layout of focus group room and viewing room.

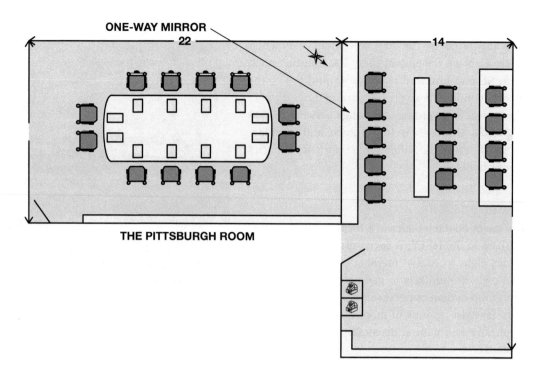

A focus group should be homogeneous in terms of demographics, psychographics, and product usage characteristics. Commonality among group members avoids conflicts and interactions among group members on side issues. Thus, a women's group should not combine married homemakers with small children; young, unmarried working women; and elderly divorced or widowed women because their lifestyles are substantially different. If the marketing research project covers distinct segments, then focus groups should be conducted separately for each segment.

The focus group participants should be carefully screened to meet certain criteria. The participants must have had adequate experience with the object or issue being discussed. People who have already participated in numerous focus groups should not be included. These so-called professional respondents are atypical, and their participation leads to serious validity problems.

Research Recipe

A focus group should be homogeneous in terms of demographics, psychographics, and product usage characteristics. If the marketing research project covers distinct segments, then conduct focus groups separately for each segment.

The physical setting for the focus group is also important. A relaxed, informal atmosphere encourages spontaneous comments. Light refreshments should be served before the session and made available throughout. Although a focus group may last from one to three hours, a duration time of 1.5 hours is typical. This period of time is needed to establish rapport with the participants and explore, in depth, their beliefs, feelings, ideas, attitudes, and insights regarding the topics of concern. Focus group interviews are invariably recorded, often on video, for subsequent replay, transcription, and analysis. Video recording has the advantage of capturing facial expressions and body movements, but it can increase the costs significantly. Frequently, clients observe the session from an adjacent room using a one-way mirror. Video transmission technology enables the clients to observe focus group sessions live from a remote location. For example, Stamford, Connecticut–based FocusVision Network, Inc. (**www.focusvision.com**) offers such a videoconferencing system.

The moderator plays a key role in the success of a focus group. The moderator must establish rapport with the participants, keep the discussion moving forward, and probe the respondents to elicit insights. In addition, the moderator may have a central role in the analysis and interpretation of the data. Therefore, the moderator should possess skill, experience, knowledge of the discussion topic and the marketing research project, and an understanding of the nature of group dynamics.

Research Recipe

The role of the moderator is critical to the success of a focus group and the usefulness of the findings. Therefore, choose the moderator carefully and fully inform that individual of the marketing research project.

Planning and Conducting Focus Groups

The procedure for planning and conducting focus groups is described in Figure 4.4. Planning begins by specifying the objectives of qualitative research. This involves an examination of the objectives of the marketing research project. In most instances, the problem has been defined by this stage and, if so, the general statement as well as the specific components of the problem should be carefully studied. Given the problem definition, the objectives of the qualitative research should be clearly determined. These objectives must be specified before conducting any qualitative research, be it focus groups, depth interviews, or projective techniques. In the first Research in Practice in this chapter featuring Nabisco, the objectives of qualitative research were to understand the motivations and snack purchase behavior of mothers.

The next step is to develop a detailed list of objectives for the focus group. This may take the form of a list of questions the researcher would like answered. In the case of Nabisco, the objectives for the focus group were to uncover how mothers felt about lunches and snacking for their children. Then a questionnaire to screen potential participants is prepared. Typical information obtained in the screening questionnaire includes product familiarity and knowledge, usage behavior,

FIGURE 4.4

PROCEDURE FOR CONDUCTING A FOCUS GROUP

attitudes toward and participation in focus groups, and standard demographic characteristics. In the Nabisco focus groups, the screening criteria for selecting focus group respondents consisted of mothers with young children at home who served snacks at least twice a week. Only respondents meeting these criteria were invited to the focus group sessions.

A detailed moderator's outline for use during the focus group interview should be prepared. This involves extensive discussions among the researcher, client, and moderator. This outline should specify the topics that will be discussed, the sequence in which they will be covered, and the amount of time that will be spent on each. Topics that will be explored in more detail and the use of flipcharts, other visual aids, products, and other stimuli should be identified. Use of a moderator's outline reduces some of the reliability problems inherent in focus groups, such as those caused by different moderators not covering the same content areas in comparable ways. In the case of Nabisco, the moderator's outline probed the motivations and concerns of mothers while serving snacks to their children.[2]

Research Recipe

You should always prepare a detailed moderator's outline for use during the focus group interview. This discussion guide should outline the topics that will be covered, the sequence in which they will be covered, and the amount of time that will be spent on each. Specify the topics that will be explored and the use of flipcharts, other visual aids, products, and other stimuli.

After a detailed outline is formulated, participants are recruited and the focus group interview is conducted. During the interview, the moderator must (1) establish rapport with the group members, (2) state the rules of group interaction, (3) set objectives, (4) probe the respondents and provoke intense discussion in the relevant areas, and (5) attempt to summarize the group members' responses to determine the extent of agreement.

Following the group discussion, either the moderator or an analyst reviews and analyzes the data and prepares the focus group report. The analyst not only reports specific comments and findings but also looks for consistent responses, new ideas, concerns suggested by facial expressions and body language, and other hypotheses that may or may not have received confirmation from all of the participants. Because the number of participants is small, frequencies and percentages are not usually reported in a focus group summary. Instead, reports typically include expressions like "most participants thought" or "participants were divided on this issue." Meticulous documentation and interpretation of the session lays the groundwork for the next step, which usually means doing additional research. The major findings of the focus groups for Nabisco were that families, especially mothers, were trying to portion out snack foods to their children to cut down on caloric intake. Mothers especially appreciated snacks in small portions with fewer calories. Also, convenience was very important.[3]

The number of focus groups that should be conducted on a single subject depends on (1) the nature of the issue, (2) the number of distinct market segments, (3) the number of new ideas generated by each successive group, and (4) time and cost. Resources permitting, one should conduct additional discussion groups until the moderator can anticipate what will be said. This usually happens after three or four groups are conducted on the same topic with the same segment. It is recommended that at least two groups be conducted. Nabisco conducted 10 focus groups, which is within the typical range of 6 to 15 for a large marketing research project.

Advantages and Disadvantages of Focus Groups

Focus groups are popular because of their many advantages. The immediacy and the richness of the comments, which come from real customers, make this technique highly useful. The group interaction produces a wider range of information, insights, and ideas than do individual interviews.

The comments of one person can trigger unexpected reactions from others, leading to a snowball effect in which participants respond to each other's comments. The responses are generally spontaneous and candid, providing rich insights. Ideas are more likely to arise out of the blue in a group than in an individual interview and are likely to be unique and potentially creative.

However, some of the qualities that make focus groups so strong also create some of their more serious limitations. The disadvantages of focus groups should not be overlooked. The clarity and conviction with which group members often speak lead to a tendency for researchers and managers to regard findings as conclusive rather than as exploratory. Focus groups are also difficult to moderate. The quality of the results depends heavily on the skills of the moderator; unfortunately, moderators who possess all of the desirable skills are rare. The unstructured nature of the responses makes coding, analysis, and interpretation difficult.

When properly conducted and used, focus groups have numerous applications, as illustrated by the Research in Practice featuring the Universal Music Group (UMG).

Research in Practice
Universal Music Group

Universal Music Group (**www.universalmusic.com**) owns the largest music publishing business in the world. Given the changing nature of the music industry, UMG conducted marketing research consisting of focus groups followed by a survey. The survey reached 1,162 respondents; 235 of them were between the ages of 13 and 15, and the rest were adults. The qualitative focus group research and the quantitative survey both referenced four key demographic segments: "Kids" (13- to 15-year-olds) and three distinct technology adoption groups called "Tech Vanguard," "Main Stream," and "Laggards."

The Laggards displayed a behavior that was distinct from the Kids and Tech Vanguard segments. The Laggards play lots of CDs (54 percent doing so at least weekly), but only 18 percent of Laggards listen at least weekly to music copied from CDs onto a computer, which is less than one-third of the corresponding figures for Kids and Tech Vanguard. The contrast with music downloaded from the Internet was even more stark, with 85 percent of Laggards stating either that they never listen to downloaded music or that this activity is "not applicable" to them.

The survey findings were consistent with the findings of focus groups that included Laggards, where the remarks made included:

R: "I listen to the radio or CDs (quaint or what!)."

J: "I only listen to CDs in the kitchen and radio and the same in the car, driving."

S: "I don't trust the longevity of a download—too susceptible to a hardware failure, virus, or other such mischief."

There was a similar story with music use on portable devices. Over one-half (52 percent) of all quantitative survey respondents listen either frequently or sometimes listen to music that has been loaded onto some form of portable device (iPod, phone, MP3 player, etc.). Among the Kids, this increases to 81 percent, but only 22 percent of Laggards fall into this category. The reason the Laggards are not using these technologies is nothing more complicated than simple disinterest; 64 percent of Laggards are just not interested in listening to music via portable devices, as was consistent with focus group findings:

J: "Never felt the need for an iPod, although my daughter's got one."

S: "I like music, radio, and specific CDs but not in my ears all the time and not from other people's devices."

Based on these research findings, Universal Music Group decided to work with Dell to offer preloaded music bundles. The songs were all taken from Universal Music Group's catalog and had two sizes and price points: $25 for a 50-song bundle or $45 for a 100-song bundle. There were six bundle themes (e.g., "Afternoon Delight," "The Classics," "Blues Masters," etc.) targeted specifically toward the Laggards and Main Stream segments. Because there were only six bundle themes, these segments aren't going to get bogged down in decisions, and they should be able to find their songs and get them all in one shot.

To target the other two segments (Kids and Tech Vanguard), Universal Music Group announced that it would license its music videos to the teen social-networking site **Kiwibox.com** in an attempt to attract young fans beyond Internet haunts like the youth-friendly but not youth-focused YouTube or MySpace. Therefore, it would be able to suit the Kids and Tech Vanguards, who are usually the younger generation that is online most of the time and listening to music while working.[4] <

Research Recipe

Never project the findings of focus groups to arrive at quantitative estimates for the target population. The purpose of focus groups is to enrich qualitative understanding and not to compute statistical estimates and projections.

iResearch
Nine West Going West: Penetrating the Women's Shoe Market

Visit **www.ninewest.com** and search the Internet, including social media, and your library's online databases, to obtain information on the marketing strategy of Nine West.

As the marketing manager, what marketing strategies would you formulate in helping Nine West increase its penetration of the women's shoe market? How would you use focus groups in helping Nine West increase its penetration of the women's shoe market? <

ONLINE FOCUS GROUPS

Online focus groups are becoming increasingly popular because of their convenience, cost-effectiveness, and quick turnaround compared to traditional focus groups. Using Internet technologies, marketing research companies have created virtual focus group facilities consisting of waiting rooms, focus group rooms, and client rooms. Respondents are preselected, generally from an online list of people who have expressed an interest in participating. Some are recruited through e-mail lists, Web intercepts, banner ads, or traditional methods (phone or mail). A screening questionnaire is administered online to qualify the respondents. Those who qualify are invited to participate in a focus group and receive a time, a URL, a room name, and a password via e-mail. Generally, four to six people participate in the online group. An online focus group has fewer participants than a face-to-face meeting because too many respondents can cause confusion.

Before the focus group begins, participants receive information about the group that covers details such as how to express emotions when typing. Emotions are indicated by using keyboard characters and are standard in their use on the Internet. For example, :-) and :-(represent smiling and sad faces, respectively. The emotion indicators usually are inserted into the text at the point where the emotion is meant. Emotions can also be expressed using a different font or color. The participants can also preview information about the focus group topic by visiting a website and reading information or downloading and viewing an actual TV ad on their computers. Then, just before the focus group begins, participants visit a website where they log on and get some last-minute instructions.

When it is time for the group, they move into a Web-based chat room. They go to the focus group location (a URL) and click on the "Enter Focus Room" item. To enter, they must supply the room name, username, and password that was e-mailed to them earlier. The moderator signs on early and administers a screening questionnaire as the respondents enter the waiting room to verify their identities. Once in the focus group chat room, the moderator and the participants type responses to each other in real time. The general practice is for the moderators to pose their questions in all capital letters, and the respondents are asked to use upper- and lowercase. The respondents are also asked to start their response with the question number every time so the moderator can quickly tie the response to the proper question. This makes it fast and easy to transcribe a focus group session. The group interaction lasts for about sixty to ninety minutes. A raw transcript is available as soon as the group is completed, and a formatted transcript is available within forty-eight hours. The whole process is much faster than the traditional face-to-face focus group method. Examples of companies that provide online focus groups include Harris Interactive (**www.harrisinteractive.com**) and Burke (**www.burke.com**).

R e s e a r c h   R e c i p e

Use online focus groups when the target respondents are familiar and comfortable with using the Internet. They offer convenience, cost-effectiveness, and faster turnaround times compared to traditional face-to-face focus groups.

New forms of online focus groups continue to emerge. For example, online bulletin board focus groups involve the moderator and the respondents over an extended period of time, from a few days to a few weeks. Thus, respondents can think and respond at their own convenience. An example is 20|20 Bulletin Board Focus Group (**www.2020research.com**) for holding an in-depth discussion among participants over an extended period of time. Participants enter the discussion several times over three to five days, depending on the research objectives. The extended time period allows respondents to react to and build on each other's ideas in a way that is often not possible during a typical 1.5-hour focus group session. Other forms of online qualitative research have also emerged, including blogs, message boards, online media sites, and online communities. Some of the useful insights gained from these procedures are illustrated by Ford Fusion. Online focus groups indicated that consumers were looking for a hybrid sedan that successfully blends excellent fuel economy with driving pleasure, and has a comfortable ride and agile handling. The Ford Fusion 2014 Hybrid model was designed along these specifications. The result? The all-new Ford Fusion Hybrid 2014 was a top-rated domestic sedan.

Advantages and Disadvantages of Online Focus Groups

Online focus groups offer many advantages. People from all over the country or even the world can participate, and the client can observe the group from the convenience of her or his home or office. The Internet enables the researcher to reach segments that are usually hard to contact, such as doctors, lawyers, and other professional people, and others who lead busy lives and are typically not interested in taking part in traditional focus groups.

Moderators may also be able to carry on side conversations with individual respondents, probing deeper into interesting areas. People are generally less inhibited in their responses and are more likely to express their thoughts fully online. Without travel, video recording, or facilities to arrange, the cost is much lower than for traditional focus groups: Firms are able to keep costs between one-fifth and one-half the costs of traditional focus groups. Online groups are also faster to conduct.

However, online focus groups are not without limitations. Only people that have and know how to use a computer can be interviewed online. Because the name of an individual on the Internet is often private, actually verifying that a respondent is a member of a target group is difficult. To overcome this limitation, traditional methods, such as telephone calls, are used for recruitment and verification of respondents. Body language, facial expressions, and tone of voice cannot be obtained online, and electronic emotion indicators obviously do not capture the breadth of emotion that video recording does.

Another factor that must be considered is the lack of general control over the respondent's environment and his or her potential exposure to distracting external stimuli. Because online focus groups could potentially have respondents scattered all over the world, the researchers and moderators have no idea what else the respondents might be doing while participating in the group. Only audio and visual stimuli can be tested. Products cannot be touched (e.g., clothing) or smelled (e.g., perfumes). It is difficult to get the clients as involved in online focus groups as they are in traditional focus groups.

1. To experience the steps involved in designing and analyzing online bulletin board research, go to **www.2020research.com**, select "Tools and Services" and then "QualBoard," and then play the video.
2. Visit e-FocusGroups (**www.e-focusgroups.com**) to see a demonstration of how an Online Video Focus Group works. ❮

DEPTH INTERVIEWS

Depth interviews are another method of obtaining qualitative data. We describe the general procedure for conducting depth interviews and then discuss their advantages, disadvantages, and applications.

Conducting Depth Interviews

depth interview
An unstructured, direct, personal interview in which a single respondent is questioned by a highly skilled interviewer to uncover underlying motivations, beliefs, attitudes, and feelings on a topic.

Like focus groups, depth interviews are an unstructured and direct way of obtaining information, but unlike focus groups, depth interviews are conducted on a one-to-one basis. A **depth interview** is an unstructured, direct, personal interview in which a single respondent is questioned by a highly skilled interviewer to uncover underlying motivations, beliefs, attitudes, and feelings on a topic.

A depth interview may take from thirty minutes to more than one hour. To illustrate the technique in the context of shopping in department stores, the interviewer begins by asking a general question such as "How do you feel about shopping at department stores?" The interviewer then encourages the subject to talk freely about his or her attitudes toward department stores. After asking the initial question, the interviewer uses an unstructured format. The subsequent direction of the interview is determined by the respondent's initial reply, the interviewer's questions for elaboration, and the respondent's answers. Suppose the respondent replies to the initial question by saying, "Shopping isn't fun anymore." The interviewer might then pose a question such as "Why isn't it fun anymore?" If the answer is not very revealing ("Fun has just disappeared from shopping"), the interviewer may ask a probing question, such as "Why was it fun before and what has changed?"

While the interviewer attempts to follow a rough outline, the specific wording of the questions and the order in which they are asked is influenced by the subject's replies. Probing is of critical importance in obtaining meaningful responses and uncovering hidden issues. Probing is done by asking questions such as "Why do you say that?" "That's interesting; can you tell me more?" or "Would you like to add anything else?" The value of information uncovered by probing is shown in the following example.

Research in Practice
Elizabeth Arden: Generation Appeal

Elizabeth Arden (**www.elizabetharden.com**) owns, manufactures, and licenses over 100 perfumes and distributes more than 200 fragrances to mass retailers. Brand names like Elizabeth Arden, Red Door, 5th avenue, and White Shoulders, as well as Elizabeth Taylor's White Diamonds, are marketed by the company. When perfume sales declined due to a recession in the United States from 2008 to 2010, Elizabeth Arden proved again that celebrities often add luster to a polished product.

To expand its target market to include younger teens, Elizabeth Arden conducted depth interviews with females in this age group. Depth interviews were chosen over focus groups because wearing a perfume can be a rather personal experience, and in-depth probing was needed to reveal the true underlying reasons that would attract the younger females to a perfume brand. The findings revealed that young teenage females are increasingly aspiring to become like their older teenage counterparts. And digital media, rather than TV, had become part of their lifestyle.

Armed with this information, Elizabeth Arden chose to pursue a younger crowd, with Britney Spears as their cover girl. This led the cosmetic company to introduce "Britney Spears Curious," a cosmetic line that coincidentally reached the market when the public eye was upon Spears's personal life. Promotions included a Web campaign featuring Spears entering a hotel room with her mysterious lover, and an online mobile number submission system, which returned voice messages from the celebrity herself. Word-of-mouth buzz spread like wildfire; according to Thomson-South Western, 27,000 teenagers received messages from Spears within a seven-week period. By understanding the high use of the Internet among young people, "Britney Spears Curious" was marketed online before reaching television and other media.

By capitalizing on teenage fanaticism uncovered via depth interviews, Elizabeth Arden introduced a best-selling new fragrance. As of 2014 the "Britney Spears Curious" line was still selling well and contributing to the company's bottom line.[5] ◄

As this example from Elizabeth Arden indicates, probing is effective in uncovering underlying or hidden information. Probing is an integral part of depth interviews.

The interviewer's role is critical to the success of the depth interview. The interviewer should (1) avoid appearing superior; (2) put the respondent at ease; (3) be detached and objective, yet personable; (4) ask questions in an informative manner; (5) not accept brief yes or no answers; and (6) probe the respondent.

Research Recipe

Probing is of critical importance in depth interviews and you should use it to uncover hidden information and issues. The one-on-one nature of depth interviews is very conducive to in-depth questioning of individual respondents, which cannot be done as effectively in focus groups. The interviewer plays a very important role in depth interviews.

Advantages and Disadvantages of Depth Interviews

Depth interviews can uncover greater depth of insights than focus groups. Also, depth interviews attribute the responses directly to the respondent, unlike focus groups, where it is sometimes difficult to determine which respondent made a particular response. Depth interviews result in a free exchange of information that may not be possible in focus groups because there is no social pressure to conform to a group response.

Depth interviews suffer from many of the disadvantages of focus groups and often to a greater extent. Skilled interviewers capable of conducting depth interviews are expensive and difficult to find. The lack of structure makes the results susceptible to the interviewer's influence, and the quality and completeness of the results depend heavily on the interviewer's skills. The data obtained are difficult to analyze and interpret, and the services of skilled psychologists are typically required for this purpose. The length of the interview combined with high costs means that the number of depth interviews in a project will be small. Despite these disadvantages, depth interviews do have some applications. They can be useful when detailed probing is required (e.g., automobile purchase), the topic is sensitive or subject to strong social norms (e.g., attitudes of college students toward dating), or the consumption experience is sensory or complicated (e.g., perfumes, bath soap). They are also effective with respondents who are professionals (e.g., industrial marketing research) and in interviewing respondents who are competitors (e.g., travel agents' perceptions of airline package travel programs).

Research Recipe

Conduct depth interviews when detailed probing is required, the topic is sensitive or subject to strong social norms, or the consumption experience is sensory or complicated. They are also effective with respondents who are professionals and in interviewing respondents who are competitors.

iResearch
"More People Go with Visa"?

Search the Internet, including social media as well as your library's online databases, to obtain information on why people use credit cards.

Conduct two depth interviews for determining the reasons why people use credit cards.

As the marketing manager for Visa, how would you use information on the reasons why people use credit cards to increase your market share? ‹

PROJECTIVE TECHNIQUES

projective technique
An unstructured and indirect form of questioning that encourages the respondents to project their underlying motivations, beliefs, attitudes, or feelings regarding the issues of concern.

Both focus groups and depth interviews are direct approaches in which the true purpose of the research is disclosed to the respondents or is otherwise obvious to them. Projective techniques are different from these two techniques because they attempt to disguise the purpose of the research. A **projective technique** is an unstructured, indirect form of questioning that encourages respondents to project their underlying motivations, beliefs, attitudes, or feelings regarding the issues of concern. In projective techniques, respondents are asked to interpret the behavior of others rather than describe their own behavior. In interpreting the behavior of others, respondents indirectly project their own motivations, beliefs, attitudes, or feelings into the situation and describe their own behaviors. Thus, the respondents' attitudes and underlying themes are uncovered by analyzing their responses to scenarios that are deliberately unstructured, vague, and ambiguous. The more ambiguous the situation, the more respondents project their emotions, needs, motives, attitudes, and values, as demonstrated by work in clinical psychology, on which projective techniques are based. In a landmark study, the U.S. Postal Service (USPS) used a projective technique to determine why most boys age 8 to 13 years old did not collect stamps as a hobby. A sample of boys was shown a picture on a screen of a 10-year-old boy fixing stamps in his album; they were asked to describe the scene and characterize the boy. Most respondents described the boy in the picture as a "sissy." After these findings were confirmed by survey research, the USPS undertook a successful advertising campaign directed at 8- to 13-year-olds to dispel the belief that stamp collecting was for "sissies." The campaign featured a famous quarterback who leads his team to victory on the football field and then comes home and starts fixing stamps in an album with his 10-year-old son.

Research Recipe

In describing ambiguous situations, respondents project their own underlying values, attitudes, and beliefs, which can then be uncovered by analyzing their responses. While interpreting the behavior of others, respondents indirectly project their own motivations, beliefs, attitudes, or feelings into the situation and describe their own behaviors.

The common projective techniques are word association, sentence completion, picture response and cartoon test, role playing, and third-person technique.

Word Association

In **word association**, respondents are presented with a list of words, one at a time and asked to respond to each with the first word that comes to mind. The words of interest, called test words, are interspersed throughout the list, which also contains some neutral, or filler, words to disguise the purpose of the study. For example, in the department store study, some of the test words might be: *location, parking, shopping, quality,* and *price.* The subject's response to each word is recorded verbatim and responses are timed so that respondents who hesitate or reason out (defined as taking longer than three seconds to reply) can be identified.

The underlying assumption of this technique is that association allows respondents to reveal their inner feelings about the topic of interest. It is often possible to classify the associations as favorable, unfavorable, or neutral. An individual's pattern of responses and the details of the response are used to determine the person's underlying attitudes or feelings on the topic of interest.

word association
A projective technique in which respondents are presented with a list of words, one at a time and asked to respond to each with the first word that comes to mind.

Research Recipe

Association with words allows respondents to reveal their underlying values, feelings, and beliefs. The key is that they respond with the first word that comes to mind when you present them with the test word.

Sentence Completion

Sentence completion is similar to word association. Respondents are given incomplete sentences and asked to complete them. Generally, they are asked to use the first word or phrase that comes to mind. In the context of determining attitudes toward department stores, the following incomplete sentences may be used.

sentence completion
A projective technique in which respondents are presented with a number of incomplete sentences and asked to complete them.

A person who shops at Sears is

_____

A person who receives a gift certificate good for Sak's Fifth Avenue would be

_____

J. C. Penney is most liked by

_____

When I think of shopping in a department store, I

_____

This example illustrates one advantage of sentence completion over word association: Respondents can be provided with a more directed stimulus. Sentence completion may provide more information about the subjects' feelings than word association. However, sentence completion is often clearer to the respondents, and thus many respondents may be able to guess the purpose of the study. A variation of sentence completion is paragraph completion, in which the respondents complete a paragraph beginning with the stimulus phrase.

R e s e a r c h   R e c i p e

Compared to word association, sentence completion provides more information but its purpose is clearer to respondents.

Picture Response and Cartoon Test

picture response technique
A projective technique in which the respondent is shown a picture and asked to tell a story describing it.

In the **picture response technique**, respondents are shown a picture and asked to tell a story describing it. The responses are used to evaluate attitudes toward the topic and describe the respondents, as illustrated by the United States Postal Service example given earlier in this chapter. A special form of the picture response technique is a cartoon test.

cartoon test
Cartoon characters are shown in a specific situation related to the problem. The respondents are asked to indicate the dialogue that one cartoon character might say in response to the comment(s) of another character.

In a **cartoon test**, cartoon characters are shown in a specific situation related to the problem. The respondents are asked to indicate what one cartoon character might say in response to the comments of another character. The responses indicate the respondents' feelings, beliefs, and attitudes toward the situation. Cartoon tests are simpler to administer and analyze than are picture response techniques. An example is shown in Figure 4.5.

R e s e a r c h   R e c i p e

Analyze the responses to picture response techniques and cartoon tests to uncover the respondents' feelings, beliefs, and attitudes toward the situation. Cartoon tests are simpler to administer and analyze than are picture response techniques.

Role Playing and Third-Person Techniques

role playing
Respondents in a marketing research project are asked to assume the behavior of someone else.

In **role playing**, respondents are asked to play the role or assume the behavior of someone else. The researcher assumes that the respondents will project their own feelings and beliefs into the role. These can then be uncovered by analyzing the responses.

FIGURE 4.5 |
A CARTOON TEST

In the **third-person technique**, the respondent is presented with a verbal or visual situation and is asked to relate the beliefs and attitudes of a third person rather than directly expressing personal beliefs and attitudes. This third person may be a friend, a neighbor, a colleague, or a "typical" person. Again, the researcher assumes that the respondent will project him- or herself into the situation and reveal personal beliefs and attitudes while describing the reactions of a third person. Asking the individual to respond in the third person reduces the social pressure to give an acceptable answer.

A study was performed for a commercial airline to understand why some people do not fly. When the respondents were asked, "Are you afraid to fly?" very few people said yes. The major reasons given for not flying were cost, inconvenience, and delays caused by bad weather. However, it was suspected that the answers were heavily influenced by the need to give socially desirable responses. Therefore, in a follow-up study, the respondents were asked, "Do you think your neighbor is afraid to fly?" The answers indicated that most of the neighbors who traveled by some other means of transportation were afraid to fly.

Note that asking the question in the first person ("Are you afraid to fly?") did not elicit the true response. Phrasing the same question in the third person ("Do you think your neighbor is afraid to fly?") lowered the respondent's defenses and resulted in a more truthful answer. In a popular version of the third-person technique, the researcher presents the respondent with a description of a shopping list and asks for a characterization of the purchaser.

> **third-person technique**
> *A projective technique in which the respondent is presented with a verbal or visual situation and asked to relate the beliefs and attitudes of a third person toward the situation.*

Research Recipe

When you ask individuals to respond in the third person, it lowers their defense mechanisms and reduces the social pressure to give desirable answers. As in all projective techniques, the assumption is that the individuals are responding in terms of their own underlying values, attitudes, beliefs, motivations, and perceptions.

We conclude our discussion of projective techniques by describing their advantages, disadvantages, and applications.

Advantages and Disadvantages of Projective Techniques

Projective techniques have a major advantage over the unstructured direct techniques (focus groups and depth interviews): They may elicit responses that subjects would be unwilling or unable to give if they knew the purpose of the study. In direct questioning, the respondent, at times, may intentionally or unintentionally misunderstand, misinterpret, or mislead the researcher. In these cases, projective techniques can increase the validity of responses by disguising the purpose. This is particularly true when the issues to be addressed are personal, sensitive, or subject to strong social norms. Projective techniques are also helpful when underlying motivations, beliefs, and attitudes are operating at a subconscious level.

Projective techniques suffer from many of the disadvantages of unstructured direct techniques, but to a greater extent. These techniques generally require personal interviews with highly trained interviewers. Skilled interpreters are also required to analyze the responses. Hence, they tend to be expensive. There is also a serious risk of interpretation bias. With the exception of word association, all techniques are open ended, making the analysis and interpretation difficult and subjective.

Some projective techniques, such as role playing, require respondents to engage in unusual behavior. In such cases, the researcher may assume that respondents who agree to participate are themselves unusual in some way. Therefore, they may not be representative of the population of interest. As a result, it is desirable to compare findings generated by projective techniques with the findings of the other techniques that permit a more direct assessment (focus groups and depth interviews).

> ## Research Recipe
>
> Use projective techniques when the required information cannot be obtained accurately by direct methods; however, do not use them naively, without regard to their assumptions and limitations. It is desirable that you compare findings generated by projective techniques with the findings of focus groups and depth interviews.

Like focus groups, depth interviews and almost all the projective techniques discussed in this chapter can be implemented over the Internet. For example, various companies and marketing researchers are using the picture response technique effectively. Coca-Cola can provide a picture on a website and ask respondents to write a story about it. The demographic data of the person coupled with the story can provide valuable insights into the respondent's psychographic profile and consumption behavior. The success of conducting qualitative research over the Internet lies in the respondents having access to and being comfortable with the Internet.

iResearch
Projecting Cosmetic Usage

Visit **www.clinique.com** and search the Internet, including social media as well as your library's online databases, to obtain information on the underlying reasons why women use cosmetics.

As the brand manager for Clinique, how would you use information on the reasons why women use cosmetics to formulate marketing strategies that would increase your market share? Which, if any, of the projective techniques would you use to determine the reasons why women use cosmetics? **<**

OTHER METHODS OF QUALITATIVE RESEARCH

A variety of other qualitative research procedures are also used. The more relevant ones include ethnography and netnography, and mystery shopping.

Ethnography and Netnography

ethnographic research
The study of human behavior in its natural context; it involves observation of behavior and setting along with depth interviews.

netnography
Netnography uses ethnographic techniques but uses data that is naturally found on the Internet and that is generated by online communities.

Ethnography or **ethnographic research** is a qualitative research method based on observing people in their natural environment rather than in a formal research setting. The objective is to understand a culture or phenomenon of interest. The data are collected by a variety of methods, including depth interviews and participant observation. In participant observation, the researcher becomes immersed within the culture or phenomenon and draws data from personal observations. Sometimes, audio and video recordings are also obtained. **Netnography** uses ethnographic techniques but uses data that is found on the Internet and that is generated by online communities. These data occur naturally and are not affected by the presence of the researcher. The following example illustrates ethnographic research.

Research in Practice
Kraft Singles Singles Out Moms

Kraft Singles (**www.kraftfoodsgroup.com**), the leader in processed cheese slices, was not keeping up with the market growth. Kraft had to figure out what mothers felt about Kraft Singles by conducting ethnographic research. A group of ethnographers from Strategic Frameworking (**www.strategicframeworking.com**) conducted observations and depth interviews in the homes of mothers age 25 to 64 while they were making sandwiches. These moms told the researchers that they were aware of what their children liked and disliked, and children liked the taste of Kraft Singles. They felt good giving Kraft Singles to their children because of its nutritional value, especially as a source of calcium. However, they could be persuaded to buy cheaper brands. When these findings were verified by a telephone survey, Kraft researchers focused on the two key concepts to prevent mothers from switching to a competitor's brand and instead remain loyal to Kraft brand. The two concepts showed how much children loved the taste of Kraft Singles, and emphasized that the brand provided the calcium that children needed. Advertising agency J. Walter Thompson (**www.jwt.com**) created the commercials and the campaign was a success, resulting in increased sales and market share.[6] ◁

Mystery Shopping

In mystery shopping, trained observers pose as consumers and shop at the company's stores or those of competitors to collect data about customer–employee interaction and other marketing variables, such as prices, displays, layout, and so forth. The mystery shoppers question the store employees, mentally take note of the answers, and observe the variables of interest. IntelliShop (**www.intelli-shop.com**) is a firm that specializes in mystery shopping. For more information on mystery shopping, visit **www.mysteryshop.org**.

INTERNATIONAL MARKETING RESEARCH

Because the researcher is often not familiar with the foreign product market to be examined, qualitative research is crucial in international marketing research. It may reveal the differences between the foreign and domestic markets. Focus groups can be used in many settings, particularly in industrialized countries. The moderator should not only be trained in focus group methodology but should also be familiar with the language, culture, and patterns of social interaction prevailing in that country. The focus group findings should be derived not only from the verbal content but also from nonverbal cues like voice intonations, inflections, expressions, and gestures. The size of the focus group could also vary. For example, in Asia, seven respondents produce the highest level of interaction among group members. In some countries, such as those in the Middle or Far East, people are hesitant to discuss their feelings in a group setting. In other countries such as Japan, people think it is impolite to disagree with others publicly. In these cases, depth interviews should be used. Nevertheless, focus groups remain popular in many parts of the world, as indicated by VisitBritain's research of the spa market in the United Kingdom.

Research in Practice
Spas: Status Symbol in the United Kingdom

VisitBritain (**www.visitbritain.com**) is a government-backed national tourism agency whose mission is to build the value of tourism to Britain. It also builds partnerships with, and provides insights into, other organizations that have a stake in British tourism. VisitBritain conducted extensive marketing research using focus groups of spa-going consumers to find out just how British spas are viewed.

The key insight to come out of the research was that spa experiences in the United Kingdom are regarded as a status symbol denoting pampering and treats, and are seen as a luxury item. Therefore, clients felt that one- to five-star ratings would not be appropriate because "who would use a one-, two- or three-star spa?"

The results led the agency to do away with the current star rating system and instead categorize spas by accreditations. The accreditation scheme is for all types of spas and guides potential clients to the ones that best suit their requirements, that is, medi-spa, hotel spa, resort spa, destination spa, sport-and-fitness spa, natural spa, day spa, and salon spa. Each spa needs to meet a set of minimum-entry requirements and a series of quality benchmarks in order to be accredited.

Source: UrbanImages / Alamy

The qualitative research doesn't stop there. Ongoing assessments of each spa are conducted by mystery shoppers to see how the spas are really run and to provide feedback based on customer needs. The services that VisitBritain now offers consumers shopping for spas, whether they are domestic or international travelers, have proven invaluable to the spa market. The UK spa industry has experienced significant growth since the introduction of the accreditation scheme.[7] ◀

Research Recipe

When researching international markets, the moderator should not only be trained in focus group methodology but should also be familiar with the language, culture, and patterns of social interaction prevailing in that country. The size of the focus group could vary across countries. In some cultures, people are hesitant to discuss their feelings in a group setting; in those cases, conduct depth interviews.

The use of projective techniques in international marketing research should be carefully considered. Word association, sentence completion, role playing, and the third-person technique involve the use of verbal cues. Picture response and cartoon tests employ nonverbal stimuli (pictures). Whether verbal or nonverbal stimuli are used, the equivalence of meaning across the cultures should be established.

The usual limitations of qualitative techniques also apply in the international context, perhaps to a greater extent. It is often difficult to find trained moderators and interviewers overseas. The development of appropriate coding, analysis, and interpretation procedures poses additional difficulties.

MARKETING RESEARCH AND SOCIAL MEDIA

Social networks are defined by the relationships between members. Marketing researchers can tap into these social networks for conducting qualitative research.

Focus Groups

Social networks provide you with a large audience eager to talk for free. Companies have devised clever ways to conduct a form of focus group and other forms of qualitative research using social media. Just being part of different types of social media and analyzing what people are talking about can yield a basic understanding of customers, but if companies really want something constructive to take shape from all that talking, they need to listen to the right people. For this reason—besides increasing their presence on varying social networks—companies are creating private online communities, which can play the role of extended focus groups. The members are carefully recruited, and membership is by invitation only. Expert facilitators engage the members regularly to build familiarity and a pattern so that the customers start to view the community as their own. A lively, friendly place is designed to assist customers in engaging in insightful conversations. JC Penney presents a case study of successfully using a private online community to conduct an extended form of focus group.

Research in Practice
JCPenney: Using Social Bodies to Design Body Lingerie

JCPenney, one of America's leading retailers, launched a private online community called the *Ambrielle Team*, which was dedicated to consumers of the JCPenney lingerie line. This team wanted to learn more about the Ambrielle customer and her fit concerns. This was a type of focus group that was conducted through forming a private community. The sample size was small, and the information was collected in a natural and unstructured manner. The product team members played the role of moderators and facilitated conversations toward finding the information they needed. Team members were handpicked and limited in number. Penney also gathered lifestyle, demographic, and psychographic information about members to make sure that the firm had a reasonably complete picture of each member. The Ambrielle team had a series of online discussions within the community to help JC Penney figure out the basic fit and quality issues of women. This was followed by a "wear" test to give a more definite focus to the feedback regarding specific products. After the "wear" test, members were again asked to express their views via the private discussion board, an online activity, and live online chats with the product team.

Source: Douglas C. Pizac / AP Images

Based on this customer alliance and consumer response, JCPenney made substantial product changes to the lingerie bands, straps, and overall sizing so that customer needs were better satisfied. These changes were posted for the community so the participants would know that the company had inculcated their insights and feedback into the product. Store sales of Ambrielle products increased thereafter.[8] ◄

Another way to conduct focus group research involves participant blogs. The general approach is to define a specific topic and then recruit participants to blog about that topic. Each participant is given his or her own blog to maintain. The number of participants typically ranges from eight to sixty. Blog projects tend to last from one to four weeks. Qualitative analyses of the blogs' content result in rich insights.

Depth Interviews

Burger King conducted a form of depth interview using social media. Burger King customers were secretly filmed after being told that the company's signature Whopper sandwich was being discontinued. A one-minute funny television commercial was developed using this episode. However, an eight-minute video called *Whopper Freakout* was posted on a companion website. Visitors viewing the video were encouraged to post their comments, and follow-up one-on-one interviews were held online with select respondents. The analysis of these comments and interviews revealed a consistent theme. When customers were confronted with the idea that they could no longer order a Whopper, they immediately recalled their childhood memories of Whoppers. Remarks such as "The people in this video are still eating at Burger King today because their parents brought them there as kids" were obtained. This led Burger King to build a marketing campaign for the Whopper based on childhood memories and nostalgia.

Projective Techniques

Several projective techniques can be implemented easily using social media communities. The unstructured and indirect form of questioning on social media has consumers willing to project their underlying thoughts, motivations, and feelings regarding the issues of concern. GlaxoSmithKline Consumer Healthcare used Communispace (**www.communispace.com**) social network groups to closely define the customer base for its new line of Alli weight-loss products. The research company used sentence completion online when it was trying to investigate self-image issues with overweight people. Community members were asked to complete sentences like "When you talk to yourself, you refer to yourself as _____." Members were also asked to post photos showing what they most regretted about their obesity. Analysis of the sentence completions and photos indicated that people were frustrated about being excluded from everyday activities. However, they were willing to take responsibility for their own weight loss. They were also willing to accept slow progress in return for long-term results. Alli was targeted at this segment, and Glaxo sold $155 million worth of Alli in the first six weeks of the product's introduction.

Limitations

Using social media to conduct qualitative research is not without drawbacks. Often the amount of information generated can be voluminous, drowning the company and its marketing research personnel in weeks of work. General Motors' Chevy Apprentice research effort, in which visitors contributed TV commercials assembled from video clips on a website, logged about 22,000 submissions. That amounted to a lot of video to view and analyze.

Research Recipe

You can tap into social networks for conducting qualitative research. Private online communities can play the role of extended focus groups. The members are carefully recruited, and expert facilitators engage the members regularly on issues of interest. Another way you can conduct focus group research involves participant blogs. You can use social media communities to recruit participants for focus groups, depth interviews, and projective techniques.

ETHICS IN MARKETING RESEARCH

When conducting qualitative research, ethical issues related to the respondents and the general public are of primary concern. These issues include disguising the purpose of the research and the use of deceptive procedures, video and audio recording the proceedings, comfort level of the respondents, and misusing the findings of qualitative research.

All indirect procedures require disguising the purpose of the research, at least to some extent. Often, a cover story is used to camouflage the true purpose. This can potentially violate the respondents' right to know, and it can also result in psychological harm. For example, respondents may be upset if, after responding to a series of projective techniques, they discovered that they had spent their time on a trivial issue, such as what should be the color of a can of a new orange drink, when they had been recruited to participate in a study on nutrition. To minimize such negative effects, the respondents should be informed at the start that the true purpose of the research is being disguised so that the responses are not biased. After completing the research tasks, debriefing sessions should be held in which the respondents are informed about the true purpose and given opportunities to make comments or ask questions. Deceptive procedures that violate respondents' right to privacy and informed consent should be avoided. One example of a deceptive procedure is allowing clients to observe focus groups or in-depth interviews by introducing them as participants helping with the project.

An ethical dilemma involves recording the focus group or the depth interview. Video or audio recording the respondents without their prior knowledge or consent raises ethical concerns. Ethical guidelines suggest that respondents should be informed and their consent obtained prior to the start of the proceedings, preferably at the time of recruitment. At the end of the meeting, participants should be asked to sign a written statement conveying their permission to use all recordings. This statement should disclose the true purpose of the research and all people who will have access to the recording. Participants should be given an opportunity to refuse signing such a statement. The files should be edited to completely omit the identity and comments of the respondents who have refused.

Another concern that needs to be addressed is the comfort level of the respondents. During qualitative research, particularly in depth interviews, respondents should not be pushed beyond the point where they become uncomfortable. Respondents' welfare should warrant restraint on the part of the moderator or interviewer. If a respondent feels uncomfortable and does not wish to answer more questions on a particular topic, the interviewer should not probe any further. A final issue relates to the general public and deals with the ethical implications of findings from qualitative research, as in the example from Facebook in the Research in Practice feature that follows.

Research in Practice
Facebook Faces Privacy Concerns

Unlike MySpace, another social-networking website, Facebook's membership was initially restricted to students of colleges and universities. Therefore, it seemed safe enough for students to share notes on everything, without the fear of professors, parents, and employers. But Facebook could not stay closed for long before opening its membership to everyone.

Despite the publicized incidents about violations of privacy on Facebook, focus groups reveal that many students do not take the threats to the privacy of the information they post on Facebook seriously. On one hand, many students are posting sensitive personal information on Facebook, including their full name, personal photo, date of birth, gender, hometown, personal interests, favorite music and movies, educational information, e-mail address, personal website URL, phone number, and address. On the other hand, few students take appropriate steps to protect the privacy of the posted information. For example, when asked if they would increase privacy settings if they had heard about a negative incident, more than half said yes. But of those who had heard such stories, only few actually followed through on tightening security.

These findings increase the ethical burden on Facebook to take adequate measures to prevent the identity of users from being stolen or put at risk and to protect their personal information. In fact, as recently as March 23, 2012, two German privacy watchdogs were not satisfied with Facebook's new privacy guidelines, saying that users get more duties instead of more rights, and that the social network still violated German and European privacy laws. The March 13, 2013 redesign of Facebook's timeline posed additional privacy threats. An Austrian student group discovered that "friends of friends" were able to access all of your (users) events "attended" information even if your security settings were such that this information should never have been made public. [9] <

Source: Erkan Mehmet / Alamy

Research Recipe

Respondents' welfare should be uppermost in your mind as a researcher. If a respondent feels uncomfortable and does not wish to answer more questions on a particular topic, the interviewer should not probe any further. If the true purpose of the research is disguised, inform the respondents upfront about this. After completing the research tasks, hold debriefing sessions in which the respondents are informed about the true purpose and given opportunities to make comments or ask questions. Make certain that video or audio recording of the respondents follows strict ethical guidelines.

Dell Running Case

Review the Dell case, Case 1.1, and questionnaire given toward the end of the book.

1. In gaining an understanding of the consumer decision-making process for personal computer purchases, would focus groups or depth interviews be more useful? Explain.
2. Can projective techniques be useful to Dell as it seeks to increase its penetration of U.S. households? Which projective technique(s) would you recommend?
3. Devise word association techniques to measure consumer associations that might affect attitudes toward personal computer purchases.
4. Design sentence completion techniques to uncover underlying motives for personal computer purchases.
5. How can Dell use social media to conduct qualitative research?

Summary

Qualitative and quantitative research should be viewed as complementary. Qualitative research methods may be direct or indirect. In direct methods, respondents are able to discern the true purpose of the research, while indirect methods disguise the purpose of the research. The major direct methods are focus groups and depth interviews. Focus groups are conducted in a group setting, whereas depth interviews are done one on one. Focus group interviews are the most widely used qualitative research technique.

The indirect techniques are called projective techniques because their goal is to get the respondents' motivations, beliefs, attitudes, and feelings projected onto ambiguous situations. The commonly used projective techniques include word association, sentence completion, picture response and cartoon tests, role playing, and third-person techniques. Projective techniques are particularly useful when respondents are unwilling or unable to provide the required information by direct methods. They are best used in conjunction with focus groups and depth interviews.

Qualitative research can reveal the salient differences between the domestic and foreign markets. Whether focus groups or depth interviews should be conducted and how the findings should be interpreted depends heavily on cultural differences. Social media have enhanced both the quality and quantity of qualitative research. When conducting qualitative research, the researcher and the client must respect the respondents by conducting research in a way that does not embarrass or harm the respondents.

Companion Website

This textbook includes numerous student resources that can be found at **www.pearsonglobaleditions.com/malhotra**. At this Companion website, you'll find:

- Student Resource Manual
- Demo movies of statistical procedures using SPSS and Microsoft Excel
- Screen captures of statistical procedures using SPSS and Microsoft Excel
- Data files for all datasets in SPSS and Microsoft Excel
- Additional figures and tables
- Videos and write-ups for all video cases
- Other valuable resources

⌄ Key Terms and Concepts

Qualitative research
Quantitative research
Direct approach
Indirect approach
Focus group

Depth interview
Projective technique
Word association
Sentence completion
Picture response technique

Cartoon test
Role playing
Third-person technique
Ethnographic research
Netnography

⌄ Suggested Cases and Video Cases

Running Case with Real Data and Questionnaire
    1.1 Dell

Comprehensive Critical Thinking Cases
    2.1 American Idol

Comprehensive Cases with Real Data and Questionnaires
    3.1 JPMorgan Chase   3.2 Wendy's

Online Video Cases
    4.1 Nike   5.1 Starbucks   7.1 P&G   8.1 Dunkin' Donuts
    9.1 Subaru   10.1 Intel   13.1 Marriott

⌄ Live Research: Conducting a Marketing Research Project

1. For most projects, it will be important to conduct some form of qualitative research.
2. Different teams can be assigned different responsibilities, for example, interviewing key decision makers, interviewing industry experts, conducting depth interviews with consumers, doing a focus group, analyzing social media content, and so forth. Alternatively, all the teams can work on these tasks.
3. It is essential to involve the client in qualitative research.

⌄ Acronyms

The key characteristics of a focus group may be described by the acronym FOCUS GROUPS:

F ocused (on a particular topic)

O utline prepared for discussion

C haracteristics of the moderator

U nstructured

S ize: eight to twelve participants

G roup composition: homogeneous

R ecorded: audio and video recording

O bservation: one-way mirror

U ndisguised

P hysical setting: relaxed

S everal sessions needed: one to three hours each

The main features of a depth interview may be summarized by the acronym DEPTH:

D epth of coverage

E ach respondent individually interviewed

P robe the respondent

T alented interviewer required

H idden motives may be uncovered

The main characteristics of projective techniques may be described by the acronym PROJECTIVE:

P roject themselves into the situation

R espondents assume the behavior of someone else

O vercome respondents' unwillingness or inability to answer

J udgment required in interpretation of responses

E xpress underlying motivations, beliefs, and attitudes

C onducting projective techniques requires considerable skill

T hemes are elicited

I ndirect (disguised)

V ague situations are used as stimuli

E xploratory in nature

∨ Review Questions

4-1. What are the primary differences between qualitative and quantitative research techniques?

4-2. What is qualitative research and how is it conducted?

4-3. How are qualitative research procedures classified?

4-4. Why is the focus group the most popular qualitative research technique?

4-5. Why is the focus group moderator so important in obtaining quality results?

4-6. How are focus group participants selected?

4-7. Why should one safeguard against professional focus group respondents?

4-8. Give two ways in which focus groups can be misused.

4-9. What would be an integral part of a skillful moderator's process of conducting a depth interview? Why?

4-10. What are the major advantages of depth interviews?

4-11. What are projective techniques? What are the main projective techniques?

4-12. Why do researchers sometimes resort to role plays or third person technique to collect responses instead of one-on-one interviews or direct focus groups?

4-13. When should projective techniques be employed?

4-14. Discuss the use of social media to conduct qualitative research.

∨ Applied Problems

4-15. Following the methods outlined in the text, develop a plan for conducting a focus group to determine consumers' attitudes toward and preferences for imported automobiles. Specify the objectives of the focus group.

4-16. Suppose Baskin-Robbins wants to know why some people do not eat ice cream regularly. Develop a cartoon test for this purpose. How can social media help Baskin-Robbins?

∨ Internet Exercises

4-17. Visit the website **http://www.atlasti.com/**. Explain how their most recent product utilizes netnography and how marketing researchers can benefit from it.

4-18. Visit the website **www.b2binternational.com**. How can business-to-business (B2B) research benefit from online marketing research communities?

4-19. Macy's has asked you to conduct focus groups to research how to increase their online sales to women above 50. Explain how you would conduct these focus groups and why.

4-20. *Tennis* magazine would like to recruit participants for online focus groups. How would you use a newsgroup like **https://groups.google.com/forum/?fromgroups#!forum/rec.sport .tennis** to recruit participants? How would you make use of social media?

NOTES

1. Based on **www.mondelezinternational.com/home/index.aspx**, accessed February 2, 2013.
2. For examples of moderator's outlines used in actual marketing research projects see my other books: Naresh K. Malhotra, *Basic Marketing Research: Integration of Social Media*, fourth edition, Pearson, 2012; and Naresh K. Malhotra, *Marketing Research: An Applied Orientation*, sixth edition, Pearson, 2010.
3. For examples of focus group reports in actual marketing research projects see my other books: Naresh K. Malhotra, Basic Marketing Research: Integration of Social Media, fourth edition, Pearson, 2012; and Naresh K. Malhotra, Marketing Research: An Applied Orientation, sixth edition, Pearson, 2010.
4. **www.universalmusic.com**, accessed March 22, 2013; and "A Look at Dell's Music Bundles," **www.coolfer. com/blog/archives/2008/11/a_look_at_dells.php**, accessed March 22, 2012.
5. Business Source Premier, "Jennifer Lopez & Britney Spears Fragrance Case Studies: Exploiting Star Appeal Through Celebrity Endorsed Fragrances." *Datamonitor*. September 2005, 1–17, **http://search.ebscohost .com/login.aspx?direct=true&db=buh&AN=21120567&site=ehost-live**; and **www.britneyspearsbeauty .com**, accessed May 2, 2013.
6. **www.kraftfoodsgroup.com**, accessed March 24, 2013.
7. **http://proquest.umi.com/pqdweb?index=46&did=1255655821&SrchMode=1&sid=1&Fmt=3&VInst=PR OD&VType=PQD&RQT=309&VName=PQD&TS=1177330747&clientId=30287**, accessed March 24, 2012.
8. **www.womma.org/casestudy/examples/generate-buzz/passenger-and-jcpenney-create**, accessed March 24, 2013.
9. Loek Essers, "Despite Changes, Facebook Still Violates EU Privacy Laws, German Officials Say," (March 23, 2012), **www.pcworld.com/article/252350/despite_changes_facebook_still_violates_eu_privacy_ laws_german_officials_say.html**, accessed March 23, 2012; and Andrea Gibson, "Students don't fear loss of privacy on Facebook Study find," **http://news.research.ohiou.edu/notebook/index.php?item=467**, accessed on June 20, 2009.

Online Video Case 4.1

NIKE: Associating Athletes, Performance, and the Brand

Visit **www.pearsonglobaleditions.com/malhotra** to read the video case and view the accompanying video. Nike: Associating Athletes, Performance, and the Brand highlights Nike's use of marketing research to build its brand into one of the most well-known and easily recognized brands in the world. In terms of qualitative research, the particular use of focus groups is described in the video. The case can be used to discuss the future use of qualitative research in order to strengthen Nike's image. Specific marketing research questions on this and the previous chapters are posed in the video case.

5 Survey and Observation

∨ Overview

In previous chapters, we have explained that once the marketing research problem has been defined (step 1 of the marketing research process) and an appropriate approach developed (step 2), the researcher is in a position to formulate the research design (step 3). As discussed in Chapter 3, the major types of research designs are exploratory and conclusive. Exploratory designs employ secondary data analysis (Chapter 3) and qualitative research (Chapter 4) as the major methodologies. Conclusive research designs may be classified as causal or descriptive. Causal designs will be explained in Chapter 6.

In this chapter, we focus on the major methods employed in descriptive research designs: survey and observation. As was explained in Chapter 3, descriptive research has as its major objective the description of something—usually market characteristics or functions. Survey, or communication, methods may be classified by mode of administration as traditional telephone interviews, computer-assisted telephone interviews, personal in-home interviews, mall-intercept interviews, computer-assisted personal interviews, mail interviews, mail panels, e-mail, and Internet (Web) surveys. We describe each of these methods and present consideration for selecting one or more survey methods in a given project. Next, we consider the major observational methods: personal observation and mechanical observation. The relative advantages and disadvantages of observation over survey methods are discussed. The factors involved in conducting survey and observation research when researching international markets, or conducting the research in social media, are discussed. Several ethical issues that can arise in survey research and observation methods are identified.

Figure 5.1 gives the relationship of this chapter to the marketing research process. To begin our discussion, here are some examples of these methods.

Much of the insights about consumers' future behavior are gained by simply asking consumers about their attitudes and intentions."

> **Surjya Roy, Senior Project Manager, Market Strategies, Inc., Livonia, Michigan**

⌄ Learning Objectives

After reading this chapter, the student should be able to:

1. Discuss and classify survey methods available to marketing researchers, and describe the various telephone, personal, mail, and electronic interviewing methods.

2. Compare the different methods, and evaluate which is best suited for a particular research project.

3. Explain how survey response rates can be improved.

4. Explain and classify the different observation methods used by marketing researchers and describe personal observation and mechanical observation.

5. Describe the relative advantages and disadvantages of observational methods and compare them to survey methods.

6. Discuss the considerations involved in implementing surveys and observation methods in an international setting.

7. Explain how social media can be used to implement survey and observation methods.

8. Understand the ethical issues involved in conducting survey and observation research.

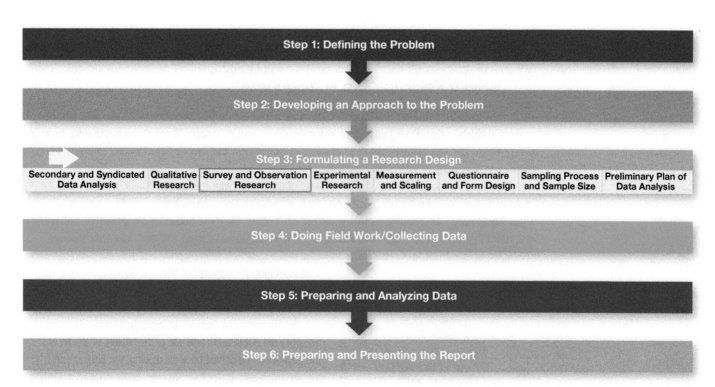

FIGURE 5.1 | RELATIONSHIP OF THIS CHAPTER TO THE MARKETING RESEARCH PROCESS

Research in Practice
Mall-Intercept Surveys: Yum!

As of 2014, Yum! Brands, Inc. (**www.yum.com**), based in Louisville, Kentucky, is the world's largest restaurant company in terms of system restaurants, with more than 38,000 restaurants in over 120 countries and territories. Its restaurant brands—KFC, Pizza Hut, and Taco Bell—are the global leaders of the chicken, pizza, and Mexican-style food categories, respectively.

The company regularly conducts mall-intercept interviews. Survey respondents get to taste new products under development and then express their opinions. As an added incentive, respondents who complete the survey are given gift cards for Yum! restaurants. As a result, Yum! has successfully launched many new products over the years. As an example, after mall-intercept interviews showed an overwhelming preference,

Source: Felicia Martinez Photography / PhotoEdit

KFC introduced Kentucky Grilled Chicken (KGC) nationwide in 2009. Kentucky Grilled Chicken, marinated and seasoned with a savory blend of six secret herbs and spices, is slow roasted for a juicy taste. Survey results further showed that, while many respondents preferred the Kentucky Grilled Chicken for health and taste reasons, they were not willing to pay more for it. Therefore, KGC was sold at the same price as Original Recipe® Chicken. In fact, customers could even mix Kentucky Grilled Chicken and Original Recipe in their bucket and enjoy ten pieces for just $9.99 plus tax. Kentucky Grilled Chicken remains a popular item on the KFC menu as of 2014.[1] ◄

Research in Practice
Heinz Ketchup: "Dip and Squeeze"

About two-thirds of all revenue at fast-food restaurants is from drive-through orders. Heinz observed how people consumed ketchup after picking up their orders at the drive-through window. These observations were made by Heinz researchers, who sat behind one-way mirrors in twenty fake minivan interiors watching consumers putting ketchup on fries, burgers, and chicken nuggets.

They found some people ripped off the corner of the packet with their teeth. Others, while driving, squirted the ketchup directly into their mouth, then added fries. Some forgo fries at the drive-through altogether to keep from creating a mess in the car. After observing these and other compensating behaviors, H. J. Heinz Co. spent three years developing a better ketchup packet named "Dip and Squeeze." Surveys conducted at fifty Chick-fil-A restaurants indicated that customers strongly preferred the new packets,

Source: Kristoffer Tripplaar / Alamy

thus validating the concept of "Dip and Squeeze." Therefore, the new package was introduced in 2011 and is gradually replacing the traditional package introduced in 1968.

As the name promises, "Dip and Squeeze" ketchup can be squeezed out through one end of the packet, or the lid of the packet can be peeled back for dipping. You squeeze on the sandwich and dip for fries. The red, bottle-shaped packets hold three times the ketchup as traditional packets. The new containers are more expensive than the old sleeves, but Heinz hopes customers learn not to grab more than one or two. The new package has been a hit with consumers.[2] ◄

Mall-intercept interviews, as well as other survey methods, are becoming increasingly popular. Observation methods are employed less frequently, but they have important uses in marketing research.

SURVEY METHODS

The **survey method** of obtaining information is based on the questioning of respondents (Figure 5.2). Respondents are asked a variety of questions regarding their behavior, intentions, attitudes, awareness, motivations, and demographic and lifestyle characteristics. These questions may be asked verbally, in writing, or via computer, and the responses may be obtained in any of these forms.

survey method
A structured questionnaire given to a population sample and designed to elicit specific information from respondents.

Typically, the questioning is structured. *Structured* here refers to the degree of standardization imposed on the data collection process. In **structured data collection**, a formal questionnaire is prepared and the questions are asked in a prearranged order. The structured survey is the most popular data collection method. It involves preparing and administering a questionnaire to the respondents (Figure 5.3).

structured data collection
Use of a formal questionnaire that presents questions in a prearranged order.

In a typical questionnaire, most questions are **fixed alternative questions**, which require the respondent to select from a predetermined set of responses. Consider, for example, the following question designed to measure attitude toward Disney theme parks:

fixed-alternative questions
Questions that require respondents to choose from a set of predetermined answers.

	Disagree				Agree
Visiting Disney theme parks is fun.	1	2	3	4	5

The survey method has several advantages. First, the questionnaire is simple to administer. Second, the data obtained are reliable because the responses are limited to the alternatives stated. The use of fixed response questions reduces the variability in the results that may be caused by differences in interviewers. Finally, coding, analysis, and interpretation of data are relatively simple.

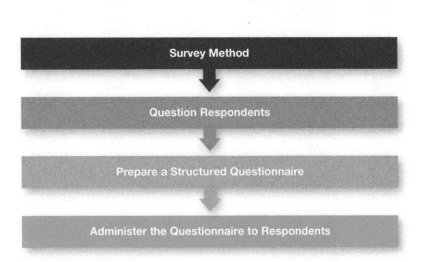

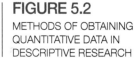

FIGURE 5.2
METHODS OF OBTAINING QUANTITATIVE DATA IN DESCRIPTIVE RESEARCH

FIGURE 5.3
THE SURVEY METHOD

The disadvantages are that respondents may be unable or unwilling to provide the desired information. For example, with questions about motivations to visit theme parks, respondents may not be consciously aware of their motives for choosing a Disney vacation. Therefore, they may be unable to provide accurate answers to questions about their motives. Respondents may be unwilling to respond if the information requested is sensitive or personal. Also, structured questions and fixed response alternatives may result in loss of validity for certain types of data such as beliefs and feelings. Finally, wording questions properly is not easy (see Chapter 8 on questionnaire design). Despite these disadvantages, however, the survey approach is by far the most common method of primary quantitative data collection in marketing research.

R e s e a r c h   R e c i p e

The structured survey involving the administration of a questionnaire is the most popular data collection method. You will find it simple to administer and it results in reliable data. Coding, analysis, and interpretation of data are also simple. It is versatile and you can use it in a variety of situations.

Survey methods can be classified based on the mode used to administer the questionnaire. This classification scheme helps distinguish among survey methods.

SURVEY METHODS CLASSIFIED BY MODE OF ADMINISTRATION

Survey questionnaires may be administered in four major modes: (1) telephone interviews, (2) personal interviews, (3) mail interviews, and (4) electronic (see Figure 5.4). Telephone interviews may be further classified as traditional telephone interviewing or computer-assisted

FIGURE 5.4
CLASSIFICATION OF SURVEY
METHODS

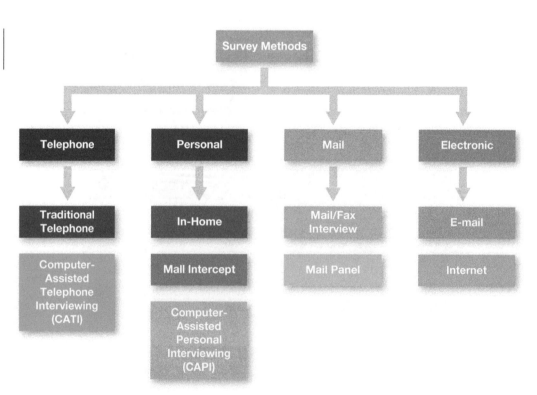

telephone interviewing (CATI). Personal interviews may be conducted in the respondent's home, as mall-intercept interviews, or as computer-assisted personal interviewing (CAPI).

The third major method is the mail interview, which takes the form of an ordinary mail survey or a survey conducted using a mail panel. Finally, electronic interviews can be conducted via e-mail or administered on the Internet. Of these methods, Internet interviews are the most popular survey method in the United States. Mail interviews are the least popular. We now describe each of these methods.

TELEPHONE METHODS

As stated earlier, telephone interviews vary in terms of the degree of computer assistance supporting the interview.

Traditional Telephone Interviews

Traditional telephone interviews involve phoning a sample of respondents and asking them a series of questions. The interviewer uses a paper questionnaire and records the responses with a pencil. Telephone interviews are generally conducted from centrally located research facilities. Telephone research centers are specifically equipped to accommodate large groups of interviewers. These facilities proliferated because of the cost and control advantages they offered. The low cost of telecommunication services has made nationwide telephone interviewing from a central location practical.

Field service supervisors can closely monitor the telephone conversations. This monitoring helps to control interviewer bias that results from variation in the way in which the questions are asked and the responses are recorded. Data quality is enhanced with on-the-spot review of completed questionnaires. Finally, the research budget, both in terms of labor costs and time restrictions, can be managed more easily when the interviewers are assembled in one location.

Computer-Assisted Telephone Interviewing

Computer-assisted telephone interviewing (CATI) uses a computerized questionnaire administered to respondents over the telephone. The interviewer sits in front of a computer screen and wears a headset. The computer screen replaces a paper-and-pencil questionnaire, and the headset substitutes for a telephone. CATI from a central location is now much more popular than the traditional telephone method. More than 90 percent of all telephone interviews in the United States are conducted using a CATI system.

Upon command, the computer dials the telephone number to be called. When contact is made, the interviewer reads the questions posed on the computer screen and records the respondent's answers directly into the computer memory bank. CATI combines the interview with the editing and data-entry steps to produce a highly efficient and accurate survey process. Because the responses are entered directly into the computer, interim and update reports can be compiled instantaneously as the data are collected.

CATI software has built-in logic, which also enhances data accuracy. The program will personalize questions and control for logically incorrect answers, such as percentage answers that do not add up to 100 percent. The software has built-in branching logic, which will skip questions that are not applicable or will probe for more detail when warranted. For example, if a respondent answered yes to the question "Have you ever purchased Nike athletic shoes?" an entire series of questions related to the experience with Nike shoes would follow. If the respondent answered no, however, that line of questioning would be skipped.

Advantages and Disadvantages of Telephone Interviewing

Telephone interviewing, in a computer-assisted format, remains a popular survey method. This popularity can be traced to several factors. Interviews can be completed quickly because the travel time associated with personal interviews is eliminated. **Sample control**, or the ability to reach the units specified in the sample, is good when proper sampling and callback procedures are followed. Control of the field force (interviewers) is good because the interviewers can be supervised from a central location. The control is even better in CATI because these systems allow the supervisor to monitor an interview without the interviewer or the respondent being aware of it. Moreover, the monitoring can be done from a remote location. The **response rate**, the percentage of total attempted interviews that are completed, also is good. And telephone surveys are not very expensive.

However, telephone interviews do have some inherent disadvantages (see Table 5.1). The questioning is restricted to the spoken word and the respondents cannot see the questionnaire. Interviewers cannot use physical stimuli, such as advertisements, visual illustrations or product demonstrations, and they cannot ask complex questions. This limits the applicability of telephone techniques for certain types of research, such as new product or advertising research.

Personal rapport and commitment are difficult to establish due to lack of face-to-face interaction between the interviewer and the respondent. Respondents can easily escape the interview process, either by cutting the interview short or simply hanging up the phone. This results in less tolerance for lengthy interviews over the phone and limits the quantity of data that can be collected.

Computer-assisted telephone interviewing (CATI) uses a computerized questionnaire administered to respondents over the telephone, as shown.
Source: Juice Images / Alamy.

sample control
The ability of the survey mode to reach effectively and efficiently the units specified in the sample.

response rate
The percentage of the total attempted interviews that are completed.

Research in Practice
Verizon: Friends and Family

As of 2014, Verizon Wireless (**www.verizon.com**) operates one of the nation's most reliable and largest wireless voice and data network, serving more than 80 million customers. To boost its subscriber count, Verizon commissioned a telephone survey. The Verizon Wireless survey was conducted by KRC Research (**www.krcresearch.com**) and polled a nationally representative sample of 769 adults age 18 and over who have a wireless phone.

According to the survey's results, a surprising number of customers (78 percent) would most prefer to have family members in their unlimited wireless calling network compared to customers (2 percent) who would include their bosses or coworkers. Forty-four percent out of the 78 percent of the survey respondents who chose to add their family members would most want their spouse or significant other in their unlimited calling network. Based on these findings, Verizon Wireless introduced the Friends and Family calling plan that gives unlimited calling to selected numbers at no additional charge. Friends and Family is available on Nationwide Single Line plans with 900 Anytime Minutes or more, as well as Nationwide Family SharePlans with 1,400 Anytime Minutes or more, at no additional monthly cost. Verizon has seen an increase in its subscriber base following the introduction of the plan.[3] ◀

R e s e a r c h   R e c i p e

CATI combines interviewing with the editing and data-entry steps to produce a highly efficient and accurate survey process. The software has built-in logic for branching and checking logically incorrect answers, and can personalize the questions for each respondent.

Table 5.1 > Relative Advantages of Different Survey Methods

Method	Advantages	Disadvantages
Telephone	Fast High sample control Good control of field force Good response rate Moderate cost	No use of physical stimuli Limited to simple questions Quantity of data is low
In-Home	Complex questions can be asked Good for physical stimuli Very good sample control High quantity of data Very good response rate	Low control of field force High social desirability Potential for interviewer bias Most expensive May take longer
Mall-intercept	Complex questions can be asked Very good for physical stimuli Very good control of environment Very good response rate	High social desirability Potential for interviewer bias Quantity of data is moderate High cost
CAPI	Complex questions can be asked Very good for physical stimuli Very good control of environment Very good response rate Low potential for interviewer bias	High social desirability Quantity of data is moderate High cost
Mail	No field force problems No interviewer bias Moderate/High quantity of data Low social desirability Low cost	Limited to simple questions Low sample control for cold mail No control of environment Low response rate for cold mail Low speed
Mail Panel	No field force problems No interviewer bias Low/moderate cost High quantity of data Good sample control Low social desirability	Limited to simple questions Low/moderate speed No control of environment
Electronic: E-mail	Low cost No interviewer bias High speed Low social desirability Contact hard-to-reach respondents	Moderate quantity of data Low sample control No control of environment Low response rate Security concerns
Electronic: Internet	Visual appeal and interactivity No interviewer bias Low cost Low social desirability Very high speed Personalized, flexible questioning Contact hard-to-reach respondents	Moderate quantity of data Low sample control No control of environment Low response rate

Research Recipe

Computer-assisted telephone interviewing (CATI) is fast and offers good sample control and control of field force. It has good response rate and moderate cost. However, it is limited in terms of use of physical stimuli, type of questions and quantity of data.

PERSONAL METHODS

Personal interviewing methods can be categorized as in-home, mall-intercept, or computer-assisted personal interviews.

Personal In-Home Interviews

In personal in-home interviews, respondents are interviewed face to face in their homes. The interviewer's task is to contact the respondents, ask the questions, and record the responses. Paper questionnaires were originally used, but they are being replaced by handheld computers. In recent years, the use of personal in-home interviews has declined.

Advantages and Disadvantages of In-Home Interviewing

In-home interviewing offers many advantages. It enables the interviewer to provide clarifications to the respondent due to face-to-face contact, thus allowing for complex questions. It permits the use of physical stimuli, such as visual aids, charts, and maps, and it allows the interviewer to display or demonstrate the product. It provides very good sample control, too, because homes can be selected without generating a list of all the homes in a given area. The homes can be selected by instructing the interviewer to start at a given location, travel in a certain direction, and select every nth (e.g., every eighth) home. A large quantity of data can be collected because the respondents are interviewed in their own homes, and they are more willing to participate for a longer period of time. The response rate is very good, particularly if respondents have been notified about the interview in advance.

In-home interviewing has lost favor due to social, labor, control, and cost factors. Changes in the family, particularly related to the dominance of two-income earners, leaves few people at home during the day. Interviewer supervision and control is difficult because the interviewers are traveling door to door. Consequently, problems with the questionnaire or with the style of the interviewer become more difficult to detect and correct. **Social desirability**, the tendency of respondents to give answers that are socially desirable but incorrect, is high when there is face-to-face contact between the interviewer and the respondent. This factor also leads to a high potential for **interviewer bias**. Interviewers can influence the answers by facial expression, intonation, or simply the way they ask the questions. This method also is the most expensive. Nevertheless, the method is still being used by syndicated firms (see Chapter 3) that need to collect a large amount of information. An example is provided by the Futures Company (**www.thefuturescompany.com**), which conducts personal in-home surveys to gather data on lifestyles and social trends.

social desirability
The tendency of respondents to give answers that might not be accurate but that might be desirable from a social standpoint.

interviewer bias
The error due to the interviewer not following the correct interviewing procedures.

Research Recipe

In-home interviewing has lost favor due to control and cost factors, but it is still being used by syndicated firms. It enables the interviewer to show stimuli and provide clarifications to the respondent, thus allowing for complex questions in the questionnaire. You can collect a large quantity of data because the respondents are interviewed in their own homes.

Despite their many applications, the use of personal in-home interviews is declining, while mall intercepts are becoming more frequent.

Mall-Intercept Personal Interviews

In mall-intercept personal interviews, respondents are approached and interviewed in shopping malls. The process involves stopping the shoppers, screening them for appropriateness, and either administering the survey on the spot or inviting them to a research facility located in the mall to complete the interview. For example, in a survey for a cellular phone manufacturer, a shopper is intercepted and asked about his or her age, education, and income. If these characteristics match the client's target population, the individual is then questioned on product usage. Some usage of cellular phones is a prerequisite for inclusion in the sample. Only those who have experience with cellular phones are invited to a test facility located in the mall to evaluate several new prototype designs under consideration.

Although the sample is composed only of individuals who shop in that retail mall, this is not a serious limitation in most cases. Although not representative of the population in general, shopping mall customers do constitute a major share of the market for many products.

Advantages and Disadvantages of Mall Intercepts

A major advantage of mall-intercept interviews is that it is more efficient for the respondent to come to the interviewer than for the interviewer to go to the respondent. The popularity of this method is evidenced by the several hundred permanent mall-research facilities located across the United States. Complex questions can be asked because of the face-to-face contact. Mall intercepts are especially appropriate when the respondents need to see, handle, or consume the product before they can provide meaningful information. The respondents can conveniently interact with the product in a central facility located in the mall. This was illustrated in the first Research in Practice in this chapter, when KFC used this technique to determine consumers' responses to Kentucky Grilled Chicken (KGC) prior to introduction.

In mall-intercept personal interviews, respondents are approached and interviewed in shopping malls, as shown.
Source: Dennis MacDonald / Alamy

Mall-intercept interviewing was chosen because it allowed the respondents to taste KGC in a test area in the mall before they responded to the survey. The researcher has very good control of the environment in which the data are being collected, and the response rate is high.

The main disadvantages are the potential for social desirability and interviewer bias due to face-to-face contact between the interviewer and the respondent. The quantity of data that can be collected is only moderate because people are generally in a hurry while shopping. The cost of mall-intercept interviewing is high.

Research Recipe

Mall intercepts are especially appropriate when the respondents need to see, handle, or consume the product before they can provide meaningful information. Although the sample is composed only of individuals who shop in that retail mall, this is not a serious limitation in most cases.

Computer–Assisted Personal Interviewing

In computer-assisted personal interviewing (CAPI), the third form of personal interviewing, the respondent sits in front of a computer terminal and answers a questionnaire on the screen. Several user-friendly electronic packages can aid in designing easy and understandable questions. Help screens and courteous error messages are also provided. The colorful screens and on- and off-screen stimuli contribute to the respondent's interest and involvement in the task. This method has

In computer-assisted personal interviewing (CAPI), the respondent is positioned in front of a computer and answers a questionnaire on the screen, as shown.

Source: Dennis MacDonald / Alamy

been classified as a personal-interview technique because an interviewer is usually present to serve as host and to guide the respondent as needed.

This approach is used in shopping malls, preceded by the intercept and screening process described earlier. It is also used to conduct business-to-business research at trade shows or conventions. For example, UPS could measure its image and test the effectiveness of its UPS Business Solutions by administering a CAPI survey at the expedited package delivery trade show. The process of interacting with the computer is simplified to minimize respondent effort and stress; touch-screen technology is often employed. Thus, the use of open-ended questions that require typing is minimized.

Advantages and Disadvantages of CAPI

CAPI seems to hold respondent interest and has several advantages. Complex questions can be asked, and the computer automatically performs skip patterns and conducts logic checks. Interviewer bias is reduced because the computer administers the interview. Like mall intercepts, CAPI can be useful when the survey requires the use of physical stimuli. It also offers excellent control of the data collection environment and results in a high response rate.

Its main disadvantages, which are shared with mall-intercept interviews, are the effects of high social desirability, moderate quantity of data, and high cost.

Research in Practice
CAPI with a Gentle Touch

TouchScreen Solutions (**www.touchscreensolutions.com.au**), operating under the TouchScreen Research trading name, is Australia's leading provider of CAPI services using touch-screen technology. Touch-screen data collection is used for two primary applications:

1. Short-term surveys, where specific target markets physically come together, such as at exhibitions, trade shows, medical conferences, shopping centers, and public gatherings.

2. Long-term surveys, where the target market comes to the client's premises, such as at banks, airport lounges, and hotels.

Touch screens can be placed on counters and points of sale or in waiting rooms, and they are useful for collecting surveys quickly and easily as sales transactions are processed or while customers wait for service.

TouchScreen Research has helped several clients do CAPI-based survey research. Clients come from industries that range from banking (e.g., ANZ Bank) to pharmaceuticals (e.g., GlaxoSmithKline).[4] ◄

Research Recipe

You can use CAPI in shopping malls, trade shows, and other central locations. It is similar to mall intercepts and shares many of its advantages and disadvantages. The main difference is that in CAPI, the questionnaire is administered to the respondent by the computer, rather than by the interviewer as in mall intercepts.

ESPN: All Sports?

Visit **www.espn.com** and search the Internet, including social media as well as your library's online databases, to obtain information on consumers' perceptions of ESPN. What are the advantages and disadvantages of personal interviews in conducting a survey to obtain information on consumers' perceptions of ESPN? Which, if any, method of personal interviewing would you recommend for administering the survey?

As the marketing manager for ESPN, how would you use information on consumers' perceptions of ESPN to formulate marketing strategies that would increase your audience? **<**

MAIL METHODS

Mail interviews, the third major form of survey administration, can be conducted with independently compiled mailing lists or by using a mail panel.

Mail Interviews

The traditional mail interview is a mail survey that is sent to individuals who meet a specified demographic profile but who have not been contacted beforehand to participate in the survey. Because respondents have not been contacted beforehand, it is called a cold survey. A typical mail interview package consists of the outgoing envelope, cover letter, questionnaire, postage-paid return envelope, and possibly an incentive. Those individuals motivated to do so complete and return the questionnaire through the mail. There is no verbal interaction between the researcher and the respondent. Individuals are selected for cold surveys through mailing lists that the client maintains internally or has purchased commercially. Commercial mailing lists typically contain some demographic and psychographic information that assists in the targeting process. Regardless of its source, a mailing list should be current and closely related to the population of interest.

The time involved and the response rate can be improved by faxing the questionnaire instead of mailing it. In **fax surveys**, the questionnaire is transmitted by a fax machine to respondents. The respondents can then return the completed questionnaire by faxing it to a designated (toll-free) number or, sometimes, by mail. Fax surveys share many characteristics with mail surveys; however, they can provide faster, and often higher, response rates. Because many households do not have fax machines, this method is not suitable for household surveys. It can be used in a variety of surveys with commercial and other institutional respondents, however.

fax survey
A survey in which the questionnaire is transmitted by fax machine to respondents. The respondents can then return the completed questionnaire by faxing it to a designated (toll-free) number or, sometimes, by mail.

Mail Panels

In contrast to cold mail interviews, **mail panels** consist of a large and nationally representative sample of individuals who have agreed to participate in periodic survey research (see Chapter 3). Incentives in the form of cash or gifts are often offered to the individuals who agree to participate. Once the individuals have been admitted to the panel, detailed demographic and lifestyle data are collected on each household. The researcher uses this information to select targeted mailing lists within the panel based on client needs. TNS (**www.tns-global.com**) is an example of a marketing research organization that maintains mail panels. Mail panels can be used to reach general as well as targeted samples.

mail panels
A large and nationally representative sample of households that have agreed to participate periodically in mail questionnaires, product tests, and survey research.

Advantages and Disadvantages of Mail Surveys

Mail surveys are an economical and efficient way to reach consumers. Cold mail surveys are low cost, and the cost of mail panels is only moderately higher. The problems of interviewer bias and the expense of field staff management are eliminated. Social desirability is low because there is no personal contact with the respondent during data collection. A moderate amount of data can be collected through cold mail surveys, whereas mail panels permit the collection of large quantities of data.

These clear advantages are offset, however, by problems regarding lack of control over the interviewing process. Unlike telephone and personal interviewing, there is no personal contact, and the respondent might feel less compelled to either participate or candidly complete the questionnaire. This problem is particularly acute with cold mail interviews. With cold mail interviews, the researcher has little control over who answers the questionnaire, how they answer it, and how quickly they return it. This results in low sample control, low response speed, and no control over the data collection environment. Thus, it is difficult to assess the quality and validity of the data.

nonresponse bias
Bias that arises when actual respondents differ from those who refuse to participate in ways that affect the survey results.

Finally, response rates to cold mail surveys are low, and nonresponse introduces a serious bias in the data. Those individuals who choose not to participate in mail interviews might have very different demographic and psychographic profiles than responders, resulting in **nonresponse bias**. Individuals with higher income and educational levels, or individuals inexperienced or uninterested in the research topic, all tend to have lower response rates. Mail panels are successful in boosting response rates, and the problem of nonresponse bias is also reduced.

Despite its shortcomings, the relative ease and low cost of mail interviews continue to make this a viable research option. Mail panels can be used to obtain information from the same respondents repeatedly. Thus, they can be used to implement a longitudinal design (Chapter 3).

Research in Practice
Mail Targets Female

Seventeen magazine (**www.seventeen.com**) conducted a study to determine the shopping habits of its readers. Questionnaires were mailed to 2,000 members of *Seventeen*'s Consumer Panel, representing a cross-section of the 13- to 21-year-old female market. Of these, 1,315 were returned, for a completion rate of 65.8 percent. The results were balanced by age and geographic area with census data so that they reflect all females age 13 to 21 in the United States. Some of the major findings were:

- Nine out of ten shopped at a large mall.
- Almost two-thirds shopped in a small shopping center.
- Over half shopped at a single standing store.

The magazine used these results to target advertisers and obtain higher advertising revenues. Several marketers, such as clothing, cosmetics, and personal-care brands, target females in this age group. *Seventeen* magazine uses its mail panel to conduct periodic surveys. This helps it to stay in touch with its target market and keep abreast of changes. As a result, *Seventeen* is the number one magazine in the female teenage market as of 2014.[5] <

Research Recipe

Cold mail surveys are inexpensive, but the response rate is low. The nonresponse can introduce a serious bias because the characteristics of those who respond may differ from the characteristics of those who do not respond. Mail panels cost more but have much higher response rates that mitigate the possibility of nonresponse bias.

iResearch
Outback: Backing Decisions with Survey Research

As the marketing manager for Outback, how would you use information on consumers' preferences for casual restaurants to formulate marketing strategies that would increase your sales and market share?

Visit **www.outback.com** and search the Internet, including social media as well as your library's online databases, to obtain information on consumers' preferences for casual restaurants. What are the advantages and disadvantages of using mail, mail panel, or fax in conducting a survey to obtain information on consumers' preferences for casual restaurants? Which, if any, of these methods would you recommend for conducting a survey for Outback? ‹

ELECTRONIC METHODS

Electronic surveys can be conducted via electronic mail (e-mail), if the respondents' addresses are known, or by posting the survey to a website.

E-mail Surveys

E-mail surveys are questionnaires distributed through electronic mail. If the addresses are known, the survey can simply be mailed electronically to respondents included in the sample. E-mail usage in the United States is very high, particularly in business firms where almost everyone has access to e-mail. Using batch-type e-mail, researchers send e-mail surveys to potential respondents who use e-mail. Respondents key in their answers and send an e-mail reply. Typically, a computer program is used to prepare the questionnaire and the e-mail address list and to prepare the data for analysis. Note that comments as well as numeric or multiple-choice responses can be collected. Respondent anonymity is difficult to maintain, however, because a reply to an e-mail message includes the sender's address. For the same reason, security and privacy issues can also be a concern.

E-mail surveys are especially suited to projects for which the e-mail lists are readily available, such as surveys of employees, institutional buyers, and consumers who frequently contact the organization via e-mail (e.g., frequent fliers of an airline). E-mail letters can also be used to ask respondents to participate in an Internet survey and provide them with a link and password to the website where the survey is posted.

Internet Surveys

An Internet survey is a questionnaire posted on a website that is self-administered by the respondent. The questions are displayed on the screen, and the respondents provide answers by clicking an icon, keying an answer, or highlighting a phrase. Web survey systems are available for constructing and posting Internet surveys. At any time, the researcher can obtain survey completion statistics, descriptive statistics of the responses, and graphical display of the data. Compared to e-mail surveys, Internet surveys offer more flexibility, greater interactivity, personalization, automatic skip patterns, and visual appeal. Several websites, including SurveyMonkey (**www.surveymonkey .com**) and Zoomerang (**www.zoomerang.com**), allow users to design surveys online without downloading the software. The survey is administered on the design site's server. Some sites offer data tabulation services as well. Qualtrics (**www.qualtrics.com**) software is another popular package for designing electronic surveys.

Internet panels are gaining in popularity and can be an efficient source of obtaining Internet samples (as discussed in more detail in Chapter 9). In fact, many marketing research suppliers and syndicated firms have replaced their traditional mail panels with Internet panels. Internet panels take less time and cost less to build and maintain compared to mail panels. Several companies offer Internet panels that can be used by other researchers—for a fee—to draw Internet samples. Such firms include Harris Interactive (**www.harrisinteractive.com**), Survey Sampling International (**www.surveysampling.com**), and Toluna (**us.toluna.com**). The advantages and disadvantages of electronic surveys relative to other survey methods are discussed in more detail in the next section.

Advantages and Disadvantages of Electronic Methods

Both e-mail and Internet methods survey thousands of potential respondents simultaneously and quickly. Of the two, Internet surveys can be conducted more quickly; the data collected can be analyzed speedily, almost in real time, making it the most popular method in the United States. The incremental cost of reaching additional respondents is marginal; thus, much larger samples can be accommodated compared to the other methods.

Both methods are cost effective. The cost savings compared to other survey methods can be dramatic for large samples. Both methods are good for contacting hard-to-reach respondents because the survey can be answered at a time and place convenient to each respondent. Thus, high-income professionals, such as doctors, lawyers, and CEOs, can be reached. These groups are well represented online.

Internet surveys, and to some extent e-mail surveys, can be personalized easily. In addition to personalizing the name, the questions themselves can be personalized based on the respondent's answers to the previous questions, for example, "If your favorite brand of toothpaste, Crest, were not available, which brand would you buy?" Internet surveys can be programmed to perform skip patterns automatically (for example, "If the answer to Question 3 is no, go to Question 9"). Internet surveys are interactive and can utilize color, sound, graphics, and animation, much like computer-assisted personal interviewing.

Callbacks are easier to make in e-mail surveys and Internet surveys that draw respondents from a panel. The computer software can automatically send e-mail reminders to respondents who have not answered the survey. The electronic method shares many of the advantages of the mail method, including the absence of field force problems and interviewer bias. They also have low social desirability.

Both methods have some disadvantages as well. Both suffer from respondent selection bias in that only people with access to e-mail or the Internet can be included in the sample. This bias is further accentuated by the fact that heavy users of these media have a higher probability of being included in the sample. These individuals might differ from the target population in ways that might bias the results. Another potential problem is that if no controls are imposed, the same respondent can answer again and again. In addition, some Internet users might consider e-mail surveys to be a form of spam.

The electronic methods also share many of the disadvantages of mail surveys. Only simple questions can be asked, sample control is low, the data collection environment cannot be controlled, and response rates are low. Only moderate quantities of data can be obtained. In spite of these disadvantages, the Internet holds tremendous promise that is increasing with the increased penetration of the Internet in homes.

Research in Practice
Internet Survey Illuminates the Lumia 800

Nokia (**www.nokia.com**) is constantly conducting research to monitor the changing lifestyles of consumers and to design its cell phones accordingly. The company commissioned M/A/R/C Research (**www.marcresearch.com**) to conduct an Internet survey of 500 adults in the United States between the ages of 18 and 54, who are employed either full-time or part-time. The survey found that people actually spill work into bathroom time; 53 percent of working Americans are interrupted by phone calls or e-mails that are work-related when they are in the bathroom. The survey also showed that people also experienced office-related intrusions in other areas of their lives: 24 percent allowed a call or e-mail to interrupt them while in the throes of passion, and 23 percent allowed a call or e-mail to interrupt them on a date. All these interruptions happen because 59 percent of the working population of America never turns off their cell phones. Another interesting finding was that 75 percent of working Americans agree that technology plays a primary role in helping them balance their work and home life. Based on these findings, Nokia started developing new cell phone models that could be used for both work and fun and marketed them with the slogan "Life in Balance." In late 2011, Nokia introduced the Nokia Lumia 800, which featured a head-turning design and superior social and Internet performance, with one-touch social network access, easy grouping of contacts, integrated communication threads, and Internet Explorer 9. The Nokia Lumia 800 was available in white beginning in February 2012. The Lumia 800 has been a success because it met a need in the marketplace. As of 2013, several different Lumia phones were available.[6] <

Research Recipe

You can conduct Internet surveys quickly and cost effectively; you can analyze the data collected speedily, almost in real time. The incremental cost of reaching additional respondents is marginal; thus, much larger samples can be accommodated compared to the other methods. However, the electronic methods (e-mail and Internet) share many of the disadvantages of mail surveys.

SOME OTHER SURVEY METHODS

Researchers have developed several variations based on the basic survey methods just described. The more popular of these other methods are presented in Table 5.2.

Table 5.2 > Some Other Survey Methods

Method	Advantages/Disadvantages	Comment
Completely automated telephone surveys (CATS)	Shares the advantages and disadvantages of CATI	Can be useful for short, in-bound surveys initiated by the respondent
Wireless phone interview (voice-based format)	Shares the advantages and disadvantages of CATS	Can be useful for point-of-purchase survey if respondent cooperation is obtained
Wireless phone interview (text-based format)	Shares the advantages and disadvantages of e-mail Interview but should be much shorter	Can be useful for point-of-purchase survey if respondent cooperation is obtained
In-office interview	Shares the advantages and disadvantages of in-home interview	Useful for interviewing busy managers
Central location interview	Shares the advantages and disadvantages of mail intercepts	Examples include trade shows, conferences, exhibitions, purchase intercept
Kiosk-based computer interviewing	Shares the advantages and disadvantages of CAPI	Visit **www.touchscreenresearch .com.au** for more information
Fax interview	Shares the advantages and disadvantages of mail survey except it is faster with higher response rate	Useful in some business surveys
Drop-off survey	Shares the advantages and disadvantages of mail surveys with higher costs and higher response rates	Can be useful for local market surveys

> ## Research Recipe
>
> Wireless phone interview (both voice-based and text-based formats) are useful for point-of-purchase surveys if respondent cooperation is obtained. You can do these surveys by making use of panels.

iResearch
Internet Surveys

The following websites demonstrate Internet surveys for respondents as well as researchers.

1. To experience what an Internet survey is like, go to Web Online Surveys at **www.web-online-surveys.com**. Select "Sample," and take the short "Website Survey."

2. To examine Internet surveys for a variety of applications, go to **www.createsurvey.com** and click on Demo.

3. To get a feel for building your own electronic survey, access the Qualtrics (**www.qualtrics.com**) software and go through the "Online Training Programs" or click "Request Demo." ❮

Remember, however, that not all survey methods are appropriate in a given situation. Therefore, the researcher should conduct a comparative evaluation to determine which methods are appropriate.

CRITERIA FOR SELECTING A SURVEY METHOD

When evaluating the various survey methods within the context of a specific research project, you have to consider the salient factors relevant to data collection. Often, certain factors dominate, leading to a particular survey method as the natural choice. For example, if a new perishable food product has to be tested, respondents would have to taste the product before answering the questionnaire. This would involve interviewing at central locations, leading to mall intercept or CAPI as a natural choice. If no method is clearly superior, the choice must be based on an overall consideration of the advantages and disadvantages of the various methods. We offer the following guidelines:

1. If complex and diverse questions have to be asked, one of the personal methods (in-home, mall intercept, or CAPI) is preferable. Internet surveys are an option, too, but the other self-administered methods (mail, mail panels, and e-mail) might not be appropriate because it is not possible to clarify respondent questions in an interactive manner. Telephone surveys are limited because the respondent cannot see the questionnaire and the interviewer–respondent contact is not face to face.

2. From the perspective of the use of physical stimuli, personal methods (in-home, mall intercept, and CAPI) are preferable.

3. If sample control is an issue, cold mail (but not mail panel), fax, and electronic methods are at a disadvantage.

4. Control of the data collection environment favors the use of central location (mall intercept and CAPI) interviewing.

5. The need for a high quantity of data favors the use of in-home surveys and mail panels, and makes the use of telephone interviewing inappropriate.

6. A low response rate is a disadvantage of the cold mail and electronic methods.

7. If social desirability is an issue, mail, mail-panel, fax, and Internet surveys are best.

8. If interviewer bias is an issue, the use of mail (cold and panel), fax, and electronic interviewing (e-mail and Internet) is favored.

9. Speed favors Internet, e-mail, telephone, and fax methods.

10. When cost is a factor, consider the following, from least costly to most costly: cold mail, fax, electronic (e-mail and Internet), mail panel, telephone, mall intercept, CAPI, and in-home methods.

Often, these methods are combined to enhance the quality of the data in a cost-effective manner. This is likely when the research project is large in scope, as in the case of Oscar Mayer in the Research in Practice. Caution should be exercised, however, when using different methods in the same domestic marketing research project, which is referred to as using mixed-mode surveys. The method used can affect the responses obtained, and hence responses obtained by different methods might not be comparable. The results of studies examining the effect of survey methods on respondents are not very consistent. The Oscar Mayer example illustrates the selection of survey modes.

Research in Practice
New Product Development at Oscar Mayer Uses Old but Proven Methods

New product development at Oscar Mayer, a brand of Kraft (**www.kraftbrands.com/oscarmayer**), starts by using prior research and external secondary data to form questions such as these:

Who is your target buyer(s)?
What product are they currently using?
What is their big problem with it?
How will you solve this problem?

Once these questions are considered, a prototype of the new product idea is formed and tested in focus groups. The feedback from these groups allows the inventors to make adjustments to their products and in essence fine-tune the idea. Next, quantitative testing is used in the form of questionnaires mailed to households. Mail survey is used because it enables Oscar Mayer to collect the required quantity of data at a very low cost and eliminates the potential for interviewer bias. The major drawback of low response rates is overcome by offering suitable incentives. Once information is received from these consumers, the data are compared to the normative database of prior research for evaluation. Once evaluated, the information is used to create options for the product in areas such as composition, packaging, size, or shape. These various designs are tested at the marketing research facility by bringing in approximately 200 target market consumers to give their opinions and rate the product variations. Central location interviewing at the marketing research facility is chosen because the "use of physical stimuli" criterion dominates, and it is necessary for the respondents to see, handle, and even taste the product. The information obtained at this stage is used to help choose among the possible product configurations. This combination of survey methods has helped Oscar Mayer introduce successful new products, such as Deli Creations, which contain everything you need to create delicious, hot, and "melty" sandwiches in a microwave minute. In 2013, Oscar Mayer successfully introduced Selects Chicken Breast Franks made with high quality cuts of chicken breast and no artificial preservatives. Thanks to survey research![7] ◄

R e s e a r c h   R e c i p e

If complex and diverse questions have to be asked or physical stimuli have to be used, and high response rates are desired, use one of the personal methods (in-home, mall intercept, or CAPI). Speed favors Internet, e-mail, telephone, and fax methods. When cost is a factor, consider the following, from least costly to most costly: cold mail, fax, electronic (e-mail and Internet), mail panel, telephone, mall intercept, CAPI, and in-home methods.

IMPROVING SURVEY RESPONSE RATES

Regardless of the survey method chosen, researchers should attempt to improve response rates. This can be done through prior notification, incentives, follow-up, and other methods such as personalization (Figure 5.5).

Prior Notification

Prior notification consists of sending a letter or e-mail or making a telephone call to potential respondents to notify them of the imminent arrival of a mail, telephone, personal, or electronic survey. Prior notification increases response rates for samples of the general public because it reduces surprise and uncertainty and creates a more cooperative atmosphere.

Incentives

prepaid incentive
Coupons, money, or some other incentive to participate that is included with the survey or questionnaire.

promised incentive
Coupons, money, or some other incentive to participate that is sent only to those respondents who complete the survey by the specified deadline.

Offering monetary as well as nonmonetary incentives to potential respondents can increase response rates. Monetary incentives can be prepaid or promised. A **prepaid incentive** is included with the survey or questionnaire; thus all potential respondents get it whether they respond or not. A **promised incentive** is sent only to those respondents who complete the survey by the specified deadline. The most commonly used nonmonetary incentives are premiums and rewards, such as pens, pencils, books, and offers of survey results. In the first Research in Practice feature, Yum! Brands used promised incentives to increase respondent co-operation and response rates. Gifts cards for Yum! restaurants are given to all respondents who complete the survey.

Prepaid incentives have been shown to increase response rates to a greater extent than promised incentives. The amount of incentive can vary from $0.25 to $50.00 or more, with a dollar being the most common in consumer surveys. The amount of the incentive has a positive relationship with response rate, but the cost of large monetary incentives might outweigh the value of the additional information obtained.

FIGURE 5.5 |
IMPROVING RESPONSE
RATES

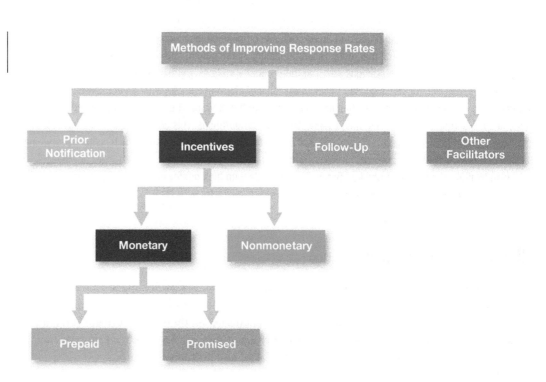

> **Research Recipe**
>
> Prepaid incentives increase response rates to a greater extent than promised incentives, with a dollar being the most common in consumer surveys. Hence, use this form of incentive.

Follow-Up

Follow-up, or contacting nonrespondents periodically after the initial contact, is particularly effective in decreasing refusals in mail surveys. The researcher might send a postcard or letter to remind nonrespondents to complete and return the questionnaire. Two or three mailings might be needed in addition to the original one. With proper follow-up, the response rate in mail surveys can be increased to 80 percent or more. Follow-up can also be done by telephone, e-mail, or personal contact.

> **Research Recipe**
>
> Follow-up, or contacting nonrespondents periodically after the initial contact, is particularly effective in decreasing refusals in mail surveys. You can do follow-up by mail, telephone, e-mail, or personal contact.

Other Facilitators of Response

Some other methods, such as personalization or sending letters addressed to specific individuals, can also be effective in increasing response rates.

> **Research Recipe**
>
> You should use multiple methods to improve survey response rates. For example, prior notification, incentives and follow-up can all be used in a survey.

OBSERVATION METHODS

Observation methods are the second type of methodology used in descriptive research (Chapter 3). **Observation** involves recording the behavioral patterns of people as well as data on objects and events in a systematic manner to obtain information about the phenomenon of interest. The observer does not question or communicate with the people being observed. Information can be recorded as the events occur or from records of past events. The major observation methods are personal observation and mechanical observation.

observation
The recording of people's behavioral patterns and of objects and events in a systematic manner to obtain information about the phenomenon of interest.

> **Research Recipe**
>
> In observation you record the data of interest without questioning or communicating. The major observation methods are personal observation and mechanical observation.

Personal Observation

In **personal observation**, a trained observer collects the data by recording behavior exactly as it occurs. (A Research in Practice feature earlier in this chapter showed how Heinz used personal observation to introduce "Dip and Squeeze" ketchup packets.) The observer does not

personal observation
An observational research method in which human observers record the phenomenon being observed as it occurs.

humanistic inquiry
A special form of personal observation in which the researcher is immersed in the system under study.

attempt to control or manipulate the phenomenon being observed but simply records what takes place. For example, a researcher might record traffic counts and observe traffic flows in a department store. This information could aid in determining store layout, the location of individual departments, shelf locations, and merchandise displays. **Humanistic inquiry** is a special form of personal observation in which the researcher is immersed in the system under study. This is in contrast to the traditional scientific method, in which the researcher is a dispassionate observer. In yet another application, called on-site observation, observers are positioned in supermarkets and presented as shoppers who need advice from another shopper in making purchase decisions.

The main advantage of personal observation is that it is highly flexible because the observer can record a wide variety of phenomena (Table 5.3). It is also highly suitable for use in natural settings. For example, the sales manager of General Motors can observe the attitudes of dealers toward a new inventory policy at one of the regular sales meetings.

The main disadvantage is that the method is unstructured: An observation form is generally not used for recording the behavior as it occurs. Rather, the observer records the phenomenon after completing the observation in a free, unstructured format. This leads to high observation bias and recording bias. Also the data and their interpretation are highly subjective, leading to high analysis bias, i.e., bias in data analysis and interpretation.

Research in Practice
Where Does North America Shop?

In shopping mall research, license plate studies are used to establish the primary trading area of a shopping mall. These studies help marketers determine where their customers live. Observers record the license plate numbers of the automobiles in a parking lot. These numbers are fed into a computer and paired with automobile registration data. This results in a map of customers located by census tract or Zip code. Such a map, along with other demographic data, can help a shopping mall determine new locations, decide on billboard space, and target direct marketing effort. License plate studies cost less ($5,000 to $25,000) and are believed to be quicker and more reliable than direct communication methods such as interviews with shoppers.

Mall of America (also known as the Megamall) is a super-regional shopping mall located in the Twin Cities suburb of Bloomington, Minnesota. The mall receives 40 million visitors a year. A license plate analysis showed that these visitors come not only from Minnesota but from several different parts of the United States and Canada. This led to the positioning of Mall of America as a place where North America shops.[8] ◄

Research Recipe

Personal observation is a highly flexible method and you can use it in natural settings. However, it is characterized by high observation bias, recording bias, and analysis bias.

Table 5.3 ❯ Relative Advantages of Observation Methods

Method	Advantages	Disadvantages
Personal observation	Most flexible Highly suitable in natural settings	High observation bias High analysis bias
Mechanical observation	Low observation bias Low to medium analysis bias	Can be intrusive Not always suitable in natural settings

Mechanical Observation

Mechanical observation, as one would expect, involves the use of a mechanical device to record behavior. These devices might or might not require respondents' direct participation. Such devices are particularly useful for recording continuous behavior, such as traffic flow in a grocery store. Nielsen's (**www.nielsen.com**) peoplemeter is an example of indirect observational devices that do not require active participation on the part of the respondents. Respondents do not need to change their behavior in any way to be involved in this type of observational study. The peoplemeter is attached to a television and continually records not only the channels the television is tuned to, but also who is watching. Arbitron (**www.arbitron.com**) has developed the portable peoplemeter, a wearable device that measures what television and radio programming a person watches or listens to during her or his waking hours. The PreTesting Group (**www.pretesting.com**) uses the People Reader, which unobtrusively records reading material and reader's eye movements to determine the reader's habits as well as the stopping power and the brand recall associated with different sizes of ads.

Other common examples of indirect mechanical observation include turnstiles that record the number of people entering or leaving a building and traffic counters placed across streets to determine the number of vehicles passing certain locations. On-site cameras (still or video) are increasingly used by retailers to assess the impact of package designs, counter space, floor displays, and traffic-flow patterns. The Universal Product Code (UPC) is a built-in source for mechanical observation. For those retailers equipped with optical scanners, the UPC system allows for the automatic collection of consumer purchase information, classifying it by product category, brand, store type, price, and quantity (see scanner data in Chapter 3).

The Internet can be a very good source for observation and can provide valuable information. The observations can be made in a variety of ways. The primary observations can be made by the number of times a webpage is visited. The time spent on the page can also be measured through more advanced techniques, such as a timer that starts when a person visits a page and clicks on a certain icon. The timer then stops when the person clicks the next icon. Various other links can be provided by the researcher on the webpage, and the research can observe which links are accessed more often. This will provide the researcher with important data on the information needs of the individuals and also the interests of the target segment.

mechanical observation
An observational research method in which mechanical devices, rather than human observers, record the phenomenon being observed.

Research in Practice
Be Careful What You Watch. Nielsen Is Watching You!

The Nielsen Company integrates audience measurement across TVs, PCs, and mobile phones to help clients create precise cross-platform plans. Mechanical observation using electronic-metering technology is at the heart of the Nielsen ratings process. The company has recruited a panel of TV families representative of homes throughout the United States. Their viewing is measured by TV meters and local peoplemeters, which capture information on what's being viewed and when. For example, the peoplemeter is attached to the televisions of panel households. The peoplemeter mechanically and continuously monitors television-viewing behavior, including when the set is turned on, and what channels are viewed and for how long. These data are stored in the peoplemeter and transmitted to a central computer. Nielsen also collects more than 2 million paper diaries from across the country in which similar information is recorded.

Using this information, the company produces the Nielsen Ratings, which are coupled with detailed analysis of consumer viewing behavior and demographic information. Which members of a household are watching which shows? Which family characteristics, such as pet ownership, income, and education, correlate with viewing choices? (See the section on media panels in Chapter 3.) Information of this kind enables clients such as P&G, Coca-Cola, and other advertisers to refine their campaigns based on demographics, time of day, and audience composition.[9] ◄

Many mechanical observation devices require the direct involvement of the participants. Physical responses to sights, sounds, smells, or any sensory stimuli are an important area of observational research. Advertising or other promotional changes, such as special sales, can elicit a physical response in consumers that cannot be observed by merely looking at them. Specialized equipment designed to monitor heart and breathing rates, skin temperature, and other physiological changes is used in these situations. Because these measurements cost more than verbal reports of the respondent's reaction, they are used only when it is assumed that the respondent cannot, or will not, respond accurately to questioning. All of the physiological measurement devices operate on the assumption that the cognitive and emotional responses to stimuli elicit predictable differences in physical response. This assumption has not yet been clearly demonstrated, however.

The main advantage of mechanical observation is low observation bias: The behavior is recorded mechanically and not by an observer. The data are analyzed according to prespecified norms and guidelines, resulting in low analysis bias. The main disadvantages are that some of these methods can be intrusive or expensive, and they might not be suitable in natural settings, such as the marketplace (Table 5.3).

Research Recipe

Mechanical observation devices fall into two categories: those that do not require direct participation by the respondents (e.g., turnstiles, UPC scanners), and those that do (e.g., specialized equipment designed to monitor heart and breathing rates, skin temperature, and other physiological changes). All mechanical devices have low observation, recording, and analysis bias.

iResearch
The Smithsonian: Attracting the Smiths

The Smithsonian Institution is America's national educational facility, with nineteen museums, nine research centers, and 155 affiliates around the world. Visit **www.smithsonianmag.com/** and search the Internet, including social media as well as your library's online databases, to obtain information on the criteria that consumers use for selecting a museum.

If the Smithsonian wants to determine how many people it attracts on a daily basis and what are the most popular exhibits, can the observation method be used? If so, which observation method would you use? As the marketing manager for the Smithsonian, how would you use information on criteria that consumers use for selecting museums to formulate marketing strategies that would increase attendance and market share? ‹

A COMPARISON OF SURVEY AND OBSERVATION METHODS

With the exception of scanner data and certain types of media panels, marketing research is seldom conducted solely with observational methods. However, observational data do offer some unique advantages. When combined with survey techniques, observation can deliver excellent results, as demonstrated by H. J. Heinz Co. in the second Research in Practice feature in this chapter.

The findings of personal observation were used to develop "Dip and Squeeze" and surveys were used to validate the new package before it was introduced nationally.

Relative Advantages of Observation

Observational data collection methods offer several advantages. First, many of these methods do not require conscious respondent participation, which minimizes nonresponse errors. Although ethical questions surround the practice of observation without consent, even conscious participation requires less effort from the respondent than that required with other research techniques.

Interviewer bias resulting from interaction with the respondent or subjective interpretation of the questionnaire is minimized because the observer has to record only what is occurring. The errors inherent in self-reported behavior are eliminated given that the observer records only actual behavior; the observer does not have to ask any questions of the respondent.

Data regarding product preferences or reactions to marketing materials from children or pets can best be collected using observational techniques. Observation is also useful in situations investigating unconscious behavior patterns or behaviors that individuals might be unwilling to discuss honestly.

Observational techniques are best applied to phenomena that occur frequently or are of short duration. In these types of applications, observational methods might cost less and be faster than survey methods.

Relative Disadvantages of Observation

Observational data provide insight into what behavior is occurring, but not why it is occurring. Attitudes, motivations, and values are all lost in the observational method. Highly personal behaviors related to personal hygiene or intimate family interactions are not available for observation.

Individuals have a tendency to observe only what they want to, and that might cause an observer to overlook important aspects of behavior. This perceptual difference among observers threatens the integrity of the observation approach.

Finally, observational techniques can be adopted for only frequent behaviors of short duration. Behaviors occurring infrequently or spanning a long period of time (e.g., individual car purchases over time) are too expensive to record using this technique.

To sum up, observation can potentially provide valuable information when used properly. From a practical standpoint, it is best to view observation methods as complementary to survey methods rather than as being in competition with them.

R e s e a r c h   R e c i p e

When combined with surveys, observation methods can result in rich insights. Hence, use these methods in a complementary way.

iResearch
Kroger Plans on Unplanned Purchases

As the marketing manager for Kroger, how would you use information on consumer behavior related to supermarket shopping to formulate marketing strategies that would increase your market share?

Visit **www.kroger.com** and search the Internet, including social media as well as your library's online databases, to obtain information on consumer behavior related to supermarket shopping. Kroger wants to determine to what extent consumers plan their product and brand purchases before entering the store and to what extent these decisions are made in the store. How will you combine the survey and observation methods to obtain this information? ❮

INTERNATIONAL MARKETING RESEARCH

Selecting appropriate interviewing methods for international marketing research is much more difficult because of the challenges of conducting research in foreign countries. Given the differences in the economic, structural, informational, technological, and sociocultural environments, the feasibility and popularity of the different interviewing methods vary widely. In the United States and Canada, nearly all households have telephones. As a result, telephone interviewing remains popular despite losing its dominant status to Internet surveys. This is also true in some European countries, such as Sweden. In many other European countries, however, not all households have telephones. In some developing countries, only a few households have them.

In-home personal interviews are the dominant mode of collecting survey data in many European countries, such as Switzerland, and in newly industrialized countries (NICs) or developing countries. Although mall intercepts are being conducted in some European countries, such as Sweden, they are not popular in other European countries or in developing countries. In contrast, central location/street interviews constitute the dominant method of collecting survey data in France and the Netherlands.

Due to their low cost, mail interviews continue to be used in most developed countries where literacy is high and the postal system is well developed. Some examples are the United States, Canada, Denmark, Finland, Iceland, Norway, Sweden, and the Netherlands. In Africa, Asia, and South America, however, the use of mail surveys and mail panels is low because of illiteracy and the large proportion of the population living in rural areas. Mail panels are used extensively only in a few countries outside the United States, such as Canada, the United Kingdom, France, Germany, and the Netherlands. However, the use of panels might increase with the advent of new technology. Likewise, although a website can be accessed from anywhere in the world, access to the Web or e-mail is limited in many countries, particularly developing countries. Hence, the use of electronic surveys may not be feasible, especially for interviewing households. European marketing research firms have been slower to adopt electronic interviewing because Internet penetration in Europe has lagged that in the United States.

Different incentives are more or less effective in improving response rates in different countries. In Japan, it is more appropriate to use gifts with business surveys rather than cash as incentives. The same is true for household surveys in Mexico. Some methods may be more effective in some countries than others. When collecting data from different countries, it is desirable to use survey methods with equivalent levels of effectiveness rather than necessarily using the identical method.

Research in Practice
Coca-Cola Adopts an Environmental Approach in China

TNS Global conducted a survey of 10,000 Chinese who were randomly selected from an online panel about environmental and ethical issues in buying products. The survey found that 89 percent of Chinese respondents said that they had refrained from buying a product in the past because the manufacturer had failed to follow environmental and ethical standards. This compared with 65 percent of consumers globally and only 54 percent of Japanese who said the same thing. This greatly concerned the Coca-Cola Company, which uses a lot of water, a scarce resource in China, to produce its soft drinks. The company, which had been accused of excessive water usage in India, wanted to avoid making the same mistake in China. Therefore, the Coca-Cola Company told the Chinese community in Beijing that the company will "replace every drop" of water and also work together in a joint campaign with the World Wildlife Fund (WWF) to protect the Yangtze River and six other rivers. These actions boosted the company's image in China, which remains one of its fastest growing markets as of 2014.[10] ◄

As in the case of surveys, the selection of an appropriate observation method in international marketing research should also take into account the differences in the economic, structural, informational and technological, and sociocultural environment (see Chapter 1).

Research Recipe

The effectiveness of survey methods could vary across countries. When collecting data from different countries, use survey methods with equivalent levels of effectiveness rather than necessarily use the same method.

MARKETING RESEARCH AND SOCIAL MEDIA

Social media can be used to conduct surveys as well as observations.

Surveys

Many social sites today present an excellent platform for allowing researchers the widespread ability to disseminate questionnaires and thereby retrieve quantitative feedback on a large scale. The use of social media overcomes the need for a physical presence of interviewers to solicit information from the public, and this helps keep costs low, thus allowing greater sample size. When implemented correctly, the collection of survey data through social media sites can be automated, which also allows the researcher to customize the study's reach to various segments of consumers. Research questions can be varied conveniently with little restriction.

Online surveys conducted through social media platforms encourage committed and credible feedback due to the inherent relevance and anonymity for the consumer. Should this fail, the virtual nature of these tools also allows subtle motivational factors to be used when soliciting quantitative data. For example, electronic coupons can be given to consumers as they leave the survey site after completing the survey. Coupled with the simplicity with which electronic content can be created and implemented, we see that conducting surveys through social media becomes highly viable and cost effective. Short surveys can be administered on the social media site itself, for example, a Facebook page. For longer surveys, a link can be provided on the social media site that directs the user to the survey site, as in the survey conducted by the Captura Group in the Research in Practice that follows.

Research in Practice
Captura Group: Capturing Expectations of the U.S. Government

The Captura Group (**www.capturagroup.com**) is a specialist marketing research firm that primarily targets the American Hispanic online market. The company implemented and fielded a social media survey with the objective of understanding how the public viewed access to U.S. government information. This survey was commissioned due to rising volumes of negative public sentiment concerning the organization of government departments and agencies in the post-9/11 climate. With the enactment of the U.S.A. Patriot Act and various other laws, the United States found itself in the late 2000s creating more agencies to overcome lapses in security. As of 2013, there were more than 1,000 individual departments or agencies in the federal government, and that number continues to grow. As a result, U.S. citizens faced increasing bureaucratic red tape whenever they had to obtain information regarding state and government matters. Many departments and agencies had overlapping degrees of jurisdiction.

The survey was conducted as follows:

Respondent facts:	• Average age of 42 • 501 people started the survey, with 385 completing it (78.5 percent) • 50/50 male: female ratio • 58 percent of respondents were familiar with the U.S. government
Social media platforms Accessible:	Eleven, including MySpace, blogs, Twitter, Yahoo! Answers, and so on

Analysis of the survey results revealed the following trends:

- The majority of respondents are interested in accessing government information via social media.
- The credibility of online government information is critical for respondents.
- Facebook is the preferred social media site among respondents.
- Respondents are very interested in having conversations with the government.
- Relevant and timely content is critical; the channel used is secondary.
- Sixty percent of respondents are interested in government information on nongovernment sites.

After viewing the results, the Obama administration admitted that the current governmental organization was overly complex and still flawed, with many loopholes. It has since tried to revamp the organization of its departments and agencies in lieu of the post-9/11 climate to make government more accessible and less complicated to the average citizen.[11] **<**

Observation

trace analysis
An observational approach in which data collection is based on physical traces, or evidence, of past behavior.

In a real sense, the comments, photos, videos, audio recordings, and other stimuli posted voluntarily by consumers on their social media sites are traces of their behaviors that can be observed. An analysis of these items constitutes a form of observation known as **trace analysis**. Some researchers consider participant blogs and online research communities to be examples of e-ethnography or netnography (online ethnographic research, as described in Chapter 4). It is also possible to observe the behavior of interest to the researcher more directly in the virtual world, as done by Starwood for Aloft Hotels.

When Starwood Hotels & Resorts considered launching a new range of design hotels under the brand name Aloft, it decided to build the first hotel virtually within Second Life. This helped the company obtain vital consumer feedback on the desired hotel design and concept. Consumers were invited on Second Life to interact in the virtual Aloft Hotel. Marketing researchers mechanically observed their behaviors and preferences. They were able to observe how the avatars moved through spaces and what areas and furniture were more popular in Second Life. The findings led to several design changes, including the decision to build radios in the guest rooms' showers. Aloft hotels were opened in 2008. They offer—to both business and leisure travelers—a blend of modern elements from the classic American tradition. As of 2014, Aloft had more than a hundred hotels around the world, including Asia, Europe, and the Middle East, as well as Central and South America, and they are still expanding.

Research Recipe

You can administer short surveys on a social media site itself, for example, a Facebook page. For longer surveys, provide a link on the social media site that directs the user to the survey site. The comments, photos, videos, audio recordings, and other stimuli posted voluntarily by consumers on their social media sites are traces of their behaviors that can be observed. You can observe the behavior of interest more directly in the virtual world, for example, Second Life.

ETHICS IN MARKETING RESEARCH

Respondents' anonymity, discussed in the context of qualitative research in Chapter 4, is an important issue in both survey and observational research. Researchers have an ethical obligation to avoid disclosing the identities of respondents to anyone outside the research organization, including the client. Only when researchers notify respondents in advance and obtain their consent prior to administering the survey can an exception be made and the respondents' identities revealed to the client. Even in such cases, prior to disclosing identification information, the researcher should obtain an assurance from the client that the respondents' trust will be maintained and their identities will not be used for sales efforts or misused in other ways. Ethical lapses in this respect by unscrupulous researchers and marketers have resulted in a serious backlash for marketing research.

The researcher has the responsibility to use an appropriate survey method in an ethical and legal way. For instance, federal legislation prohibits unsolicited faxed surveys. In many states, totally automated outgoing (initiated by the researcher) telephoning is illegal.

Researchers should not place respondents in stressful situations. Disclaimers such as "There are no right or wrong answers; we are only interested in your opinion" can relieve much of the stress inherent in a survey. Finally, surveys should not be used for unethical purposes such as sugging and frugging. See the Research in Practice for more information about these unethical practices.

Research in Practice
Sugging and Frugging Are Unethical

Sometimes direct marketing and telemarketing firms contact consumers under the pretense of conducting survey research but with the real motive of generating sales leads. Such surveys ask information about interest in the marketer's products, the respondent's background and demographic variables, and the respondent's desire for more information. Information on respondents who show interest or request more information is passed on to the company's salespeople with instructions to pursue these hot leads. Clearly, the purpose of these surveys is not scientific investigation but generating sales leads. This practice is called sugging. Frugging is a similar practice and involves soliciting funds under the guise of research. Both sugging and frugging are unethical and hurt the cause of marketing research. The marketing research industry has taken an aggressive stand against both these practices.[12] **<**

Often the behavior of people is observed without their knowledge because informing the respondents may alter their behavior. However, not informing the respondents can violate the respondents' privacy. One guideline is that people should not be observed for research in situations where they would not expect to be observed by the public. For example, observing people in public places like a mall or a grocery store is appropriate if certain procedures are followed. Notices should be posted in these areas stating that they are under observation for marketing research purposes. After the data have been collected, the researcher should obtain the necessary permission from the respondents. If any of the respondents refuse to grant permission, the observation records pertaining to them should be destroyed. These guidelines should also be applied when using cookies on the Internet to observe people's Web browsing behavior.

Research Recipe

The researcher has the ethical responsibility to avoid placing respondents in stressful situations. Use disclaimers such as "There are no right or wrong answers; we are only interested in your opinion" that can relieve much of the stress inherent in a survey. You should conduct surveys and observations in strictly ethical ways.

Dell Running Case

Review the Dell case, Case 1.1, and the questionnaire given toward the end of the book.

1. The Dell survey was administered by posting it on a website and sending an e-mail invitation to respondents. Evaluate the advantages and disadvantages of this method. Do you think that this method was the most effective?

2. Compare the various survey methods for conducting the Dell survey. Could Dell have used social media? If so, how?

3. Can Dell use the observation method to determine consumers' preferences for PCs and notebook computers? If so, which observation method would you recommend and why?

4. Visit a store selling PCs and notebooks (e.g., Best Buy, Sears, etc.). If this store wants to conduct a survey to determine consumer preferences for PCs and notebook computers, which survey method would you recommend and why?

Summary

Surveys and observations are the two primary methods of conducting quantitative, descriptive research. Surveys involve the questioning of respondents, whereas respondent behavior is simply recorded in observation.

Surveys involve the administration of a questionnaire and can be classified based on the method or mode of administration as traditional telephone interviews, computer-assisted telephone interviewing (CATI), in-home personal interviews, mall-intercept interviews, computer-assisted personal interviewing (CAPI), mail surveys, mail panels, or electronic surveys administered by e-mail or Internet. Of these methods, Internet interviews are the most popular in the United States. However, each method has some general advantages and disadvantages. Although these data collection methods are usually thought of as distinct and competitive, they should not be considered mutually exclusive. It is possible to employ them productively in combination.

The major observational methods are personal observation and mechanical observation. Compared to surveys, the relative advantages of observational methods are (1) they permit measurement of actual behavior, (2) there is no reporting bias, and (3) there is less potential for interviewer bias. Also, certain types of data can be obtained best, sometimes only, by observation. The relative disadvantages of observation are (1) very little can be inferred about motives, beliefs, attitudes, and preferences; (2) there is potential for observer bias; (3) most methods are time-consuming and expensive; (4) it is difficult to observe some forms of behavior; and (5) there is potential for unethical behavior. With the exception of scanner data and certain types of media panels, observation is rarely used as the sole method of obtaining primary data, but it can be used productively in conjunction with survey methods.

An important consideration in selecting the methods of administering surveys internationally is to ensure equivalence and comparability across countries. Social media have added a new dimension to survey as well as observation research; they constitute an important domain in which both survey and observation can be implemented. Misuse of surveys as a guise for selling, failing to maintain the anonymity of respondents, and observing behavior without respondents' knowledge or consent are major ethical issues in implementing survey and observation methods.

⌄ Companion Website

This textbook includes numerous student resources that can be found at **www.pearsonglobaleditions.com/malhotra**. At this Companion website, you'll find:

● Student Resource Manual
● Demo movies of statistical procedures using SPSS and Microsoft Excel
● Screen captures of statistical procedures using SPSS and Microsoft Excel
● Data files for all datasets in SPSS and Microsoft Excel
● Additional figures and tables
● Videos and write-ups for all video cases
● Other valuable resources

⌄ Key Terms and Concepts

Survey method	Interviewer bias	Observation
Structured data collection	Fax survey	Personal observation
Fixed alternative questions	Nonresponse bias	Humanistic inquiry
Mail panel	Social desirability	Mechanical
Sample control	Prepaid incentive	observation
Response rate	Promised incentive	Trace analysis

⌄ Suggested Cases and Video Cases

Running Case with Real Data and Questionnaire
    1.1 Dell

Comprehensive Critical Thinking Cases
    2.1 American Idol

Comprehensive Cases with Real Data and Questionnaires
    3.1 JPMorgan Chase
    3.2 Wendy's

Online Video Cases
    5.1 Starbucks 7.1 P&G 8.1 Dunkin' Donuts 9.1 Subaru
    10.1 Intel 13.1 Marriott

⌄ Live Research: Conducting a Marketing Research Project

As a class, discuss the various survey methods and select one that is appropriate for the project. In addition to the criteria given in this chapter, certain practical constraints might have to be considered if the students must collect data. Examples include the following:

1. A budget for making telephone calls should be supplied if a telephone survey is to be done.
2. If a CATI system is not available, the telephone method can be limited to traditional telephone.
3. Students will not be allowed to conduct mall-intercept interviews unless permission is obtained from mall management. Some malls have signed exclusive contracts with marketing research firms for data collection.

4. It might not be practical to do in-home personal interviews covering a large geographic area or even a local region.
5. There might not be enough time for a mail survey, and a mail panel might be prohibitively expensive unless there is an adequate budget for the project.
6. E-mail addresses might not be available or might be very difficult to get.
7. Mechanical observation devices can be impractical to obtain and use.

The survey/data collection method selected should be discussed and approved by the client.

∨ Acronyms

The classification of survey methods by mode of administration may be described by the acronym METHODS:

M ail panels

E lectronic interviews

T elephone interviews

H ome (in-home personal) interviewing

O n-site mall interviews

D irect-mail interviews

S oftware for CATI/CAPI

∨ Review Questions

5-1. Explain briefly how the topics covered in this chapter fit into the framework of the marketing research process.
5-2. What are mixed-mode surveys and when are they used?
5-3. What are the relevant factors for evaluating which survey method is best suited to a particular research project?
5-4. What are cold surveys? How are they different from mail panels?
5-5. What are the advantages of internet surveys over mail surveys?
5-6. Name the types of mechanical observation, and explain how they work.
5-7. What are the relative advantages and disadvantages of observation?

∨ Applied Problems

5-8. Describe a marketing research problem in which both survey and observation methods could be used for obtaining the information needed. Is the use of social media appropriate in your case?
5-9. The campus food service would like to determine how many people eat in the student cafeteria. List the ways in which this information could be obtained. Which method is best?
5-10. Locate and answer an Internet survey for which you would qualify as a respondent. How would you evaluate this survey based on the discussion in this chapter?
5-11. Locate an Internet survey and examine the content of the questionnaire carefully. What are the relative advantages and disadvantages of administering the same survey using CATI or mall-intercept interviewing?

∨ Internet Exercises

5-12. Visit the website **www.questionform.com** and design a survey to measure customer preference for the iPad over other available tablets. Publish the survey on available social media platforms and summarize the findings and response rate.

5-13. What observation techniques does Strategy Analytics (**www.strategyanalytics.com**) utilize for its AppOptix service and how does it operate? What industry does it potentially serve?

NOTES

1. **www.kfc.com**, accessed May 6, 2013; and "Kentucky Grilled Chicken," **www.kfc.com/food/chicken/ky-grilled.asp**, accessed November 4, 2013.
2. **www.heinz.com**, accessed May 16, 2013; and Sarah Nassauer, "Old Ketchup Packet Heads for Trash," *Wall Street Journal* (Monday, September 19, 2011): B1–B2.
3. **www.verizonwireless.com**, accessed March 17, 2013; and Viscusi, S., "Verizon Wireless Helps Friends & Family Save Money and Stay in Touch," **http://fixed-mobile-convergence.tmcnet.com/topics/mobile-communications/articles/50546-verizon-wireless-helps-friends-family-save-money-stay.htm**, accessed March 17, 2013.
4. **www.touchscreenresearch.com.au**, accessed April 2, 2013.
5. **www.seventeen.com/**, accessed March 3, 2013.
6. **www.nokia.com**, accessed January 5, 2013.
7. **www.kraftbrands.com/oscarmayer**, accessed February 3, 2013.
8. **www.mallofamerica.com**, accessed January 15, 2013.
9. **www.nielsen.com**, accessed February 26, 2013.
10. ViewsWire, *China company: Coca-Cola's new formula*. Retrieved March 4, 2012, from Factiva Database.
11. **www.slideshare.net/jedsundwall/social-media-survey-results**, accessed May 7, 2013.
12. "The Code of Marketing Research Standards," **www.marketingresearch.org**, accessed January 10, 2013; and Diane K. Bowers, "Sugging Banned, At Last," *Marketing Research: A Magazine of Management & Applications*, 7(4) (Fall/Winter 1995): 40.

Online Video Case 5.1

STARBUCKS: Staying Local While Going Global Through Marketing Research

Visit **www.pearsonglobaleditions.com/malhotra** to read the video case and view the accompanying video. Starbucks: Staying Local While Going Global Through Marketing Research describes how Starbucks has gathered useful feedback and marketing research information from customers, leading to the introduction of several successful new products and penetration into new global markets. The case can be used to discuss the various benefits and limitations of descriptive research and particularly the use of both survey and observation methods. Specific marketing research questions on this and the previous chapters are posed in the video case.

6 Experimentation and Causal Research

⌄ Overview

We introduced causal designs in Chapter 3, where we discussed their relationship to exploratory and descriptive designs, and defined experimentation as the primary method employed in causal designs. This chapter explores the concept of causality further. We identify the necessary conditions for causality, examine the role of validity in experimentation, and consider the procedures for controlling extraneous variables. We present a classification of experimental designs and consider specific designs, along with the relative merits of laboratory and field experiments. The considerations involved in conducting experimental research when researching international markets and the impact of social media are discussed. Several ethical issues that arise in experimentation are identified. Figure 6.1 gives the relationship of this chapter to the marketing research process. We begin with an example.

While experiments cannot prove causality, experimentation is the best method for making causal inferences."

> Lynd Bacon, CEO and Founder, Loma Buena Associates, Woodside, California.

∨ Learning Objectives

After reading this chapter, the student should be able to:

1. Explain the concept of causality as defined in marketing research, and distinguish between the ordinary meaning and the scientific meaning of causality.

2. Discuss the conditions for causality, and whether a causal relationship can be demonstrated conclusively.

3. Define and differentiate the two types of validity: internal validity and external validity.

4. Describe and evaluate experimental designs and the differences among pre-experimental, true experimental, and statistical designs.

5. Compare and contrast the use of laboratory versus field experimentation and experimental versus nonexperimental designs in marketing research.

6. Understand why the internal and external validity of field experiments conducted overseas is generally lower than in the United States.

7. Describe how social media can facilitate causal research.

8. Describe the ethical issues involved in conducting causal research and the role of debriefing in addressing some of these issues.

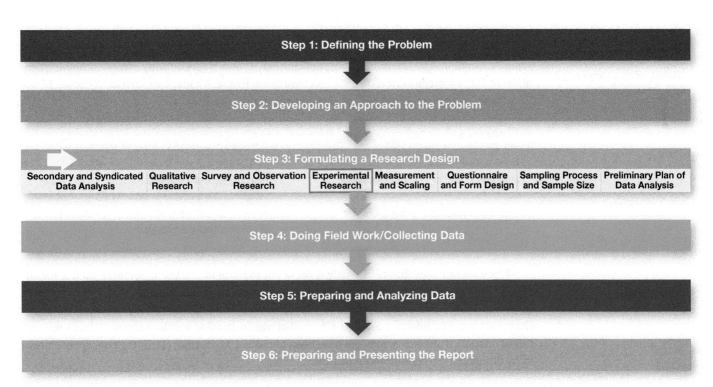

FIGURE 6.1 | RELATIONSHIP OF THIS CHAPTER TO THE MARKETING RESEARCH PROCESS

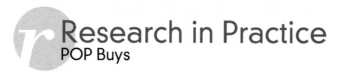

Research in Practice
POP Buys

Rite Aid Drug Company (**www.riteaid.com**) conducted an experiment to examine the effectiveness of in-store radio advertisements to induce point-of-purchase (POP) buys. Twenty statistically compatible drugstores were selected based on store size, geographical location, traffic-flow count, and age. Half of these stores were randomly selected as test stores, whereas the other half served as control stores. The test stores aired the radio advertisements; the control stores' POP radio systems were removed. Tracking data in the form of unit volume and dollar sales were obtained for seven days before the experiment, during the course of the four-

Source: Kristoffer Tripplaar / Alamy

week experiment, and seven days after the experiment. The products monitored varied from inexpensive items to small kitchen appliances. Results indicated that sales of the advertised products in the test stores at least doubled. Based on this evidence, Rite Aid concluded that in-store radio advertising was highly effective in inducing POP buys and decided to continue it.

Anheuser-Busch, Pepsi, Pfizer, Procter & Gamble, and Ralston-Purina sponsored this study. All these companies sell products that can benefit from point-of-purchase advertising. Based on these results, these firms decided to increase their POP promotional budget.[1] ◄

CONCEPT OF CAUSALITY

causality
The occurrence of X increases the probability of the occurrence of Y.

Experimentation is commonly used to infer causal relationships. The concept of **causality** requires some explanation. The scientific concept of causality is complex. Causality means something very different to the average person on the street than to a scientist. A statement such as "*X* causes *Y*" will have the following meaning to an ordinary person and to a scientist.

Ordinary Meaning	Scientific Meaning
X is the only cause of *Y*.	*X* is only one of a number of possible causes of *Y*.
X must always lead to *Y* (*X* is a deterministic cause of *Y*).	The occurrence of *X* makes the occurrence of *Y* more probable (*X* is a probabilistic cause of *Y*).
It is possible to prove that *X* is a cause of *Y*.	We can never prove that *X* is a cause of *Y*. At best, we can infer that *X* is a cause of *Y*.

The scientific meaning of causality is more appropriate to marketing research than is the ordinary meaning. Marketing effects are caused by multiple variables, and the relationship between cause and effect tends to be probabilistic. We can never prove causality (i.e., demonstrate it conclusively); we can only infer a cause-and-effect relationship. In other words, it is possible that the true causal relation, if one exists, may not have been identified. We further clarify the concept of causality by discussing the conditions for causality.

R e s e a r c h   R e c i p e

The scientific notion of causality acknowledges that marketing effects are caused by multiple variables and that the relationship between cause and effect tends to be probabilistic. You can only infer a cause-and-effect relationship; you can never prove it.

CONDITIONS FOR CAUSALITY

Before making causal inferences, or assuming causality, three conditions must be satisfied: (1) concomitant variation, (2) time order of occurrence of variables, and (3) elimination of other possible causal factors. These conditions are necessary but not sufficient to demonstrate causality. No one of these three conditions, not even all three conditions combined, can demonstrate decisively that a causal relationship exists. These conditions are explained in more detail in the following sections.

Concomitant Variation

Concomitant variation is the extent to which a cause, X, and an effect, Y, occur together or vary together in the way predicted by the hypothesis under consideration. It is the extent to which X and Y are associated or correlated. For example, the management of a department store believes that sales are highly dependent on the quality of in-store service. This hypothesis could be examined by assessing concomitant variation. Here, the causal factor X is in-store service, and the effect factor Y is store sales. A concomitant variation supporting the hypothesis would imply that stores with satisfactory in-store service would also have satisfactory sales. Likewise, stores with unsatisfactory service would exhibit unsatisfactory sales. If, on the other hand, the opposite pattern was found, we would conclude that the hypothesis was untenable.

concomitant variation
A condition for inferring causality, which requires that a cause, X, and an effect, Y, occur together or vary together as predicted by the hypothesis under consideration.

Suppose we collect data on 100 stores and indeed find that stores with satisfactory in-store service also have satisfactory sales. Based on this evidence, can we conclude that high quality of in-store service causes high store sales? Certainly not! All that can be said is that association makes the hypothesis more tenable; it does not prove it. What about the effect of other possible causal factors such as store size? Larger stores will have higher sales than smaller stores. So unless the effect of other factors, such as store size, that affect stores sales is considered (controlled), we cannot say anything definitively about the relationship between in-store service and store sales.

The time order of the occurrence of variables provides additional insights into causality.

Time Order of Occurrence of Variables

The time order of occurrence condition states that the causing event must occur either before or simultaneously with the effect; it cannot occur afterward. By definition, an effect cannot be produced by an event that occurs after the effect has taken place. However, it is possible for each event in a relationship to be both a cause and an effect of the other event. In other words, a variable can be both a cause and an effect in the same causal relationship. To illustrate, customers who shop frequently in a department store are more likely to have the charge or credit card for that store. Also, customers who have the charge card for a department store are likely to shop there frequently. Thus, each may be the cause of the other.

Consider the in-store service and sales of a department store. If in-store service is the cause of sales, then improvements in service must be made before, or at least simultaneously with, an increase in sales. These improvements might consist of training or hiring more sales personnel. Then, in subsequent months, the sales of the department store should increase. Alternatively, the sales might increase simultaneously with the training or hiring of additional sales personnel. On the other hand, suppose a store experienced an appreciable increase in sales and then decided to use some of that money to retrain its sales personnel, leading to an improvement in service. In this case, in-store service cannot be a cause of increased sales. Rather, just the opposite hypothesis might be plausible.

Absence of Other Possible Causal Factors

The absence of other possible causal factors means that the factor or variable being investigated should be the only possible causal explanation. In-store service may be a cause of sales if we can be sure that changes in all other factors affecting sales, namely, pricing, advertising, level of distribution, product quality, competition, and so on, were held constant or otherwise controlled.

In an after-the-fact examination of a situation, we can never confidently rule out all other causal factors. In contrast, with experimental designs, it is possible to control for some of the other causal factors. It is also possible to balance the effects of some of the uncontrolled variables so that only random variations resulting from these uncontrolled variables will be measured. These aspects are discussed in more detail later in this chapter. The difficulty of establishing a causal relationship is illustrated by the following example.

Research in Practice
Which Comes First?

Recent statistical data show that consumers increasingly make buying decisions in the store while they are shopping. Some studies indicate that as much as 80 percent of buying decisions are made at point of purchase (POP). POP buying decisions have increased concurrently with increased advertising efforts in the stores. These advertisements include radio advertisements, ads on shopping carts and grocery bags, ceiling signs, and shelf displays. It is estimated that brand and retail owners spent more than $1 billion in 2013 trying to influence the consumer at the point of purchase. It is difficult to ascertain from these data whether the increased POP decision making is the result of increased advertising efforts in the store, or whether the increase in store advertising results from attempts to capture changing consumer attitudes toward purchasing and to capture sales from the increase in POP decision making. It is also possible that both variables may be causes and effects in this relationship.[2] ◄

If it is difficult to establish cause-and-effect relationships, as the preceding example indicates, what is the role of evidence obtained in experimentation?

Role of Evidence

Evidence of concomitant variation, time order of occurrence of variables, and elimination of other possible causal factors, even if combined, still do not demonstrate conclusively that a causal relationship exists. If all the evidence is strong and consistent, however, it may be reasonable to conclude that there is a causal relationship. Accumulated evidence from several investigations increases our confidence that a causal relationship exists. Confidence is further enhanced if the evidence is interpreted in light of intimate conceptual knowledge of the problem situation. Controlled experiments can provide strong evidence on all three conditions.

Research Recipe

Before you can make causal inferences, three conditions must be satisfied: (1) concomitant variation, (2) time order of occurrence of variables, and (3) elimination of other possible causal factors. These conditions are necessary but not sufficient to demonstrate causality. Even all three conditions combined cannot demonstrate conclusively that a causal relationship exists, but their occurrence can make a causal inference plausible.

iResearch
Internet Use and Information Availability

As the head of the Federal Trade Commission (FTC), what are your concerns about the increased availability of information on the Internet?

Search the Internet, including social media as well as your library's online databases, to obtain information on Internet usage by consumers. What conditions are necessary for you to conclude that increased use of the Internet by consumers is increasing the availability of information on the Internet? <

WHAT IS EXPERIMENTATION?

Experimentation is the research technique used in causal research (Figure 6.2). It is the primary method for establishing cause-and-effect relationships in marketing (see Chapter 3). As seen from Figure 6.2, experiments can be conducted in the field or in the laboratory. A **field experiment** involves measurement of behavior, attitudes, or perceptions in the environment in which they occur. Thus, field experiments are conducted in natural settings. The opening Research in Practice about Rite Aid presents an example of a field experiment. On the other hand, a **laboratory experiment** is conducted is an artificial environment. Advertising testing and test kitchens in central-location theaters are examples of laboratory experiments used in marketing research.

Experiments can be described in terms of independent, dependent, and extraneous variables; test units; and random assignment to experimental and control groups.

field experiment
An experiment conducted in actual market conditions, that is in a natural environment.

laboratory experiment
An experiment conducted in an artificial environment in which the researcher constructs the desired conditions.

DEFINITIONS AND CONCEPTS

In this section, we define some basic concepts and illustrate those using examples, including the Research in Practice about Rite Aid given earlier in this chapter.

Independent Variables

Independent variables are variables or alternatives that are manipulated (i.e., the levels of these variables are changed by the researcher) and whose effects are measured and compared. These variables, also known as treatments, may include price levels, package designs, and advertising themes. In the example given in the Research in Practice called "POP Buys," the independent variable or treatment consisted of in-store radio advertising. In-store radio advertising was manipulated to have two levels: present versus absent.

independent variables
Variables that are manipulated by the researcher and whose effects are measured and compared.

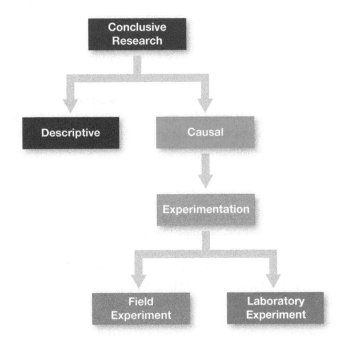

FIGURE 6.2
EXPERIMENTATION AS
CONCLUSIVE RESEARCH

Test Units

test units
Individuals, organizations, or other entities whose responses to independent variables or treatments are being studied.

Test units are individuals, organizations, or other entities whose responses to the independent variables or treatments are being examined. Test units may include consumers, stores, or geographic areas. The test units were stores in the Rite Aid example.

Dependent Variables

dependent variables
Variables that measure the effect of the independent variables on the test units.

Dependent variables are the variables that measure the effect of the independent variables on the test units. These variables may include sales, profits, and market shares. The dependent variable was sales in the Rite Aid example.

Extraneous Variables

extraneous variables
Variables, other than the independent variables, that influence the response of the test units.

Extraneous variables are all variables other than the independent variables that affect the response of the test units. These variables can confound the dependent variable measures in a way that weakens or invalidates the results of the experiment. Extraneous variables include store size, store location, and competitive effort. In the Rite Aid example, store size, geographical location, traffic-flow count, and age of the stores were extraneous variables that had to be controlled.

Random Assignment to Experimental and Control Groups

random assignment
The process of randomly assigning test units and treatments to the experimental and control groups. It is one of the most common techniques used to control for the effect of extraneous variables on the dependent variable.

Random assignment involves randomly assigning test units to the experimental and control groups and is one of the most common techniques used to control for the effect of extraneous variables on the dependent variable. Random assignment to experimental and control groups attempts to minimize the influence of extraneous factors such as age, income, or brand preference by spreading them equally across the groups under study.

experimental group
The group exposed to the manipulated independent variable.

When an experiment is being conducted, at least one group will be exposed to the manipulated independent variable. This is called the **experimental group** (EG). The results of this experimental group might be compared to another experimental group at a differing level of manipulation or to a control group (CG). The **control group** is not exposed to the independent variable manipulation. It provides a point of comparison when examining the effects of these manipulations on the dependent variable. In the Rite Aid example, the stores were randomly assigned to the two groups. One group was randomly chosen to be the experimental group (which was exposed to radio advertising) and the other served as the control group (which received no radio advertising).

control group
The group that is not exposed to the independent variable manipulation. It provides a point of comparison when examining the effects of these manipulations on the dependent variable.

Experiment

experiment
The process of manipulating one or more independent variables and determining their effect on one or more dependent variables measured on the test units, while controlling for the extraneous variables.

An **experiment** is formed when the researcher manipulates one or more independent variables and determines their effect on one or more dependent variables measured on the test units, while controlling for the effect of extraneous variables (Figure 6.3). The Rite Aid research project qualifies as an experiment based on this definition.

Experimental Design

experimental design
The set of experimental procedures specifying (1) the test units and sampling procedures, (2) independent variables, (3) dependent variables, and (4) how to control the extraneous variables.

An **experimental design** is a set of procedures specifying (1) the test units and how these units are to be divided into homogeneous subsamples, (2) what independent variables or treatments are to be manipulated, (3) what dependent variables are to be measured, and (4) how the extraneous variables are to be controlled. In the opening Research in Practice feature about Rite Aid, the experimental design required random selection of half the stores as test stores; the other half served as control stores. The test stores aired the radio advertisements; the control stores' POP radio systems were removed.

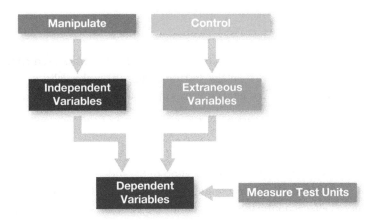

FIGURE 6.3
WHAT IS AN EXPERIMENT?

Research Recipe

An experiment is the primary method for establishing cause-and-effect relationships in marketing. To conduct an experiment, you manipulate one or more independent variables and then determine the effects that those manipulated variables have on the dependent variables measured on the test units while controlling the influence of outside or extraneous variables. Experiments can be described in terms of independent, dependent, and extraneous variables; test units; and random assignment to experimental and control groups.

DEFINITION OF SYMBOLS

To facilitate our discussion of extraneous variables and specific experimental designs, we define a set of symbols that are commonly used in marketing research.

X = the exposure of a group to an independent variable, treatment, or event, the effects of which are to be determined.

O = the process of observation or measurement of the dependent variable on the test units or group of units.

R = the random assignment of test units or groups to separate treatments.

In addition, the following conventions are adopted:

- Movement from left to right indicates movement through time.
- Horizontal alignment of symbols implies that all those symbols refer to a specific treatment group.
- Vertical alignment of symbols implies that those symbols refer to activities or events that occur simultaneously, that is, at the same time.

For example, the symbolic arrangement

$$X \qquad O_1 \qquad O_2$$

means that a given group of test units was exposed to the treatment variable (X), and the response was measured at two different points in time, O_1 and O_2.

Likewise, the symbolic arrangement

$$R \qquad X_1 \qquad O_1$$
$$R \qquad X_2 \qquad O_2$$

means that two groups of test units were randomly assigned to two different treatment groups at the same time, and the dependent variable was measured in the two groups simultaneously.

VALIDITY IN EXPERIMENTATION

When conducting an experiment, a researcher has two goals: (1) draw valid conclusions about the effects of independent variables on the test units and (2) make valid generalizations to a larger population of interest. The first goal concerns internal validity, the second, external validity (Figure 6.4).

Internal Validity

internal validity
A measure of the accuracy of an experiment. It measures if the manipulation of the independent variables, or treatments, actually caused the effects on the dependent variable(s).

Internal validity refers to whether the manipulation of the independent variables or treatments actually caused the observed effects on the dependent variables. Thus, internal validity refers to whether the observed effects on the test units could have been caused by variables other than the treatment. If the observed effects are influenced or confounded by extraneous variables, it is difficult to draw valid inferences about the causal relationship between the independent and dependent variables. Internal validity is the basic minimum that must be present in an experiment before any conclusion about treatment effects can be made. Without internal validity, the experimental results are confounded. Control of extraneous variables is a necessary condition for establishing internal validity.

External Validity

external validity
A determination of whether the cause-and-effect relationships found in the experiment can be generalized.

External validity refers to whether the cause-and-effect relationships found in the experiment can be generalized. In other words, can the results be generalized beyond the experimental situation and, if so, to what populations, settings, times, independent variables, and dependent variables can the results be projected? Threats to external validity arise when the specific set of experimental conditions do not realistically take into account the interactions of other relevant variables in the real world.

It is desirable to have an experimental design that has both internal and external validity, but in applied marketing research, we often have to trade one type of validity for another. To control for extraneous variables, a researcher may conduct an experiment in an artificial environment, often called a laboratory environment. This enhances internal validity of these experiments, called laboratory experiments (Figure 6.2). However, it may limit the generalizability of the results, thereby reducing external validity. For example, fast-food chains test customers' preferences for new formulations of menu items in test kitchens. Can the effects measured in this environment be generalized to fast-food outlets? In contrast, experiments conducted in fast-food outlets, that is, actual fast-food restaurants, would be conducted in a field environment and called field experiments. In

FIGURE 6.4 |
VALIDITY IN
EXPERIMENTATION

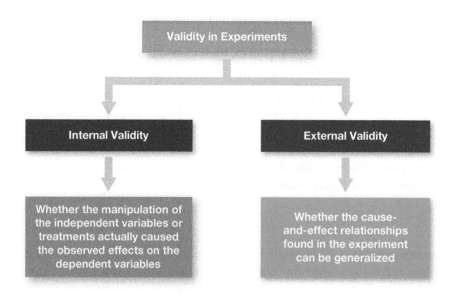

field experiments, the researcher has much less control over extraneous variables that might affect internal validity. If internal validity can be maintained, however, the results can be generalized more easily than those obtained in a laboratory setting. The Rite Aid example presented earlier in this chapter is an example of a field experiment having high external validity.

In spite of these deterrents to external validity, if an experiment lacks internal validity, it may not be meaningful to generalize the results. Factors that threaten internal validity may also threaten external validity, the most serious of these being extraneous variables.

CONTROLLING EXTRANEOUS VARIABLES

Extraneous variables represent alternative explanations of experimental results. They pose a serious threat to the internal and external validity of an experiment. Unless they are controlled for, they affect the dependent variable and thus confound the results. For this reason, they are also called **confounding variables**. Extraneous variables can be controlled by randomization.

Randomization refers to the random assignment of test units to experimental groups by using random numbers. Treatment conditions are also randomly assigned to experimental groups. For example, respondents are randomly assigned to one of three experimental groups. One of the three versions of a test commercial, selected at random, is administered to each group. As a result of random assignment, extraneous factors can be represented equally in each treatment condition. Randomization is the preferred procedure for ensuring the prior equality of experimental groups. However, randomization may not be effective when the sample size is small because randomization merely produces groups that are equal on average. It is possible, though, to check whether randomization has been effective by measuring the possible extraneous variables and comparing them across the experimental groups. In the Rite Aid experiment given earlier in this chapter, half of the stores were randomly selected as test stores, and the other half served as control stores. In general, extraneous variables can also be controlled by adopting specific experimental designs that use randomization, as described in the next section.

A CLASSIFICATION OF EXPERIMENTAL DESIGNS

The three broad categories of experimental designs are pre-experimental, true experimental, and statistical design (Figure 6.5). **Pre-experimental designs** are characterized by a lack of randomization. In **true experimental designs**, the researcher can randomly assign subjects and experimental groups. Therefore, these designs provide a larger degree of control over extraneous variables.

A **statistical design** is a series of basic experiments that allows for statistical control and analysis of extraneous variables. Statistical designs are classified on the basis of their characteristics and use.

confounding variables
Synonymous with extraneous variables. Used to illustrate that extraneous variables can confound the results by influencing the dependent variable.

pre-experimental designs
Designs that do not control for extraneous factors by randomization.

true experimental designs
Experimental designs distinguished by the fact that the researcher can randomly assign test units to experimental groups and also randomly assign treatments to experimental groups.

statistical design
An experimental design that allows for the statistical control and analysis of extraneous variables.

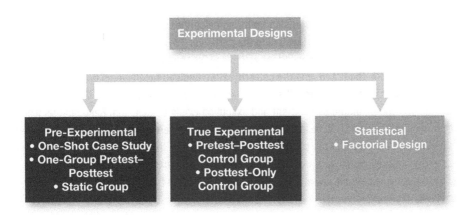

FIGURE 6.5
A CLASSIFICATION OF EXPERIMENTAL DESIGNS

The effectiveness of Nike advertising that makes use of celebrities can be assessed by using appropriate experimental designs.
Source: Stephen Shaver / UPI / Landov

one-shot case study

A pre-experimental design in which a single group of test units is exposed to a treatment X, and then a single measurement on the dependent variable is taken. Test units are not assigned at random.

We will illustrate the various experimental designs in the context of measuring the effectiveness of Nike advertising. Nike makes heavy use of celebrities in its advertising, including sports stars such as Kobe Bryant and Michael Jordan. Should Nike continue to feature celebrities in its advertising? Is this advertising effective? Experimental research that measures advertising effectiveness can provide useful information. We begin our discussion with the pre-experimental designs.

PRE-EXPERIMENTAL DESIGNS

Pre-experimental designs lack randomization. This section describes three specific designs: the one-shot case study, the one-group pretest–posttest design, and the static group.

One-Shot Case Study

Also known as the after-only design, the **one-shot case study** can be represented symbolically as

$$X \qquad O_1$$

A single group of subjects is exposed to a treatment (X), and then a single measurement on the dependent variable is taken (O_1). This type of design is constructed using a nonrandom sampling process in which the subjects are self-selected or selected arbitrarily by the researcher. Without randomization, the observed dependent variables are subject to the influences of several extraneous variables.

The one-shot case study lacks a control group. Without a control group, there is no point of comparison for the results. Due to lack of randomization and the absence of a control group, this design is clearly weak in terms of internal validity. For this reason, the one-shot case study is more appropriate for exploratory rather than conclusive research (see Chapter 3).

Research in Practice
One Shot at Nike Advertising

To assess the effectiveness of Nike advertising featuring celebrities, telephone interviews would be conducted with respondents who report watching the particular TV program on which the commercial was aired the previous night (X). The dependent variables (Os) are unaided and aided recall, and attitudes toward the advertisement, the brand, and the celebrity. First, unaided recall would be measured by asking the respondents whether they recall seeing a commercial for athletic shoes. If they recall the Nike commercial, details about commercial content and execution would be solicited. Respondents who do not recall the test commercial would be asked if they saw a Nike commercial (aided recall). For those who have an unaided or aided recall of the commercial, attitudes toward the commercial, the brand advertised, and the celebrity featured would be measured. The results of these experimental measures can be compared with normal scores for these types of questions to assess the effectiveness of the advertising and the celebrity featured. ‹

One-Group Pretest–Posttest Design

The **one-group pretest–posttest design** can be symbolized as

$$O_1 \qquad X \qquad O_2$$

In this design, a group of subjects is measured once before the experimental treatment (O_1) and once after (O_2). Again, this design lacks a control group for comparison. The treatment effect (TE) is computed as $O_2 - O_1$. Although this design is considered better than a one-shot case study, the validity of conclusions is questionable because extraneous variables are largely uncontrolled due to lack of randomization and the lack of a control group. The following example shows how this design is used.

one-group pretest–posttest design
A pre-experimental design in which a group of test units is measured twice, before and after exposure to the treatment. Test units are not assigned at random.

Research in Practice
Can Nike Perform in a Theater?

Firms such as GfK (**www.gfk.com**) commonly use the one-group pretest–posttest design to measure the effectiveness of test commercials. Respondents are recruited to central theater locations in various test cities. The respondents are interviewed, and their attitudes toward Nike advertising, the brand, and the celebrity (O_1) are measured. Then they watch a TV program containing the Nike commercial (X) and other filler commercials. After viewing the TV program, the respondents are again interviewed regarding their attitudes toward Nike advertising, the brand, and the celebrity (O_2). The effectiveness of the test commercial is determined by the difference between O_2 and O_1. ◄

Static Group Design

The **static group** is a two-group experimental design in which one of the groups acts as a control group (CG). Only one group, the experimental group (EG), receives the experimental treatment. The subjects are not assigned randomly, and measurements are made on both groups following the treatment (posttest). This design is expressed symbolically as:

$$\begin{array}{lll} \text{EG:} & X & O_1 \\ \text{CG:} & & O_2 \end{array}$$

The treatment effect would be measured as the difference between the control group and the experimental group ($O_1 - O_2$). The lack of randomization leaves the experiment open to some extraneous effects. The two groups might differ before the treatment.

In practice, the control group is often defined as the group receiving the current level of marketing activity rather than as a group that receives no treatment at all. In many cases, it is impossible to reduce marketing input (e.g., price) to zero.

static group
A pre-experimental design in which there are two groups: the experimental group (EG), which is exposed to the treatment, and the control group (CG). Measurements on both groups are made only after the treatment, and test units are not assigned at random.

Research in Practice
Is Nike Advertising Static?

A static group comparison to measure the effectiveness of a Nike commercial would be conducted as follows. Two groups of respondents would be recruited on the basis of convenience. Only the experimental group would be exposed to the TV program that contains the Nike commercial (X). Attitudes toward Nike advertising, the brand, and the celebrity would then be measured in both the experimental group (O_1) and the control group (O_2). The effectiveness of the Nike commercial would be measured as the difference between the experimental and control group ($O_1 - O_2$). ◄

Fox News Format: A Foxy Business

Visit **www.foxnews.com** and search the Internet, including social media as well as your library's online databases, to obtain information on consumers' preferences for network news channels. Fox News wants to determine which one of three new formats it should implement. Would you recommend a pre-experimental design? If so, which one would you recommend?

As the marketing manager of Fox News, how would you use information on consumers' preferences for network news channels to formulate marketing strategies that would increase your audience and market share? ‹

TRUE EXPERIMENTAL DESIGNS

True experimental designs are differentiated from pre-experimental designs by the fact that subjects are randomly assigned to groups. Treatment conditions are also randomly assigned to groups. For example, respondents are randomly assigned to one of three experimental groups. One of the three versions of a test commercial, selected at random, is administered to each group. As a result of random assignment, extraneous factors can be represented equally in each group or treatment condition. As stated earlier, randomization is the preferred procedure for ensuring the prior equality of experimental groups. True experimental designs include the pretest–posttest control group design and the posttest-only control group design.

Pretest–Posttest Control Group Design

pretest–posttest control group design

A true experimental design in which the experimental group is exposed to the treatment but the control group is not. There is random assignment and pretest and posttest measures are taken on both groups.

In the **pretest–posttest control group design**, subjects are randomly assigned to either the experimental or the control group. A pretreatment measure is taken on each group. After administering the treatment to the experimental group, both groups are measured again. This design is symbolized as follows:

$$\text{EG:} \quad R \quad O_1 \quad X \quad O_2$$
$$\text{CG:} \quad R \quad O_3 \quad \quad O_4$$

The treatment effect (TE) is measured as:

$$(O_2 - O_1) - (O_4 - O_3)$$

The use of a control group and randomization in this design controls for most extraneous variables. The extraneous effects are presumed to be represented equally in both the control and experimental groups. Thus, the difference between the control and experimental groups is thought to reflect only the treatment.

Research in Practice
Nike Pre- and Postmortem

An experiment for measuring the effectiveness of Nike's advertising using a pretest–posttest control group design would be conducted as follows. A sample of respondents would be distributed randomly, half to the experimental group and half to the control group. A pretest questionnaire would be administered to the respondents in both groups to obtain a measurement on attitudes toward Nike advertising, the brand, and the celebrity. Only the respondents in the experimental group would be exposed to the TV program containing the Nike commercial. Then a questionnaire would be administered to respondents in both groups to obtain posttest measures on attitudes toward Nike advertising, the brand, and the celebrity. ◀

As this example shows, the pretest–posttest control group design involves two groups and two measurements on each group. A simpler design is the posttest-only control group design.

Posttest–Only Control Group Design

The **posttest-only control group design** does not involve any premeasurement. Subjects are randomly assigned to either the experimental or the control group. After administering the treatment to the experimental group, both groups are measured. It can be symbolized as follows:

$$\begin{array}{llll} \text{EG:} & R & X & O_1 \\ \text{CG:} & R & & O_2 \end{array}$$

The treatment effect is the difference between the experimental and control group measurements:

$$\text{TE} = O_1 - O_2$$

The simplicity of this design offers time, cost, and sample-size advantages. For these reasons, it is the most popular experimental design in marketing research. However, this design is not without limitations. Although randomization is used to equalize groups, without a pretest, there is no way to verify group similarity. Without a pretest, researchers are also unable to examine changes in individual subjects over the course of the study. Note that, except for premeasurement, the implementation of this design is very similar to that of the pretest–posttest control group design. The Rite Aid example discussed earlier in this chapter provided an application. The stores were randomly assigned to the experimental group and the control group. No premeasurements were taken. Only the stores in the experimental group were exposed to radio advertising. Measurements on the sales of advertised items were obtained in the experimental group (O_1) and control group (O_2) stores. The increase in sales due to radio advertising was determined as ($O_1 - O_2$).

posttest-only control group design
A true experimental design in which the experimental group is exposed to the treatment but the control group is not and no pretest measure is taken. There is random assignment and posttreatment measures are taken on both groups.

Research Recipe

True experimental designs involve randomization. You randomly assign subjects to groups, and also randomly assign treatment conditions to groups. True experimental designs include the pretest–posttest control group design and the posttest-only control group design. The posttest-only control group design is the most popular experimental design in marketing research because it offers time, cost, and sample-size advantages.

STATISTICAL DESIGNS

Statistical designs consist of series of basic experiments that allow for statistical control and analysis of extraneous variables. In other words, several basic experiments are conducted simultaneously. Thus, statistical designs are influenced by the same sources of invalidity that affect the basic designs (pre-experimental or true experimental) being used. Statistical designs offer the following advantages:

1. The effects of more than one independent variable can be measured.
2. Specific extraneous variables can be statistically controlled.
   The most common statistical designs are the factorial designs.

Factorial Design

factorial design

A statistical experimental design used to measure the effects of two or more independent variables at various levels and to allow for interactions between variables.

interaction

An interaction occurs when the simultaneous effect of two or more variables is different from the sum of their separate effects.

A **factorial design** is used to measure the effects of two or more independent variables at various levels. It allows for the measurement of interactions between variables. An **interaction** is said to take place when the simultaneous effect of two or more variables is different from the sum of their separate effects. For example, an individual's favorite drink might be coffee and her favorite temperature level might be cold, but she might not prefer cold coffee, leading to an interaction.

A factorial design can also be thought of as a table. In a two-factor design, each level of one variable represents a row, and each level of another variable represents a column. Factorial designs involve a cell for every possible combination of treatment variables, as in the example that follows.

Research in Practice
Factoring Humor and Information in Nike Commercials

Suppose that in the Nike case, the researcher is interested in examining the effect of humor and the effect of various levels of brand information on advertising effectiveness. Three levels of humor (no humor, some humor, and high humor) are to be examined. Likewise, brand information is to be manipulated at three levels (low, medium, and high). The resulting table would be three rows (levels of information) by three columns (levels of humor), producing nine possible combinations, or cells, as laid out in Table 6.1. The respondents would be randomly assigned to one of the nine cells. Respondents in each cell would receive a specific treatment combination. For example, respondents in the upper left-hand corner cell would view a commercial that had no humor and low brand information. After exposure to a treatment combination, measures would be obtained on attitudes toward Nike advertising, the brand, and the celebrity from respondents in each cell. ◀

Statistical procedures are used to analyze the treatment effects. The main disadvantage of a factorial design is that the number of treatment combinations increases multiplicatively with an increase in the number of variables or levels. This is not often a serious limitation, however, because the researcher can control both the number of variables and the levels.

Table 6.1 > An Example of a Factorial Design

Amount of Brand Information	Amount of Humor		
	No Humor	Medium Humor	High Humor
Low			
Medium			
High			

Research Recipe

Statistical designs consist of series of basic experiments that allow you statistical control and analysis of extraneous variables. The most common form is a factorial design. You can think of a factorial design as a table. It is used to measure the effects of two or more independent variables at various levels and allows for the measurement of interactions between variables.

SELECTING AN EXPERIMENTAL DESIGN

Selecting an experimental design often involves a trade-off in terms of control. Designs that offer the greatest degree of internal validity typically are conducted in highly artificial environments that can threaten the generalizability or external validity of the experimental results.

One solution to finding the optimum combination of internal and external validity might be to use differing experimental designs at differing points in the study. For example, designs that offer tight internal validity (i.e., laboratory experiments) could be used during the early stages of the research effort. In this way, a more reliable measure of the true treatment effect could be secured. Because research in the early phases tends to be exploratory, pre-experimental designs may suffice. During later stages of the study, more natural settings (i.e., field experiments) could be used to enable generalization of results. True experimental and factorial designs are favored in the later stages.

Research Recipe

You can attain high internal and external validity by using different designs at different stages of the research project. Laboratory experiments that offer tight internal validity could be used during the early stages of the research, and pre-experimental designs may suffice. Field experiments could be used during later stages of the project to enable generalization of results. True experimental and factorial designs are more appropriate during the later stages.

iResearch
Canon Is Sensitive to Price Sensitivity

Visit **www.bestbuy.com** and identify the price ranges of the digital cameras by Canon and other brands. Search the Internet, including social media as well as your library's online databases, to obtain information on consumers' price sensitivity for digital cameras.

Canon wants to determine consumers' price sensitivity for its new advanced digital camera. Design an appropriate experiment. Would you recommend a true experimental design? If yes, which one?

As the marketing manager of Canon cameras, how would you use information on consumers' price sensitivity for digital cameras to formulate pricing strategies that would increase your market share? <

EXPERIMENTATION ON THE WEB

The Internet can provide a mechanism for controlled experimentation in a laboratory-type environment. Continuing with the example of testing the effectiveness of Nike's advertising, various Nike advertisements or commercials can be posted at various websites. Matched or randomly selected respondents can be recruited to visit these sites, with each group visiting only one site. If any pretreatment measures have to be obtained, the respondents answer a questionnaire posted on the site. They are then exposed to a particular Nike advertisement or a commercial at that site. After viewing the advertisement or commercial, the respondents answer additional questions, thus providing posttreatment measures. Control groups can be implemented in a similar way. All of the experimental designs that we have considered can be implemented in this manner.

Internet experiments can also be used to test the effectiveness of alternative Web designs. Visitors are randomly exposed to different Web designs, and their purchases are tracked over time, keeping the other marketing variables constant. Thus, the most effective design can be determined and implemented on the company's website.

EXPERIMENTAL VERSUS NONEXPERIMENTAL DESIGNS

In Chapter 3, we discussed three types of research designs: exploratory, descriptive, and causal. Of these, only causal designs are truly appropriate for inferring cause-and-effect relationships. Although descriptive survey data are often used to provide evidence of "causal" relationships, these studies do not meet all the conditions required for causality. For example, it is difficult in descriptive studies to establish the prior equivalence of the respondent groups with respect to both the independent and dependent variables. On the other hand, an experiment can establish this equivalence by random assignment of test units to groups. In descriptive research, it is also difficult to establish time order of occurrence of variables. In an experiment, however, the researcher controls the timing of the measurements and the introduction of the treatment. Finally, descriptive research offers little control over other possible causal factors.

We do not wish to undermine the importance of descriptive research designs in marketing research. As we mentioned in Chapter 3, descriptive research constitutes the most popular research design in marketing research, and we do not want to imply that it should never be used to examine causal relationships. Indeed, some authors have suggested procedures for drawing causal inferences from descriptive (nonexperimental) data. Rather, our intent is to alert the reader to the limitations of descriptive research for examining causal relationships. We also want to make the reader aware of the limitations of experimentation.

Research Recipe

Use only causal designs making use of experiments for inferring cause-and-effect relationships; descriptive surveys are limited in this respect.

LIMITATIONS OF EXPERIMENTATION

Although experimentation is becoming increasingly important in marketing research, it does have the following limitations: time, cost, and administration of an experiment.

Time

Many types of field experiments become increasingly accurate with time. For example, to observe the long-term effect of a promotional campaign or a product introduction, purchase behavior must be observed over multiple purchase cycles. The accuracy of such behavioral information tends to increase with the passage of time. This added precision must be weighed against the costs of delaying a product rollout or the launch of a new advertising campaign.

Cost

The Rite Aid experiment in the first Research in Practice feature ran for six weeks.

New-product research in field environments can be extremely expensive. It is much more expensive than laboratory experiments, which typically occur on a small scale and use a limited number of subjects. To field-test a new product, management must consider more than just the direct costs of data collection and analysis. Production must be initiated on a limited scale; point-of-sale promotional campaigns as well as mass advertising must be developed and introduced on a limited basis. Limited distribution channels might also have to be opened. This type of experiments can easily cost millions of dollars.

Administration

Controlling the effects of extraneous variables is an essential aspect of experimental research. Achieving the desired level of control becomes increasingly difficult as the research moves from the laboratory to the field. Field experiments often interfere with a company's ongoing operations, and obtaining cooperation from the retailers, wholesalers, and others involved can be difficult. Also, competitors might deliberately contaminate the results of a field experiment. These limitations of administering an experiment were evident in the Rite Aid experiment.

APPLICATION: TEST MARKETING

Test marketing, also called market testing, is an application of a controlled experiment done in limited but carefully selected parts of the marketplace called **test markets**. It involves a replication of a planned national marketing program in the test markets. Often, the marketing mix variables (independent variables) are varied in test marketing, and the sales (dependent variables) are monitored so that an appropriate national marketing strategy can be identified. The two major objectives of test marketing are to (1) determine market acceptance of the product and (2) test alternative levels of marketing mix variables.

test marketing
An application of a controlled experiment done in limited but carefully selected test markets. It involves a replication of the planned national marketing program for a product in the test markets.

test markets
A carefully selected part of the marketplace that is particularly suitable for test marketing.

Research in Practice
Big Mac Extended

McDonalds test-marketed the Mac Snack Wrap in a few markets in the United States—Phoenix, Arizona; Houston, Texas; Milwaukee, Wisconsin; and Michigan City, Indiana; as well as in Canada. The price was $1.49. The new wrap is just like the standard Big Mac, but instead all of the ingredients are stuffed inside a warm flour tortilla. When the test market results were favorable, the Mac Snack Wrap was introduced in North America.[3]

INTERNATIONAL MARKETING RESEARCH

If field experiments are difficult to conduct in the United States, the challenge they pose is greatly increased in the international arena. In many countries, the marketing, economic, structural, and information and technological environments (see Chapter 1) are not developed to the extent that they are in the United States. For example, in many countries, the television stations are owned and operated by the government, with severe restrictions on television advertising. This makes field experiments manipulating advertising levels extremely difficult. Consider, for example, M&M/Mars, which has set up massive manufacturing facilities in Russia and advertises its candy bars on television. Yet the sales potential has not been realized. Is Mars advertising too much, too little, or just right? While the answer could be determined by conducting a field experiment that manipulated the level of advertising, such causal research may not be easy to implement given the Russian government's control of Russian television stations.

Likewise, the lack of major supermarkets in the Baltic States makes it difficult for Procter & Gamble to conduct field experiments to determine the effect of in-store promotions on the sales of its detergents. In some countries in Asia, Africa, and South America, a majority of the population lives in small towns and villages. Yet basic infrastructure such as roads, transportation, and warehouse facilities are lacking, making it difficult to achieve desired levels of distribution. Even when experiments are designed, it is difficult to control for the time order of occurrence of variables and the absence of other possible causal factors, two of the necessary conditions for causality. Because the researcher has far less control over the environment, control of extraneous variables is particularly problematic. And it may not be possible to address this problem by adopting the most appropriate experimental design because environmental constraints may make that design impractical.

Thus, the internal and external validity of field experiments conducted overseas is generally lower than in the United States. Although we have pointed out the difficulties of conducting field experiments in other countries, we do not wish to imply that such causal research cannot or should not be conducted. Some form of test marketing is generally possible, as the following example indicates.

Research in Practice
Flawless Quality and Exclusivity at More Than $100,000 Apiece

Source: Sandro Campardo/AP Images

Lange Uhren GmbH, maker of A. Lange & Söhne watches (**www.alange-soehne.com**), has succeeded in the global economy. The reason is its market savvy. Test marketing was done in the United States, Japan, and France to determine an effective positioning and pricing strategy for the watches. In each country, the price and the positioning strategy were varied and consumer response was assessed. The results, which were similar across countries, indicated that a prestige positioning with a premium price would be most effective. The eastern Germany area, where the company is located, is well known for superior craftsmanship. Lange Uhren used a well-trained workforce and the new marketing platform to rekindle this tradition. The new positioning strategy is based on flawless quality and exclusivity, which are portrayed uniquely in each cultural context. The watches are sold by only twenty-two retailers worldwide for more than $100,000 each. The strategy has been successful, and the company has weathered even the difficult economic environment from 2009 to 2012. Business was back to normal in 2014.[4] <

Research Recipe

You may find it difficult to conduct field experiments in many developing countries because these countries lack marketing and basic infrastructure. For these reasons, the internal and external validity of field experiments conducted overseas is generally lower than in the United States.

MARKETING RESEARCH AND SOCIAL MEDIA

Both the virtual and real social worlds can be used for experimental research purposes. In virtual worlds, one can use Second Life (**www.secondlife.com**) as a tool to conduct standard marketing research experiments at a lower cost. Incentives in the form of Linden dollars can be used to gain the cooperation of Second Life residents and improve response rates. The researcher can also give nonmonetary incentives such as free virtual products and services; these virtual incentives could be clothing or scripts that add certain features to avatars. The French market research firm Repères (**www.reperes.net**) is one of the leading research providers within this domain.

The virtual world is especially well suited for laboratory-type experiments. In a virtual environment, it is a lot simpler and much less costly to manipulate the independent variable and control for mediating variables than it is in the real world. All of the experimental designs that we have discussed in this chapter can be implemented within the context of a virtual world. This is also true of test marketing. However, opinions, tastes, and preferences in virtual worlds may not be the same as in a real setting. Therefore, each new idea generated within virtual worlds needs to be subjected to a thorough reality test before actually being implemented.

All of the experimental designs that we have discussed in this chapter can also be implemented within the context of the real social world. Compared to the field, experimentation in social media offers the advantages of ease of implementation and lower cost. The internal validity may be satisfactory in most cases because extraneous variables can generally be controlled. However, external validity will not be as high as that of field experiments. A study conducted by Procter & Gamble (P&G) provides an illustration of using social media for experimentation.

Research in Practice
Old Spice Experiments with a New Way of Reaching Consumers

In 2013, the competition for Procter & Gamble's Old Spice body wash for men had become so fierce that Old Spice's share in the male body wash segment was starting to slip. To make things more difficult, Unilever announced that it would be launching a big campaign for Dove Men+Care body wash.

P&G required an in-depth understanding of the key customer segment to drive more effective product and service innovation. Hence, the company decided to experiment with posting YouTube videos (the treatment, X) to check consumer response and reaction to its new advertisement campaign. The dependent variables used to measure consumer response included the following: (1) On day one, the campaign received almost 6 million views; (2) on day two, Old Spice had eight of the eleven most popular videos online; and (3) at the end of the campaign, Old Spice's YouTube channel reported more than 11 million views and over 160,000 subscribers. Proctor & Gamble now had data on 160,000 people they didn't have before, and they used that data to formulate effective marketing strategies for Old Spice body wash for men. This is an example of a one-shot case study, a pre-experimental design that was implemented successfully in social media.[5] ◄

Source: Bob Daemmrich / Alamy

Research Recipe

You can conduct laboratory-type experiments in virtual space on sites such as Second Life. In the virtual world, it is a lot simpler and much less costly to manipulate the independent variable and control for mediating variables than it is in the real world. However, you should test ideas generated within the virtual world in the real world before you implement them. You can also implement all these designs in the real social world. The internal validity may be satisfactory in most cases, but external validity will not be as high as that of field experiments.

ETHICS IN MARKETING RESEARCH

demand artifacts

Responses given because the respondents attempt to guess the purpose of the experiment and respond accordingly.

It is often necessary to disguise the purpose of the experiment in order to produce valid results. One reason is to reduce **demand artifacts**: Responses given because respondents attempt to guess the purpose of the experiment and respond accordingly. Disguising the purpose of the research should be done in a manner that does not violate the rights of the respondents. One way to handle this ethical dilemma is to inform the respondents, at the beginning, that the experiment has been disguised. They should also be given a description of the research task and told that they can leave the experiment at any time. After the data have been collected, the true purpose of the study and the nature of the disguise should be fully explained to the respondents, and they should be given an opportunity to withdraw their information. This procedure is called **debriefing**. Disclosure in this way does not bias the results. There is evidence indicating that data collected from subjects informed of the disguise and those not informed is similar. Debriefing can alleviate stress and make the experiment a learning experience for the respondents.

debriefing

After an experiment is completed, informing test subjects what the experiment was about and how the experimental manipulations were performed.

One additional ethical concern is the responsibility of the researcher to use an appropriate experimental design for the problem and thus control errors caused by extraneous variables. As the following example illustrates, determining the most appropriate experimental design for the problem requires not only an initial evaluation but also continuous monitoring.

Research in Practice
Correcting Errors Early: A Stitch in Time Saves Nine

A marketing research firm specializing in advertising research is examining the effectiveness of a television commercial for Nike athletic shoes. A one-group pretest–posttest design is used. Attitudes held by the respondents toward Nike athletic shoes are obtained prior to the respondents being exposed to a sports program and several commercials, including the one for Nike. Attitudes are again measured after the respondents view the program and the commercials. Initial evaluation based on a small sample found the one-group pretest–posttest design adopted in this study to be susceptible to demand artifacts. Because time and financial constraints make redesigning the study difficult at best, the research continues without correction.

Continuing a research project after knowing errors were made in the early stages is not ethical behavior. Experimental design problems should be disclosed immediately to the client. Decisions whether to redesign or accept the flaw should be made jointly. ❮

Dell Running Case

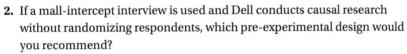

Review the Dell case, Case 1.1, and questionnaire given toward the end of the book.

1. Is causal research necessary in this case? If so, which experimental designs would you recommend and why? If not, describe a scenario in which causal research would be necessary. Can the latter experimental design be implemented in social media? If so, how?

2. If a mall-intercept interview is used and Dell conducts causal research without randomizing respondents, which pre-experimental design would you recommend?

3. Can you think of any way in which the static group design can be randomized to increase its validity?

Summary

The scientific notion of causality says that we can never prove that X causes Y. At best, we can only infer that X is one of the causes of Y in that it makes the occurrence of Y probable. Three conditions must be satisfied before causal inferences can be made: (1) concomitant variation, which implies that X and Y must vary together in a hypothesized way; (2) time order of occurrence of variables, which implies that X must precede or occur simultaneously with Y; and (3) elimination of other possible causal factors, which implies that competing explanations must be ruled out. Experiments provide the most convincing evidence of all three conditions. An experiment is formed when the researcher manipulates one or more independent variables and determines their effect on one or more dependent variables measured on the test units, while controlling for the effect of extraneous variables.

In designing an experiment it is important to consider internal and external validity. Internal validity refers to whether the manipulation of the independent variables actually caused the effects on the dependent variables. External validity refers to the generalizability of experimental results. For the experiment to be valid, the researcher must control the threats imposed by extraneous variables.

Experimental designs may be classified as pre-experimental, true experimental, and statistical. An experiment may be conducted in a laboratory environment or under actual market conditions in a real-life setting. Only causal designs encompassing experimentation are appropriate for inferring cause-and-effect relationships.

While experiments have limitations in terms of time, cost, and administration, they are becoming increasingly popular in marketing. Test marketing is an important application of experimental design.

The internal and external validity of field experiments conducted overseas is generally lower than in the United States. Development in many countries is not as advanced as it is in the United

States, and the researcher lacks control over many of the marketing variables. This makes it difficult to implement experimental procedures. Using social media, such as virtual reality, the researcher can create an environment that represents the field (marketplace) and yet exercise the degree of control possible only in a laboratory setting. The ethical issues involved in conducting causal research include disguising the purpose of the experiment. Debriefing can be used to address some of the ethical issues.

∨ Companion Website

This textbook includes numerous student resources that can be found at **www.pearsonglobaleditions.com/malhotra**. At this Companion website, you'll find:

- Student Resource Manual
- Demo movies of statistical procedures using SPSS and Microsoft Excel
- Screen captures of statistical procedures using SPSS and Microsoft Excel
- Data files for all datasets in SPSS and Microsoft Excel
- Additional figures and tables
- Videos and write-ups for all video cases
- Other valuable resources

∨ Key Terms and Concepts

Causality	Interaction	Pretest–posttest control group design
Concomitant variation	Internal validity	
Independent variables	External validity	Posttest-only control group design
Test units	Pre-experimental designs	
Dependent variables		Factorial design
Extraneous variables	True experimental designs	Laboratory experiment
Confounding variables		
Experiment	Statistical design	Field experiment
Random assignment	One-shot case study	Demand artifacts
Experimental group	One-group pretest–posttest design	Test marketing
Control group		Test markets
Experimental design	Static group	Debriefing

∨ Suggested Cases and Video Cases

Running Case with Real Data and Questionnaire

    1.1 Dell

Comprehensive Critical Thinking Cases

    2.1 American Idol

Comprehensive Cases with Real Data and Questionnaires

    3.1 JPMorgan Chase   3.2 Wendy's

Online Video Cases

    6.1 AFLAC   7.1 P&G   9.1 Subaru   13.1 Marriott

⌄ Live Research: Conducting a Marketing Research Project

If an experiment is to be conducted, an experimental design should be chosen based on class discussion. The choice of an experimental design might have to be tempered by several considerations:

1. It might not be possible to control for certain extraneous variables.
2. There might be only limited flexibility to manipulate the independent variables (e.g., advertising or sales effort cannot be reduced to the zero level).
3. Random assignment of test units to the treatment conditions might not be possible.
4. The choice of dependent variables might be limited by measurement considerations.

The experimental design selected should be discussed and approved by the client.

⌄ Acronyms

The salient characteristics of an experiment may be described by the acronym EXPT:

E xtraneous variables

X independent variables

P re- or postmeasurements on the dependent variable

T est units

⌄ Review Questions

6-1. What are the requirements for inferring a causal relationship between two variables?
6-2. What is one way of having the optimum combination of internal and external validity during experimental research?
6-3. What is the most common statistical design? Explain it.
6-4. Differentiate between experimental and control groups.
6-5. List the steps involved in implementing the posttest-only control group design. Describe the design symbolically.
6-6. What advantages do statistical designs have over basic designs?
6-7. What is one way of measuring whether randomization has been effective?
6-8. Should descriptive research be used for investigating causal relationships? Why or why not?
6-9. What is test marketing?
6-10. How can social media be used to conduct an experiment?

⌄ Applied Problems

6-11. A pro-life group wanted to test the effectiveness of an anti-abortion commercial. Two random samples, each of 250 respondents, were recruited in Atlanta. One group was shown the anti-abortion commercial. Then attitudes toward abortion were measured for respondents in both groups.
  a. Identify the independent and dependent variables in this experiment.
  b. What type of design was used?
  c. Can this design be implemented in social media? How?

6-12. In the experiment just described, suppose the respondents had been selected by convenience rather than randomly. What type of design would result?

6-13. State the type of experiment being conducted in the following situations.

a. A major distributor of office equipment is considering a new sales presentation program for its salespeople. The largest sales territory is selected, the new program is implemented, and the effect on sales is measured.

b. Procter & Gamble wants to determine if a new package design for Tide is more effective than the current design. Twelve supermarkets are randomly selected in Chicago. In six of them, which are randomly selected, Tide is sold in the new packaging. In the other six, the detergent is sold in the old package. Sales for both groups of supermarkets are monitored for three months.

6-14. Describe a specific situation for which each of the following experimental designs is appropriate. Defend your reasoning.

a. One-group pretest–posttest design

b. Pretest–posttest control group design

c. Posttest-only control group design

d. Factorial design

⌄ Internet Exercises

6-15. Survey the relevant literature and write a short paper on the role of the computer in controlled experiments in marketing research.

6-16. Hardees is developing a new dessert menu. How could a web-based market experiment be prepared to test customer acceptance of the items included on the menu?

6-17. Facebook is planning to change the layout of its homepage for user accounts and wants to test the new layout before releasing it. What type of experiment would be most suitable and how would it be applied?

6-18. Microsoft has developed a new version of its spreadsheet EXCEL but is not sure what the user reaction will be. Design an Internet-based experiment to determine user reaction to the new and the previous versions of EXCEL.

6-19. Explain how you would implement a posttest-only control group design on the Internet to measure the effectiveness of a new print ad for Toyota Camry.

NOTES

1. **www.riteaid.com**, accessed February 3, 2013; Michelle L. Kirsche, "POPAI Study Confirms Importance of POP Ads," *Drug Store News* 26(13) (October 11, 2004): 4–5; Anonymous, "In-Store Promo Drives Soda Sales, Study Says," *Drug Store News,* 23(18) (December 17, 2001): 81; Robert Dwek, "Prediction of Success," *Marketing* (POP & Field Marketing Supplement) (April 17, 1997): XII–XIII; and "POP Radio Test Airs the Ads in Store," *Marketing News* (October 24, 1986): 16.

2. **www.popai.com**, accessed March 2, 2013; "Does spending money on point of sale drive sales?" **www.retail-week.com/in-business/retail-surgery/does-spending-money-on-point-of-sale-drive-sales/5026519.article**, accessed April 10, 2012.

3. **www.mcdonalds.com/us/en/home.html**, accessed March 17, 2013; and **http://blogs.houstonpress.com/hairballs/2009/03/smaller_big_mac.php**, accessed March 17, 2012.

4. **www.alange-soehne.com**, accessed January 5, 2013; Frank S. Costanza, "Exports Boost German Jewelry Industry," *National Jeweler,* 45(8) (April 16, 2001): 57; and David Woodruff and Karen Nickel, "When You Think Deluxe, Think East Germany," *Business Week,* May 26, 1997: 124E2.

5. Simon Small, "Old Spice Campaign Case Study," **http://from.simontsmall.com/index.php/2010/08/12/old-spice-campaign-case-study/**; accessed March 30, 2013; and "How Old Spice Revived a Campaign That No One Wanted to Touch," **http://mashable.com/2011/11/01/old-spice-campaign/**, accessed November 8, 2013.

Online Video Case 6.1

AFLAC: Marketing Research Quacks a Duck

Visit **www.pearsonglobaleditions.com/malhotra** to read the video case and view the accompanying video. AFLAC: Marketing Research Quacks a Duck describes the crucial role of marketing research in designing the right advertising campaign and the resulting impact on brand recognition for AFLAC. In particular, the AFLAC duck commercials were tested against alternatives in experimental design situations. This case can be used to discuss the use of alternative experimental designs in evaluating advertising effectiveness. Specific marketing research questions on this and the previous chapters are posed in the video case.

Measurement and Scaling

❯ Overview

Once the type of research design has been determined and the exploratory and conclusive methods of research specified (Chapters 3 through 6), the researcher can move on to the next phase of the research design: deciding on measurement and scaling procedures. This chapter describes the concepts of scaling and measurement and discusses four primary scales of measurement: nominal, ordinal, interval, and ratio. We next describe both comparative and noncomparative scaling techniques and explain them in detail. The comparative techniques consist of paired comparison, rank order, and constant sum. The noncomparative techniques are comprised of continuous and itemized rating scales. We discuss the popular itemized rating scales (the Likert, semantic differential, and Stapel scales), as well as the construction of multi-item rating scales. We show how scaling techniques should be evaluated in terms of reliability and validity, and consider how the researcher selects a particular scaling technique. The considerations involved in implementing the scales of measurement when researching international markets and when conducting research in social media are discussed. Several ethical issues that can arise in measurement and scaling are identified. Figure 7.1 gives the relationship of this chapter to the marketing research process.

"When we analyze research results, we must believe that the measurements provide realistic representations of opinions and behaviors and properly capture how a respondent's data relates to all other respondents."

> Greg Van Scoy, Senior Vice President, Client Services, Burke, Inc., Cincinnati, Ohio.

∨ Learning Objectives

After reading this chapter, the student should be able to:

1. Introduce the concepts of measurement and scaling and show how scaling may be considered an extension of measurement.

2. Discuss the primary scales of measurement and differentiate nominal, ordinal, interval, and ratio scales.

3. Classify scaling techniques as comparative and noncomparative, and describe the comparative techniques of paired comparison, rank order, and constant sum.

4. Describe the noncomparative scaling techniques; distinguish between continuous and itemized rating scales; and explain Likert, semantic differential, and Stapel scales.

5. Discuss the variations involved in constructing itemized rating scales.

6. Discuss the criteria used for scale evaluation and explain how to assess reliability and validity.

7. Discuss the considerations involved in implementing scales of measurement in an international setting.

8. Explain how social media can be used to implement comparative and noncomparative scaling techniques.

9. Understand the ethical issues involved in selecting scales of measurement.

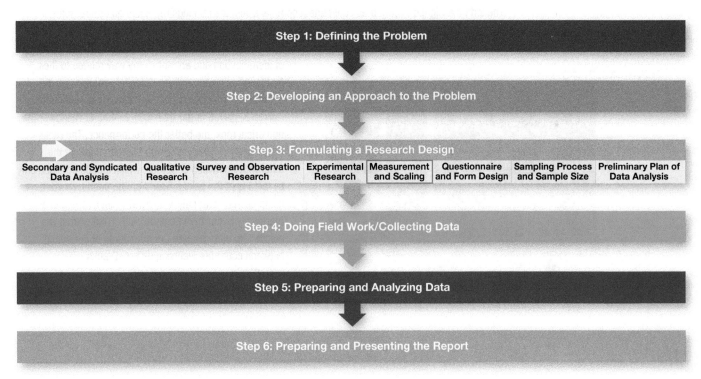

FIGURE 7.1 | RELATIONSHIP OF THIS CHAPTER TO THE MARKETING RESEARCH PROCESS

Research in Practice
Scaling the World of Football

According to Federation Internationale de Football Association's (FIFA) (**www.fifa.com**) June 2013 men's rankings, Spain was at the top with 1614 points and Germany was in the second spot with 1416 points. The top ten countries in men's football (known as soccer in the United States) were:

| ID | Team | Ranking as of June 2013 | |
		Rank	Points
A	Spain	1	1614
B	Germany	2	1416
C	Argentina	3	1287
D	Croatia	4	1222
E	Netherlands	5	1158
F	Portugal	6	1137
G	Colombia	7	1123
H	Italy	8	1097
I	England	9	1095
J	Ecuador	10	1066

The letters assigned to countries constitute a nominal scale, the rankings represent an ordinal scale, whereas the points awarded denote an interval scale. Thus, country G refers to Colombia, which was ranked 7 and received 1123 points. Note that the letters assigned to denote the countries simply serve the purpose

Source: epa european pressphoto agency b.v. / Alamy

of identification and are not in any way related to their football-playing capabilities. Such information can be obtained only by looking at the ranks. Thus, Netherlands, ranked 5, played better than Italy, ranked 8. The lower the numerical rank, the better the performance. The ranks do not give any information on the magnitude of the differences between countries, which can be obtained only by looking at the points. Based on the points awarded, it can be seen that Italy, with 1097 points, played only marginally better than England, with 1095 points. The points help us to discern the magnitude of difference between countries receiving different ranks.[1] **<**

Assigning rankings and ratings (points) to football teams are examples of the important role of measurement and scaling in marketing research.

MEASUREMENT AND SCALING

measurement

The assignment of numbers or other symbols to characteristics of objects according to certain set rules.

Measurement means assigning numbers or other symbols to characteristics of objects according to certain set rules. Note that what we measure is not the object, but some characteristic of it. Thus, we do not measure consumers—only their perceptions, attitudes, preferences, or other relevant characteristics. In marketing research, numbers are usually assigned for two reasons. First, numbers permit statistical analysis of the resulting data. Second, numbers facilitate the communication of measurement rules and results.

The most important aspect of measurement is that the researcher specifies rules for assigning numbers to the characteristics. The assignment process must be such that there is a one-to-one correspondence between the numbers and the characteristics being measured. For example, the same dollar figures are assigned to households with identical annual incomes. Only then can the numbers be associated with specific characteristics of the measured object, and vice versa. In addition, the rules for assigning numbers should be standardized and applied uniformly. They must not change over objects (e.g., stores) or time (e.g., quarter to quarter in quarterly surveys of customer satisfaction).

Scaling may be considered an extension of measurement. **Scaling** involves creating a continuum upon which measured objects are located. To illustrate, consider a scale for locating consumers according to the characteristic "attitude toward fast-food restaurants." Each respondent is assigned a number indicating an unfavorable attitude (measured as 1), a neutral attitude (measured as 2), or a favorable attitude (measured as 3) toward a specific fast-food restaurant. Measurement is the actual assignment of 1, 2, or 3 to each respondent for each restaurant. Scaling is the process of placing the respondents on a continuum with respect to their attitude toward fast-food restaurants. Suppose we measured attitudes toward five fast-food restaurants and then added the score of each respondent across the five restaurants to arrive at a total or overall attitude score. The total or overall score would vary from 5 (for a respondent who gave a rating of 1 to each of the five restaurants) to 15 (for a respondent who gave a rating of 3 to each of the five restaurants). In our example, scaling is the process by which respondents would be assigned an overall attitude score varying from 5 to 15. In the first Research in Practice feature in this chapter, measurement was the assignment of points to countries based on their performance in football. Scaling involved creating a continuum from 1066 to 1614 points upon which the top ten countries were located.

scaling
The generation of a continuum upon which measured objects are located.

Research Recipe

Measurement is usually the assignment of numbers to characteristics of objects according to certain set rules. You measure some characteristic of the object and not the object itself. Scaling may be considered an extension of measurement and involves creating a continuum upon which measured objects are located.

PRIMARY SCALES OF MEASUREMENT

There are four primary scales of measurement: nominal, ordinal, interval, and ratio (Figure 7.2). These scales are illustrated in Figure 7.3, and their properties are summarized in Table 7.1 and discussed in the following sections. We illustrate all the primary scales in measuring preference and patronage of fast-food restaurants as given in Table 7.2

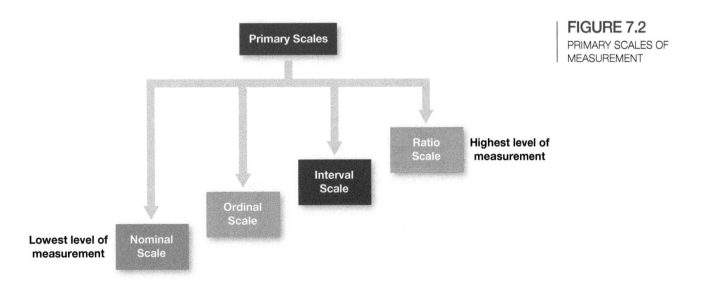

FIGURE 7.2
PRIMARY SCALES OF MEASUREMENT

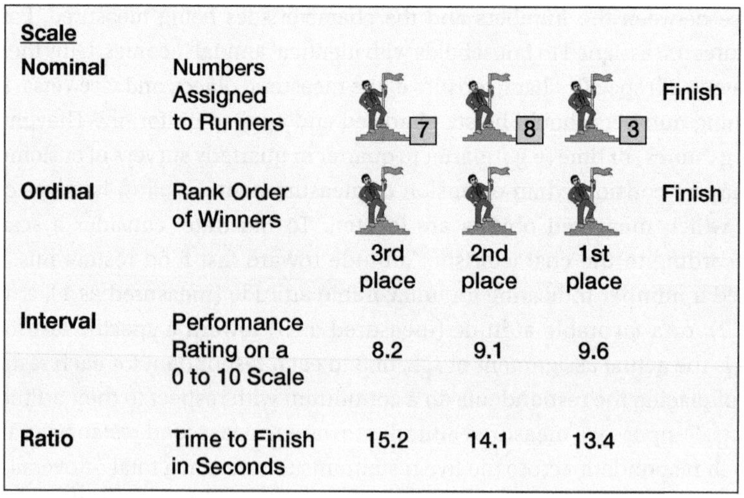

FIGURE 7.3
PRIMARY SCALES
OF MEASUREMENT
ILLUSTRATED

Scale					
Nominal	Numbers Assigned to Runners	7	8	3	Finish
Ordinal	Rank Order of Winners	3rd place	2nd place	1st place	Finish
Interval	Performance Rating on a 0 to 10 Scale	8.2	9.1	9.6	
Ratio	Time to Finish in Seconds	15.2	14.1	13.4	

nominal scale
A scale whose numbers serve only as labels or tags for identifying and classifying objects, with a strict one-to-one correspondence between the numbers and the objects when used for identification.

Nominal Scale

A **nominal scale** is a figurative labeling scheme in which the numbers serve only as labels or tags for identifying and classifying objects. For example, the numbers assigned to respondents in a study constitute a nominal scale. When a nominal scale is used for the purpose of identification, there is a strict one-to-one correspondence between the numbers and the objects. Each number is assigned to only one object, and each object has only one number assigned to it. Common examples include Social Security numbers and numbers assigned to baseball players. Thus a Social Security number can be assigned to one and only one individual, and each individual can be assigned one and only one Social Security number. In marketing research, nominal scales are used for identifying respondents, brands, attributes, restaurants, and other people and objects. In the first Research in Practice feature in this chapter, the letters A through J assigned to the ten countries constituted a nominal scale.

When used for classification purposes, the nominally scaled numbers serve as labels for classes or categories. For example, based on gender, you might classify the males as group 1 and the females as group 2. The classes are mutually exclusive and collectively exhaustive. Thus, a person will be classified as either a male or a female, but he or she cannot be classified into both categories because these categories are mutually exclusive. Also, every person will be classified as either a male or a female because these classes are collectively exhaustive; we cannot have a person who does not fall into either of these categories. The objects in each class are viewed as equivalent with respect to the characteristic

Table 7.1 > Primary Scales of Measurement

Primary Scale	Basic Characteristics	Common Examples	Marketing Examples
Nominal	Numbers Identify and classify objects	Social Security numbers; numbering of football players	Brand numbers; store types; sex classification
Ordinal	Numbers indicate the relative positions of the objects but not the magnitude of differences between them	Quality rankings; rankings of teams in a tournament	Preference rankings; market position; social class
Interval	Differences between objects can be compared; zero point is arbitrary	Temperature (Fahrenheit; Celsius)	Attitudes; opinions; index numbers
Ratio	Zero point is fixed; ratios of scale values can be computed	Length; weight	Age; income; costs; sales; market shares

Table 7.2 > Illustration of Primary Scales of Measurement

Nominal Scale		Ordinal Scale		Interval Scale		Ratio Scale	
Store Number	Store Name	Preference Ranking		Preference Ratings		Amount Spent in the Last 2 Months	
				1–7	11–17	Dollars	Cents
1.	Burger King	4	79	4	14	10	1000
2.	McDonald's	2	25	7	17	50	5000
3.	Subway	5	82	3	13	0	0
4.	KFC	3	30	6	16	25	2500
5.	Pizza Hut	1	10	7	17	75	7500

represented by the nominal number. Thus, all males are considered equivalent with respect to gender, as indeed are all females. All objects in the same class have the same number (i.e., all males are assigned the number 1 and all females are assigned the number 2) and no two classes have the same number (no male can be assigned a number 2 and no female can be assigned the number 1).

The numbers in a nominal scale do not reflect the amount of the characteristic possessed by the objects. For example, a high Social Security number does not imply that the person is in some way superior to those with lower Social Security numbers, or vice versa. The same applies to numbers assigned to classes. Thus, males (assigned a number 1) are in no way superior or inferior to females (assigned a number 2). The numbers 1 and 2 merely denote whether a person is a male or female, respectively. The nominal scale represents the lowest level of measurement and is illustrated in the following.

In a fast-food restaurant project, numbers 1 through 5 were assigned to the five restaurants considered in the study (see Table 7.2). Thus, restaurant number 4 referred to KFC. It did not imply that KFC was in any way superior or inferior to McDonald's, which was assigned the number 2. Any reassignment of the numbers, such as transposing the numbers assigned to KFC and McDonald's, would have no effect on the numbering system because the numerals do not reflect any characteristics of the restaurants.

Research Recipe

In a nominal scale, the numbers serve only as labels or tags for identifying and classifying objects. When used for identification, there is strict one-to-one correspondence between the numbers and objects. When used for classification, the numbers serve as labels for classes or categories. Note that the numbers do not reflect the amount of the characteristic possessed by the objects.

Ordinal Scale

An **ordinal scale** is a ranking scale in which numbers are assigned to objects to indicate the relative extent to which the objects possess some characteristic. An ordinal scale allows you to determine whether an object has more or less of a characteristic than another object, but not how much more or less. Thus an ordinal scale indicates relative position, not the magnitude of the differences between the objects. The object ranked first has more of the characteristic compared to the object ranked second, but whether the object ranked second is a close second or a poor second is not known. Measurements of this type include "greater than" or "less than" judgments from the respondents. Thus, an ordinal scale conveys more information than a nominal scale that does not contain "greater than" or "less than" judgments. Common examples of ordinal scales include quality rankings, rankings of teams in a tournament, socioeconomic class, and occupational status. In marketing research, ordinal scales are used to measure relative attitudes, opinions, perceptions, and preferences. Another common form of ordinal scales is categorical scales (nominal scales) that show order, or more or less

ordinal scale
A ranking scale in which numbers are assigned to objects to indicate the relative extent to which some characteristic is possessed. Thus, it is possible to determine whether an object has more or less of a characteristic than another object.

of a characteristic such as education levels, age categories, income categories, and so on. In the first Research in Practice feature in this chapter, the rank order of countries with Spain ranked number 1, Germany 2, and so on with Ecuador ranked 10 constituted an ordinal scale.

In an ordinal scale, equivalent objects receive the same rank. Ordinal scales can be transformed in any way as long as the basic ordering of the objects is maintained because the differences in numbers are void of any meaning other than order. Such transformations result in equivalent scales.

Table 7.2 gives a particular respondent's preference rankings (see the first column under Preference Ranking). Respondents ranked five fast-food restaurants in order of preference by assigning a rank of 1 to the most preferred restaurant, a rank of 2 to the second most preferred restaurant, and so on. The lower number indicates that the restaurant is preferred to one with a higher number. Note that Pizza Hut (ranked 1), is preferred to McDonald's (ranked 2), but how much it is preferred we do not know. Also, it is not necessary that we assign numbers from 1 to 5 to obtain a preference ranking. The second ordinal scale, which assigns a number 10 to Pizza Hut, a number 25 to McDonald's, 30 to KFC, and so on, is an equivalent scale, as it was obtained by transforming the first scale while maintaining the order (see the second column under Preference Ranking). This transformation is based on the rule that the lower the numerical rank, the higher the preference. The first scale, i.e., 1, 2, 3, 4, and 5 and the second scale, i.e., 10, 25, 30, 79, and 82, result in the same ordering of the restaurants according to preference and are therefore equivalent. This equivalence can be seen as follows. 1 is less than 2 and 10 is less than 25; 2 is less than 3 and 25 is less than 30; 3 is less than 4 and 30 is less than 79; 4 is less than 5 and 79 is less than 82. Both scales are based on the same rule, that is, the lower the numerical rank, the higher the preference and both result in the same rank order. As noted earlier, the differences in numbers are void of any meaning other than order. As a further illustration, *Fortune* magazine uses ordinal scaling to determine the world's most admired companies. See the next Research in Practice.

Research in Practice
The World's Most Admired Companies

The value of the World's Most Admired Companies rankings, as with *Fortune* magazine's list of America's most admired, lies in their having been bestowed by the people who are closest to the action: senior executives and directors in each industry, and financial analysts who are in a position to study and compare the competitors in each field. *Fortune* asked them to rate companies on the eight criteria used to rank America's most admired: innovativeness, overall quality of management, value as a long-term investment, responsibility to the community and the environment, ability to attract and keep talented people, quality of products or services, financial soundness, and wise use of corporate assets. For global ranking, *Fortune* added another criterion to reflect international scope: a company's effectiveness in doing business globally. A company's overall ranking is based on the average of the scores of all the criteria attributes. The 2013 World's Most Admired Companies were:

ID	Company	Rank
A	Apple	1
B	Google	2
C	Amazon.com	3
D	Coca-Cola	4
E	Starbucks	5
F	IBM	6
G	Southwest Airlines	7
H	Berkshire Hathaway	8
I	Walt Disney	9
J	FedEx	10

In this example, the ID letters used to identify the companies represent a nominal scale. Thus, I denotes Walt Disney and F refers to IBM. The number ranks represent an ordinal scale. Thus, Amazon.com, ranked 3, received higher evaluations than IBM, ranked 6. Such rankings are useful because they represent summary measures of the esteem in which companies are held. Note that all the top ten companies are American, which underscores the dominance of the United States in global business.[2] <

Research Recipe

In an ordinal scale, the numbers are assigned to objects to indicate the relative extent to which the objects possess some characteristic. The numbers allow you to determine whether an object has more or less of a characteristic than some other object, but not how much more or less. The numbers are void of any meaning other than order. Thus, any order-preserving transformation of the scale results in an equivalent scale.

iResearch
Increasing Customer Satisfaction with Burger King

Visit **www.bk.com** and search the Internet, including social media as well as your library's online databases, to obtain information on customer satisfaction with fast-food restaurants.

As the marketing director for Burger King, what marketing strategies would you formulate to enhance customer satisfaction? How would you use nominal and ordinal scales to measure customer satisfaction with the major fast-food restaurants such as Burger King? <

Interval Scale

In an **interval scale**, numerically equal distances on the scale represent equal values in the characteristic being measured. An interval scale contains all the information of an ordinal scale, but it also allows you to compare the differences between objects. The difference between any two adjacent scale values is identical to the difference between any other two adjacent values of an interval scale. There is a constant or equal interval between scale values. The difference between 1 and 2 is the same as the difference between 2 and 3, which is the same as the difference between 5 and 6. Thus, an interval scale conveys more information than an ordinal scale that does not contain information on distance. A common example in everyday life is a temperature scale. In marketing research, attitudinal data obtained from rating scales are often treated as interval data. For example, asking respondents to express their degree of agreement with the statement "I like Starbucks coffee" on a 5-point scale (1 = strongly disagree, 5 = strongly agree) will measure their attitude toward Starbucks coffee. Interval scales are widely used in marketing research to obtain data from respondents and are the most popular of all the primary scales. In the first Research in Practice feature in this chapter, the points assigned to the countries with Spain receiving the highest points amounting to 1614 and Ecuador receiving 1066, the lowest, constituted an interval scale. In an interval scale, the location of the 0 point or the origin is not fixed. Both the origin and the units of measurement are arbitrary. Hence, it is permissible to shift the origin, for example, by adding a constant, and that will result in an equivalent scale. Because the 0 point is not fixed, it is not meaningful to take ratios of scale values. We illustrate this property of the interval scale by examining the information in Table 7.2, which shows a respondent's preferences for the five restaurants expressed on a 1 to 7 rating scale (see the first column under Preference Ratings). We can see that, although KFC received a preference rating of 6 and Subway a preference rating of 3, this does not mean that KFC is preferred two times as much as Subway. The ratings are then transformed to an equivalent 11 to 17 scale by shifting the

interval scale
A scale in which the numbers are used to rate objects. The numerically equal distances on the scale represent equal distances in the characteristic being measured.

origin from 1 to 11. This can be done by adding 10 to each scale value (see the second column under Preference Ratings). Thus, 1 becomes 11, 2 becomes 12, 3 becomes 13, and so on, and seven becomes 17. The transformed ratings for KFC and Subway become 16 and 13, and the ratio is no longer 2 to 1.

Research Recipe

In an interval scale, numerically equal distances on the scale represent equal values in the characteristic being measured. The difference between any two adjacent scale values is identical to the difference between any other two adjacent values of an interval scale. Thus, an interval scale allows you to compare the differences between objects. Both the 0 point (origin) and the units of measurement are arbitrary. Therefore, it is permissible to shift the origin, for example, by adding a constant, and that will result in an equivalent scale. Because the 0 point or origin is not fixed, it is not meaningful to take ratios of scale values in an interval scale; the ratios of scale values will change when the origin is shifted.

Ratio Scale

ratio scale
The highest measurement scale conveying the most information. It allows the researcher to identify or classify objects, rank-order the objects, and compare intervals or differences. It is also meaningful to compute ratios of scale values.

A **ratio scale** possesses all the properties of the nominal, ordinal, and interval scales, plus an absolute 0 point. Thus, the ratio scale represents the highest level of measurement conveying the most information. In ratio scales, we can identify or classify objects, rank the objects, and compare intervals or differences. Unlike the nominal, ordinal, and interval scales, it is also meaningful to compute ratios of scale values. Not only is the difference between 2 and 5 the same as the difference between 14 and 17, but also 14 is seven times as large as 2 in an absolute sense. Common examples of ratio scales include height, weight, age, and income that are measured as exact numbers rather than as categories. In marketing, sales, costs, market share, and the number of customers are variables measured on a ratio scale. While not shown in the first Research in Practice feature in this chapter, the annual dollar amount spent on football in each of these countries would comprise a ratio scale.

Ratio scales allow only proportionate transformations that involve multiplication by a positive constant. One cannot add an arbitrary constant, unlike the case of an interval scale. An example of this transformation is provided by the conversion of yards to feet (multiplication by 3) or dollars to cents (multiplication by 100). The comparisons between the lengths of objects are identical whether made in yards or feet. Ratio scales are not as popular as interval scales for obtaining information because respondents find it more taxing to provide ratio scale information than they do interval scale data.

The ratio scale is further illustrated in the context of the fast-food restaurant example. In Table 7.2, a respondent is asked to indicate the dollar amounts spent in each of the five restaurants during the last two months. Note that, because this respondent spent $50 in McDonald's and only $10 in Burger King, this respondent spent five times as much in McDonald's as in Burger King. Also, the 0 point is fixed because 0 means that the respondent did not spend anything at that restaurant. Multiplying these numbers by 100 to convert dollars to cents results in an equivalent scale.

Research Recipe

A ratio scale possesses all the properties of the nominal, ordinal, and interval scales, and it has an absolute 0 point. Hence, it is meaningful to compute ratios of scale values. Ratio scales allow only proportionate transformations. You cannot add an arbitrary constant, unlike the case of an interval scale. The ratio scale represents the highest level of measurement that conveys the most information.

COMPARATIVE AND NONCOMPARATIVE SCALING TECHNIQUES

The scaling techniques commonly employed in marketing research can be classified into comparative and noncomparative scales (see Figure 7.4). **Comparative scales** involve the direct comparison of two or more objects; objects are evaluated in relation to other objects in the stimulus set. For example, respondents might be asked whether they prefer Coke or Pepsi. Comparative scale data must be interpreted in relative terms and have only ordinal or rank-order properties. For this reason, comparative scaling is also referred to as nonmetric scaling (nonmetric data have only ordinal properties). As shown in Figure 7.4, comparative scales include paired comparisons, rank order, and constant sum scales. In **noncomparative scales**, also referred to as monadic or metric scales, objects are evaluated independently of each other. The resulting data are generally assumed to be interval scaled. Metric data have interval or ratio properties. For example, respondents might be asked to evaluate Coke on a 1 to 7 preference scale (1 = not at all preferred, 7 = greatly preferred). Similar evaluations would be obtained independently for Pepsi. The noncomparative scales consist of continuous and itemized scales (Likert, semantic differential, and Stapel scales). We consider first comparative scaling techniques and then noncomparative scaling techniques.

comparative scales
One of two types of scaling techniques in which there is direct comparison of stimulus objects with one another.

noncomparative scales
One of two types of scaling techniques in which each object is scaled independently of the other objects in the stimulus set.

Research Recipe

Comparative scales involve the direct comparison of two or more objects; objects are evaluated relative to other objects in the stimulus set. You must interpret comparative scale data in relative terms because such data have only ordinal or rank-order properties. In contrast, in noncomparative scales, objects are evaluated independently of each other. The resulting data are generally assumed to be interval scaled.

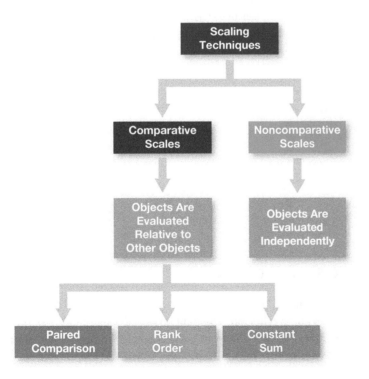

FIGURE 7.4
A CLASSIFICATION OF SCALING TECHNIQUES

COMPARATIVE SCALING TECHNIQUES

Paired Comparison Scaling

paired comparison scaling
A comparative scaling technique in which a respondent is presented with two objects at a time and asked to select one object in the pair according to some criterion. The data obtained are ordinal in nature.

As its name implies, in **paired comparison scaling**, a respondent is presented with two objects and asked to select one according to some criterion. The data obtained are ordinal in nature. A respondent may state that she shops in JC Penney more than in Sears, likes Total cereal better than Kellogg's Product 19, or likes Crest more than Colgate. Paired comparison scales are frequently used when the stimulus objects are physical products. Paired comparison scaling is a widely used comparative scaling technique.

Paired comparison data can be analyzed by calculating the percentage of respondents who prefer one stimulus over another. Paired comparison scaling is useful when the number of brands is limited because it requires direct comparison and overt choice. With a large number of brands, however, the number of comparisons becomes unwieldy. Paired comparisons bear little resemblance to the marketplace situation that involves selection from multiple alternatives. Also respondents may prefer one object over certain others, but they may not like it in an absolute sense (that is, it is disliked less). The following Research in Practice provides further insights into paired comparison scaling.

Research in Practice
Paired Comparison Scaling

The most common method of taste testing is paired comparison. The consumer is asked to sample two different products and select the one with the most appealing taste. The test is done in private, either in homes or other predetermined sites. A minimum of 1,000 respondents is considered an adequate sample.

A blind taste test for products, where imagery, self-perception, and brand reputation are very important factors in the consumer's purchasing decision, may not be a good indicator of performance in the marketplace. The introduction of Yoplait Lactose Free yogurt in 2012 illustrates this point. The new yogurt was favored over other yogurt brands in blind paired comparison taste tests, but its introduction was less than stellar. ◀

Source: Steve Cukrov / Alamy

Research Recipe

In paired comparison scaling, you present respondents with two objects and ask them to select one according to some criterion. The data obtained are ordinal in nature and you analyze them by calculating the percentage of respondents who prefer one stimulus over another. Paired comparison scaling is useful when the number of brands is limited.

Rank-Order Scaling

After paired comparisons, the most popular comparative scaling technique is rank-order scaling. Rank-order scaling is similar to the ordinal scale discussed earlier in the section on primary scales. In **rank-order scaling**, respondents are presented with several objects simultaneously and asked to order or rank them according to some criterion. For example, respondents may be asked to rank brands of toothpaste according to overall preference. These rankings are typically obtained by asking the respondents to assign a rank of 1 to the most preferred brand, 2 to the second most preferred, and so on, until a rank of n is assigned to the least preferred brand. Like paired comparison, this approach is also comparative in nature, and it is possible that the respondent may dislike, in an absolute sense, the brand ranked first. Rank-order scaling also results in ordinal data. See Table 7.2 for an illustration, which uses rank-order scaling to derive an ordinal scale. In the first Research in Practice feature in this chapter, the ranking of countries with Spain ranked number 1, Germany 2, and so on with Ecuador ranked 10 constituted a rank-order scale.

Rank-order scaling is commonly used to measure preferences for brands as well as attributes. Compared to paired comparisons, this type of scaling process more closely resembles the shopping environment. It also takes less time because the respondents have to make fewer judgments compared to paired comparisons. Another advantage is that most respondents easily understand the instructions for ranking. The major disadvantage is that this technique produces only ordinal data.

rank-order scaling
A comparative scaling technique in which respondents are presented with several objects simultaneously and asked to order or rank them according to some criterion.

Research Recipe

In rank-order scaling, you present respondents with several objects simultaneously and ask them to order or rank the objects according to some criterion. Like paired comparison, this approach is comparative in nature producing ordinal data, and it is possible that the respondent may dislike, in an absolute sense, the brand ranked first. Unlike paired comparisons, this type of scaling process closely resembles the shopping environment. It also takes less time because the respondents have to make fewer judgments compared to paired comparisons.

Constant Sum Scaling

In **constant sum scaling**, respondents allocate a constant sum of units, such as points, dollars, or chips, among a set of stimulus objects with respect to some criterion. Respondents may be asked to allocate 100 points (or any other fixed number of points, say, 10) to attributes of a fast-food restaurant in a way that reflects the importance they attach to each attribute. If an attribute is unimportant, the respondent assigns it 0 points. If an attribute is twice as important as some other attribute, it receives twice as many points. The sum of all the points is 100; hence, the name of the scale.

We illustrate this procedure by giving the points allocated by a respondent to reflect the importance attached to four attributes of fast-food restaurants as follows.

constant sum scaling
A comparative scaling technique in which respondents are required to allocate a constant sum of units such as points, dollars, chits, stickers, or chips among a set of stimulus objects with respect to some criterion.

Attribute	Points Allocated
Quality	40
Service	20
Cleanliness	10
Value	30
Total	100

The attributes are scaled by counting the points assigned to each one by the respondent. This respondent attaches the greatest importance to quality, followed by value and then service, with cleanliness being the least important. Such information cannot be obtained from rank-order data.

Note that the constant sum also has an absolute 0:20 points are twice as many as 10 points, and the difference between 10 and 20 points is the same as the difference between 20 and 30 points. For this reason, constant sum scale data are sometimes treated as metric. While this may be appropriate in the limited context of the stimuli scaled, these results are not generalizable to other stimuli not included in the study. Thus, strictly speaking, the constant sum should be considered an ordinal scale because of its comparative nature and the resulting lack of generalizability. It can be seen that the allocation of points in the preceding example is influenced by the specific attributes included in the evaluation task. If a fifth attribute, for example, convenience of location, is added, the allocation obtained with the four attributes is no longer valid. The respondent will have to perform the entire evaluation task anew.

The main advantage of the constant sum scale is that it allows for fine discrimination among stimulus objects without requiring too much time. However, it has two primary disadvantages. Respondents may allocate more or fewer units than those specified. For example, a respondent may allocate 108 or 94 points rather than the specified 100. The researcher must modify such data in some way or eliminate this respondent from analysis. Another potential problem is rounding error if too few units are used. On the other hand, the use of a large number of units may be too taxing for the respondent and can cause confusion and fatigue.

Research Recipe

In constant sum scaling, you ask respondents to allocate 100 points to attributes of a product in a way that reflects the importance they attach to each attribute. If an attribute is unimportant, it should be assigned 0 points. If an attribute is twice as important as some other attribute, it should receive twice as many points. The sum of all the points should be 100. The main advantage of the constant sum scale is that it allows for fine discrimination among stimulus objects. Its main disadvantages are that some respondents may allocate more or fewer units than those specified, and rounding errors or fatigue.

iResearch
Coaching Consumer Preferences for Coach

Visit **www.coach.com** and search the Internet, including social media as well as your library's online databases, to obtain information on consumer preferences for leather goods. How would you use comparative scales to measure consumer preferences for leather goods?

As the marketing director for Coach, how would you use information on consumer preferences for leather goods to increase your market share? ‹

NONCOMPARATIVE SCALING TECHNIQUES

Respondents using a noncomparative scale do not compare the object being rated to either another object or some specified standard, such as "your ideal brand." They evaluate only one object at a time, and for this reason noncomparative scales are often referred to as monadic scales. In evaluating the objects, the respondents employ whatever rating standard seems

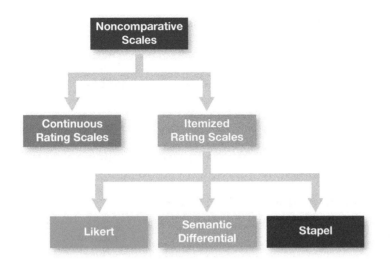

FIGURE 7.5

A CLASSIFICATION OF
NONCOMPARATIVE RATING
SCALES

Table 7.3 > Basic Noncomparative Scales

Scale	Basic Characteristics	Examples	Advantages	Disadvantages
Continuous Rating Scale	Place a mark on a continuous line	Reaction to TV commercials	Easy to construct	Scoring can be cumbersome unless computerized
Itemized Rating Scales				
Likert Scale	Degree of agreement on a 1 (strongly disagree) to 5 (strongly agree) scale	Measurement of attitudes	Easy to construct, administer, and understand	More time consuming
Semantic Differential	Seven-point scale with bipolar labels	Brand, product, and company images	Versatile	Difficult to construct bipolar adjectives
Stapel Scale	Unipolar ten-point scale, −5 to +5, without a neutral point (zero)	Measurement of attitudes and images	Easy to construct and administer over telephone	Confusing and difficult to apply

appropriate to them. As shown in Figure 7.5, noncomparative techniques consist of continuous and itemized rating scales, which are described in Table 7.3 and discussed in the following sections.

Continuous Rating Scale

In a **continuous rating scale**, also referred to as a graphic rating scale, respondents rate the objects by placing a mark at the appropriate position on a line that runs from one extreme of the criterion variable to the other. Thus, the respondents are not restricted to selecting from marks previously set by the researcher. The form of the continuous scale may vary considerably. For example, the line may be vertical or horizontal; scale points, in the form of numbers or brief descriptions, may be provided. The scale points, if provided, may be few or many. Three versions of a continuous rating scale are illustrated as follows:

continuous rating scale
A noncomparative measurement scale in which respondents rate the objects by placing a mark at the appropriate position on a line that runs from one extreme of the criterion variable to the other. The form may vary considerably.

How would you rate McDonald's as a fast-food restaurant?

Version 1

Probably   Probably
the worst - - - - - - - | - the best

Version 2

Probably   Probably
the worst - - - - - - - | - the best
           0   10   20   30   40   50   60   70   80   90   100

Version 3

             Very bad   Neither good   Very good
                              nor bad

Probably   Probably
the worst - - - - - - - | - the best
           0   10   20   30   40   50   60   70   80   90   100

Once the respondent has provided the ratings, the researcher divides the line into as many categories as desired and assigns scores based on the categories into which the ratings fall. In the fast-food restaurant project example, the respondent exhibits an unfavorable attitude toward McDonald's. These scores are typically treated as interval data.

The advantage of continuous scales is that they are easy to construct. However, scoring is cumbersome and unreliable. Continuous scales also provide little new information. Hence, their use in marketing research has been limited. Recently, however, with the increased popularity of computer-assisted personal interviewing, Internet surveys, and other technologies, their use is becoming more frequent, as illustrated by the following Research in Practice.

Research in Practice
Continuous Measurement and Analysis of Perceptions: The Perception Analyzer

The Perception Analyzer (**www.perceptionanalyzer.com**) by Dialsmith is a computer-supported, interactive feedback system composed of wireless or wired handheld dials for each participant; a console (computer interface); and special software that edits questions, collects data, and analyzes participant responses. Members of focus groups use it to record their emotional response to television commercials instantly and continuously. Each participant is given a dial and instructed to continuously record his or her reaction to the material being tested. As the respondents turn the dials, the information is fed to a computer. Thus, the researcher can determine the second-by-second response of the respondents as the commercial is run. This response can be superimposed on the commercial to see the respondents' reactions to the various frames and parts of the commercial.

The Perception Analyzer was recently used to measure responses to a series of slice-of-life television commercials for McDonald's. The researchers found that mothers and daughters had different responses to different aspects of the commercial. Using the emotional response data, the researchers could determine which commercial had the greatest emotional appeal across mother–daughter segments. McDonald's marketing efforts proved successful, with 2012 revenues of $27.567 billion.[3] **<**

Research Recipe

In a continuous rating scale, respondents rate the objects by placing a mark at the appropriate position on a line that runs from one extreme of the criterion variable to the other. Thus, the respondents are not restricted to selecting from marks previously set by the researcher. Continuous scales are useful where the scoring process is automated, as in computer-assisted personal interviewing and Internet surveys.

iResearch
Developing Blockbuster Movies Is Not a Mickey Mouse Business

Visit **www.disney.com** and search the Internet, including social media as well as your library's online databases, to obtain information on consumer movie-viewing habits and preferences.

How would you measure audience reaction to a new movie slated for release by the Walt Disney Company?

As the marketing director for Disney movies, how would you develop "blockbuster" movies? ◀

Itemized Rating Scales

In an **itemized rating scale**, the respondents are provided with a scale that has a number or brief description associated with each category. The categories are ordered in terms of scale position, and the respondents are required to select the specified category that best describes the object being rated. Itemized rating scales are widely used in marketing research. We first describe the commonly used itemized rating scales—the Likert, semantic differential, and Stapel scales (see Figure 7.5)—and then examine variations in the use of itemized rating scales.

itemized rating scale
A noncomparative measurement scale having numbers and/or brief descriptions associated with each category. The categories are ordered in terms of scale position.

LIKERT SCALE　Named after its developer, Rensis Likert, the **Likert scale** is widely used. This rating scale requires the respondents to indicate a degree of agreement or disagreement with each of a series of statements about the stimulus objects. Typically, each scale item (statement) has five response categories, ranging from "strongly disagree" to "strongly agree." We illustrate with a Likert scale for evaluating attitudes toward McDonald's.

Likert scale
A noncomparative measurement scale that typically has five response categories ranging from "strongly disagree" to "strongly agree," which requires the respondents to indicate a degree of agreement or disagreement with each of a series of statements related to the stimulus objects.

Instructions　Listed below are different opinions about McDonald's. Please indicate how strongly you agree or disagree with each by using the following scale and circling the appropriate number:

　1 = Strongly disagree

　2 = Disagree

　3 = Neither agree nor disagree

　4 = Agree

　5 = Strongly agree

Form

	Strongly disagree	Disagree	Neither agree nor disagree	Agree	Strongly agree
1. McDonald's sells high-quality food.	1	②	3	4	5
2. McDonald's has poor in-store service.	1	②	3	4	5
3. I like to eat in McDonald's.	1	2	③	4	5
4. McDonald's does not offer a good variety of menu items.	1	2	3	④	5
5. McDonald's is where America eats.	①	2	3	4	5
6. I do not like the advertising done by McDonald's.	1	2	3	④	5
7. McDonald's charges fair prices.	1	②	3	4	5

Note that some statements are positive (e.g., statement 1) in that they reflect positively on McDonald's, while others are negative (e.g., statement 2) and reflect negatively on McDonald's. There is a reason for having both positive and negative statements. This controls the tendency of some respondents, particularly those with very positive or very negative attitudes, to mark the right- or left-hand sides of the scale without reading the statements. To conduct the analysis, each statement is assigned a numerical score, ranging from 1 to 5. (Sometimes each statement may be assigned a score ranging from –2 to +2.) The analysis can be conducted on an item-by-item basis (profile analysis), or a total (summated) score can be calculated for each respondent by summing across items (statements). Suppose the Likert scale in the fast-food restaurant example was used to measure attitudes toward McDonald's as well as Burger King. Profile analysis would involve comparing the two restaurants in terms of the average respondent ratings for each item, such as quality of food, in-store service, variety of menu items, and so on. The summated approach is most frequently used; as a result, the Likert scale is also referred to as a summated scale. When using this approach to determine the total score for each respondent on each restaurant, it is important to use a consistent scoring procedure so that a high (or low) score consistently reflects a favorable response. This requires that the categories assigned to the negative statements by the respondents be scored by reversing the scale. Note that for a positive statement, an agreement reflects a favorable response, whereas for a negative statement, a disagreement represents a favorable response. Accordingly, a "strongly agree" response to a positive statement and a "strongly disagree" response to a negative statement would both receive scores of 5. In the scale shown above, if a higher score is to denote a more favorable attitude, the scoring of items 2, 4, and 6 will be reversed. The respondent in the fast-food restaurant project example has an attitude score of 16 (2 + 4 + 3 + 2 + 1 + 2 + 2). For the second statement, because it is negative, although the respondent has circled 2, the score assigned is 4. Likewise, the circled numbers for statements 4 and 6 are also reversed. Each respondent's total score for each restaurant is calculated. Note that across seven items, the total scores will be in a range from 7 to 35. A respondent with the highest total score will have the most favorable attitude toward McDonald's, whereas a respondent with the lowest total score will have the least favorable attitude toward McDonald's.

The Likert scale has several advantages. It is easy to construct and administer. Respondents readily understand how to use the scale, making it suitable for mail, telephone, electronic, or personal interviews. The major disadvantage of the Likert scale is that it takes longer to complete than other itemized rating scales because respondents have to read each statement (or the interviewer has to read each statement to them). The following example shows another use of a Likert scale in marketing research.

Research in Practice
Satisfied Salespeople Stay Longer

A study investigated the hypothesis that salespeople's job satisfaction (JS) is related positively to the length of time they stay in a company. Job satisfaction was measured by multiple statements or items using the standard Likert scale. One of the items used to measure JS is as follows:

	Strongly disagree	Disagree	Neutral	Agree	Strongly agree
I get a feeling of accomplishment from the work I am doing.	1	2	3	4	5

The survey data provided support for the hypothesis. The study concluded that sales managers should spend more effort on recruiting, training, and supporting salespeople to increase intrinsic job satisfaction and thereby reduce sales force turnover.[4] <

Source: goodluz / Fotolia

Research Recipe

The Likert scale requires respondents to indicate a degree of agreement or disagreement with each of a series of statements, some of which are positive and some negative. Typically, the scale has five response categories ranging from "strongly disagree" to "strongly agree." You can conduct the analysis on an item-by-item basis (profile analysis), or you can calculate a total (summated) score for each respondent by summing across items (statements). When calculating a summated score, the categories assigned to the negative statements by the respondents must be scored by reversing the scale.

SEMANTIC DIFFERENTIAL SCALE   The **semantic differential scale** is a 7-point rating scale with end points associated with bipolar labels or descriptors. In a typical application, respondents rate objects on a number of itemized, 7-point rating scales bounded or anchored at each end by one of two bipolar adjectives, such as *cold* and *warm*. We illustrate this scale by presenting a respondent's evaluation of McDonald's on five attributes.

semantic differential scale
A noncomparative 7-point rating scale with end points associated with bipolar labels that have semantic meaning.

Instructions   This part of the study measures what certain fast-food restaurants mean to you by having you judge them on a series of descriptive scales bounded or anchored at each end by one of two bipolar adjectives. Please mark (with an X) the blank that best indicates how accurately one or the other adjective describes what the restaurant means to you. Please be sure to mark every scale; do not omit any scale.

Form

MCDONALD'S IS:

Powerful	:—:—:—:—: X :—:—:	Weak
Unreliable	:—:—:—:—:—: X :—:	Reliable
Modern	:—:—:—:—:—:—: X :	Old-fashioned
Cold	:—:—:—:—:—: X :—:	Warm
Careful	:—: X :—:—:—:—:—:	Careless

The respondents mark the blank that best indicates how they would describe the object being rated. Thus, in our example, McDonald's is evaluated as somewhat weak, reliable, very old-fashioned, warm, and careful. The negative adjective or phrase sometimes appears at the left side of the scale and sometimes at the right. This controls the tendency of some respondents, particularly those with very positive or very negative attitudes, to mark the right- or left-hand sides of the scale without reading the labels, as in the Likert scale.

Individual items on a semantic differential scale may be scored on either a −3 to +3 or a 1 to 7 scale. The resulting data are commonly analyzed through profile analysis. In profile analysis, mean values on each rating scale are calculated and compared by plotting or by statistical analysis. This helps determine the overall differences and similarities among the objects. To assess differences across segments of respondents, the researcher can compare mean responses of different segments. On the other hand, in cases when the researcher requires an overall comparison of objects, such as determining restaurant preference, the individual item scores are added to arrive at a total score, as already illustrated for the Likert scale.

Its versatility makes the semantic differential a popular rating scale in marketing research. It has been widely used in comparing brand, product, and company images. It has also been used to develop advertising and promotion strategies and in new product development studies. Several modifications of the basic scale have been proposed.

R e s e a r c h   R e c i p e

The semantic differential scale is a 7-point rating scale with end points associated with bipolar labels or descriptors. The negative descriptor sometimes appears at the left side of the scale and sometimes at the right. You can analyze the data by profile analysis or by calculating a summated score, as in the case of the Likert scale.

Stapel scale

A noncomparative vertical scale for measuring attitudes that consists of a single adjective in the middle of an even-numbered range of values, usually ten.

STAPEL SCALE   The **Stapel scale**, named after its developer, Jan Stapel, is a unipolar rating scale with ten categories numbered from −5 to +5, without a neutral point (0). This scale is usually presented vertically. Respondents are asked to indicate how accurately or inaccurately each term describes the object by selecting an appropriate numerical response category. The higher the number, the more accurately the term describes the object, as shown in the McDonald's example. In this example, McDonald's is evaluated as not having high-quality food and having somewhat poor service.

Instructions   Please evaluate how accurately each word or phrase describes each of the fast-food restaurants. Select a plus number for the phrases you think describe the restaurant accurately. The more accurately you think the phrase describes the restaurant, the larger the plus number you should choose. You should select a minus number for phrases you think do not describe it accurately. The less accurately you think the phrase describes the restaurant, the larger the minus number you should choose. You can select any number, from +5 for phrases you think are very accurate to −5 for phrases you think are very inaccurate. Please indicate your response by circling the appropriate number.

Form

MCDONALD'S

+5	+5
+4	+4
+3	+3
+2	(+2)
+1	+1

(Continued on the next page)

High-Quality Food	Poor Service
−1	−1
−2	−2
−3	−3
(−4)	−4
−5	−5

The data obtained by using a Stapel scale can be analyzed in the same way as Likert or semantic differential data. The Stapel scale produces results similar to the semantic differential scale. The Stapel scale's advantages are that it does not require a pretest of the adjectives or phrases to ensure true bipolarity, and it can be administered over the telephone. However, some researchers believe the Stapel scale is confusing and difficult to apply. Of the three itemized rating scales considered, the Stapel scale is used least. However, this scale merits more attention than it has received.

Research Recipe

The Stapel scale is a unipolar rating scale with ten categories numbered from −5 to +5, without a neutral point (0). Present this scale vertically. Analyze the data in a manner similar to that for Likert or semantic differential scales. Of the three itemized rating scales considered, the Stapel scale is used least.

VARIATIONS IN NONCOMPARATIVE ITEMIZED RATING SCALES Noncomparative itemized rating scales need not be used as originally proposed but can take many different forms. For example, the number of categories in a Likert scale need not be five, the number in the semantic differential scale need not be seven, and the Stapel scale does not need to have ten categories. In fact, the number of categories in scales commonly used in marketing research varies from five to ten. More categories allow for finer discrimination among stimulus objects but also impose greater workload on the respondents. Therefore, a trade-off has to be made. The general guideline is to use as few categories as possible and yet obtain the required degree of discrimination.

The number of categories could be odd or even. With an odd number of categories, the middle scale position is generally designated as neutral or impartial. The presence, position, and labeling of a neutral category can have a significant influence on the response. The decision to use an odd or even number of categories depends on whether some of the respondents may be neutral on the response being measured. If a neutral or indifferent response is possible from at least some of the respondents, an odd number of categories should be used. If, on the other hand, the researcher wants to force a response or believes that no neutral or indifferent response exists, a rating scale with an even number of categories should be used.

A number of options are available with respect to scale form or configuration. Scales can be presented vertically or horizontally. Categories can be expressed by boxes, discrete lines, or units on a continuum and may or may not have numbers assigned to them. If numerical values are used, they may be positive, negative, or both. Several possible configurations are presented in Figure 7.6. Table 7.4 presents some commonly used scales. Although these particular scales have five categories, the number of categories can be varied based on the researcher's judgment. Finally, different types of itemized rating scales can be used in a single questionnaire.

FIGURE 7.6
RATING SCALE
CONFIGURATIONS

A variety of scale configurations may be employed to measure the comfort of Nike shoes. Some examples include:

Nike shoes are:

(1) Place an "X" on one of the blank spaces.

Very
Uncomfortable   _____   _____   _____   _____   _____   _____   _____   Very
Comfortable

(2) Circle the number.

Very   **1**   **2**   **3**   **4**   **5**   **6**   **7**   Very
Uncomfortable   Comfortable

(3) Place an "X" on one of the blank spaces.

_____ Very Uncomfortable
_____ Uncomfortable
_____ Neither Uncomfortable nor Comfortable
_____ Comfortable
_____ Very Comfortable

(4) Place an "X" on one of the blank spaces.

_____   _____   _____   _____   _____   _____   _____

Very Uncomfortable	Uncomfortable	Somewhat Uncomfortable	Neither Comfortable nor Uncomfortable	Somewhat Comfortable	Comfortable	Very Comfortable

(5) Circle the number.

   −3   −2   −1   0   1   2   3

Very   Neither   Very
Uncomfortable   Comfortable   Comfortable
                                    nor
                               Uncomfortable

Table 7.4 > Some Commonly Used Scales in Marketing

Construct	Scale Descriptors
Attitude	Very Bad, Bad, Neither Bad nor Good, Good, Very Good
Importance	Not at All Important, Not Important, Neutral, Important, Very Important
Satisfaction	Very Dissatisfied, Dissatisfied, Neither Dissatisfied nor Satisfied, Satisfied, Very Satisfied
Purchase Frequency	Never, Rarely, Sometimes, Often, Very Often

R e s e a r c h   R e c i p e

The three itemized rating scales can take different forms. The number of categories varies typically from five to ten but you can use more or less than this range. The number of categories can be odd or even. The scale form or configuration can vary widely. You can use different types of itemized rating scales in a single questionnaire.

iResearch
Rockport: Competing for Dress Shoes

Visit **www.rockport.com** and search the Internet, including social media as well as your library's online databases, to obtain information on consumers' preferences for dress shoes. Develop an itemized scale to measure consumers' preferences for dress shoes.

As the marketing manager for Rockport, how would you use information on consumers' preferences for dress shoes to increase your market share? ❮

MULTI-ITEM SCALES

Itemized rating scales discussed earlier form the basic components of multi-item rating scales. As the name implies, multi-item scales consist of multiple items that need to be evaluated in order to obtain a given measurement. This was illustrated by the Likert scale measuring attitudes toward McDonald's that consisted of seven items. Likewise, the semantic differential and Stapel scales illustrated earlier in the context of McDonald's are also multi-item scales consisting of five and two items, respectively. The development of multi-item rating scales requires considerable technical expertise. The opinion leadership scale, given in the Research in Practice feature in the next section on Scale Evaluation, is another example of a multi-item scale.

SCALE EVALUATION

A multi-item scale should be evaluated for accuracy and applicability. As shown in Figure 7.7, this involves an assessment of reliability and validity of the scale. Both reliability and validity can be understood in terms of measurement, systematic, and random errors.

Measurement error is the variation in the information sought by the researcher and the information generated by the measurement process employed. There are two sources of measurement error: systematic error and random error. **Systematic error** affects the measurement in a constant way. It represents stable factors that affect the observed score in the same way each time the measurement is made. Examples of systematic error are mechanical factors such as poor printing, overcrowding of items in the questionnaire, and poor design. **Random error**, on the other hand, is not constant. It represents transient factors that affect the observed score in different ways each time the measurement is made. Examples of random error are personal factors such as health, emotions, and fatigue. The distinction between systematic and random error is crucial to our understanding of reliability and validity.

measurement error
The variation in the information sought by the researcher and the information generated by the measurement process employed.

systematic error
Error that affects the measurement in a constant way; stable factors that affect the observed score in the same way each time the measurement is made.

random error
Measurement error that arises from random changes or differences in respondents or measurement situations.

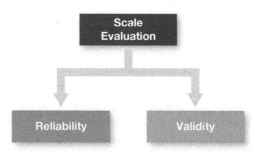

FIGURE 7.7
SCALE EVALUATION

Reliability

reliability
The extent to which a scale produces consistent results if repeated measurements are made on the characteristic.

Reliability refers to the extent to which a scale produces consistent results if repeated measurements are made. Systematic sources of error do not have an adverse impact on reliability because they affect measurement in a constant way and do not lead to inconsistency. In contrast, random error produces inconsistency, leading to lower reliability. Reliability can be defined as the extent to which a measure is free from random error. If there is no random error, the measure is perfectly reliable. Reliability is assessed by determining the association between scores obtained from different administrations of the scale. If the association is high, the scale yields consistent results and is therefore reliable.

Research in Practice
Dell Measures Opinion Leadership to Stay a Leader

Opinion leaders are those whose opinions influence other people. Their opinions are especially important in the adoption of computer-related products and services. In a survey of recent purchasers of Dell PCs and notebook computers, opinion leadership was measured using the following 7-point Likert-type scales (1 = disagree completely, 7 = agree completely).

Opinion Leadership

1. When it comes to computer-related products, my friends are very likely to ask my opinion.
2. I am often used as a source of advice about computer-related products by friends and neighbors.
3. I often tell my friends what I think about computer-related products.

It has been found that this scale has good reliability. Early adopters of computer-related products tend to be younger males who are opinion leaders, seek novel information, and have a lot of computer experience. Information technology companies like Dell, Microsoft, IBM, and others need to ensure positive reactions from early product adopters and should focus marketing efforts on these individuals when introducing new products.[5] ◄

Validity

validity
The extent to which differences in observed scale scores reflect true differences among objects on the characteristic being measured rather than systematic or random error.

The **validity** of a scale may be defined as the extent to which differences in observed scale scores reflect true differences among objects on the characteristic being measured, rather than systematic or random error. Perfect validity requires that there be no measurement error, that is, no systematic error and no random error. Validity can be assessed by determining whether a scale performs as expected in relation to other selected variables. These variables may include demographic and psychographic characteristics, attitudinal and behavioral measures, or scores obtained from other scales. For example, a researcher may develop short forms of standard personality scales. The original scales and the short versions would be administered simultaneously to a group of respondents and the results compared to assess validity.

Relationship Between Reliability and Validity

The relationship between reliability and validity can be understood in terms of measurement error. If a measure is perfectly valid, it is also perfectly reliable. In this case, there is no measurement error. Thus, there is no systematic error and no random error. Thus, perfect validity implies perfect reliability. If a measure is unreliable, it cannot be perfectly valid because, at a minimum, random error is present. Systematic error may also be present. Thus, unreliability implies invalidity. If a measure is perfectly reliable, it may or may not be perfectly valid because systematic error may still be present, although random error is zero. While lack of reliability constitutes negative evidence for validity, reliability does not in itself imply validity. Reliability is a necessary but not sufficient condition for validity.

Research Recipe

The distinction between systematic and random error is crucial to understanding reliability and validity. Reliability is the extent to which the measure is free from random error. You can assess reliability by determining the association between scores obtained from different administrations of the scale. If the association is high, the scale is reliable. Validity is the extent to which the measure is free from both random and systematic errors. You can assess validity by determining whether a scale performs as expected in relation to other selected variables. While lack of reliability constitutes negative evidence for validity, reliability does not in itself imply validity.

CHOOSING A SCALING TECHNIQUE

In addition to theoretical considerations and evaluation of reliability and validity, certain practical factors should be considered in selecting scaling techniques for a particular marketing research problem. These factors include the level of information (nominal, ordinal, interval, or ratio) desired, the capabilities of the respondents, context, time, cost, and scales used in the past. For example, if a certain type of scale has been used to measure a variable in the past, let's say, a 10-point Likert-type scale to measure customer satisfaction, the same scale might have to be used again to allow a comparison of the findings with past results or industry norms (e.g., the American Customer Satisfaction Index).

As a general rule, using the scaling technique that will yield the highest level of information feasible in a given situation will permit the use of the greatest variety of statistical analyses. Also, regardless of the type of scale used, whenever feasible, several scale items should be used to measure the characteristic of interest. This provides more accurate measurement than a single-item scale. In many situations, it is desirable to use more than one scaling technique.

Research Recipe

Whenever feasible, use several scale items to measure the characteristic of interest. This provides more accurate measurement than a single-item scale. In many situations, it is desirable to use more than one scaling technique.

INTERNATIONAL MARKETING RESEARCH

In the four primary scales, the level of measurement increases from nominal to ordinal to interval to ratio scale. This increase in measurement level is obtained at the cost of complexity. From the viewpoint of the respondents, nominal scales are the simplest to use, whereas the ratio scales are the most complex. Respondents in many developed countries, because of higher education and consumer sophistication levels, are quite used to providing responses on interval and ratio scales. It has been argued that respondents in many developing countries experience difficulty in expressing the gradation required by interval and ratio scales. Therefore, preferences can be measured best by using ordinal scales. In particular, the use of binary scales (e.g., preferred/not preferred), the simplest type of ordinal scale, has been recommended. For example, while measuring preferences for athletic shoes in the United States, Nike could ask consumers to rate their preferences for wearing athletic shoes on specified occasions using a 7-point interval scale. However, consumers in rural West Africa could be shown a pair of athletic shoes and simply asked whether or not they would prefer to wear the athletic shoes for a specific occasion (e.g., when shopping, exercising, working, relaxing on a holiday, etc.). The advantage of selecting the primary scales to match the profile of the target respondents is well illustrated by the Dunkin' Donuts survey of Italians.

Research in Practice
Dunkin' Donuts Goes Italian

In 2011 to 2013, Italy was facing a big debt problem and Italians were going through a difficult economic period. Dunkin' Donuts sponsored a survey to determine how the tough economic environment had affected the lifestyles of Italians. The questionnaire included a series of lifestyles statements, and the respondents were asked to express their (dis)agreement using Likert-type scales. These scales were used because they had been effective in previous lifestyle research in Italy. The findings indicated that Italians had become increasingly value-conscious and were hunting for coupons and special offers, they had become very concerned about their privacy, and mobile phone usage in general and Short Message Service (SMS) usage in particular had increased significantly.

As a result, Dunkin' Donuts launched an SMS-based marketing campaign. Customers were able to get coupons for Dunkin' Donuts by using their mobile handsets to respond to advertisements displayed on store notice boards and billboards and aired on the radio. By sending a short message to the published numbers, users received an immediate reply featuring a coupon or a special offer redeemable at local outlets. This two-month mobile interactive campaign resulted in a 9 percent increase in sales in Italy for Dunkin' Donuts.[6] ◄

Special attention should be devoted to determining equivalent verbal descriptors in different languages and cultures. The end points of the scale are particularly prone to different interpretations. In some cultures, the number 1 may be interpreted by the respondents as best, while in others it may be interpreted as worst, regardless of how it is scaled by the researcher. It is important that the researcher employs the scale end points and the verbal descriptors in a manner that is consistent with the culture.

R e s e a r c h   R e c i p e

Respondents in many developing countries may be unable to express the gradation required by interval and ratio scales. Therefore, measure preferences by using ordinal scales. The use of binary scales (e.g., preferred/not preferred), the simplest type of ordinal scale, is recommended. It is important that you employ the scale end points and the verbal descriptors in a manner that is consistent with the culture.

MARKETING RESEARCH AND SOCIAL MEDIA

All the primary scales and all the comparative and noncomparative scales that we have discussed in this chapter can be implemented easily in social media. Even continuous scales can be used efficiently given the computerized nature of measurement. No additional requirements are imposed by social media. The principles underlying scaling and measurement and the comparative scaling techniques also remain the same. An analysis of social media content can shed light on the level of measurement that is appropriate in a given project. It can also provide guidance on the type of scaling techniques (comparative or noncomparative) to use. It is quite feasible to employ more than one scaling method to measure a given construct or variable to obtain evidence on validity. The use of rating scales in social media can yield rich dividends, as exemplified by Future Shop of Canada.

Research in Practice
Future Shop Has Social Media in Its Future

Future Shop is Canada's largest consumer electronics retailer. The company is using social media conversations not only to learn about its customers, but also to support and sell products. The company was initially built on the high-touch model in which sales associates were taught to be valued customer advisers. Recently, the company has duplicated this real-world experience online. Visitors to the Future Shop website (**www.futureshop.ca**) are greeted by a video image of a sales associate who offers to help guide their experience. Customers can ask questions of the avatar and get answers from a growing database of advice that is contributed by other customers and sales associates. Future Shop has co-developed a rating system with Lithium Technologies, a leading provider of Social CRM solutions (**www.lithium.com**) that obtains feedback from customers on each other's comments and on the quality of information given by sales associates. The ratings are obtained using Likert-type scales. Likert scales are chosen for their simplicity and ease of administration online. Customer contributors can earn discounts and status in the community, while sales associates can earn cash. Since implementing this system, the website traffic has increased dramatically. So has the effectiveness of Future Shop's in-store selling. "We actually see people walking in [the store] with printouts and asking for specific experts they've met online," said the company.[7] ◄

Finally, some specific measures have been developed to evaluate social media sites based on information that is available to the public. The more commonly used measures include longevity, output (frequency, quantity), inbound links, Technorati, Bloglines or Blogpulse rankings, number of friends or followers, number of comments, and media citations.

Research Recipe

An analysis of social media content can shed light on the level of measurement (nominal, ordinal, interval, or ratio) that is appropriate in a given project. It can also provide guidance on the type of scaling techniques (comparative or noncomparative) to use. You can employ more than one scaling method to measure a given variable to obtain evidence on validity.

ETHICS IN MARKETING RESEARCH

The researcher has the ethical responsibility to use scales that have reasonable reliability and validity. The findings generated by scales that are unreliable or invalid are questionable at best and raise serious ethical issues. The researcher should not bias the scales to slant the findings in any particular direction. This is easy to do by either biasing the wording of the statements (Likert-type scales), the scale descriptors, or other aspects of the scales. Consider the use of scale descriptors. The descriptors used to frame a scale can be chosen to bias results in a desired direction, for example, to generate a positive view of the client's brand or a negative view of a competitor's brand. To project the client's brand favorably, respondents are asked to indicate their opinion of the brand on several attributes using 7-point scales anchored by the descriptors extremely bad to good. In such a case, respondents are reluctant to rate the product as extremely bad. In fact, respondents who believe the product to be only mediocre will end up responding favorably. Try this yourself. How would you rate BMW automobiles on the following attributes?

Reliability:	Extremely bad	1	2	3	4	5	6	7	Good
Performance:	Extremely bad	1	2	3	4	5	6	7	Good
Quality:	Extremely bad	1	2	3	4	5	6	7	Good
Prestige:	Extremely bad	1	2	3	4	5	6	7	Good

Did you find yourself rating BMW cars positively? Using this same technique, it is possible to negatively bias evaluations of competitors' brands, for example, Mercedes, by providing a mildly negative descriptor against a strong positive descriptor, as in the following.
How would you rate Mercedes automobiles on the following attributes?

Reliability:	Somewhat bad	1	2	3	4	5	6	7	Extremely good
Performance:	Somewhat bad	1	2	3	4	5	6	7	Extremely good
Quality:	Somewhat bad	1	2	3	4	5	6	7	Extremely good
Prestige:	Somewhat bad	1	2	3	4	5	6	7	Extremely good

The researcher has a responsibility to both the client and the respondents to ensure the applicability and usefulness of the scale, as we see in the following example.

Research in Practice
Scaling Ethical Dilemmas

In a study designed to measure ethical judgments of marketing researchers, scale items from a previously developed and tested scale were used. After a pretest was conducted on a convenience sample of sixty-five marketing professionals, however, it became apparent that some original scale items were worded in a way that did not reflect current usage. Therefore, these items were updated. For example, an item that was gender-specific, such as, "He pointed out that…" was altered to read "The project manager pointed out that…." In the original scale, subjects were requested to show their approval or disapproval of the stated action (item) of a marketing research director with regard to specific scenarios. Realizing that a binary or dichotomous scale would be too restrictive, approval or disapproval was indicated by having respondents supply interval-level data via 5-point scales with descriptive anchors of 1 = Disapprove, 2 = Disapprove somewhat, 3 = Neither approve nor disapprove, 4 = Approve somewhat, and 5 = Approve. In this way, scaling dilemmas were resolved.[8] ◄

R e s e a r c h   R e c i p e

The researcher has the ethical responsibility to use scales that have reasonable reliability and validity. You should not deliberately bias the scales to slant the findings in any particular direction.

Dell Running Case

Review the Dell case, Case 1.1, and questionnaire given toward the end of the book.

1. What primary scales of measurement have been employed in the Dell questionnaire? Illustrate each type.
2. Illustrate the use of rank-order and constant sum scales in a customer perception survey by Dell.
3. Design Likert, semantic differential, and Stapel scales to measure consumers' preferences for Dell computers.
4. Develop Likert-type scales to measure preferences for Dell and two other competing brands in social media.

 # Summary

Measurement is the assignment of numbers or other symbols to characteristics of objects according to set rules. Scaling involves the generation of a continuum upon which measured objects are located. The four primary scales of measurement are nominal, ordinal, interval, and ratio. Of these, the nominal scale is the most basic in that the numbers are used only for identifying or classifying objects. In the ordinal scale, the next higher-level scale, the numbers indicate the relative position of the objects but not the magnitude of differences between them. The interval scale permits a comparison of the differences between the objects. Because it has an arbitrary 0 point, however, it is not meaningful to calculate ratios of scale values on an interval scale. The highest level of measurement is represented by the ratio scale in which the 0 point is fixed. The researcher can compute ratios of scale values using this scale. The ratio scale incorporates all the properties of the lower-level scales.

Scaling techniques can be classified as comparative or noncomparative. Comparative scaling involves a direct comparison of stimulus objects. Comparative scales include paired comparisons, rank order, and constant sum. The data obtained by these procedures have only ordinal properties.

In noncomparative scaling, each object is scaled independently of the other objects in the stimulus set. The resulting data are generally assumed to be interval or ratio scaled. Noncomparative rating scales can be either continuous or itemized. The itemized rating scales are further classified as Likert, semantic differential, or Stapel scales. Several variations of the original itemized scales are commonly used in marketing research.

Multi-item scales consist of a number of rating scale items. These scales should be evaluated in terms of reliability and validity. Reliability is the extent to which the measure is free from random error. Validity is the extent to which the measure is free from both random and systematic errors.

The choice of particular scaling techniques in a given situation should be based on theoretical and practical considerations. As a general rule, the scaling technique used should be the one that will yield the highest level of information feasible. Also, multiple measures should be obtained.

Respondents in many developed countries, because of higher education and consumer sophistication levels, are quite used to providing responses on interval and ratio scales. In developing countries, however, preferences can be measured best by using ordinal scales. Special attention should be devoted to determining equivalent verbal descriptors in different languages and cultures. All of the comparative and noncomparative scaling techniques discussed in this chapter can be implemented easily in social media. Ethical considerations require that the appropriate type of scales be used in order to get the data needed to answer the research questions and test the hypotheses. The researcher has a responsibility to both the client and respondents to ensure the applicability and usefulness of the scales.

⌄ Companion Website

This textbook includes numerous student resources that can be found at
www.pearsonglobaleditions.com/malhotra. At this Companion website, you'll find:

- Student Resource Manual
- Demo movies of statistical procedures using SPSS and Microsoft Excel
- Screen captures of statistical procedures using SPSS and Microsoft Excel
- Data files for all datasets in SPSS and Microsoft Excel
- Additional figures and tables
- Videos and write-ups for all video cases
- Other valuable resources

⌄ Key Terms and Concepts

Measurement	Noncomparative scales	Semantic differential scale
Scaling	Paired comparison scaling	Stapel scale
Nominal scale	Rank-order scaling	Measurement error
Ordinal scale	Constant sum scaling	Systematic error
Interval scale	Continuous rating scales	Random error
Ratio scale	Itemized rating scale	Reliability
Comparative scales	Likert scale	Validity

⌄ Suggested Cases and Video Cases

Running Case with Real Data and Questionnaire
    1.1 Dell

Comprehensive Critical Thinking Cases
    2.1 American Idol

Comprehensive Cases with Real Data and Questionnaires
    3.1 JPMorgan Chase   3.2 Wendy's

Online Video Cases
    7.1 P&G   8.1 Dunkin' Donuts
    9.1 Subaru   13.1 Marriott

⌄ Live Research: Conducting A Marketing Research Project

1. As a class, discuss the level of measurement (nominal, ordinal, interval, or ratio) that is appropriate for the key variables.
2. Discuss which, if any, of the comparative techniques are appropriate.

3. Continuous measures are generally more difficult to implement.
4. As a class, discuss the type of itemized rating scales (Likert, semantic differential, or Stapel) that are appropriate for the key variables.
5. Consider the practical constraints, especially time, cost, and capabilities of the respondents and scales used in the past.

∨ Acronyms

The four primary types of scales may be described by the acronym FOUR:

F igurative: nominal scale

O rdinal scale

U nconstrained 0 point: interval scale

R atio scale

The different comparative and noncomparative scales may be represented by the acronym SCALES:

S emantic differential scale

C onstant sum scale

A rranged in order: rank-order scale

L ikert scale

E ngaged: paired comparison scale

S tapel scale

∨ Review Questions

7-1. What is measurement?

7-2. What are the primary scales of measurement?

7-3. Describe the differences between a nominal and an ordinal scale.

7-4. What are the implications of having an arbitrary 0 point in an interval scale?

7-5. What are the advantages of a ratio scale over an interval scale? Are these advantages significant?

7-6. Can the primary scales of measurement be implemented in social media? Explain your reasoning.

7-7. What is a comparative rating scale?

7-8. What is a paired comparison?

7-9. What are some advantages of rank-order scaling over paired comparison scaling?

7-10. Describe the constant sum scale. How is it different from the other comparative rating scales?

7-11. What is a semantic differential scale? For what purposes is this scale used?

7-12. Describe the Stapel scale.

7-13. Briefly explain itemized rating scales and how they differ from the continuous rating scale.

7-14. Discuss the use of social media in implementing itemized rating scales.

7-15. Briefly explain the two types of measurement errors.

7-16. What is reliability?

7-17. What is validity?

7-18. What is the relationship between reliability and validity?

7-19. How would you select a particular scaling technique?

⌄ Applied Problems

7-20. Identify the type of scale (nominal, ordinal, interval, or ratio) being used in each of the following. Explain your reasoning.

    a. I like to solve crossword puzzles.

Disagree				Agree
1	2	3	4	5

    b. How old are you? _____

    c. Please rank the following activities in terms of your preference by assigning ranks 1 to 5.

        i. Reading magazines _____
        ii. Watching television _____
        iii. Dating _____
        iv. Shopping _____
        v. Eating out _____

    d. What is your Social Security number? _____

    e. On an average weekday, how much time do you spend doing your homework and class assignments?

        i. Less than 15 minutes _____
        ii. 15 to 30 minutes _____
        iii. 31 to 60 minutes _____
        iv. 61 to 120 minutes _____
        v. More than 120 minutes_____

    f. How much money did you spend last month on entertainment? _____

7-21. Develop a Likert, semantic differential, and Stapel scale for measuring store loyalty.

7-22. Develop a multi-item scale to measure students' attitudes toward internationalization of the management curriculum. How would you assess the reliability and validity of this scale?

7-23. Develop a Likert scale for measuring the attitude of students toward the Internet as a source of general information. Administer your scale to a small sample of ten students and improve it. How would you implement this scale in social media?

7-24. The following scale was used in a recent study to measure attitude toward new technology. Please tell me how much you agree or disagree with the following statements as they describe how you view new technology. Use a scale of 1 to 5, where 1 = strongly disagree and 5 = strongly agree.

    I'm a person who avoids new technology.
    I'm a technology buff who keeps up with the latest equipment.
    I take a wait-and-see approach to new technology until it is proven.
    I'm the kind of person friends turn to for advice on buying new technology.

    a. How would you score this scale to measure attitude toward new technology?

    b. Develop an equivalent semantic differential scale to measure attitude toward new technology.

    c. Develop an equivalent Stapel scale to measure attitude toward new technology.

    d. Which scale form is most suited for a telephone survey?

∨ Internet Exercises

7-25. Visit the website **www.gartner.com**. What type of scaling are they using in their surveys ranking vendor performances? Why did you choose this answer?

7-26. Surf the internet to find examples of surveys using semantic differential scales. Write a report describing the context in which these scales are being used.

7-27. Search the Internet including social media to identify the top five selling automobile brands during the last calendar year. Rank-order these brands according to sales.

7-28. Design Stapel scales to measure customer perception of Pepsi soft drinks in terms of appearance and taste.

7-29. Design semantic differential scales to measure the perception of FedEx overnight delivery service and compare it to that offered by UPS. Relevant information may be obtained by visiting the websites of these two companies (**www.fedex.com**, **www.ups.com**).

7-30. Visit the websites of two marketing research firms conducting surveys. Analyze one survey of each firm to evaluate the itemized rating scales being used.

7-31. Surf the Internet including social media to find two examples each of Likert, semantic differential, and Stapel scales. Write a report describing the context in which these scales are being used.

NOTES

1. **www.fifa.com**, accessed June 21, 2013.
2. Fortune magazine website, **http://money.cnn.com/magazines/fortune/**, accessed March 19, 2013.
3. **www.mcdonalds.com**, accessed March 5, 2013; and **www.perceptionanalyzer.com**, accessed March 5, 2013.
4. Jamie Madsen, "Seven Simple Ways to Increase Employee Satisfaction," **www.jobscience.com/company/7-simple-ways-increase-employee-satisfaction/**, accessed November 8, 2013. John P Walsh and Shu-Fen Tseng, "The Effects of Job Characteristics on Active Effort at Work," *Work & Occupations* 25(1) (February 1998): 74–96; George H. Lucas, Jr., A. Parasuraman, Robert A. Davis, and Ben M. Enis, "An Empirical Study of Salesforce Turnover," *Journal of Marketing*, 51 (July 1987): 34–59.
5. Naresh K. Malhotra, *Marketing Research: An Applied Orientation*, Sixth Edition (Upper Saddle River, NJ: Pearson Education, 2010).
6. Based on PlusOne, "How SMS Is Building Business," **www.plusone.com.au/smsstudies.php**, accessed March 3, 2013.
7. Paul Gillin, *Secrets of Social Media Marketing* (Fresno, CA: Quill Driver Books, 2009).
8. Gael McDonald, "Cross-Cultural Methodological Issues in Ethical Research," *Journal of Business Ethics,* 27(1/2) (September 2000): 89–104; I. P. Akaah, "Differences in Research Ethics Judgments Between Male and Female Marketing Professionals," *Journal of Business Ethics,* 8 (1989): 375–381. See also Anusorn Singhapakdi, Scott J. Vitell, Kumar C. Rallapalli, and Kenneth L. Kraft, "The Perceived Role of Ethics and Social Responsibility: A Scale Development," *Journal of Business Ethics,* 15(11) (November 1996): 1131–1140.

Online Video Case 7.1

PROCTER & GAMBLE: Using Marketing Research to Build Brands

Visit **www.pearsonglobaleditions.com/malhotra** to read the video case and view the accompanying video. Procter & Gamble: Using Marketing Research to Build Brands presents P&G's strong culture of understanding its consumers by conducting marketing research and innovating to meet their needs and desires. The case can be used to illustrate the use of the primary type of scales in measuring consumer preferences for toothpaste and diaper brands. Specific marketing research questions on this and the previous chapters are posed in the video case.

8 Questionnaire and Form Design

∨ Overview

Questionnaire or form design is an important step in formulating a research design. Once the researcher has specified the nature of the research design (Chapters 3 through 6) and determined the scaling procedures (Chapter 7), a questionnaire or an observational form can be developed. This chapter discusses the importance of questionnaires and observational forms. Next, we describe the objectives of a questionnaire and the steps involved in designing questionnaires. We provide several guidelines for developing sound questionnaires. We also consider the design of observational forms. The considerations involved in designing questionnaires when conducting international marketing research and research in social media are discussed. Several ethical issues that arise in questionnaire design are identified. Figure 8.1 gives the relationship of this chapter to the marketing research process.

∨ Learning Objectives

After reading this chapter, the student should be able to:

1. Explain the purpose of a questionnaire and its objectives.
2. Describe the process of designing a questionnaire, the steps involved, and the guidelines that must be followed at each step.
3. Discuss the observational form of data collection.
4. Discuss the use of software for designing questionnaires.
5. Explain the considerations involved in designing questionnaires for international marketing research.
6. Explain how social media interface with questionnaire design.
7. Understand the ethical issues involved in questionnaire design.

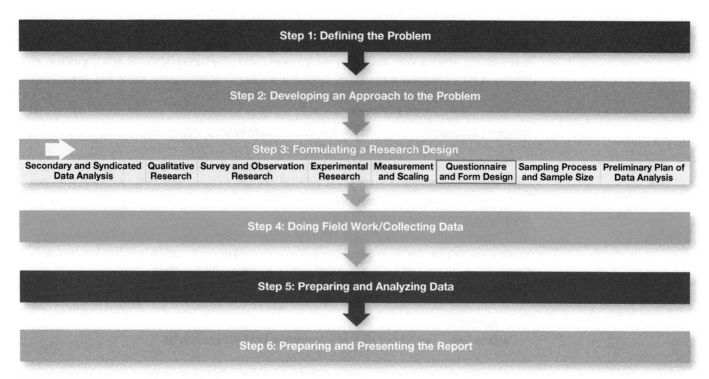

Step 1: Defining the Problem

Step 2: Developing an Approach to the Problem

Step 3: Formulating a Research Design

| Secondary and Syndicated Data Analysis | Qualitative Research | Survey and Observation Research | Experimental Research | Measurement and Scaling | Questionnaire and Form Design | Sampling Process and Sample Size | Preliminary Plan of Data Analysis |

Step 4: Doing Field Work/Collecting Data

Step 5: Preparing and Analyzing Data

Step 6: Preparing and Presenting the Report

FIGURE 8.1 | RELATIONSHIP OF THIS CHAPTER TO THE MARKETING RESEARCH PROCESS

Research in Practice
The Consensus on Census 2010 Questionnaires

A census is a snapshot of the entire population at a single point in time. Conducted every ten years since 1790 by the United States Census Bureau (**www.census.gov**), the U.S. Census determines how many people reside within the country's borders, who they are, and where they live. After careful pretesting that involved several waves, the Census 2010 questionnaire was sent to every housing unit in the country. The person who filled out the form provided the household information and answered questions about every household member, including him or her on:

- Name
- Sex
- Age/birth date
- Hispanic ethnicity
- Race
- Relationship to the person filling out the form
- Other residence, for example, military or college residence, if the residents sometimes live at another address

In every decennial census since 1940, two questionnaires have been used to collect information: a short form, with only basic questions such as age, sex, race, and Hispanic origin; and a long form, with the basic short-form questions plus about fifty additional questions on socioeconomic and housing characteristics. For the first time since 1940, however, the Census 2010 was a short-form-only census. The decennial long form has been replaced by the American Community Survey (ACS). The ACS is a nationwide, continuous survey designed to provide reliable and timely demographic, housing, social, and economic data every year.

Each question—how it was worded, how many and which categories were included—was carefully considered and pretested. The information was either required by law to provide constitutionally mandated information or it was collected to help ensure the accuracy and completeness of the census.

The Census 2010 incorporated two important new operations. For the first time, the Census Bureau sent out replacement questionnaires after an initial period of time, and the bureau also mailed out bilingual (English and Spanish) questionnaires to selected areas. Both of these operational changes increased mail response rates and reduced the nonresponse follow-up workload.

The Census 2010 questionnaire also added two new administrative questions designed to improve the accuracy and completeness of the data. Although these questions were not required by federal law, they were included to help respondents evaluate how many people are living in the household:

- Were there any additional people staying here April 1, 2010, that you did not include in Question 1? (see question 2)
- Does Person X sometimes live or stay somewhere else? (see question 10)

As a result of these efforts, the quality of Census 2010 data collection processes improved. There were fewer duplicate records (people counted twice) and a higher share of records with usable data. The 2010 short-form design appeared to be effective—there was a participation rate of 72 percent compared with 69 percent using the combined short and long form design in 2000.[1]

United States Census 2010

U.S. DEPARTMENT OF COMMERCE
Economics and Statistics Administration
U.S. CENSUS BUREAU

This is the official form for all the people at this address.
It is quick and easy, and your answers are protected by law.

Use a blue or black pen.

Start here

The Census must count every person living in the United States on April 1, 2010.

Before you answer Question 1, count the people living in this house, apartment, or mobile home using our guidelines.

- Count all people, including babies, who live and sleep here most of the time.

The Census Bureau also conducts counts in institutions and other places, so:

- Do not count anyone living away either at college or in the Armed Forces.
- Do not count anyone in a nursing home, jail, prison, detention facility, etc., on April 1, 2010.
- Leave these people off your form, even if they will return to live here after they leave college, the nursing home, the military, jail, etc. Otherwise, they may be counted twice.

The Census must also include people without a permanent place to stay, so:

- If someone who has no permanent place to stay is staying here on April 1, 2010, count that person. Otherwise, he or she may be missed in the census.

1. How many people were living or staying in this house, apartment, or mobile home on April 1, 2010?

Number of people = _____

2. Were there any additional people staying here April 1, 2010 that you did not include in Question 1?
Mark X all that apply.

- ☐ Children, such as newborn babies or foster children
- ☐ Relatives, such as adult children, cousins, or in-laws
- ☐ Nonrelatives, such as roommates or live-in baby sitters
- ☐ People staying here temporarily
- ☐ No additional people

3. Is this house, apartment, or mobile home —
Mark X ONE box.

- ☐ Owned by you or someone in this household with a mortgage or loan? Include home equity loans.
- ☐ Owned by you or someone in this household free and clear (without a mortgage or loan)?
- ☐ Rented?
- ☐ Occupied without payment of rent?

4. What is your telephone number? We may call if we don't understand an answer.
Area Code + Number

___ - ___ - ___

OMB No. 0607-0919-C: Approval Expires 12/31/2011.

Form **D-61** (1-25-2008)

5. Please provide information for each person living here. Start with a person living here who owns or rents this house, apartment, or mobile home. If the owner or renter lives somewhere else, start with any adult living here. This will be Person 1.
What is Person 1's name? Print name below.

Last Name _____

First Name _____ MI ___

6. What is Person 1's sex? Mark X ONE box.
- ☐ Male ☐ Female

7. What is Person 1's age and what is Person 1's date of birth?
Please report babies as age 0 when the child is less than 1 year old.
Print numbers in boxes.

Age on April 1, 2010 | Month | Day | Year of birth

→ NOTE: Please answer BOTH Question 8 about Hispanic origin and Question 9 about race. For this census, Hispanic origins are not races.

8. Is Person 1 of Hispanic, Latino, or Spanish origin?
- ☐ No, not of Hispanic, Latino, or Spanish origin
- ☐ Yes, Mexican, Mexican Am., Chicano
- ☐ Yes, Puerto Rican
- ☐ Yes, Cuban
- ☐ Yes, another Hispanic, Latino, or Spanish origin — Print origin, for example, Argentinean, Colombian, Dominican, Nicaraguan, Salvadoran, Spaniard, and so on. ↗

_____

9. What is Person 1's race? Mark X one or more boxes.
- ☐ White
- ☐ Black, African Am., or Negro
- ☐ American Indian or Alaska Native — Print name of enrolled or principal tribe. ↗

_____

- ☐ Asian Indian ☐ Japanese ☐ Native Hawaiian
- ☐ Chinese ☐ Korean ☐ Guamanian or Chamorro
- ☐ Filipino ☐ Vietnamese ☐ Samoan
- ☐ Other Asian — Print race, for example, Hmong, Laotian, Thai, Pakistani, Cambodian, and so on. ↗
- ☐ Other Pacific Islander — Print race, for example, Fijian, Tongan, and so on. ↗

_____

- ☐ Some other race — Print race. ↗

_____

10. Does Person 1 sometimes live or stay somewhere else?
- ☐ No ☐ Yes — Mark X all that apply.
  - ☐ In college housing ☐ For child custody
  - ☐ In the military ☐ In jail or prison
  - ☐ At a seasonal or second residence ☐ In a nursing home
  - ☐ For another reason

→ If more people were counted in Question 1, continue with Person 2.

QUESTIONNAIRES AND OBSERVATIONAL FORMS

As was discussed in Chapter 5, survey and observation are the two basic methods for obtaining quantitative primary data in descriptive research. Both of these methods require some procedure for standardizing the data collection process so that the data obtained can be analyzed in a uniform and coherent manner. If forty different interviewers conduct personal interviews or make observations in different parts of the country, the data they collect will not be comparable unless the interviewers follow specific guidelines and ask questions and record answers in a standard way. A standardized questionnaire or form will serve this purpose, ensure comparability of the data, increase speed and accuracy of recording, and facilitate data processing.

Research Recipe

A questionnaire standardizes the data collection process. It ensures comparability of the data, increases speed and accuracy of recording, and facilitates data processing. Hence, always use a questionnaire when conducting surveys on a large sample.

iResearch
How Important Is a Questionnaire?

Sprite is the third most popular soft drink brand, behind Coke and Pepsi. College students are heavy users of soft drinks.

As the brand manager for Sprite, what information do you need to target this segment? Search the Internet, including social media as well as your library's online databases, to obtain information that will assist you, the brand manager of Sprite, in targeting the student segment.

You and a fellow student each interview a different respondent (another student) to determine preferences for soft drinks, but neither of you construct a questionnaire. How comparable are the data each of you obtain? Develop a formal questionnaire jointly, and each of you administer it to another respondent. Are the data both of you obtain more comparable than before? What does this teach you about the importance of a questionnaire? **<**

QUESTIONNAIRE DEFINITION

questionnaire
A structured technique for data collection that consists of a series of questions, written or verbal, that a respondent answers.

A **questionnaire** is a formalized set of questions for obtaining information from respondents. Typically, a questionnaire is only one element of a data collection package, which might also include (1) field work procedures, such as instructions for selecting, approaching, and questioning respondents (see Chapter 10); (2) some reward, gift, or payment offered to respondents; and (3) communication aids, such as maps, pictures, advertisements, and products (in personal interviews) and return envelopes (in mail surveys). Regardless of the form of administration, a questionnaire is characterized by some specific objectives.

OBJECTIVES OF A QUESTIONNAIRE

Any questionnaire has three main objectives. First, it must translate the information needed into a set of specific questions that the respondents can and will answer, in other words, that the respondents are both able and willing to answer. Developing questions that respondents can and will answer and that will yield the desired information is difficult. Two apparently similar ways of posing a question may yield different information. Hence, this objective is a challenge.

Second, a questionnaire must uplift, motivate, and encourage the respondent to become involved in the interview, to cooperate, and to complete the interview. Incomplete interviews have limited usefulness at best. In designing a questionnaire, the researcher should strive to minimize respondent fatigue, boredom, incompleteness, and nonresponse. A well-designed questionnaire can motivate the respondents and increase the response rate, as illustrated by the Census 2010 questionnaire that had a higher participation rate as compared to 2000 in the first Research in Practice feature in this chapter.

Third, a questionnaire should minimize response error. **Response error** is the error that arises when respondents give inaccurate answers or their answers are misrecorded or misanalyzed. A questionnaire can be a major source of response error. Minimizing this error is an important objective of questionnaire design.

response error
The type of error that arises when respondents give inaccurate answers or their answers are misrecorded or are analyzed incorrectly.

> ## Research Recipe
>
> Design your questionnaire to achieve three main objectives: (1) It must translate the information needed into a set of specific questions that the respondents are able and willing to answer; (2) it must uplift and motivate the respondent to become involved in the interview, to cooperate, and to complete the interview; and (3) it should minimize response error.

QUESTIONNAIRE DESIGN PROCESS

This section presents guidelines useful to beginning researchers in designing questionnaires. Although these rules can help you avoid major mistakes, the fine-tuning of a questionnaire comes from the creativity of a skilled researcher.

Questionnaire design will be presented as a series of steps (see Figure 8.2): (1) Specify the information needed, (2) specify the type of interviewing method, (3) determine the content of individual questions, (4) overcome the respondent's inability and/or unwillingness to answer, (5) decide on the question structure, (6) determine the question wording, (7) arrange the questions in proper order, (8) choose the form and layout, (9) reproduce the questionnaire, and (10) pretest the questionnaire.

We will present guidelines for each step. In practice, the steps are interrelated and the development of a questionnaire will involve some iteration and looping. For example, the researcher may discover that respondents misunderstand all the possible wordings of a question. This may require a loop back to the earlier step of deciding on the question structure. Following the steps and guidelines presented in this chapter should result in good questionnaires. For examples of well-designed questionnaires, see Cases 1.1 Dell, 3.1 JPMorgan Chase, and 3.2 Wendy's. The questionnaires in these cases were designed by professional marketing research firms.

Specify the Information Needed and the Interviewing Method

The first step in questionnaire design is to specify the information needed, a task that has already been done earlier. As was discussed in Chapter 2, this is one component of developing an approach to the problem (step 2 of the marketing research process). It is helpful to review components of the problem and the approach, particularly the information needed. In the first Research in Practice, the information needed in the Census 2010 was clearly identified.

The second step in questionnaire design is to specify the interviewing method, something that has already been done at an earlier stage. An appreciation of how the type of interviewing method influences questionnaire design can be obtained by considering how the questionnaire is administered under each method (see Chapter 5). In personal in-home and mall-intercept interviews,

FIGURE 8.2 |
QUESTIONNAIRE DESIGN
PROCESS

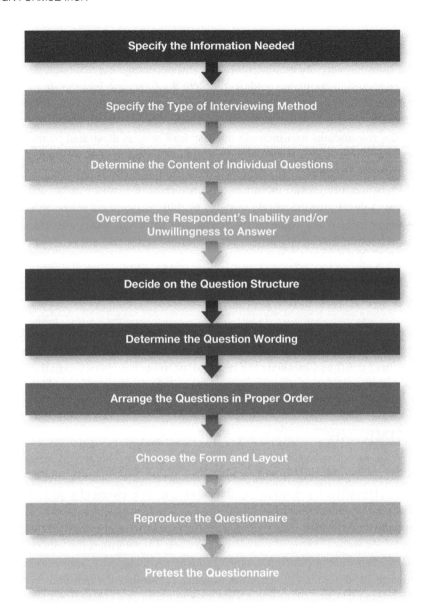

respondents see the questionnaire and interact face to face with the interviewer. Thus, lengthy, complex, and varied questions can be asked. In telephone interviews, the respondents interact with the interviewer but not face to face and they do not see the questionnaire. This limits the type of questions that can be asked to short and simple ones. Mail questionnaires are self-administered, so the questions must be simple, and detailed instructions must be provided. In computer-assisted personal interviews (CAPI) and computer-assisted telephone interviews (CATI), complex skip patterns and randomization of questions to eliminate order bias can be accommodated easily. Internet questionnaires share many of the characteristics of CAPI, but e-mail questionnaires have to be simpler. Questionnaires designed for personal and telephone interviews should be written in a conversational style.

The type of interviewing method also influences the content of individual questions.

Research Recipe

Design the questionnaire to obtain all the information that is needed and to be compatible with the survey method(s) that will be used.

Determine the Content of Individual Questions

Once the information needed is specified and the type of interviewing method has been chosen, the next step is to determine individual question content: what to include in individual questions.

IS THE QUESTION NECESSARY? Every question in a questionnaire should contribute to the information needed or serve some specific purpose. If there is no satisfactory use for the data resulting from a question, that question should be eliminated. As illustrated in the first Research in Practice, the questions in the Census 2010 were either required by law to provide constitutionally mandated information or they were collected to help ensure the accuracy and completeness of the census (questions 2 and 10).

In certain situations, however, questions may be asked that are not directly related to the information that is needed but nevertheless serve some purpose. It is useful to ask some neutral questions at the beginning of the questionnaire to establish involvement and rapport, particularly when the topic of the questionnaire is sensitive or controversial. Sometimes filler questions are asked to disguise the purpose or sponsorship of the project. Rather than limiting the questions to the brand of interest, questions about competing brands may also be included to disguise the sponsorship. For example, a survey on personal computers sponsored by Hewlett Packard (HP) may also include filler questions related to Dell and Apple.

ARE SEVERAL QUESTIONS NEEDED INSTEAD OF ONE? Once we have ascertained that a question is necessary, we must make sure that it is sufficient to get the desired information. Sometimes, several questions are needed to obtain the required information in an unambiguous manner. Consider the following question:

"Do you think Sprite is a tasty and refreshing soft drink?"

(Incorrect)

A yes answer will presumably be clear, but what if the answer is no? Does this mean that the respondent thinks that Sprite is not tasty, that it is not refreshing, or that it is neither tasty nor refreshing? Such a question is called a **double-barreled question** because two or more questions are combined into one. To obtain the required information unambiguously, two distinct questions should be asked:

double-barreled question
A single question that attempts to cover two issues. Such questions can be confusing to respondents and can result in ambiguous responses.

"Do you think Sprite is a tasty soft drink?" and
"Do you think Sprite is a refreshing soft drink?"

(Correct)

> **R e s e a r c h   R e c i p e**
>
> Every question should be necessary and serve a distinct purpose. You may need more than one question to obtain the required information in an unambiguous manner. Avoid double barreled questions.

iResearch
Old Navy: Quality and Style Are Never Old

Visit **www.oldnavy.com** and search the Internet, including social media as well as your library's online databases, to obtain information on Old Navy's marketing program.

As the CEO of Old Navy, what would you do to improve consumers' perceptions of the quality of your brand?

Formulate a double-barreled question to determine consumer perceptions of the quality and style of Old Navy clothing. Then reformulate your question to obtain unambiguous answers. ◄

Overcome the Respondent's Inability to Answer

Researchers should not assume that respondents are able to provide accurate or reasonable answers to all questions. The respondents will be unable to respond accurately if they are not informed or unable to articulate their responses.

IS THE RESPONDENT INFORMED?

Respondents are often asked about topics on which they are not informed. A husband may not be informed about monthly expenses for groceries and department store purchases if it is the wife who makes these purchases, or vice versa. Research has shown that respondents will often answer questions even though they are uninformed.

In situations where not all respondents are likely to be informed about the topic of interest, questions that measure familiarity, product use, and past experience should be asked before questions about the topics themselves. Such questions enable the researcher to filter out respondents who are not adequately informed. A "don't know" option appears to reduce uninformed responses without reducing the overall response rate or the response rate for questions about which the respondents have information. Hence, this option should be provided when the researcher expects that respondents may not be adequately informed about the subject of the question. Also, in some cases it may be appropriate to give the respondents relevant information about the brand or product before asking them to express their opinions. The ability of the respondents can also be enhance by asking questions in a way that will help them remember or respond. The Census 2010 questionnaire added two new questions (questions 2 and 10) to help respondents accurately evaluate how many people are living in the household.

CAN THE RESPONDENT ARTICULATE HIS OR HER RESPONSES?

Respondents may be unable to articulate certain types of responses. For example, if asked to describe the atmosphere of the department store they would prefer to patronize, most respondents may be unable to phrase their answers. On the other hand, if the respondents are provided with alternative descriptions of store atmosphere, they will be able to indicate the one they like the best. If respondents are unable to articulate their responses to a question, they are likely to ignore that question and may refuse to respond to the rest of the questionnaire. Thus, respondents should be given aids, such as pictures, maps, and descriptions, to help them articulate their responses.

Research Recipe

You can enhance the ability of respondents to answer by (1) giving them relevant information; (2) asking questions in a way that will help them remember or respond; and (3) providing them with aids such as descriptions, pictures, and maps.

Overcome the Respondent's Unwillingness to Answer

Even if respondents are able to answer a particular question, they may be unwilling to do so either because too much effort is required or the information requested is sensitive.

EFFORT REQUIRED OF THE RESPONDENT

Most respondents are unwilling to devote a lot of effort to providing information. Hence, the researcher should minimize the effort required of the respondents by providing the response options, as seen in the Census 2010 questionnaire in the first Research in Practice. Suppose the researcher is interested in determining from which departments in a store the respondent purchased merchandise on the most recent shopping trip. This information can be obtained in at least two ways. The researcher could ask the respondent to list all the departments from which merchandise was purchased on the most recent shopping trip, or the researcher could provide a list of departments and ask the respondent to check the applicable ones:

> Please list all the departments from which you purchased merchandise on your most recent shopping trip to a department store.
>
> (Incorrect)
>
> In the list that follows, please check all the departments from which you purchased merchandise on your most recent shopping trip to a department store.

   1. Women's dresses   _____
   2. Men's apparel   _____
   3. Children's apparel   _____
   4. Cosmetics   _____
        .
        .
        .
   17. Jewelry   _____
   18. Other (please specify) _____

(Correct)

The second option is preferable because it requires less effort from respondents.

SENSITIVE INFORMATION   Respondents are unwilling to disclose, at least accurately, sensitive information because this may cause embarrassment or threaten the respondent's prestige or self-image. If pressed for the answer, respondents may give biased responses, especially during personal interviews (see Chapter 5). Sensitive topics include money, family life, political and religious beliefs, and involvement in accidents or crimes. Respondents may be encouraged to provide sensitive information that they are otherwise unwilling to give by using the following desensitizing techniques:

1. Place sensitive topics at the end of the questionnaire. By then, initial mistrust has been overcome, rapport has been created, the legitimacy of the project has been established, and respondents are more willing to give information.
2. Preface the question with a statement that the behavior of interest is common. For example, before requesting information on credit card debt, say, "Recent studies show that most Americans are in debt." This technique is called the use of counterbiasing statements.
3. Ask the question using the third-person technique (see Chapter 4). In other words, phrase the question as if it referred to other people.
4. Provide response categories rather than asking for specific figures. Do not ask, "What is your household's annual income?" Instead, ask the respondent to check the appropriate income category: under $25,000, $25,001–$50,000, $50,001–$75,000, or over $75,000. In personal interviews, give the respondents cards that list the numbered choices. The respondents then indicate their responses by number.

Research Recipe

You can enhance the willingness of respondents to answer by (1) reducing the effort required, for example, by listing the response options; and (2) using desensitizing techniques when trying to obtain sensitive information.

Decide on the Question Structure

A question may be unstructured or structured. In the following sections, we define unstructured questions and discuss their relative advantages and disadvantages, and then consider the major types of structured questions: multiple-choice, dichotomous, and scales (Figure 8.3).

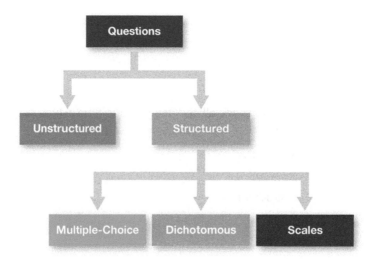

FIGURE 8.3
TYPES OF QUESTIONS

unstructured questions
Open-ended questions that respondents answer in their own words.

UNSTRUCTURED QUESTIONS **Unstructured questions** are open-ended questions that respondents answer in their own words. They are also referred to as free-response or free-answer questions. The following are some examples:

- What is your occupation?
- Who is your favorite singer?

Open-ended questions are good as first questions on a topic. They enable the respondents to express general attitudes and opinions that can help the researcher interpret their responses to structured questions. Unstructured questions have a much less biasing influence on response than structured questions. Hence, unstructured questions are useful in exploratory research.

A principal disadvantage of unstructured questions is that potential for interviewer bias is high. Whether the interviewers record the answers verbatim or write down only the main points, the data depend on the skills of the interviewers. Voice recorders should be used if verbatim reporting is important. Another major disadvantage of unstructured questions is that the coding of responses is costly and time consuming. The coding procedures required to summarize responses in a format useful for data analysis and interpretation can be extensive. By their very nature, unstructured or open-ended questions give extra weight to respondents who are more articulate. Also, unstructured questions are not suitable for self-administered questionnaires (mail, CAPI, e-mail, and Internet) because respondents tend to be more brief when they are writing rather than speaking.

In general, open-ended questions are useful in exploratory research and as opening questions. Otherwise, their disadvantages outweigh their advantages in a large survey. It is for this reason that the Census 2010 questionnaire did not contain any open-ended questions.

structured questions
Questions that prespecify the set of response alternatives and the response format. A structured question could be multiple-choice, dichotomous, or scale.

STRUCTURED QUESTIONS **Structured questions** specify the set of response alternatives and the response format. A structured question may be multiple-choice, dichotomous, or scale.

Multiple-Choice Questions In multiple-choice questions, the researcher provides a choice of answers and respondents are asked to select one or more of the alternatives given. Consider the following question.

Do you intend to buy a new car within the next six months?
_____ Definitely will not buy
_____ Probably will not buy
_____ Undecided
_____ Probably will buy
_____ Definitely will buy
_____ Other (please specify)

For other examples of multiple choice questions, see the Census 2010 questionnaire given in the first Research in Practice, for example question 3. Several of the issues discussed in Chapter 7 with respect to itemized rating scales also apply to multiple-choice answers. The response alternatives should include the set of all possible choices. The general guideline is to list all alternatives that may be of importance and include an alternative labeled "Other (please specify)," as shown previously and in the Census 2010 questionnaire. The response alternatives should be mutually exclusive. Respondents should also be able to identify one, and only one, alternative unless the researcher specifically allows two or more choices (for example, "Please indicate all the brands of soft drinks that you have consumed in the past week" or question 2 in the Census 2010).

Multiple-choice questions overcome many of the disadvantages of open-ended questions because interviewer bias is reduced and because these questions are administered quickly. Also, coding and processing of data are much less costly and time consuming. In self-administered questionnaires, respondent cooperation is improved if the majority of the questions are structured.

Multiple-choice questions are not without disadvantages. Considerable effort is required to design effective multiple-choice questions. Exploratory research using open-ended questions may be required to determine the appropriate response alternatives. It is difficult to obtain information on alternatives not listed. Even if an "Other (please specify)" category is included, respondents tend to choose among the listed alternatives. In addition, showing respondents the list of possible answers produces biased responses.

Dichotomous Questions A **dichotomous question** has only two response alternatives: yes or no, agree or disagree, and so on. See also question 6 of the Census 2010 questionnaire in the first Research in Practice. Often, the two alternatives of interest are supplemented by a neutral alternative, such as "no opinion," "don't know," "both," or "none." The question asked before about intentions to buy a new car as a multiple-choice question can also be asked as a dichotomous question.

dichotomous question
A structured question with only two response alternatives, such as yes or no.

Do you intend to buy a new car within the next six months?
_____ Yes
_____ No

The decision to use a dichotomous question should be guided by whether the respondents approach the issue as a yes-or-no question. The general advantages and disadvantages of dichotomous questions are very similar to those of multiple-choice questions. Dichotomous questions are the easiest type of questions to code and analyze, but they have one acute problem: The response can be influenced by the wording of the question. To illustrate, the statement, "Individuals are more to blame than social conditions for crime and lawlessness in this country," produced agreement from 59.6 percent of the respondents. However, on a matched sample that responded to the opposite statement, "Social conditions are more to blame than individuals for crime and lawlessness in this country," 43.2 percent (as opposed to 40.4 percent expected based on agreement with the opposite statement) agreed. To overcome this problem, the question should be framed in one way on one-half of the questionnaires and in the opposite way on the other half. This is referred to as the split-ballot technique.

Scales Scales were discussed in detail in Chapter 7. To illustrate the difference between scales and other kinds of structured questions, consider the question about intentions to buy a new car. One way of framing this using a scale is as follows:

Do you intend to buy a new car within the next six months?

Definitely will not buy	Probably will not buy	Undecided	Probably will buy	Definitely will buy
1	2	3	4	5

This is only one of several scales that could be used to ask this question (see Chapter 7). As shown in the Census 2010 questionnaire and in the following Research in Practice, a survey may contain different types of questions.

Research in Practice
Foresight Research Provides Sight for Chrysler 300 C

Chrysler wanted to determine how its 300 C cars would be accepted by the customers of the chauffeured transportation industry. The company hired Foresight Research (**www.foresightresearch.com**) to conduct the needed research. Foresight designed a self-administered questionnaire that was distributed by the drivers of two major chauffeuring services in Detroit and Los Angeles to the passengers in livery company vehicles to complete. The sample size was 165.

The structured questionnaire contained survey questions that included different types of question structures. Some of the questions included the following:

- How often do you use chauffeured transportation services? (multiple-choice)
- Do you know the make of the vehicle you are riding in today? (dichotomous: yes or no)
- If this same make of vehicle were dispatched for your next chauffeured transportation experience, would you have any objection? (dichotomous: yes or no)
- Taking into consideration everything about this car, how satisfied are you overall with the vehicle? (10-point scale, 1 being highly dissatisfied, 10 being highly satisfied)
- How satisfied are you with each of these vehicle elements? (10-point scale—rear seat passenger roominess, luxury feel of interior, exterior styling, sound/quietness, trunk size)
- How would you describe your overall experience of riding in this vehicle? (unstructured: open-ended)

The research findings showed that at least 90 percent of the Chrysler 300 C passengers surveyed would have no objection to having another Chrysler 300 C dispatched to them; 91 percent of passengers were overall satisfied with the vehicle dispatched, and none were dissatisfied. Most comments about the Chrysler 300 C were positive, reflecting a view of the vehicle as comfortable, quiet, roomy, and sufficiently luxurious. Negative comments on the Chrysler 300 C were mainly due to insufficient trunk size. Overall, respondents recognized and accepted the Chrysler 300 C as an executive car. Encouraged by these findings, Chrysler successfully penetrated the chauffeured transportation industry. The 2013 Chrysler 300 C had a starting manufacturer suggested retail price (MSRP) of $36,145. ◄

Source: Ryu Seung-il/Polaris/Newscom

Research Recipe

Use unstructured questions in exploratory research. For large, descriptive surveys, use multiple-choice and dichotomous questions, and scales. Your survey may contain different types of questions.

Determine the Question Wording

Question wording is the translation of the desired question content and structure into words that respondents can clearly and easily understand. Deciding on question wording is perhaps the most critical and difficult task in developing a questionnaire. If a question is worded poorly, respondents may refuse to answer it or may answer it incorrectly. The first condition, in which respondents refuse to answer, is known as item nonresponse and can increase the complexity of data analysis. The second condition leads to response error, discussed earlier in this chapter. Unless the respondents and the researcher assign exactly the same meaning to the question, the results will be biased. The Census 2010 questionnaire in the first Research in Practice demonstrates clarity of question wording.

To avoid these problems, we offer the following guidelines: (1) define the issue, (2) use ordinary words, (3) use unambiguous words, (4) avoid leading questions, and (5) use positive and negative statements.

DEFINE THE ISSUE   A question should clearly define the issue being addressed. Beginning journalists are admonished to define the issue in terms of *who, what, when, where, why,* and *way* (the six Ws). *Who, what, when,* and *where* are particularly important and can also serve as guidelines for defining the issue in a question. Consider the following question:

Which brand of shampoo do you use?

(Incorrect)

On the surface, this question may seem well-defined, but we may reach a different conclusion when we examine it under the microscope of *who, what, when,* and *where. Who* in this instance refers to the respondent. It is not clear, though, whether the researcher is referring to the brand the respondent uses personally or the brand used by the household. *What* is the brand of shampoo. However, what if more than one brand of shampoo is used? Should the respondent mention the most preferred brand, the brand used most often, the brand used most recently, or the brand that comes to mind first? *When* is not clear; does the researcher mean last time, last week, last month, last year, or ever? As for *where,* it is implied that the shampoo is used at home, but this is not stated clearly. Our analysis may be summarized as follows.

The Ws	Defining the Question
Who	**The Respondent** It is not clear whether this question relates to the individual respondent or the respondent *and* the respondent's household.
What	**The Brand of Shampoo** It is unclear how the respondent is to answer this question if more than one brand is used.
When	**Unclear** The timeframe is not specified in this question. The respondent could interpret it as meaning the shampoo used this morning, this week, over the past year, or ever.
Where	**Not Specified** At home, at the gym, on the road?

A better wording for this question would be the following:

Which brand or brands of shampoo have you personally used at home during the last month? In case of more than one brand, please list all the brands that apply.

(Correct)

USE ORDINARY WORDS   Ordinary words should be used in a questionnaire, and they should match the vocabulary level of the respondents. When choosing words, keep in mind that the average person in the United States has a high school, not a college, education. For certain respondent groups, the education level is even lower. For example, the author did a project for a major telecommunications firm that operates primarily in rural areas of the United States. The average educational level in these areas was less than high school, and many respondents had only a fourth- to sixth-grade education. Technical jargon should also be avoided. Most respondents do not understand technical marketing words. For example, instead of asking,

"Do you think the distribution of soft drinks is adequate?"

(Incorrect)

ask,

"Do you think soft drinks are readily available when you want to buy them?"

(Correct)

USE UNAMBIGUOUS WORDS   The words used in a questionnaire should have a single meaning that is known to all respondents. A number of words that appear to be unambiguous have different meanings to different people. These words include *usually, normally, frequently, often, regularly, occasionally*, and *sometimes*. Consider the following question:

In a typical month, how often do you shop in department stores?
_____ Never
_____ Occasionally
_____ Sometimes
_____ Often
_____ Regularly

(Incorrect)

The answers to this question are fraught with response bias because the words used to describe category labels have different meanings for different respondents. Three respondents who shop once a month may check three different categories: "occasionally," "sometimes," and "often." A much better wording for this question would be the following:

In a typical month, how often do you shop in department stores?
_____ Less than once
_____ One or two times
_____ Three or four times
_____ More than four times

(Correct)

Note that this question provides a consistent frame of reference for all respondents. Response categories have been objectively defined, and respondents are no longer free to interpret them in their own way.

All-inclusive or all-exclusive words may also be understood differently by different people and should be avoided. Some examples of such words are *all, always, any, anybody, ever*, and *every*. To illustrate, *any* could mean "every," "some," or "one only" to different respondents, depending on how they interpret it.

The U.S. Census Bureau took great pains to use ordinary and unambiguous words in the Census 2010 questionnaires, which not only improved the response rate but also resulted in more accurate data (see the first Research in Practice feature in this chapter).

leading question
A question that gives the respondent a clue about what answer is desired or leads the respondent to answer in a certain way.

acquiescence bias (yea-saying)
This bias is the result of some respondents' tendency to agree with the direction of a leading question (yea-saying).

AVOID LEADING OR BIASING QUESTIONS   A **leading question** is one that clues the respondent to what answer is desired or leads the respondent to answer in a certain way. Some respondents have a tendency to agree with whatever way the question is leading them to answer. This tendency is known as **yea-saying** and results in a bias called **acquiescence bias**. Consider the following question, which is meant to determine Americans' preferences for domestic or imported automobiles:

Do you think that patriotic Americans should buy imported automobiles when that would put American labor out of work?
_____ Yes
_____ No
_____ Don't know

(Incorrect)

This question would lead respondents to a no answer. After all, how can patriotic Americans put American labor out of work? Therefore, this question would not accurately determine the preferences of Americans for imported versus domestic automobiles. A better question would be:

> Do you think that Americans should buy imported automobiles?
> _____ Yes
> _____ No
> _____ Don't know
>
>   (Correct)

Bias may also arise when respondents are given clues about the sponsor of the project. Respondents tend to respond favorably toward the sponsor. The question, "Is Colgate your favorite toothpaste?" is likely to bias the responses in favor of Colgate. A more unbiased way of obtaining this information would be to ask, "What is your favorite brand of toothpaste?" and see if Colgate is mentioned.

BALANCE DUAL STATEMENTS: POSITIVE AND NEGATIVE Many questions, particularly those measuring attitudes and lifestyles, are worded as statements to which respondents indicate their degree of agreement or disagreement. Evidence indicates that the response obtained is influenced by the directionality of the statements: whether they are stated positively or negatively. In these cases, it is better to use dual statements, some of which are positive and the others negative. Two different questionnaires could be prepared. One questionnaire would contain half negative and half positive statements in an interspersed way. The direction of these statements would be reversed in the second questionnaire. An example of dual statements was provided in the summated Likert scale in Chapter 7 that was designed to measure attitudes toward McDonald's; some statements about McDonald's were positive and others were negative.

Research Recipe

You can improve the wording of a question by (1) defining the issue in terms of *who*, *what*, *when*, and *where*; (2) using ordinary words that match the vocabulary and educational levels of the respondents; (3) using unambiguous words; (4) avoiding leading questions that lead the respondents to answer in a certain way; and (5) using positive and negative statements.

iResearch
FedEx: The Big Caters to the Small

Visit **www.fedex.com** and search the Internet, including social media as well as your library's online databases, to obtain information on the overnight package delivery market. Write a brief report.

As the marketing director for FedEx, how would you penetrate the important small-business market for overnight package delivery?

Evaluate the wording of the following question asked of small-business owners and CEOs: "If FedEx were to introduce a new overnight delivery service for small businesses, how likely are you to adopt it?" ‹

Arrange the Questions in Proper Order

OPENING QUESTIONS The opening questions can be crucial in gaining the confidence and cooperation of respondents. The opening questions should be interesting, simple, and non-threatening. Questions that ask respondents for their opinions can be good opening questions because most people like to express their opinions. Sometimes such questions are asked even though they are unrelated to the research problem and their responses are not analyzed. In some instances, it is necessary to screen or qualify the respondents, or determine whether a respondent is eligible to participate in the interview. In these cases, the screening or qualifying questions serve as the opening questions, as in the Research in Practice about Wendy's.

Research in Practice
Wendy's: Qualifying Customers Leads to Unqualified Success

An online survey for Wendy's had to be restricted to consumers who were between the ages of 18 and 45. Hence, age was the first question that was asked, and the answer was used to qualify the potential respondent, as illustrated in the following:

1. To begin, which of the following categories includes your age? (CHOOSE ONE RESPONSE ONLY.)

    (1) Under 18 [TERMINATE]

    (2) 18–24

    (3) 25–29

    (4) 30–34

    (5) 35–39

    (6) 40–45

    (7) 46 or older [TERMINATE]

    (8) Refused [TERMINATE]

See Case 3.2 for the rest of the questionnaire. Having a targeted sample by qualifying the potential respondents resulted in findings that were geared to this specific segment. This enabled Wendy's to formulate marketing strategies to penetrate the 18- to 45-year-old segment successfully. **<**

basic information
Information that relates directly to the marketing research problem.

classification information
Socioeconomic and demographic characteristics used to classify respondents.

identification information
Information obtained in a questionnaire that includes the respondent's name, postal address, e-mail address, and phone number.

TYPE OF INFORMATION   The type of information obtained in a questionnaire may be classified as: (1) basic information, (2) classification information, and (3) identification information. **Basic information** relates directly to the research problem. **Classification information**, consisting of socioeconomic and demographic characteristics, is used to classify the respondents and understand the results. **Identification information** includes the respondent's name, postal address, e-mail address, and telephone number. Identification information may be obtained for a variety of purposes, including verifying that the respondents listed were actually interviewed, remitting promised incentives, and so on. As a general guideline, basic information should be obtained first, followed by classification, and, finally, identification information. The basic information is of greatest importance to the research project and should be obtained first, before the risk of alienating the respondents by asking a series of personal questions. The questionnaire given in Applied Problem 8-20 (at the end of this chapter) incorrectly obtains identification (name) and some classification (demographic) information in the beginning.

DIFFICULT QUESTIONS   Difficult questions or questions that are sensitive, embarrassing, complex, or dull should be placed late in the sequence. After rapport has been established and the respondents become involved, they are less likely to object to these questions. Thus, in a department store project, information about credit card debt was asked at the end of the section on basic information. Likewise, income should be the last question in the classification section, and the respondent's telephone number should be the final item in the identification section.

EFFECT ON SUBSEQUENT QUESTIONS   Questions asked early in a sequence can influence the responses to subsequent questions. As a rule of thumb, general questions should precede specific questions. This prevents specific questions from biasing responses to general questions. Consider the following sequence of questions:

> Q1: What considerations are important to you in selecting a department store?
> Q2: In selecting a department store, how important is convenience of location?
>
> (Correct)

Note that the first question is general, whereas the second is specific. If these questions were asked in the reverse order, respondents would be clued about convenience of location and would be more likely to give this response to the general question.

Going from general to specific is called the **funnel approach**, as illustrated in Figure 8.4. The funnel approach is particularly useful when information has to be obtained about respondents' general choice behavior and their evaluations of specific products. Sometimes the inverted funnel approach may be useful. In this approach, questioning begins with specific questions and concludes with the general questions. The respondents are compelled to provide specific information before making general evaluations. This approach is useful when respondents have no strong feelings or have not formulated a point of view.

LOGICAL ORDER   Questions should be asked in a logical order, as in the Census 2010 questionnaire in the first Research in Practice. All of the questions that deal with a particular topic should be asked before beginning a new topic. When switching topics, brief transitional phrases should be used to help respondents switch their train of thought.

Branching questions should be designed carefully. **Branching questions** are questions that direct respondents to different places in the questionnaire based on how they respond to the question at hand. These questions ensure that all possible contingencies are covered. They also help reduce interviewer and respondent error and encourage complete responses. Skip patterns based on the branching questions can become quite complex. The general order of questions is outlined in Table 8.1.

funnel approach
A strategy for ordering questions in a questionnaire in which the sequence starts with general questions that are followed by progressively specific questions in order to prevent specific questions from biasing general questions.

branching questions
Questions used to guide an interviewer (or respondent) through a survey by directing the interviewer (or respondent) to different spots on the questionnaire depending on the respondent's answers.

FIGURE 8.4
THE FUNNEL APPROACH TO ORDEREING QUESTIONS

Broad or General Questions

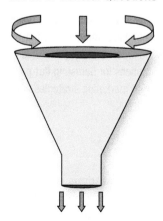

Narrow or Specific Questions

Table 8.1 > The General Ordering of Questions in a Questionnaire

Question Type	Nature	Function	Example
Qualifying/Screening Questions	Focus on respondent inclusion criteria	To determine if a respondent is eligible to participate in the survey	Who in your household does most of the shopping for groceries?
Introductory Questions/ warm-ups	Broad, easy questions	To break the ice and put the respondent at ease	How often do you shop for groceries?
Main Questions: Easy	Related to the information needed but easy to answer	To focus on the survey topic and reassure the respondent that the survey is easy	How important Is each of the following factors in selecting a supermarket?
Main questions: More difficult	Related to the information needed but may be difficult to answer	To obtain the rest of the information needed	How would you rank order the following eight supermarkets in terms of your preference to shop?
Psychographics/ Lifestyles	Not relevant in all surveys	To obtain personality related information	Please indicate your degree of dis/agreement with the following statements
Demographics	Personal information	To classify the respondents	What is your occupation?
Identification Information	Name, address, telephone	To identify the respondent	Name:

Research Recipe

When ordering the questions, follow these guidelines: (1) Opening questions should be interesting, simple and nonthreatening; (2) obtain basic information first, followed by classification information, followed by identification information; (3) difficult and sensitive questions should be placed late in the sequence; (4) consider the effect on subsequent questions and use the funnel approach; and (5) follow a logical order.

iResearch
Is the Flat-Panel Television Market Flat?

Search the Internet, including social media as well as your library's online databases, to obtain information on consumers' perceptions, preferences, and purchase intentions for flat-panel televisions.

Specify the information needed and the order in which you would obtain information on consumers' perceptions, preferences, and purchase intentions for Samsung flat-panel televisions.

As the vice president for marketing, what marketing strategies would you formulate to increase Samsung's penetration of the flat-panel television market? <

Choose the Form and Layout

The format, spacing, and positioning of questions can have a significant effect on the results, as illustrated by the Census 2010 questionnaire in the first Research in Practice in this chapter. This is particularly important for self-administered questionnaires. It is good practice to divide a questionnaire into several parts. Several parts may be needed for questions pertaining to the basic information. The questions in each part should be numbered, particularly when branching questions are used. Numbering of questions also makes the coding of responses easier. This can be seen in the Census 2010 questionnaire in the first Research in Practice.

The questionnaires themselves should be numbered serially. This facilitates the control of questionnaires in the field as well as the coding and analysis. Numbering makes it easy to account for the questionnaires and to determine if any have been lost. A possible exception to this rule is mail questionnaires. If these are numbered, respondents assume that a given number identifies a particular respondent. Some respondents may refuse to participate or may answer differently under these conditions. However, recent research suggests that this loss of anonymity has little, if any, influence on the results.

Research Recipe

Observe the following guidelines while deciding on the form and layout of a questionnaire: (1) Divide the questionnaire into parts and number the questions in each part, and (2) number the questionnaires serially.

Reproduction of the Questionnaire

How a questionnaire is reproduced for administration can influence the results. For example, if the questionnaire is reproduced on poor-quality paper or is otherwise shabby in appearance, the respondents will think the project is unimportant and the quality of response will be adversely affected. Therefore, the questionnaire should be reproduced on good-quality paper and have a professional appearance, as in the Census 2010 questionnaire.

Each question should be reproduced on a single page (or double-page spread). A researcher should avoid splitting a question, including its response categories. Split questions can mislead the interviewer or the respondent into thinking that the question has ended at the end of a page. This will result in answers based on incomplete questions.

Vertical response columns should be used for individual questions. It is easier for interviewers and respondents to read down a single column rather than sideways across several columns. Sideways formatting and splitting, done frequently to conserve space, should be avoided. The tendency to crowd questions together to make the questionnaire look shorter should be avoided because it can lead to errors.

Research Recipe

Follow these guidelines in reproducing the questionnaire: (1) It should be reproduced on good-quality paper and have a professional appearance, (2) each question should be reproduced on a single page or double-page spread (avoid splitting a question), (3) vertical response columns should be used for individual questions, and (4) do not crowd questions together to make the questionnaire look shorter.

Pretest the Questionnaire

Pretesting refers to the testing of the questionnaire on a small sample of respondents to identify and eliminate potential problems or bugs. Even the best questionnaire can be improved by pretesting. As a general rule, a questionnaire should not be used in the field without adequate pretesting. A pretest should be extensive, as illustrated by the Census 2010 questionnaire in this chapter's first Research in Practice. All aspects of the questionnaire should be tested, including question content, wording, sequence, form and layout, question difficulty, and instructions. The respondents in the pretest should be similar to those who will be included in the actual survey in terms of background characteristics, familiarity with the topic, and attitudes and behaviors of

pretesting
The testing of the questionnaire on a small sample of respondents for the purpose of improving the questionnaire by identifying and eliminating potential problems.

interest. In other words, respondents for the pretest and for the actual survey should be drawn from the same population.

Pretests are best done by personal interviews, even if the actual survey is to be conducted by mail, telephone, or electronic means, because interviewers can observe respondents' reactions and attitudes. After the necessary changes have been made to the survey, another pretest should be conducted by mail, telephone, or electronic means if those methods are to be used in the actual survey. The latter pretests should reveal problems peculiar to the interviewing method. To the extent possible, a pretest should involve administering the questionnaire in an environment and context similar to that of the actual survey.

Ordinarily, the pretest sample size is small, varying from fifteen to thirty respondents for the initial testing, depending on the heterogeneity of the target population. The sample size can increase substantially if the pretesting involves several stages or waves. The questionnaire should be revised to correct for the problems identified during pretesting. After each significant revision of the questionnaire, another pretest should be conducted using a different sample of respondents. Sound pretesting involves several stages, as in the Census 2010 questionnaire in the first Research in Practice. One pretest is a bare minimum. Pretesting should be continued until no further changes are needed. Finally, the responses obtained from the pretest should be coded and analyzed. Table 8.2 summarizes the questionnaire design process in the form of a checklist.

Table 8.2 > Questionnaire Design Checklist

Step 1   Specify The Information Needed
1. Ensure that the information obtained fully addresses all the components of the problem.
2. Have a clear idea of the target population.

Step 2   Type of Interviewing Method
1. Review the type of interviewing method determined based on considerations discussed in Chapter 5.

Step 3   Individual Question Content
1. Is the question necessary?
2. Are several questions needed instead of one to obtain the required information in an unambiguous manner?
3. Do not use double-barreled questions.

Step 4   Overcoming Inability and Unwillingness to Answer
1. Is the respondent informed?
2. If respondents are not likely to be informed, questions that measure familiarity, product use, and past experience should be asked before questions about the topics themselves.
3. Can the respondent remember?
4. Can the respondent articulate?
5. Minimize the effort required of the respondents.
6. Make the request for information seem legitimate.
7. Is the information sensitive?

Step 5   Choosing Question Structure
1. Open-ended questions are useful in exploratory research and as opening questions.
2. Use structured questions whenever possible.
3. In multiple-choice questions, the response alternatives should include the set of all possible choices and should be mutually exclusive.
4. In a dichotomous question, if a substantial proportion of the respondents can be expected to be neutral, include a neutral alternative.
5. Consider the use of the split ballot technique to reduce order bias in dichotomous and multiple-choice questions.
6. If the response alternatives are numerous, consider using more than one question.

Step 6	Choosing Question Wording

1. Define the issue in terms of who, what, when, where, why, and way (the six Ws).
2. Use ordinary words. Words should match the vocabulary level of the respondents.
3. Avoid ambiguous words: usually, normally, frequently, often, regularly, occasionally, sometimes, etc.
4. Avoid leading questions that clue the respondent to what the answer should be.
5. Use positive and negative statements.

Step 7	Determine the Order of Questions

1. 1. The opening questions should be interesting, simple, and nonthreatening.
2. Qualifying questions should serve as the opening questions.
3. Basic information should be obtained first, followed by classification, and finally, identification information.
4. Difficult, sensitive, or complex questions should be placed late in the sequence.
5. General questions should precede the specific questions.
6. Questions should be asked in a logical order.

Step 8	Form and Layout

1. Divide a questionnaire into several parts.
2. Questions in each part should be numbered.
3. The questionnaires themselves should be numbered serially.

Step 9	Reproduction of the Questionnaire

1. The questionnaire should have a professional appearance.
2. Booklet format should be used for long questionnaires.
3. Each question should be reproduced on a single page (or double-page spread).
4. The tendency to crowd questions to make the questionnaire look shorter should be avoided.

Step 10	Pretesting

1. Pretesting should be done always.
2. All aspects of the questionnaire should be tested, including question content, wording, sequence, form and layout, question difficulty, and instructions.
3. The respondents in the pretest should be similar to those who will be included in the actual survey.
4. Begin the pretest by using personal interviews.
5. Pretest should also be conducted by mail, telephone, or electronically if those methods are to be used in the actual survey.
6. A variety of interviewers should be used for pretests.
7. The pretest sample size is small, varying from 15 to 30 respondents for the initial testing.
8. After each significant revision of the questionnaire, another pretest should be conducted, using a different sample of respondents.
9. The responses obtained from the pretest should be coded and analyzed.

Research Recipe

Pretest every questionnaire extensively. Test all aspects of the questionnaire, including question content, wording, sequence, form and layout, question difficulty, and instructions. The respondents for the pretest should be drawn from the population for the actual survey. Use personal interviews for the initial pretest and then follow up with a pretest using the survey method if that is different. Continue pretesting in waves of fifteen to thirty respondents until no further changes are needed. Finally, code and analyze the responses obtained from the pretest.

SOFTWARE FOR QUESTIONNAIRE DESIGN

Software is available for designing questionnaires administered over the Internet or other modes (e.g., telephone, personal interviews, or mail). Although we describe the use of the software for constructing Internet questionnaires, the functions are essentially similar for questionnaires constructed for other modes. The software helps develop and disseminate the questionnaire and, in many cases, retrieve and analyze the collected data, and prepare a report. In addition, these software programs have a variety of features that facilitate questionnaire construction. Some commonly used survey software programs include Qualtrics (**www.qualtrics.com**), SurveyPro 5 (**www.apian.com**), Vovici (**www.vovici.com**), and SSI Web by Sawtooth Software (**www.sawtoothsoftware.com**).

Free/Low-Cost Survey Sites

Several websites allow users to create and file their own surveys for free or at a low cost. Zoomerang (**www.zoomerang.com**) by MarketTools (**www.markettools.com**), SurveyMonkey (**www.surveymonkey.com**), PollDaddy (**www.polldaddy.com**), Kwik Surveys (**www.kwiksurveys .com**), FreeOnlineSurveys.com (**freeonlinesurveys.com**), eSurveypro (**www.esurveyspro.com**), FreePollKit (**www.freepollkit.com**), and Impressity (**www.impressity.com**) are some of the firms offering free basic plans. They allow anyone to create and administer online surveys. Low-cost Web-based services include CreateSurvey (**www.createsurvey.com**), SurveyGizmo (**www .surveygizmo.com**), and Checkbox (**www.checkbox.com**).

OBSERVATIONAL FORMS

Forms for recording observational data are easier to construct than questionnaires. The researcher need not be concerned with the psychological impact of the questions and the way they are asked. The researcher need only develop a form that identifies the required information clearly; makes it easy for the field worker to record the information accurately; and simplifies the coding, entry, and analysis of data. The form and layout as well as the reproduction of observational forms should follow the same guidelines discussed for questionnaires. Finally, like questionnaires, observational forms also require adequate pretesting.

INTERNATIONAL MARKETING RESEARCH

The questionnaire or research instrument should be adapted to the specific cultural environment and should not be biased in terms of any one culture. This requires careful attention to each step of the questionnaire design process. The information needed should be clearly specified. It is important to account for any differences in underlying consumer behavior; decision-making process; and psychographic, lifestyle, and demographic variables. In the context of demographic characteristics, information on marital status, education, household size, occupation, income, and dwelling unit may have to be specified differently for different countries because these variables may not be directly comparable across countries. For example, household definition and size varies greatly, given the extended family structure in some countries and the practice of two or even three families living under the same roof.

Although personal interviewing is the dominant survey method in international marketing research, different interviewing methods may be used in different countries. Hence, the questionnaire may have to be suitable for administration by more than one method. The questionnaire may have to be translated for administration in different cultures. The researcher must ensure that the questionnaires in different languages are equivalent.

The use of unstructured or open-ended questions may be desirable if the researcher lacks knowledge about the determinants of response in other countries. Unstructured questions also reduce cultural bias because they do not impose any response alternatives. However, unstructured questions are more affected by differences in educational levels than are structured questions. They should be used with caution in countries with high illiteracy rates. Unstructured and structured questions can be employed in a complementary way to provide rich insights, as in the following Research in Practice feature.

Research in Practice
The Theme: Singapore's Theme Restaurants

Singapore is comprised of over sixty islets and has a population of almost 4 million people (as of 2014) (**www.visitsingapore.com**). Globally, it is known for its diverse restaurant industry. Of the 27,000 food-service establishments, 21 percent are classified as restaurants. A study was conducted on the following four theme restaurants in Singapore: Hard Rock Café, Planet Hollywood, Celebrities Asia, and House of Mao (visit **www.asiacuisine.com.sg** for a description of these restaurants).

A questionnaire was pretested with twenty diners who had eaten at all four of the theme restaurants. Some revisions were made to the questionnaire based on the comments from those respondents. The survey was then administered to 300 participants in a questionnaire format that was designed to find out the participants' perceptions of the theme restaurants. The participants were chosen at random using a mall-intercept method and by asking the participants if they had been a customer in a theme restaurant in the past year. If their answer was yes, they were asked to participate and then fill out a four-page survey. The survey was divided into two sections: Section A asked about the participant's general perception of the theme restaurants, and section B asked the respondent to rate each of the four restaurants on a 5-point scale on nine different attributes. Respondents were also asked several open-ended questions at the end of the questionnaire, for example, Do you think more theme restaurants will open in Singapore in the future? and Do you think these restaurants will be successful?

Source: Tim Chong/Reuters / Landov

Most respondents felt more theme restaurants would open in Singapore and most were neutral about their success. House of Mao received the highest rating in theme concept, and Hard Rock Café received the highest rating in overall experience meeting expectations. Hard Rock Café had the best overall ratings on the nine attributes. Based on this survey, there is room for growth in the theme restaurant industry in Singapore.[2] ◄

Research Recipe

You should adapt the questionnaire to the specific cultural environment; it should not be biased in terms of any one culture. It may have to be suitable for administration by more than one survey method. The questionnaire may have to be translated into different languages; in such cases, ensure that the different forms of the questionnaire are equivalent.

MARKETING RESEARCH AND SOCIAL MEDIA

Analysis of social media can provide a good understanding of the underlying issues pertaining to the problem at hand. Such an understanding can be invaluable in designing an appropriate questionnaire for use in traditional or social media surveys. As we discussed earlier in this chapter, some of the challenges in questionnaire design involve determining the content, structure, and wording of individual questions. To devise questions that are appropriate in terms of content, structure, and wording, research skills have to be applied from the respondents' viewpoints. The same is true for deciding on the order of questions. Social media are effective and accessible domains for capturing viewpoints of the target respondents. For questionnaires used in surveys conducted in social media, the general principles and guidelines remain the same as discussed in this chapter.

Research in Practice
Bottled Innovation

Source: AP Photo/Cafe Press

Sigg USA (**www.mysigg.com**) is a manufacturer of eco-friendly aluminum water bottles. The company makes bottles that customers can reuse instead of throwing them away in a landfill. Sigg wanted to conduct a survey to determine consumers' views on eco-friendliness. However, designing a questionnaire turned out to be a challenge because it was not clear what questions should be asked, and what should be the content, structure, and wording of the questions. So Sigg worked with Gold Mobile (**www.gold-mobile.com**), a social media marketing agency, to create a contest called "What Does Eco-Friendly Mean to You?" The agency targeted its promotion to eco-friendly specialty sites like Hugg, a social bookmarking service for eco-enthusiasts. It also sponsored the contest on InHabitat, a community for design and architecture professionals with interest in eco-friendly trends. Ecology bloggers noticed the presence on InHabitat, which led to more than 100 mentions of the contest. Ultimately, more than 160 entries were submitted, providing rich insights into what *eco-friendly* meant to consumers and more than enough information to design a survey questionnaire.

A dominant theme that emerged was that eco-friendliness meant protection of nature, from oceans to the open prairies. The survey findings not only helped Sigg to develop innovative eco-friendly bottle designs but also an effective marketing platform to target the eco-friendly consumers. Sigg launched "Celebrate America," a limited-release collection of their famous bottles. The collection consists of six eco-friendly special Sigg bottle designs by American artists, including Keith Haring and Drew Brophy. The images on the bottles celebrate daily life in the United States, from coast to coast and from the big surf to the open prairies.[3] ◄

Research Recipe

Analysis of social media can assist you in designing questions that are appropriate in terms of content, structure, and wording and in deciding on the order of questions. Follow the same general principles and guidelines for questionnaires administered in social media.

ETHICS IN MARKETING RESEARCH

Several ethical issues related to the researcher–respondent relationship and the researcher–client relationship may have to be addressed in questionnaire design. Of particular concern are the use of overly long questionnaires, combining questions of more than one client in the same questionnaire or survey (piggybacking), and deliberately biasing the questionnaire.

Respondents are volunteering their time and should not be overburdened by a questionnaire that solicits too much information. The researcher should avoid overly long questionnaires. An overly long questionnaire may vary in length or completion time, depending on variables such as the topic of the survey, the effort required, the number of open-ended questions, the frequency of the use of complex scales, and the method of administration. According to the guidelines of the Marketing Research and Intelligence Association of Canada (mria-arim.ca), with the exception of in-home personal interviews, questionnaires that take more than thirty minutes to complete are generally considered overly long. Personal in-home interviews can take up to sixty minutes without overloading the respondents.

An important researcher–client issue is piggybacking, which occurs when a questionnaire contains questions pertaining to more than one client. This is often done in omnibus panels (see Chapter 3) that different clients can use to field their questions. Piggybacking can substantially reduce costs and can be a good way for clients to collect primary data that they would not be able to afford otherwise. In these cases, all clients must be aware of and consent to the arrangement. Unfortunately, piggybacking is sometimes used without the client's knowledge for the sole purpose of increasing the research firm's profit. This practice is unethical.

Finally, the researcher has the ethical responsibility of designing the questionnaire to obtain the required information in an unbiased manner. Deliberately biasing the questionnaire in a desired direction—for example, by asking leading questions—cannot be condoned. In deciding the question structure, the most appropriate rather than the most convenient option should be adopted, as illustrated in the Research in Practice about ethics in international marketing. Also, the questionnaire should be thoroughly pretested before field work begins or an ethical breach has occurred.

Research in Practice
Questioning International Marketing Ethics

In designing a questionnaire, open-ended questions may be most appropriate if the response categories are not known. In a study designed to identify ethical problems in international marketing, a series of open-ended questions was used. The objective of the survey was to elicit the most frequently encountered ethical problems, in order of priority, by Australian firms that engage in international marketing activities. After reviewing the results, the researcher tabulated and categorized them into ten categories that occurred most often: traditional small-scale bribery; large-scale bribery; gifts, favors, and entertainment; pricing; inappropriate products or technology; tax evasion practices; illegal or immoral activitives; questionable commissions to channel members; cultural differences; and involvement in political affairs. The sheer number of categories indicates that international marketing ethics should probably be questioned more closely! The use of structured questions in this case, although more convenient, would have been inappropriate and would have raised ethical concerns because the researcher lacked knowledge about constructing suitable response categories before the survey was administered.[4] ‹

> ## Research Recipe
>
> Do not construct questionnaires that are overly long. Your questionnaire should not take more than thirty minutes to complete except for in-home personal interviews. Personal in-home interviews can take up to sixty minutes. Piggybacking should not be done without the client's knowledge. Deliberately biasing the questionnaire in a desired direction is unethical.

Dell Running Case

Review the Dell case, Case 1.1, and questionnaire given toward the end of the book.

1. Critically evaluate the Dell questionnaire using the principles discussed in this chapter.
2. Draft a questionnaire to measure student preferences for notebook computers.
3. Evaluate the questionnaire you have developed using the principles discussed in this chapter.
4. Develop a revised questionnaire to measure student preferences for notebook computers.
5. What did you learn in the questionnaire revision process?
6. Administer your revised questionnaire in social media. You can post the questionnaire or a link to it on your Facebook account and invite your friends to respond. Summarize your experience.

 **Summary**

To collect quantitative primary data, a researcher must design a questionnaire or an observational form. A questionnaire has three objectives. It must translate the information needed into a set of specific questions the respondents can and will answer. It must motivate respondents to complete the interview. It must also minimize response error.

The questionnaire design process begins by specifying (1) the information needed and (2) the type of interviewing method. The next step is (3) to decide on the content of individual questions. Each question should overcome the respondents' inability and/or unwillingness to answer (step 4). Respondents may be unable to answer if they are not informed or cannot articulate the response. The unwillingness of the respondents to answer must also be overcome. Respondents may be unwilling to answer if the question requires too much effort or solicits sensitive information. Next comes the decision regarding the question structure (step 5). Questions can be unstructured (open-ended) or structured to varying degrees. Structured questions include multiple-choice questions, dichotomous questions, and scales.

Determining the wording of each question (step 6) involves defining the issue, using ordinary words, using unambiguous words, and using dual statements. The researcher should avoid leading questions. Once the questions have been worded, the order in which they will appear in the questionnaire must be decided (step 7). Special consideration should be given to opening questions, type of information, difficult questions, and the effect on subsequent questions. The questions should be arranged in a logical order.

The stage is now set for determining the form and layout of the questions (step 8). Several factors are important in reproducing the questionnaire (step 9). These factors include appearance, fitting each question on one page or double-page spread, response category format, and avoiding overcrowding. Last but not least is pretesting (step 10). Important issues are the extent of pretesting, the nature of the respondents, the type of interviewing method, the type of interviewers, sample size, and editing and analysis.

The design of observational forms requires explicit decisions about what is to be observed and how that behavior is to be recorded.

The questionnaire should be adapted to the specific cultural environment and should not be biased in terms of any one culture. Also, the questionnaire may have to be suitable for administration by more than one method because different interviewing methods may be used in different countries. Questionnaires translated into different languages should be equivalent.

Analysis of social media can assist in designing questions that are appropriate in terms of content, structure, and wording and in deciding on the order of questions. Several ethical issues related to the researcher–respondent relationship and the researcher–client relationship may have to be addressed.

∨ Companion Website

This textbook includes numerous student resources that can be found at **www.pearsonglobaleditions.com/malhotra**. At this Companion website, you'll find:

- Student Resource Manual
- Demo movies of statistical procedures using SPSS and Microsoft Excel
- Screen captures of statistical procedures using SPSS and Microsoft Excel
- Data files for all datasets in SPSS and Microsoft Excel
- Additional figures and tables
- Videos and write-ups for all video cases
- Other valuable resources

∨ Key Terms and Concepts

questionnaire	dichotomous question	classification information
response error	acquiescence bias	identification information
double-barreled question	(yea-saying)	funnel approach
unstructured questions	leading question	branching questions
structured questions	basic information	pretesting

⌄ Suggested Cases and Video Cases

Running Case with Real Data and Questionnaire
1.1 Dell

Comprehensive Critical Thinking Cases
2.1 American Idol

Comprehensive Cases with Real Data and Questionnaires
3.1 JPMorgan Chase   3.2 Wendy's

Online Video Cases
8.1 Dunkin' Donuts   9.1 Subaru   13.1 Marriott

⌄ Live Research: Conducting a Marketing Research Project

1. Each team can develop a questionnaire following the principles discussed in this chapter. The best features of each questionnaire can be combined to develop the project questionnaire.
2. Each team should be assigned a few pretest interviews.
3. If a questionnaire has already been prepared, it should be critically evaluated by the class.

⌄ Acronyms

The objectives and steps involved in developing a questionnaire may be defined by the acronym QUESTIONNAIRE:

Objectives	**Q**	uestions that respondents can and will answer
	U	plift the respondent
	E	rror elimination
Steps	**S**	pecify the information needed
	T	ype of interviewing method
	I	ndividual question content
	O	vercoming inability and unwillingness on the part of the respondents to answer
	N	onstructured versus structured questions
	N	onbiased question wording
	A	rrange the questions in proper order
	I	dentify form and layout
	R	eproduce the questionnaire
	E	liminate problems and bugs by pretesting

The guidelines for question wording may be summarized by the acronym WORDS:

W *ho, what, when, where, why*, and *way*

O rdinary words

R *egularly, normally, usually*, and so on, should be avoided

D ual statements (positive and negative)

S pecifying how to answer (i.e., using leading questions) should not be done

The guidelines for deciding on the order of questions may be summarized by the acronym ORDER:

O pening questions: simple

R udimentary or basic information should be obtained first

D ifficult questions should be asked toward the end

E xamine the influence on subsequent questions

R eview the sequence to ensure a logical order

⌄ Review Questions

8-1. What are the three main objectives of any questionnaire?

8-2. Explain how the mode of administration affects questionnaire design.

8-3. What are the different methods of administering a questionnaire?

8-4. What is a double-barreled question?

8-5. What is a split-ballot technique and what is it used for?

8-6. What are the reasons that respondents are unwilling to answer specific questions?

8-7. What are the advantages and disadvantages of unstructured questions?

8-8. What are the issues involved in designing multiple-choice questions?

8-9. What are the guidelines available for deciding on question wording?

8-10. What is a leading question? Give an example.

8-11. What is the proper order for questions intended to obtain basic, classification, and identification information?

8-12. What are counterbiasing questions and what are they used for?

8-13. Describe the issues involved in pretesting a questionnaire.

8-14. How can social media aid in developing a questionnaire?

8-15. What are the ethical issues in developing a questionnaire?

⌄ Applied Problems

8-16. Search the Internet including social media to obtain information on flying and passengers' airline preferences. Develop three double-barreled questions related to flying and passengers' airline preferences. Also develop corrected versions of each question.

8-17. List at least ten ambiguous words that should not be used in framing questions.

8-18. Do the following questions define the issue? Why or why not?

    a. What is your favorite brand of toothpaste?

    b. How often do you go on a vacation?

    c. Do you consume orange juice?

        1. Yes   **2.** No

8-19. Design an open-ended question to determine whether households engage in gardening. Also develop a multiple-choice and a dichotomous question to obtain the same information. Which form is the most desirable?

8-20. A new graduate hired by the marketing research department of AT&T is asked to prepare a questionnaire to determine household preferences for cell phone plans. The questionnaire is to be administered in mall-intercept interviews. Using the principles of questionnaire design, critically evaluate the questionnaire prepared by this new graduate, which follows.

CELL PHONE PLAN SURVEY

1. Name _____
2. Age _____
3. Marital status _____
4. Income _____

5. Which, if any, of the following cell phone plans do you have?

   1. _____ AT&T   2. _____ Verizon   3. _____ Sprint
   4. _____ T-Mobile   5. _____ Other(s)

6. How frequently do you use a cell phone to make international calls?

   Infrequently   Very Frequently

         1   2   3   4   5   6   7

7. What do you think of the individual cell phone plans offered by AT&T?
   _____

8. Suppose your household were to select a cell phone plan. Please rate the importance of the following factors in selecting a plan.

	Not Important			Very Important	
a. Cost per month	1	2	3	4	5
b. Number of minutes	1	2	3	4	5
c. Number of rollover minutes	1	2	3	4	5
d. Unlimited nights/weekends	1	2	3	4	5
e. Quality of cell phone service	1	2	3	4	5
f. Quality of customer service	1	2	3	4	5

9. How important is it for a cell phone company to offer other services, such as Internet access and TV?

   Not important   Very Important
         1   2   3   4   5   6   7

10. Do you have children living at home? _____

    Thank you for your help.

⌄ Internet Exercises

8-21. Nissan is changing the design of one of its highest-selling cars, the Murano, and is conducting an internet survey to determine whether the design change would affect customer perception of the car as a family car. Design a structured survey to obtain required information. You can visit **http://www.nissan-global.com/** for more information.

8-22. Develop the questionnaire in Internet Exercise 8-21 using an electronic questionnaire design package that is available for free (see the websites mentioned in this chapter in the subsection entitled Free/Low-Cost Survey Sites). Administer this questionnaire to ten students using a notebook computer.

8-23. Develop a structured and an unstructured questionnaire to measure the importance of online retail shopping for working mothers. Distribute a copy of each to 10 different individuals and compare your results.

8-24. Visit the website of one of the online marketing research firms (e.g., Toluna at **us.toluna .com/default.aspx** or **www.toluna.com**). Locate a survey administered currently at this site. Critically analyze the questionnaire using the principles discussed in this chapter. Note that you will have to register in order to take the survey.

NOTES

1. **www.census.gov**, accessed January 11, 2013; **www.prb.org**, accessed January 11, 2013.
2. **www.visitsingapore.com**, accessed January 22, 2013; Donald J. MacLaurin and Tanya L. MacLaurin, "Customer Perceptions of Singapore's Theme Restaurants," Cornell Hotel and Restaurant Administration Quarterly (June 2000) 41(3): 75–85.
3. Paul Gillin, Secrets of Social Media Marketing (Fresno, CA: Quill Driver Books, 2009).
4. M. Evans, M. Robling, F. Maggs Rapport, H. Houston, P. Kinnersley, C. Wilkinson, "It Doesn't Cost Anything Just to Ask, Does It? The Ethics of Questionnaire-Based Research," **jme.bmj.com/cgi/content/abstract/28/1/41**, accessed March 1, 2013; John Tsalikis and Bruce Seaton, "Business Ethics Index: Measuring Consumer Sentiments Toward Business Ethical Practices." Journal of Business Ethics, 64(4), (April 2006): 317–326; Janet K. Mullin Marta, Anusorn Singhapakdi, Ashraf Attia, and Scott J. Vitell, "Some Important Factors Underlying Ethical Decisions of Middle-Eastern Marketers," International Marketing Review 21(1) (2004): 53; Mark A. Davis, "Measuring Ethical Ideology in Business Ethics: A Critical Analysis of the Ethics Position Questionnaire," Journal of Business Ethics, 32(1) (July 2001): 35–53; R. W. Armstrong, "An Empirical Investigation of International Marketing Ethics: Problems Encountered by Australian Firms," Journal of Business Ethics, 11 (1992): 161–171.

Online Video Case 8.1

DUNKIN' DONUTS: Dunking the Competition

Visit **www.pearsonglobaleditions.com/malhotra** to read the video case and view the accompanying video. Dunkin' Donuts: Dunking the Competition highlights the emphasis that Dunkin' Donuts places on using marketing research to make the customers critical stakeholders who provide feedback and insight and help direct the innovation process. The company conducts research using survey questionnaires and taste testing in many different markets. The case can be used as a springboard to develop a questionnaire for assessing consumer preferences for fast coffee shops. Specific marketing research questions on this and the previous chapters are posed in the video case.

9 Sampling Design and Procedures

⌄ Overview

Sampling is one of the components of a research design. The formulation of the research design is the third step of the marketing research process. At this stage, the information needed to address the marketing research problem has been identified and the nature of the research design (exploratory, descriptive, or causal) has been determined (Chapters 3 through 6). Furthermore, the scaling and measurement procedures have been specified (Chapter 7), and the questionnaire has been designed (Chapter 8). The next step is to design suitable sampling procedures. Sampling design involves several basic questions: (1) Should a sample be taken? (2) If so, what process should be followed? (3) What kind of sample should be taken? and (4) How large should it be?

This chapter introduces the fundamental concepts of sampling and the qualitative considerations necessary to answer these questions. We address the question of whether or not to sample and describe the steps involved in sampling. Next, we present nonprobability and probability sampling techniques. We discuss the use of sampling techniques in international marketing research and research in social media, identify the relevant ethical issues, and describe the use of the Internet and computers for sampling.

Figure 9.1 gives the relationship of this chapter to the marketing research process. We begin with an example of the MTV generation, which illustrates the usefulness of sampling.

∨ Learning Objectives

After reading this chapter, the student should be able to:

1. Differentiate a sample from a census and identify the conditions that favor the use of a sample versus a census.

2. Discuss the sampling design process: definition of the target population, determination of the sampling frame, selection of sampling technique(s), determination of sample size, and execution of the sampling process.

3. Classify sampling techniques as nonprobability and probability sampling techniques.

4. Describe the nonprobability sampling techniques of convenience, judgmental, quota, and snowball sampling.

5. Describe the probability sampling techniques of simple random, systematic, stratified, and cluster sampling.

6. Identify the conditions that favor the use of nonprobability sampling versus probability sampling.

7. Understand the sampling design process and the use of sampling techniques in international marketing research.

8. Describe how the representativeness of social media samples can be improved.

9. Identify the ethical issues related to the sampling design process and the use of appropriate sampling techniques.

10. Explain the use of the Internet and computers in sampling design.

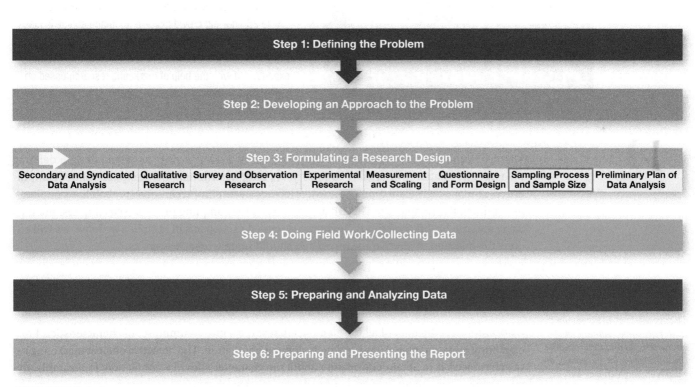

FIGURE 9.1 | RELATIONSHIP OF THIS CHAPTER TO THE MARKETING RESEARCH PROCESS

Research in Practice
Sampling the MTV Generation

As of 2014, MTV (**www.mtv.com**) included favorites such as MTV, MTV Geek!, MTV Tr3s, MTV2, MTVU, and other networks around the world. MTV uses a free-flowing corporate culture and a group of power brands to earn big profits for parent Viacom (**www.viacom.com**).

The days were not always so rosy for the network, however. Market research by MTV spotted trouble in the 18- to 24-year-old group that had initially helped to give MTV its hip image. Ratings began to slip as users complained that there was no longer music on MTV.

Telephone surveys were conducted with 1,000 people in the 18- to 24-year-old group. The sample was chosen by selecting households based on computerized random-digit dialing, that is, household telephone numbers generated randomly by a computer. If the household had more than one 18- to 24-year-old, one person was selected using the next birthday method. The interviewer asked which of the eligible persons in the household had the next birthday and included that person in the sample. The results of this survey showed that MTV needed a makeover.

Source: Dave King / Dorling Kindersley Limited

In response, MTV launched music hours shown live from Times Square. New shows were created. The *Video Music Awards* were revamped. Veejays became more authentic and not TV-pretty. The objective of this makeover was to give MTV a cleaner, more pensive image to keep its viewers happy. The 18- to 24-year-old crowd is important to the network because it is this group that younger teens and the 25- to 35-year-old crowd looks to for image and style ideas. Stagnant Nielsen ratings and upset advertisers suddenly got a wakeup call. As of 2014, MTV is continuing to grow and expand, and with the help of marketing research based on appropriate sampling procedures, it should be able to stay hip for generations to come.[1] ◄

The Research in Practice about MTV illustrates the various aspects of sampling design: defining the target population (Americans 18 to 24 years old), determining the sampling frame (computerized random-digit dialing procedures), selecting a sampling technique (probability sampling), determining the sample size (1,000), and executing the sampling process (selecting respondents using the next birthday method). Before we discuss these aspects of sampling in detail, we will address the question of whether the researcher should sample or take a census.

SAMPLE OR CENSUS

population
The aggregate of all the elements that share some common set of characteristics and that comprise the universe for the purpose of the marketing research problem.

census
A complete enumeration of the elements of a population or study objects.

sample
A subgroup of the elements of the population selected for participation in the study.

A **population** is the total of all the elements that share some common set of characteristics. Each marketing research project has a uniquely defined population. The objective of most marketing research projects is to obtain information about the characteristics of a population, for example, the proportion of consumers loyal to a particular brand of toothpaste. The researcher can obtain information about population characteristics by taking either a census or a sample. A **census** involves a complete count of all elements in a population. A **sample** is a subgroup of the population selected for the marketing research project.

Budget and time limits are obvious constraints favoring the use of a sample. A census is both costly and time-consuming to conduct. A census is unrealistic if the population is large, as it is for most consumer products. In the case of many industrial products, however, the population is small, thus making a census feasible as well as desirable. For example, in investigating the use of certain machine tools by U.S. automobile manufacturers, a census would be preferred to a sample. Another reason for preferring a census in this case is that variance, or variability, in the characteristic of interest is large. For example, machine tool usage at Ford will vary greatly from the usage at Honda. Small population sizes as well as high variance in the characteristic to be measured favor a census.

If the cost of sampling errors is high (e.g., if the sample omitted a major manufacturer like Ford, the results could be misleading), a census, which eliminates such errors, is desirable. **Sampling errors** are errors resulting from the particular sample selected being an imperfect representation of the population of interest. **Nonsampling errors**, on the other hand, can be attributed to sources other than sampling. They result from a variety of causes, including errors in problem definition, approach, scaling, questionnaire design, survey methods, interviewing techniques, and data preparation and analysis. The high cost of nonsampling errors (e.g., interviewing errors because of lack of supervision), on the other hand, would favor sampling. A census can greatly increase nonsampling errors to the point that these errors exceed the sampling errors of a sample. Nonsampling errors are found to be the major contributor to total error, whereas random sampling errors have been relatively small in magnitude. Hence, in most cases involving large populations, accuracy considerations would favor a sample over a census. This is one of the reasons that the U.S. Bureau of the Census checks the accuracy of various censuses by conducting sample surveys. However, it is not always possible to reduce nonsampling error sufficiently to compensate for sampling error, as would be the case in a study involving U.S. automobile manufacturers In general, in marketing research projects dealing with consumers or households, a census is not feasible and a sample should be taken. This was the case in the MTV survey of people in the 18- to 24-year-old group in the first Research in Practice. However, in many business-to-business or industrial marketing situations where the population size is small, a census is feasible as well as desirable.

sampling errors
Errors resulting from the particular sample selected being an imperfect representation of the population of interest.

nonsampling errors
Errors that can be attributed to sources other than sampling, such as errors in problem definition, approach, scaling, questionnaire design, survey methods, field work, and data preparation and analysis.

Research Recipe

As a general rule, select a sample in a consumer survey where the population size is large. In a business/organizational survey involving a small population, attempt a census.

iResearch
Boeing: Spreading Its Wings

Search the Internet, as well as your library's online databases, to determine the population of all airlines operating in the United States. If a survey of airlines is to be conducted to determine their future plans to purchase and/or lease airplanes, would you take a sample or a census? Explain.

As the CEO of Boeing, how would you use information about the future plans of airlines to purchase and/or lease airplanes to formulate your marketing strategy? ‹

THE SAMPLING DESIGN PROCESS

The sampling design process includes five steps, which are shown sequentially in Figure 9.2. These steps are closely interrelated and relevant to all aspects of the marketing research project, from problem definition to the presentation of the results. Therefore, sample design decisions should be integrated with all other decisions in a research project.

FIGURE 9.2
SAMPLING DESIGN
PROCESS

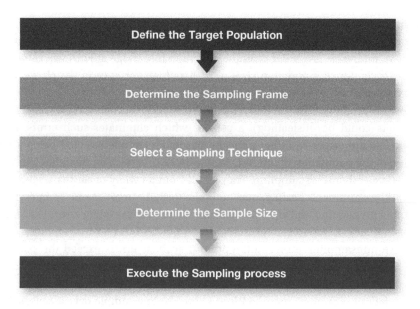

Define the Target Population

target population
The collection of elements or objects that possesses the information sought by the researcher and about which inferences are to be made.

Sampling design begins by specifying the target population. The **target population** is the collection of elements or objects that possesses the information sought by the researcher and about which inferences are to be made. Inference involves projection or generalization of the sample results to the target population, as illustrated in the section entitled A Classification of Sampling Techniques. The target population must be defined precisely. Imprecise definition of the target population will result in research that is ineffective at best and misleading at worst. Defining the target population involves translating the problem definition into a precise statement of who should and should not be included in the sample.

element
The object that possesses the information sought by the researcher and about which inferences are to be made.

sampling unit
The basic unit containing the elements of the population to be sampled.

The target population should be defined in terms of elements, sampling units, extent, and time. An **element** is the object about which or from which the information is desired. In survey research, the element is usually the respondent. A **sampling unit** is an element, or a unit containing the element, that is available for selection at some stage of the sampling process, for example, a household. Suppose that Revlon wanted to assess consumer response to a new line of lipsticks and wanted to sample females over 18 years of age. It may be possible to sample females over the age of 18 directly, in which case a sampling unit would be the same as an element. Alternatively, the sampling unit might be households. In the latter case, households would be sampled and all females over age 18 in each selected household would be interviewed or one selected from each sampled household, for example, by using the next birthday method, as illustrated in the MTV Research in Practice. Here, the sampling unit and the population element are different. *Extent* refers to the geographical boundaries, and the *time* frame is the time period under consideration. Defining the target population is illustrated in Figure 9.3. In the MTV Research in Practice, the element consisted of people in the 18- to 24-year-old group, the sampling unit was households, the extent was the United States, and the time frame was the period of the survey.

Determine the Sampling Frame

sampling frame
A representation of the elements of the target population. It consists of a list or set of directions for identifying the target population.

A **sampling frame** is a representation of the elements of the target population. It consists of a list or set of directions for identifying the target population. Examples of a sampling frame include the telephone book, an association directory listing the firms in an industry, a mailing list purchased from a commercial organization, a city directory, or a map. If a list cannot be compiled, then at least some directions for identifying the target population should be specified, such as random-digit dialing procedures in telephone surveys (see the first MTV Research in Practice feature in this chapter).

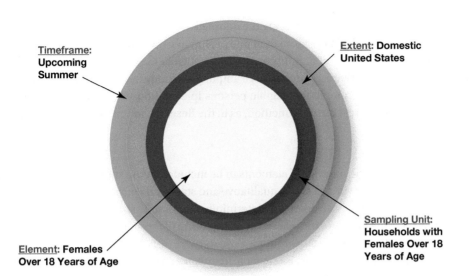

FIGURE 9.3

DEFINING THE TARGET POPULATION

Often it is possible to compile or obtain a list of population elements, but the list may omit some elements of the population or include other elements that do not belong. Therefore, the use of a list will lead to sampling frame error, as illustrated in Figure 9.4. In some instances, the discrepancy between the population and the sampling frame is small enough to ignore. In most cases, however, the researcher should recognize and treat the sampling frame error.

Research Recipe

Define the target population in terms of elements, sampling units, extent, and time. Select an appropriate sampling frame that minimizes the sampling frame error.

Select a Sampling Technique

The most important decision about the choice of sampling technique is whether to use probability or nonprobability sampling. Given the importance of this decision, the issues involved are discussed in great detail later in this chapter.

If the sampling unit is different from the element, it is necessary to specify precisely how the elements within the sampling unit should be selected. In in-home personal interviews and telephone interviews, merely specifying the address or the telephone number may not be sufficient.

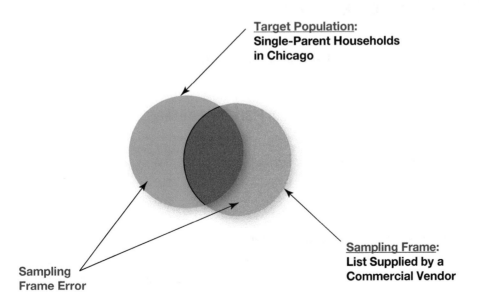

FIGURE 9.4

SAMPLING FRAME ERROR

For example, should the person answering the doorbell or the telephone be interviewed, or someone else in the household? Often, more than one person in a household may qualify. For example, both the male and female head of household may be eligible to participate in a study examining family leisure activities. When a probability sampling technique is being employed, a random selection must be made from all the eligible persons in each household. A simple procedure for random selection is the next birthday method, as in the Research in Practice feature about MTV.

Determine the Sample Size

sample size
The number of elements to be included in a study.

Sample size refers to the number of elements to be included in the study. Determining the sample size is complex and involves several qualitative and statistical considerations. Important qualitative factors that should be considered in determining the sample size include (1) the importance of the decision, (2) the nature of the research, (3) the nature of the analysis, (4) sample sizes used in similar studies, and (5) resource constraints.

In general, for more important decisions, more information is necessary and the information should be obtained more precisely. This calls for larger samples, but as the sample size increases, each unit of information is obtained at greater cost and less benefit. The nature of the research also has an impact on the sample size. For exploratory research designs, such as those using qualitative research, the sample size is typically small. For conclusive research, such as descriptive surveys, larger samples are required.

If sophisticated analysis of the data using advanced statistical techniques is required, the sample size should be large. The same applies if the data are to be analyzed in great detail. Thus, a larger sample would be required if the data are being analyzed at the subgroup or segment level than if the analysis is limited to the aggregate or total sample. Sample size is influenced by the average size of samples in similar studies. Table 9.1 gives an idea of sample sizes used in different marketing research studies. These sample sizes have been determined based on experience and can serve as rough guidelines, particularly when nonprobability sampling techniques are used.

The sample size decision should be guided by a consideration of the resource constraints. In any marketing research project, money and time are limited. Other constraints include the availability of qualified personnel for data collection. Based on all the foregoing considerations, the sample size in the MTV survey in the first Research in Practice was determined to be 1,000.

The statistical considerations involve the variability (variance) of the characteristic being measured and other considerations. Statistically, a sample of 400 (385 to be more precise) is sufficient to yield estimates of percentages that meet commonly acceptable statistical standards.[2] Thus, the sample size of 1,000 in the MTV survey more than met statistical standards.

Research Recipe

Determine the sample size based on the importance of the decision, the nature of the research, the nature of the analysis, sample sizes used in similar studies, resource constraints, and statistical considerations.

Table 9.1 > Sample Sizes Used in Marketing Research Studies

Type of Study	Minimum Size	Typical Range
Problem-identification research (e.g., market potential]	500	1,000–2,500
Problem-solving research (e.g., pricing)	200	300–500
Product tests	200	300–500
Test marketing studies	200	300–500
TV/radio/print advertising (per commercial or ad tested)	150	200–300
Test-market audits	10 stores	10–20 stores
Focus groups	2 groups	10–15 groups

Execute the Sampling Process

Execution of the sampling process requires a detailed specification of how the sampling design decisions with respect to the population, sampling frame, sampling unit, sampling technique, and sample size are to be implemented. If households are the sampling units, an operational definition of a household is needed. Procedures should be specified for vacant housing units and for callbacks in case no one is at home. Detailed information must be provided for all sampling design decisions. In the MTV Research in Practice execution involved selecting households based on computerized random-digit dialing procedures and selecting 18- to 24-year-old respondents using the next birthday method. We illustrate further with a survey done for the Florida Department of Tourism.

Research in Practice
Tourism Department Telephones Birthday Boys and Girls

A telephone survey was conducted for the Florida Department of Tourism to gain an understanding of the travel behavior of in-state residents. The households were stratified by north, central, and south Florida regions. A computerized random-digit sample was used to reach these households. Households were screened to locate family members who met four qualifications:

1. Age 25 or older.
2. Live in Florida at least seven months of the year.
3. Have lived in Florida for at least two years.
4. Have a Florida driver's license.

To obtain a representative sample of qualified individuals, the households were selected based on randomly generated telephone numbers using a computer program. A random method was also used to select the respondent from within a household. All household members meeting the four qualifications were listed and the person with the next birthday was selected. Repeated callbacks were made to reach that person. The steps in the sampling design process were as follows:

1. *Target population:* adults meeting the four qualifications (element) in a household with a working telephone number (sampling unit) in the state of Florida (extent) during the survey period (time).
2. *Sampling frame:* computer program for generating random telephone numbers.
3. *Sampling unit:* working telephone numbers.
4. *Sampling technique:* stratified sampling. The target population was geographically stratified into three regions: north, central, and south Florida.
5. *Sample size:* 868.
6. *Execution:* allocate the sample among strata; use computerized random-digit dialing; list all the members in the household who meet the four qualifications; select one member of the household using the next birthday method.[3] <

Source: Peter Titmuss / Alamy

A CLASSIFICATION OF SAMPLING TECHNIQUES

Sampling techniques may be broadly classified as nonprobability and probability. **Nonprobability sampling** relies on the personal judgment of the researcher rather than chance to select sample elements. The researcher can arbitrarily or consciously decide what elements to include in the sample. Nonprobability samples may yield good estimates of the

nonprobability sampling
Sampling techniques that do not use chance selection procedures. Rather, they rely on the personal judgment of the researcher.

FIGURE 9.5
NONPROBABILITY
SAMPLING TECHNIQUES

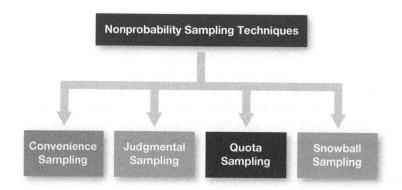

population characteristics. However, they do not allow for objective evaluation of the sampling errors. Because there is no way of determining the probability of selecting any particular element for inclusion in the sample, the estimates obtained are not statistically projectable to the population; that is, one cannot derive inferences about the population based on the sample results. Thus, if 35 percent of the people in a sample selected by nonprobability sampling express preference for a new service, we cannot conclude that 35 percent of the target population will have the same preference. Commonly used nonprobability sampling techniques include convenience sampling, judgmental sampling, quota sampling, and snowball sampling (Figure 9.5).

probability sampling
A sampling procedure in which each element of the population has a fixed probabilistic chance of being selected for the sample.

In **probability sampling**, sampling units are selected by chance. Because sample elements are selected by chance, it is possible to determine the accuracy of the sample estimates of the characteristics of interest, for example, the percentage expressing preference for a new service. This permits the researcher to make inferences or projections about the target population from which the sample was drawn. Thus, if 35 percent of the people in a sample selected by probability sampling express preference for a new service, we can conclude that it is likely that 35 percent of the target population will have the same preference. Probability sampling techniques consist of simple random sampling, systematic sampling, stratified sampling, and cluster sampling (Figure 9.6). First, however, we discuss nonprobability sampling techniques.

R e s e a r c h   R e c i p e

Nonprobability sampling techniques rely on the judgment of the researcher, and you can arbitrarily or consciously decide what elements to include in the sample. Because there is no way of determining the probability of selecting any particular element for inclusion in the sample, you should not project the estimates obtained from nonprobability sampling to the target population. In probability sampling, sampling units are selected by chance and you can make projections to the target population from which the sample was drawn.

FIGURE 9.6
PROBABILITY SAMPLING
TECHNIQUES

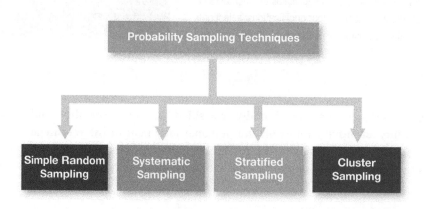

NONPROBABILITY SAMPLING TECHNIQUES

Convenience Sampling

Convenience sampling attempts to obtain a sample of convenient elements. The selection of sampling units is left primarily to the interviewer. Often, respondents are selected because they happen to be in the right place at the right time. Examples of convenience sampling include (1) use of students, church groups, and members of social organizations; (2) mall-intercept interviews without qualifying the respondents; (3) department stores using charge account lists; and (4) "people on the street" interviews.

Convenience sampling is the least expensive and least time-consuming of all sampling techniques. The sampling units are accessible, easy to measure, and cooperative. In spite of these advantages, this form of sampling has serious limitations. Many potential sources of selection bias are present, including respondent self-selection (that is, respondents can influence their selection or nonselection). Convenience samples are not representative of any definable population. Hence, it is not meaningful to generalize the sample results to any population from a convenience sample, and convenience samples are not appropriate for marketing research projects involving population inferences. Convenience samples are not recommended for descriptive or causal research, but they can be used in exploratory research for generating ideas, insights, or hypotheses. Convenience samples can be used for focus groups, pretesting questionnaires, or pilot studies. Even in these cases, caution should be exercised in interpreting the results.

convenience sampling
A nonprobability sampling technique that attempts to obtain a sample of convenient elements. The selection of sampling units is left primarily to the interviewer.

Research Recipe

Convenience sampling is the least expensive and least time-consuming of all sampling techniques, but it has serious limitations. You can use it in exploratory research for generating ideas, insights, or hypotheses.

Judgmental Sampling

Judgmental sampling is a form of convenience sampling in which the population elements are selected based on the judgment of the researcher. The researcher, exercising judgment or expertise, chooses the elements to be included in the sample because he or she believes that they are representative of the population of interest or are otherwise appropriate. Common examples of judgmental sampling include (1) test markets selected to determine the potential of a new product, (2) purchase engineers selected in industrial marketing research because they are considered to be representative of their respective companies, and (3) bellwether precincts selected in voting behavior research. The use of this technique is illustrated in the context of Carl's Jr. test-marketing its Foot-long Cheeseburger.

judgmental sampling
A form of convenience sampling in which the population elements are selected based on the judgment of the researcher.

Research in Practice
Test-Marketing the Foot-long Cheeseburger

Carl's Jr. test-marketed it's Foot-long Cheeseburger in fifty Carl's Jr. restaurants in southern California and fifty Hardee's units in Indiana. These locations were selected because the researcher felt they would provide a good general indicator of initial response to the new product. Note that Carl's Jr. was only looking to evaluate the initial response to the Foot-long Cheeseburger, not to make projections of how much it would sell nationally. ❮

In the Research in Practice about Carl's Jr., judgment was used to select specific test markets and specific restaurants within those test markets. Judgmental sampling is inexpensive, convenient, and quick. However, it does not allow direct generalizations to a specific population. Judgmental sampling is subjective, and its value depends entirely on the researcher's judgment, expertise, and creativity. It may be useful if broad population inferences are not required. As in the

Research in Practice about Carl's Jr., judgment samples are frequently used in commercial marketing research projects. An extension of this technique involves the use of quotas.

> ## R e s e a r c h   R e c i p e
>
> Judgmental sampling is subjective and its value depends entirely on the researcher's judgment, expertise, and creativity. You can use it in a variety of applications, including the selection of test markets.

Quota Sampling

quota sampling
A nonprobability sampling technique that is a two-stage judgmental sampling. The first stage consists of developing control categories or quotas of population elements. In the second stage, sample elements are selected based on convenience or judgment.

Quota sampling may be viewed as two-stage judgmental sampling. The first stage consists of developing control categories, or quotas, of population elements. To develop these quotas, the researcher lists relevant control characteristics and determines the distribution of these characteristics in the target population. The relevant control characteristics, which may include sex, age, and race, are identified on the basis of judgment. Often, the quotas are assigned so that the proportion of the sample elements possessing the control characteristics is the same as the proportion of population elements with these characteristics. In other words, the quotas ensure that the composition of the sample is the same as the composition of the population with respect to the characteristics of interest. In the second stage, sample elements are selected based on convenience or judgment. Once the quotas have been assigned, there is considerable freedom in selecting the elements to be included in the sample. The only requirement is that the elements selected fit the control characteristics. This technique is illustrated in the Research in Practice about magazine readership in metropolitan areas.

Research in Practice
Does Metropolitan Magazine Readership Measure Up?

A study is undertaken to determine the readership of certain magazines by the adult population of a metropolitan area with a population of 1.86 million. A quota sample of 1,000 adults is selected. The control characteristics are sex, age, and race. Based on the composition of the adult population of the community, the quotas are assigned as follows:

Control Characteristic	Population Composition Percentage	Sample Composition Percentage	Sample Composition Number
Sex			
Male	48	48	480
Female	52	52	520
	100	100	1,000
Age			
18–30	27	27	270
31–45	39	39	390
45–60	16	16	160
Over 60	18	18	180
	100	100	1,000
Race			
White	59	59	590
Black	35	35	350
Other	6	6	60
	100	100	1,000

Even if the sample composition mirrors that of the population with respect to the control characteristics, there is no assurance that the sample is representative. If a characteristic that is relevant to the problem is overlooked, the quota sample will not be representative. Relevant control characteristics are often omitted because practical difficulties are associated with trying to include many control characteristics. Because the elements within each quota are selected based on convenience or judgment, many sources of selection bias are potentially present. The interviewers may choose to go to selected areas where eligible respondents are more likely to be found. They may avoid people who look unfriendly or are not well dressed, or those who live in undesirable locations. Quota sampling does not permit assessment of sampling error.

Quota sampling attempts to obtain representative samples at a relatively low cost. Its advantages are the lower costs and greater convenience to the interviewers in selecting elements for each quota. Recently, tighter controls have been imposed on interviewers and interviewing procedures that tend to reduce selection bias, and guidelines have been suggested for improving the quality of mall-intercept quota samples. Under certain conditions, quota sampling obtains results close to those for conventional probability sampling.

Research Recipe

Quota sampling may be viewed as two-stage judgmental sampling. In the first stage you develop control categories, or quotas, of population elements. In the second stage, you select sample elements based on convenience or judgment. Although there is no assurance, quotas can improve the representativeness of the sample.

Snowball Sampling

In **snowball sampling**, an initial group of respondents is selected, usually at random. After being interviewed, these respondents are asked to identify others who belong to the target population of interest. Subsequent respondents are selected based on the referrals. This process may be carried out in waves by obtaining referrals from referrals, thus leading to a snowball effect. Even though probability sampling is used to select the initial respondents, the final sample is a nonprobability sample. The referrals will have demographic and psychographic characteristics that are more similar to the persons referring them than would occur by chance.

A major objective of snowball sampling is to estimate characteristics that are rare in the population. Examples include users of particular government or social services, such as food stamps, whose names cannot be revealed; special census groups, like widowed males under age 35; and members of a scattered minority population. Snowball sampling is used in industrial buyer–seller research to identify buyer–seller pairs. The major advantage of snowball sampling is that it substantially increases the likelihood of locating the desired characteristic in the population. It also results in relatively low sampling variance and costs. Snowball sampling is illustrated in the following Research in Practice.

snowball sampling
A nonprobability sampling technique in which an initial group of respondents is selected randomly. Subsequent respondents are selected based on the referrals or information provided by the initial respondents. This process may be carried out in waves by obtaining referrals from referrals.

Research in Practice
Survey Snowball

To study the demographic profile of marketing research interviewers in Ohio, a sample of interviewers was generated using a variation of snowball sampling. Initial contact with interviewers was made by placing classified advertisements in newspapers in seven major metropolitan areas. These notices asked experienced marketing research interviewers willing to answer twenty-five questions about their job to write to the author. These responses were increased through a referral system: Each interviewer was asked for the names and addresses of other interviewers. Eventually this process identified interviewers from many communities throughout the state who had not seen the original newspaper notices. Only 27 percent of returned questionnaires resulted from the classified notices; the remainder could be traced to referrals and referrals from referrals.[4] ◄

In the preceding Research in Practice, note the nonrandom selection of the initial group of respondents through classified advertisements. This procedure was more efficient than random selection. In other cases, random selection of respondents through probability sampling techniques is more appropriate.

Research Recipe

In snowball sampling, you select an initial group of respondents, usually at random. You select subsequent respondents based on the referrals from initial respondents. This technique is useful for estimating characteristics that are rare in the population.

iResearch
Unisex Shirts: Sampling Gender Inequalities Affirmatively

As the vice president of marketing for Polo Ralph Lauren, what information would you need to determine whether the company should launch nationally a new line of unisex shirts it has developed?

Visit **www.polo.com** and search the Internet, including social media as well as your library's online databases, to obtain information on Polo Ralph Lauren's marketing strategy. Polo Ralph Lauren would like to determine initial consumer reaction to a new line of unisex shirts it has developed. If nonprobability sampling is to be used, which sampling technique would you recommend and why? **<**

PROBABILITY SAMPLING TECHNIQUES

Probability sampling techniques vary in terms of sampling efficiency. Sampling efficiency reflects a trade-off between sampling cost and precision. Precision refers to the level of uncertainty about the characteristic being measured. Precision is inversely related to sampling errors but positively related to cost. The greater the precision, the lower the sampling errors and the greater the cost, and most studies require a trade-off. The researcher should strive for the most efficient sampling design, subject to the budget allocated. The efficiency of a probability sampling technique may be assessed by comparing it to that of simple random sampling.

Simple Random Sampling

In **simple random sampling (SRS)**, each element in the population has a known and equal probability of selection, and every element is selected independently of every other element. The sample is drawn by a random procedure from a sampling frame. This method is equivalent to a lottery system in which names are placed in a container, the container is shaken, and the names of the winners are then drawn in an unbiased manner.

To draw a simple random sample, the researcher first compiles a sampling frame in which each element is assigned a unique identification number. Then random numbers are generated to determine which elements to include in the sample. The random numbers may be generated with a computer routine or a table. This was illustrated in the MTV Research in Practice where a computer program was used to randomly generate household telephone numbers.

SRS has many desirable features. It is easy to understand. The sample results may be projected to the target population. Most approaches to statistical inference assume that the data have been collected by simple random sampling. However, SRS suffers from at least four significant limitations. First, it is often difficult to construct a sampling frame that will permit a simple random sample to be drawn. Second, SRS can result in samples that are very large or spread over

simple random sampling (SRS)

A probability sampling technique in which each element in the population has a known and equal probability of selection. Every element is selected independently of every other element, and the sample is drawn by a random procedure from a sampling frame.

large geographic areas, thus increasing the time and cost of data collection. Third, SRS often results in lower precision than other probability sampling techniques. In fact, the efficiency of other probability sampling techniques is often assessed by comparing it to that of simple random sampling (SRS). Fourth, SRS may or may not result in a representative sample. Although samples drawn will represent the population well on average, a given simple random sample may grossly misrepresent the target population. This is more likely if the size of the sample is small. For these reasons, SRS is not widely used in marketing research. Procedures such as systematic sampling are more popular.

Research Recipe

In simple random sampling (SRS), each element in the population has a known and equal probability of selection, and you select every element independently of every other element. This technique is equivalent to a lottery system. You assess the efficiency of a probability sampling technique by comparing it to that of SRS.

Systematic Sampling

In **systematic sampling**, the sample is chosen by selecting a random starting point and then picking every ith element in succession from the sampling frame. The sampling interval, i, is determined by dividing the population size N by the sample size n and rounding to the nearest integer. For example, there are 100,000 elements in the population, and a sample of 1,000 is desired. In this case, the sampling interval, i, is 100. A random number between 1 and 100 is selected. If this number is 23, for example, the sample consists of elements 23, 123, 223, 323, 423, 523, and so on.[5]

systematic sampling
A probability sampling technique in which the sample is chosen by selecting a random starting point and then picking every ith element in succession from the sampling frame.

Systematic sampling is different from SRS in that only the initial element is selected randomly and the remaining elements are selected systematically, that is, by adding i to the previous element number. In SRS, all the elements are selected randomly.

For systematic sampling, the researcher assumes that the population elements are ordered in some respect. When the ordering of the elements is related to the characteristic of interest, systematic sampling increases the representativeness of the sample. If firms in an industry are arranged in increasing order of annual sales, a systematic sample will include some small and some large firms. A simple random sample may be unrepresentative because it may contain, for example, only small firms or a disproportionate number of small firms. If the ordering of the elements produces a cyclical pattern, systematic sampling may decrease the representativeness of the sample. To illustrate, consider the use of systematic sampling to generate a sample of monthly department store sales from a sampling frame containing monthly sales for the last sixty years. If a sampling interval of 12 is chosen, the resulting sample would not reflect the month-to-month variation in sales. Let's say that a random number from 1 to 12 is selected, and let's say that 3 is the number selected, representing the month of March. Thus, the sample will consist of 3, 15 (3 + 12), 27 (3 + [2 × 12]), and the month of March will be selected for each of the sixty years. In this case, the monthly variation in sales for each year would not be reflected in the sample.

Systematic sampling is less costly and easier than SRS because random selection is done only once. The random numbers do not have to be matched with individual elements, as in SRS. Another relative advantage is that systematic sampling can even be used without knowledge of the composition (elements) of the sampling frame. For example, every ith person leaving a department store or mall can be intercepted. For these reasons, systematic sampling is often employed in consumer mail, telephone, and mall-intercept interviews, as illustrated by the Research in Practice about *Tennis* magazine.

Research in Practice
Tennis Magazine's Systematic Sampling Returns a Smash

Tennis magazine conducted a mail survey of its subscribers to gain a better understanding of its market. Systematic sampling was employed to select a sample of 1,472 subscribers from the publication's domestic circulation list. If we assume that the subscriber list had 1,472,000 names, the sampling interval would be 1,000 (1,472,000/1,472). A number from 1 to 1,000 was drawn at random. Beginning with that number, every 1,000th subscriber was selected.

A brand-new dollar bill was included with the questionnaire as an incentive to respondents. A postcard alerting respondents was mailed one week before the survey. A second, follow-up questionnaire was sent to the whole sample ten days after the initial questionnaire. There were seventy-six post office returns, so the net effective mailing was 1,396. Six weeks after the first mailing, 778 completed questionnaires were returned, yielding a response rate of 56 percent.[6] ◄

Research Recipe

In systematic sampling, you select only the initial element randomly; the remaining elements are selected systematically. This form of sampling increases the representativeness of the sample when the elements are ordered in a way related to the characteristics of interest. It may decrease the representativeness of the sample if the elements are ordered in a cyclical manner.

Stratified Sampling

stratified sampling
A probability sampling technique that uses a two-step process to first partition the population into subpopulations, or strata. Then elements are selected from each stratum by a random procedure.

Stratified sampling is a two-step process in which the population is first partitioned into subpopulations, or strata. The strata should be mutually exclusive and collectively exhaustive in that every population element should be assigned to one and only one stratum and no population elements should be omitted. Next, elements are selected from each stratum by a random procedure, usually simple random sampling (SRS). Technically, only SRS should be employed in selecting the elements from each stratum. In practice, sometimes systematic sampling and other probability sampling procedures are employed. Stratified sampling differs from quota sampling in that the sample elements are selected probabilistically rather than based on convenience or judgment. A major objective of stratified sampling is to increase precision without increasing cost.

The variables used to partition the population into strata are referred to as stratification variables. The criteria for the selection of these variables consist of homogeneity (similarity), heterogeneity (dissimilarity), relatedness, and cost. The elements within a stratum should be as homogeneous (similar) as possible, but the elements in different strata should be as heterogeneous (different) as possible. The stratification variables should also be closely related to the characteristic of interest. The more closely these criteria are met, the greater the effectiveness in controlling extraneous sampling variation. Finally, the variables should decrease the cost of the stratification process by being easy to measure and apply.

Variables commonly used for stratification include demographic characteristics (as illustrated in the example for quota sampling), type of customer (credit card versus non–credit card), size of firm, or type of industry. It is possible to use more than one variable for stratification, although more than two are seldom used because of pragmatic and cost considerations. The selection of stratification variables is illustrated with an example from the American Express National Travel Forecast survey.

Research in Practice
Tracking Travel by Telephone

The American Express National Travel Forecast survey was conducted by GfK US (**www.gfk.com**), through OmniTel, a weekly telephone omnibus survey (see Chapter 3 for a description of omnibus surveys/panels). A total of 1,030 people (525 women, 505 men) were interviewed. The variables used for stratification were sex, age, income, and census region. The survey found that Americans in the age group of 25 to 49 years, who are most likely to have children at home, were most interested in visiting Orlando, Florida. With the elderly (65 or older), Washington, DC, was particularly popular. Younger Americans age 18 to 34 were most likely to rank vacations as a top priority. Because travel preferences varied with age, age was indeed a useful stratification variable. However, the other stratification variables, namely, sex, income, and census region, did not have a significant effect on travel preferences. Hence, sampling costs could have been decreased without decreasing precision by stratifying on the basis of age alone.[7] <

Stratified sampling can ensure that all the important subpopulations are represented in the sample because all the strata are included in the sample. This is particularly important if the distribution of the characteristic of interest in the population is skewed. For example, because most households have annual incomes less than $50,000, the distribution of household incomes is skewed. Very few households have annual incomes of $300,000 or more. If a simple random sample is taken, households with incomes of $300,000 or more may not be adequately represented. Stratified sampling would guarantee that the sample contains a certain number of these households. Stratified sampling combines the simplicity of SRS with potential gains in precision. Therefore, it is a popular sampling technique.

Research Recipe

Stratified sampling is a two-step process in which you first partition the population into subpopulations, or strata. Next, you select elements from each stratum by a random procedure, usually simple random sampling. A major objective of stratified sampling is to increase precision without increasing cost; hence, it is a popular technique.

Cluster Sampling

In **cluster sampling**, the target population is first divided into mutually exclusive and collectively exhaustive subpopulations, or clusters. Then a random sample of clusters is selected, based on a probability sampling technique such as simple random sampling. For each selected cluster, either all the elements are included in the sample or a sample of elements is drawn probabilistically. If all the elements in each selected cluster are included in the sample, the procedure is called one-stage cluster sampling. If a sample of elements is drawn probabilistically from each selected cluster, the procedure is two-stage cluster sampling.

The key distinction between cluster sampling and stratified sampling is that, in cluster sampling, only a sample of subpopulations (clusters) is chosen, whereas in stratified sampling, all the

cluster sampling
First, the target population is divided into mutually exclusive and collectively exhaustive subpopulations called clusters. Then a random sample of clusters is selected based on a probability sampling technique such as simple random sampling. For each selected cluster, either all the elements are included in the sample or a sample of elements is drawn probabilistically.

subpopulations (strata) are selected for further sampling. The objectives of the two methods are also different. The objective of cluster sampling is to increase sampling efficiency by decreasing costs. The objective of stratified sampling is to increase precision. With respect to homogeneity and heterogeneity, the criteria for forming clusters are just the opposite of that for strata. Elements within a cluster should be as heterogeneous (different) as possible, but clusters themselves should be as homogeneous (similar) as possible. Ideally, each cluster should be a small-scale representation of the population. In cluster sampling, a sampling frame is needed only for those clusters selected for the sample. A common form of cluster sampling is **area sampling**, in which the clusters consist of geographic areas, such as counties, housing tracts, or blocks. The following Research in Practice illustrates two-stage area sampling.

area sampling

A common form of cluster sampling in which the clusters consist of geographic areas such as counties, housing tracts, blocks, or other area descriptions.

Research in Practice
Blocks with Bucks

A marketing research project investigated the behavior of affluent consumers. A simple random sample of 800 block groups was selected from a listing of neighborhoods with average incomes exceeding $100,000 in the states ranked in the top half by income according to census data. Commercial list organizations supplied head-of-household names and addresses for approximately 95 percent of the census-tabulated homes in these 800 block groups. From the 213,000 enumerated households, 9,000 were selected by simple random sampling. The survey found that the affluent households spend a greater proportion of their incomes on luxury goods and therefore represent a primary target market for luxury good marketers such as Louis Vuitton Moet Hennessy (LVMH), the largest luxury good producer in the world, with over fifty brands, including Louis Vuitton, the brand with the world's first designer label.[8] ‹

Cluster sampling is the most cost-effective probability sampling technique. This advantage must be weighed against several limitations. Cluster sampling results in relatively imprecise samples, and it is difficult to form heterogeneous clusters because, for example, households in a block tend to be similar rather than dissimilar. It can be difficult to compute and interpret statistics based on clusters.

Research Recipe

In cluster sampling, you first divide the target population into mutually exclusive and collectively exhaustive subpopulations, or clusters. Then you randomly select a sample of clusters based on a probability sampling technique such as SRS. For each selected cluster, either you include all the elements in the sample (one-stage cluster sampling) or you draw a random sample of elements (two-stage cluster sampling). The objective of cluster sampling is to increase sampling efficiency by decreasing costs.

iResearch
Herbal Essences: Introducing New Products Is of the Essence

As the marketing chief of Herbal Essences, how would you determine which new shampoos should be introduced into the market?

Search the Internet, including social media as well as your library's online databases, to determine the size of the shampoo market in the United States. Herbal Essences would like to determine the demand for a new shampoo. If a survey is to be conducted using probability sampling, which sampling technique should be used and why? ‹

CHOOSING NONPROBABILITY VERSUS PROBABILITY SAMPLING

The choice between nonprobability and probability sampling should be based on considerations such as the nature of the research, relative magnitude of nonsampling versus sampling errors, and statistical and operational considerations. In exploratory research, the findings are treated as preliminary, and the use of probability sampling may not be warranted. On the other hand, in conclusive research, where the researcher wishes to use the results to estimate overall market shares or the size of the total market, probability sampling is favored. Probability samples allow statistical projection of the results to a target population. This was the case in the MTV Research in Practice. The survey findings had to be projected to the entire population of 18- to 24- year-old people. Thus probability sampling, specifically simple random sampling, was employed and a computer program was used to randomly generate household telephone numbers.

If nonsampling errors are likely to be an important factor, then nonprobability sampling may be preferable because the use of judgment may allow greater control over the sampling process. On the other hand, if sampling errors are more important, probability sampling is favored. Probability sampling is preferable from a statistical viewpoint because it is the basis of most common statistical techniques.

However, probability sampling is sophisticated and requires statistically trained researchers. It generally costs more and takes longer than nonprobability sampling. In many marketing research projects, it is difficult to justify the additional time and expense. Therefore, in practice, the objectives of the study dictate which sampling method will be used.

Research Recipe

Use nonprobability sampling for exploratory research, when nonsampling errors are larger than sampling errors, and costs are important. On the other hand, use probability sampling for conclusive research, when sampling errors are larger than nonsampling errors, and statistical considerations are important.

INTERNET SAMPLING

The use of online sampling is growing with the increasing penetration of the Internet. Nonprobability as well as probability sampling techniques can be implemented on the Internet. The respondents can be recruited beforehand or tapped online, randomly or otherwise. Nonprobability sampling is commonly implemented on the Internet by tapping every visitor. Tapping every visitor to a website is obviously an example of convenience sampling. Based on the researcher's judgment, certain qualifying criteria can be introduced to prescreen the respondents. Even quotas can be imposed. However, the extent to which the quotas will be met is limited by the number as well as the characteristics of the visitors to the site. Probability sampling techniques can be implemented by randomly recruiting respondents and emailing them invitations to the web site where the survey is posted. In this case, the survey is posted in a hidden location on the Web and is protected by a password. Hence, uninvited Web surfers are unable to access it. Alternatively, random pop-ups can be used to invite Web surfers to the survey.

Research Recipe

You can implement nonprobability as well as probability sampling techniques on the Internet. You can recruit the respondents beforehand or tap them online. Recruiting or tapping visitors to a web site nonrandomly results in nonprobability sampling; randomly doing so will result in probability sampling.

INTERNATIONAL MARKETING RESEARCH

Implementing the sampling design process in international marketing research is seldom an easy task. Several factors should be considered in defining the target population. The relevant element (respondent) may differ from country to country. In the United States, children play an important role in the purchase of children's cereals. In countries with authoritarian child-rearing practices, however, the mother may be the relevant element. Women play a key role in the purchase of automobiles and other durables in the United States; in male-dominated societies, such as in the Middle East, such decisions are made by men. Accessibility also varies across countries. In Mexico, houses cannot be entered by strangers because of boundary walls and servants. Dwelling units may be unnumbered and streets unidentified, making it difficult to locate designated households.

Developing an appropriate sampling frame is a difficult task. In many countries, particularly in developing countries, reliable information about the target population may not be available from secondary sources. Government data may be unavailable or highly biased. Population lists may not be available commercially. The time and money required to compile these lists may be prohibitive. For example, in Saudi Arabia, there is no officially recognized census of the population, no elections and hence no voter registration records, and no accurate maps of population centers. In this situation, the interviewers could be instructed to begin at specified starting points and to sample every nth dwelling until the specified number of units has been sampled.

Given the lack of suitable sampling frames; the inaccessibility of certain respondents, such as women in some cultures; and the dominance of personal interviewing, probability sampling techniques are uncommon in international marketing research. However, the increased penetration of the Internet and the availability of online panels in most countries are enabling researchers to overcome many of the traditional hurdles, as indicated by the MasterCard Research in Practice.

Research in Practice
MasterCard Masters Asia and the Pacific Region

MasterCard Worldwide (**www.mastercard.com**) is widely recognized not only as one of the best global payment solutions companies, but also as a global knowledge leader. Recently, MasterCard partnered with IPSOS (**www.ipsos.com**), one of the largest survey-based research groups, to conduct marketing research on online shopping in Asia and the Pacific region. The purpose was to gain more insights about e-commerce patterns and trends as well as examine the future growth for credit cards.

An online survey was conducted that involved 4,157 individuals, age 18 to 49, in eight key markets of MasterCard in Asia and the Pacific region. The sample was selected through IPSOS Asia online panels and restricted to individuals with bank accounts who accessed the Internet at least once a week. In each country, panelists meeting these qualifications were selected using simple random sampling (SRS). The sample size was comparable across countries, as shown below:

Hong Kong $(n = 541)$

China $(n = 519)$

Australia $(n = 517)$

Singapore $(n = 515)$

South Korea $(n = 520)$

Japan $(n = 507)$

India $(n = 517)$

Thailand $(n = 521)$

The survey results showed that online shopping was popular in Asia and the Pacific region, with 63 percent of people surveyed saying that they shop online. The survey also identified the key drivers of online purchases, which are Internet penetration, income levels, and cultural factors. However, security was the top concern among the online shoppers in Asia and the Pacific region: 65 percent of Internet users were reluctant to shop online because of security reasons. The specific figures for each country were as follows: China, 87 percent; Thailand, 75 percent; Hong Kong, 74 percent; and India, 73 percent. However, online shoppers from more developed countries like South Korea and Japan were not too worried about this issue: Only 26 percent of South Koreans and 31 percent of Japanese were concerned with security. Despite some security concerns, credit cards were the preferred mode of payment for online shoppers in the region. In response to these findings, MasterCard launched a concentrated effort to address the security concerns. For example, the company upgraded the security infrastructure of its system of paying. The company hosted payment system seminars in the region to address the security issue. During the seminar, the company highlighted its commitment to providing the safest and most secure and reliable payment card in consumers' wallets. Since then, business for MasterCard has been booming in Asia and the Pacific region.[9] <

Research Recipe

Probability sampling techniques are uncommon in international marketing research given the lack of suitable sampling frames, the inaccessibility of certain respondents, and the dominance of personal interviewing. However, you can conveniently use probability sampling techniques when sampling respondents from online panels.

iResearch
PC Usage in the United States and India

As the global marketing manager for Intel, the computer microprocessor manufacturer, would you adopt the same or different marketing strategies in the United States and India?

Search the Internet, including social media as well as your library's online databases, to obtain information on the usage or nonusage of personal computers by households in the United States and India. Intel wants to conduct cross-cultural research to determine the similarities and differences between the two countries in the household usage or nonusage of personal computers. Should the same or different sampling techniques be used in the two countries? Which technique(s) should be used? <

MARKETING RESEARCH AND SOCIAL MEDIA

General social media content available in the public domain may not be representative or even appropriate in all cases. The sampling frame is biased and limited because only consumers who are online and engaged in social media are represented. Even so, consumers who are heavy users of social media have a greater probability of being sampled. Yet there are ways to improve the representativeness of information gleaned from general social media analysis and monitoring.

- Instead of targeting an entire site, select sections of sites that suit the brand's profile. Careful screening can result in a more targeted and representative sample.
- Narrow your search results by designing search queries that mine social media content with consumer-, category-, or brand-related terms.
- Use text analysis that detects age, gender, geography, or other characteristics that distinguish different types of voices and then filter the results to reflect your target population more accurately. This information may be obtained from publicly available social media profile information of the individuals posting comments.

Research in Practice
Simple Random Sampling Results in Sophisticated Market Segmentation

Umbria, now part of J.D. Power and Associates (**www.jdpower.com**), used its text-mining technology to segment the market for an apparel client. A large number of comments pertaining to apparel were first collected from a variety of social media sites. Simple random sampling (SRS) was then used to select a manageable but representative subset.

Source: J.D. Power & Associates

SRS was chosen because the sampling frame was readily available and the results were projectable. The selection of a representative sample facilitated a more detailed analysis than might have been possible on all the comments collected. Text mining was used to analyze the selected comments to arrive at six segments: Fit Finders, Self-Expressives, Bargain Seekers, Label Whores, Style Gurus, and Dissenters. These labels were quite descriptive of the segments. For example, Fit Finders are Generation Xers who want jeans that complement their changing physiques. Self-Expressives want to customize their jeans by distressing them or adding patches and embroidery. The client used these findings to design and market products tailor-made for each segment, which in turn resulted in a sophisticated segmentation scheme and a successful marketing strategy.[10] <

Research Recipe

You can improve the representativeness of information gleaned from general social media in several ways. These include selecting sections of sites that suit the brand's profile; narrowing search results by designing search queries that mine social media content with consumer-, category-, or brand-related terms; and filtering the results using demographics to reflect your target population more accurately.

ETHICS IN MARKETING RESEARCH

The researcher has several ethical responsibilities to both the client and the respondents in the sampling process. Pertaining to the client, the researcher must develop a sampling design that is appropriate for controlling the sampling and nonsampling errors that were discussed in this chapter. When appropriate, probability sampling should be used. When nonprobability sampling is used, effort should be made to obtain a representative sample. It is unethical and misleading to treat nonprobability samples as probability samples and to project the results to a target population. As the following Research in Practice demonstrates, appropriate definition of the population and the sampling frame, and application of the correct sampling techniques are essential if the research is to be conducted and the findings are to be used ethically.

Research in Practice
Systematic Sampling Reveals Systematic Gender Differences in Ethical Judgments

In an attempt to explore differences in research ethics judgments between male and female marketing professionals, data were obtained from 420 respondents. The population was defined as marketing professionals, and the sampling frame was the American Marketing Association directory. The respondents were selected from the directory based on a systematic sampling plan. Attempts were made to overcome nonresponse by mailing a cover letter and a stamped preaddressed return envelope along with the questionnaire *and* by promising to provide each respondent with a copy of the research study results. Results of the survey showed that female marketing professionals, in general, demonstrated higher levels of research ethical judgments than their male counterparts.[11] **<**

Researchers must be sensitive to preserving the anonymity of the respondents when conducting business-to-business research, employee research, and other projects in which the population size is small. When the population size is small, it is easier to discern the identities of the respondents than when the samples are drawn from a large population. Sampling details that are too revealing or verbatim quotations in reports to the client can compromise the anonymity of the respondents. In such situations, the researcher has the ethical obligation to protect the identities of the respondents, even if it means limiting the level of sampling detail that is reported to the client and other parties.

Research Recipe

Appropriate definition of the population and the sampling frame, and application of the correct sampling techniques are essential if the research is to be conducted ethically. You have the ethical responsibility to preserve the anonymity of the respondents when conducting business-to-business research, employee research, and projects where the population size is small.

Dell Running Case

Review the Dell case, Case 1.1, and the questionnaire given toward the end of the book.

1. As the marketing manager of Dell personal computers, what marketing programs will you design to target families?
2. Search the Internet, including social media as well as your library's online databases, to obtain information that will assist you in targeting families.
3. Dell wants to conduct a telephone survey to determine how it can convince more families to purchase its PCs and notebooks. Design the sampling process.
4. Discuss the advantages and disadvantages of Dell using social media samples to obtain information on consumers' preferences for notebook computers.

Summary

Information about the characteristics of a population may be obtained by conducting either a sample or a census. Budget and time limits, large population size, and small variance in the characteristic of interest favor the use of a sample. Sampling is also preferred when the cost of sampling error is low, and the cost of nonsampling error is high. The opposite set of conditions favor the use of a census.

Sampling design begins by defining the target population in terms of elements, sampling units, extent, and time. Then the sampling frame should be determined. A sampling frame is a representation of the elements of the target population. It consists of a list or directions for identifying the target population. At this stage, it is important to recognize any sampling frame errors that may exist. The next step involves selecting a sampling technique and determining the sample size. In addition to quantitative analysis, several qualitative considerations should be taken into account in determining the sample size. Finally, execution of the sampling process requires detailed specifications for each step in the sampling process.

Sampling techniques may be classified as nonprobability and probability techniques. Nonprobability sampling techniques rely on the researcher's judgment. Consequently, they do not permit an objective evaluation of the precision of the sample results, and the estimates obtained are not statistically projectable to the population. The commonly used nonprobability sampling techniques include convenience sampling, judgmental sampling, quota sampling, and snowball sampling.

In probability sampling techniques, sampling units are selected by chance. Each sampling unit has a nonzero chance of being selected. It is also possible to determine the precision of the sample estimates and to make projections to the target population. Probability sampling techniques include simple random sampling, systematic sampling, stratified sampling, and cluster sampling. The choice between probability and nonprobability sampling should be based on the nature of the research, relative magnitude of sampling and nonsampling errors, and statistical and operational considerations.

When conducting international marketing research, a researcher faces several challenges that can be addressed if an online survey is used appropriately. There are ways in which one can improve the representativeness of social media samples. It is unethical and misleading to treat nonprobability samples as probability samples and to project the results to a target population. The Internet and computers can be used to make the sampling design process more effective and efficient.

∨ Companion Website

This textbook includes numerous student resources that can be found at **www.pearsonglobaleditions.com/malhotra**. At this Companion website, you'll find:

- Student Resource Manual
- Demo movies of statistical procedures using SPSS and Microsoft Excel
- Screen captures of statistical procedures using SPSS and Microsoft Excel
- Data files for all datasets in SPSS and Microsoft Excel
- Additional figures and tables
- Videos and write-ups for all video cases
- Other valuable resources

∨ Key Terms and Concepts

population	sampling frame	simple random sampling (SRS)
census	sample size	
sample	nonprobability sampling	systematic sampling
sampling errors	probability sampling	stratified sampling
nonsampling errors	convenience sampling	cluster sampling
target population	judgmental sampling	area sampling
element	quota sampling	
sampling unit	snowball sampling	

⌄ Suggested Cases and Video Cases

Running Case with Real Data and Questionnaire
1.1 Dell

Comprehensive Critical Thinking Cases
2.1 American Idol

Comprehensive Cases with Real Data and Questionnaires
3.1 JPMorgan Chase   3.2 Wendy's

Online Video Cases
9.1 Subaru   13.1 Marriott

⌄ Live Research: Conducting a Marketing Research Project

1. A census might be feasible in a business-to-business project where the size of the population is small, but it is not feasible in most consumer projects.
2. Define the target population (element, sampling unit, extent, and time), and discuss a suitable sampling frame.
3. Probability sampling techniques are more difficult and time-consuming to implement, and their use might not be warranted unless the results are being projected to a population of interest.

⌄ Acronyms

The sampling design process and the steps involved may be represented by the acronym SAMPLE:

S ampling design process

A mount: sample size determination

M ethod: sampling technique selection

P opulation definition

L ist: sampling frame determination

E xecution of the sampling process

⌄ Review Questions

9-1. What is the major difference between a sample and a census?
9-2. Under what conditions would a sample be preferable to a census? A census preferable to a sample?
9-3. Describe the sampling design process.
9-4. How should the target population be defined?
9-5. What is a sampling unit? How is it different from the population element?
9-6. What qualitative factors should be considered in determining the sample size?
9-7. What are the disadvantages of nonprobability sampling techniques?
9-8. What is the least expensive and least time-consuming of all sampling techniques? What are the major limitations of this technique?
9-9. What are the advantages and disadvantages of judgmental sampling?

9-10. What is the relationship between quota sampling and judgmental sampling?

9-11. What are the distinguishing features of simple random sampling?

9-12. Describe the procedure for selecting a systematic random sample.

9-13. Describe stratified sampling. What are the criteria for the selection of stratification variables?

9-14. What is the major advantage of snowball sampling?

9-15. What are the advantages of systematic sampling over simple random sampling?

9-16. What considerations are relevant in selecting a sampling technique in international marketing research?

9-17. How can the representativeness of social media samples be improved?

9-18. What are the ethical issues involved in sampling?

∨ Applied Problems

9-19. Define the appropriate target population and the sampling frame in each of the following situations:

    a. The manufacturer of a new cereal brand wants to conduct in-home product usage tests in Chicago.

    b. A national chain store wants to determine the shopping behavior of customers who have its store charge card.

    c. A local television station wants to determine households' viewing habits and programming preferences.

    d. The local chapter of the American Marketing Association wants to test the effectiveness of its new member drive in Atlanta, Georgia.

9-20. A manufacturer would like to survey users to determine the demand potential for a new power press. The new press has a capacity of 500 tons and costs $275,000. It is used for forming products from lightweight and heavyweight steel and can be used by automobile, construction equipment, and major appliance manufacturers.

    a. Identify the population and sampling frame that could be used.

    b. Describe how a simple random sample can be drawn using the identified sampling frame.

    c. Could a stratified sample be used? If so, how?

    d. Could a cluster sample be used? If so, how?

    e. Which sampling technique would you recommend? Why?

∨ Internet Exercises

9-21. A company decides to send email surveys on its new car polishing spray to random people, asking them to forward it to 10 of their contacts after they are finished. What form of sampling did the company decide to apply and what are the limitations of this choice in this case?

9-22. How can quota sampling being applied through a website like **www.linkedin.com**?

9-23. Using a computer program, generate a set of 1,000 random numbers for selecting a simple random sample.

9-24. Describe how you can use **www.yellowpages.com** to create a sample in the state of New York by using systematic sampling technique.

NOTES

1. **www.mtv.com**, accessed January 7, 2013; Marc Gunther, "This Gang Controls Your Kids' Brains," *Fortune* (October 27, 1997): 1–10.
2. To see the statistical details for this calculation, refer to Chapter 12 in Naresh K. Malhotra, *Marketing Research: An Applied Orientation*, Sixth Edition (Upper Saddle River, NJ: Pearson, 2010).
3. **www.myflorida.com**, accessed February 3, 2013; "The Many Faces of Florida," *Association Management* (A Guide to Florida Supplement) (April 1997): 3; "Florida Travel Habits Subject of Phone Survey," *Quirk's Marketing Research Review* (May 1987): 10, 11, 31, 56, 60.
4. "Survey Interviewers and Statistical Clerks", online at **www.servicecanada.gc.ca/eng/qc/job_futures/statistics/1454.shtml**, accessed June 28, 2013; Gale D. Muller and Jane Miller, "Interviewers Make the Difference," *Marketing research: A Magazine of Management & Applications* 8(1) (Spring 1996): 8–9; Raymond F. Barker, "A Demographic Profile of Marketing Research Interviewers," *Journal of the Market Research Society* (July 1987): 279–292.
5. When the sampling interval, *i*, is not a whole number, the easiest solution is to use as the interval the nearest whole number below or above *i*. If rounding has too great an effect on the sample size, add or delete the extra cases.
6. **www.tennis.com**, accessed February 10, 2013; Mark Adams, "Court Marshall," *Mediaweek* 6(12) (March 18, 1996): 22; "Readership Survey Serves Tennis Magazine's Marketing Needs," *Quirk's Marketing Research Review* (May 1988): 75–76.
7. **www.americanexpress.com**, accessed January 15, 2013; "Purchasing Smarts Pay Off in Travel Buying," *Purchasing* 121(9) (December 12, 1996): 30–31; "Vacations High Priority Among Americans, Survey Shows," *Quirk's Marketing Research Review* (May 1988): 16–19.
8. **http://en.wikipedia.org/wiki/Luxury_good#Luxury_brands**, accessed January 12, 2013; Thomas J. Stanley and Murphy A. Sewall, "The Response of Affluent Consumers to Mail Surveys," *Journal of Advertising Research* (June–July 1986): 55–58.
9. **www.mastercard.com**, accessed June 28, 2013; **www.mastercard.com/us/company/en/insights/pdfs/2008/Asia_Pacific_Online_Shop.pdf**, accessed March 10, 2013.
10. **www.jdpower.com**, accessed January 15, 2013; Paul Gillin, *Secrets of Social Media Marketing* (Fresno, CA: Quill Driver Books, 2009).
11. Khalizani Khalid, "The Ethical Reasoning Variations of Personal Characteristics," *International Journal of Development and Sustainability* 1(1) (June 2012) 8-30, online at **http://isdsnet.com/ijds-v1n1-2.pdf**, accessed June 28, 2013; Satish P. Deshpande, "Managers' Perception of Proper Ethical Conduct: The Effect of Sex, Age, and Level of Education," *Journal of Business Ethics* 16(1) (January 1997): 79–85; I. P. Akaah, "Differences in Research Ethics Judgments Between Male and Female Marketing Professionals," *Journal of Business Ethics*, 8(1989): 375–381.

Online Video Case 9.1

SUBARU: "Mr. Survey" Monitors Customer Satisfaction

Visit **www.pearsonglobaleditions.com/malhotra** to read the video case and view the accompanying video. Subaru: "Mr. Survey" Monitors Customer Satisfaction presents an interesting overview of Joe Barstys's role at Subaru and the importance and utility of surveys in building customer loyalty. About 500,000 mail surveys (with a high response rate) a year plus Internet surveys have helped Subaru get continuous feedback on key parameters that shape customer experience resulting in high brand loyalty. The case can be used to discuss how sample size can be determined for a questionnaire study in measuring consumers' evaluation of Subaru brands. Specific marketing research questions on this and the previous chapters are posed in the video case.

10 Data Collection and Preparation

⌄ Overview

field work

The process of making contact with the respondents, administering the questionnaires or observational forms, recording the data, and turning in the completed forms for processing. Also called data collection.

field workers

Interviewers, supervisors, and other personnel involved in the data collection process.

Field work or data collection is the fourth step in the marketing research process. It follows problem definition and development of the approach (Chapter 2), and formulation of the research design (Chapters 3 through 9). During **field work**, also called data collection, the field workers make contact with the respondents, administer the questionnaires or observational forms, record the data, and turn in the completed forms for processing. **Field workers** are interviewers, supervisors, and other personnel involved in the data collection process. A personal interviewer administering questionnaires door to door, an interviewer intercepting shoppers in a mall, a telephone interviewer calling from a central location, a worker mailing questionnaires from an office or posting them on a website, and an observer counting customers in a particular section of a store are all field workers.

After the field work is conducted, the researcher can move on to data preparation and analysis, the fifth step of the marketing research process. Before the raw data contained in the questionnaires can be subjected to statistical analysis, they must be converted into a form suitable for analysis. The quality of statistical results depends on the care exercised in the data preparation phase. Inadequate attention to data preparation can seriously compromise statistical results, leading to biased findings and incorrect interpretation.

This chapter covers the fourth and fifth steps of the marketing research process. It describes the nature of field work and the general field work/data collection process. This process involves the selection, training, and supervision of field workers; the validation of field work; and the evaluation of field workers. Then we describe the data preparation process, which begins with checking the questionnaires for completeness. We discuss the editing of data and provide guidelines for handling illegible, incomplete, inconsistent, ambiguous, or otherwise unsatisfactory responses. We also describe coding, transcribing, and data cleaning, emphasizing the treatment of missing responses, the statistical adjustment of data, and the selection of a data analysis strategy. We briefly discuss data collection and preparation in the context of international marketing research and conducting research in social media, and identify the relevant ethical issues.

Help for running the SPSS and Excel programs used in this chapter is provided in four ways: (1) detailed step-by-step instructions are given later in the chapter; (2) you can download (from the Companion website for this book) computerized demonstration movies illustrating these step-by-step instructions; (3) you can download screen captures with notes illustrating these step-by-step instructions; and (4) you can refer to the Student Resource Manual that is posted on the Companion website for this book.

Figure 10.1 gives the relationship of this chapter to the marketing research process. To begin, we present a brief example that highlights the nature of field work or data collection.

✔ Learning Objectives

After reading this chapter, the student should be able to:

1. Describe the field work or data collection process and explain the selection, training, and supervision of field workers, the validation of field work, and the evaluation of field workers.

2. Discuss the training of field workers in making the initial contact, asking the questions, probing, recording the answers, and terminating the interview.

3. Discuss the supervision of field workers in terms of quality control and editing, sampling control, control of cheating, and central office control.

4. Describe the evaluation of field workers in areas of cost and time, response rates, quality of interviewing, and the quality of data.

5. Discuss the nature and scope of data preparation, and the data preparation process.

6. Explain questionnaire checking and editing, and treatment of unsatisfactory responses by returning to the field, assigning missing values, and discarding unsatisfactory responses.

7. Describe the guidelines for coding questionnaires, including the coding of structured and unstructured questions.

8. Discuss the data-cleaning process and the methods used to treat missing responses: substitution of a neutral value, casewise deletion, and pairwise deletion.

9. State the reasons for and methods of statistically adjusting data: variable respecification and recoding.

10. Describe the procedure for selecting a data analysis strategy and the factors influencing the process.

11. Explain the issues related to data collection and data preparation when conducting international marketing research.

12. Explain field work and data preparation in relation to social media.

13. Discuss the ethical aspect of data collection and data preparation.

14. Describe the SPSS and Excel programs available for data entry, variable respecification, and variable recoding.

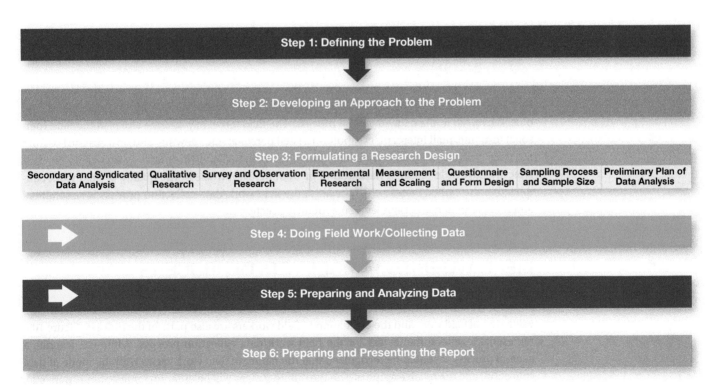

FIGURE 10.1 | RELATIONSHIP OF THIS CHAPTER TO THE MARKETING RESEARCH PROCESS

Research in Practice
Refusing Refusals

Founded in 1957, the Marketing Research Association (MRA) is the leading and largest association of the marketing research profession (**www.marketingresearch.org**). In an MRA survey that interviewed more than 3,700 U.S. consumers, nearly 45 percent said they had refused to participate in a survey over the past year. MRA offers several guidelines related to field work to help reduce refusal rates:

Source: Marketing Research Association. Used with permission.

- Interviewers should be carefully, selected, trained and supervised.
- Interviewer evaluation programs should be routinely administered so that field workers will be effective at their jobs.
- Courtesy should be exercised when deciding what hours of the day to call respondents. MRA recommends calling between 9 A.M. and 9 P.M.
- If mall respondents indicate the time is not convenient, an appointment should be made to conduct the interview later.
- The subject matter should be disclosed to the respondents if this can be done without biasing the data. The more information people are given, the less reason they have to be suspicious.
- Field workers should make the interviews as positive, pleasant and appealing as possible.[1] ◄

THE NATURE OF FIELD WORK OR DATA COLLECTION

Data collection involves the use of some kind of field force, namely, interviewers, supervisors, and others involved in the data collection process. The field force may operate either in the field (personal in-home, mall intercept, computer-assisted personal interviewing, and observation) or from an office (telephone, mail, e-mail, and Internet surveys). The field workers who collect the data typically have little research background or training. Nevertheless, the quality of field work conducted in the United States is high because the field work/data collection process is streamlined and well controlled, as discussed in the following section.

FIELD WORK/DATA COLLECTION PROCESS

All field work involves the selection, training, and supervision of persons who collect data. The validation of field work and the evaluation of field workers are also parts of the process. Figure 10.2 represents a general framework for the field work/data collection process. While we describe a general process, it should be recognized that the nature of field work varies with the mode of data collection, and the relative emphasis on the different steps will be different for telephone, personal, mail, and electronic interviews.

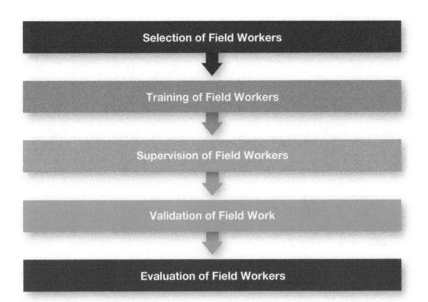

FIGURE 10.2
THE FIELD WORK/DATA
COLLECTION PROCESS

Selection of Field Workers

The first step in the field work process is the selection of field workers. The importance of careful selection was emphasized by the Marketing Research Association in the first Research in Practice feature in this chapter. The researcher should: (1) develop job specifications for the project, taking into account the mode of data collection; (2) decide what characteristics the field workers should have; and (3) recruit appropriate individuals. Interviewers' background characteristics, opinions, perceptions, expectations, and attitudes can affect the responses they elicit. To the extent possible, interviewers should be selected to match respondents' characteristics. The job requirements will also vary with the nature of the problem and the type of data collection method. Field workers are generally paid an hourly rate or on a per-interview basis. The typical interviewer is a married woman age 35 to 54 years, with an above-average education and an above-average household income.

R e s e a r c h   R e c i p e

To the extent possible, select interviewers to match respondents' characteristics, the nature of the problem, and the type of data collection method. The more characteristics the interviewer and the respondent have in common, the greater the probability of a successful interview.

Training of Field Workers

Training of field workers is critical to the quality of data collected. Training may be conducted in person at a central location, or by mail or via the Internet if the interviewers are geographically dispersed. Training ensures that all interviewers administer the questionnaire in the same manner so that the data can be collected uniformly. Training should cover making the initial contact, asking the questions, probing, recording the answers, and terminating the interview (Figure 10.3).

The initial contact can result in cooperation or the loss of potential respondents. Interviewers should be trained to make opening remarks that will convince potential respondents that their participation is important. Interviewers should be instructed on handling objections and refusals. For example, if the respondent says, "This is not a convenient time for me," the interviewer should

FIGURE 10.3
TRAINING FIELD WORKERS

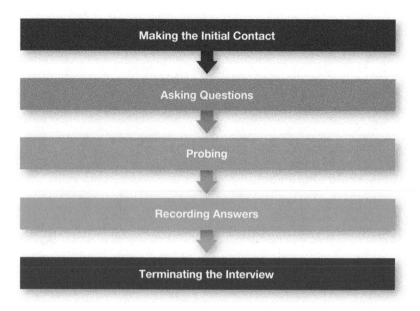

respond, "What would be a more convenient time for you? I will call back then." Similar guidelines were provided by the Marketing Research Association in the first Research in Practice feature in this chapter.

The interviewers absolutely must ask questions as they are written, strictly following the wording and the order. Even a slight change in the wording, sequence, or manner in which a question is asked can distort its meaning and bias the response.

probing
A motivational technique used when asking survey questions to induce the respondents to enlarge on, clarify, or explain their answers and to help the respondents focus on the specific content of the interview.

Probing involves motivating respondents to enlarge on, clarify, or explain their answers. Probing also helps respondents focus on the specific content of the interview and provide only relevant information. Probing should not introduce any bias. Some commonly used probing techniques include repeating the question, repeating the respondent's reply, and using a pause.

Although recording respondent answers seems simple, several mistakes are common. All interviewers should use the same format and conventions to record the interviews and edit completed interviews. While the rules for recording answers to structured questions vary with each specific questionnaire, the general rule is to check the box that reflects the respondent's answer. The general rule for recording answers to unstructured questions is to record the responses verbatim.

Before terminating the interview, the interviewer should answer the respondent's questions about the project. The respondent should be left with a positive feeling about the interview. It is important to thank the respondent and express appreciation.

Research Recipe

Train interviewers in terms of making the initial contact, asking the questions, probing, recording the answers, and terminating the interview. Interviewers should be trained to make opening remarks that will convince potential respondents that their participation is important. The interviewers absolutely must ask questions as they are written. Train interviewers in probing to motivate respondents to enlarge on, clarify, or explain their answers without introducing any bias. The general rule is to check the box that reflects the respondent's answer for structured questions and record the responses verbatim for unstructured questions. The interviewer should answer the respondents' questions about the project and leave them with a positive experience.

iResearch
Beyond Cosmetic Changes: Selecting and Training Field Workers

As the brand manager for Clinique, what information would help you to formulate marketing strategies to increase Clinique's sales? Visit **www.clinique.com** and search the Internet, including social media as well as your library's online databases, to obtain information on women's cosmetics usage. How would you select and train field workers to conduct a mall-intercept survey to determine women's cosmetics usage in a project for Clinique? ‹

Supervision of Field Workers

Supervision of field workers means making sure that they are following the procedures and techniques in which they were trained. The importance of careful supervision was emphasized by the Marketing Research Association in the first Research in Practice feature in this chapter. Supervision involves quality control and editing, sampling control, control of cheating, and central office control (see Figure 10.4).

Quality control of field workers requires checking to see if the field procedures are implemented properly. If any problems are detected, the supervisor should discuss them with the interviewers and provide additional training as necessary. To understand the interviewers' problems, the supervisors should also do some interviewing. Supervisors should collect questionnaires and other forms, and edit them daily.

An important aspect of supervision is **sampling control**, which attempts to ensure that the interviewers are following the sampling plan strictly rather than selecting sampling units based on convenience or accessibility. To control sampling issues, supervisors should keep daily records of the number of calls made, respondents who are not at home, refusals, and completed interviews for each interviewer, and the total for all interviewers under their control.

sampling control
An aspect of supervision that ensures that the interviewers follow the sampling plan strictly rather than select sampling units based on convenience or accessibility.

Cheating involves falsifying part of a question or the entire questionnaire. An interviewer may falsify part of an answer to make it acceptable or may fake answers. The most blatant form of cheating occurs when the interviewer falsifies the entire questionnaire, merely filling in fake answers without contacting the respondent. Cheating can be minimized through proper training, supervision, and validation of field work.

Supervisors provide quality and cost control information to the central office so that an overall progress report can be maintained. In addition to the controls initiated in the field, other controls may be added at the central office to identify potential problems. Central office control includes tabulation of quota variables, important demographic characteristics, and answers to key questions.

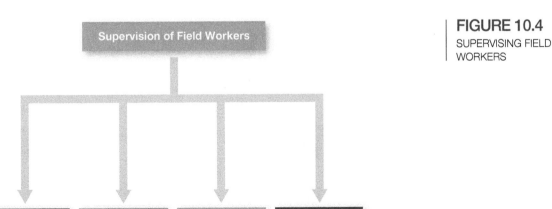

FIGURE 10.4
SUPERVISING FIELD WORKERS

> ## Research Recipe
>
> Supervision involves quality control and editing, sampling control, control of cheating, and central office control. Ensure that the field work procedures are implemented properly, interviewers are following the sampling plan strictly rather than selecting sampling units based on convenience or accessibility, there is no cheating, and quality and cost controls are maintained.

Validation of Field Work

Validation of field work means verifying that the field workers are submitting authentic interviews. To validate the study, the supervisors call 10 to 25 percent of the respondents to inquire whether the field workers actually conducted the interviews. The supervisors ask about the length and quality of the interview, reaction to the interviewer, and basic demographic data. The demographic information is cross-checked against the information reported by the interviewers on the questionnaires.

Evaluation of Field Workers

It is important to evaluate field workers to provide them with feedback on their performance as well as to identify the better field workers and build a better, high-quality field force. The importance of careful evaluation was emphasized by the Marketing Research Association in the first Research in Practice feature in this chapter. The evaluation criteria should be clearly communicated to the field workers during their training. The evaluation of field workers should be based on the criteria of cost and time, response rates, quality of interviewing, and quality of data (see Figure 10.5).

The interviewers can be compared in terms of the total cost (salary and expenses) per completed interview. If the costs differ by city size, comparisons should be made only among field workers working in comparable cities. The field workers should also be evaluated on how they spend their time. Time should be broken down into categories such as actual interviewing, travel, and administration.

response rate
The number of attempted interviews that are completed.

Response rate may be defined as the number of attempted interviews that are completed. It is important to monitor response rates on a timely basis so that corrective action can be taken if these rates are too low. Supervisors can help interviewers with an inordinate number of refusals by listening to the introductions they use and providing immediate feedback. When all the interviews are over, different field workers' percentage of refusals can be compared to identify the better ones.

To evaluate interviewers on the quality of interviewing, the supervisor must directly observe the interviewing process. The supervisor can do this in person, or the field worker can

FIGURE 10.5
EVALUATING FIELD
WORKERS

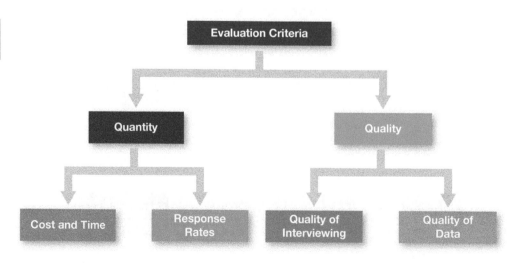

video-record the interview. The quality of interviewing should be evaluated in terms of (1) the appropriateness of the introduction, (2) the precision with which the field worker asks questions, (3) the ability to probe in an unbiased manner, (4) the ability to ask sensitive questions, (5) interpersonal skills displayed during the interview, and (6) the manner in which the interview is terminated.

The completed questionnaires of each interviewer should be evaluated for the quality of data. Some indicators of data quality are (1) the recorded data are legible; (2) all instructions, including skip patterns, are followed; (3) the answers to unstructured questions are recorded verbatim; (4) the answers to unstructured questions are meaningful and complete enough to be coded; and (5) questions that are not answered, called item nonresponse, occur infrequently.

Research Recipe

Evaluate field workers based on the criteria of cost and time, response rates, quality of interviewing, and quality of data. Compare interviewers in terms of the total cost per completed interview and response rates. The supervisor must directly observe the interviewing process, and the completed questionnaires of each interviewer should be evaluated for the quality of data.

iResearch
Ford: Extending Its Field to China

As the international marketing manager for Ford Motors, what information would you like in order to formulate marketing strategies to increase your sales in China? Visit **www.ford.com** and search the Internet, including social media as well as your library's online databases, to obtain information on Chinese consumers' preferences for cars. How would you select, train, and supervise field workers conducting an in-home survey in China to determine consumers' preferences for cars? ‹

THE DATA PREPARATION PROCESS

Once the data have been collected, they need to be prepared and made suitable before any analysis is conducted. The data preparation process is shown in Figure 10.6. The entire process is guided by the preliminary plan of data analysis that was formulated in the research design phase (Chapter 3), which should be reviewed. The next step is to check for acceptable questionnaires. This is followed by editing, coding, and transcribing the data. The data are cleaned, and a treatment for missing responses is prescribed. Often, statistical adjustment of the data may be necessary to make them suitable for analysis. The researcher should then select an appropriate data analysis strategy. The final data analysis strategy differs from the preliminary plan of data analysis due to the information and insights gained since the preliminary plan was formulated. These steps are discussed in some detail.

Questionnaire Checking

Data preparation should begin as soon as the first batch of questionnaires is received from the field, while the field work is still going on. Thus, if any problems are detected, the field work can be modified to incorporate corrective action. The initial step in questionnaire checking involves a check of all questionnaires for completeness and interviewing quality. If quotas or cell group sizes have been imposed, the acceptable questionnaires should be classified and counted

FIGURE 10.6

DATA PREPARATION
PROCESS

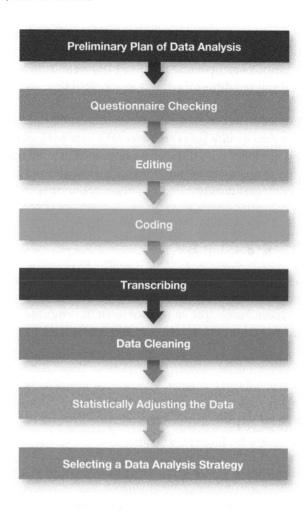

accordingly. Any problems in meeting the sampling requirements should be identified and corrective action taken, such as conducting additional interviews in the underrepresented cells, before the data are edited.

Editing

editing

A review of the questionnaires with the objective of increasing accuracy and precision.

Editing is the review of the questionnaires with the objective of increasing accuracy and precision. It consists of screening questionnaires to identify illegible, incomplete, inconsistent, or ambiguous responses. At this stage, the researcher makes a preliminary check for consistency. Certain obvious inconsistencies can be easily detected. For example, a respondent reports an annual income of less than $20,000 yet indicates frequent shopping at prestigious department stores like Neiman-Marcus.

Unsatisfactory responses are commonly handled by returning to the field to get better data, assigning missing values, or discarding unsatisfactory respondents (see Figure 10.7). The questionnaires with unsatisfactory responses may be returned to the field, where the interviewers recontact the respondents. This approach is particularly attractive for business and industrial marketing surveys, where the sample sizes are small and the respondents are easy to identify.

If returning the questionnaires to the field is not feasible, the researcher may assign missing values to unsatisfactory responses. For example, for responses obtained on a 1 to 5 Likert scale (see Chapter 7), 9 may be assigned as a missing value to scale items that were left blank by the respondents. The treatment of missing values is discussed later in this chapter. If neither of the preceding two options is feasible, the respondents with unsatisfactory responses are simply discarded. If the researcher decides to discard unsatisfactory respondents, the procedure adopted to identify these respondents and their number should be reported.

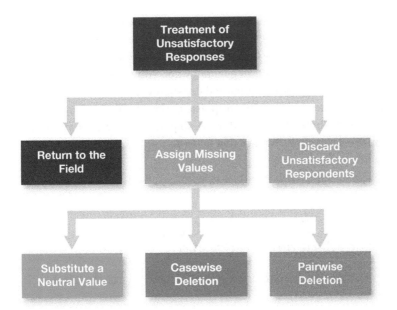

FIGURE 10.7
TREATMENT OF
UNSATISFACTORY
RESPONSES

Research Recipe

Begin questionnaire checking as soon as the first batch of questionnaires is received from the field, while the field work is still going on. Editing consists of screening questionnaires to identify illegible, incomplete, inconsistent, or ambiguous responses. Handle unsatisfactory responses by returning to the field to get better data, assigning missing values, or discarding unsatisfactory respondents.

Coding

Coding means assigning a code, usually a number, to each possible response to each question. The code includes an indication of the column position (field) and data record it will occupy. For example, the sex of respondents may be coded as 1 for females and 2 for males. A field represents a single item of data, such as the sex of the respondent. A record consists of related fields, such as sex, marital status, age, household size, occupation, and so on. All the demographic and personality characteristics of a respondent may be contained in a single record.

coding
Assigning a code to represent a specific response to a specific question along with the data record and column position that the code will occupy.

The respondent code and the record number should appear on each record in the data. If possible, standard codes should be used for missing data. For example, a code of 9 (or –9) could be used for a single-digit variable (responses coded on a scale of 1 to 7), 99 for a double-digit variable (responses coded on a scale of 1 to 11), and so forth. The missing value codes should be distinct from the codes assigned to the legitimate responses.

If the questionnaire contains only structured questions or very few unstructured questions, it is precoded. This means that codes are assigned before field work is conducted. If the questionnaire contains unstructured questions, codes are assigned after the questionnaires have been returned from the field (postcoding). We provide some guidelines on the coding of structured questions followed by coding of unstructured questions (see Chapter 8).

CODING STRUCTURED QUESTIONS   Coding structured questions is relatively simple because the response options are predetermined. The researcher assigns a code for each response to each question and specifies the appropriate record and columns in which the response codes are to appear. For example,

In the last month, have you bought a product or service over the Internet?

1. Yes   2. No (P)

For this question, a yes response is coded 1 and a no response receives a 2. The letter in parentheses indicates that the code assigned will appear in column P for this respondent, for example, in an Excel spreadsheet. Because only one response is allowed and there are only two possible responses (1 or 2), a single column is sufficient. In general, when you are entering data in a spreadsheet, a single column is sufficient to code a structured question with a single response. In questions that permit multiple responses, each possible response option should be assigned a separate column. Such questions include those about brand ownership or usage, television viewing, and magazine readership, as in the Research in Practice that follows.

Research in Practice
Reading Magazine Readership

Which magazines have you read during the last two months? (Check as many as apply.)

Time	❑	(D)
Newsweek	❑	(E)
BusinessWeek	❑	(F)
Forbes	❑	(G)
Fortune	❑	(H)
The Economist	❑	(I)
Other magazines	❑	(J)

Suppose a respondent checked *Time, Newsweek,* and Other magazines. On the record for this respondent, a 1 will be entered in the columns lettered D, E, and J, respectively. All the other columns (F, G, H, and I) will receive a 0. ◄

CODING UNSTRUCTURED QUESTIONS Coding unstructured or open-ended questions is more complex. Respondents' verbatim responses are recorded on the questionnaire. Codes are then developed and assigned to these responses by analyzing the data of a few respondents. The following guidelines are suggested for coding unstructured questions and questionnaires in general.

Category codes should be mutually exclusive and collectively exhaustive. Categories are mutually exclusive if each response fits into one, and only one, category code. Categories should not overlap. Categories are collectively exhaustive if every response fits into one of the assigned category codes. This can be achieved by adding an additional category code of "other" or "none of the above." However, only a few (10 percent or less) of the responses should fall into this category. The vast majority of the responses should be classified into meaningful categories.

codebook

A book containing coding instructions and the necessary information about variables in the data set.

CODEBOOK A **codebook** contains coding instructions and the necessary information about variables in the data set. A codebook guides the coders in their work and helps the researcher to properly identify and locate the variables. Even if the questionnaire has been precoded, it is helpful to prepare a formal codebook. A codebook generally contains the following information: (1) column number, (2) record number, (3) variable number, (4) variable name, (5) question number, and (6) instructions for coding. Figure 10.8 is an excerpt from a codebook developed for the data of Table 10.1.

Column Number	Variable Number	Variable Name	Question Number	Coding Instructions
1	1	ID		1 to 20 as coded
2	2	Preference	1	Input the number circled. 1 = Weak Preference 7 = Strong Preference
3	3	Quality	2	Input the number circled. 1 = Poor 7 = Excellent
4	4	Variety	3	Input the number circled. 1 = Poor 7 = Excellent
5	5	Value	4	Input the number circled. 1 = Poor 7 = Excellent
6	6	Service	5	Input the number circled. 1 = Poor 7 = Excellent
7	7	Income	6	Input the number circled. 1 = Less than $20,000 2 = $20,000 to 34,999 3 = $35,000 to 49,999 4 = $50,000 to 74,999 5 = $75,000 to 99,999 6 = $100,00 or more

FIGURE 10.8
A CODEBOOK EXCERPT

Table 10.1 > Department Store Preference

Id	Preference	Quality	Variety	Value	Service	Income
1	2	2	3	1	3	6
2	6	5	6	5	7	2
3	4	4	3	4	5	3
4	1	2	1	1	2	5
5	7	6	6	5	4	1
6	5	4	4	5	4	3
7	2	4	3	2	3	5
8	3	3	4	2	3	4
9	7	6	7	6	5	2
10	2	3	2	2	2	5
11	2	3	2	1	3	6
12	6	6	6	6	7	5
13	4	4	3	3	4	3
14	1	1	3	1	2	4
15	7	7	5	5	4	2
16	5	5	4	5	5	3
17	2	3	1	2	2	4
18	4	4	3	3	2	3
19	7	5	5	7	5	5
20	3	2	2	3	3	3

SPSS Data File

Excel Data File

Research Recipe

For structured questions, assign a code for each response to each question and specify the appropriate record and columns in which the response codes are to appear. For unstructured questions, category codes should be mutually exclusive and collectively exhaustive, and they should be developed by analyzing the data of a few respondents.

Transcribing

Transcribing data involves transferring the coded data from the questionnaires or coding sheets onto disks or directly into computers by keypunching and developing a data file. Besides keypunching, the data can be transferred by using mark sense forms, optical scanning, computerized sensory analysis, or other means. A familiar example of optical scanning is the transcription of the Universal Product Code (UPC) data at supermarket checkout counters. Technological advances have resulted in the automation of the data transcription process. If the data have been collected via computer-assisted telephone interview (CATI), computer-assisted personal interview (CAPI), or Internet surveys, transcribing is unnecessary because the data are entered directly into the computer as they are collected.

DEVELOPING A DATA FILE Transcribed data can be entered into a spreadsheet program such as Excel. Most analysis programs can import data from a spreadsheet. In this case, the data for each respondent for each field is a cell. Typically, each row of the (Excel) spreadsheet contains the data of one respondent or case. The columns contain the variables, with one column for each variable or response. These concepts are illustrated in Table 10.1. This table gives the data from a pretest sample of twenty respondents on preferences for department stores.

Each respondent was asked to rate his or her preference to shop in a familiar department store (1 = weak preference, 7 = strong preference) and to rate the department store in terms of quality of merchandise, variety, value, and service (1 = poor, 7 = excellent). Annual household income was obtained and coded as: 1 = less than $20,000, 2 = $20,000 to 34,999, 3 = $35,000 to 49,999, 4 = $50,000 to 74,999, 5 = $75,000 to 99,999, 6 = $100,000 or more. The codebook for coding these data is given in Figure 10.8. Note that, in addition to the data of Table 10.1, the codebook also contains information on several other codes that are not shown.

If the data of Table 10.1 are entered using either Excel or SPSS, the resulting data files will resemble Table 10.1. You can verify this by downloading Excel and SPSS files for Table 10.1 from the Companion website for this book. Note that the SPSS data file has two views: the data view and the variable view. The data view gives a listing of the data and resembles Table 10.1. The variable view gives a listing of the variables showing the type, labels or description, values, and underlying coding for each variable, as shown in Table 10.2. Clicking on the Values column of the SPSS file opens a "Value Labels" dialog box. Value labels are unique labels assigned to each possible value of a variable. For example, 1 equals weak preference and 7 equals strong preference. If descriptors were used for the other preference values, those other preference values would also be assigned the corresponding "Value Labels." For descriptions of the other columns of Table 10.2, see the section on "Detailed Steps: Data Entry" under SPSS Windows.

In Table 10.1, as well as in the corresponding Excel and SPSS files, the columns represent the fields, and the rows represent the records or respondents because there is one record per respondent. Notice that there are seven columns. The first column contains the respondent ID, and the second column contains the preference for the department store. Columns three to six contain the evaluations of the department store on quality of merchandise, variety, value, and service, respectively. Finally, the seventh column contains the respondent's income, coded as specified in the codebook. Each row contains all the data of a single respondent and represents a record. The table has twenty rows, or records, indicating that data for twenty respondents are stored in this data file. Databases consist of one or more interrelated files. For example, a database might contain all the customer satisfaction surveys conducted quarterly for the last five years.

Table 10.2 > SPSS Variable View of the Data of Table 10.1

SPSS Data File

	Name	Type	Width	Decimals	Label	Values	Missing	Columns	Align	Measure	Role
1	ID	Numeric	8	0	Respondent Identification Number	None	None	8	Right	Nominal	Input
2	Preference	Numeric	8	0	Preference for the Department Store	{1, Weak Preference}...	None	8	Right	Scale	Input
3	Quality	Numeric	8	0	Quality of Merchandize	{1, Poor}...	None	8	Right	Scale	Input
4	Variety	Numeric	8	0	Variety of Merchandize	{1, Poor}...	None	8	Right	Scale	Input
5	Value	Numeric	8	0	Value for Money	{1, Poor}...	None	8	Right	Scale	Input
6	Service	Numeric	8	0	In-store Service	{1, Poor}...	None	8	Right	Scale	Input
7	Income	Numeric	8	0	Household Income	{1, Less than $20,000}...	None	8	Right	Ordinal	Input

Research Recipe

You can enter data into a spreadsheet program, such as Excel; the data for each respondent for each field is a cell. Typically, each row of the (Excel) spreadsheet contains the data of one respondent or case.

You can also enter data into SPSS. The SPSS data file has two views: the data view and the variable view. The data view gives a listing of the data, while the variable view gives a listing of the variables showing the type, labels or description, values, and underlying coding for each variable.

iResearch
Are There Any Patriotic Feelings Toward the New England Patriots?

As the marketing director for the New England Patriots, what information would help you to formulate marketing strategies to increase the attendance at the Patriots home games?

Visit **www.nfl.com** and search the Internet, including social media as well as your library's online databases, to obtain information on why people attend professional football games. A survey was administered to attendees at a Patriots home game to determine why they were attending. What guidelines will you follow in checking the questionnaire, editing, and coding? <

Data Cleaning

Data cleaning includes consistency checks and treatment of missing responses. While preliminary consistency checks have been made during editing, the checks at this stage are more thorough and extensive because they are made by computer.

data cleaning
Thorough and extensive checks for consistency and treatment of missing responses or values.

consistency checks
The part of the data-cleaning process that identifies data that are out of range, are logically inconsistent, or have extreme values. Data with values not defined by the coding scheme are inadmissible.

CONSISTENCY CHECKS   **Consistency checks** identify data that are out of range, are logically inconsistent, or have extreme values. Out-of-range data values are inadmissible and must be corrected. For example, if respondents have been asked to express their degree of agreement with a series of lifestyle statements on a 1 to 5 Likert scale (Chapter 7), and if 9 has been designated for missing values, data values of 0, 6, 7, and 8 are out of range. Computer packages like SPSS and Excel can be programmed to identify out-of-range values for each variable and print out the respondent code, variable code, variable name, record number, column number, and out-of-range value. This makes it is easy to check each variable systematically for out-of-range values. The correct responses can be determined by going back to the edited and coded questionnaire.

Responses can be logically inconsistent in various ways. For example, a respondent may indicate that she charges her shopping to a store charge card, although she does not have one. Or a respondent reports both unfamiliarity with, and frequent usage of, the same product. The necessary information (respondent code, variable code, variable name, record number, column number, and inconsistent values) can be printed to locate these responses and take corrective action.

Finally, extreme values should be examined closely. Not all extreme values result from errors, but they may point to problems with the data. For example, an extremely low evaluation of a brand may be the result of the respondent indiscriminately circling 1s (on a 1 to 7 rating scale) on all attributes of this brand.

missing responses
Values of a variable that are unknown because these respondents did not provide unambiguous answers to the question or their answers were not properly recorded. Also called missing values.

TREATMENT OF MISSING RESPONSES   **Missing responses**, also referred to as *missing values*, represent values of a variable that are unknown, either because respondents did not provide unambiguous answers or their answers were not properly recorded. Treatment of missing responses poses problems, particularly if the proportion of missing responses is more than 10 percent. The following options are available for the treatment of missing responses (see Figure 10.7).

1. *Substitute a Neutral Value* A neutral value, typically the mean response to the variable, is substituted for the missing responses. Thus, the mean of the variable remains unchanged and other statistics, such as correlations, are not affected much. While this approach has some merit, the logic of substituting a mean value (say, 4) for respondents who, if they had answered, might have used either high ratings (6 or 7) or low ratings (1 or 2) is questionable.

casewise deletion
A method for handling missing responses or values in which cases or respondents with any missing values are discarded from the analysis.

2. *Casewise Deletion* In **casewise deletion**, cases, or respondents, with any missing responses are discarded from the analysis. Because many respondents may have some missing responses, this approach could result in a small sample. Throwing away large amounts of data is undesirable because it is costly and time-consuming to collect data. Respondents with missing responses could differ from respondents with complete responses in systematic ways. If so, casewise deletion could seriously bias the results.

pairwise deletion
A method of handling missing responses or values in which all cases, or respondents, with any missing values are not automatically discarded; rather, for each calculation, only the cases or respondents with complete responses are considered.

3. *Pairwise Deletion* In **pairwise deletion**, instead of discarding all cases with any missing values, the researcher uses only the cases, or respondents, with complete responses for each calculation. As a result, different calculations in an analysis may be based on different sample sizes. This procedure may be appropriate when (1) the sample size is large, (2) there are few missing responses, and (3) the variables are not highly related. However, this procedure can produce results that are unappealing or are not even feasible.

The different procedures for the treatment of missing responses may yield different results particularly when the responses are not missing at random and the variables are related. Hence, missing responses should be kept to a minimum. The researcher should carefully consider the implications of the various procedures before selecting a particular method for the treatment of nonresponse.

Research Recipe

Data cleaning includes consistency checks and treatment of missing responses. Consistency checks identify data that are out of range, are logically inconsistent, or have extreme values. Missing responses represent values of a variable that are unknown. Treat such responses by substituting a neutral value such as the mean or by using casewise deletion or pairwise deletion.

Statistically Adjusting the Data

Procedures for statistically adjusting the data consist of (1) variable respecification and (2) recoding. These adjustments are not always necessary, but they can enhance the quality of data analysis.

VARIABLE RESPECIFICATION **Variable respecification** involves the transformation of data to create new variables or modify existing ones. The purpose of respecification is to create variables that are consistent with the objectives of the study. Respecification often involves summing the items of a Likert-type scale to create a summed score. For example, in Chapter 7, a Likert scale consisting of seven statements was used to measure attitude toward McDonald's. These seven statements need to be summed, after reversing the scoring of the negative statements, to arrive at a total attitudinal score. The process of reversing the scoring for the negative statements, as well as the process of summing, involves variable respecification.

variable respecification
The transformation of data to create new variables or the modification of existing variables so that they are more consistent with the objectives of the study.

Another common form of variable respecification is **standardization**. To standardize a scale X_i, we first subtract the mean, $\overline{X}$, from each score and then divide by the standard deviation, s_x. Thus, the standardized scale will have a mean of 0 and a standard deviation of 1. This is essentially the same as the calculation of z scores (see Chapter 12). Standardization allows the researcher to compare variables that have been measured using different types of scales. Mathematically, standardized scores, z_i, may be obtained as:

standardization
The process of correcting data to reduce them to the same scale by subtracting the sample mean and dividing by the standard deviation. A standardized variable will have a mean of 0 and a standard deviation of 1.

$$z_i = (X_i - \overline{X})/s_x$$

RECODING Once the data have been coded, transcribed, and cleaned, it might be necessary to redefine the categories of a categorical variable, such as income. For example, if there are too few respondents in the lowest income category, this category can be combined or merged with the next lowest category. This is referred to as **recoding**. Recoding involves redefining the values of a variable and includes forming categories or redefining the categories of a categorical variable. Both variable respecification and recoding using SPSS and Excel are illustrated later in this chapter.

recoding
Recoding involves redefining the values of a variable and includes forming categories or redefining the categories of a categorical variable.

Research Recipe

Variable respecification involves the transformation of data to create new variables or modify existing ones that are consistent with the objectives of the study. A common form of variable respecification is the summing of items to create a summed score. Another example is standardization, in which the standardized variable will have a mean of 0 and a standard deviation of 1. To standardize a variable, first subtract the mean from each score and then divide by the standard deviation. Recoding involves redefining the values of a variable and includes forming categories or redefining the categories of a categorical variable.

Visit **www.lexus.com** and search the Internet, including social media as well as your library's online databases, to obtain information on the criteria that buyers use in selecting a luxury car brand. Demographic and psychographic data were obtained in a survey designed to explain the choice of a luxury car brand. What kind of consistency checks, treatment of missing responses, and variable respecification should be conducted?

As the marketing manager for Lexus, what information would you like to have in order to formulate marketing strategies to increase your market share? **<**

Selecting a Data Analysis Strategy

The selection of a data analysis strategy must begin with a consideration of the earlier steps in the process: problem definition (Step 1), development of an approach (Step 2), and research design (Step 3). The preliminary plan of data analysis prepared as part of the research design should be used as a springboard. Changes may be necessary in light of additional information generated in subsequent stages of the research process.

The next step is to consider the known characteristics of the data. The measurement scales used exert a strong influence on the choice of statistical techniques (see Chapter 7). In addition, the type of insights desired may favor certain techniques. It is also important to take into account the properties of the statistical techniques, particularly their purpose and underlying assumptions. For example, some statistical techniques are appropriate for examining differences in variables (*t* tests), while others are appropriate for assessing the association between variables (correlations and regression, all discussed in Chapter 12). The insights into the data obtained during data preparation can be valuable for selecting a strategy for analysis.

Finally, the researcher's background and philosophy affect the choice of a data analysis strategy. The experienced, statistically trained researcher will employ a range of techniques appropriate for analyzing the data from a given project.

> ### Research Recipe
>
> Select a data analysis strategy based on the earlier steps of the marketing research process, known characteristics of the data, properties of statistical techniques, and the background and philosophy of the researcher. The measurement scales used exert a strong influence on the choice of statistical techniques, and the type of insights desired may favor certain techniques. It is also important to take into account the properties of the statistical techniques, particularly their purpose and underlying assumptions.

INTERNATIONAL MARKETING RESEARCH

The selection, training, supervision, and evaluation of field workers are critical in international marketing research. Local field work agencies are unavailable in many countries. Therefore, it may be necessary to recruit and train local field workers or import trained foreign workers. The use of local field workers is desirable because they are familiar with the local language and culture. They can thus create an appropriate climate for the interview and be sensitive to the concerns of the respondents. Extensive training and close supervision may be required. As observed in many countries, interviewers tend to help the respondent with the answers and select household or sampling units based on personal considerations rather than the sampling plan. Finally, interviewer cheating may be more of a problem in many foreign countries than in the United States. Validation of field work is critical. Proper application of field work procedures can greatly reduce these difficulties and result in consistent and useful findings.

Before analyzing the data, the researcher should ensure that the units of measurement are comparable across countries or cultural units. For example, the data may have to be adjusted to establish currency equivalents or metric equivalents to achieve consistent results.

Research in Practice
A Worldwide Scream for Ice Cream

Häagen-Dazs, the hyper-rich U.S. ice cream, is the latest hot American export. Its sales in Asia, Britain, France, and Germany are increasing at a phenomenal rate. By 2015, consumers worldwide are expected to eat well over $2 billion worth of Häagen-Dazs products annually. Over half the sales will come from the international market. How did this come about? The strategy for whetting foreign appetites is simple. Marketing research conducted in several European (e.g., Britain, France, and Germany) and several Asian (e.g., Japan, Singapore, and Taiwan) countries revealed that consumers were hungry for a high-quality ice cream with a premium image and were willing to pay a premium price for it. These consistent findings emerged after the price of ice cream in each country was respecified to a common basis. Respecification was necessary because the prices were specified in different local currencies, and a common basis was needed for comparison across countries. Also, in each country, the premium price had to be defined in relation to the prices of competing brands. Price respecification accomplished both these objectives.

Source: Directphoto.org / Alamy

Based on these findings, Häagen-Dazs first introduced the brand at a few high-end retailers; it then built company-owned stores in high-traffic areas; it finally rolled into convenience stores and supermarkets. It maintained the premium-quality brand name by starting first with a few high-end retailers. It also supplied free freezers to retailers. Hungry for quality product, British citizens shelled out $5.00 a pint—double or triple the price of home brands. Back in the United States, Häagen-Dazs remains popular, although it faces intense competition and raised health awareness on the part of consumers. This added to the impetus to enter foreign markets.[2] <

Research Recipe

While conducting international research, it may be necessary to recruit and train local field workers or import trained foreign workers. Before analyzing the data, you should ensure that the units of measurement are comparable across countries or cultural units.

MARKETING RESEARCH AND SOCIAL MEDIA

Interviewers conducting telephone or personal interviews are generally employed on a part-time or contract basis. However, research staff members who collect and analyze data from social media are normally full-time employees of the research firm. A limited number of operational staff or field workers, as few as two or three, may be assigned to a social media project. These factors make the selection, training, supervision, validation, and evaluation of field workers much more streamlined, although many of the issues involved are the same as encountered in traditional field work.

Another challenge that a researcher faces is working closely with the client in making additional field work decisions. When collecting qualitative data, several decisions have to be made, and these should be arrived at jointly by the researcher and the client. These decisions involve determining the type and specification of the social media channels to be monitored; developing a standardization of terms, conversation types, and content types; establishing a standardized coding scheme; and setting benchmarks. Thus, a crucial part of the organization of field work is forming a core team of people drawn from both the client and research organizations.

Social media data collection and analysis can be a very dynamic process. Unlike traditional data collection, respondents do not merely respond to questions or stimuli. Rather, they generate the data and edit it via their communal participation. In short, social media respondents co-create; thus, respondents become participants in a shared enterprise, retaining the rights to set the agenda rather than simply responding to it. Although the data preparation process remains essentially similar to that discussed earlier, there are certain unique aspects to social media data collection, as illustrated in the research project undertaken by KDPaine & Partners for Georgia Tech.

Research in Practice
Georgia Tech: Using Social Media to Make Social Comparisons

KDPaine & Partners provided custom research to measure the effectiveness of social media and traditional public relations. The research firm undertook a project to determine specifically what presence and activity Georgia Tech (**www.gatech.edu**) and its peer institutions had in social media. The field work was organized as follows: Two senior members of Georgia Tech's communications/marketing team; the CEO of KDPaine & Partners, LLC; the KDPaine director of research; and the KDPaine education team leader formed a core team working together to determine goals, methodology, and the timeline for the

Source: jackweichen / Shutterstock

project. Following the development of goals and the project vision, the KDPaine director of research and the education team leader finalized coding instructions. Once instructions were completed, the education team leader conducted training on test items for readers (field workers) until they reached acceptable reliability standards for all major variables. Then, the KDPaine director of research and the education team leader determined and acquired the desired population and sample sizes. Once the desired sample was achieved and the coders were trained, official reading of social media sites (data collection) began with intercoder reliability tests (which involve comparisons of coding done by different readers) being administered intermittently to ensure accuracy. Every month, results were compiled and reported on to set benchmarks and were examined over time. Team meetings were held regularly between Georgia Tech and KDPaine to discuss the efficacy of the field work methodology and the ensuing results.

In 2012, KDPaine & Partners merged with Salience Insight (**salienceinsight.com**), the media insight division of News Group International, a global provider of business intelligence and media resource services.[3] ◀

Research Recipe

The selection, training, supervision, validation, and evaluation of field workers is much more streamlined when conducting field work in social media, although many of the issues involved are the same as those encountered in traditional field work. Jointly with the client make decisions that involve determining the type and specification of the social media channels to be monitored; developing standardization of terms, conversation types, and content types; establishing a standardized coding scheme; and setting benchmarks. Unlike traditional data collection, respondents do not merely respond to questions or stimuli; they generate the data and edit it via their communal participation.

ETHICS IN MARKETING RESEARCH

The data, whether collected by the internal marketing research department or by an external field work agency, should be obtained by following high ethical standards. The researchers and field workers should make the respondents feel comfortable by addressing their apprehensions. One way in which the comfort level of the respondents can be increased is by providing them with adequate information about the research firm and the project, addressing their questions, and clearly stating the responsibilities and expectations of the field workers and the respondents at the start of the interview. The respondents should be told that they are not obligated to answer questions that make them uncomfortable, and that they can terminate the interview at any point should they experience discomfort. The researcher and field workers have an ethical responsibility to respect the respondents' privacy, feelings, and dignity. The respondents should be left with a positive and pleasant experience. This will enhance goodwill and future cooperation from respondents. The aspect was emphasized by the Marketing Research Association in the first Research in Practice feature in this chapter.

The researchers and the field work agencies are also responsible to the clients for following the accepted procedures for the selection, training, supervision, validation, and evaluation of field workers. They must ensure the integrity of the data collection process. The field work procedures should be documented carefully and made available to the clients. Appropriate actions by researchers and field work agencies can go a long way in addressing ethical concerns associated with field work, as illustrated by the Research in Practice feature about Burke.

Research in Practice
Burke: Raising the Ethical Bar in Data Collection

Information provided while responding to an 800 number, using a credit card, or purchasing a product is often used to compile lists of customers and potential customers. These lists are rarely sold to telemarketing and direct marketing organizations. The public perception is different, however, and many people feel that marketers and marketing researchers misuse the information they collect. This misperception is giving marketing research a negative image.

In an effort to correct this misperception, many marketing researchers and field work agencies are addressing these issue head-on at the start of an interview. Burke (**www.burke.com**) is one of the premier international research and consulting firms. When contacting potential respondents, Burke provides them with information about the firm (Burke) and the marketing research project. The respondents are assured that Burke operates within a code of ethics. Some marketing research firms and field work agencies provide potential respondents with toll-free numbers that they can call to obtain more information or verify the information given by the field workers. Such actions make the respondents more comfortable and informed, and result in higher-quality data for the clients.[4] ◄

Ethical issues that arise during the data preparation and analysis step of the marketing research process pertain mainly to the researcher. While checking, editing, coding, transcribing, and cleaning, researchers should try to get some idea about the quality of the data. An attempt should be made to identify respondents who have provided data of questionable quality. Consider, for example, a respondent who checks the 7 response to all twenty items measuring attitude toward spectator sports on a Likert scale that ranges from 1 to 7. Apparently, this respondent did not realize that some of the statements were negative and some were positive. Thus, this respondent indicates an extremely favorable attitude toward spectator sports on all the positive statements and an extremely negative attitude on the statements that were reversed. Decisions about whether such respondents should be discarded (i.e., not included in the analysis) can raise ethical concerns. A good rule of thumb is to make such decisions during the data preparation phase before conducting any analysis.

In contrast, suppose the researcher conducted the analysis without first attempting to identify unsatisfactory respondents. The analysis does not reveal the expected relationship, however; that is, the analysis does not show that attitude toward spectator sports influences attendance at spectator sports. The researcher then decides to examine the quality of the data obtained. In checking the questionnaires, a few respondents with unsatisfactory data are identified. In addition to the type of unsatisfactory responses mentioned earlier, there were other questionable patterns as well. To illustrate, some respondents had checked all responses as 4, the "neither agree nor disagree" response, to all twenty items measuring attitude toward spectator sports. When the questionnaires from these respondents are eliminated and the reduced data set is analyzed, the expected results—showing a positive influence of attitude on attendance at spectator sports—are obtained. Discarding respondents after analyzing the data raises ethical concerns, particularly if the report does not state that the initial analysis was inconclusive. The procedure used to identify unsatisfactory respondents and the number of respondents discarded should be clearly disclosed.

Research Recipe

The researchers and field workers should make the respondents feel comfortable by addressing their apprehensions and providing them with adequate information about the research firm and the project. They should respect the respondents' privacy, feelings, and dignity. They are also responsible to the clients for following the accepted procedures for the selection, training, supervision, validation, and evaluation of field workers. Ethical issues that arise during the data preparation and analysis step of the marketing research process pertain mainly to the researcher. You should clearly disclose the procedure used to identify unsatisfactory respondents and the number of respondents discarded.

SOFTWARE APPLICATIONS

Major statistical packages, such as SPSS (**www.spss.com**) and Excel (**www.microsoft.com/ office/excel**), have websites that can be accessed for a variety of information. These packages also contain options for handling missing responses and for statistically adjusting the data. In addition, a number of statistical packages can now be found on the Internet. Although some of these programs do not offer integrated data analysis and management, they can be very useful for conducting specific statistical analyses. In this book, special emphasis is placed on SPSS and Excel.

EXHIBIT 10.1
Instructions for Running Computerized Demonstration Movies

For best results while viewing the SPSS and Excel demonstrations, the "Display" resolution of your computer should be set to 1,280 by 1,024 pixels. To check that, click on the "Display" icon under your computer's Control Panel. Although we give instructions for running SPSS demonstrations, those for Excel are very similar. To run a demonstration movie on this book's Companion website, simply click on the relevant file. To download the demonstration movies and run them on your computer, please follow these instructions.

For each procedure, you can download either a single Adobe Acrobat document (.pdf) or a set of HTML files contained in a folder. Downloading the Adobe Acrobat document (.pdf) is simple, and you will need Acrobat 9 or higher to run it. To download HTML files, pick the folder with the appropriate name. For example, to run a variable respecification on the data of Table 10.1, use the "IBM SPSS 20 Ch10 Variable Respecification" folder. Each folder will have several files. It is important that you download all the files in a folder and save them in one separate folder. All the files in a folder are required to run the demonstration. All the files in each folder should be downloaded and saved in the same separate folder. The file that you should select to run the demonstration movie is the one that has the ".htm" extension appended to its name. For example, if you want to run a demonstration of variable respecification on the data of Table 10.1 using SPSS, then double-click the file "IBM SPSS 20 Chp10 Variable Respecification demo movie" in the "IBM SPSS 20 Ch10 Variable Respecification" folder. Once you double-click, Internet Explorer (or your default Web browser) will be loaded, and the demonstration movie will start automatically. Note that the other files also need to be in the same folder.

If you want to stop the demonstration movie at any specific point in the demonstration, simply click the ▮▮ button. The demonstration stops at that point. That button now changes form, and looks like ▶ . To continue viewing the demonstration from that point on, simply click the ▶ button. To fast-forward the demonstration, you can click the ▷ button. Click it multiple times if you need to fast-forward through longer intervals. To rewind the demonstration, simply click the ◁ button. Click it multiple times if you need to rewind through longer intervals. At any time, if you want to replay the demonstration, right from the beginning, then simply click the ↺ button. Finally, you can also move the slide _____ left or right to navigate through the demonstration. The slider achieves the same purpose as that of the fast-forward and rewind buttons.

SPSS and Excel Computerized Demonstration Movies

We have developed computerized demonstration movies that give step-by-step instructions for running all the SPSS and Excel programs that are discussed in this book. These demonstration movies can be downloaded from the Companion website for this book. The instructions for running these demonstration movies are given in Exhibit 10.1.

SPSS and Excel Screen Captures with Notes

The step-by-step instructions for running the various SPSS and Excel programs discussed in this book are also illustrated in screen captures with appropriate notes. These screen captures can be downloaded from the Companion website for this book.

SPSS WINDOWS

Using the base module of SPSS, out-of-range values can be selected using the SELECT IF command. These cases, with the identifying information (subject ID, variable name, and variable value), can then be printed using the LIST or PRINT commands. The PRINT command saves

active cases to an external file. If a formatted list is required, the SUMMARIZE command can be used.

Detailed Steps: Overview

Detailed step-by-step instructions for running the SPSS programs for the data analysis presented in this chapter can be downloaded from the Companion website for this book in two forms: (1) computerized demonstration movies and (2) screen captures with notes. You can also refer to the Student Resource Manual. In addition, these steps are illustrated in the following sections. These steps are given for IBM SPSS STATISTICS 20 and IBM SPSS STATISTICS 21; they are essentially the same in both of these versions. The steps in the earlier versions are about the same, with minor differences in the labeling of some of the boxes.

Detailed Steps: Data Entry

We illustrate the use of SPSS in entering the data of Table 10.1. In SPSS, data are organized by rows and columns. Each row represents a respondent or a case. The columns represent variables. The steps involved are as follows.

1. Double-click on the IBM SPSS Statistic 21 icon.
2. By default, the program is set to OPEN AN EXISTING DATA SOURCE. As you are inputting coded data for the first time, click on TYPE IN DATA button. Click OK.
3. To create variables, click on the VARIABLE VIEW tab on the lower left corner of the screen. You will see the VARIABLE VIEW screen.
4. By default, the columns are organized as: NAME, TYPE, WIDTH, DECIMALS, LABEL, VALUES, MISSING, COLUMNS, ALIGN, MEASURE, and ROLE. Under the NAME column, type in ID in row 1, Preference in row 2, Quality in row 3, Variety in row 4, Value in row 5, Service in row 6, and Income in row 7.
5. TYPE referring to Type of Data is set to NUMERIC, the default option. WIDTH is set to 8, also the default option.
6. Set DECIMALS to 0. If you click on the first row under DECIMALS, up and down arrows will appear. Click the down arrow twice and DECIMALS will be set to 0. Simply copy the first cell and paste it on all the cells under DECIMALS in rows 2 to 7.
7. In the LABEL column, enter a descriptive label for each variable. For example, for ID, type "Respondent Identification Number;" for Preference, type "Preference for the Department Store;" and so on. See Table 10.2 for other labels.
8. Clicking on the VALUES column of the SPSS file opens a VALUE LABELS dialog box. Value labels are unique labels assigned to each possible value of a variable. For example, for "Preference" in row 2, 1 denotes weak preference and 7 denotes strong preference. In the VALUE LABELS dialog box, type 1 for VALUE and type in "Weak Preference" for LABEL. Click ADD. Then, type 7 for VALUE and "Strong Preference" for LABEL and again click ADD. Then click OK. Similarly add value labels for the other variables. See Table 10.2.
9. Leave MISSING column as is, with NONE as the default option.
10. COLUMNS is set to a width of 8, the default option.
11. ALIGN all input data to the RIGHT, the default option.
12. MEASURE refers to the type of scale and is set to SCALE for interval and ratio scale data. Click on the entry in the first row and then click on the down arrow to the NOMINAL setting. Click on the entry in the second row and then click on the down arrow to the SCALE setting. Simply copy the second cell and paste it on all the cells under MEASURE in rows 3 to 6. Income should be set as ORDINAL.
13. ROLE is set to INPUT, the default option, as the data are input into the file.

14. Click on the DATA VIEW box in the lower left corner. Key in the responses of the respondents, with all the responses of a respondent entered in a single row.
15. Save your file. Either click on FILE and then SAVE or SAVE AS.

Detailed Steps: Variable Respecification

We illustrate the use of the base module in creating a new variable using the data of Table 10.1. Open the SPSS data file for Table 10.1. We want to create a variable called *overall evaluation of the department store (Overall)* that is the sum of the ratings on quality, variety, value, and service. Thus,

Overall = Quality + Variety + Value + Service

These steps are as follows.

1. Select TRANSFORM.
2. Click COMPUTE VARIABLE.
3. Type "overall" into the TARGET VARIABLE box.
4. Click "Quality of Merchandise[quality]" and move it to the NUMERIC EXPRESSION box.
5. Click the "+" sign.
6. Click "Variety of Merchandise[variety]" and move it to the NUMERIC EXPRESSION box.
7. Click the "+" sign.
8. Click "Value for Money[value]" and move it to the NUMERIC EXPRESSION box.
9. Click the "+" sign.
10. Click "In-Store Service[service]" and move it to the NUMERIC EXPRESSION box.
11. Click TYPE & LABEL under the TARGET VARIABLE box and type "Overall Evaluation." Click CONTINUE.
12. Click OK.

Detailed Steps: Variable Recoding

We also want to illustrate the recoding of a variable to create a new variable using the data of Table 10.1. Income category 1 occurs only once and income category 6 occurs only twice. Therefore, we want to combine income categories 1 and 2 and categories 5 and 6 and create a new income variable "rincome" labeled "Recoded Income." Note that "rincome" has only four categories, which are coded as 1 to 4. Open the SPSS data file for Table 10.1.

1. Select TRANSFORM.
2. Select RECODE INTO DIFFERENT VARIABLES.
3. Click "Household Income[income]" and move it to the INPUT VARIABLE → OUTPUT VARIABLE box.
4. Type "rincome" into the OUTPUT VARIABLE NAME box.
5. Type "Recoded Income" into the OUTPUT VARIABLE LABEL box.
6. Click the OLD AND NEW VALUES box.
7. Under OLD VALUES, on the left, click RANGE. Type 1 and 2 in the range boxes. Under NEW VALUES, on the right, click VALUE and type 1 into the value box. Click ADD.
8. Under OLD VALUES, on the left, click VALUE. Type 3 in the value box. Under NEW VALUES, on the right, click VALUE and type 2 into the value box. Click ADD.
9. Under OLD VALUES, on the left, click VALUE. Type 4 in the value box. Under NEW VALUES, on the right, click VALUE and type 3 in the value box. Click ADD.
10. Under OLD VALUES, on the left, click RANGE. Type 5 and 6 in the range boxes. Under NEW VALUES, on the right, click VALUE and type 4 in the value box. Click ADD.
11. Click CONTINUE.
12. Click CHANGE.
13. Click OK.

EXCEL

Although Excel is an effective spreadsheet program, it lacks the qualities of a relational database that SPSS offers. As a result, distributions of variables cannot be directly produced, and data recoding must be done through if-then statements.

Detailed Steps: Overview

Detailed step-by-step instructions for running the Excel programs for the data analysis presented in this chapter can be downloaded from the Companion website for this book in two forms: (1) computerized demonstration movies and (2) screen captures with notes. In addition, these steps are illustrated in the following sections for Excel 2007, Excel 2010, and Excel 2013; they are essentially the same in these versions. The steps in earlier versions are about the same, with minor differences in how "Data Analysis" is accessed and the labeling of some of the boxes.

Detailed Steps: Data Entry

We illustrate the use of Excel in entering the data of Table 10.1. In Excel, data are organized by rows and columns. Each row represents a respondent or a case. The columns represent variables. The steps involved are as follows:

1. Double-click on the Excel icon or open a blank workbook.
2. In the first row, type in ID in column 1, Preference in column 2, Quality in column 3, Variety in column 4, Value in column 5, Service in column 6, and Income in column 7. You may have to adjust the width of some of the columns.
3. Key in the responses of the respondents starting with row 2, with all the responses of a respondent entered in a single row. Thus, the data for the twenty respondents will be entered in rows 2 to 21.
4. Save your file. Click on FILE and then SAVE or SAVE AS.

Detailed Steps: Variable Respecification

We illustrate the use of Excel in creating a new variable using the data of Table 10.1. We want to create a variable called *overall evaluation of the department store (Overall)* that is the sum of the ratings on quality, variety, value, and service. Once you open Table 10.1 (Excel file), the steps are as follows.

1. Click on the cell H1.
2. Type "New Variable" in cell H1.
3. Type "=C2+D2+E2+F2" in cell H2.
4. Click on the "Accept formula value" or "Enter" symbol (✓).
5. Next, right-click on cell H2. An Excel pop-up menu will be displayed.
6. Select the COPY menu item.
7. Next, select (highlight) cells H3 through H21.
8. Right-click in any one of these highlighted cells. An Excel pop-up menu will be displayed.
9. Select the PASTE menu item.
10. The values for the new variable are now displayed in the cells H2 to H21.

Detailed Steps: Variable Recoding

We also want to illustrate the recoding of a variable using Excel to create a new variable using the data of Table 10.1. We will be recoding income into four categories (as explained earlier using SPSS). Open the Excel data file for Table 10.1.

1. Click on the cell H1.
2. Type "RINCOME" in cell H1.

3. Carefully type the formula
   "=IF(G2=6,4,IF(G2=5,4,IF(G2=4,3,IF(G2=3,2,IF(G2=2,1,IF(G2=1,1,1))))))"
   correctly in cell H2.
4. Click on the "Accept formula value" or "Enter" symbol (✓).
5. Next, right-click on cell H2. An excel pop-up menu will be displayed.
6. Select the COPY menu item.
7. Next, select (highlight) cells H3 through H21.
8. Right-click in any one of these highlighted cells. An excel pop-up menu will be displayed.
9. Select the PASTE menu item.
10. The recoded values for the new variable are now displayed in the cells H2 to H21.

Dell Running Case

Review the Dell case, Case 1.1, and questionnaire given toward the end of the book.

What's it like to shop for notebook computers? Design a questionnaire to determine students' shopping behavior for notebook computers. Administer the survey to five different students on your campus.

1. How did you feel approaching these respondents?
2. What seemed to be the most challenging part of the survey for the respondents?
3. If other students were employed to collect the data for this survey project, how should they be trained?
4. If other students were employed to collect the data for this survey project, how should they be supervised?
5. Administer the questionnaire you designed by posting it or a link to it on your Facebook account and inviting your friends to participate in the survey. What field work–related issues did you encounter?

Go to the Companion website for this book, download the Dell data file, and answer the following questions.

6. Recode the respondents' answers based on total hours per week spent online (q1) into two groups: five hours or fewer (light users) and six hours or more (heavy users).
7. Recode the respondents' answers based on total hours per week spent online (q1) into three groups: five hours or fewer (light users), six to ten hours (medium users), and eleven hours or more (heavy users).
8. Form a new variable that denotes the total number of things that people have ever done online based on q2_1 to q2_7. Note the missing values for q2_1 to q2_7 are coded as 0.
9. Recode q4 (overall satisfaction) into two groups: Very satisfied (rating of 1), and somewhat satisfied or dissatisfied (ratings of 2, 3, and 4).
10. Recode q5 (would recommend) into two groups: definitely would recommend (rating of 1), and probably would or less likely to recommend (ratings of 2, 3, 4, and 5).
11. Recode q6 (likelihood of choosing DELL) into two groups: definitely would choose (rating of 1), and probably would or less likely to choose (ratings of 2, 3, 4, and 5).
12. Recode q9_5per (q9A) into three groups: definitely or probably would have purchased (ratings of 1 and 2), might or might not have purchased (rating of 3), and probably or definitely would not have purchased (ratings of 4 and 5).

13. Recode q9_10per (q9B) into three groups: definitely or probably would have purchased and might or might not have purchased (ratings of 1, 2, and 3), probably would not have purchased (rating of 4), and definitely would not have purchased (rating of 5).

14. Recode the demographics as follows:

   a. Combine the two lowest education (q11) categories into a single category. Thus, some high school or less and high school graduate will be combined into a single category labeled "High school graduate or less."

   b. Recode age (q12) into four new categories: 18 to 29, 30 to 39, 40 to 49, and 50 or older.

   c. Combine the two lowest income (q13) categories into a single category labeled "Under $30,000."

Summary

Researchers have two major options for collecting data: developing their own organizations or contracting with field work agencies. In either case, data collection involves the use of field workers consisting of interviewers, supervisors, and others involved in data collection. To the extent possible, interviewers should be selected to match respondents' characteristics, the nature of the problem, and the type of data collection method. They should be trained in important aspects of field work, including making the initial contact, asking the questions, probing, recording the answers, and terminating the interview. Supervision of field workers involves quality control and editing, sampling control, control of cheating, and central office control. Validation of field work can be accomplished by calling 10 to 25 percent of those who have been identified as interviewees and inquiring whether the interviews took place. Field workers should be evaluated on the basis of cost and time, response rates, quality of interviewing, and quality of data collection.

Data preparation begins by reviewing the preliminary plan of data analysis followed by a preliminary check of all questionnaires for completeness and interviewing quality. Then more thorough editing takes place. Editing consists of screening questionnaires to identify illegible, incomplete, inconsistent, or ambiguous responses. Such responses may be handled by returning questionnaires to the field, assigning missing values, or discarding the unsatisfactory respondents.

The next step is coding. A numerical or alphanumeric code is assigned to represent a specific response to a specific question, along with the column position that code will occupy. The coded data are transcribed onto disks, or entered into computers via keypunching, optical scanning, computerized sensory analysis, or other technologies.

Cleaning the data requires consistency checks and treatment of missing responses. Options available for treating missing responses include substitution of a neutral value such as the mean, casewise deletion, and pairwise deletion. Statistical adjustments such as variable respecification, and recoding often enhance the quality of data analysis. The selection of a data analysis strategy should be based on the earlier steps of the marketing research process, known characteristics of the data, properties of statistical techniques, and the background and philosophy of the researcher.

The selection, training, supervision, and evaluation of field workers are even more critical in international marketing research because local field work agencies are not available in many countries. Before analyzing the data in international marketing research, the researcher should ensure that the units of measurement are comparable across countries or cultural units.

The selection, training, supervision, validation, and evaluation of field workers is much more streamlined when conducting field work in social media, although many of the issues involved are the same as those encountered in traditional field work. Unlike traditional data collection, respondents using social media do not merely respond to questions or stimuli; they generate the data and edit it via their communal participation.

Ethical issues include making the respondents feel comfortable in the data collection process so that their experience is positive. Every effort must be undertaken to ensure that the data collected are of high quality. Ethical issues also arise during data preparation, particularly the discarding of unsatisfactory respondents

∨ Companion Website

This textbook includes numerous student resources that can be found at **www.pearsonglobaleditions.com/malhotra**. At this Companion website, you'll find:

- Student Resource Manual
- Demo movies of statistical procedures using SPSS and Microsoft Excel
- Screen captures of statistical procedures using SPSS and Microsoft Excel
- Data files for all datasets in SPSS and Microsoft Excel
- Additional figures and tables
- Videos and write-ups for all video cases
- Other valuable resources

∨ Key Terms and Concepts

field work	coding	casewise deletion
field workers	codebook	pairwise deletion
probing	data cleaning	variable
sampling control	consistency	respecification
response rate	checks	standardization
editing	missing responses	recoding

∨ Suggested Cases and Video Cases

Running Case with Real Data and Questionnaire
1.1 Dell

Comprehensive Critical Thinking Cases
2.1 American Idol

Comprehensive Cases with Real Data and Questionnaires
3.1 JPMorgan Chase 3.2 Wendy's

Online Video Cases
10.1 Intel 11.1 Marriott 12.1 Marriott 13.1 Marriott

⌄ Live Research: Conducting a Marketing Research Project

1. The students conducting field work should be appropriately trained. Follow the guidelines in the chapter.
2. The team leaders can conduct fewer interviews but also act as supervisors. They should be trained in supervision.
3. The callback procedures should be specified. An example of such a procedure is the instruction to abandon a telephone number after three callback attempts.
4. If in-home interviews are to be conducted in the local area, each interviewer (student) can be assigned a specific part of a census track.
5. The project coordinators should number the questionnaires and keep track of any quotas.
6. The team leaders should be responsible for the initial editing of the questionnaires.
7. Each student should be responsible for coding her or his questionnaires and for data entry. It is recommended that the data be entered into an Excel spreadsheet using the coding scheme developed by the instructor or one of the teams.
8. The project coordinators should assemble all the student files into one data file, conduct the computer checks, and clean up the data.
9. The data analysis strategy should be specified by the instructor and discussed in class.

⌄ Acronyms

In the field work/data collection process, the organization VESTS the field workers with skills:

V alidation of field work

E valuation of field workers

S election of field workers

T raining of field workers

S upervision of field workers

The areas in which field workers should be trained may be summarized by the acronym TRAIN:

T erminating the interview

R ecording the answers

A sking the questions

I nitial contact development

N osy behavior: probing

The data preparation process may be summarized by the acronym DATA PREP:

D ata cleaning

A djusting the data statistically

T ranscribing

A nalysis strategy

P ost–field work questionnaire checking

R ecording numerical or alphanumerical values: coding

E diting

P reliminary plan of data analysis

∨ Review Questions

10-1. What options are available to researchers for collecting data?

10-2. Describe the field work/data collection process.

10-3. What are the guidelines for asking questions?

10-4. What is probing?

10-5. How can supervisors validate the field work of interviewers?

10-6. What aspects are involved in the supervision of field workers?

10-7. What is validation of field work? How is this done?

10-8. Describe the criteria that should be used for evaluating field workers.

10-9. Describe the data preparation process.

10-10. What activities are involved in the preliminary checking of questionnaires that have been returned from the field?

10-11. What is meant by editing a questionnaire?

10-12. How would you treat unsatisfactory responses that are discovered in editing?

10-13. Describe the guidelines for the coding of unstructured questions.

10-14. What is a codebook and what is it used for?

10-15. What options are available for the treatment of missing data?

10-16. When should the data preparation process start and why?

10-17. What considerations are involved in selecting a data analysis strategy?

10-18. Compare the field work in social media research to traditional field work.

∨ Applied Problems

10-19. Write some interviewer instructions for in-home personal interviews to be conducted by students. How would your instructions change if the survey is administered in social media?

10-20. Comment on the following field situations and make recommendations for corrective action.

    a. One of the interviewers has an excessive rate of refusals in in-home personal interviewing.

    b. In a CATI situation, many phone numbers are giving a busy signal during the first dialing attempt.

    c. An interviewer reports that, at the end of the interviews, many respondents asked if they had answered the questions correctly.

    d. While validating the field work, a respondent reports that she cannot remember being interviewed over the telephone, but the interviewer insists that the interview was conducted.

10-21. Shown below is part of a questionnaire used to determine consumer preferences for digital cameras. Set up a coding scheme for the following three questions (Q9, Q10, and Q11). Note that the first eight questions are not included.

Q9. Please rate the importance of the following features you would consider when shopping for a new digital camera.

		Not so important				Very important
a.	Megapixel	1	2	3	4	5
b.	F-stop	1	2	3	4	5
c.	Optical zoom	1	2	3	4	5
d.	Auto focus	1	2	3	4	5

Q10. If you were to buy a new digital camera, which of the following outlets would you visit? Please check as many as apply.

- **a.** _____ Drugstore
- **b.** _____ Camera store
- **c.** _____ Discount/mass merchandiser
- **d.** _____ Consumer electronics store
- **e.** _____ Internet stores/shopping sites
- **f.** _____ Other

Q11. Where do you get most of your photo processing done? Please check only one option.

- **a.** _____ Drugstore
- **b.** _____ Mini-labs
- **c.** _____ Camera stores
- **d.** _____ Discount/mass merchandiser
- **e.** _____ Consumer electronics store
- **f.** _____ Mail order/Internet
- **g.** _____ Kiosk/other

⌄ Internet Exercises

10-22. Visit the website of the marketing research company GMI (**http://www.gmi-mr.com/**) and write a brief report on the methods they use to ensure effective data processing for their clients.

10-23. Visit the website of Alpha Analytics (**www.alpha-analytics.com/home**). Briefly describe their data cleaning and validation techniques and how they are applied.

10-24. Design an electronic survey, using an online website, to determine if there is a relation between health awareness and purchasing organic food. Use the survey to determine if a difference in gender affects this relationship. Distribute the survey to a representative sample and write a report on the findings.

NOTES

1. **www.marketingresearch.org**, accessed January 10, 2013; Reg Baker, "Nobody's Talking," *Marketing Research: A Magazine of Management & Applications* 8(1) (Spring 1996): 22–24; "Study Tracks Trends in Refusal Rates," *Quirk's Marketing Research Review* (August–September 1989): 16–18, 42–43.
2. **www.haagendazs.com**, accessed January 17, 2013; David Kilburn, "Häagen-Dazs Is Flavor of Month," *Marketing Week* 20(23) (September 4, 1997): 30; and Mark Maremont, "They're All Screaming for Häagen-Dazs," *Business week* (October 14, 1991).
3. **www.gatech.edu**, accessed January 17, 2013; Society for New Communications Research, "Division: Academic, Category: Online Reputation Management, Georgia Institute of technology," Report, 2009.
4. **www.burke.com**, accessed February 12, 2013.

Online Video Case 10.1

INTEL: Building Blocks Inside Out

Visit **www.pearsonglobaleditions.com/malhotra** to read the video case and view the accompanying video. Intel: Building Blocks Inside Out demonstrates the critical role that marketing research has played in Intel's phenomenal growth. Marketing research was instrumental in developing the Intel brand, designing the "Intel Inside" campaign, and crafting the new logo with "Leap ahead" tag line. This case can be used as a springboard for students to analyze the field work process in a mall-intercept survey to determine consumer preferences for an ultra-light notebook that uses a newly designed chip. It also incorporates the data preparation process. Furthermore, it is a comprehensive case that also contains questions for the first nine chapters.

Data Analysis: Frequency Distribution, Hypothesis Testing, and Cross-Tabulation

∨ Overview

Once the data have been prepared for analysis (see Chapter 10), the researcher should conduct some basic analyses. Often, this involves computing frequency counts, percentages, and averages and constructing tables that examine the joint occurrence of different values of two variables. This chapter describes basic data analysis techniques, including frequency distribution, hypothesis testing, and cross-tabulation.

First, the chapter describes the frequency distribution of a single variable and explains how it provides an indication of the number of out-of-range, missing, or extreme values, as well as insight into the central tendency and variability of the underlying distribution. Next, a general procedure for hypothesis testing is presented. The use of cross-tabulation for understanding the associations between variables taken two at a time is then considered. Although the nature of the association can be observed from tables, statistics are available for testing the significance and strength of the association. Figure 11.1 briefly explains the step of the marketing research process on which this chapter concentrates.

Help for running the SPSS and Excel programs used in this chapter is provided in four ways: (1) detailed, step-by-step instructions are given later in the chapter; (2) you can download (from the Companion website for this book) computerized demonstration movies illustrating these step-by-step instructions; (3) you can download screen captures with notes illustrating these step-by-step instructions; and (4) you can refer to the Student Resource Manual that is posted on the Companion website for this book.

Many commercial marketing research projects do not go beyond basic data analysis. These findings are often displayed using tables and graphs, as discussed further in Chapter 13. Although the findings of basic analysis are valuable in their own right, the insights gained from the basic analysis are also invaluable in interpreting the results obtained from more sophisticated statistical techniques. Therefore, before conducting more advanced statistical analysis, it is useful to do some basic analysis. To provide you with a flavor of these techniques, we illustrate the use of frequency distribution.

Cross-tabulation still remains the most frequently used data analysis technique for marketers. However, cross-tabulation alone leaves a lot of information unexplored and does not exploit the predictive value of research. For that, you need to go beyond cross-tabulation to more sophisticated statistical techniques."

> **William Neal, Senior Executive Officer, SDR Consulting, Atlanta, Georgia**

∨ Learning Objectives

After reading this chapter, the student should be able to:

1. Understand why preliminary data analysis is desirable and the type of insights that can be obtained from such analysis.

2. Explain what is meant by frequency counts and what measures are associated with such analysis.

3. Describe the general procedure for hypothesis testing and the steps involved.

4. Discuss how cross-tabulation analysis should be conducted and the associated statistics.

5. Understand the chi-square statistic and the purpose for which it is used.

6. Discuss the other statistics used to assess the association between two variables and when these statistics are used.

7. Describe the SPSS and Excel programs available for conducting frequency and cross-tabulation analyses.

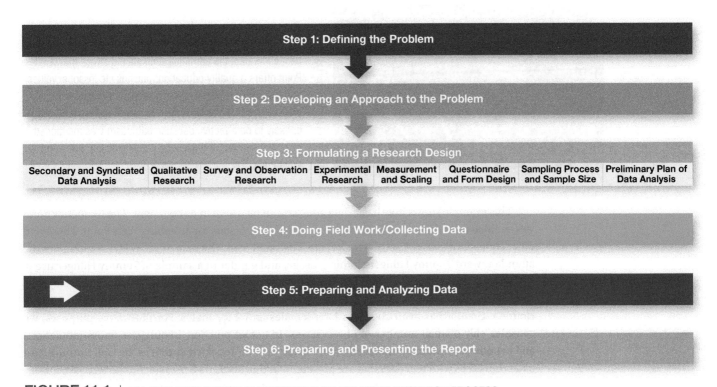

Step 1: Defining the Problem

Step 2: Developing an Approach to the Problem

Step 3: Formulating a Research Design

| Secondary and Syndicated Data Analysis | Qualitative Research | Survey and Observation Research | Experimental Research | Measurement and Scaling | Questionnaire and Form Design | Sampling Process and Sample Size | Preliminary Plan of Data Analysis |

Step 4: Doing Field Work/Collecting Data

Step 5: Preparing and Analyzing Data

Step 6: Preparing and Presenting the Report

FIGURE 11.1 | RELATIONSHIP OF THIS CHAPTER TO THE MARKETING RESEARCH PROCESS

Research in Practice
West Point: Patriotism, It Ain't

In a survey of 1,150 teens planning to attend college, 168 said they would consider attending the U.S. military academy at West Point. The frequency distribution of the main reason they would consider attending is given in the following table.

Reason	Number	Percentage
Quality education/academics	44	26
Teaches life lessons/values/discipline	35	21
Prepare for career (military or otherwise)	34	20
Want to join the military	17	10
Patriotism	13	8
Excellent reputation	12	7
Other Reasons	13	8
Total	168	100

Source: Jon Arnold Images Ltd / Alamy

The number of applications to the U.S. military academy at West Point has been declining over the years. To recruit the best cadidates, the administration should stress that West Point offers a quality education; teaches life lessons, values, and discipline; and will prepare cadets for a career of their choice. A patriotic appeal, such as those used in the past, is unlikely to be effective because patriotism was mentioned by only 8 percent of those who would consider attending West Point.[1] **<**

This example shows how basic data analysis can be useful in its own right. The frequency analysis enabled us to draw specific conclusions about the reasons for attending West Point. These and other concepts discussed in this chapter are illustrated using the data of Table 11.1, which gives the attitude toward Tommy Hilfiger clothing, usage, and gender of a sample of Tommy Hilfiger users. Attitude is measured on a 7-point Likert-type scale (1 = very unfavorable, 7 = very favorable). The users have been coded as 1, 2, or 3, representing light, medium, or heavy users of Tommy Hilfiger clothing. Gender has been coded as 1 for females and 2 for males. For illustrative purposes, we consider only a small number of observations. In actual practice, frequencies, cross-tabulations and hypotheses tests are performed on much larger samples, such as that in the Dell running case and other cases with real data that are presented in this book. As a first step in the analysis, it is often useful to examine the frequency distributions of the relevant variables.

FREQUENCY DISTRIBUTION

Marketing researchers often need to answer questions about a single variable, for example:

- What percentage of the market consists of heavy users, medium users, light users, and nonusers?
- What is the income distribution of brand users? Is this distribution skewed toward low-income brackets?

Table 11.1 > Usage and Attitude Toward Tommy Hilfiger

SPSS Data File

Excel Data File

No	User Group	Sex	Attitude
1.	3	2	7
2.	1	1	2
3.	1	1	3
4.	3	2	6
5.	3	2	5
6.	2	2	4
7.	2	1	5
8.	1	1	2
9.	2	2	4
10.	1	1	3
11.	3	2	6
12.	3	2	6
13.	1	1	2
14.	3	2	6
15.	1	2	4
16.	1	2	3
17.	3	1	7
18.	2	1	6
19.	1	1	1
20.	3	1	5
21.	3	2	6
22.	2	2	2
23.	1	1	1
24.	3	1	6
25.	1	2	3
26.	2	2	5
27.	3	1	7
28.	2	1	5
29.	1	1	9
30.	2	2	5
31.	1	2	1
32.	1	2	4
33.	2	1	3
34.	2	1	4
35.	3	1	5
36.	3	1	6
37.	3	2	6
38.	3	2	5
39.	3	2	7
40.	1	1	4
41.	1	1	2
42.	1	1	1
43.	1	1	2
44.	1	1	3
45.	1	1	1

FIGURE 11.2
CONDUCTING FREQUENCY
ANALYSIS

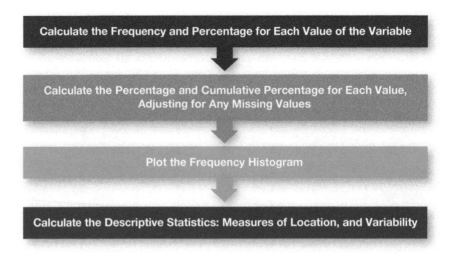

frequency distribution

A mathematical distribution with the objective of obtaining a count of the number of responses associated with different values of one variable and to express these counts in percentage terms.

The answers to these kinds of questions can be determined by examining frequency distributions. In a **frequency distribution**, one variable is considered at a time. The objective is to obtain a count of the number of responses associated with different values of the variable. The relative occurrence, or relative frequency, of different values of the variable is expressed in percentages, as in the first Research in Practice in this chapter about West Point. A frequency distribution for a variable produces a table of frequency counts, percentages, and cumulative percentages for all the values associated with that variable. The steps involved in conducting frequency analysis are given in Figure 11.2.

Table 11.2 provides the frequency distribution of attitude toward Tommy Hilfiger clothing based on Table 11.1 and obtained by using a statistical package (SPSS or Excel). In this table, the first column contains the labels assigned to the different categories of the variable. The second column (Value) indicates the code or value assigned to each label or category. The third column (Frequency) gives the number of respondents for each value, including the missing values.

For example, of the forty-five respondents who participated in the Tommy Hilfiger survey, six have a value of 2, denoting an unfavorable attitude. One respondent did not answer and thus has a missing value, denoted by 9. The fourth column (Percentage) displays the percentage of respondents checking each value. These percentages are obtained by dividing the frequencies in column 3 by 45. The next column (Valid Percentage) shows percentages calculated by excluding the cases with missing values, in this example, by dividing the frequencies in column 3 by

SPSS Output File

Excel Output File

Table 11.2 > Frequency Distribution of Attitude Toward Tommy Hilfiger

Value Label	Value	Frequency	Percentage	Valid Percentage	Cumulative Percentage
Very unfavorable	1	5	11.1	11.4	11.4
	2	6	13.3	13.6	25.0
	3	6	13.3	13.6	38.6
	4	6	13.3	13.6	52.3
	5	8	17.8	18.2	70.5
	6	9	20.0	20.5	90.9
Very favorable	7	4	8.9	9.1	100.0
Missing	9	1	2.2	Missing	
	Total	**45**	**100.0**	**100.0**	

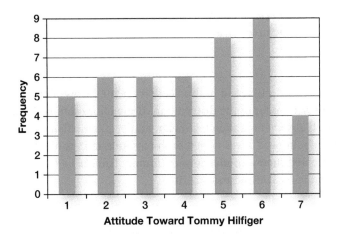

FIGURE 11.3
FREQUENCY HISTOGRAM

SPSS Output File

Excel Output File

44 (i.e., 45 − 1). As can be seen, eight respondents (18.2 percent) have an attitude value of 5. If there were no missing values, columns 4 and 5 would be identical. The last column represents cumulative percentages after adjusting for missing cases. The cumulative percentage for a value denotes the percentage of responses that are less than or equal to that value. The cumulative percentage corresponding to the value of 5 is 70.5 percent. In other words, 70.5 percent of the respondents have a value of 5 or less. The data of Table 11.1, as well as the SPSS and Excel outputs, with explanatory notes, can be downloaded from the Companion website for this book.

A frequency distribution helps determine the extent of illegitimate responses. Values of 0 and 8 would be illegitimate responses, or errors. The cases with these values can be identified and corrective action can be taken. The presence of *outliers*, cases with extreme values, can also be detected. In the case of a frequency distribution of household size, a few isolated families with household sizes of nine or more might be considered outliers. A frequency distribution also indicates the shape of the empirical distribution of the variable. The frequency data can be used to construct a histogram, or a vertical bar chart, in which the values of the variable are portrayed along the *x*-axis and the absolute or relative frequencies of the values are placed along the *y*-axis.

Figure 11.3 is a histogram of the attitude data in Table 11.2. From the histogram, one can examine whether the observed distribution is consistent with an expected or assumed distribution. Because numbers are involved, a frequency distribution can be used to calculate descriptive or summary statistics. Some of the statistics associated with frequency distribution are discussed in the next section. The first Research in Practice feature in this chapter provided an illustration of frequency analysis in determining the motivations for attending the U.S. military academy at West Point.

Research Recipe

A frequency distribution considers one variable at a time and produces a table of frequency counts, percentages, and cumulative percentages for all the values associated with that variable. A frequency distribution indicates the shape of the empirical distribution of the variable and helps you to determine the extent of illegitimate responses and the presence of outliers.

STATISTICS ASSOCIATED WITH FREQUENCY DISTRIBUTION

As illustrated in the previous section, a frequency distribution is a convenient way of looking at the values of a variable. A frequency table is easy to read and provides basic information, but sometimes this information might be too detailed and the researcher must summarize it by the use of descriptive statistics. The most commonly used statistics associated with frequencies are measures of location (mean, mode, and median) and measures of variability (range and standard deviation).

Measures of Location

measures of location
A statistic that describes a location within a data set. Measures of central tendency describe the center of the distribution.

The **measures of location** discussed in this section are measures of central tendency because they tend to describe the center of the distribution. If the entire sample is changed by adding a fixed constant to each observation, then the mean, mode, and median change by the same fixed amount. Suppose the number 10 was added to the attitude ratings of all the $(45 - 1 = 44)$ respondents who expressed their attitudes toward Tommy Hilfiger in Table 11.1. In this case, the mean, mode, and median will all increase by 10.

mean
A measure of central tendency given as the average; that value obtained by summing all elements in a set and dividing by the number of elements.

MEAN   The **mean**, or average value, is the most commonly used measure of central tendency or center of a distribution. It is used to estimate the average when the data have been collected using an interval or ratio scale (see Chapter 7). The data should display some central tendency, with most of the responses distributed around the mean.

The mean, $\overline{X}$, is given by

$$\overline{X} = \sum_{i=1}^{n} X_i / n$$

where

X_i = observed values of the variable X

n = number of observations (sample size)

Thus, to calculate the mean, we sum all the observed values of the variable and divide by the number of observations. Generally, the mean is a robust measure and does not change markedly as data values are added or deleted. For the frequency counts given in Table 11.2, the mean value is calculated, using SPSS or Excel, as:

$$\overline{X} = 4.11$$

mode
A measure of central tendency given as the value that occurs the most in a sample distribution.

MODE   The **mode** is the value that occurs most frequently. It represents the highest peak of the distribution. The mode is a good measure of location when the variable is inherently categorical or has otherwise been grouped into categories. The mode in Table 11.2 is 6 because this value occurs with the highest frequency, that is, nine times (see also the histogram in Figure 11.3).

median
A measure of central tendency given as the value above which half of the values fall and below which half of the values fall.

MEDIAN   The **median** of a sample is the middle value when the data are arranged in ascending or descending rank order (see Chapter 7). If the number of data points is even, the median is usually estimated as the midpoint between the two middle values—by adding the two middle values and dividing their sum by 2. The middle value is the value where 50 percent of the values are greater than that value, and 50 percent are less. Thus, the median is the 50th percentile. The median is an appropriate measure of central tendency for ordinal data. In Table 11.2, the middle value is the average of the twenty-second and twenty-third observations when the data are arranged in ascending or descending order. This average is 4, and so the median is 4. The median can be determined easily by using cumulative percentages in the frequency table. Note that at a value of 4, the cumulative percentage is 52.3 percent, but for a value of 3, it is 38.6 percent. Therefore, the 50 percent point occurs at the value of 4.

As you can see from Table 11.2, the three measures of central tendency for this distribution are different (mean = 4.11, mode = 6, median = 4). This is not surprising because each measure defines central tendency in a different way. The three values are equal only when the distribution is symmetric. In a symmetric distribution, the values are equally likely to plot on either side of the center of the distribution, and the mean, mode, and median are equal (see Figure 11.4).

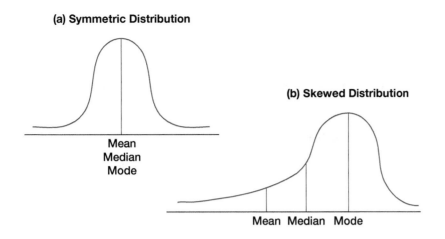

FIGURE 11.4

SYMMETRIC VERSUS
SKEWED DISTRIBUTIONS

An advantage of calculating all three measures of central tendency is that we can determine whether the distribution is symmetric or asymmetric. The asymmetry of the distribution of Table 11.2 can also be seen from the histogram of Figure 11.3.

If the distribution is asymmetric, which measure should be used? The answer depends on the level of measurement of the variable (see Chapter 7). If the variable is measured on a nominal scale, the mode should be used. If the variable is measured on an ordinal scale, the median is appropriate. If the variable is measured on an interval or ratio scale, the mode is a poor measure of central tendency. This can be seen from Table 11.2. Although the modal value of 6 has the highest frequency of nine, it represents only 20.5 percent of the sample. In general, for interval or ratio data, the median is a better measure of central tendency than the mode, although it, too, ignores available information about the variable. The actual values of the variable above and below the median are ignored. The mean is the most appropriate measure of central tendency for interval or ratio data. The mean makes use of all the information available because all of the values are used in computing it.

Measures of Variability

The **measures of variability** indicate the dispersion of a distribution. The most common, which are calculated on interval or ratio data, are the range, variance, and standard deviation.

measures of variability
Statistics that indicate the distribution's dispersion.

RANGE   The **range** measures the spread of the data. It is simply the difference between the largest and smallest values in the sample. As such, the range is directly affected by outliers.

range
The difference between the largest and smallest values of a distribution.

$$\text{Range} = X_{\text{largest}} - X_{\text{smallest}}$$

If all the values in the data are multiplied by a constant, the range is multiplied by the same constant. The range in Table 11.2 is $7 - 1 = 6$.

VARIANCE AND STANDARD DEVIATION   The difference between the mean and an observed value is called the *deviation from the mean*. The **variance** is the mean squared deviation from the mean, that is, the average of the square of the deviations from the mean for all the values. The variance can never be negative. When the data points are clustered around the mean, the variance is small. When the data points are scattered, the variance is large. The variance helps us to understand how similar or different the data points are. If the data points are similar, the variance is small and their distribution is clustered tightly around the mean. If the data points are very different in value, the variance is large and their distribution is spread more widely around the mean. If all the data values are multiplied by a constant, the variance is multiplied by the square of the constant.

variance
The mean squared deviation of all the values from the mean.

The **standard deviation** is the square root of the variance. Thus, the standard deviation is expressed in the same units as the data, whereas the variance is expressed in squared units. The standard deviation serves the same purpose as the variance in helping us to understand how clustered or spread the distribution is around the mean value.

standard deviation
The square root of the variance.

The standard deviation of a sample, s_x, is calculated as

$$s_x = \sqrt{\sum_{i=1}^{n} \frac{(X_i - \overline{X})^2}{n - 1}}$$

For the data given in Table 11.2, the sample variance is calculated, using SPSS or Excel, as:

$$s_x^2 = 3.59$$

The standard deviation, therefore, is calculated as

$$\text{Standard deviation} = s_x = \sqrt{3.59}$$
$$= 1.90$$

In contrast to the sample variance that is denoted by s^2, the population variance is denoted by σ^2 (see Table 11.3).

Research Recipe

The most commonly used measures of location associated with frequencies are mean, mode, and median. The three values are equal only when the distribution is symmetric. If the distribution is asymmetric, the appropriate measure of location depends on the level of measurement of the variable. If the variable is measured on a nominal scale, use the mode. If the variable is measured on an ordinal scale, the median is appropriate. If the variable is measured on an interval or ratio scale, use the mean because it is the most appropriate measure of central tendency. The most commonly used measures of variability are range and standard deviation, both assume the data are interval or ratio scaled.

 iResearch
Subway Customers: Who Are the Heavyweights?

As the marketing director for Subway, how would you target heavy users of fast-food restaurants?
   Visit **www.subway.com** and search the Internet, including social media as well as your library's online databases, to obtain information on the heavy users of fast-food restaurants. In a survey for Subway, information was obtained on the number of visits to Subway per month. How would you identify the heavy users of Subway, and what statistics would you compute to summarize the number of visits to Subway per month? <

Table 11.3 > Symbols for Population and Sample Variables

Variable	Population	Sample
Mean	μ	$\overline{X}$
Proportion	π	p
Variance	σ^2	s^2
Standard deviation	σ	s
Size	N	n
Standard error of the mean	$\sigma_{\overline{x}}$	$s_{\overline{x}}$
Standard error of the proportion	σ_p	s_p
Standardized variate (z)	$\dfrac{X - \mu}{\sigma}$	$\dfrac{X - \overline{X}}{s_x}$

INTRODUCTION TO HYPOTHESIS TESTING

Hypotheses were defined and illustrated in Chapter 2. Recall that hypotheses are unproven statements or propositions of interest to the researcher. Hypotheses are declarative and can be tested statistically. Often, hypotheses are possible answers to research questions. Basic analysis invariably involves some hypothesis testing. The following are examples of hypotheses generated in marketing research:

- The average number of computers owned is 1.8 per household.
- The department store is being patronized by more than 10 percent of the households.
- The heavy and light users of a brand differ in terms of psychographic characteristics.
- One hotel has a more upscale image than its close competitor.
- Familiarity with a restaurant results in greater preference for that restaurant.

The next section describes a general procedure for hypothesis testing that can be applied to test a wide range of hypotheses.

A GENERAL PROCEDURE FOR HYPOTHESIS TESTING

The following steps are involved in hypothesis testing (see Figure 11.5):

1. Formulate the null hypothesis H_0 and the alternative hypothesis H_1.
2. Select an appropriate statistical test and the corresponding test statistic.

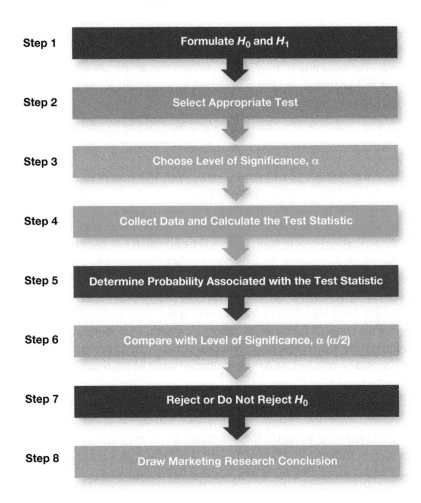

Step 1 Formulate H_0 and H_1

Step 2 Select Appropriate Test

Step 3 Choose Level of Significance, α

Step 4 Collect Data and Calculate the Test Statistic

Step 5 Determine Probability Associated with the Test Statistic

Step 6 Compare with Level of Significance, α ($\alpha/2$)

Step 7 Reject or Do Not Reject H_0

Step 8 Draw Marketing Research Conclusion

FIGURE 11.5

A GENERAL PROCEDURE FOR HYPOTHESIS TESTING

3. Choose the level of significance (α).
4. Determine the sample size and collect the data. Calculate the value of the test statistic.
5. Determine the probability associated with the test statistic calculated from the sample data under the null hypothesis.
6. Compare the probability associated with the test statistic with the appropriate level of significance based on the α value selected in Step 3.
7. Make the statistical decision to reject or not reject the null hypothesis.
8. Arrive at a conclusion. Express the statistical decision in terms of the marketing research problem.

Step 1: Formulating the Hypothesis

null hypothesis

A statement suggesting no expected difference or effect. If the null hypothesis is not rejected, no changes will be made.

The first step is to formulate the null and alternative hypotheses. A **null hypothesis** is a statement of the status quo, one of no difference or no effect. If the null hypothesis is not rejected, no changes will be made. An **alternative hypothesis** is one in which some difference or effect is expected. Accepting the alternative hypothesis leads to changes in opinions or actions. Thus, the alternative hypothesis is the opposite of the null hypothesis.

alternative hypothesis

A statement suggesting some difference or effect is expected. Accepting the alternative hypothesis leads to changes in opinions or actions.

The null hypothesis is always the hypothesis that is tested. The null hypothesis refers to a specified value of the population parameter (e.g., μ, σ, π), not a sample statistic (e.g., $\overline{X}$). Table 11.3 gives the symbols for the commonly used population and sample variables. A null hypothesis might be rejected, but it can never be accepted based on a single test. A statistical test can have one of two outcomes. One is that the null hypothesis is rejected and the alternative hypothesis is accepted. The other outcome is that the null hypothesis is not rejected based on the evidence. However, it would be incorrect to conclude that, because the null hypothesis is not rejected, it can be accepted as valid. In classical hypothesis testing, there is no way to determine whether the null hypothesis is true.[2]

In marketing research, the null hypothesis is formulated so that its rejection leads to the acceptance of the desired conclusion. The alternative hypothesis represents the conclusion for which evidence is sought. For example, Tommy Hilfiger is considering the introduction of a new return policy. The policy will be introduced if it is preferred by more than 40 percent of customers. The appropriate way to formulate the hypotheses is as follows:

$$H_0: \pi \leq 0.40$$

$$H_1: \pi > 0.40$$

where π denotes the proportion of customers in the population who prefer the new policy. Here, the null hypothesis H_0 is that the proportion of customers in the population who prefer the new policy is less than or equal to 0.40, whereas the alternative hypothesis H_1 is that the proportion of customers in the population who prefer the new policy is greater than 0.40. If the null hypothesis H_0 is rejected, then the alternative hypothesis H_1 will be accepted and the new return policy introduced. If H_0 is not rejected, however, the new return policy should not be introduced unless additional evidence is obtained.

one-tailed test

A test of the null hypothesis where the alternative hypothesis is expressed directionally.

The test of the null hypothesis is a **one-tailed test** because the alternative hypothesis is expressed directionally: The proportion of customers who express a preference is greater than 0.40. However, suppose the researcher wanted to determine whether the new return policy is different (superior or inferior) from the current policy, which is preferred by 40 percent of customers. Then a **two-tailed test** would be required, and the hypotheses would be expressed as

two-tailed test

A test of the null hypothesis where the alternative hypothesis is not expressed directionally but is bidirectional.

$$H_0: \pi = 0.40$$

$$H_1: \pi \neq 0.40$$

In commercial marketing research, the one-tailed test is used more often than a two-tailed test. Typically, there is some preferred direction for the conclusion for which evidence is sought. For example, the higher the profits, sales, and product quality, the better.

In the Tommy Hilfiger example considered here, the test is a one-sample test of proportion. The data would be collected from only one sample as illustrated in step 4.

Research Recipe

Always formulate the hypotheses so that the null hypothesis is a statement of the status quo, one of no difference or no effect. However, the alternative hypothesis should be one in which some difference or effect is expected; accepting the alternative hypothesis leads to changes in opinions or actions. Thus, the alternative hypothesis should be the opposite of the null hypothesis.

The null hypothesis is always the hypothesis that is tested, and it refers to a specified value of the population parameter (e.g., μ, σ, π), not a sample statistic (e.g., $\overline{X}$). If the alternative hypothesis is expressed directionally, use a one-tailed test. On the other hand, if the alternative hypothesis is bidirectional, use a two-tailed test.

Step 2: Selecting an Appropriate Test

To test the null hypothesis, it is necessary to select an appropriate statistical technique. The researcher should take into consideration how the test statistic is computed and the sampling distribution that the sample statistic (e.g., the mean) follows. The **test statistic** measures how close the sample has come to the null hypothesis. The test statistic often follows a well-known distribution, such as the normal, t, or chi-square distribution. Guidelines for selecting an appropriate test or statistical technique are discussed later in this chapter, as well as in Chapter 12.

In our Tommy Hilfiger example, the z statistic, which follows the standard normal distribution, would be appropriate. The **normal distribution** is bell-shaped and symmetrical. Its mean, median, and mode are identical. This statistic, used to conduct the **z test** that is based on the standard normal distribution, would be computed as follows for proportions:

$$z = \frac{p - \pi}{\sigma_p}$$

where p denotes the proportion of customers in the sample who prefer the new return policy, π is the proportion in the population under the null hypothesis, and σ_p is the standard deviation that is given by:

$$\sigma_p = \sqrt{\frac{\pi(1 - \pi)}{n}}$$

Note that the formula for z is essentially the formula for standardization discussed in Chapter 10.

test statistic
A measure of how close the sample has come to the null hypothesis. It often follows a well-known distribution, such as the normal, t, or chi-square distribution.

normal distribution
The normal distribution is bell-shaped and symmetric. Its measures of central tendency are identical.

z test
A hypothesis test using the standard normal distribution.

Step 3: Choosing Level of Significance

Whenever an inference is made about a population, there is a risk that an incorrect conclusion will be reached. Two types of error can occur.

TYPE I ERROR   **Type I error** occurs when the sample results lead to the rejection of the null hypothesis when it is, in fact, true. In our example, a type I error would occur if we concluded, based on the sample data, that the proportion of customers preferring the new return policy was greater than 0.40 when, in fact, it was less than or equal to 0.40. The probability of type I error (α) is also called the **level of significance**. The type I error is controlled by establishing the tolerable level of risk of rejecting a true null hypothesis. The selection of a particular risk level should depend on the cost of making a type I error. Typically, a value of 0.05 is selected for α.

type I error
An error that occurs when the sample results lead to the rejection of a null hypothesis that is, in fact, true. Also known as alpha *(α) error.*

level of significance
The probability of making a type I error, denoted by α.

type II error

An error that occurs when the sample results lead to nonrejection of a null hypothesis that is, in fact, false. Also known as beta (β) error.

power of a test

The probability of rejecting the null hypothesis when it is, in fact, false and should be rejected. It is (1 − β).

TYPE II ERROR **Type II error** occurs when the sample results do not lead to the rejection of the null hypothesis when it is, in fact, false. In our example, the type II error would occur if we concluded, based on sample data, that the proportion of customers preferring the new return policy was less than or equal to 0.40 when, in fact, it was greater than 0.40. The probability of type II error is denoted by β. Unlike α, which is specified by the researcher, the magnitude of β depends on the actual value of the population parameter (i.e., mean or proportion). The complement of the probability of a type II error, $(1 − β)$, is called the **power of a test**. It is the probability of rejecting the null hypothesis when it is, in fact, false and should be rejected.

Research Recipe

Type I error occurs if the sample results lead to the rejection of the null hypothesis when it is, in fact, true. The probability of type I error (α) is called the level of significance. Typically set α at 0.05. Type II error occurs if the null hypothesis is not rejected when it is, in fact, false. Its probability, β, depends on the actual value of the population parameter. The power of a test is $(1 − β)$.

Step 4: Data Collection

Sample size is determined as explained in Chapter 9. The required data are collected and the value of the test statistic computed. In our example, suppose 500 customers were surveyed and 220 expressed a preference for the new return policy. Thus, the value of the sample proportion is $p = 220/500 = 0.44$.

The value of σ_p can be determined as follows:

$$\sigma_p = \sqrt{\frac{\pi(1 − \pi)}{n}}$$

$$= \sqrt{\frac{(0.40)(0.6)}{500}}$$

$$= 0.0219$$

The test statistic z can be calculated as follows:

$$z = \frac{p − \pi}{\sigma_p}$$

$$= \frac{0.44 − 0.40}{0.0219}$$

$$= 1.83$$

Step 5: Determining the Probability

Using standard normal tables, the probability of obtaining a z value of 1.83 can be calculated as 0.0336 (see Figure 11.6). Most computer programs, including SPSS and Excel, automatically calculate this value. It is also called the **p value** and is the probability of observing a value of the test statistic as extreme as, or more extreme than, the value actually observed, assuming that the null hypothesis is true. Some statistical packages refer to the p value as $\leq$ PROB or PROB $=$.

p value

The probability of observing a value of the test statistic as extreme as, or more extreme than, the value actually observed, assuming that the null hypothesis is true.

Steps 6 and 7: Comparing the Probability and Making the Decision

The probability associated with the calculated or observed value of the test statistic calculated from the sample data is 0.0336. This is the probability of getting a p value of 0.44 when $\pi = 0.40$. This is less than the level of significance of 0.05. Hence, the null hypothesis is rejected. Note that, in a one-tailed test, if the probability associated with the calculated or observed value of the

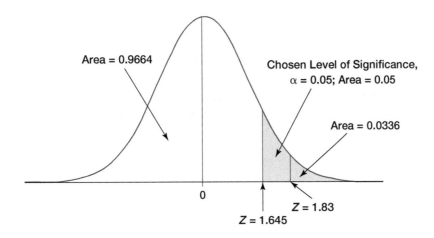

FIGURE 11.6

PROBABILITY OF *Z* WITH
A ONE-TAILED TEST

test statistic is *less than* the level of significance (α), the null hypothesis is rejected because the rejection region for rejecting the null hypothesis lies in only one direction (Figure 11.7[a]). In a two-tailed test, however, the alternative hypothesis is not directional but rather is bidirectional. Hence, in a two-tailed test, if the probability associated with the calculated or observed value of the test statistic is *less than* the level of significance divided by two ($\alpha/2$), the null hypothesis is rejected (Figure 11.7[b]). Hence, a two-tailed test is more conservative than the corresponding one-tailed test. If a hypothesis is rejected using a two-tailed test, then it will also be rejected using the corresponding one-tailed test. Logically, if the probability associated with the calculated or observed value of the test statistic is *less than* $\alpha/2$, it is also *less than* α. This can also be seen from Figure 11.7.

Research Recipe

In a one-tailed test, if the probability associated with the calculated or observed value of the test statistic is *less than* the level of significance (α), reject the null hypothesis. In a two-tailed test, however, if the probability associated with the calculated or observed value of the test statistic is *less than* the level of significance divided by two ($\alpha/2$), then reject the null hypothesis. Thus, if a hypothesis is rejected using a two-tailed test, then it will also be rejected using the corresponding one-tailed test.

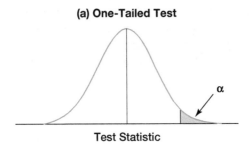

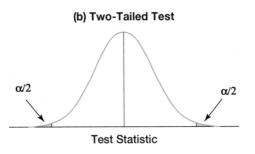

Step 8: Marketing Research Conclusion

The conclusion reached by hypothesis testing must be expressed in terms of the marketing research problem and the managerial action that should be taken. In our example, we conclude that there is evidence that the proportion of customers preferring the new return policy is significantly greater than 0.40. Hence, the recommendation would be to introduce the new return policy. Another illustration of hypothesis testing is provided by the Research in Practice about Holiday Inn.

Research in Practice
Holiday Inn: The "In" Thing

The Holiday Inn hotel chain is part of the InterContinental Hotels Group (IHG). As of 2014, IHG (**www.ihg.com**) had more than 4,150 hotels in almost 100 countries around the world. Although IHG has a room capacity of 18.8 million rooms, it holds only 3 percent of the market share. In an attempt to increase its market share, IHG was considering opening other hotel chains for middle-class hotel customers that would have more stylish rooms. Management analysis indicated that this would be feasible if more than 20 percent of the target customers preferred stylish rooms. The following hypotheses were formulated:

$$H_0: \pi \leq 0.20$$
$$H_1: \pi > 0.20$$

Note that this is a one-tailed test. IHG recruited TNS (**www.tnsglobal.com**) to survey 14,000 travelers on three continents. The findings of this study showed that a surprising 40 percent of middle-class hotel customers cared about style and design in their hotel rooms, leading to the rejection of the null hypothesis.

In response to this finding, IHG introduced a few different kinds of "branded" hotels, such as Holiday Indigo, Nickelodeon Family Suites, Holiday Inn Sunspree Resorts, and Holiday Inn Garden Court. The main aim of these chains is to capitalize on mid-market customers who are willing to spend on luxury and service. Each chain is personalized and unique, fighting against the "sea of sameness" into which the hotel industry has sunk. By conducting hypothesis testing, IHG has discovered the needs of its customers in a changing market. It will be able to cater to these needs and differentiate its hotels to stand above the competition.[3] ◂

Source: BirchTree / Alamy

A CLASSIFICATION OF HYPOTHESIS-TESTING PROCEDURES

Hypotheses testing can be related to either an examination of associations or an examination of differences (see Figure 11.8). In tests of associations, the null hypothesis is that there is no association between the variables (H_0: ... is *not* related to...). In tests of differences, the null hypothesis is that there is no difference (H_0: ... is *not* different from...). Tests of differences could relate to means or proportions. First, we discuss hypotheses related to associations in the context of cross-tabulations.

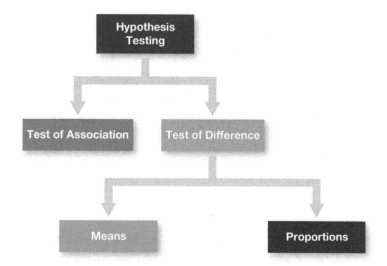

FIGURE 11.8

A BROAD CLASSIFICATION OF HYPOTHESIS-TESTING PROCEDURES

CROSS-TABULATION

Although answers to questions related to a single variable are interesting, they often raise additional questions about how to link that variable to other variables. To introduce the frequency distribution, we posed two representative marketing research questions. For each of these, a researcher might pose additional questions to relate these variables to other variables. For example:

- Is product use (measured in terms of heavy users, medium users, light users, and nonusers) related to interest in outdoor activities (high, medium, and low)?
- Is the income (high, medium, and low) of brand users related to the geographic region in which they live (north, south, east, and west)?

The answers to such questions can be determined by examining cross-tabulations. Whereas a frequency distribution describes one variable at a time, a **cross-tabulation** describes two or more variables simultaneously. Cross-tabulation results in tables that reflect the joint distribution of two or more variables with a limited number of categories or distinct values. The categories of one variable are cross-classified with the categories of one or more other variables. Thus, the frequency distribution of one variable is subdivided according to the values or categories of the other variables. Note that cross-tabulation examines association between variables, not causation. To examine causation, the causal research design framework should be adopted (see Chapters 3 and 6).

cross-tabulation
A statistical technique that describes two or more variables simultaneously and results in tables that reflect the joint distribution of two or more variables that have a limited number of categories or distinct values.

Suppose Tommy Hilfiger was interested in determining whether gender was associated with the degree of usage of Tommy Hilfiger clothing. In Table 11.1, the respondents were divided into three categories of light (denoted by 1), medium (2), or heavy users (3) of Tommy Hilfiger clothing based on reported usage. There were nineteen light users, ten medium users, and sixteen heavy users. Although data on attitude were missing for one respondent, information on usage and gender was available for all respondents. Gender was coded as 1 for females and 2 for males. The sample included twenty-four females and twenty-one males.

The cross-tabulation is shown in Table 11.4. A cross-tabulation includes a cell for every combination of the categories of the two variables. The number in each cell shows how many respondents gave that combination of responses. In Table 11.4, fourteen respondents were females and light users. The marginal totals (column totals and row totals) in this table indicate that, of the forty-five respondents with valid responses on both the variables, nineteen were light users, ten were medium users, and sixteen were heavy users, confirming the classification procedure adopted.

SPSS Output File

Excel Output File

Table 11.4 > A Cross-Tabulation of Gender and Usage of Tommy Hilfiger Clothing

USAGE	GENDER		Row Total
	Female	Male	
Lights Users	14	5	19
Medium Users	5	5	10
Heavy Users	5	11	16
Column Total	24	21	

contingency table
A cross-tabulation table; it contains a cell for every combination of categories of the two variables.

bivariate cross-tabulation
A cross-tabulation with two variables.

Twenty-one respondents were males and twenty-four were females. Note that this information could have been obtained from a separate frequency distribution for each variable. In general, the margins of a cross-tabulation show the same information as the frequency tables for each of the variables. Cross-tabulation tables also are called **contingency tables**. We will discuss cross-tabulation for two variables, the most common form in which this procedure is used.

Cross-tabulation with two variables is also known as **bivariate cross-tabulation**. Consider again the cross-classification of gender and usage of Tommy Hilfiger clothing given in Table 11.4. Is usage of Tommy Hilfiger clothing related to gender? It might be. We see from Table 11.4 that disproportionately more of the males are heavy users and disproportionately more of the females are light users. Computation of percentages can provide more insights.

Because two variables have been cross-classified, percentages could be computed either column-wise, based on column totals (see Table 11.5), or row-wise, based on row totals (see Table 11.6).

Which of these tables is more useful? The answer depends on which variable will be considered as the independent variable and which as the dependent variable. The general rule is to compute the percentages in the direction of the independent variable, across the dependent variable. In our analysis, gender would be considered as the independent variable and usage as the dependent variable. Therefore, the correct way of calculating percentages is as shown in Table 11.5. Note

SPSS Output File

Excel Output File

Table 11.5 > Usage of Tommy Hilfiger Clothing by Gender

USAGE	GENDER	
	Female	Male
Light Users	58.4%	23.8%
Medium Users	20.8%	23.8%
Heavy Users	20.8%	52.4%
Column Total	100.0%	100.0%

SPSS Output File

Excel Output File

Table 11.6 > Gender by Usage of Tommy Hilfiger Clothing

USAGE	GENDER		Row Total
	Female	Male	
Light Users	73.7%	26.3%	100.0%
Medium Users	50.0%	50.0%	100.0%
Heavy Users	31.2%	68.8%	100.0%

that, although 52.4 percent of the males are heavy users, only 20.8 percent of females are heavy users. This seems to indicate that, compared to females, males are more likely to be heavy users of Tommy Hilfiger clothing. The recommendation to management might be to promote more heavily to women to increase their usage rate or to promote more heavily to men to prevent brand loyalty erosion. Obviously, additional variables would need to be analyzed before management would act on such variables. Nevertheless, this illustrates how hypotheses testing should be linked to recommended managerial actions.

Note that computing percentages in the direction of the dependent variable across the independent variable, as shown in Table 11.6, is not meaningful in this case. Table 11.6 implies that heavy usage of Tommy Hilfiger clothing causes people to be males, which obviously is not meaningful. The corresponding SPSS and Excel outputs for this cross-tabulation with explanatory notes can be downloaded from the website for this book. As another example, consider the study of older models in the Research in Practice feature that follows.

Research in Practice
Old Is Gold, but Some Marketers Treat It as Dust

A study examined whether older models are depicted in a negative light in TV commercials. Television commercials emanating from the three major networks, one local station, and five cable companies were analyzed by the researchers. The results were as follows in terms of the number and percentage of models of different age groups that were depicted in a positive or negative light:

Depiction of the Model	Age of the Model (Years)					
	Under 45		45–64		65 and over	
	Number	Percentage	Number	Percentage	Number	Percentage
Positive Depiction	415	83.1	64	66.0	28	54.0
Negative Depiction	85	16.9	33	34.0	24	46.0
Total	500	100	97	100	52	100

Note that as the age of the model increases, the percentages in the negative-depiction column increase. Therefore, the study concluded that older models do tend to be depicted in a negative manner. Thus, some marketers might be pursuing self-defeating strategies by depicting older consumers unfavorably. Marketers should note that older consumers represent a large and growing segment that controls substantial income and wealth.[4] ‹

Source: Advertising Archives

> ### Research Recipe
>
> A cross-tabulation describes two or more variables simultaneously and results in tables that reflect the joint distribution of two or more variables with a limited number of categories or distinct values. Cross-tabulation examines association between variables, not causation, and the pattern of the association can be interpreted by calculating percentages. Compute the percentages in the direction of the independent variable, across the dependent variable.

STATISTICS ASSOCIATED WITH CROSS-TABULATION

This section focuses on the statistics commonly used for assessing the statistical significance and strength of association of cross-tabulated variables. The statistical significance of the observed association is commonly measured by the chi-square statistic, which is discussed first. The strength of association, or degree of association, is important from a practical or managerial perspective. Generally, the strength of an association is of interest only if the association is statistically significant. The strength of the association can be measured by the phi correlation coefficient, the contingency coefficient, and Cramer's *V*.

Chi-Square

chi-square statistic
The statistic used to test the statistical significance of the observed association in a cross-tabulation. It assists in determining whether a systematic association exists between the two variables.

The **chi-square statistic** (χ^2) is used to test the statistical significance of the observed association in a cross-tabulation. It can be used in determining whether a systematic association exists between two variables. The null hypothesis, H_0, is that there is no association between the variables. The statistical software you use will automatically calculate the value of the chi-square statistic.

To determine whether a systematic association exists, the probability of obtaining a value of chi-square as large as or larger than the one calculated from the cross-tabulation is estimated (see Step 5 in Figure 11.5). An important characteristic of the chi-square statistic is the number of degrees of freedom (df) associated with it. Unlike the normal distribution, the **chi-square distribution** is a skewed distribution, the shape of which depends solely on the number of degrees of freedom (Figure 11.9). As the number of degrees of freedom increases, the chi-square distribution becomes more symmetrical. In the case of a chi-square statistic associated with a cross-tabulation, the number of degrees of freedom is equal to the product of the number of rows (*r*) less one and the number of columns (*c*) less one. That is, df $= (r - 1) \times (c - 1)$. The null hypothesis (H_0) of no association between the two variables will be rejected only when the probability associated with the test statistic is less than the significance level (α), given the appropriate degrees of freedom, as shown in Figure 11.9. (See Steps 6 and 7 in Figure 11.5.)

chi-square distribution
A skewed distribution whose shape depends solely on the number of degrees of freedom. As the number of degrees of freedom increases, the chi-square distribution becomes more symmetrical.

For the cross-tabulation given in Table 11.4, there are $(3 - 1) \times (2 - 1) = 2$ degrees of freedom. The calculated chi-square statistic has a value of 6.33, and the associated probability is

FIGURE 11.9
CHI-SQUARE TEST OF ASSOCIATION

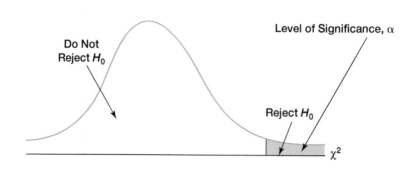

0.042 (determined by SPSS or Excel). Because the associated probability is less than 0.05, the null hypothesis of no association is rejected, indicating that the association is statistically significant at the 0.05 level.

The chi-square statistic should be estimated only on counts of data. When the data are in percentage form, they should first be converted to absolute counts or numbers. Normally, the strength of association is not meaningful and hence is not calculated when the null hypothesis of no association is not rejected. If there is no relationship between the two variables, there can be no strength. If the association is statistically significant, as determined by the chi-square test, the strength of the association can be measured by the phi correlation coefficient, the contingency coefficient, or Cramer's *V*.

Phi Coefficient

The **phi coefficient** (ϕ) is used as a measure of the strength of association in the special case of a table with two rows and two columns (a 2 × 2 table). It takes the value of 0 when there is no association, which would be indicated by a chi-square value of 0 as well. When the variables are perfectly associated, phi assumes the value of 1, and all the observations fall just on the main or minor diagonal. (In some computer programs, phi assumes a value of –1 rather than 1 when there is perfect negative association.) In the more general case involving a table of any size, the strength of association can be assessed by using the contingency coefficient.

phi coefficient
A measure of the strength of association in the special case of a table with two rows and two columns (a 2 × 2 table).

Contingency Coefficient

The phi coefficient is specific to a 2 × 2 table; the **contingency coefficient** (*C*) can be used to assess the strength of association in a table of any size. The contingency coefficient varies between 0 and 1. The 0 value occurs in the case of no association (i.e., the variables are statistically independent), but the maximum value of 1 is never achieved. Rather, the maximum value of the contingency coefficient depends on the size of the table (number of rows and number of columns). For this reason, it should be used only to compare tables of the same size.

contingency coefficient
A measure of the strength of association in a table of any size, whose maximum value depends on the size of the table.

In our case, the null hypothesis was rejected; thus, it is meaningful to calculate the contingency coefficient. The value of the contingency coefficient for Table 11.4 is 0.351, as determined by using SPSS or Excel. This value of *C* indicates that the association is low to moderate.

Cramer's V

Cramer's *V* is a modified version of the phi correlation coefficient, ϕ, and is used in tables larger than 2 × 2. When phi is calculated for a table larger than 2 × 2, it has no upper limit. Cramer's *V* is obtained by adjusting phi such that *V* ranges from 0 to 1. A large value of *V* merely indicates a high degree of association. It does not indicate how the variables are associated. As a rule of thumb, values of *V* below 0.3 indicate low association, values between 0.3 and 0.6 indicate low to moderate association, and values above 0.6 indicate strong association.

Cramer's *V*
A measure of the strength of association used in tables larger than 2 × 2, whose value ranges from 0 to 1.

The value of Cramer's *V* for Table 11.4 is 0.375. Thus, the association is low to moderate.

Given that the null hypothesis was rejected and we have determined the strength of association as low to moderate, we can interpret the pattern of relationship by looking at the percentages in Table 11.5. There is a low to moderate association between gender and usage of Tommy Hilfiger clothing. Males tend to be heavy users, whereas females tend to be light users.

CROSS-TABULATION IN PRACTICE

When conducting cross-tabulation analysis in practice, it is useful to follow these steps (see Figure 11.10):

1. Construct the cross-tabulation table.
2. Test the null hypothesis to see that there is no association between the variables using the chi-square statistic (see the procedure described in Figure 11.5).

FIGURE 11.10

HYPOTHESIS TESTING IN
CROSS-TABULATION

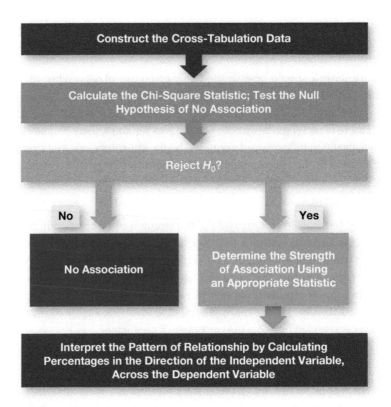

3. If you fail to reject the null hypothesis, there is no relationship.
4. If H_0 is rejected, determine the strength of the association using an appropriate statistic (phi-coefficient, contingency coefficient, or Cramer's V) as discussed earlier in this chapter.
5. If H_0 is rejected, interpret the pattern of the relationship by computing the percentages in the direction of the independent variable, across the dependent variable. Draw marketing conclusions.

Research Recipe

Use the chi-square statistic (χ^2) to test the statistical significance of the observed association in a cross-tabulation with the number of degrees of freedom equal to the product of the number of rows (r) less one and the number of columns (c) less one. That is, $df = (r - 1) \times (c - 1)$. If the null hypothesis of no association between the variables is rejected, then measure the strength of the association by the phi correlation coefficient, the contingency coefficient, or Cramer's V. Use the phi coefficient for a 2×2 table and Cramer's V for a larger table. Use the contingency coefficient only to compare tables of the same size.

iResearch
Analyzing Cosmetic Usage Is No Cosmetic Effort

Visit **www.loreal.com** and search the Internet, including social media as well as your library's online databases, to obtain information on the heavy users, light users, and nonusers of cosmetics. How would you analyze the data to determine whether the heavy users, light users, and nonusers of cosmetics differ in terms of demographic characteristics?

As the marketing director for L'Oréal, what marketing strategies would you adopt to reach the heavy users, light users, and nonusers of cosmetics? **<**

SOFTWARE APPLICATIONS

SPSS and Excel have programs for computing frequency distributions, performing cross-tabulations, and testing hypotheses. We discuss the use of these statistical packages to conduct frequency analysis and cross-tabulation in the following sections. Hypotheses testing for examining differences is discussed in Chapter 12.

SPSS and Excel Computerized Demonstration Movies

We have developed computerized demonstration movies that give step-by-step instructions for running all the SPSS and Excel programs that are discussed in this chapter. These demonstration movies can be downloaded from the Companion website for this book. The instructions for running these demonstration movies are given in Exhibit 10.1.

SPSS and Excel Screen Captures with Notes

The step-by-step instructions for running the various SPSS and Excel programs discussed in this chapter are also illustrated in screen captures with appropriate notes. These screen captures can be downloaded from the Companion website for this book.

SPSS WINDOWS

This section gives the detailed steps for running the SPSS programs for conducting the analysis discussed in this chapter.

Detailed Steps: Overview

Detailed step-by-step instructions and demonstrations for running the SPSS programs for the data analysis presented in this chapter can be downloaded from the Companion website for this book in two forms: (1) computerized demonstration movies and (2) screen captures with notes. You can also refer to the Student Resource Manual. In addition, these steps are illustrated in the following sections. These steps are given for IBM SPSS STATISTICS 20 and IBM SPSS STATISTICS 21; they are essentially the same in both of these versions. The steps in the earlier versions are about the same, with minor differences in the labeling of some of the boxes.

Detailed Steps: Frequencies

Detailed steps are presented for running frequencies on attitude toward Tommy Hilfiger (see Table 11.1) and for plotting the histogram (see Figure 11.3). Open the SPSS data file for Table 11.1.

1. Select ANALYZE on the SPSS menu bar.
2. Click DESCRIPTIVE STATISTICS, and select FREQUENCIES.
3. Move the variable "Attitude toward Tommy Hilfiger [attitude]" to the VARIABLE(S) box.
4. Click STATISTICS.
5. Select MEAN, MEDIAN, MODE, STD. DEVIATION, VARIANCE, and RANGE.
6. Click CONTINUE.
7. Click CHARTS.
8. Click HISTOGRAMS, then click CONTINUE.
9. Click OK.

Detailed Steps: Cross-Tabulations

We give detailed steps for running the cross-tabulation of gender and usage of Tommy Hilfiger clothing given in Table 11.4 and for calculating the chi-square, contingency coefficient, and Cramer's *V*. Open the SPSS data file for Table 11.1.

1. Select ANALYZE on the SPSS menu bar.
2. Click DESCRIPTIVE STATISTICS, and select CROSSTABS.
3. Move the variable "User Group [usergr]" to the ROW(S) box.
4. Move the variable "Sex [sex]" to the COLUMN(S) box.
5. Click CELLS.
6. Select OBSERVED under COUNTS, and select COLUMN under PERCENTAGES.
7. Click CONTINUE.
8. Click STATISTICS.
9. Click CHI-SQUARE, PHI, and CRAMER'S *V.*
10. Click CONTINUE.
11. Click OK.

EXCEL

This section gives the detailed steps for running the Excel programs for conducting the analysis discussed in this chapter.

Detailed Steps: Overview

Detailed step-by-step instructions and demonstrations for running the Excel programs for the data analysis presented in this chapter can be downloaded from the Companion website for this book in two forms: (1) computerized demonstration movies and (2) screen captures with notes. You can also refer to the Student Resource Manual. In addition, these steps are illustrated in the following sections. These steps are given for Excel 2007, Excel 2010, and Excel 2013; they are essentially the same in these versions. The steps in the earlier versions are about the same, with minor differences in how "Data Analysis" is accessed and the labeling of some of the boxes.

Detailed Steps: Frequencies

We give detailed steps for running frequencies on attitude toward Tommy Hilfiger (see Table 11.1) using Excel. Open the Excel data file for Table 11.1.

1. In column E, insert a new column labeled "BIN." Fill cells E2 to E8 with 1 to 7.
2. Select DATA tab.
3. In the ANALYSIS group, select DATA ANALYSIS.
4. The DATA ANALYSIS Window pops up.
5. Select HISTOGRAM from the DATA ANALYSIS Window.
6. Click OK.
7. The HISTOGRAM pop-up window appears on screen.
8. The HISTOGRAM window has two portions:
   a. INPUT
   b. OUTPUT OPTIONS
9. The INPUT portion asks for two inputs.
   a. Under INPUT, click in the INPUT RANGE box and select (highlight) all forty-five rows (cells D2 to D46) under ATTITUDE. "$D$2: $D$46" should appear in the input range box.
   b. In the BIN RANGE box, select (highlight) all seven rows (cells E2 to E8) under BIN. "$E$2:$E$8" should appear in the BIN RANGE box.

10. In the OUTPUT OPTIONS of the pop-up window, select the following options:
    a. NEW WORKBOOK
    b. CUMULATIVE PERCENTAGE
    c. CHART OUTPUT
11. Click OK.
12. Note that the default chart output size is very small. Click the histogram diagram and drag it on the corners to enlarge it so that you can see it better.

Detailed Steps: Cross-Tabulations

We show the detailed steps for running the cross-tabulation of sex and usage of Tommy Hilfiger clothing given in Table 11.4. Open the Excel data file for Table 11.1.

1. Select INSERT (Alt + N).
2. Click on PIVOT TABLE. The CREATE PIVOT TABLE window pops up.
3. Select columns A to D and rows 1 to 46; "$A$1:$D$46" should appear in the range box.
4. Select NEW WORKSHEET in the CREATE PIVOT TABLE window.
5. Click OK
6. Drag variables into the layout on the left in the following format:

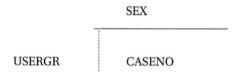

SEX

USERGR   CASENO

7. Right-click on SUM OF CASENO in the lower-right corner. Select "VALUE FIELD SETTINGS."
8. Under "SUMMARIZE VALUE FIELD BY" select COUNT.
9. Click OK.

Dell Running Case

Review the Dell case, Case 1.1 and questionnaire given toward the end of the book. Go to the Companion website for this book and download the Dell data file.

1. Calculate the frequency distribution for each variable in the data file. Examine the distribution to get a feel for the data.
2. Cross-tabulate the recoded questions: q4 (overall satisfaction with Dell), q5 (would recommend Dell), and q6 (likelihood of choosing Dell) with the recoded demographic characteristics. Interpret the results.
3. Cross-tabulate the recoded questions on price sensitivity (q9_5per (q9A) and q9_10per (q9B)) with the recoded demographic characteristics. Interpret the results.

Summary

Basic data analysis provides valuable insights and guides the rest of the data analysis as well as the interpretation of the results. A frequency distribution should be obtained for each variable in the data. This analysis produces a table of frequency counts, percentages, and cumulative percentages for all the values associated with that variable. It indicates the extent of out-of-range, missing, or extreme values. The mean, mode, and median of a frequency distribution are measures of central tendency. The variability of the distribution is described by the range and the variance or standard deviation.

The general procedure for hypothesis testing involves eight steps. Formulate the null and the alternative hypotheses, select an appropriate test statistic, choose the level of significance (α), calculate the value of the test statistic, and determine the probability associated with the test statistic calculated from the sample data under the null hypothesis. Compare the probability associated with the test statistic with the level of significance specified. Make the decision to reject or not reject the null hypothesis, and arrive at a marketing research conclusion.

Cross-tabulations are tables that reflect the joint frequency distribution of two or more variables. In cross-tabulation, the cell percentages can be computed either column-wise, based on column totals, or row-wise, based on row totals. The general rule is to compute the percentages in the direction of the independent variable, across the dependent variable. The chi-square statistic provides a test of the statistical significance of the observed association in a cross-tabulation. The phi coefficient, contingency coefficient, and Cramer's V provide measures of the strength of association between the variables.

∨ Companion Website

This textbook includes numerous student resources that can be found at **www.pearsonglobaleditions.com/malhotra**. At this Companion website, you'll find:

- Student Resource Manual
- Demo movies of statistical procedures using SPSS and Microsoft Excel
- Screen captures of statistical procedures using SPSS and Microsoft Excel
- Data files for all datasets in SPSS and Microsoft Excel
- Additional figures and tables
- Videos and write-ups for all video cases
- Other valuable resources

∨ Key Terms and Concepts

frequency distribution	alternative hypothesis	p value
measures of location	one-tailed test	cross-tabulation
mean	two-tailed test	contingency table
mode	test statistic	bivariate cross-tabulation
median	normal distribution	chi-square statistic
measures of variability	z test	chi-square distribution
range	type I error	phi coefficient
variance	level of significance	contingency coefficient
standard deviation	type II error	Cramer's V
null hypothesis	power of a test	

∨ Suggested Cases and Video Cases

Running Case with Real Data and Questionnaire
1.1 Dell

Comprehensive Cases with Real Data and Questionnaires
3.1 JPMorgan Chase   3.2 Wendy's

Online Video Cases
11.1 Marriott   12.1 Marriott   13.1 Marriott

⌄ Live Research: Conducting a Marketing Research Project

1. Each team can conduct the entire analysis, or the data analysis can be split between or among teams, with different teams conducting a different type of analysis. It is helpful to run a frequency count for every variable. This gives a good feel for the data.
2. Calculate the measures of location (mean, median, and mode) and measures of variability (range and standard deviation) for each variable.
3. Relevant associations can be examined by conducting cross-tabulations. Procedures should be specified for categorizing interval or ratio-scaled variables. In this process, it is helpful to examine the frequency distributions.

⌄ Acronyms

The statistics associated with frequencies can be summarized by the acronym FREQUENCIES:

F requency histogram

R ange

E stimate of location: mean

Q uotients: percentages

U ndulation: variance

E stimate of location: mode

N umbers or counts

C umulative percentage

I ncorrect and missing values

E stimate of location: median

S hape of the distribution

The salient characteristics of cross-tabulations can be summarized by the acronym TABULATE:

T wo variables at a time

A ssociation and not causation is measured

B ased on cell counts

U derstood easily by managers

L imited number of categories

A ssociated statistics

T wo ways to calculate percentages

E xamine pattern of relationship

✕ Review Questions

11-1. What is an advantage of calculating all three measures of central tendency?

11-2. Describe the procedure for computing frequencies.

11-3. What measures of location are commonly computed for frequencies?

11-4. Why is the range value affected by outliers?

11-5. What does the variance tell us about data points?

11-6. What is the difference between null and alternative hypothesis?

11-7. What is the general rule for computing percentages in cross-tabulation?

11-8. Briefly describe the test statistic.

11-9. Differentiate between Type I and Type II errors.

11-10. What statistics are available for determining the strength of association in cross-tabulation?

11-11. Discuss the reasons for the frequent use of cross-tabulations. What are some of its limitations?

✕ Applied Problems

11-12. In each of the following situations, formulate the null and alternative hypotheses.

    a. A new product will be introduced if it is preferred by more than 70 percent of the consumers in the target market.

    b. A new commercial will be aired if the average preference for it exceeds 5.8 on a 7-point scale.

    c. A company will start selling its products online if more than 55 percent of the consumers express a preference for online purchasing.

    d. The average price of a pair of jeans available in the marketplace exceeds $45.

    e. Less than 40 percent of the people approve of Barak Obama's presidency.

    f. The mean familiarity with banks is different than 4.0 on a 7-point scale.

11-13. In each of the following situations, indicate the statistical analysis you would conduct and the appropriate test or test statistic that should be used.

    a. Respondents in a survey of 1,000 households were classified as heavy, medium, light, or nonusers of ice cream. They also were classified as being in high-, medium-, or low-income categories. Is the consumption of ice cream related to income level?

    b. In a survey using a representative sample of 2,000 households from the TNS consumer panel, the respondents were asked whether they preferred to shop at Sears. The sample was divided into small and large households based on a median split of household size. Does preference for shopping in Sears vary by household size?

11-14. The current advertising campaign for a major soft-drink brand would be changed if less than 30 percent of the consumers like it.

    a. Formulate the null and alternative hypotheses.

    b. Discuss the type I and type II errors that could occur in hypothesis testing.

11-15. A major department store chain is having a sale on refrigerators. The number of refrigerators sold during this sale at a sample of ten stores was:

    80 110 0 40 70 80 100 50 80 30

    a. What are the mean, mode, and median? Which measure of central tendency is most appropriate in this case and why?

    b. What are the variance and the standard deviation?

    c. Construct a histogram, and discuss whether this variable is normally distributed.

11-16. In a study measuring households' familiarity with downloading pictures from the Internet, the following results were obtained (1 = not at all familiar, 7 = very familiar).

Level of Familiarity	Number of Households
1	22
2	26
3	34
4	40
5	32
6	28
7	18

    a. Convert the number of households into percentages.
    b. Calculate the cumulative percentages.
    c. Construct a histogram with familiarity on the *x*-axis and frequency on the *y*-axis.
    d. What are the mean, median, and mode of the distribution?

11-17. A research project examining the impact of income on the consumption of gourmet foods was conducted. Each variable was classified into three levels of high, medium, and low. The following results were obtained.

		Income		
		Low	Medium	High
Consumption of	Low	25	15	10
Gourmet	Medium	10	25	15
Foods	High	15	10	25

What is the pattern of the relationship between income and consumption of gourmet food?

11-18. A pilot survey was conducted with thirty respondents to examine Internet usage for personal (nonprofessional) reasons. The following table contains the resulting data giving each respondent's sex (1 = male, 2 = female); familiarity with the Internet (1 = very unfamiliar, 7 = very familiar); Internet usage in hours per week; attitude toward Internet and toward technology, both measured on a 7-point scale (1 = very unfavorable, 7 = very favorable); and whether the respondent shopped or banked online (1 = yes, 2 = no).

Respondent Number	Sex	Familiarity	Internet Usage	Attitude Toward Internet	Attitude Toward Technology	Usage of Internet: Shopping	Usage of Internet: Banking
			Internet Usage Data				
1	1	7	14	7	6	1	1
2	2	2	2	3	3	2	2
3	2	3	3	4	3	1	2
4	2	3	3	7	5	1	2
5	1	7	13	7	7	1	1
6	2	4	6	5	4	1	2
7	2	2	2	4	5	2	2
8	2	3	6	5	4	2	2
9	2	3	6	6	4	1	2
10	1	9	15	7	6	1	2

SPSS Data File

Excel Data File

(*Continued*)

				Attitude	Attitude	Usage of	Usage of
				Internet Usage Data			
Respondent Number	Sex	Familiarity	Internet Usage	Attitude Toward Internet	Attitude Toward Technology	Usage of Internet: Shopping	Usage of Internet: Banking
11	2	4	3	4	3	2	2
12	2	5	4	6	4	2	2
13	1	6	9	6	5	2	1
14	1	6	8	3	2	2	2
15	1	6	5	5	4	1	2
16	2	4	3	4	3	2	2
17	1	6	9	5	3	1	1
18	1	4	4	5	4	1	2
19	1	7	14	6	6	1	1
20	2	6	6	6	4	2	2
21	1	6	9	4	2	2	2
22	1	5	5	5	4	2	1
23	2	3	2	4	2	2	2
24	1	7	15	6	6	1	1
25	2	6	6	5	3	1	2
26	1	6	13	6	6	1	1
27	2	5	4	5	5	1	1
28	2	4	2	3	2	2	2
29	1	4	4	5	3	1	2
30	1	3	3	7	5	1	2

a. Obtain the frequency distribution of familiarity with the Internet. Calculate the relevant statistics.

b. For the purpose of cross-tabulation, classify respondents as light or heavy users. Those reporting five hours or less usage should be classified as light users and the remaining as heavy users. Run a cross-tabulation of sex and Internet usage. Interpret the results. Is Internet usage related to one's sex?

NOTES

1. **www.usma.edu**, accessed July 5, 2013; Harvard Business School, "The U.S. Military Academy at West Point," Case number 9-512-012.
2. Technically, a null hypothesis cannot be accepted. It can be either rejected or not rejected. This distinction is inconsequential, however, in applied research.
3. **www.ihg.com**, accessed October 11, 2013; "Holiday Inn Brand Experience," **www.ihg.com/holidayinn/hotels/us/en/global/exp/exp_home**, accessed October 11, 2013.
4. Abbey Klaassen, "Ads for the People, by the People," *Advertising Age*, 77(9) (February 27, 2006): 1–59; Robin T. Peterson and Douglas T. Ross, "A Content Analysis of the Portrayal of Mature Individuals in Television Commercials," *Journal of Business Ethics*, 16 (1997): 425–433.

Online Video Case 11.1

MARRIOTT: Marketing Research Leads to Expanded Offerings

Visit **www.pearsonglobaleditions.com/malhotra** to read the video case and view the accompanying video. Marriott: Marketing Research Leads to Expanded Offerings suggests that Marriott's sustained vast expansion over the last several decades is due in large part to marketing research. This case can be used as a springboard for students to conduct comparisons in consumer perceptions about Marriott and three competing hotel chains. In light of the chapter's objectives, it has questions on what analyses should be performed using frequency distribution and cross-tabulation. It is a comprehensive case that also contains questions for the first ten chapters.

Data Analysis: Hypothesis Testing Related to Differences, Correlation, and Regression

⌄ Overview

Chapter 11 described basic data analysis, covering frequency distributions, cross-tabulation, and the general procedure for hypothesis testing, including tests for association. As explained in that chapter, hypothesis-testing procedures are classified as tests of associations or tests of differences. This chapter presents tests for examining hypotheses related to differences.

The tests presented in this chapter assume that the data are at least interval scaled (Chapter 7) and hence are called parametric tests. We first discuss the case for difference in mean for one sample followed by hypothesis testing for two samples. We also examine hypothesis testing associated with differences in proportions and describe correlation and regression analyses. Figure 12.1 explains the steps of the marketing research process on which this chapter concentrates.

Help for running the SPSS and Excel programs used in this chapter is provided in four ways: (1) detailed step-by-step instructions are given later in the chapter; (2) you can download (from the Companion website for this book) computerized demonstration movies illustrating these step-by-step instructions; (3) you can download screen captures with notes illustrating these step-by-step instructions; and (4) you can refer to the Student Resource Manual that is posted on the Companion website for this book.

To provide you with a flavor of hypothesis testing related to differences, we illustrate the use of two-independent-samples t tests.

⌄ Learning Objectives

After reading this chapter, the student should be able to:

1. Understand the role of the t distribution in testing hypotheses that are related to differences.

2. Explain how to test the hypothesis related to one sample.

3. Describe how hypothesis testing changes when there are two independent samples rather than one, and when testing for difference in proportions rather than means.

4. Discuss how to test the hypothesis for paired samples.

5. Explain the basic concepts of correlation and regression analyses.

6. Describe the SPSS and Excel programs available for conducting hypotheses testing related to differences, correlation and regression analyses.

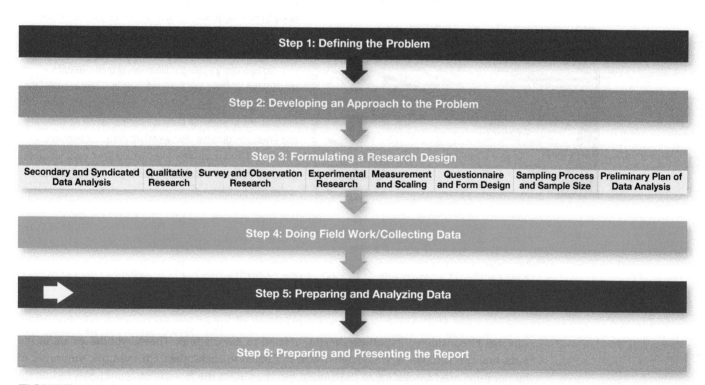

Step 1: Defining the Problem

Step 2: Developing an Approach to the Problem

Step 3: Formulating a Research Design

| Secondary and Syndicated Data Analysis | Qualitative Research | Survey and Observation Research | Experimental Research | Measurement and Scaling | Questionnaire and Form Design | Sampling Process and Sample Size | Preliminary Plan of Data Analysis |

Step 4: Doing Field Work/Collecting Data

Step 5: Preparing and Analyzing Data

Step 6: Preparing and Presenting the Report

FIGURE 12.1 | RELATIONSHIP OF THIS CHAPTER TO THE MARKETING RESEARCH PROCESS

Research in Practice
Gender Differences in Millennials' Online Reviews

Millennials, also called Generation Y, are people born between 1981 and 1994. They are heavy users of social media and have infuenced its development so that social media is now an important source of product information. A survey was conducted of 227 millennials in a behavioral lab at a major U.S. university during spring 2011. The respondents were asked to indicate the positive and negative reviews they post online on a scale of 0 to 10, where 0 denoted never and 10 denoted very frequently. The differences between males and females were examined using two-independent-samples *t* tests. The following results were obtained.

Average Postings of Online Reviews

Type of Review	Males	Females
All reviews*	5.14	3.81
Positive reviews	4.96	3.98
Negative reviews*	4.35	3.05

*Gender scores are significantly different for this type. Significance = 0.05.

Contrary to popular thinking, respondents were more likely to post positive reviews rather than negative reviews. Compared to females, males were more likely to post reviews of all types and were also more likely to post negative reviews. However, the differences between males and females were not significant for positive reviews.

Source: Nicholas Kamm/Getty Images, Inc.

Companies targeting millennials should carefully monitor the reviews that are posted online. This is one of the reasons for the success of Amazon (**www.amazon.com**). Amazon encourages the postings of reviews on its website and leverages positive reviews while using the negative reviews to focus on quality improvements. Amazon has also designed differential marketing startegies to reach out to males and females.[1] <

HYPOTHESES TESTING RELATED TO DIFFERENCES

Chapter 11 considered hypotheses testing related to associations. These hypotheses are of the form that two variables are associated with or related to each other. For example, the values of homes purchased are related to the buyers' incomes. Here the focus is on hypotheses testing related to differences. These hypotheses are of the form that two variables are different from each other, for example, people living in the suburbs have higher incomes than people living in the downtown areas. A classification of hypothesis-testing procedures for examining differences is presented in Figure 12.2. These procedures are related to examining differences in means or proportions.

First, we focus on hypothesis-testing procedures examining differences in means. These procedures are also called **parametric tests** because they assume that the variables of interest are metric. Metric variables are measured on an interval or ratio scale (see Chapter 7), for example, that the average household spends more than $100 per month on cellular phone services. Here,

parametric tests
Hypothesis-testing procedures that assume the variables of interest are measured on at least an interval scale.

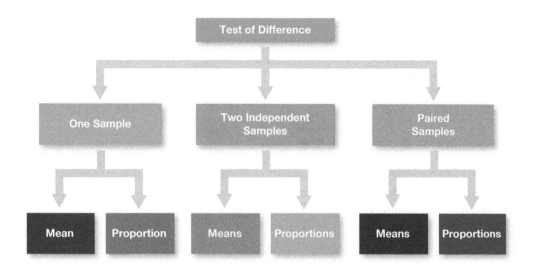

FIGURE 12.2
HYPOTHESIS TESTS
RELATED TO DIFFERENCES

the monthly expenditure on cellular phone services is measured on a ratio scale. The most popular parametric test is the *t* test conducted for examining hypotheses about means. The *t* test can be conducted on the means of one sample or two samples of observations. In the case of two samples, the samples can be independent or paired. The first Research in Practice feature in this chapter provided an application of a *t* test for the difference in means of two independent samples—males and females. All *t* tests are based on the *t* distribution.

Research Recipe

Hypotheses related to differences compare two variables that are different from each other. Conduct the *t* test for examining hypotheses about means of one sample or two samples of observations. In the case of two samples, the samples can be independent or paired.

The *t* Distribution

Parametric tests provide inferences for making statements about the means of parent populations. A **t test** is commonly used for this purpose. This test is based on the Student's *t* statistic. The **t statistic** is calculated by assuming that the variable is normally distributed, the mean is known, and the population variance is estimated from the sample. Assume that the random variable X is normally distributed, with a known mean μ and unknown population variance σ^2, which is estimated by the sample variance s^2 (see Table 11.3 in Chapter 11 for a definition of the symbols associated with the sample and the population). The standard deviation of the sample mean, $\overline{X}$, also called **standard error**, of mean (see Table 11.3 in Chapter 11), is estimated as

$$s_{\overline{x}} = s/\sqrt{n}$$

Thus,

$$t = (\overline{X} - \mu)/s_{\overline{x}}$$

is *t* distributed with $n - 1$ degrees of freedom, where n is the sample size.

The **t distribution** is similar to the normal distribution in appearance. Both distributions are bell-shaped and symmetric. However, the *t* distribution has more area in the tails and less in the center than the normal distribution because population variance σ^2 is unknown and is estimated by the sample variance s^2. Given the uncertainty in the value of s^2, the observed values of *t* are more variable than those of *z*. Thus, we must go a larger number of standard deviations from zero to encompass a certain percentage of values from the *t* distribution than is the case with the

t test
A hypothesis test using the t distribution, which is used when the mean is known, the standard deviation is unknown and is estimated from the sample.

t statistic
A statistic that assumes the variable has a symmetric, bell-shaped distribution; the mean is known (or assumed to be known); and the population variance is estimated from the sample.

standard error
The standard deviation of the mean or proportion.

t distribution
A symmetric bell-shaped distribution that is defined by $n - 1$ degrees of freedom.

normal distribution. As the number of degrees of freedom increases, however, the t distribution approaches the normal distribution. In fact, for large samples of 120 or more, the t distribution and the normal distribution are nearly indistinguishable. Although normality is assumed, the t test is quite robust to departures from normality.

R e s e a r c h   R e c i p e

Conduct a t test based on the t statistic, which is calculated by assuming that the variable is normally distributed, the mean is known, and the population variance is unknown but is estimated from the sample. The degrees of freedom are $n - 1$.

Hypothesis Testing Based on the t Statistic

For the special case when the t statistic is used, the general procedure for hypothesis testing discussed in Chapter 11 (see Figure 11.5) is applied, as shown in Figure 12.3.

1. Formulate the null (H_0) and the alternative (H_1) hypotheses.
2. Select the appropriate formula for the t statistic.
3. Select a significance level, α, for testing H_0. Typically, the 0.05 level is selected.
4. Take one or two samples and compute the mean and standard deviation for each sample. Calculate the t statistic assuming H_0 is true. Calculate the degrees of freedom.

FIGURE 12.3
CONDUCTING t TESTS

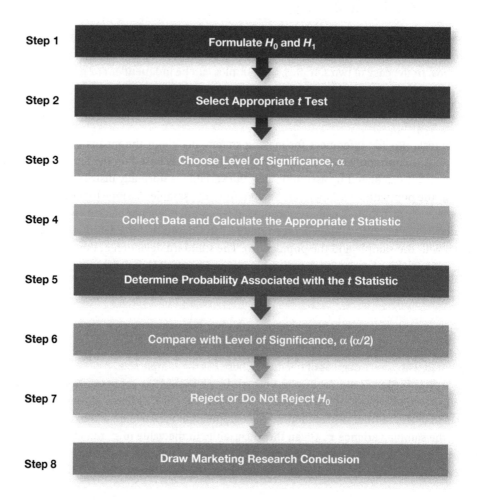

Step 1 — Formulate H_0 and H_1

Step 2 — Select Appropriate t Test

Step 3 — Choose Level of Significance, α

Step 4 — Collect Data and Calculate the Appropriate t Statistic

Step 5 — Determine Probability Associated with the t Statistic

Step 6 — Compare with Level of Significance, α ($\alpha/2$)

Step 7 — Reject or Do Not Reject H_0

Step 8 — Draw Marketing Research Conclusion

5. Estimate the probability of observing a value of the test statistic as extreme as, or more extreme than, the value actually observed, assuming that the null hypothesis is true. This is also called the p value. In SPSS and Excel, this probability is determined automatically by the software.
6. Compare the probability computed in Step 5 with the significance level selected in Step 3. Note that the p value should be compared to either α or $\alpha/2$. It should be compared to α for a one-tailed test and $\alpha/2$ for a two-tailed test. (See Figure 11.7 in Chapter 11.)
7. Make the statistical decision to reject or not reject the null hypotheses. If the probability computed in Step 5 (p value) is smaller than the appropriate significance level (α or $\alpha/2$) stated in Step 6, reject H_0. If the probability is larger, do not reject H_0. Failure to reject H_0 does not necessarily imply that H_0 is true. It only means that the true state is not significantly different from that assumed by H_0.[2]
8. Express the conclusion reached by the t test in terms of the marketing research problem.

Research Recipe

If the probability associated with the t statistic, the p value, is smaller than the appropriate significance level (α or $\alpha/2$), reject H_0. If the probability is larger, do not reject H_0. Compare the p value to α for a one-tailed test and $\alpha/2$ for a two-tailed test.

The general procedure for conducting t tests is illustrated in the following sections by using the data of Table 12.1. This table contains data from two samples, each consisting of ten respondents.

Table 12.1 > Preference for Yellowstone Before and After Visiting the Park

Preference for Yellowstone			
No.	Sample	Before	After
1.	1	7	9
2.	1	6	8
3.	1	5	8
4.	1	6	9
5.	1	4	7
6.	1	6	8
7.	1	5	7
8.	1	4	7
9.	1	7	9
10.	1	5	7
11.	2	3	7
12.	2	4	8
13.	2	4	7
14.	2	3	6
15.	2	6	8
16.	2	5	8
17.	2	4	9
18.	2	3	6
19.	2	3	7
20.	2	5	9

SPSS Data File

Excel Data File

t tests can be used to examine differences in preferences for the Yellowstone National Park.
Source: michael langley / Fotolia

Sample 1 consists of teenagers (ages 13 to 19), whereas sample 2 consists of adults 20 years old or older. The respondents were asked to indicate their preferences for Yellowstone National Park immediately before and immediately after their visits, using a 10-point scale. For illustrative purposes, we consider only a small number of observations. In actual practice, hypotheses tests are performed on much larger samples, such as that in the Dell running case and other cases with real data that are presented in this book. We begin with the one-sample case.

ONE-SAMPLE TEST

In marketing research, the researcher is often interested in making statements about a single variable against a known or given standard. The following are examples of such statements:

- At least 65 percent of customers will like the new package design.
- The average monthly household expenditure on groceries exceeds $500.

These statements can be translated into null hypotheses that can be tested using a one-sample test, such as the *z* test or the *t* test. In the case of a *t* test for a single mean, the researcher is interested in testing whether the population mean conforms to a given hypothesis (H_0). In the first Research in Practice feature in this chapter, the hypothesis that the mean rating of males for all reviews exceeded 5.0 would be tested using the one-sample *t* test.

Mean

The one-sample *t* test is illustrated using the data of Table 12.1. The null hypothesis H_0, based on a previous survey, is that the mean preference for sample 1 (teenagers) before entering Yellowstone National Park (PREFERENCE 11) will be 5.0. It is possible that the preference for Yellowstone National Park could have increased or decreased since the last survey, and hence the alternative hypothesis H_1 is that the mean preference for sample 1 before entering the park is different than 5.0. The hypotheses are as follows:

$$H_0: \mu = 5.0$$
$$H_1: \mu \neq 5.0$$

This one-sample *t* test was conducted using a statistical program. The results are described in Table 12.2. The corresponding SPSS and Excel outputs, with explanatory remarks, can be downloaded from the Companion website for this book. It can be seen from Table 12.2 that the mean preference of sample 1 before entering the park is 5.5 with a standard deviation of 1.08. The value

SPSS Output File

Excel Output File

Table 12.2 ❯ One-Sample *t* Test

Variable	Number of Cases	Mean	SD	SE of Mean
VAR00002	10	5.5000	1.080	.342

Test Value = 5

Mean Difference	*t* value	df	Two-Tail Sig.
.50	1.46	9	.177

of t is 1.46. With 9 ($n - 1$) degrees of freedom, the probability of getting a more extreme value of t (i.e., the p value) is 0.177, which is greater than 0.025 for a two-tailed test. Hence, the null hypothesis cannot be rejected. In other words, the mean preference of sample 1 before entering the park is no different from 5.0. Based on the results then, the preference of teenagers has not changed since the last survey. Note that 5.5 is not significantly different than 5.0. This is due to a relatively large standard deviation and the relatively small sample size.

Research Recipe

In the one-sample t test for a single mean, compare the sample mean to the mean value posited by the null hypothesis. The t statistic has $n - 1$ degrees of freedom.

Proportion

Such hypotheses relate to the proportion or percentage pertaining to a single population. Examples might be "the proportion of brand-loyal users of Coca-Cola exceeds 0.2" or "70 percent of the households eat out at least once a week." The procedure for testing a hypothesis associated with a proportion for one sample was illustrated in Chapter 11 in the section titled A General Procedure for Hypothesis Testing. As was shown in Chapter 11, the one-sample test for a single proportion is based on the z statistic, which follows the standard normal distribution. The population mean as well as the variance are assumed to be known under the null hypothesis. Refer to Chapter 11 for more details.

Research Recipe

Conduct the one-sample test for a single proportion using the z statistic, which follows the standard normal distribution. The population mean as well as the variance are assumed to be known under the null hypothesis.

TWO-INDEPENDENT-SAMPLES TEST

As seen in Figure 12.2, the two samples can be either independent or paired. The hypotheses and the related tests could pertain to examining differences in means or proportions.

Samples drawn randomly from different populations are termed **independent samples**. Several hypotheses in marketing relate to parameters from two different populations:

- High-income consumers spend more on entertainment than low-income consumers do.
- The proportion of households with an Internet connection in the United States exceeds that in Germany.

independent samples
Two samples that are not experimentally related. The measurement of one sample has no effect on the values of the other sample.

In each of the foregoing hypotheses, we have two different populations: high-income and low-income consumers, and the United States and Germany. Samples drawn randomly from these populations will be independent samples. In the first Research in Practice dealing with millennials' online reviews, males and females constituted two independent samples. For the purpose of analysis, data pertaining to different groups of respondents (e.g., males and females) are generally treated as independent samples even though the data may pertain to the same survey. As in the case for one sample, the hypotheses can relate to means or proportions. The first hypothesis listed in the introduction to this section relates to means, whereas the second relates to proportions.

Means

In the case of means for two independent samples, the hypotheses take the following form:

$$H_0: \mu_1 = \mu_2$$
$$H_1: \mu_1 \neq \mu_2$$

The null hypothesis H_0 states that the two population means are equal, whereas the alternative hypothesis H_1 states that they are unequal. The procedure for conducting the t test for two independent samples is described in Figure 12.4. The two populations are sampled, and the means and variances are computed based on samples of sizes n_1 and n_2. If both populations are found to have the same variance, a pooled variance estimate is computed from the two sample variances, and the appropriate value of t can be calculated using the formula given earlier. In this case, the degrees of freedom are $(n_1 + n_2 - 2)$.

If the two populations have unequal variances, an exact t cannot be computed for the difference in sample means. In these cases, an approximation to t is computed. The number of degrees of freedom in this case is usually not an integer, but a reasonably accurate probability can be obtained by rounding to the nearest integer.

An **F test** of sample variance can be performed if it is not known whether the two populations have equal variance. In this case, the hypotheses are

$$H_0: \sigma_1^2 = \sigma_2^2$$
$$H_1: \sigma_1^2 \neq \sigma_2^2$$

F test

A statistical test of the equality of the variances of two populations.

FIGURE 12.4

CONDUCTING t TEST
FOR TWO INDEPENDENT
SAMPLES

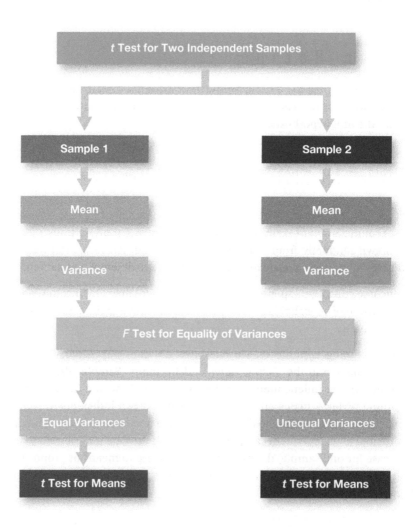

The null hypothesis H_0 states that the two population variances are equal, whereas the alternative hypothesis H_1 is that they are unequal. The **F statistic** is computed from the sample variances by dividing the larger sample variance by the smaller sample variance. The **F distribution** is defined by two sets of degrees of freedom—those in the numerator and those in the denominator. These degrees of freedom for the numerator are $n_1 - 1$ for sample 1, and $n_2 - 1$ for the denominator for sample 2, where sample 1 is the sample with the larger variance. If the probability of F (the p value) is greater than the significance level $\alpha/2$, H_0 is not rejected and t based on the pooled variance estimate can be used. However, if the probability of F is less than or equal to $\alpha/2$, H_0 is rejected and t based on a separate variance estimate is used.

F statistic
A statistic that is calculated as the ratio of two sample variances by dividing the larger sample variance by the smaller sample variance.

F distribution
A frequency distribution that depends on two sets of degrees of freedom: the degrees of freedom in the numerator and the degrees of freedom in the denominator.

Using the data of Table 12.1, we can examine whether the teenagers have a different preference (PREFERENCE 11) than adults (PREFERENCE 21) before entering the park. A two-independent-samples t test is conducted. Because the difference could be in either direction, a two-tailed test is used. This two-sample t test was conducted using statistical software, and the results are presented in Table 12.3; the corresponding SPSS and Excel outputs with explanatory notes can be downloaded from the Companion website for this book.

The value of the F statistic for testing the equality of variances is

$$F_{9,9} = 1.05$$

Note that the F test of sample variances has a probability of 0.472 that exceeds 0.025. Accordingly, the null hypothesis of equal variances cannot be rejected, and the t test based on the pooled variance estimate should be used.

Under the null hypothesis, the value of the t statistic is 3.14 with $20 - 2 = 18$ degrees of freedom. This gives us a probability of 0.006, which is less than the significance level of $0.05/2 = 0.025$ for a two-tailed test. Therefore, the null hypothesis of equal means is rejected, and the conclusion is that the teenagers and adults differ in their preferences for Yellowstone National Park before entering the park. Table 12.3 also shows the t test using separate variance estimates because most computer programs automatically conduct the t test both ways.

Suppose we want to determine whether teenagers have a higher preference for Yellowstone National Park compared to adults. In this case, a one-tailed rather than a two-tailed test should be used. The hypotheses are as follows:

$$H_0: \mu_1 \leq \mu_2$$
$$H_1: \mu_1 > \mu_2$$

The null hypothesis H_0 is that the preference for Yellowstone National Park for teenagers is less than or equal to the preference of adults. The alternative hypothesis H_1 is that teenagers have a

Table 12.3 ❯ *t* Tests for Independent Samples

Variable Sample	Number of Cases	Mean	SD	SE of Mean
Teenagers	10	5.5000	1.080	.342
Adults	10	4.0000	1.054	.333

Mean Difference = 1.5000
Levene's Test for Equality of Variances: $F = 1.05$ $P = .472$

t Test for Equality of Means

Variances	*t* value	df	2-Tail Sig	SE of Diff
Equal	3.14	18	.006	.477
Unequal	3.14	17.99	.006	.477

SPSS Output File

Excel Output File

higher preference for Yellowstone National Park compared to adults. The t statistic is calculated in exactly the same way as in the two-tailed test. However, the level of significance is α for a one-tailed test (see Figure 11.7). In this case also, the p value is less than 0.05, leading to a similar conclusion as that arrived at earlier.

A two-tailed test is more conservative than the corresponding one-tailed test. If a hypothesis is rejected using a two-tailed test, then it will also be rejected using the corresponding one-tailed test. As explained in Chapter 11, the level of significance is α for a one-tailed test and $\alpha/2$ for a two-tailed test (see Figure 11.7). For another application of the t test, consider the differences between Generation Xers and Baby Boomers in a quest for luxury in the Research in Practice feature.

Research in Practice
Generation Xers Versus Baby Boomers in a Quest for Luxury

The American Express Platinum Luxury Survey was conducted among a random cross-section of 500 wealthy U.S. consumers: 250 Baby Boomers (born between 1946 and 1964) and 250 Gen Xers (born between 1964 and 1980), both drawn from the same income group, with an annual household income of $125,000 to $199,999. The survey was administered through several channels, including one-on-one interviews at luxury stores. The survey found that Generation Xers' annual spending far exceeds that of Baby Boomers in a number of luxury-good categories:

- 60 percent more than Baby Boomers on fragrance, cosmetics, and beauty products ($3,235 versus $2,017)
- 47 percent more on fashion accessories ($6,066 versus $4,116)
- 36 percent more on men's and women's clothing ($23,027 versus $16,924)
- 32 percent more on wines and liquors ($3,922 versus $2,966)
- 33 percent more for entertainment ($3,629 versus $2,722)
- 17 percent more for personal/health services ($3,324 versus $2,838)

Two-sample t tests indicated that all of these differences were statistically significant at the 0.05 level. The conclusion was that luxury high-end products, such as those marketed by Gucci, Louis Vuitton, Hermes, Cartier, Christian Dior, and so on, should be targeted at Generation Xers, while at the same time maintaining relationships through marketing campaigns or continual quality service with the Baby Boomers.[3] <

Source: Inga Ivanova / Shutterstock

Research Recipe

In two-independent-samples t test for means, you should first test for the equality of the two population variances using the F test. The F statistic is computed from the sample variances by dividing the larger sample variance with the smaller sample variance. The degress of freedom for the numerator are $n_1 - 1$, and for the denominator they are $n_2 - 1$, where n_1 is the size of the sample with the larger variance.

If the null hypothesis of equal variances is not rejected, then use t based on the pooled variance estimate. If the null hypothesis is rejected, however, then use t based on a separate variance estimate. The degrees of freedom are $(n_1 + n_2 - 2)$.

In Research in Practice feature about Generation Xers and Baby Boomers, we tested the difference between means. A similar test is available for testing the difference between proportions for two independent samples.

Proportions

A case involving proportions for two independent samples is illustrated in Table 12.4, which gives the number of users and nonusers of jeans in the United States and Hong Kong. Is the proportion of users the same in the U.S. and Hong Kong samples?

The null and alternative hypotheses are:

$$H_0: \pi_1 = \pi_2$$
$$H_1: \pi_1 \neq \pi_2$$

The null hypothesis H_0 states that the two population proportions are equal, whereas the alternative hypothesis H_1 is that they are unequal. A z test is used as in testing the proportion for one sample (see Chapter 11). A significance level of $\alpha = 0.05$ is selected. Given the data of Table 12.4 and using a statistical software program, the test statistic can be calculated as:

$$z = 0.2/0.04583 = 4.36$$

Given a two-tailed test, the p value should be compared to $\alpha/2$, or 0.025. The probability associated with the z value (the p value) is less than 0.025. Therefore, the null hypothesis is rejected, and the proportion of users (0.80 for the United States and 0.60 for Hong Kong) is significantly different for the two samples.

As an alternative to the parametric z test considered earlier, one could also use the cross-tabulation procedure to conduct a chi-square test, especially if the samples are not large. In this case, we have a 2 × 2 table. One variable is used to denote the sample, and the value 1 is assumed for sample 1 and the value 2 for sample 2. The other variable is the dichotomous variable of interest. The t test in this case is equivalent to a chi-square test for independence in a 2 × 2 contingency table. For large samples, the t distribution approaches the normal distribution; thus, the t test and the z test are equivalent.

Table 12.4 > Comparing Jean Users for the United States and Hong Kong

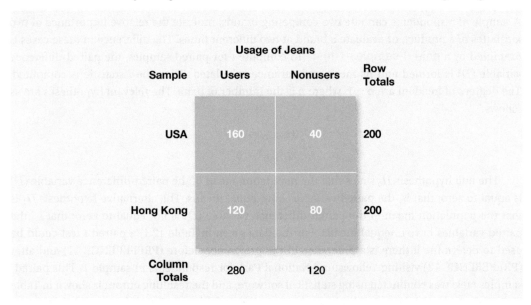

Sample	Usage of Jeans		Row Totals
	Users	Nonusers	
USA	160	40	200
Hong Kong	120	80	200
Column Totals	280	120	

iResearch
Who Are the Expert and Novice Users of Digital Cameras?

If you are the marketing director for Nikon, how would you segment the digital camera market?

Visit **www.nikon.com** and search the Internet, including social media as well as your library's online databases, to obtain information on digital camera usage in U.S. households. As a marketing research analyst working for Nikon, how would you determine whether the two digital camera usage segments (experts and novices) differ in terms of ten psychographic characteristics, each measured on a 7-point scale? **<**

PAIRED-SAMPLES TEST

paired samples
In hypothesis testing, the observations are paired so that the two sets of observations relate to the same respondents.

In many marketing research applications, the observations for two groups are not selected from independent samples. Rather, the observations relate to **paired samples** in that the two sets of observations relate to the same respondents. Examples of hypotheses related to paired samples include the following:

● Shoppers consider brand name to be more important than price when purchasing fashion clothing.
● The proportion of a bank's customers who have a checking account exceeds the proportion who have a savings account.

Each of the foregoing hypotheses relates to the same set of people. The first hypothesis relates to means, whereas the second relates to proportions.

Means

paired-samples *t* test
A test for differences in the means of paired samples.

A sample of respondents can rate two competing brands, indicate the relative importance of two attributes of a product, or evaluate a brand at two different times. The difference in these cases is examined by a **paired-samples *t* test**. To compute t for paired samples, the paired-difference variable (D) is formed and its mean and variance calculated. Then the t statistic is computed. The degrees of freedom are $n - 1$, where n is the number of pairs. The relevant hypotheses are as follows:

$$H_0: \mu_D = 0$$
$$H_1: \mu_D \neq 0$$

The null hypothesis H_0 states that the population mean of the paired-difference variable (D) is equal to zero; that is, the paired variables have equal means. The alternative hypothesis H_1 is that the population mean of the paired-difference variable (D) is not equal to zero; that is, the paired variables have unequal means. For the data given in Table 12.1, a paired t test could be used to determine if there is a difference in the preference before (PREFERENCE 11) and after (PREFERENCE 12) visiting Yellowstone National Park for respondents in sample 1. This paired-samples t test was conducted using statistical software, and the resulting output is shown in Table 12.5. We can see that the mean difference between the variables is -2.4, with a standard deviation

Table 12.5 ❯ *t* Tests for Paired Samples

Variable	Number of pairs	Corr	2-tail Sig	Mean	SD	SE of Mean
Preference Before				5.5000	1.080	0.342
	10	.881	.001			
Preference After				7.9000	.876	0.277

SPSS Output File

Excel Output File

Paired Differences

Mean	SD	SE of Mean	t-value	df	2-tail Sig
−2.4000	0.516	0.163	−14.70	9	.000

of 0.516 and a standard error of 0.163. The *t* statistic has a value of -14.7 with $10 - 1 = 9$ degrees of freedom; this has a probability (*p* value) of less than 0.001. Because the *p* value is less than 0.025, the null hypothesis is rejected. Therefore, the preferences of teenagers before and after visiting Yellowstone National Park are significantly different. A comparison of the mean preference before and the mean preference after visiting the park reveals that the preference is higher after visiting Yellowstone National Park. Thus, visitors like what they see.

The corresponding SPSS and Excel outputs, with explanatory notes, can be downloaded from the Companion website for this book. A one-tailed test would have the same value for the *t* statistic, but the level of significance would be α rather than $\alpha/2$ (see Figure 11.7). Thus, if we wanted to test whether the preferences after visiting the park were significantly greater than before the visit, a one-tailed test would also lead to the rejection of the null hypothesis.

$$H_0: \mu_D \leq 0$$
$$H_1: \mu_D > 0$$

where

$$D = \text{preference after the visit} - \text{preference before the visit}$$

Note that the computer program tested the difference as Before − After; hence, the negative mean difference and the negative *t* value in the output given in Table 12.5. The Research in Practice feature provides another application in the context of determining the effectiveness of Cole Haan advertising.

Research in Practice
Cole Haan Touts Comfort and Style

In 2014, Cole Haan (**www.colehaan.com**) was touting the style and walking comfort of its shoes. The commercials, as well as the print ads, were carefully tested before they were released to the media. A group of 200 men were asked to respond to a series of ten scales designed to measure attitude toward Cole Haan shoes. They were then exposed to the commercial as part of an entertaining program. After the program, attitude toward Cole Haan shoes was again measured using the same ten scales (see the one-group pretest-posttest design in Chapter 6). A paired *t* test indicated a significant increase in attitude after exposure to the commercial. The commercials and the print ads not only fared well in the test, they were also successful in achieving sales growth.[4] ❮

Table 12.6 > A Summary of Hypothesis Testing

Sample	Test/Comments
One Sample	
Means	*t* test, if variance is unknown
	z test, if variance is known
Proportions	*z* test
Two Independent Samples	
Means	Two-group *t* test
	F test for equality of variances
Proportions	*z* test
	Chi-square test
Paired Samples	
Means	Paired *t* test
Proportions	Chi-square test

Research Recipe

To conduct a *t* test for means of paired samples, form the paired-difference variable (D) and calculate its mean and variance. Then compute the *t* statistic. The degrees of freedom are $n - 1$, where n is the number of pairs.

Proportions

The difference in proportions for paired samples can be tested by the chi-square test, which was explained in Chapter 11. Here, one variable denotes the sample, assuming a value of 1 for the first measurement on the sample and a value of 2 for the second measurement on the same sample. The other variable is the proportion of interest, again coded as 1 and 2 (or as 0 and 1). The various hypothesis-testing procedures for examining differences in means and proportions are summarized in Table 12.6.

Research Recipe

To conduct a *t* test for proportions of paired samples, use the chi-square test.

iResearch
Gap: Independent and Paired (*t* Tests)

As the marketing director for Gap, how would you improve Gap's image and competitive position?

Visit **www.gap.com** and search the Internet, including social media as well as your library's online databases, to obtain information on the factors that consumers use to evaluate competing brands of casual clothes. How do these factors compare with the ones in the next sentence? The users and nonusers of Gap evaluated the brand using Likert-type scales on four factors: comfort, durability, style, and image. How would you analyze these data using two-independent-samples and paired-samples *t* tests? <

CORRELATION

The **product moment correlation** is the most widely used statistic that summarizes the strength and direction of linear association between two metric (interval- or ratio-scaled; see Chapter 7) variables, say, *X* and *Y*. It is used to determine whether a linear or straight-line relationship exists between *X* and *Y*, as well as the degree to which one variable, *X*, is related to another variable, *Y*. Because it was originally proposed by Karl Pearson, it also is known as the Pearson correlation coefficient. Other terms used to refer to the product moment correlation are *simple correlation, bivariate correlation, correlation coefficient,* or merely *correlation*. The product moment correlation is denoted by *r* and varies between −1.0 and +1.0, with values near +1.0 indicating a very positive association and those near −1.0 a very negative relationship.

product moment correlation (*r*)
A statistic summarizing the strength of linear association between two metric variables.

When it is computed for a population rather than a sample, the product moment correlation is denoted by ρ, the Greek letter rho. The statistical significance of the relationship between two variables measured by using *r* can be conveniently tested. Based on the principles outlined earlier in this chapter, the null hypothesis H_0 is that rho is zero and the alternative hypothesis H_1 is that rho is not equal to zero. The test statistic has a *t* distribution with $n - 2$ degrees of freedom. If the *p* value is less than 0.025 for a two-tailed test, the null hypothesis is rejected, leading to the conclusion that the linear relationship between the two variables is significant. The sign of *r* (+ or −) indicates whether the relationship is positive or negative, and the magnitude of *r* indicates the strength of the relationship.

As an example, suppose a researcher wants to explain attitudes toward motorcycles (attitude) in terms of the number of years the respondent has owned a motorcycle (duration). The attitude is measured on an 11-point scale (1 = do not like motorcycles, 11 = very much like motorcycles), and the duration of motorcycle ownership is measured in terms of the number of years the respondent has owned one or more motorcycles. The researcher also collects information on importance attached to performance on an 11-point scale. In a pretest of twelve respondents, the data shown in Table 12.7 were obtained.

SPSS Output File

Excel Output File

Using statistical software, such as SPSS or Excel, the correlation coefficient between attitude and duration based on the data of Table 12.7 is calculated as 0.9361 and is statistically significant (*p* value is less than 0.025). The corresponding SPSS and Excel outputs with explanatory notes can be downloaded from the Companion website for this book. In this example, the value of *r*, 0.9361, is close to 1.0, which means that the number of years a respondent has owned

Table 12.7 > Explaining Attitude Toward Motorcycles

SPSS Data File

Excel Data File

Respondent Number	Attitude Toward Motorcycle	Duration of Motorcycle Ownership	Importance Attached to Performance
1	6	10	3
2	9	12	11
3	3	12	4
4	3	4	1
5	10	12	11
6	4	6	1
7	5	3	7
8	2	2	4
9	11	18	3
10	9	9	10
11	10	17	3
12	2	2	5

a motorcycle is strongly associated with the respondent's attitude toward motorcycles. Thus, the length of time a person has owned a motorcycle is related to the attitude toward motorcycles. Furthermore, the positive sign of r implies a positive relationship; the longer the duration of motorcycle ownership, the more favorable the attitude, and vice versa. For example, if Tom has owned a motorcycle much longer than Bob, Tom is likely to have a much more favorable attitude toward motorcycles than Bob. Over many years of ownership, Tom sees his motorcycle as a treasured possession. In contrast, Bob has only recently purchased a motorcycle and has yet to develop such strong feelings toward it.

Research Recipe

Calculate the product moment correlation to summarize the strength and direction of association between two metric variables and to determine whether a linear or straight-line relationship exists between them. The product moment correlation is an absolute number and varies between -1.0 and $+1.0$, with a value near 1.0 (or -1.0) indicating a strong positive (or negative) association. Test the statistical significance of the association by using a t test with $n - 2$ degrees of freedom.

REGRESSION ANALYSIS

regression analysis
A statistical procedure for analyzing associative relationships between a metric dependent variable and one or more metric independent variables.

Regression analysis is a procedure for analyzing associative relationships between a metric dependent variable and one or more metric independent variables. **Bivariate regression** is a procedure for deriving a mathematical equation, in the form of a straight line, between a single metric dependent variable and a single metric independent variable. In bivariate regression we have only one independent variable, whereas in the case of **multiple regression**, we have two or more (multiple) independent variables. For example, bivariate regression can answer the following question: Can the variation in market share be accounted for by the size of the sales force? However, multiple regression would be used to explain whether the variation in market shares can be accounted for by the size of the sales force, the amount of advertising expenditure, and the amount of sales promotion budget. Although the independent variables can explain the variation in the dependent variable, this does not necessarily imply causation (see Chapters 3 and 6 for causal research).

bivariate regression
A procedure for deriving a mathematical relationship, in the form of an equation, between a single metric dependent variable and a single metric independent variable.

multiple regression
A statistical technique that simultaneously develops a mathematical relationship between a single metric dependent variable and two or more metric independent variables.

Multiple Regression Model

The general form of the multiple regression model is as follows:

$$Y = \beta_0 + \beta_1 X_1 + \beta_2 X_2 + \beta_3 X_3 + \ldots + \beta_k X_k + e$$

and is estimated by the following equation:

$$\hat{Y} = a + b_1 X_1 + b_2 X_2 + b_3 X_3 + \ldots + b_k X_k$$

Y is the dependent variable, X_1 to X_k are the independent variables, β_is are the coefficients, and e is the error term. The number of independent variables is k and the sample size is n. $\hat{Y}$ is the predicted value of the dependent variable. The parameter a represents the intercept, and the bs are the partial regression coefficients. The statistical software estimates the parameters (a and bs) in such a way as to minimize the total error. This process also maximizes the correlation between the actual values of Y and the predicted values of $\hat{Y}$. When both the independent and the dependent variables are standardized (see Chapter 10 for standardization), the intercept assumes a value of 0. The term **beta coefficient**, or *beta weight*, is used to denote the standardized regression

beta coefficient
Used to denote the standardized regression coefficient. Also known as beta weight.

coefficient. Standardization is sometimes desirable because it is easier to compare the beta coefficients than it is to compare the unstandardized or raw coefficients.

Strength of Association

The strength of association in multiple regression is measured by the square of the multiple correlation coefficient, R^2, which is also called the **coefficient of multiple determination**. The multiple correlation coefficient, R, can also be viewed as the simple correlation coefficient, r, between Y and $\hat{Y}$. R^2 cannot decrease as more independent variables are added to the regression equation. Diminishing returns do set in, however, so that after the first few variables, the additional independent variables do not make much of a contribution. For this reason, R^2 is adjusted for the number of independent variables and the sample size to calculate **adjusted R^2**. This adjustment is negative so that the value of adjusted R^2 cannot be higher than R^2.

coefficient of multiple determination
In multiple regression, the strength of association is measured by the square of the multiple correlation coefficient, R^2, which is called the coefficient of multiple determination.

adjusted R^2
The value of R^2 adjusted for the number of independent variables and the sample size. The value of adjusted R^2 cannot be higher than R^2.

Significance Testing

Significance testing involves testing the significance of the overall regression equation as well as specific partial regression coefficients. The null hypothesis for the overall test is that the coefficient of multiple determination in the population, R^2_{pop}, is zero. The overall test can be conducted by using an F statistic, which has an F distribution with k and $(n - k - 1)$ degrees of freedom.

If the overall null hypothesis is rejected, one or more population partial regression coefficients have a value different from 0. To determine which specific coefficients (b_is) are nonzero, additional tests are necessary. Testing for the significance of the b_is can be done by using t tests based on a t distribution with $(n - k - 1)$ degrees of freedom. Both the t test and the F test were discussed earlier in this chapter.

For the data of Table 12.7, we explain the attitude toward motorcycles in terms of duration of motorcycle ownership and importance attached to performance. The results of multiple regression analysis are depicted in Table 12.8. The corresponding SPSS and Excel outputs with explanatory notes can be downloaded from the Companion website for this book. The intercept has a value of 0.3373. The partial regression coefficient for duration (X_1) is 0.4811.

Table 12.8 > Multiple Regression

Multiple R	.9721
R^2	.9450
Adjusted R^2	.9330
Standard Error	.8597

Analysis of Variance

	df	Sum of Squares	Mean Square
Regression	2	114.2643	57.1321
Residual	9	6.6524	.7392
$F = 77.2936$		Significance of $F = .0000$	

Variables in the Equation

Variable	b	SE_b	Beta (B)	T	Sig. T
Importance	.2887	.08608	.3138	3.353	.0085
Duration	.4811	.05895	.7636	8.160	.0000
(Constant)	.3373	.56736		.595	.5668

SPSS Output File

Excel Output File

The corresponding beta coefficient is 0.7636. The partial regression coefficient for importance attached to performance (X_2) is 0.2887, with a beta coefficient of 0.3138. The estimated regression equation is:

$$\hat{Y} = 0.3373 + 0.4811X_1 + 0.2887X_2$$

or

$$\text{Attitude} = 0.3373 + 0.4811\,(\text{duration}) + 0.2887\,(\text{importance})$$

The value of R^2 is 0.9450 and is significant; the adjusted R^2 is estimated as 0.9330. Of course, R^2 should be significant, and higher values of R^2 are more desirable than lower values. Note that the value of adjusted R^2 is close to R^2. This suggests that both independent variables contribute toward explaining the variation in attitude toward motorcycles. Indeed, the results in Table 12.8 show that the coefficients for both independent variables are significant. Therefore, both the duration of motorcycle ownership and the importance attached to performance are important in explaining attitude toward motorcycles. If any of the regression coefficients are not significant, however, they should be treated as zero.

Research Recipe

In regression analysis, there is only one metric dependent variable. In bivariate regression there is only one metric independent variable, whereas in the case of multiple regression, we have two or more (multiple) metric independent variables. In multiple regression, measure the strength of association by the square of the multiple correlation coefficient, R^2, which is also called the coefficient of multiple determination. R^2 is adjusted for the number of independent variables and the sample size to calculate adjusted R^2. This adjustment is negative so that the value of adjusted R^2 cannot be higher than R^2.

Determine the significance of the overall regression equation by the F test with k and $(n - k - 1)$ degrees of freedom. If the overall regression is significant, test for the significance of the individual b_is by using t tests with $(n - k - 1)$ degrees of freedom.

SOFTWARE APPLICATIONS

Both SPSS and Excel have programs for conducting all the tests discussed in this chapter. We describe in detail how to conduct them.

SPSS and Excel Computerized Demonstration Movies

We have developed computerized demonstration movies that give step-by-step instructions for running all the SPSS and Excel programs that are discussed in this chapter. These demonstration movies can be downloaded from the Companion website for this book. The instructions for running these demonstration movies are given in Exhibit 10.1.

SPSS and Excel Screen Captures with Notes

The step-by-step instructions for running the various SPSS and Excel programs discussed in this chapter are also illustrated in screen captures with appropriate notes. These screen captures can be downloaded from the Companion website for this book.

SPSS WINDOWS

We give an overview of the detailed steps involved in conducting these analyses using SPSS. Then we provide detailed, step-by-step instructions for conducting a one-sample t test, a two-independent-samples t test, a paired-samples t test, correlation and regression.

Detailed Steps: Overview

Detailed, step-by-step instructions for running the SPSS programs for the data analysis presented in this chapter can be downloaded from the Companion website for this book in two forms: (1) computerized demonstration movies and (2) screen captures with notes. In addition, these steps are illustrated in the following sections. You can also refer to the Student Resource Manual. These steps are given for IBM SPSS STATISTICS 20 and IBM SPSS STATISTICS 21; they are essentially the same in both of these versions. The steps in the earlier versions are about the same with minor differences in the labeling of some of the boxes.

Detailed Steps: One-Sample t Test

Provided here are the detailed steps for running a one-sample test on the data of Table 12.1. The null hypothesis is that the mean preference for sample 1 before entering the park is 5.0. Open the SPSS data file for Table 12.1.

1. Select DATA from the SPSS menu bar.
2. Click SELECT CASES.
3. Check IF CONDITION IS SATISFIED. Then click the IF button.
4. Move SAMPLE [sample] into the SELECT CASES: IF box. Click "=" and then click "1."
5. Click CONTINUE.
6. Check FILTER OUT UNSELECTED CASES.
7. Click OK.
8. Select ANALYZE from the SPSS menu bar.
9. Click COMPARE MEANS and then ONE-SAMPLE *T TEST*.
10. Move Preference Before Visiting [pref1] into the TEST VARIABLE(S) box.
11. Type "5" in the TEST VALUE box.
12. Click OK.

Detailed Steps: Two-Independent-Samples t Test

Next are the detailed steps for running a two-independent-samples t test on the data of Table 12.1. The null hypothesis is that the mean preference for adults and teenagers before visiting Yellowstone National Park is the same. Open the SPSS data file for Table 12.1. First, make sure all cases are included.

    Menu Bar
        DATA
            Select CASES.
                Select ALL CASES.
                    Click OK.

Perform the analysis as follows:

1. Select ANALYZE from the SPSS menu bar.
2. Click COMPARE MEANS and then INDEPENDENT-SAMPLES *T TEST*.
3. Move "Preference Before Visiting [pref1]" into the TEST VARIABLE(S) box.
4. Move "Sample [sample]" into the GROUPING VARIABLE box.

5. Click DEFINE GROUPS.
6. Type "1" in the GROUP 1 box and "2" in the GROUP 2 box.
7. Click CONTINUE.
8. Click OK.

Detailed Steps: Paired–Samples *t* Test

Next are the detailed steps for running a paired-samples *t* test on the data of Table 12.1. The null hypothesis is that there is no difference in the mean preference of teenagers before and after visiting Yellowstone National Park. Open the SPSS data file for Table 12.1.

1. Select DATA from the SPSS menu bar.
2. Click SELECT CASES.
3. Check IF CONDITION IS SATISFIED. Then click the IF button.
4. Move "SAMPLE[sample]" into the SELECT CASES: IF box. Click "=" and then click "1."
5. Click CONTINUE.
6. Check FILTER OUT UNSELECTED CASES.
7. Click OK.
8. Select ANALYZE from the SPSS menu bar.
9. Click COMPARE MEANS and then PAIRED-SAMPLES T TEST.
10. Select "Preference Before Visiting [pref1]" and then select "Preference After Visiting [pref2]." Move these variables into the PAIRED VARIABLES: box.
11. Click OK.

Detailed Steps: Correlation

The following are the detailed steps for running a correlation between attitude toward motorcycles and duration of motorcycle ownership given in Table 12.7. Open the SPSS data file for Table 12.7.

1. Select ANALYZE from the SPSS menu bar.
2. Click CORRELATE and then BIVARIATE.
3. Move "Attitude [attitude]" and "Duration [duration]" into the VARIABLES: box.
4. Check PEARSON under CORRELATION COEFFICIENTS.
5. Check ONE-TAILED under TEST OF SIGNIFICANCE.
6. Check FLAG SIGNIFICANT CORRELATIONS.
7. Click OK.

Detailed Steps: Bivariate and Multiple Regression

The following are the detailed steps for running a bivariate regression with attitude toward motorcycles as the dependent variable and duration of motorcycle ownership as the independent variable using the data of Table 12.7. Open the SPSS data file for Table 12.7.

1. Select ANALYZE from the SPSS menu bar.
2. Click REGRESSION and then LINEAR.
3. Move "Attitude [attitude]" into the DEPENDENT box.
4. Move "Duration [duration]" into the INDEPENDENT(S) box.
5. Select ENTER in the METHOD box (default option).
6. Click STATISTICS and check ESTIMATES under REGRESSION COEFFICIENTS.
7. Check MODEL FIT.
8. Click CONTINUE.
9. Click OK.

The steps for running multiple regression are similar, except for step 4. In step 4, move "Duration [duration]" and "Importance [important]" into the INDEPENDENT(S) box.

EXCEL

We give an overview of the detailed steps involved in conducting these analyses using Excel. Then we provide detailed, step-by-step instructions for conducting a one-sample t test, a two-independent-samples t test, a paired-samples t test, correlation, and regression.

Detailed Steps: Overview

Detailed, step-by-step instructions for running the Excel programs for the data analysis presented in this chapter can be downloaded from the Companion website for this book in two forms: (1) computerized demonstration movies and (2) screen captures with notes. In addition, these steps are illustrated in the following sections for Excel 2007, Excel 2010, and Excel 2013; they are essentially the same in these versions. The steps in the earlier versions are about the same, with minor differences in how "Data Analysis" is accessed and the labeling of some of the boxes.

Detailed Steps: One-Sample t Test

The following are detailed steps for running a one-sample test on the data of Table 12.1. The null hypothesis is that the mean preference for sample 1 before entering the park is 5.0. Open the Excel data file for Table 12.1.

1. Add a column with the name "Dummy" beside PREF2 and fill the first ten rows (cells E2 to E11) with "5".
2. Select DATA tab.
3. In the ANALYSIS tab, select DATA ANALYSIS.
4. The DATA ANALYSIS window pops up.
5. Select T-TEST: PAIRED TWO SAMPLE FOR MEANS in DATA ANALYSIS window.
6. Click OK.
7. T-TEST: PAIRED TWO SAMPLE FOR MEANS window appears on the screen.
8. T-TEST: PAIRED TWO SAMPLE FOR MEANS window has two parts:
   a. INPUT
   b. OUTPUT OPTIONS
9. The INPUT portion asks for two inputs:
   a. Click in the VARIABLE 1 RANGE box. Select (highlight) the first ten rows of data under PREF1. $C$2:$C$11 should appear on VARIABLE 1 RANGE.
   b. Click in the VARIABLE 2 RANGE box. Select (highlight) the first ten rows of data under Dummy; $E$2:$E$11 should appear on VARIABLE 2 RANGE.
   c. Leave HYPOTHESIZED MEAN DIFFERENCE and LABELS blank.
   d. The default value of ALPHA is 0.05 and it is seen in the ALPHA box. Let the ALPHA value remain as is.
10. In the OUTPUT OPTIONS pop-up window, select NEW WORKBOOK.
11. Click OK.

Detailed Steps: Two-Independent-Samples t Test

The following are detailed steps for running a two-independent-samples t test on the data of Table 12.1. The null hypothesis is that the mean preference for adults and teenagers before visiting Yellowstone National Park is the same. Open the Excel data file for Table 12.1.

1. Select DATA tab.
2. In the ANALYSIS group, select DATA ANALYSIS.
3. The DATA ANALYSIS window pops up.
4. Select T-TEST: TWO-SAMPLE ASSUMING EQUAL VARIANCES in the DATA ANALYSIS window.

5. Click OK.
6. The T-TEST: TWO-SAMPLE ASSUMING EQUAL VARIANCES window pops up.
7. This window has two parts:
   a. INPUT
   b. OUTPUT OPTIONS
8. The INPUT portion asks for two inputs:
   a. Click in the VARIABLE 1 RANGE box. Select (highlight) the first 10 rows of data under PREF1. $C$2:$C$11 should appear on VARIABLE 1 RANGE.
   b. Click in the VARIABLE 2 RANGE box. Select (highlight) the last 10 rows of data under PREF1. $C$12:$C$21 should appear on VARIABLE 2 RANGE.
   c. Leave HYPOTHESIZED MEAN DIFFERENCE and LABELS blank.
   d. The default value of ALPHA is 0.05 and it is seen in the ALPHA box. Let the ALPHA value remain as is.
9. In the OUTPUT OPTIONS pop-up window, select NEW WORKBOOK.
10. Click OK.

Detailed Steps: Paired–Samples *t* Test

The following are detailed steps for running a paired-samples *t* test on the data of Table 12.1. The null hypothesis is that there is no difference in the mean preference of teenagers before and after visiting Yellowstone National Park. Open the Excel data file for Table 12.1.

1. Select DATA tab.
2. In the ANALYSIS tab, select DATA ANALYSIS.
3. The DATA ANALYSIS window pops up.
4. Select T-TEST: PAIRED TWO SAMPLE FOR MEANS in the DATA ANALYSIS window.
5. Click OK.
6. The T-TEST: PAIRED TWO SAMPLE FOR MEANS window pops up.
7. T-TEST: PAIRED TWO SAMPLE FOR MEANS window has two parts:
   a. INPUT
   b. OUTPUT OPTIONS
8. The INPUT portion asks for two inputs:
   a. Click in the VARIABLE 1 RANGE box. Select (highlight) the first ten rows of data under PREF1; $C$2:$C$11 should appear on VARIABLE 1 RANGE.
   b. Click in the VARIABLE 2 RANGE box. Select (highlight) the first ten rows of data under PREF2; $D$2:$D$11 should appear on VARIABLE 2 RANGE.
   c. Leave HYPOTHESIZED MEAN DIFFERENCE and LABELS blank.
   d. The default value of ALPHA is 0.05 and it is seen in the ALPHA box. Let the ALPHA value remain as is.
9. In the Output portion of the pop-up window, select NEW WORKBOOK.
10. Click OK.

Detailed Steps: Correlation

The following are the detailed steps for running a correlation between attitude toward motorcycles and duration of motorcycle ownership given in Table 12.7. Open the Excel data file for Table 12.7.

1. Select DATA tab.
2. In the ANALYSIS tab, select DATA ANALYSIS.
3. DATA ANALYSIS window pops up.
4. Select CORRELATION from the DATA ANALYSIS window.
5. Click OK.
6. The CORRELATION pop-up window appears on the screen.

7. The CORRELATION window has two portions:
    a. INPUT
    b. OUTPUT OPTIONS
8. The INPUT portion asks for the following inputs:
    a. Click in the INPUT RANGE box. Select (highlight) all rows of data under ATTITUDE and DURATION. $B$2:$C$13 should appear on INPUT RANGE.
    b. Click on COLUMNS beside GROUPED BY.
    c. Leave LABELS IN FIRST ROW as blank.
9. In the OUTPUT OPTIONS pop-up window, select NEW WORKBOOK.
10. Click OK.

Detailed Steps: Bivariate and Multiple Regression

The following are the detailed steps for running a bivariate regression with attitude toward motorcycles as the dependent variable and duration of motorcycle ownership as the independent variable using the data in Table 12.7. Open the Excel data file for Table 12.7.

1. Select DATA tab.
2. In the ANALYSIS tab, select DATA ANALYSIS
3. DATA ANALYSIS window pops up.
4. Select REGRESSION from the DATA ANALYSIS window.
5. Click OK.
6. The REGRESSION pop-up window appears on the screen.
7. The REGRESSION window has four portions:
    a. INPUT
    b. OUTPUT OPTIONS
    c. RESIDUALS
    d. NORMAL PROBABILITY
8. The INPUT portion asks for the following:
    a. Click in the INPUT Y RANGE box. Select (highlight) all the rows of data under ATTITUDE. $B$2:$B$13 should appear in INPUT Y RANGE box.
    b. Click in the INPUT X RANGE box. Select (highlight) all the rows of data under DURATION. $C$2:$C$13 should appear in INPUT X RANGE box.
    c. Leave LABELS and CONSTANT IS ZERO as blanks. CONFIDENCE LEVEL should be 95% (default).
9. In the OUTPUT OPTIONS, select NEW WORKBOOK.
10. Click OK

The steps for running multiple regression are similar, except for step 8b. In step 8b, click in the INPUT X RANGE box. Select (highlight) all the rows of data under Duration and Importance. $C$2:$D$13 should appear on INPUT X RANGE.

Dell Running Case

Review the Dell case, Case 1.1, and the questionnaire given toward the end of the book. Go to the Companion website for this book and download the Dell data file.

1. The mean response on which of the evaluations of Dell (q8_1 to q8_13) exceeds 5 (the midpoint of the scale)?
2. Are the two overall satisfaction groups derived based on the recoding of q4, as specified in Chapter 10, different in terms of each of the evaluations of Dell (q8_1 to q8_13)?

3. Are the two likely to recommend groups derived based on the recoding of q5, as specified in Chapter 10, different in terms of each of the evaluations of Dell (q8_1 to q8_13)?

4. Are the two likelihood of choosing Dell groups derived based on the recoding of q6, as specified in Chapter 10, different in terms of each of the evaluations of Dell (q8_1 to q8_13)?

5. Is the mean of responses to q8_1 (Makes ordering a computer system easy) and q8_2 (Lets customers order computer systems customized to their specifications) different?

6. Is the mean of responses to q8_9 ("Bundles" its computers with appropriate software) and q8_10 ("Bundles" its computers with Internet access) different?

7. Is the mean of responses to q8_6 (Has computers that run programs quickly) and q8_7 (Has high-quality computers with no technical problems) different?

8. Can the overall satisfaction (q4) be explained in terms of all thirteen evaluations of Dell (q8_1 to q8_13) when the independent variables are considered individually? When the independent variables are considered simultaneously? Interpret the results.

9. Can the likelihood of choosing Dell (q6) be explained in terms of all thirteen evaluations of Dell (q8_1 to q8_13) when the independent variables are considered individually? When the independent variables are considered simultaneously? Interpret the results.

 # Summary

Hypotheses related to differences in the population means can be tested using the t distribution. Hypothesis testing based on the t statistic follows the general procedure for hypothesis testing, which was discussed in Chapter 11. The t distribution is similar to the normal distribution in appearance. As the number of degrees of freedom increases, the t distribution approaches the normal distribution. The t statistic is calculated by assuming that the variable is normally distributed, the mean is known, and the population variance is estimated from the sample.

Different forms of the t test are suitable for testing hypotheses based on one sample, two independent samples, or paired samples. In testing hypotheses based on one sample, use the t test if the population variance is unknown and the z test if the variance is known. The z test is used for testing the proportion based on one sample.

Samples drawn randomly from different populations are termed independent samples. For the purpose of analysis, data pertaining to different groups of respondents (e.g., males and females) are generally treated as independent samples even though the data may pertain to the same survey. In testing for the difference between means based on two independent samples, use the two-group t test, but the correct form to use depends on whether the variances are equal or unequal for the two populations. Use the F test to test for the equality of variances. The difference in proportions may be tested using the z test or the chi-square test.

The samples are paired when the two sets of observations relate to the same respondents. In this case, the difference between means should be tested using the paired t test. However, the difference between proportions should be tested using the chi-square test.

The product moment correlation measures the linear association between two metric variables. Bivariate regression derives a mathematical equation, in the form of a straight line, between a single metric dependent variable and a single metric independent variable. Multiple regression involves a single metric dependent variable and two or more (multiple) independent variables that are also metric. The strength of association is measured by the coefficient of multiple determination, R^2. The significance of the overall regression equation may be tested by the overall F test. Individual partial regression coefficients can be tested for significance using the t test.

⌄ Companion Website

This textbook includes numerous student resources that can be found at **www.pearsonglobaleditions.com/malhotra.** At this Companion website, you'll find:

- Student Resource Manual
- Demo movies of statistical procedures using SPSS and Microsoft Excel
- Screen captures of statistical procedures using SPSS and Microsoft Excel
- Data files for all datasets in SPSS and Microsoft Excel
- Additional figures and tables
- Videos and write-ups for all video cases
- Other valuable resources

⌄ Key Terms and Concepts

parametric tests	F statistic	multiple regression
t test	F distribution	beta coefficient
t statistic	paired samples	(beta weight)
standard error	paired-samples t test	coefficient of multiple
t distribution	product moment correlation	determination
independent samples	regression analysis	adjusted R^2
F test	bivariate regression	

⌄ Suggested Cases and Video Cases

Running Case with Real Data and Questionnaire
1.1 Dell

Comprehensive Cases with Real Data and Questionnaires
3.1 JPMorgan Chase   3.2 Wendy's

Online Video Cases
12.1 Marriott   13.1 Marriott

∨ Live Research: Conducting a Marketing Research Project

1. The differences between groups are of interest in most projects. These differences can be examined by using an independent-samples t test for two groups.
2. Often each respondent evaluates many stimuli. For example, each respondent might evaluate different brands or provide importance ratings for different attributes. In such cases, differences between pairs of stimuli can be examined using the paired-samples t test.
3. It is desirable to calculate product moment correlations between all interval-scaled variables. This gives an idea of the correlations between variables.
4. Multiple regressions should be run when examining the association between a single dependent variable and several independent variables.

∨ Acronym

The major characteristics of t tests can be summarized by the acronym T TEST:

T   distribution is similar to the normal distribution

T   est of difference: means or proportions

E   stimate of variance from the sample

S   ingle sample

T   wo samples: independent or paired

∨ Review Questions

12-1. Present a classification of hypothesis-testing procedures.
12-2. Describe the general procedure for conducting a t test.
12-3. What are the tests that could be used in a two-independent-samples t test for proportions?
12-4. How is t test conducted for two independent samples?
12-5. What is the difference between the t distribution and the normal distribution?
12-6. Describe the procedure for examining a hypothesis related to proportions of two independent samples.
12-7. How can the strength of association be measured in a multiple regression model?
12-8. Describe the procedure for examining a hypothesis related to proportions of paired samples.
12-9. What does the product moment correlation determine?
12-10. What is bivariate regression?
12-11. What is the difference between bivariate regression and multiple regression?

∨ Applied Problems

12-12. In each of the following situations, indicate the statistical analysis you would conduct and the appropriate test or test statistic that should be used.
    a. Consumer preferences for Coca-Cola were obtained on an 11-point Likert scale. The same consumers were then shown a commercial about Coca-Cola. After the

      commercial, preferences for Coca-Cola were measured again. Has the commercial been successful in inducing a change in preferences?

    b. Respondents in a survey of 1,000 households were asked to indicate their frequency of domestic air travel on an interval scale. They were also classified as being in high- or low-income categories. Is the frequency of domestic air travel related to income level?

    c. In a telephone survey using a representative sample of 3,000 households, the respondents were asked to indicate their preference for fast-food restaurants using a 7-point Likert scale. The sample was divided into small and large households based on the number of people in the household. Does preference for fast-food restaurants vary by household size?

12-13. The current advertising campaign for a major automobile brand will be changed if fewer than 70 percent of the consumers like it.

    a. Formulate the null and alternative hypotheses.

    b. Which statistical test would you use? Why?

12-14. A major computer manufacturer is having a sale on computers. The number of computers sold during this sale at a sample of ten stores was 800, 1,100, 0, 400, 700, 800, 1,000, 500, 800, and 300.

    a. Is there evidence that an average of more than 500 computers per store were sold during this sale? Conduct the appropriate test using SPSS or Excel. Use $\alpha = 0.05$.

    b. What assumption is necessary to perform this test?

12-15. After receiving complaints from readers, your campus newspaper decides to redesign its front page. A new format B is developed and tested against the current format, A. A total of 100 students are randomly selected, and fifty students are randomly assigned to each format condition. The students are asked to evaluate the effectiveness of the format on an 11-point scale (1 = poor, 11 = excellent). Is the new format better than the current format?

    a. State the null hypothesis.

    b. What statistical test should you use?

12-16. Conduct the following analyses for the Internet usage data given in Applied Problem 11-18 in Chapter 11.

    a. Test the hypothesis that the mean familiarity with the Internet exceeds 4.0.

    b. Is the Internet usage different for males compared to females? Formulate the null and alternative hypotheses, and conduct the test.

    c. Is the proportion of respondents using the Internet for shopping the same for males and females? Formulate the null and alternative hypotheses, and conduct the test.

    d. Do the respondents differ in their attitude toward the Internet and attitude toward technology? Formulate the null and alternative hypotheses, and conduct the test.

12-17. In a pretest, 30 respondents were asked to express their preference for an outdoor lifestyle (V1) using a 7-point scale (1 = not at all preferred, 7 = greatly preferred). They were also asked to indicate the importance of the following variables on a 7-point scale (1 = not at all important, 7 = very important).

      V2 = enjoying nature
      V3 = enjoying the weather
      V4 = living in harmony with the environment
      V5 = exercising regularly
      V6 = meeting other people

The sex of the respondent (V7) was coded as 1 = female and 2 = male. The location of residence (V8) was coded as 1 = midtown/downtown, 2 = suburbs, and 3 = countryside. The data obtained are given in the following table.

SPSS Data File

Excel Data File

Respondent Number	V1	V2	V3	V4	V5	V6	V7	V8
1	7	3	6	4	5	2	1	1
2	1	1	1	2	1	2	1	1
3	6	2	5	4	4	5	1	1
4	4	3	4	6	3	2	1	1
5	1	2	2	3	1	2	1	1
6	6	3	5	4	6	2	1	1
7	5	3	4	3	4	5	1	1
8	6	4	5	4	5	1	1	1
9	3	3	2	2	2	2	1	1
10	2	4	2	6	2	2	1	1
11	6	4	5	3	5	5	1	2
12	2	3	1	4	2	1	1	2
13	7	2	6	4	5	6	1	2
14	4	6	4	5	3	3	1	2
15	1	3	1	2	1	4	1	2
16	6	6	6	3	4	5	2	2
17	5	5	6	4	4	6	2	2
18	7	7	4	4	7	7	2	2
19	2	6	3	7	4	3	2	2
20	3	7	3	6	4	4	2	2
21	1	5	2	6	3	3	2	3
22	5	6	4	7	5	6	2	3
23	2	4	1	5	4	4	2	3
24	4	7	4	7	4	6	2	3
25	6	7	4	2	1	7	2	3
26	3	6	4	6	4	4	2	3
27	4	7	7	4	2	5	2	3
28	3	7	2	6	4	3	2	3
29	4	6	3	7	2	7	2	3
30	5	6	2	6	7	2	2	3

Using a statistical package of your choice, answer the following questions. In each case, formulate the null and the alternative hypotheses and conduct the appropriate statistical test(s).

a. Does the mean preference for an outdoor lifestyle exceed 3.0?

b. Does the mean importance of enjoying nature exceed 3.5?

c. Does the mean preference for an outdoor lifestyle differ for males and females?

d. Does the importance attached to V2 through V6 differ for males and females?

e. Do the respondents attach more importance to enjoying nature than they do to enjoying the weather?

f. Do the respondents attach more importance to enjoying the weather than they do to meeting other people?

g. Do the respondents attach more importance to living in harmony with the environment than they do to exercising regularly?

12-18. Conduct the following analyses for the Internet usage data given in Applied Problem 11-18 in Chapter 11.

a. Find the simple correlations between the following sets of variables: Internet usage and attitude toward the Internet, Internet usage and attitude toward technology, and attitude toward the Internet and attitude toward technology. Interpret the results.

b. Run a bivariate regression, with Internet usage as the dependent variable and attitude toward the Internet as the independent variable. Interpret the results.

c. Run a bivariate regression, with Internet usage as the dependent variable and attitude toward technology as the independent variable. Interpret the results.

d. Run a multiple regression, with Internet usage as the dependent variable, and attitude toward the Internet and attitude toward technology as the independent variables. Interpret the results.

12-19. Conduct the following analyses for the preference of the outdoor-lifestyle data given in Applied Problem 12-17 of this chapter.

a. Calculate the simple correlations between V1 to V6 and interpret the results.

b. Run a bivariate regression, with preference for an outdoor lifestyle (V1) as the dependent variable and the importance of enjoying nature (V2) as the independent variable. Interpret the results.

c. Run a multiple regression, with preference for an outdoor lifestyle as the dependent variable and V2 to V6 as the independent variables. Interpret the results. Compare the coefficients for V2 obtained in the bivariate and the multiple regressions.

NOTES

1. W. Glynn Mangold and Katherine Taken Smith, "Selling to Millennials with Online Reviews," *Business Horizons* (March–April 2012):141–153.
2. Technically, a null hypothesis cannot be accepted. It can be either rejected or not rejected. This distinction, however, is inconsequential in applied research.
3. **www.americanexpress.com**, accessed January 17, 2013; American Express, "American Express Platinum Luxury Survey Shows Wealthy Gen X Consumers Are Mighty in Luxury Buying Power, Spending More Than Baby Boomer Population," **www.prnewswire.com/news-releases/american-express-platinum-luxury-survey-shows-wealthy-gen-x-consumers-are-mighty-in-luxury-buying-power-spending-more-than-baby-boomer-population-54546962.html**, accessed November 15, 2013.
4. Based on **www.colehaan.com**, accessed January 17, 2013.

Online Video Case 12.1

MARRIOTT: Marketing Research Leads to Expanded Offerings

Visit **www.pearsonglobaleditions.com/malhotra** to read the video case and view the accompanying video. Marriott: Marketing Research Leads to Expanded Offerings highlights Marriott's discovery from focus groups and survey research that it could have many types of hotels serving different market segments, and that these market segments, although all providing the same basic needs, would not compete with each other. This case can be used as a springboard for students to conduct comparisons in consumer perceptions about Marriott and three competing hotel chains. In light of the chapter's objectives, it has questions on various hypotheses the researcher can test and what correlation and regression analyses should be performed. It is a comprehensive case that also contains questions for the first eleven chapters.

Report Preparation and Presentation

∨ Overview

Report preparation and presentation constitutes the sixth and final step of the marketing research project. It follows problem definition, developing an approach, research design formulation, field work, and data preparation and analysis. This chapter describes the importance of this final step as well as a process for report preparation and presentation. Figure 13.1 explains the relationship of this chapter to the steps of the marketing research process.

We provide guidelines for report preparation, including report writing and preparing tables and graphs. Oral presentation of the report is discussed. Research follow-up, including assisting the client and evaluating the research process, is described. The chapter also discusses special considerations for report preparation and presentation in international marketing research, use of social media, and ethics. To give the reader an idea of what to expect, we begin with an example of United Airlines.

∨ Learning Objectives

After reading this chapter, the student should be able to:

1. Understand the process that should be followed in preparing and presenting the final report.

2. Explain the guidelines available for writing a report that includes graphs and tables.

3. Describe how an oral presentation should be made and some of the principles involved.

4. Discuss the importance of follow-up with the client, and the assistance that should be given to the client in implementing and evaluating the research project.

5. Explain how the report preparation and presentation process differs in international marketing research.

6. Describe how social media facilitate and enhance report preparation and presentation.

7. Discuss the ethical issues related to the interpretation and reporting of the research process and findings.

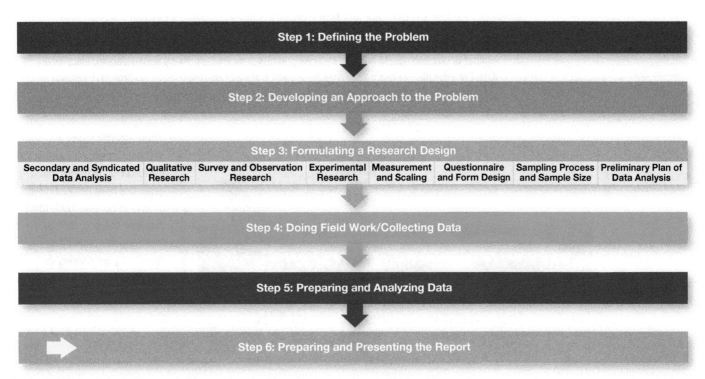

FIGURE 13.1 | RELATIONSHIP OF THIS CHAPTER TO THE MARKETING RESEARCH PROCESS

Research in Practice
United: Reporting the Friendly Skies

United Airlines (**www.united.com**) is the largest airline in the world following its merger with Continental Airlines on October 1, 2010. The airline puts a premium on customer satisfaction. For its in-flight customer satisfaction tracking program, United surveys passengers on some 900 flights per month using a four-page scannable questionnaire. It administers 192,000 questionnaires in nine languages to people traveling to forty different countries. The survey covers passenger satisfaction with the entire air travel process: reservations, airport service, flight attendants, meal service, and the aircraft itself.

The marketing research department at United prepares a monthly report summarizing the customer satisfaction data for about 100 people worldwide, including airport, country, and regional managers; executive management; and others at United's headquarters. The report is thorough and includes all of the following: title page, table of contents, executive summary, problem definition, approach, research design, data analysis, results, and conclusions and recommendations. Several tables and graphs are included to enhance the clarity of the findings. The report findings are also available online.

After issuing the monthly report, the marketing research department handles several requests from internal customers (i.e., various departments within United Airlines) for additional analysis. For example, the marketing department might request a breakdown of customer satisfaction rating by demographic characteristics for a specific route (city pair), such as Chicago to Los Angeles. Because the data can be linked to operational data, such as arrival and departure times and number of passengers, United's researchers can dig deep to answer questions from internal customers. Alex Maggi, United's senior staff analyst for market research, says:

> We have often used the data to identify the reasons why some ratings might differ from one airport to another or one segment to another, by looking at customer mix, by linking survey data to operational data. For example, we can take ratings for a given flight and link them to the on-time performance of the flight in that market and we can show that when on-time performance went down, so did the ratings in specific categories.

Source: Iconic New York / Alamy

This monthly report on customer satisfaction and the follow-up activities that it generates have helped United Airlines to become much more customer focused, thereby improving its competitive positioning and making its friendly skies even friendlier.[1] <

IMPORTANCE OF THE REPORT AND PRESENTATION

report
A written and/or oral presentation of the research process, results, recommendations, and/or conclusions to a specific audience.

A **report** is a written and/or oral presentation of the research process, results, recommendations, and/or conclusions to a specific audience. The written report and the oral presentation are the tangible products of the research effort, and the report serves as a historical record of the project. If inadequate attention is paid to this step, the value of the project to management will be greatly diminished. The involvement of many marketing managers in the project is limited to the written report and the oral presentation. These managers evaluate the quality of the entire project based on the quality of the report and presentation. Management's decision to undertake marketing research in the future or to use the particular research supplier again will be influenced by the perceived usefulness of the report and the presentation. For these reasons, report preparation and presentation assume great importance.

Research Recipe

Never underestimate the importance of the report and its presentation. Many managers' exposure to and evaluation of the entire project may be based on the quality of the report and presentation.

THE REPORT PREPARATION AND PRESENTATION PROCESS

Figure 13.2 illustrates the report preparation and presentation process. The process begins with interpreting the results of data analysis in light of the marketing research problem, approach, research design, and field work.

Instead of merely summarizing the statistical results, the researcher should present the findings so that they can be used directly as input into decision making. Wherever appropriate, conclusions should be drawn and recommendations that management can act upon should be made. Before writing the report, the researcher should discuss the major findings, conclusions, and recommendations with the client's key decision makers. These discussions play a major role in ensuring that the report meets the client's needs and is ultimately accepted. These discussions should confirm specific dates for the delivery of the written report and other data.

The entire marketing research project should be summarized in a single written report or in several reports addressed to different readers. For example, a report prepared for top management should emphasize the strategic aspects of the research project rather than the operating details. However, a report prepared for operating managers should stress the operating details. Generally, an oral presentation supplements these written documents. After the presentation, the client should be given an opportunity to reflect on the report and the project. After that, the researcher

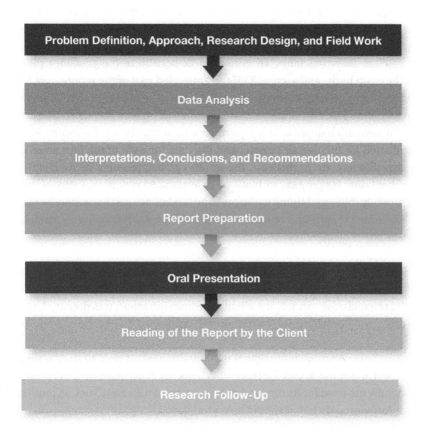

FIGURE 13.2
THE REPORT PREPARATION AND PRESENTATION PROCESS

should take the necessary follow-up actions. This was illustrated in the first Research in Practice feature in this chapter, in which United's marketing research department handles several requests for additional data analysis. The researcher should assist the client in understanding the report, implementing the findings, undertaking further research, and evaluating the research process in retrospect.

Research Recipe

Prepare the report for a specific audience. It may be necessary to prepare several reports addressed to different readers. As the researcher, you should be intimately involved in report preparation and presentation.

REPORT PREPARATION

Researchers differ in the way they prepare a research report. The personality, background, expertise, and responsibility of the researcher, along with the decision maker (DM) to whom the report is addressed, interact to give each report a unique character. In short or repetitive projects, an extensive formal written report of the type described here might not be prepared. Nonetheless, the guidelines for formatting and writing reports and designing tables and graphs generally should be followed.

Report Format

Report formats are likely to vary with the researcher or the marketing research firm conducting the project, the client for whom the project is being conducted, and the nature of the project itself. Hence, we give guidelines from which the researcher can develop a format for the research project at hand. Most formal research reports, as described in the first Research in Practice feature in this chapter about United Airlines, include most of the elements contained in Table 13.1.

As you can see from the table, sections I to IX constitute the prefatory part, sections X through XVI the main body, and section XVII the appended part of the report. This format closely follows the earlier steps of the marketing research process. The format should be flexible, however, so that it can accommodate the unique features of a specific project. For instance, the results might be presented in several chapters of the report. In a national survey, for example, data analysis might be conducted for the overall sample, and the data for each of the four geographic regions might be analyzed separately. In this case, the results can be presented in five chapters instead of one. On the other hand, for projects with online or automated reporting, many of the elements of Table 13.1, especially those pertaining to the prefatory and appended parts, may be omitted. This is also true of less formal reports and reports prepared by internal marketing research departments. We briefly describe the elements of Table 13.1.

TITLE PAGE   The title page should include the title of the report, information (name, postal address, e-mail address, website URL, and telephone numbers) about the researcher or organization conducting the research, the name of the client for whom the report was prepared, and the date of release. The title should also indicate the nature of the project.

letter of transmittal
A letter that delivers the report to the client and summarizes the researcher's overall experience with the project without mentioning the findings.

LETTER OF TRANSMITTAL   A formal report generally contains a **letter of transmittal** that delivers the report to the client and summarizes the researcher's overall experience with the project. The letter should also identify the need for further action on the part of the client, such as implementation of the findings or further research that should be undertaken.

Table 13.1 >

I. Title page
II. Letter of transmittal
III. Letter of authorization
IV. Table of contents
V. List of tables
VI. List of graphs
VII. List of appendixes
VIII. List of exhibits
IX. Executive summary
    a. Major findings
    b. Conclusions
    c. Recommendations

                  Prefatory Part

X. Problem definition
    a. Background to the problem
    b. Statement of the problem
XI. Approach to the problem
XII. Research design
    a. Type of research design
    b. Information needs
    c. Data collection from secondary sources
    d. Data collection from primary sources
    e. Scaling techniques
    f. Questionnaire development and pretesting
    g. Sampling techniques
    h. Field work
XIII. Data analysis
    a. Methodology
    b. Plan of data analysis
XIV. Results
XV. Limitations and caveats
XVI. Conclusions and recommendations

                  Main Body

XVII. Exhibits
    a. Questionnaires and forms
    b. Statistical output
    c. Lists
    d. Bibliography

                  Appended Part

LETTER OF AUTHORIZATION The client writes a letter of authorization to the researcher before work on the project begins. It authorizes the researcher to proceed with the project and specifies its scope and the terms of the contract.

TABLE OF CONTENTS The table of contents should list the topics covered and the appropriate page numbers. In most reports, only the major headings and subheadings are included. Separate lists of tables, graphs, appendixes, and exhibits follow the table of contents.

EXECUTIVE SUMMARY The executive summary is an extremely important part of the report because this is often the only portion of the report that executives read. The summary should describe, as concisely as possible, the problem, the approach, the research design, major results, conclusions, and recommendations.

PROBLEM DEFINITION   This section of the report provides background on the problem; highlights discussions with the decision makers and industry experts; and discusses the secondary data analysis, the qualitative research that was conducted, and the factors that were considered. It should contain a clear statement of the management decision problem and the marketing research problem (see Chapter 2).

APPROACH TO THE PROBLEM   This section should discuss the broad approach that was adopted in addressing the problem. It should also contain a description of the analytical framework and models formulated, and the research questions and hypotheses, and it should identify the information needed.

RESEARCH DESIGN   The section on research design should specify the details of how the research was conducted (see Chapters 3 through 10). This should include the nature of the research design adopted, data collection from secondary and primary sources, scaling techniques, questionnaire development and pretesting, sampling techniques, and field work. These topics should be presented in a nontechnical, easy-to-understand manner. The technical details should be included in an appendix. This section of the report should justify the specific methods selected.

DATA ANALYSIS   This section should describe the plan of data analysis and justify the data analysis strategy and techniques used. The techniques used for analysis should be described in simple, nontechnical terms.

RESULTS   This section is normally the longest part of the report and can comprise several chapters. Often, the results are presented not only at the aggregate level, but also at the subgroup (market segment, geographical area, etc.) level. The results should be organized in a coherent and logical way. The presentation of the results should be geared directly to the components of the marketing research problem and the information needs that were identified. The details should be presented in tables and graphs and the main findings discussed in the text.

LIMITATIONS AND CAVEATS   All marketing research projects have limitations caused by time, budget, and other organizational constraints that might be serious enough to warrant discussion. This section should be written with great care and a balanced perspective. On the one hand, the researcher must make sure that management does not rely too much on the results or use them for unintended purposes, such as projecting them to unintended populations. On the other hand, this section should not erode confidence in the research or unduly minimize its importance.

CONCLUSIONS AND RECOMMENDATIONS   Presenting a mere summary of the statistical results is not sufficient. The researcher should interpret the results in light of the problem being addressed to arrive at major conclusions. Based on the results and conclusions, the researcher might make recommendations to the decision makers. Sometimes marketing researchers are not asked to make recommendations because they research only one area and thus do not understand the bigger picture at the client firm. If recommendations are made, they should be feasible, practical, actionable, and directly usable as inputs into managerial decision making. Conclusions and recommendations should be discussed with the client before finalizing them. It is very important that the report of a conclusive research project (see Chapter 3) be written so that the findings can be used as input into managerial decision making. Otherwise the report is unlikely to get the attention it deserves from management, as illustrated by the following Research in Practice feature.

Research in Practice
Does Management Read Marketing Research Reports?

Every profession has its nagging doubts. Teachers sometimes wonder if their students are really learning anything; police officers occasionally question whether they are actually reducing crime. Once in a while, marketing researchers have a sneaking suspicion that no one is reading their reports.

Determined to resolve this doubt, one marketing researcher inserted a very undignified photo of himself from a recent office party in the middle of his report. Weeks went by as the report was passed through brand and category management with no response. Finally, the senior vice president of advertising called to ask if the marketing researcher needed a vacation. Evidently, this senior vice president was the only one who had read the report in detail.

Source: Carsten Reisinger / Fotolia

Who is responsible when research reports are ignored—the research department or management? According to a study recently released by the Advertising Research Foundation (**thearf.org**) and the American Marketing Association (**www.marketingpower.com**), most marketing managers truly believe that marketing research can be valuable. They also claim that most of what they read is not delivering the kind of information they need to make business decisions. Thus, the responsibility of writing readable reports lies with marketing researchers.[2] <

Research Recipe

Report formats are likely to vary with the researcher or the marketing research firm conducting the project, the client for whom the project is being conducted, and the nature of the project itself. Most formal research reports prepared by external marketing research firms should include most of the elements of Table 13.1.

Report Writing

A report should be written for specific readers—the marketing managers who will use the results. The report should take into account the readers' technical sophistication and interest in the project, as well as the circumstances under which they will read the report and how they will use it.

Technical jargon should be avoided. The researcher is often required to cater to the needs of several audiences with different levels of technical sophistication and interest in the project. Such conflicting needs can be met by including different sections in the report for different readers or separate reports entirely.

The report should be easy to follow. It should be structured logically and written clearly. An excellent check on the clarity of a report is to have two or three people who are unfamiliar with the project read it and offer critical comments. Several revisions of the report might be needed before the final document emerges.

Objectivity is a virtue that should guide report writing. The report should accurately present the methodology, results, and conclusions of the project without slanting the findings to conform to management's expectations.

It is important to reinforce key information in the text with tables, graphs, pictures, maps, and other visual devices. Visual aids can greatly facilitate communication and add to the clarity and impact of the report. The appearance of a report is also important. The report should be professionally reproduced with quality paper, printing, and binding. Guidelines for tabular and graphical presentation are discussed next.

> ## Research Recipe
>
> Write the report objectively for specific readers. It should be easy to follow and should include tables, graphs, and other visual aids.

Visit **www.gallup.com** and search for recent reports posted on this website. What can you learn about report writing from these reports? Critically evaluate, from a researcher's perspective, the format of one of the reports posted at this website. As the marketing manager (or the reader) for whom the report was meant, how useful do you find the report you considered? **<**

Guidelines for Tables

Statistical tables are a vital part of the report and deserve special attention (see the first Research in Practice feature on United Airlines in this chapter). We illustrate the guidelines for tables using the data for Hewlett-Packard sales reported in Tables 13.2 and 13.3. The numbers in parentheses in the following paragraphs refer to the numbered sections of Table 13.2.

TITLE AND NUMBER   Every table should have a number (1a) and title (1b). The title should be brief, but it should clearly describe the information provided. Arabic numbers are used to identify tables so that they can be referred to easily in the text.

ARRANGEMENT OF DATA ITEMS   Data should be arranged in a table to emphasize the most significant aspect of the data. For example, when the data pertain to time, the items should be arranged by appropriate time period. When order of magnitude is most important, the data items should be arranged in that order (2a). If ease of locating items is critical, an alphabetical arrangement is most appropriate.

BASIS OF MEASUREMENT   The basis or unit of measurement should be clearly stated (3a).

leaders
Dots or hyphens that are used in a table to lead the eye horizontally; they impart uniformity and improve readability.

LEADERS, RULINGS, SPACES   **Leaders**—dots or hyphens used to lead the eye horizontally—impart uniformity and improve readability (4a). Instead of horizontal or vertical rules, use so-called white spaces (4b) to set off data items. Skipping lines after different sections of the data can also assist the eye. Horizontal rules (4c) are often used after the headings.

EXPLANATIONS AND COMMENTS: HEADINGS, STUBS, AND FOOTNOTES   Explanations and comments clarifying the table can be provided in the form of captions, stubs, and footnotes. Designations placed over the vertical columns are called *headings* (5a). Designations placed in the left-hand column are called **stubs** (5b). Information that cannot be incorporated into the table should be explained by footnotes (5c). Letters or symbols should be used for footnotes rather than numbers. The footnotes should come after the main table but before the source note.

stubs
Designations placed in the left-hand column of a table.

SOURCES OF THE DATA   If the data contained in the table are secondary, the source of the data should be cited (6a).

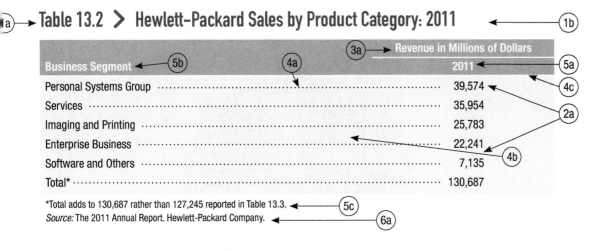

Table 13.2 > Hewlett-Packard Sales by Product Category: 2011

Business Segment	Revenue in Millions of Dollars 2011
Personal Systems Group	39,574
Services	35,954
Imaging and Printing	25,783
Enterprise Business	22,241
Software and Others	7,135
Total*	130,687

*Total adds to 130,687 rather than 127,245 reported in Table 13.3.
Source: The 2011 Annual Report. Hewlett-Packard Company.

Table 13.3 > Hewlett-Packard Sales: 2007 to 2011

Year	Net Revenue (Millions of Dollars)
2007	104,286
2008	118,364
2009	114,552
2010	126,033
2011	127,245

Source: The 2009–2011 Annual Reports, Hewlett-Packard Company.

Research Recipe

Every table should have a number and a title. Arrange the data to emphasize the most significant aspect. Clearly state the basis or unit of measurement. Use leader lines of dots or hyphens to lead the eye horizontally, impart uniformity, and improve readability. Explanations and comments clarifying the table can be provided in the form of captions, stubs, and footnotes. Cite the source of the data, if the data contained in the table are secondary.

Guidelines for Graphs

As a general rule, graphic aids should be used whenever practical, as in the first Research in Practice feature on United Airlines in this chapter. Graphical display of information can complement the text and tables to enhance clarity of communication and impact. As the saying goes, a picture is worth a thousand words. The guidelines for preparing graphs are similar to those for tables. Therefore, this section focuses on the different types of graphical aids. Several of these are illustrated using the data from Table 13.2 and other data for Hewlett-Packard (HP) reported in Table 13.3.[3]

GEOGRAPHIC AND OTHER MAPS   Geographic and other maps, such as product positioning maps, can communicate relative location and other comparative information. Geographic maps can pertain to countries, states, counties, sales territories, and other divisions. For example, suppose the researcher wanted to display the percentage of HP revenues by business segment for each state in the United States. This information could be communicated in a map in which each state was divided into five areas, proportionate to the percentage sales for each of HP's major product lines: personal systems, services, imaging and printing, enterprise business, and software and others. Each area could be displayed in a different color or pattern.

FIGURE 13.3

PIE CHART OF 2011
HEWLETT-PACKARD
REVENUES BY BUSINESS
SEGMENT

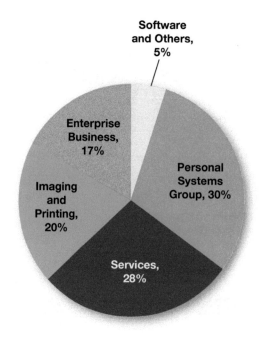

pie chart
A round chart divided into sections. Also called a round chart.

line chart
A chart that connects a series of data points using continuous lines.

pictograph
A graphical depiction that makes use of small pictures or symbols to display the data.

PIE CHARTS   In a **pie chart**, also called a *round chart*, the area of each section, as a percentage of the total area of the circle, reflects the percentage associated with the value of a specific variable. A pie chart is not useful for displaying relationships over time or relationships among several variables. As a general guideline, a pie chart should not contain more than seven sections. Figure 13.3 shows a pie chart for HP revenues by business segment for 2011, as presented in Table 13.2.

LINE CHARTS   A **line chart** connects a series of data points using continuous lines. This is an attractive way of illustrating trends and changes over time. Figure 13.4 shows a line chart for HP revenues from 2007 to 2011 based on Table 13.3. Several series can be compared on the same chart, and forecasts, interpolations, and extrapolations can be shown. If several series are displayed simultaneously, each line should have a distinctive color or form.

PICTOGRAPHS   A **pictograph** uses small pictures or symbols to display the data. Figure 13.5 presents a pictograph for HP revenues from 2007 to 2011. As can be seen from the figure, pictographs do not depict results precisely. Therefore, caution should be exercised when using them.

FIGURE 13.4

LINE CHART OF
HEWLETT-PACKARD'S
TOTAL REVENUES

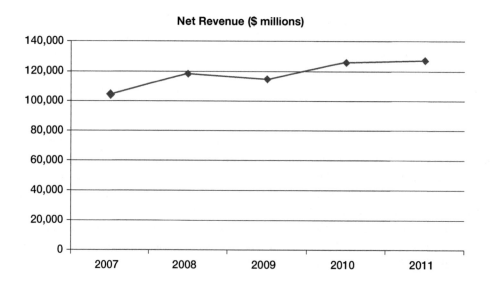

2011	$$$$$$$$$$$$$$
2010	$$$$$$$$$$$$$$
2009	$$$$$$$$$$$$
2008	$$$$$$$$$$$$
2007	$$$$$$$$$$$

FIGURE 13.5
PICTOGRAPH OF
HEWLETT-PACKARD
SALES

HISTOGRAMS AND BAR CHARTS   A **bar chart** displays data in various bars that can be positioned horizontally or vertically. Bar charts can be used to present absolute and relative magnitudes, differences, and changes. The **histogram** is a vertical bar chart where the height of the bars represents the relative or cumulative frequency of occurrence of a specific variable (see Figure 13.6).

SCHEMATIC FIGURES AND FLOWCHARTS   Schematic figures and flowcharts take on a number of different forms. They can be used to display the steps or components of a process, as in Figure 13.2, or they can be used as classification diagrams. Examples of classification charts for classifying secondary and syndicated data were provided in Chapter 3 (Figures 3.6 to 3.9).

bar chart
A chart that displays data in bars positioned horizontally or vertically.

histogram
A vertical bar chart in which the height of the bars represents the relative or cumulative frequency of occurrence of a specific variable.

Research Recipe

Geographic maps can pertain to countries, states, counties, sales territories, and other divisions. As a general guideline, a pie chart should not contain more than seven sections. A line chart connects a series of data points using continuous lines and is an attractive way of illustrating trends and changes over time. Pictographs do not depict results precisely and you should use them with caution. Use histograms and bar charts to present absolute and relative magnitudes, differences, and changes. Use schematic figures and flowcharts to display the steps or components of a process or use them as classification diagrams.

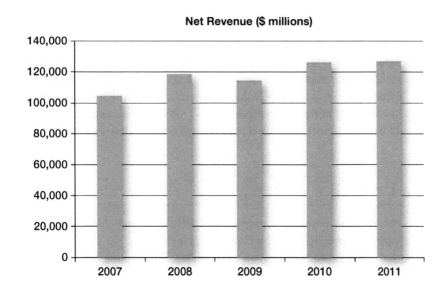

Net Revenue ($ millions)

FIGURE 13.6
HISTOGRAM OF
HEWLETT-PACKARD'S
TOTAL REVENUES

iResearch
Reporting Pepsi-Cola

Visit **www.pepsi.com** and search the Internet for the company's latest annual report. Critically evaluate the use of graphs in Pepsi-Cola's latest annual report. What additional graphs would you construct?

As the vice president of marketing, how useful do you find the graphs in Pepsi-Cola's latest annual report? **<**

ORAL PRESENTATION AND DISSEMINATION

The researcher should present the entire marketing research project to the managers of the client firm. This presentation will help the managers understand and accept the written report. Any preliminary questions that the managers might have can be addressed in the presentation. Because many executives form their first and lasting impressions about the project based on the presentation, its importance cannot be overemphasized. The key to an effective presentation is preparation. A written script or detailed outline should be prepared following the format of the written report. The presentation must be geared to the audience. For this purpose, the researcher should determine audience members' backgrounds, interests, and involvement in the project, as well as the extent to which they are likely to be affected by it. For example, a presentation prepared for the advertising department should put more emphasis on advertising decisions, including budget, media, copy, and execution details. The presentation should be rehearsed several times before it is made to managers.

Visual aids, such as tables and graphs, should be displayed with a variety of media. It is important to maintain eye contact and interact with audience members during the presentation. Sufficient opportunity should be provided for questions, both during and after the presentation. The presentation should be made interesting and convincing with the use of appropriate stories, examples, experiences, and quotations. Filler words such as *uh, y'know*, and *all right* should be avoided.

The **"tell 'em" principle** is effective for structuring a presentation. This principle states: (1) tell 'em what you're going to tell 'em, (2) tell 'em, and (3) tell 'em what you've told 'em. Another useful guideline is the **"KISS 'em" principle**; KISS stands for **K**eep **I**t **S**imple and **S**traightforward.

Body language is also important. It helps speakers to convey their ideas more emphatically. Body language can reinforce the issue or the point the speaker is trying to communicate to the audience. The speaker should vary the volume, pitch, voice quality, articulation, and rate of his or her voice while speaking. The presentation should terminate with a strong closing. To stress its importance, a top-level manager in the client's organization should sponsor the presentation.

The dissemination of the research results should go beyond the oral presentation. The marketing research report, or at least sections of it, should be widely distributed to key executives within the client firm and be made available on demand, for example, by online distribution. (This was illustrated in the first Research in Practice feature in this chapter, in which United Airlines makes its monthly customer satisfaction report available online.) After dissemination, key executives in the client firm should be given time to read the report in detail before follow-up activities are initiated.

"tell 'em" principle
An effective guideline for structuring a presentation. This principle states: (1) tell 'em what you're going to tell 'em, (2) tell 'em, and (3) tell 'em what you've told 'em.

"KISS 'em" principle
A principle of report presentation that states **K**eep **I**t **S**imple and **S**traightforward.

Research Recipe

The key to an effective presentation is preparation. Display visual aids, such as tables and graphs, with a variety of media. Both the "tell 'em" principle and the "KISS 'em" principle" should be followed. Vary the volume, pitch, voice quality, articulation, and rate of your voice while speaking.

RESEARCH FOLLOW-UP

The researcher's task does not end with the oral presentation. Two other tasks remain. First, the researcher should help the client understand and implement the findings and take any follow-up actions. Second, while it is still fresh in her or his mind, the researcher should evaluate the entire marketing research project.

Assisting the Client

After the client has read the report in detail, questions might arise. The client might not understand parts of the report, particularly those dealing with technical matters. The researcher should provide any help that is needed, as is routinely done by the marketing research department of United Airlines (see the first Research in Practice in this chapter). Sometimes the researcher helps implement the findings. Often, the client retains the researcher to help select a new product or advertising agency, develop a pricing policy, segment the market, or take other marketing actions. An important reason for client follow-up is to discuss further research projects. For example, the researcher and management might agree to repeat the study after two years.

Evaluating the Research Project

Although marketing research is scientific, it also involves creativity, intuition, and expertise. Hence, every marketing research project provides an opportunity for learning, and the researcher should critically evaluate the entire project to obtain new insights and knowledge. The key question to ask is: Could this project have been conducted more effectively and/or efficiently? This question, of course, raises several more specific questions. Could the problem have been defined differently and thus enhance the value of the project to the client or reduce the costs? Would a different approach have yielded better results? Was the research design the best? What about the mode of data collection? Should mall intercepts have been used instead of telephone interviews? Was the sampling plan the most appropriate? Were the sources of possible design error correctly anticipated and kept under control, at least in a qualitative sense? If not, what changes could have been made? How could the selection, training, and supervision of field workers have been altered to improve data collection? Was the data analysis strategy effective in yielding information useful for decision making? Were the conclusions and recommendations appropriate and useful to the client? Was the report adequately written and presented? Was the project completed within the time and budget allocated? If not, what went wrong? The insights gained from such an evaluation will benefit the researcher and subsequent projects.

> **R e s e a r c h   R e c i p e**
>
> You should help the client understand and implement the findings and take any follow-up actions. You should also evaluate the entire marketing research project.

INTERNATIONAL MARKETING RESEARCH

The guidelines presented earlier in this chapter apply to international marketing research as well, although report preparation can be complicated by the need to prepare reports for management in different countries and in different languages. In such a case, the researcher should prepare different versions of the report, each geared to specific readers. The reports should be comparable, although the formats might differ. The guidelines for oral presentation are also similar to those given earlier, with the added proviso that the presenter should be sensitive to cultural norms. For example, telling jokes, which is frequently done in the United States, is not appropriate in all cultures.

Most marketing decisions are made from facts and figures arising out of marketing research. But these figures have to pass the test and limits of logic, subjective experience, and gut feelings of decision makers. The subjective experience and gut feelings of managers can vary widely across countries; thus, different recommendations might be made for implementing the research findings in different countries. This is particularly important when making innovative or creative recommendations, as illustrated by the Research in Practice about McDonald's in Australia.

Research in Practice
McDonald's Is Up Down Under

PlusOne Marketing (**www.plusone.com.au**) is an integrated agency in Australia providing a range of innovative services like marketing, media, and communications. In a report prepared for McDonald's Australia, the company recommended that the fast-food giant launch a short message service (SMS) voucher campaign. This recommendation was based on an online survey of 1,000 people that showed that a majority of the respondents preferred vouchers to gift cards. Seventy-seven percent of respondents wanted to use their vouchers for treats. Consumers view vouchers as a guilt-free way of spending on themselves without having to dip into their savings or their salary. Another finding influencing this recommendation was that mobile phone usage in general and SMS usage in particular had increased significantly in Australia. The report prepared had tables and graphs highlighting these facts.

Source: Mark Baker / AP Images

Based on the recommendations, McDonald's Australia ran an SMS voucher campaign in Bundaberg, Queensland, that was integrated with a competition run through a local radio station. Listeners entered the radio competition by sending an SMS. In response, they received a confirmation of their entry with an SMS voucher attached. They could take this voucher to a Bundaberg McDonald's restaurant and receive one of three offers. The customers were also asked to reply to the SMS voucher with a "Y" to receive more McDonald's offers, which most recipients did. McDonald's saw very healthy SMS voucher redemption rates and a healthy increase in sales and profits.[4] ◄

Research Recipe

It may be necessary to prepare different reports in different languages for managers in different countries. The reports should be comparable, although the formats might differ. In making the oral presentation, you should be sensitive to cultural norms. Different recommendations might be made for implementing the research findings in different countries.

MARKETING RESEARCH AND SOCIAL MEDIA

Social media, particularly blogs and Twitter, can play a crucial role in disseminating the report, the results of a marketing research project, and the decisions made by the company based on the findings. The Nielsen Wire is the Nielsen Company's blog and features important information from its mass of publications and research units, covering the latest daily updates in consumer behavior and media, and marketing trends. The Nielsen Company also does a fine job of using its Twitter platform, posting their latest studies, global news, and insights pertaining to the latest research done by the company. Google also makes extensive use of social media to inform the public of their new initiatives and other information about the company. Google bought a blog platform known as Blogspot (**www.blogger.com**) to allow individuals and companies to disseminate information to others at little to no cost at all. Google has its own blog (**www.googleblog.blogspot.com**), which it uses to keep its consumers updated with information, insights, and updates to their technology. It also integrates the Google culture into the blogging world. Blogs can provide an avenue for a company to obtain consumer reaction to the research findings as well as consumer feedback on the decisions made and actions taken by the company based on the research findings.

Social media research results can be presented effectively using charts and graphs such as the Twitter trends' statistics graph. Social media community members' stories can often be effective illustrations of statistical findings when used in reports or executive presentations. These points are illustrated by the Research in Practice about Johnson & Johnson.

Research in Practice
Who Cried in the End? Johnson & Johnson and Not the Moms!

Johnson & Johnson is a well-known *Fortune* 500 company. Its products include St. Joseph aspirin; Band Aid; Baby Powder; Tylenol; and, last but not least, Motrin. Of the many pain-relieving products, Motrin is one that eases the aches that mothers experience from holding their babies in carriers such as slings and wraps. However, this product caused a huge outrage within the community of moms.

A commercial on YouTube posted by Johnson & Johnson stated:

"They say that babies who are carried close to their mothers' bodies cry less than others"

and then asked:

"Do moms that wear their babies cry more than those who don't?"

As many as 27,000 views of the Motrin commercial were generated in just 21 hours. Mothers who saw the Motrin ad were infuriated and felt that they were judged for being moms. They expressed their disagreement with the commercial by coming together on Twitter. At first, this seemed like a minor issue; however, when the Twitter trends' statistics graph was generated, it proved otherwise. The chart that follows clearly illustrates the trends of Motrin compared to other popular tweets mentioning brands like Apple and Microsoft. The immediate, obvious surge in the number of mentions for Motrin, above and beyond the mentions for Apple and Microsoft, emerged after the outrage over the Motrin ad, a stark contrast from its previously unnoticeable nonmentions.

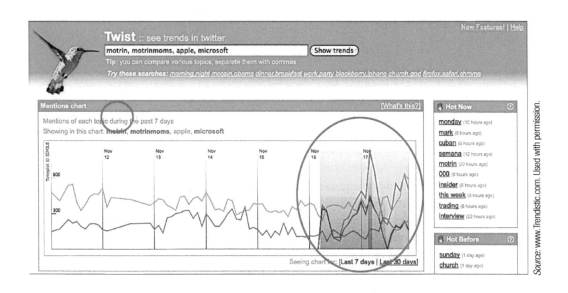

In this case, moms who were angry came together on Twitter to discuss and comment, and later had the intention even to boycott Motrin for coming up with such an offensive commercial. Examples of a few comments and "voices" are reproduced here.

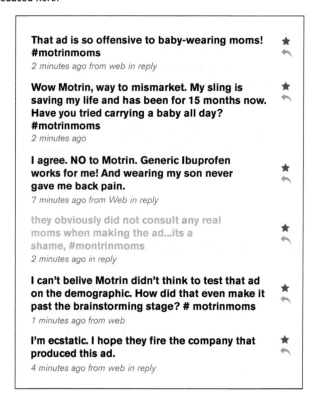

The power of Twitter trends' statistics graph, backed by qualitative comments, was so convincing that Johnson & Johnson removed the commercial for Motrin as soon as it could. This shows that companies should listen to their consumers and pay attention to information about their brand that is found on social media.[5] ‹

Research Recipe

Social media can play an important role in disseminating the report and the results of a marketing research project and the decisions made by the company based on the findings. Use social media community members' stories to effectively illustrate statistical findings in reports and executive presentations.

ETHICS IN MARKETING RESEARCH

Several ethical issues arise during report preparation and presentation, including ignoring pertinent data when drawing conclusions or making recommendations, not reporting relevant information (such as low response rates), deliberately misusing statistics, falsifying figures, altering research results, and misinterpreting the results with the objective of supporting a personal or corporate viewpoint. These issues should be addressed in a satisfactory manner, and the researchers should prepare reports that accurately and fully document the details of all the procedures and findings.

Like researchers, clients also have the responsibility for full and accurate disclosure of the research findings and are obligated to employ these findings honorably. For example, a client who distorts the research findings to make a more favorable claim in advertising can negatively affect the public. Ethical issues also arise when client firms, such as tobacco companies, use marketing research findings to formulate questionable marketing programs.

Research in Practice
Tobacco Industry Is a "Smoking Gun"

It is well known that tobacco smoking is responsible for 30 percent of all cancer deaths in the United States. It is also a leading cause of heart disease and is associated with colds, gastric ulcers, chronic bronchitis, emphysema, and other diseases. Should tobacco companies be ethically responsible for this situation? Is it ethical for these companies to employ marketing research to create glamorous images for cigarettes that have a strong appeal to the target market?

Based on the findings of extensive research, it is estimated that advertising by the tobacco industry plays a part in inducing 3,000 teenagers to become smokers each day in the United States. Advertising for Camel cigarettes through the Old Joe (Joe Camel) cartoon advertisements increased Camel's share of the illegal children's market segment for cigarettes, from 0.5 percent to 32.8 percent, representing sales estimated at $500 million per year.

These detrimental effects were not limited to the United States. Not only was the tobacco industry enticing children to smoke, it also targeted other less-informed populations, such as those living in less-developed countries. This raises the question of whether tobacco companies employed these tactics in an effort to replace those U.S. smokers who quit or died.[6] <

Research Recipe

Ignoring pertinent data when drawing conclusions or making recommendations, not reporting relevant information (such as low response rates), deliberately misusing statistics, falsifying figures, altering research results, and misinterpreting the results with the objective of supporting a personal or corporate viewpoint are ethical breaches that you should avoid at all times. Clients also have the responsibility for full and accurate disclosure of the research findings and are obligated to employ these findings ethically.

SOFTWARE APPLICATIONS

The major statistical packages have procedures for constructing tables and graphs and for preparing reports. In SPSS, GRAPHS can be accessed from the menu bar. Also, a separate program called REPORTING can be used to present results in the desired format. Excel has extensive charting capabilities that can be accessed through the INSERT tab on the menu bar. Excel through Microsoft Office provides a direct link to Word and PowerPoint for report preparation and presentation.

Dell Running Case

Review the Dell case, Case 1.1, and the questionnaire given toward the end of the book.

1. Write a report for Dell management that summarizes the results of your analyses. Prepare a set of charts using Excel. How can you use social media to enhance your report?
2. What recommendations do you have for Dell managers?
3. Can you make a compelling business presentation in ten minutes? Develop a ten-minute presentation for Dell management using no more than ten PowerPoint slides.
4. Share your final presentation with a group of fellow students (representing Dell managers) in a formal setting.
5. What was the most challenging part of preparing, rehearsing, and making this presentation?
6. What will you do differently in your next presentation as a result of what you have learned in this experiential learning exercise?

 Summary

Report preparation and presentation is the final step in the marketing research project. This process begins with a review of the earlier steps of the marketing research process. Special emphasis should be placed on interpretation of data analysis results and conclusions and recommendations. Next, the formal report is written and an oral presentation is made. After managers have read the report, the researcher should conduct a follow-up, assisting management and undertaking a thorough evaluation of the marketing research project.

In international marketing research, report preparation can be complicated by the need to prepare reports in different languages for management in different countries. The use of social media and available software can greatly facilitate and enhance report preparation, presentation, and dissemination. Social media community members' stories can often be effective illustrations of statistical findings in reports or presentations. Several ethical issues are pertinent, particularly those related to the interpretation and reporting of the research process and findings to the client and to the subsequent ways the client uses these results.

∨ Companion Website

This textbook includes numerous student resources that can be found at **www.pearsonglobaleditions.com/malhotra**. At this Companion website, you'll find:

- Student Resource Manual
- Demo movies of statistical procedures using SPSS and Microsoft Excel
- Screen captures of statistical procedures using SPSS and Microsoft Excel
- Data files for all datasets in SPSS and Microsoft Excel
- Additional figures and tables
- Videos and write-ups for all video cases
- Other valuable resources

∨ Key Terms and Concepts

report	pie chart	histogram
letter of transmittal	line chart	"tell 'em" principle
leaders	pictograph	"KISS 'em" principle
stubs	bar chart	

∨ Suggested Cases and Video Cases

Running Case with Real Data and Questionnaire
1.1 Dell

Comprehensive Critical Thinking Cases
2.1 American Idol

Comprehensive Cases with Real Data and Questionnaires
3.1 JPMorgan Chase   3.2 Wendy's

Online Video Cases
13.1 Marriott

∨ Live Research: Conducting a Marketing Research Project

1. The individual parts of the report can be assigned to teams, with each team writing a specific part. Each team also prepares the PowerPoint slides for that part.
2. The project coordinators should be responsible for compiling the final report and the presentation.
3. Make liberal use of graphs.
4. A presentation of the project should be made to the client, with each team presenting its part.
5. If each team has worked on the entire report, compile the final report by combining the best parts of the various team reports. This task can be handled by the project coordinators under the supervision of the instructor. The team to make the client presentation can be selected by the instructor based on class presentations by individual teams.

∨ Acronyms

The guidelines for report writing can be described by the acronym REPORT:

R eaders (should be written for specific readers)

E asy to follow

P resentable and professional appearance

O bjective

R einforce text with tables and graphs

T erse

The guidelines for constructing tables can be described by the acronym TABLES:

T itle and number

A rrangement of data items

B asis of measurement

L eaders, rules, spaces

E xplanations and comments: headings, stubs, and footnotes

S ources of data

GRAPHS can be used as an acronym to guide the construction of graphs:

G eographic and other maps

R ound or pie chart

A ssembly or line charts

P ictographs

H istograms and bar charts

S chematic figures and flowcharts

The guidelines for making a presentation can be summarized by the acronym PRESENTATION:

P reparation

R ehearse your presentation

E ye contact

S tories, experiences, examples, and quotations

E quipment: multimedia

N o filler words

"T ell 'em" principle

A udience analysis

T erminate with a strong closing

I nteract with the audience

O utline or script should be prepared

N umber-one-level manager should sponsor it

∨ Review Questions

13-1. Describe the process of report preparation.

13-2. Describe a commonly used format for writing marketing research reports.

13-3. Describe the following parts of a report: title page, table of contents, executive summary, problem definition, research design, data analysis, and conclusions and recommendations.

13-4. What is the difference between a letter of transmittal and letter of authorization?

13-5. Why is the executive summary an important part of the report?

13-6. What are the main factors considered when writing a report?

13-7. How should the data items be arranged in a table?

13-8. What is a pie chart? What type of information is suitable for a pie chart? What type of information is not suitable for a pie chart?

13-9. Describe a line chart. What kind of information is commonly displayed using this type of chart?

13-10. Describe the role of pictographs. What is the relationship between bar charts and histograms?

13-11. What are the final two steps a researcher should do after presenting the research findings to the decision makers?

13-12. What are the key factors behind a successful report presentation?

13-13. Describe the evaluation of a marketing research project in retrospect.

13-14. How can social media be used to enhance report preparation and presentation?

∨ Applied Problems

13-15. The following passage is taken from a marketing research report prepared for a group of entrepreneurs without much formal business education who run a small family-owned business:

> To measure the image of the hotel industry, two different scaling techniques were employed. The first was a series of semantic differential scales. The second consisted of a set of Likert scales. The use of two different techniques for measurement could be justified based on the need to assess the convergent validity of the findings. Data obtained using both these techniques were treated as interval-scaled. Pearson product moment correlations were computed between the sets of ratings. The resulting correlations were high, indicating a high level of convergent validity.

Rewrite this paragraph so that it is suitable for inclusion in the report for this audience.

13-16. Graphically illustrate the consumer decision-making process described in the following paragraph:

> The consumer first becomes aware of the need. Then the consumer simultaneously searches for information from several sources: retailers, advertising, word of mouth, independent publications, social media, and the Internet. Next, the consumer develops a criterion for evaluating the available brands in the marketplace. Based on this evaluation, the consumer selects the most preferred brand.

13-17. For the data given in Tables 13.2 and 13.3, use a graphics package or a spreadsheet, such as Excel, to construct the following graphs:
   a. Pie chart
   b. Line chart
   c. Bar chart

∨ Internet Exercises

13-18. What are the most powerful social media networks that researchers could obtain data from about customer feedback and loyalty and why?

13-19. Visit the website **www.nielsen.com** and choose one of the reports published. Write a brief analysis of the findings and solutions presented by the report.

NOTES

1. **www.united.com**, accessed March 11, 2013; "United Airlines Enhances Easy Check-in Self-Service Units," *Airline Industry Information* (December 5, 2003): 1; Steve Raabe, "United Airlines Passengers Report Improvement in Customer Service," *Knight Ridder Tribune Business News* (December 20, 2002): 1; Joseph Rydholm, "Surveying the Friendly Skies," *Quirk's Marketing Research Review* (May 1996): 11, 33–35.
2. "How to Write a Good Market Research Report," **www.allaboutmarketresearch.com/articles/art080.htm**, accessed April 16, 2013; Gillian Christie, "Golden Rules of Writing Well," *Chartered Accountants Journal*, 86(11) (December 2007): 60–61; Naomi R. Henderson, "In Defense of Clients," *Marketing Research: A Magazine of Management and Applications*, 15(2) (Summer 2003): 38; Jeannine Bergers Everett, "Value-Added Research Begins Where the Marketplace Meets Management," *Marketing Research: A Magazine of Management and Applications*, 9(1) (Spring 1997): 33–36.
3. **www.hp.com**, accessed March 22, 2013.
4. Based on PlusOne, "How SMS is building business," **www.plusone.com.au/smsstudies.php**, accessed March 13, 2013.
5. A. Kapin, "Motrin's Pain: Viral Video Disaster," **www.fastcompany.com/blog/allyson-kapin/radical-tech/motrins-pain-viral-video-disaster**, accessed July 10, 2013; C. L. Owens, "Johnson & Johnson— Presentation Transcript," **www.slideshare.net/guest901f5569/johnson-johnson-2591972**, accessed July 10, 2013; M. Roumen, "The Motrin Case: The Voice of the Crowd," **www.viralblog.com/social-media/the-motrin-case-the-voice-of-the-crowd**, accessed July 10, 2013.
6. **www.tma.org**, accessed March 3, 2013; Anonymous, "States to Sue Reynolds American over Cigarette Ad," *Wall Street Journal* (Eastern edition), 250(132) (December 5, 2007): B4; Lindsey Tanner, "Tobacco Firms Put on Pressure," *Marketing News*, 36(19) (September 16, 2002): 44; Elise Truly Sautter and Nancy A. Oretskin, "Tobacco Targeting: The Ethical Complexity of Marketing to Minorities," *Journal of Business Ethics*, 16(10) (July 1997): 1011–1017; Kenman L. Wong, "Tobacco Advertising and Children: The Limits of First Amendment Protection," *Journal of Business Ethics*, 15(10) (October 1996): 1051–1064; S. Rapp, "Cigarettes: A Question of Ethics," *Marketing* (November 5, 1992): 17. See also Waymond Rodgers and Susana Gago, "Biblical Scriptures Underlying Six Ethical Models Influencing Organizational Practices," *Journal of Business Ethics*, 64 (2006): 125–136.

Online Video Case 13.1

MARRIOTT: Marketing Research Leads to Expanded Offerings

Visit **www.pearsonglobaleditions.com/malhotra** to read the video case and view the accompanying video. Marriott: Marketing Research Leads to Expanded Offerings highlights Marriott's success in using marketing research to develop a segmentation strategy of targeting different customers with different needs by providing different products and options. This case can be used as a springboard for students to present their results (with graphs and tables) regarding comparisons in consumer perceptions about Marriott and three competing hotel chains. It is a comprehensive case that also contains questions for the first twelve chapters.

CASE 1.1   DELL DIRECT

SPSS Data File   Excel Data File

Dell, Inc. is a holding company that conducts its business worldwide through its subsidiaries. It designs, develops, manufactures, markets, sells, and supports a wide range of products that are customized to individual customer requirements. Its products include mobility products, personal computers, software and peripherals, servers and networking, services, and storage.

Michael Dell, the flamboyant founder and chairman of Dell, started college at the University of Texas as a pre-med student but found time to establish a business selling random-access memory (RAM) chips and disk drives for IBM PCs. Dell bought products at cost from IBM dealers, who were required at the time to order large monthly quotas of PCs from IBM. Dell then resold his stock through newspapers and computer magazines at 10 to 15 percent below retail. By April 1984, Dell was grossing about $80,000 a month—enough to persuade him to drop out of college. Soon he started making and selling IBM clones under the brand name PC's Limited. Dell sold his machines directly to consumers, not through retail outlets as most other manufacturers did. By eliminating the retail markup, Dell could sell PCs at about 40 percent of the price of an IBM.

Michael Dell renamed his company Dell Computer and added international sales offices in 1987. In 1988, the company started selling to larger customers, including government agencies. That year (1988), Dell Computer went public. In 1996, Dell started selling PCs and notebook computers through its website. This channel of order confirmation and shipping and handling is still the bread-and-butter means of addressing Dell's consumers' and enterprise customers' requirements. In 1997, Dell entered the market for workstations and strengthened its consumer business by separating it from its small-business unit and launching a leasing program for consumers. To diversify its revenue sources, in 2001, Dell expanded its storage offerings when it agreed to resell systems from EMC. To grow its services unit, Dell acquired Microsoft software support specialist Plural in 2002.

Despite its success at grabbing PC market share, Dell continues to attack new markets. It has put increasing emphasis on server computers and storage devices for enterprises. Furthering its push beyond PCs, Dell has introduced a handheld computer, a line of Ethernet switches, and consumer electronics such as digital music players and liquid crystal display (LCD) televisions. It originally partnered with Lexmark to develop a line of Dell-branded printers, and it has formed additional partnerships to grow its printing line quickly. On the services front, Dell has mirrored its straightforward approach to hardware sales, embracing a fixed-price model for offerings such as data migration and storage systems implementation. Dell is currently looking to international revenue to supplant sales in the PC-saturated U.S. market.

Dell has thrived as downward-spiraling prices and commoditization washed over the PC industry, benefiting the company's customers and bashing its competitors. Instead of battling the tide by attempting to erect proprietary systems, as HP and IBM often did, Dell used its low-cost, direct-sales model to ride the wave. In 2008, Dell announced PartnerDirect, a global program that brought its existing partner initiatives under one umbrella. Dell intends to expand the program globally. Continuing its strategy and efforts of better meeting customers' needs and demands, it began offering select products in retail stores in several countries in the Americas, Europe, and Asia during fiscal 2008. These actions represent the first steps in its retail strategy, which will allow Dell to extend its business model to reach customers that it had not been able to reach directly.

From 2009 to 2014, Dell got serious about ramping its solutions skills and capabilities with organic and inorganic investments in key intellectual property and talent. In 2009, the company acquired Perot Systems and launched a new business called Dell™ Services that gave customers end-to-end integrated technology (IT) services to help lower their total cost of IT ownership. Dell entered the smartphone market with the Mini 3i from China Mobile. In February 2011, it acquired Compellent Technologies, Inc., and in August 2011, it acquired Force10 Networks. In February 2012, Dell acquired AppAssure and followed that with the acquisition of Clerity Solutions in April 2012. On May 6, 2013, Dell announced the acquisition of Enstratius, a provider of software and consulting services that delivers hybrid-cloud and single-cloud management capabilities. By 2014, the company had its best solutions portfolio ever.

With intense competition for market share and customer patronage in 2014, Dell conducted a survey of recent purchasers of Dell PCs and notebooks. Dell wants to understand its consumers' primary use of its computers for Internet and other uses. Dell also wants to understand the satisfaction that its consumers derive from Dell products. Dell wants to estimate its customers' probability of repeat buying of Dell products and the extent to which its current customers will recommend Dell to their friends and family. Finally, Dell wants to understand if there is any correlation on any of these identified usage factors and the underlying demographic aspects of the classification of its customers. The following questionnaire was the one it used and the data file can be downloaded from the website for this book.

Questions

The questions are given in the Dell Running Case contained in the text chapters.

References

1. **www.gartner.com**, accessed July 3, 2013.
2. **www.dell.com**, accessed July 3, 2013.

Note: This case was prepared for class discussion purposes only and does not represent the views of Dell or its affiliates. The problem scenario is hypothetical and the name of the actual company has been disguised. However, the questionnaire and the data provided are real. Some questions have been deleted, while the data for other questions are not provided because of proprietary reasons.

DELL COMPUTERS

Internet Interview

Thank you for your interest in our study.

Burke is an independent marketing research firm that has been commissioned by DELL Computers to get the honest opinions of recent purchasers of DELL personal computer systems. You will be asked to offer your views about DELL and describe your Internet usage.

This survey should take only a few minutes of your time. By completing this survey, you will be automatically entered into a drawing for $100 gift certificates that can be used at a variety of major online retailers. If you don't complete the survey, you may qualify for the drawing by writing to the address contained on the email inviting you to participate in this project.

Unless you give us your permission at the end of the survey to release your name to DELL along with your responses, your individual responses will be kept confidential.

INTERNET USAGE

Q1   Approximately how many total hours per week do you spend online? This would be the total from all the locations you might use.

Less than 1 hour ☐ –1
1 to 5 hours ☐ –2
6 to 10 hours ☐ –3
11 to 20 hours ☐ –4
21 to 40 hours ☐ –5
or 41 hours or more ☐ –6

Q2A   Following is a list of things people can do online. Please indicate which of these you have ever done on the Internet.
[Rotate responses.]

Don't Know = 0

		Yes	No
_____	Communicated with others via newsgroups or chat rooms	☐–1	☐–2
_____	Looked for a job	☐–1	☐–2
_____	Planned or booked trips	☐–1	☐–2
_____	Downloaded a picture or graphic	☐–1	☐–2
_____	Downloaded sounds or audio clips	☐–1	☐–2
_____	Looked up information about a TV show or movie	☐–1	☐–2
_____	Downloaded a video clip	☐–1	☐–2

Q3   What other type of things do you use the Internet for?

DELL SATISFACTION AND LOYALTY

Q4   Overall, how satisfied are you with your DELL computer system?

Very satisfied ☐ –1
Somewhat satisfied ☐ –2
Somewhat dissatisfied ☐ –3
or Very dissatisfied ☐ –4

Q5   How likely would you be to recommend DELL to a friend or relative?

Definitely would recommend ☐ –1
Probably would ☐ –2
Might or might not ☐ –3
Probably would not ☐ –4
or Definitely would not recommend ☐ –5

Q6   If you could make your computer purchase decision again, how likely would you be to choose DELL?

Definitely would ☐ –1
Probably would ☐ –2
Might or might not ☐ –3
Probably would not ☐ –4
or Definitely would not ☐ –5

Q7   Deleted (open-ended question) _____

COMPUTER MANUFACTURER IMPORTANCE/PERFORMANCE RATINGS

Q8   The following set of statements refers to personal computer manufacturers. For each statement, please first indicate to what extent you agree that **DELL Computers** meets that requirement.

To do this, please use a scale from 1 to 9, where a "1" means you **do not agree at all** with the statement, and a "9" means you **agree completely**. Of course, you may use any number between 1 and 9 that best describes how much you agree or disagree with the statement.

Don't Know = 0

A.   How much do you agree that **DELL Computers** (*insert statement*)?

(Rotate statements.)

	Rating
Makes ordering a computer system easy	_____
Lets customers order computer systems customized to their specifications	_____
Delivers its products quickly	_____
Prices its products competitively	_____
Features attractively designed computer system components	_____
Has computers that run programs quickly	_____
Has high-quality computers with no technical problems	_____
Has high-quality peripherals (e.g., monitor, keyboard, mouse, speakers, disk drives)	_____
"Bundles" its computers with appropriate software	_____
"Bundles" its computers with Internet access	_____
Allows users to assemble components easily	_____
Has computer systems that users can readily upgrade	_____
Offers easily accessible technical support	_____

Q9A   If the price of the DELL computer system you purchased had been **5**% higher, and all other personal computer prices had been the same, how likely would you have been to have purchased your DELL computer system?

Definitely would have purchased ☐ –1
Probably would have purchased ☐ –2
Might or might not have purchased ☐ –3
Probably would not have purchased ☐ –4
or Definitely would not have purchased ☐ –5

Q9B   If the price of the DELL computer system you purchased had been **10**% higher, and all other personal computer prices had been the same, how likely would you have been to have purchased your DELL computer system?

Definitely would have purchased ☐ –1
Probably would have purchased ☐ –2
Might or might not have purchased ☐ –3
Probably would not have purchased ☐ –4
or Definitely would not have purchased ☐ –5

EARLY ADOPTER ATTRIBUTES

Q10   Following is a series of statements that people may use to describe themselves. Please indicate how much you agree or disagree that they describe you. To do this, please use a scale of 1 to 7 where a "1" means you **disagree completely** and a "7" means you **agree completely**. Of course, you may use any number between 1 and 7.

Don't Know = 0

The first/next statement is (*insert statement*). What number from 1 to 7 best indicates how much you agree or disagree that this statement describes you?

Rating

Market Maven Items

I like introducing new brands and products to my friends. _____

I like helping people by providing them with information about many kinds of products. _____

People ask me for information about products, places to shop, or sales. _____

My friends think of me as a good source of information when it comes to new products or sales. _____

Innovativeness

I like to take a chance. _____

Buying a new product that has not yet been proven is usually a waste of time and money. _____

If people would quit wasting their time experimenting, we would get a lot more accomplished. _____

I like to try new and different things. _____

I often try new brands before my friends and neighbors do. _____

I like to experiment with new ways of doing things. _____

Opinion Leadership

When it comes to computer-related products, my friends are very likely to ask my opinion. _____

I am often used as a source of advice about computer-related products by friends and neighbors. _____

I often tell my friends what I think about computer-related products. _____

DEMOGRAPHICS

Q11 These next questions are about you and your household and will just be used to divide our interviews into groups.

What was the last grade of school you completed?

Some high school or less □ –1
High school graduate □ –2
Some college/technical school □ –3
College graduate or higher □ –4

Q12 Which of the following best describes your age?

18 to 19 □ –1
20 to 24 □ –2
25 to 29 □ –3
30 to 34 □ –4
35 to 39 □ –5
40 to 44 □ –6
45 to 49 □ –7
50 to 54 □ –8
55 to 59 □ –9
60 to 64 □ –10
65 to 69 □ –11
70 to 74 □ –12
75 to 79 □ –13
80 or older □ –14

Q13 Which of the following best describes your household's total yearly income before taxes?

Under $20,000 □ –1
$20,000-$29,999 □ –2
$30,000-$49,999 □ –3
$50,000-$74,999 □ –4
$75,000-$99,999 □ –5
$100,000 or over □ –6

No Answer = 0

Q14 Are you ...?

Male □ –1
Female □ –2

This completes all the questions.
Thank you very much for your assistance with this interview!

CASE 2.1   *AMERICAN IDOL*

A Big Hit for Marketing Research?

"This could be more of a challenge than we previously thought," Melissa Marcello told her business associate Julie Litzenberger. After nodding in agreement, Litzenberger put down her cup of coffee at the Vienna, Virginia, Starbucks coffee shop near her firm's headquarters.

Both Marcello and Litzenberger were far along their career paths as researchers in 2013 when they met at Starbucks. Marcello was CEO of a research agency and Litzenberger led the public relations division at marketing communications agency Sage Communications (**www.sagecommunications.com**). Both were based in the Washington, DC area.

Litzenberger took the last bite of her cinnamon scone before sipping her latte. She nodded again to Marcello across the table for two before answering. "Research studies that are the most successful in moving the needle are the studies where the research firm uses scientific and credible methods, poses the right questions, and provides the client company with the insights needed to sufficiently reduce risk in decision making," Litzenberger said. "In short, improving decision making is what effective marketing research is about."

Over the years, Marcello and Litzenberger had witnessed prospective client companies voicing resistance to pursuing marketing research. Skeptics of professional marketing research sometimes would say that they "already knew enough about customers to make decisions." Other times, skeptics would assail the sampling methods of studies in an attempt to dismiss the results. And in other instances, skeptics would merely claim that finding the answers to such questions about customers would be too expensive to obtain. In sum, professionally done marketing research was presented as being impractical.

Marcello and Litzenberger were attempting to overcome a challenge in client development. Specifically, they were attempting to obtain evidence to confront skeptics of professionally done marketing research without compromising the privacy of previous clients with whom they had worked. It was inappropriate for them to share the results of previous studies with anyone other than the clients who had contracted them for those studies.

While considering dozens of ideas over the past three weeks of project development brainstorming sessions, Marcello and Litzenberger were now focused on one project for demonstrating the usefulness of marketing research to prospective clients. The research question was: "What still needs to be known about the viewers and voters for contestants of the popular TV show *American Idol*?"

American Idol (**www.americanidol.com**) is an annual televised singing competition that began its first season in 2002. The program has always sought to discover the best young singer in the United States. Each year, a series of nationwide auditions are followed by a series of telecasts featuring the singers who advance to the next week's show based on public voting. Throughout the show's history, three or four judges have critiqued the singing of surviving contestants each week, and good-guy Ryan Seacrest has hosted the show each year. Judges for the twelfth season (2013) were Mariah Carey, Randy Jackson, Nicki Minaj, and Keith Urban.

Ratings for the *American Idol* finale for 2013 plunged to an all-time low for the twelve-year old show. According to Nielsen Co.

(**www.nielsen.com**), 14.3 million viewers watched as Candice Glover won over Kree Harrison. That was a 33 percent drop from 2012. *American Idol* experienced declining viewership also in 2012 (eleventh) season. *Idol* delivered 21.49 million viewers, according to Fox's time-zone-adjusted national ratings, down 24 percent from 29.29 million for 2011. The 2010 season finale had 24.22 million viewers watching Lee DeWyze and Crystal Bowersox, compared to the previous year (2009), which had 28.84 million viewers. Despite these issues, there was lack of third-party research to gain more insight into who the viewers actually were or their motivations for voting for *American Idol* contestants.

"Are we kidding ourselves?" Marcello challenged Litzenberger. "Who would care about a study investigating *American Idol* viewers?"

"How about the sponsors of the show?" Litzenberger quickly countered. "Pepsi Cola passed on sponsoring the show during its development, but Coca-Cola decided to take a risk and invested $10 million to become a sponsor in *American Idol*'s first season. That's a lot of cola and that was a lot of risk to take in the volatile world of broadcast television!"

"You're right," Marcello said. "I later read in *USA Today* that Kelly Clarkson might have been voted the first American Idol, but Coke was the real winner. So maybe Pepsi was the real loser. Coke and Ford now spend tens of millions each year not only to be sponsors, but also to have tie-in promotions."

"But just how durable is the show's concept?" Litzenberger asked after finishing her latte. "What if we find that voters are mostly pre-teen girls? What if we find that adults don't vote for the contestants or adults don't have confidence in the judges' opinions?"

"The news media should find such answers more delicious than that slice of pumpkin bread I see in that glass case over there by the cash register," Marcello said. "Journalists will almost always cover what they regard as relevant and quantifiable trends in popular culture."

Litzenberger leaned forward. "So how do you propose that we do such a study?"

"We've devoted hours to this question at my firm for more than a week. Here's our best thinking on it as of today," Marcello said. "We could place about six questions on ORC International's CARAVAN (**www.orcinternational.com**) national omnibus telephone survey to find out more about who, among adults 18 or older living in the United States, watched and voted during the 2013 season of *American Idol*. Such an omnibus survey could be done by telephone during three days in late May 2013."

"Okay, but what about sampling?" Litzenberger said. "You know we might get attacked on this. It could be really expensive, too. Can we afford it?"

"If we do it this way, we can afford it," Marcello said. "It will run about $1,000 per question. We'll have the Opinion Research Corporation ask our questions along with those of other sponsoring companies to a randomly selected national sample of 1,045 adults comprised about evenly of men and women. With a total sample size of more than 1,000, we will be able to say with 95 percent certainty that the results would be accurate to within plus or minus 3 percent. This exceeds acceptable standards for a survey about media preferences."

"So if only 10 percent of our sample reported voting for *American Idol* contestants, we would be able to say with 95 percent confidence that the actual percentage of the adult population who voted was somewhere between 7 and 13 percent?" Litzenberger asked.

"You've got it," Marcello affirmed. "Of course, it could be a lower or a much higher percentage. Nobody really knows now. Anybody who says otherwise is merely speculating."

Silence now overcame these two researchers as they reflected on the future courses of action they could take. They could drop the whole idea of demonstrating the usefulness of marketing research. They could pursue this *American Idol* study. If so, what questions should be asked to respondents and why? Should they continue to consider other ideas for such a study and pursue it later? What should they do? Why?

Critical Thinking Questions

1. Marcello and Litzenberger felt it was important to conduct this study because _____.
   (State the relevant background information used to justify their work.)
2. The main purpose of Marcello and Litzenberger's study was _____.
   (State as accurately as possible the purpose for doing the study.)
3. The key questions that Marcello and Litzenberger want to address are _____.
   (Identify the key questions in the minds of the case's protagonists.)
4. The methods used to answer their key questions were _____.
   (Describe the general approach used and include details that assist in evaluating the quality of the results, for example, sample size, etc.).
5. The most important information in this article is _____.
   (Identify the facts, observations, and/or data Marcello and Litzenberger use to support their conclusions. Be quantitative.)
6. The results can be put into context by comparing them to _____.
   (Place the quantitative results into an easy-to-understand context by expressing them as percentages or by comparing them to an intuitively understood value—for example, twice the size of a football field.)
7. The main inferences/conclusions in this case are _____.
   (Identify the key conclusions that the case protagonists present.)
8. If we take this line of reasoning seriously, the implications are _____.
   (What consequences are likely to follow if people take Marcello and Litzenberger's reasoning seriously?)

Technical Questions

Chapter 1

9. How should Marcello and Litzenberger account for the role of social media in designing this research?

10. What does this case suggest is the role of marketing research in marketing decision making?

Chapter 2

11. Define the management decision problem confronting Marcello and Litzenberger and a corresponding marketing research problem. Show the linkages between the two.

Chapter 3

12. If Marcello and Litzenberger decide to conduct this study, what research design should they adopt? Relate the different phases of the research design to specific aspects of the marketing research problem.
13. What kind of secondary and syndicated data would be helpful in addressing the questions raised by Marcello and Litzenberger? What is the role played by such data?

Chapter 4

14. Discuss the role of qualitative research in gaining a better understanding of why people view *American Idol*. What insights can be gained from an analysis of social media?

Chapter 5

15. Is the telephone survey the most appropriate method in this case? If not, which survey method would you recommend?

Chapter 6

16. Why did Marcello and Litzenberger not consider doing an experiment? What aspects of *American Idol* viewers should be researched by conducting an experiment?

Chapter 7

17. Discuss the role of measurement and scaling in assessing the audience response to *American Idol*.

Chapter 8

18. Critically evaluate the wording of the following question: "Who is your favorite *American Idol*?"

Chapter 9

19. Describe the sampling process employed by Opinion Research Corporation's CARAVAN. (*Hint:* Visit www.orcinternational.com)

Chapter 10

20. If you were the supervisor in charge of the CARAVAN telephone interviewers, what challenges would you face?

Chapter 13

21. As part of the management team at Fox, which produces *American Idol*, how would you evaluate the report produced by Marcello and Litzenberger? How will the proposed study help you make decisions about the show?

References

1. **www.americanidol.com**, accessed January 5, 2013.
2. **http://en.wikipedia.org/wiki/American_Idol**, accessed July 19, 2013.
3. James Hibberd, "*American Idol* Premiere Ratings: Biggest Drop Ever" (January 19, 2012), **http://insidetv.ew.com/2012/01/19/american-idol-premiere-ratings/**, accessed April 18, 2012.
4. Adapted from Melissa Marcello and Julie Litzenberger, "Fascinating Findings," *Quirk's Marketing Research Review*, 21(3) (March 2007): 58–62.

Note: The contribution of Professor Mark Peterson in developing this case is gratefully acknowledged.

CASE 3.1   JPMORGAN CHASE

Chasing Growth Through Mergers and Acquisitions

SPSS Data File   Excel Data File

JPMorgan Chase (**www.jpmorgan.com**) is a leading global financial services firm that provides broad-range investment banking, financial services for consumers, small business and commercial banking, financial transaction processing, asset management, and private equity services. As of 2014, JPMorgan Chase operates in more than 100 countries, and it serves millions of U.S. consumers and many of the world's most prominent corporate, institutional, and government clients. JPMorgan Chase is a component of the Dow Jones Industrial Average and is one of the Big Four banks of the United States, with Bank of America, Citigroup, and Wells Fargo. The company is not only doing well currently with assets of $2.3 trillion and a promising future, but it also has a noteworthy history.

JPMorgan Chase & Co. was founded in New York in 1799. The firm is built on the foundation of nearly 1,000 predecessor institutions that have come together over the years to form today's company. Here are some highlights from its recent history and the key transactions leading up to the formation of JPMorgan Chase:

- In 1991, Chemical Banking Corp. combined with Manufacturers Hanover Corp., keeping the name Chemical Banking Corp., then the second largest banking institution in the United States.
- In 1995, First Chicago Corp. merged with National Bank of Detroit's parent NBD Bancorp., forming First Chicago NBD, the largest banking company based in the Midwest.
- In 1996, Chase Manhattan Corp. merged with Chemical Banking Corp., creating what was then the largest bank holding company in the United States.
- In 1998, Banc One Corp. merged with First Chicago NBD, taking the name Bank One Corp. Merging subsequently with Louisiana's First Commerce Corp., Bank One became the largest financial services firm in the Midwest, the fourth largest bank in the United States, and the world's largest Visa credit card issuer.
- In 2000, JPMorgan & Co. merged with Chase Manhattan Corp., in effect combining four of the largest and oldest money center banking institutions (JPMorgan, Chase, Chemical, and Manufacturers Hanover) in New York City into one firm called JPMorgan Chase & Co.
- In 2004, JPMorgan Chase merged with Bank One.
- In 2008, JPMorgan Chase & Co. acquired The Bear Stearns Companies Inc., strengthening its capabilities across a broad range of businesses, including prime brokerage, cash clearing, and energy trading globally.
- In 2008, JPMorgan Chase acquired Washington Mutual's deposits for $1.9 billion after the largest bank failure in U.S. history.
- In 2010, J.P. Morgan acquired full ownership of its U.K. joint venture, J.P. Morgan Cazenove, one of Britain's premier investment banks.

The acquisition of other companies is one of the primary methods that JPMorgan has used to grow its numbers, and it can be considered a strength in regard to how these mergers have combined to give rise to a broad range of commercial and investment banking capabilities. In 2011, JPMorgan celebrated the 90th anniversary of the firm's presence in China. In July 2013, it was the third largest bank in the world by market capitalization, behind Wells Fargo of USA and Industrial and Commercial Bank of China. JPMorgan has consistently achieved one of the best overall rankings in the *Institutional Investor* magazine's annual survey of U.S. equity analysts.

To sustain growth that is so important in its strategic and long-term plans, JPMorgan Chase conducted a study to understand its consumers, their lifestyles, and potential for customer segmentation in terms of investment products and service needs. The following questionnaire was the one it used, and the data file can be downloaded from the website for this book. The outputs and the analyses of this study should help JPMorgan Chase carve out its growth plan and implement it successfully.

Questions

Chapter 1

1. Discuss the role that social media research can play in helping JPMorgan Chase formulate sound marketing strategies.

Chapter 2

2. Management would like to expand JPMorgan Chase's market share in the consumer market even more. Define the management decision problem.
3. Define an appropriate marketing research problem based on the management decision problem you have identified.

Chapter 3

4. Formulate an appropriate research design for investigating the marketing research problem that you have defined above in question 3 for Chapter 2.
5. Use the Internet to determine the market shares of the major banks for the last calendar year.
6. What type of syndicate data will be useful to JPMorgan Chase?

Chapter 4

7. Discuss the role of focus groups versus depth interviews in helping JPMorgan Chase expand its market share. What insights can be gained from an analysis of social media?

Chapter 5

8. If a survey is to be conducted to determine consumer preferences for banks, which survey method should be used? Explain.

Chapter 6

9. Discuss the role of pre-experimental versus true experimental designs in helping JPMorgan Chase expand its product offerings.

Chapter 7

10. Illustrate the use of paired comparison and constant sum scales in measuring consumer preferences for banks. Should any of these scales be used?

11. Develop a Likert scale for measuring attitudes toward JPMorgan Chase bank.

Chapter 8

12. Critically evaluate the questionnaire developed for the JPMorgan Chase survey.

Chapter 9

13. What sampling plan should be adopted for the survey you decided to use in question 8 for Chapter 5? How should the sample size be determined?

Chapter 10

14. How would you supervise and evaluate field workers for conducting the survey that you decided to use in question 8 for Chapter 5?

15. Many of the importance items (Q1) have more than 10 percent missing values. Identify these items. How would you address these missing values?

16. Recode the following demographic characteristics into the categories specified: (a) Age (Q9) (27–57 = 1, 58–68 = 2, 69–75 = 3, 76–90 = 4); (b) Marital status (Q11) (now married = 1, all other, i.e., now not married = 2); (c) number of dependent children (Q12) (3–10 = 3); and (d) education (Q14) (combine some high school, high school graduate, and vocational or technical school into a single category, and also combine law school graduate, dental/medical school graduate, and doctorate into a single category).

17. Recode the advantage of using primary provider (Q5) into two categories (1–3 = 1 [small advantage], 4–5 = 2 [big advantage]).

18. Recode overall satisfaction with service provider (Q6_a) into three categories (2–4 = 1, 5 = 2, 6 = 3).

Chapter 11

19. Calculate an overall rating score for the primary financial provider by summing the ratings of all thirteen items in Q6 (Q6_a through Q6_m). Obtain a frequency distribution and summary statistics. Interpret the results.

20. Are the decision-making approaches (Q8) related to any of the demographic characteristics (Q9 through Q15, some recoded as specified previously for Chapter 10)?

21. Is the recoded advantage of using primary provider (Recoded Q5) related to any of the recoded demographic characteristics?

Chapter 12

22. Are the ratings of any of the importance variables (Q1_a through Q1_l) different for those who rate the advantage of their primary provider as big compared to those who rate it as small (Q5 recoded as specified previously for Chapter 10)? Formulate the null and alternative hypotheses and conduct an appropriate test.

23. Are any of the ratings of the primary financial provider (Q6_a through Q6_m) different for those who rate the advantage of their primary provider as big compared to those who rate it as small (Q5 recoded as specified previously for Chapter 10)? Formulate the null and alternative hypotheses and conduct an appropriate test.

24. Is "the performance of investments with this provider" (Q1_a) more important than "online services offered" (Q1_e)? Formulate the null and alternative hypotheses and conduct an appropriate test.

25. Is the likelihood of "recommend your primary provider to someone you know" (Q2) lower than the likelihood of "continue to use your primary provider at least at the same level as up to now" (Q3)? Formulate the null and alternative hypotheses and conduct an appropriate test.

26. Can the likelihood of "recommend your primary provider to someone you know" (Q2) be explained by the ratings of the primary financial provider (Q6_a through Q6_m) when these ratings are considered simultaneously?

27. Can the likelihood of "continue to use your primary provider at least at the same level as up to now" (Q3) be explained by the ratings of the primary financial provider (Q6_a through Q6_m) when these ratings are considered simultaneously?

Chapter 13

28. Write a report for JPMorgan Chase based on all the analyses that you have conducted. What do you recommend that JPMorgan Chase do in order to continue to grow?

29. If the survey conducted by JPMorgan Chase were to be conducted in Argentina, how should the marketing research be conducted?

References

1. www.jpmorganchase.com, accessed July 18, 2013.
2. www.jpmorganchase.com/cm/cs?pagename=Chase/ Href&urlname=jpmc/about/history, accessed July 18, 2013.
3. www.jpmorganchase.com/cm/BlobServer?blobtable=Do cument&blobcol=urlblob&blobkey=name&blobheader=ap plication/pdf&blobnocache=true&blobwhere=jpmc/about/ history/shorthistory.pdf, accessed July 18, 2013.
4. http://files.shareholder.com/downloads/ ONE/468644334x0x184756/31e544ec-a273-4228-8c2a-8e46127783f8/2007ARComplete.pdf, accessed July 18, 2013.
5. Francos, Alex. "ICBC Loses Bank Crown to U.S.," *The Wall Street Journal* (Asia Edition) (July 24, 2013):1, 22.

Note: This case was prepared for class discussion purposes only and does not represent the views of JPMorgan Chase or its affiliates. The problem scenario is hypothetical, and the name of the actual company has been disguised. However, the questionnaire and the data provided are real. Some questions have been deleted, while the data for other questions are not provided because of proprietary reasons.

ANNUAL FINANCIAL SERVICES SURVEY

Introduction

This survey asks some questions about financial services, that is, about investments and banking. The **primary financial services provider** (company) is where you have the **largest** portion of your household's investments and savings/checking assets.

Your co-operation in answering these questions is greatly appreciated.

Financial Services Provider

1. If you were selecting a **primary financial provider (company)** *today*, how important would each of the following be to you? **(X ONE Box for EACH.)**

	Extremely Important	Very Important	Somewhat Important	Somewhat Unimportant	Not Important at All
a. Performance of investments with this provider	5 ☐	4 ☐	3 ☐	2 ☐	1 ☐
b. Fees or commissions charged	5 ☐	4 ☐	3 ☐	2 ☐	1 ☐
c. Depth of products and services to meet the range of your investment needs	5 ☐	4 ☐	3 ☐	2 ☐	1 ☐
d. Ability to resolve problems	5 ☐	4 ☐	3 ☐	2 ☐	1 ☐
e. Online services offered	5 ☐	4 ☐	3 ☐	2 ☐	1 ☐
f. Multiple providers' products to choose from	5 ☐	4 ☐	3 ☐	2 ☐	1 ☐
g. Quality of advice	5 ☐	4 ☐	3 ☐	2 ☐	1 ☐
h. Knowledge of representatives or advisers you deal with	5 ☐	4 ☐	3 ☐	2 ☐	1 ☐
i. Representative knowing your overall situation and needs	5 ☐	4 ☐	3 ☐	2 ☐	1 ☐
j. Access to other professional resources	5 ☐	4 ☐	3 ☐	2 ☐	1 ☐
k. Degree to which my provider knows me	5 ☐	4 ☐	3 ☐	2 ☐	1 ☐
l. Quality of service	5 ☐	4 ☐	3 ☐	2 ☐	1 ☐

	Extremely Likely	Very Likely	Somewhat Likely	Somewhat Unlikely	Very Unlikely
2. How **likely** are you to recommend your primary provider to someone you know? **(X ONE Box.)**	5 ☐	4 ☐	3 ☐	2 ☐	1 ☐
3. How **likely** is it that you will continue to use your primary provider at least at the same level as up to now? **(X ONE Box.)**	5 ☐	4 ☐	3 ☐	2 ☐	1 ☐
4. How **likely** is it that you or your household will **drop** or **replace** your primary provider? **(X ONE Box.)**	5 ☐	4 ☐	3 ☐	2 ☐	1 ☐
5. How would you rate the **advantage** to you of using your primary provider rather than other financial services providers? **(X ONE Box.)**	**Very Big** 5 ☐	**Big** 4 ☐	**Some** 3 ☐	**Slight** 2 ☐	**None** 1 ☐

6. How would you rate the following elements of your **primary financial provider (company)**? If it is not applicable, select **"NA."**
(X ONE Box for EACH Statement.)

	Excellent	Very Good	Good	Fair	Poor	NA
a. Overall satisfaction with primary provider	6 ☐	5 ☐	4 ☐	3 ☐	2 ☐	1 ☐
b. Performance of investments with this provider	6 ☐	5 ☐	4 ☐	3 ☐	2 ☐	1 ☐
c. Fees or commissions charged	6 ☐	5 ☐	4 ☐	3 ☐	2 ☐	1 ☐
d. Depth of products and services to meet the range of your investments needs	6 ☐	5 ☐	4 ☐	3 ☐	2 ☐	1 ☐
e. Ability to resolve problems	6 ☐	5 ☐	4 ☐	3 ☐	2 ☐	1 ☐
f. Online services offered	6 ☐	5 ☐	4 ☐	3 ☐	2 ☐	1 ☐
g. Multiple providers' products to choose from	6 ☐	5 ☐	4 ☐	3 ☐	2 ☐	1 ☐
h. Quality of advice	6 ☐	5 ☐	4 ☐	3 ☐	2 ☐	1 ☐
i. Knowledge of representatives or advisers you deal with	6 ☐	5 ☐	4 ☐	3 ☐	2 ☐	1 ☐
j. Representative knowing your overall situation and needs	6 ☐	5 ☐	4 ☐	3 ☐	2 ☐	1 ☐
k. Access to other professional resources	6 ☐	5 ☐	4 ☐	3 ☐	2 ☐	1 ☐
l. Degree to which my provider knows me	6 ☐	5 ☐	4 ☐	3 ☐	2 ☐	1 ☐
m. Quality of service	6 ☐	5 ☐	4 ☐	3 ☐	2 ☐	1 ☐

7. During the past twelve months, have you or anyone in your household switched some assets (other than checking account assets) from one investment/savings **provider** to another? (Do *not* include switching money from one individual investment such as a stock or bond to another stock or bond within the same brokerage or investment company.) Please **exclude** assets in a 401(k), 403(b), 457, or similar defined contribution retirement accounts.

1 ☐ Yes   2 ☐ No

8. The following are some different approaches you and/or your household might take regarding advice and investment decision making. Please read each one and then answer the question below.

1. Using a variety of online or offline information sources, you make your own investment decisions without the assistance of an investment professional or advisor.

2. Using a variety of online or offline information sources, you make *most* of your own investment decisions but use an investment professional or advisor for specialized needs only (e.g., alternative investments or tax advice).

3. You regularly consult with an investment professional or advisor and you may also get additional information yourself, but *you* make most of the final decisions.

4. You rely upon an investment professional or advisor to make *most* or *all* of your investment decisions.

For the majority of your assets, which *one* of the previous approaches (1–4) *best* describes your preferred approach?
(Write in a number from 1–4.)

Number: _____

Your answers to the following questions will be used to help us interpret the information you have provided.

9. What is your age?

Age: _____ years

10. Are you . . . ?

1 ☐ Male   2 ☐ Female

11. What is your current marital status? **(X ONE Box.)**

1 ☐ Now married   2 ☐ Widowed   3 ☐ Divorced

4 ☐ Separated   5 ☐ Single, never married   6 ☐ Living together, not married

12. How many people in your household are dependent children? **(Write in number.)** _____

13. For the following type of financial transaction, please indicate who is *primarily* responsible, or if the responsibilities are shared. **(X ONE Box for Each.)**

	Male Head of Household	Female Head of Household	Shared Equally	Other
Investment decision making	1 ☐	2 ☐	3 ☐	4 ☐

14. What is the highest level of education you have completed? **(X ONE Box.)**

01 ☐ Some high school

02 ☐ High school graduate

03 ☐ Vocational or technical school/apprenticeship

04 ☐ Some college

05 ☐ College graduate

06 ☐ Some graduate school

07 ☐ Master's degree

08 ☐ Law school graduate

09 ☐ Dental/medical school graduate

10 ☐ Doctorate

15. What is your retirement status? **(X ONE Box.)**

1 ☐ Retired   2 ☐ Semi-Retired   3 ☐ Not Retired

CASE 3.2 WENDY'S

History and Life After Dave Thomas

 SPSS Data File

 Excel Data File

As of 2014, Wendy's (**www.wendys.com**) is the world's third largest quick-service hamburger company. The Wendy's system includes more than 6,500 franchise and company restaurants in the United States and twenty-seven other countries and U.S. territories worldwide. Wendy's restaurants offer a standard menu featuring hamburgers and chicken breast sandwiches, prepared to order with the customer's choice of condiments, as well as chicken nuggets, chili, baked potatoes, french fries, salads, desserts, soft drinks, and children's meals.

Dave Thomas, the founder of Wendy's, began his fast-food career in 1956 when he and Phil Clauss opened a barbecue restaurant in Knoxville, Tennessee. He put his restaurant experience to use in 1969 by opening his first Wendy's restaurant, naming it after his daughter. Thomas limited the menu to cooked-to-order hamburgers, chili, and shakes, charging prices slightly higher than rivals Burger King and McDonald's. The restaurants were decorated with carpeting, wood paneling, and Tiffany-style lamps to reinforce the relatively upscale theme. In the early 1970s, the company began franchising to accelerate expansion. It also founded its Management Institute to train owners and managers in Wendy's operational techniques. The first non-U.S. Wendy's opened in Canada in 1975. Wendy's went public in 1976, and by the end of that year, it boasted a collection of 500 restaurants. Its first national commercial aired in 1977. Two years later, the chain added a salad bar to its menu.

Dave Thomas retired as chairman in 1982 and took the title of senior chairman. Wendy's launched an $8 million TV ad campaign featuring Clara Peller asking, "Where's the beef?" in 1984, and its market share jumped to 12 percent. When McDonald's and Burger King responded with their own campaigns, Wendy's introduction of a breakfast menu (1985); new products, such as the Big Classic burger (1986); and the SuperBar buffet (1987) could not help reverse the erosion of the company's market share (down to 9 percent by 1987). With his honest demeanor and humble delivery, Thomas found an audience as Wendy's TV spokesperson in 1989. The company even attributed the rebound in earnings at the time to his appearances.

Wendy's reacted to growing concern about nutrition by introducing a grilled chicken sandwich in 1990. It also appealed to budget-conscious consumers with its ninety-nine-cent Super Value Menu. Wendy's had 4,000 restaurants by 1992, the same year it added packaged salads to its menu. The next year, high school dropout Thomas earned his diploma; his class voted him Most Likely to Succeed.

The death of Dave Thomas early in 2002 was a crushing blow to the company and a loss for the fast-food industry. Wendy's continued to perform well over the next three years, even after losing its founder, Dave Thomas. In November 2004, Wendy's decided to end its unsuccessful ad campaign featuring an everyman-type character, an "unofficial spokesman" called Mr. Wendy, because the campaign drew attention away from the food. This marks an ongoing dilemma

for Wendy's: how to brand the company in the post-Thomas era. The company initiated a series of ads featuring still images of Dave Thomas in late November 2005 to commemorate the chain's thirty-fifth anniversary, but the long-term question of its identity remained. During 2005, it started a campaign built around the call to action "Do What Tastes Right," which underscores Wendy's thirty-five-year heritage of serving great tasting, high-quality food. It featured a variety of different types of ads that were matched to targeted audiences. Included were advertising that promoted specific menu items as well as executions that supported the Wendy's brand as a whole.

In mid-2006, Wendy's International, Inc., created a new area of marketing to lead innovation efforts for the Wendy's brand. The expanded role of Wendy's marketing department included the establishment of an innovation and strategy group comprised of research and development, strategic insights and innovation, and operations innovation.

Wendy rolled out its strategic growth plan in October 2007 and identified ten imperatives for 2008. The imperatives are focused on "Doing What's Right for Customers." The ten imperatives build on Wendy's "Recipe for Success," which is focused on revitalizing the Wendy's brand, streamlining and improving operations, reclaiming innovation leadership, strengthening franchisee commitment, capturing new opportunities (e.g., international growth), and embracing a performance-driven culture.

In August 2008, Wendy's reached out to cash-strapped consumers with a trio of high-quality, signature sandwiches priced at ninety-nine cents. It introduced a ninety-nine-cent Double Stack cheeseburger and planned to promote this menu option aggressively, along with the company's popular ninety-nine-cent Junior Bacon Cheeseburger and ninety-nine-cent Crispy Chicken Sandwich. On September 29, 2008, Triarc Companies, Inc., the franchisor of the Arby's restaurant system, completed its previously announced merger with Wendy's International, Inc. The combined company was renamed Wendy's/Arby's Group, Inc. Triarc subsequently sold Arby's in 2011.

Shortly after its acquisition by Triarc, Wendy's undertook systematic survey research in 2009 and 2010, interviewing 10,000 consumers. The findings indicated that consumers liked the idea of fresh food with as little processing as possible and familiar ingredients. These findings led to the reinvention of Wendy's core menu. Out went the traditional iceberg lettuce topped with tomatoes and onions, and in came four new salad varieties featuring eleven different greens and new ingredients like apples, pecans, and asiago cheese. In 2011, Wendy's turned its attention to french fries, switching from a mixture of potato varieties to only Russet potatoes, sliced with the skin still on, and sprinkled with sea salt. In March 2012, Wendy's introduced its new Spicy Chicken Guacamole Club that added even more flavors with a zesty ranch sauce—and yes, guacamole—to create a big, bold tasty sandwich. More recently, Wendy's beefed up its burgers, switching to a looser grind of beef that made its burgers thicker and juicier. The company also refashioned its trademark square burgers with softer edges to give them a fresher, more appealing look. As of 2014, Wendy's brand transformation was being engineered with bold restaurant designs, innovative food, and improved customer service.

To survive the merciless fast-food industry, Wendy's conducted another survey. Wendy's wanted to study customer demographics and awareness of different competing fast-food chains; the satisfaction responses of consumers in terms of family orientation, comfort, price, quick service, healthy foods, cleanliness, and so on; and the patronage preferences of costumers in terms of eat-in or drive-through. The following questionnaire was used by Wendy's to obtain this information, and the data obtained can be downloaded from the website for this book. Based on the data collected and analysis of this study, Wendy's intends to improve its service and brand orientation.

Questions

Chapter 1

1. Discuss the role that social media research can play in helping a fast-food restaurant such as Wendy's formulate sound marketing strategies.

Chapter 2

2. Wendy's is considering further expansion in the United States. Define the management decision problem.
3. Define an appropriate marketing research problem based on the management decision problem you have identified.

Chapter 3

4. Formulate an appropriate research design for investigating the marketing research problem you defined above in question 3 for Chapter 2.
5. Use the Internet to determine the market shares of the major national fast-food chains for the last calendar year.
6. What type of syndicate data will be useful to Wendy's?

Chapter 4

7. Discuss the role of qualitative research in helping Wendy's expand further in the United States. What insights can be gained from an analysis of social media?

Chapter 5

8. Wendy's has developed a new fish sandwich with a distinctive Cajun taste. It would like to determine consumer response to this new sandwich before introducing it in the marketplace. If a survey is to be conducted to determine consumer preferences, which survey method should be used? Explain your choice.

Chapter 6

9. Discuss the role of experimentation in helping Wendy's determine its optimal level of advertising expenditures.

Chapter 7

10. Illustrate the use of primary types of scales in measuring consumer preferences for fast-food restaurants.
11. Illustrate the use of Likert, semantic differential, and Stapel scales in measuring consumer preferences for fast-food restaurants.

Chapter 8

12. Develop a questionnaire for assessing consumer preferences for fast-food restaurants.

Chapters 9

13. What sampling plan should be adopted for the survey you chose in question 8 for Chapter 5? How should the sample size be determined?

Chapter 10

14. How should the field workers be selected and trained to conduct the field work for the survey you chose in question 8 for Chapter 5?
15. How should the missing values be treated for the following demographic variables: education (D5), income (D6), employment status (D7), and marital status (D8)?
16. Recode payment method (D1) by combining Debit card, Check, and Other into one category.
17. Recode the number of people living at home (D3A) as follows: for adults age 18+, four or more should be combined into one category labeled 4+; for each of the three remaining age groups (under 5, 6–11, and 12–17), two or more should be combined into a single category labeled 2+.
18. Recode education (D5) by combining the lowest two categories and labeling it "completed high school or less."
19. Recode income (D6) by combining the highest three categories and labeling it "$100,000 or more."
20. Recode employment status (D7) by combining homemaker, retired, and unemployed into a single category.
21. Classify respondents into light, medium, and heavy users of fast food based on a frequency distribution of S3A: In the past four weeks, approximately how many times, have you, yourself, eaten food from a fast-food restaurant? Use the following classification: 1–4 times = light, 5–8 times = medium, 9 or more times = heavy.

Chapter 11

22. Run a frequency distribution for all variables except respondent ID (responid). Why is this analysis useful?
23. Cross-tabulate the fast-food consumption classification (recoded S3A; see the questions listed above for Chapter 10) with the following demographic characteristics (some recoded as specified above for Chapter 10): age (S1), gender (S2), payment method (D1), number of people living at home (D3A), education (D5), income (D6), employment (D7), marital status (D8), and region. Interpret the results.
24. Cross-tabulate the payment method (recoded D1) with the remaining demographic characteristics (some recoded as specified above for Chapter 10): age (S1), gender (S2), number of people living at home (D3A), education (D5), income (D6), employment (D7), marital status (D8), and region. Interpret the results.
25. Cross-tabulate eating there more often, less often, or about the same as a year or so ago (q8_1, q8_7, q8_26, q8_36, and q8_39) with the following demographic characteristics (some recoded as specified above for Chapter 10): age (S1), gender (S2), payment method (D1), number of people living at home (D3A), education (D5), income (D6), employment (D7), marital status (D8), and region. Interpret the results.

Chapter 12

26. Do the ratings on the psychographic statements (q14_1, q14_2, q14_3, q14_4, q14_5, q14_6, and q14_7) differ for males and females (S2)? Formulate the null and alternative hypotheses and conduct an appropriate test.

27. Do the respondents agree more with "I have been making an effort to look for fast-food choices that have better nutritional value than the foods I have chosen in the past" (q14_6) than they do with "I consider the amount of fat in the foods my kids eat at fast-food restaurants" (q14_5)? Formulate the null and alternative hypotheses and conduct an appropriate test.

28. Can each of the restaurant ratings (q9_1, q9_7, q9_26, q9_36, and q9_39) be explained in terms of the ratings on the psychographic statement (q14_1, q14_2, q14_3, q14_4, q14_5, q14_6, and q14_7) when the statements are considered simultaneously?

Chapter 13

29. Write a report for Wendy's management summarizing the results of your analyses. What recommendations do you have for Wendy's management?

30. If this survey were to be conducted in Malaysia rather than the United States, how would the research process be different?

31. Should the sample size in Malaysia be the same as the sample size in the United States? Should the same sampling procedures be used in the two countries?

References

1. **www.wendys.com**, accessed July 19, 2013.
2. Julie Jargon, "Wendy's Stages a Palace Coup: Despite Fewer U.S. Locations, Chain Set to Unseat Burger King as No. 2 in Sales," *Wall Street Journal* (December 21, 2011): B1–B2.

Note: This case was prepared for class discussion purposes only and does not represent the views of Wendy's or its affiliates. The problem scenario is hypothetical, and the name of the actual company has been disguised. However, the questionnaire and the data provided are real. Some questions have been deleted, while the data for other questions are not provided because of proprietary reasons.

Region information is not indicated in the questionnaire but is coded in the data file as: 1 = Northeast, 2 = Midwest, 3 = South, and 4 = West.

Online WENDY'S Commitment Study Questionnaire

JULY 8, 2013

RID _____

Thank you for participating in our survey.

S1. To begin, which of the following categories includes your age? (CHOOSE ONE RESPONSE ONLY.)

1 Under 18	**[TERMINATE QS1]**
2 18–24	
3 25–29	
4 30–34	
5 35–39	
6 40–45	
7 46 or older	**[TERMINATE QS1]**
– Refused	**[TERMINATE QS1]**

S2. Are you...? (CHOOSE ONE RESPONSE ONLY.)

1 Male
2 Female

S3. OMITTED

S3A. In the past four weeks, approximately how many times, have you, yourself, eaten food from a fast-food restaurant? **[ACCEPT WHOLE NUMBERS ONLY; DO NOT ACCEPT RANGE.] [RANGE: 0–99]**

_____

And Don't Know/Refused **[TERMINATE QS3A]**
[TERMINATE QS3A IF ZERO]

1. [OMITTED]
2. [OMITTED]
3. [OMITTED]

3a. You have indicated that you have heard of these restaurants. When was the last time, if ever, that you, yourself, have eaten from each one? (PLEASE SELECT ONE TIMEFRAME FOR EACH RESTAURANT.) **[FORMAT AS GRID: INCLUDE RESPONSES FROM Q1.]**

1 Within the past 4 weeks
2 More than 4 weeks to within the past 3 months
3 More than 3 months ago
4 Never

4. [OMITTED]
5. [OMITTED]
6. [OMITTED]
7. [OMITTED]

8. For each of the restaurants listed below, please indicate whether you, yourself, are eating from there more often, less often, or about the same frequency as a year or so ago. **[SHOW ONLY THOSE Q3a = 1 or 2]**

	More Often	**About the Same**	**Less Often**
Insert brands	1	2	3

9. I'd like you to rate the restaurants you, yourself, have eaten from in the past 3 months using a 10-point scale, where "10" means you think it is perfect, and "1" means you think it is terrible. Now taking into account everything that you look for in a fast-food restaurant, how would you rate each of the following? **[SHOW Q3a = 1 or 2]**

Terrible (1)	**2**	**3**	**4**	**5**	**6**	**7**	**8**	**9**	**Perfect (10)**
O	O	O	O	O	O	O	O	O	O

10. [OMITTED]
11. [OMITTED]
12. [OMITTED]

13. Sometimes it is difficult for people to make up their minds about which fast-food restaurant to go to on a given visit. Think about when you go to a fast-food restaurant. In general, which of the following statements best describes the extent to which you find it difficult to make up your mind about which fast-food restaurant to go to? (CHOOSE ONE RESPONSE ONLY.)

1 I **always know** exactly which fast-food restaurant I am going to go to.
2 I **usually know** exactly which fast-food restaurant I am going to go to.
3 I'm **usually undecided** about which fast-food restaurant I am going to go to.
4 I'm **always undecided** about which fast-food restaurant I am going to go to.

14. Below is a list of statements that may or may not be used to describe you in general. Using the scale of Disagree completely, Disagree somewhat, Neither agree nor disagree, Agree somewhat, and Agree completely or Not applicable (N/A), please indicate how strongly you agree or disagree with each statement. (CHOOSE ONE RESPONSE FOR EACH STATEMENT.)

Disagree Completely	**Disagree Somewhat**	**Neither Agree nor Disagree**	**Agree Somewhat**	**Agree Completely**	**N/A**
O	O	O	O	O	O

1 I try to stay current on the latest health and nutrition information.
2 I read nutritional labels on most products I buy.
3 I am making more of an effort to find out about the nutritional content of the foods I eat at fast-food restaurants.
4 I consider the amount of fat in the foods I eat at fast-food restaurants.
5 I consider the amount of fat in the foods my kids eat at fast-food restaurants.
6 I have been making an effort to look for fast-food choices that have better nutritional value than the foods I have chosen in the past.
7 I am eating at fast-food restaurants less often out of concern for the high fat content in the foods at fast-food restaurants.

These last few questions are for classification purposes only.

D1. Which of the following methods do you most often use when purchasing from fast-food restaurants? Do you pay…? CHOOSE ONE RESPONSE ONLY.)

1 Cash
2 Credit card
3 Debit card
4 Check
5 Other

D2. [OMITTED]

D3. [OMITTED]

D3A. How many people in each of the following age groups live in your home? (PLEASE ENTER A NUMBER FOR EACH AGE RANGE. ENTER "0" IF THERE IS NO ONE IN THAT RANGE IN YOUR HOUSEHOLD.)

A Adults age 18+ [**RANGE: 1–15**]
B Children under age 5 [**RANGE: 0–9**]
C Children age 6–11 [**RANGE: 0–9**]
D Children age 12–17 [**RANGE: 0–9**]

D4. [OMITTED]

D5. Which of the following best represents the last level of education that you, yourself, completed? (CHOOSE ONE RESPONSE ONLY.)

1 Some high school or less
2 Completed high school
3 Some college
4 Completed college
5 Post graduate
– Prefer not to answer

D6. Which of the following best describes your family's annual household income before taxes? (CHOOSE ONE RESPONSE ONLY.)

1 Under $25,000
2 $25,000 but under $50,000
3 $50,000 but under $75,000
4 $75,000 but under $100,000
5 $100,000 but under $150,000
6 $150,000 but under $200,000
7 $200,000 or more
– Prefer not to answer

D7. Which of the following best describes your employment status? (CHOOSE ONE RESPONSE ONLY.)

1 Full-time
2 Part-time
3 Retired
4 Student
5 Homemaker
6 Unemployed
– Prefer not to answer

D8. Are you…?

1 Single, Separated, Divorced, Widowed
0 Married/Living as Married
– Prefer not to answer

Thank you for taking the time to participate in our research!

	Q1
Arby's	1
Atlanta Bread Company	2
A&W	3
Baja Fresh	4
Blimpie	5

(Continued)

	Q1
Boston Chicken/Market	6
Burger King	7
Captain D's	8
Carl's Jr.	9
Checker's Drive In	10
Chick-Fil-A	11
Chipotle Mexican Grill	12
Church's	13
Del Taco	14
Domino's Pizza	15
El Pollo Loco	16
Grandy's	17
Green Burrito	18
Hardee's	19
In-N-Out Burger	20
Jack in the Box	21
KFC/Kentucky Fried Chicken	22
La Salsa	23
Little Caesars	24
Long John Silvers	25
McDonald's	26
Panda Express	27
Panera Bread	28
Papa John's	41
Pick Up Stix	29
Pizza Hut	30
Popeye's	31
Quiznos	32
Rally's	33
Rubio's	34
Sonic	35
Subway	36
Taco Bell	37
Taco Bueno	38
Wendy's	39
Whataburger	40
[OMITTED—OTHER SPECIFY]	
None	42

Index

Note: Page numbers with *t* indicate tables; those with *f* indicate figures; those with *n* indicate notes.

SUBJECT INDEX

for graph guidelines in reports (GRAPHS), 405
for marketing research (RESEARCH), 48
for presentation guidelines (PRESENTATION), 405–406
for projective techniques (PROJECTIVE), 144
for question order (ORDER), 265
for question wording (WORDS), 264
for questionnaires (QUESTIONNAIRE), 264
for report writing guidelines (REPORT), 405
for research design components (R DESIGNS), 115
for sampling design process (SAMPLE), 291
for scales of different types (SCALES), 233
for scales, primary types (FOUR), 233
for secondary data evaluation (SECOND), 115
for survey methods by mode of administration (METHODS), 176
for syndicated data (SYNDICATED), 115–116
for *t* tests (T TEST), 382
for table guidelines in reports (TABLES), 405
for training of field workers (TRAIN), 320
Activities, interests, and opinions (AIOs), 99
Adjusted R^2, 373
Administration as limitation of experimentation, 195
Advertising evaluation surveys, 99
Advertising Research Foundation, 393
Alternative hypothesis, 336, 337
Analytical framework, 70
Analytical model, 70
Approach to the problem. *See under* Marketing research problem
Area sampling, 284
Artifacts, demand, 198
Audits, 104
  physical, 104
  problem, 57–58
  retailer, 104–105
  uses, advantages, and disadvantages of, 105
  wholesaler, 104–105

Baby Boomers, 366
Bar charts in reports, 397
Basic information, 252
Beta coefficient, 372–373
Beta weight, 372
Bias
  acquiescence, 250
  interviewer, 162, 169
  nonresponse, 158
  observation, 168
Binary scales, 228
Bivariate correlation, 371
Bivariate cross-tabulation, 342
Bivariate regression, 372

Blogs, 75, 108, 129
  participant, 139
Branching questions, 253
Broad statement of the problem, 67
Business/nongovernment data, 94–95
Business Periodicals Index, 95
Buyer behavior in environmental context, 63–64

Cable TV, scanner panels with, 103
Callbacks in e-mail surveys, 160
Cartoon test, 134
Casewise deletion in treating missing responses, 308
Causality, 178, 180–183
  conditions for, 181–183
    absence of other causal factors, 181–182
    concomitant variation, 181
    role of evidence, 182
    time order of occurrence of variables, 181
  defined, 180
Causal research, 88, 146
  versus descriptive research, 88f
Census
  Census 2010, 238–239, 244
  data in, 95–96
  defined, 238, 270
Central location interviews, 161t
Chat rooms, 59
Cheating, 299
China, environmental approach in, 170
Chi-square distribution, 344
Chi-square statistic, 344–346
CI Resource Index, 95
Classification information, 252
Clients, 55
  assisting, 399
Cluster sampling, 283–284
Codebook, 304, 305
Coding in data preparation, 303–306
Coefficient of multiple determination, 373
Cold mail surveys, 157
  costs of, 158
  response rate to, 158
Comparative scaling, 213, 213f, 214–216
  constant sum scaling, 215–216
  paired comparison scaling, 214
  rank-order scaling, 215
Completely automated telephone surveys (CATS), 161t
Computer-assisted personal interviews (CAPI), 146, 155–156, 162, 242
Computer-assisted telephone interviews (CATI), 146, 151, 152, 153, 242
  advantages and disadvantages of, 156
Conclusions in report, 392
Conclusive research, 86
  classification of, 146
  differences between exploratory research and, 86t
Concomitant variation in causality, 181
Consistency checks in data collection, 308

Constant sum scaling, 215–216
Constraints in environmental context, 63
Consumer data, syndicated services for, 98–104, 98f
Consumer surveys, 97
Contingency coefficient, 345–346
Contingency tables in cross-tabulation, 342
Continuous rating scale, 217–218
Control groups, random assignment to, 184
Convenience sampling, 277
Correlation, 371–372
Correlation coefficient, 371
Costs as limitation of experimentation, 195
Cramer's *V,* 345, 346
Cross-sectional designs, 87–88, 87f
Cross-tabulation, 341–346
  bivariate, 342
  defined, 341
  in practice, 345–346
  statistics associated with, 344–345
Currency as criteria in evaluating secondary data, 91
Customer databases, 93
Customer relationship management (CRM), 92, 94
Customized services, 36–37, 36f

Data
  analysis of, 32f, 33, 38, 326–385
  business/nongovernment, 94–95
  collection of, 32, 32f, 294–301
  external, 92
  external secondary, 94–96
  internal, 92
  internal secondary, 92–94
  preparation of, 32f, 33, 301–320
  primary, 60, 89
  scanner, 103
  secondary, 60
  statistically adjusting, 309–310
  volume tracking scanner, 103
Data analysis, 326–355
  cross-tabulation in, 341–346
  in Excel. *See also* Excel
  frequency distribution in, 328–334
  hypothesis testing in, 335–341, 356–385
  in reports, 392
  selecting strategy for, 310
  in SPSS. *See also* SPSS
Database marketing, 92, 94
Data cleaning in data collection, 307–309
Data collection. *See also* Field workers
  ethics and, 313–314
  in Excel, 315, 318–319
  in hypothesis testing, 338
  in international marketing research, 310–311
  nature of, 296
  process of, 296–298
  social media and, 311–312
  software applications and, 314–319

in SPSS, 314–317
  validation of, 300
Data entry
  in Excel, 307
  in SPSS, 307
Data file, developing, 306
Data mining, 94
Data preparation process, 301–310
  coding in, 303–306
  data cleaning in, 307–309
  editing in, 302–303
  questionnaire checking in, 301–302
  selecting data analysis strategy in, 310
  statistically adjusting the data in, 309–310
  transcribing in, 306–307
Data warehouses, 94
Debriefing, 198
Decision makers, discussion with, 56–59
Decision support systems (DDS), 41
  role of marketing research in, 41, 41f
Defining the problem. *See* Problem definition
Demand artifacts, 198
Demographics, 95
Dependability as criteria in evaluating secondary data, 92
Dependent variables in experimentation, 184
Depth interviews, 118, 130–132, 135, 136
  advantages and disadvantages of, 131–132
  conducting, 130–131
  defined, 130
  ethics and, 140
  social media and, 139
Descriptive research, 87f, 87–89, 110
  versus causal research, 88f
  objectives of, 146
Dichotomous questions, 247
Differences, hypothesis testing related to, 358–371
Direct approach in qualitative research procedures, 122
Double-barreled questions, 243
Double income no kids (DINKs) lifestyle, 99
Drop-off surveys, 161t
Dual statements, balancing, 251

Economic environment, in environmental context, 65
Editing in data preparation, 302–303
Electronic scanner services, 97, 103–104
  uses, advantages, and disadvantages of, 103–104
Electronic surveys, 159–161
  advantages and disadvantages of, 160
Elements, 272
E-mail surveys, 146, 159
Emotions, keyboard characters for, 128